LIBRARY OF NEW TESTAMENT STUDIES
516

Formerly the Journal for the Study of the New Testament Supplement series

Editor
Chris Keith

Editorial Board
Dale C. Allison, John M.G. Barclay, Lynn H. Cohick, R. Alan Culpepper, Craig A. Evans, Robert Fowler, Simon J. Gathercole, Juan Hernandez Jr., John S. Kloppenborg, Michael Labahn, Love L. Sechrest, Robert Wall, Steve Walton, Catrin H. Williams

So Great a Salvation

A Dialogue on the Atonement in Hebrews

Edited by
Jon C. Laansma, George H. Guthrie, and
Cynthia Long Westfall

t&tclark

LONDON • NEW YORK • OXFORD • NEW DELHI • SYDNEY

T&T CLARK
Bloomsbury Publishing Plc

50 Bedford Square, London, WC1B 3DP, UK
1385 Broadway, New York, NY 10018, USA
29 Earlsfort Terrace, Dublin 2, Ireland

BLOOMSBURY, T&T CLARK and the T&T Clark logo
are trademarks of Bloomsbury Publishing Plc

First published in Great Britain 2019
Paperback edition first published 2021

Copyright © Jon C. Laansma, George H. Guthrie, Cynthia Long Westfall
and contributors, 2019

Jon C. Laansma, George H. Guthrie, Cynthia Long Westfall have asserted their right under the
Copyright, Designs and Patents Act, 1988, to be identified as Editors of this work.

For legal purposes the Acknowledgements on p. xvi constitute
an extension of this copyright page.

Cover design: Tjaša Krivec

All rights reserved. No part of this publication may be reproduced or
transmitted in any form or by any means, electronic or mechanical,
including photocopying, recording, or any information storage or retrieval
system, without prior permission in writing from the publishers.

Bloomsbury Publishing Plc does not have any control over, or responsibility for,
any third-party websites referred to or in this book. All internet addresses given
in this book were correct at the time of going to press. The author and publisher
regret any inconvenience caused if addresses have changed or sites have
ceased to exist, but can accept no responsibility for any such changes.

A catalogue record for this book is available from the British Library.

Library of Congress Cataloging-in-Publication Data
Names: Guthrie, George H., 1959-editor.
Title: So great a salvation: a dialogue on the atonement in Hebrews / edited
by George H. Guthrie, Jon Laansma, and Cynthia Long Westfall.
Description: 1 [edition]. | New York: T&T Clark, 2019. |
Includes bibliographical references and index.
Identifiers: LCCN 2019009768 (print) | LCCN 2019016510 (ebook) |
ISBN 9780567689115 (ePUB) | ISBN 9780567657244 (ePDF) |
ISBN 9780567656629 (hardback: alk.paper)
Subjects: LCSH: Bible. Hebrews–Criticism, interpretation, etc. |
Atonement–Biblical teaching. | Salvation–Christianity–Biblical teaching.
Classification: LCC BS2775.6.A8 (ebook) | LCC BS2775.6.A8 S6 2019 (print) |
DDC 227/.8706–dc23
LC record available at https://lccn.loc.gov/2019009768

ISBN: HB: 978-0-5676-5662-9
PB: 978-0-5677-0032-2
ePDF: 978-0-5676-5724-4
eBook: 978-0-5676-8911-5

Series: Library of New Testament Studies, 2345678X, volume 516

Library of New Testament Studies, 2345678X, volume 516

To find out more about our authors and books visit
www.bloomsbury.com and sign up for our newsletters.

πῶς ἡμεῖς ἐκφευξόμεθα τηλικαύτης ἀμελήσαντες σωτηρίας;

我们若忽略这么大的救恩，怎能逃罪呢？

tutaokokaje tusipojali wokovu mkuu kama huu?

فَكَيْفَ نُفْلِتُ نَحْنُ إِنْ أَهْمَلْنَا هَذَا الْخَلَاصَ الْعَظِيمَ جِدًّا

איך נמלט אנחנו אם לא נשים לב לישועה גדולה כזאת?

¿Cómo, pues, escaparemos nosotros, si descuidamos una salvación tan grande?

तो हम लोग ऐसे बड़े उद्धार से निश्चिन्त रहकर कैसे बच सकते हैं?

quomodo nos effugiemus si tantam neglexerimus salutem?

تو اتنی بڑی نجات سے غافل رہ کر ہم کیوں کر بچ سکتے ہیں؟

Contents

List of Abbreviations ix
Notes on Contributors xiii
Preface and Acknowledgments xvi

Introduction *Jon C. Laansma* 1

Part One Contexts

1 Atonement in Ancient Israel: The Whole Burnt Offering as Central to Israel's Cult *L. Michael Morales* 27
2 Putting Words in His Mouth: The Son Speaks in Hebrews *Karen H. Jobes* 40
3 The Origins of Hebrews' High Priest Christology: A Conundrum Revisited *Nicholas Perrin* 51
4 Jesus's Atoning Sacrifice in Hebrews and Atonement of Sin in the Greco-Roman World *Eckhard J. Schnabel* 65
5 The Epistle to the Hebrews in Patristic Trinitarian and Christological Doctrine *Khaled Anatolios* 87

Part Two Themes

6 "Mediator of a New Covenant": Atonement and Christology in Hebrews *Daniel J. Treier* 105
7 Blood, Death, and Sacrifice in the Epistle to the Hebrews According to Thomas Aquinas *Matthew Levering* 120
8 Living and Active: The Exalted Prophet in the Epistle to the Hebrews *Michael Allen* 144
9 It Is Not Finished: Jesus's Perpetual Atoning Work as the Heavenly High Priest in Hebrews *David M. Moffitt* 157
10 Plight and Solution: Hebrews and the Invitation to Rest *Mark S. Gignilliat* 176
11 Hebrews and the Jewish Law *Matthew Thiessen* 183
12 Promises to the Son: Covenant and Atonement in Hebrews *Amy Peeler* 195
13 Time and Atonement in Hebrews *George H. Guthrie* 209
14 Space and Atonement in Hebrews *Cynthia L. Westfall* 228

15 Faith in Hebrews and Its Relationship to Soteriology: An
   Interpretation in the Context of the Concept of Fides in Roman
   Culture *Gabriella Gelardini* 249
16 The Church and Atonement in Hebrews *Harold W. Attridge* 257

Bibliography 277
Index of References to Premodern Sources 300
Index of Authors 315

Abbreviations

AD	anno Domini
AB	Anchor Bible
Agr.	Cato, De Agri Cultura
Alc.	Euripides *Alcestis*,
ALGHJ	Arbeiten zur Literatur und Geschichte des hellenistischen Judentum
Amat.	Plutarch, *Amatorius*
ANE	Ancient Near East
ANRW	*Aufstieg und Niedergang der römischen Welt: Geschichte und Kultur Roms im Spiegel der neueren Forschung*
Ant.	Josephus, *Antiquities of the Jews*
Apoph. lac.	Plutarch, *Apophthegmata Laconica*
ATR	Anglican Theological Review
b. Ḥag.	*Ḥagigah*
BC	Before Christ
Barn.	*Barnabas*
BBB	Bonner biblische Beiträge
BBR	Bulletin for Biblical Research
BCE	Before the Common Era
BDAG	Bauer-Danker *Lexicon*
Bib	*Biblica*
Bibl.	Apollodorus/Ps. Apollodorus, *Bibliotheca*
BINS	Biblical Interpretation Series, Brill
BTB	Biblical Theology Bulletin
BZ	Biblische Zeitschrift
BZNW	Beihefte zur ZNW
C. Ar.	Athanasius, *Orationes contra Arianos*
C.S.C.	*Congregatio a Sancta Cruce*
CBQMS	Catholic Biblical Quarterly, Monograph Series
CBR	Currents in Biblical Research
CE	Common Era
Civ.	Augustine, *City of God*
Clem.	Seneca, *De Clementia*
Conf.	Philo, *De confusione linguarum*
Diatr.	Epictetus, *Discourses*
Dom.	Cicero, *De domo suo*
EA	*Epigraphica Anatolica*

EKKNT	Evangelisch-Katholischer Kommentar zum Neuen Testament
Ep.	Pliny the Younger, *Epistulae*
Ep.	Seneca, *Epistulae morales ad Lucilium*
ESV	English Standard Version
Eth. nic.	Aristotle, *Nicomachean Ethics*
Exod. Rab.	Exodos Rabbah
FRLANT	Forschungen zur Religion und Literatur des Alten und Neuen Testaments
FzB	Forschung zur Bibe
Gen. Rab.	Genesis Rabbah
Geogr.	Strabo, *Geographica*
GNB	Good New Bible
HBM	Hebrew Bible Monographs
Her.	Philo, *Quis rerum divinarum heres sit*
Hist.	Herodotus, *Histories*
Hist. eccl.	Eusebius, *Church History*
HNT	*Handbuch z. Neuen Testament*
HSM	Harvard Semitic Monographs
HTR	*Harvard Theological Review*
Hymn. Cer.	Callimachus, *Hymnus in Cererem*
IG	Inscriptiones Graecum
Il.	Homer, *Iliad*
Inc.	Athanasius, *On the Incarnation*
Inst.	Quintilian, *Institutio Oratoria*
IVP	InterVarsity Press
JAOS	*Journal of the American Oriental Society*
JBL	*Journal of Biblical Literature*
JETS	*Journal of the Evangelical Theological Society*
JPS	Jewish Publication Society
JR	*Journal of Religion*
JRA	*Journal of Roman Archaeology*
JSNT	*Journal for the Study of the New Testament*
JSNTSup	Journal for the Study of the New Testament, Supplement Series
JSOT	Journal for the Study of the Old Testament
JSOTSup	Journal for the Study of the Old Testament, Supplement Series
Jub.	*Jubilees*
KBNT	Kommentare und Beiträge zum Alten und Neuen Testament
KEK	Kritisch-exegetischer Kommentar über das Neue Testament
Lam. Rab.	Lamentations Rabbah
LCL	Loeb Classical Library
Leg.	Philo, *Legum allegoriae*
Leg. Gai.	Philo, *Legatio ad Gaium*
Let. Aris.	Letter of Aristeas

Lev. Rab.	Leviticus Rabbah
LNTS	Library of New Testament Studies
LSJ	H.G. Liddell, Robert Scott and H. Stuart Jones, Greek–English Lexicon
LXX	Septuagint
Metam.	Liberalis, *Metamorphoseon Synagoge*
Migr.	Philo, *De migratione Abrahami*
MT	Masoretic Text
NAB	New American Bible
NASB	New American Standard Bible
NICNT	New International Commentary on the New Testament
NIGTC	The New International Greek Testament Commentary
NIV	New International Version
NIVAC	New International Version Application Commentary
NLT	New Living Translation
NovT	*Novum Testamentum*
NovTSup	Novum Testamentum, Supplements
NPNF	*Nicene and Post-Nicene Fathers*
NRSV	New Revised Standard Version
NRTh	*La Nouvelle Revue Théologique*
NT	New Testament
NTL	New Testament Library
Num. Rab.	Numbers Rabbah
O.F.M. Cap.	Order of Friars Minor Capuchin
O.P.	Order of Preachers
Od.	Homer, *Odyssey*
OG	Old Greek
Op.	Hesiod, *Works and Days*
Opif.	Philo, *De opificio mundi*
Or.	Aristides, *Libanius of Antioch*
Or. Bas.	Gregory of Nazianzus, *Oratio in laudem Basilii*
OT	Old Testament
ÖTK	Ökumenischer Taschenbuchkommentar zum Neuen Testament
OTP	Old Testament Pseudepigrapha
Pan.	Pliny the Younger, *Panegyricus*
Pesiq. Rab.	Pesiqta Rabbati
Pirqe R. El.	Pirqe Rabbi Eliezer
Plant.	Philo, *De plantatione*
Praem. Poen.	Philo, *De praemiis et poenis*
Prob.	Philo, *Quod omnis probus liber sit*
Prom.	Aeschylus, *Prometheus Bound*
Pss. Sol	*Psalms of Solomon*
PTMS	Princeton Theological Monograph Series
Quaest. in Exod.	Philo, *Quaestiones et solutiones in Exodum*

RevThom	*Revue thomiste*
Rhet.	Dionysius Halicarnassus, *The Art of Rhetoric*
RNT	Regensburger Neues Testament
RSV	Revised Standard Version
S.J.	Studia judaica
Sacr.	Philo, *De sacrificiis Abelis et Caini*
SBG	Studies in Biblical Greek
SBL	Society of Biblical Literature
SBLDS	SBL Dissertation Serie
SBLMS	SBL Monograph Series
SBLRBS	SBL Sources for Biblical Stud
SCM	Student Christian Movement
SEG	Supplementum Epigraphicum Graecum
SJLA	Studies in Judaism in Late Antiquity
SJT	*Scottish Journal of Theology*
SNTSMS	Society for New Testament Studies Monograph Series
Sobr.	Philo, *De sobrietate*
Somn.	Philo, *De somniis*
Song Rab.	Song of Solomon Rabbah
SPB	Studia postbiblica
SPCK	Society for Promoting Christian Knowledge
Spec.	Philo, *De specialibus legibus*
STDJ	Studies on the Texts of the Desert of Judah
TDNT	Theological Dictionary of the New Testament
Theog.	Hesiod, *Theogony*
TJ	*Trinity Journal*
TNTC	Tyndale New Testament Commentaries
Tusc.	Cicero, *Tusculanae Disputationes*
TWNT	Theologisches Wörterbuch zum Neuen Testament
TynBul	*Tyndale Bulletin*
Vit. Apoll.	Philostratus, *Life of Apollonius*
VT	*Vetus Testamentum*
War	Josephus, *The Jewish War*
WBC	Word Biblical Commentary
WMANT	Wissenschaftliche Monographien zum Alten und Neuen Testament
WUNT	Wissenschaftliche Untersuchungen zum Neuen Testament
ZAW	*Zeitschrift für die alttestamentliche Wissenschaft*
1 Clem.	*1 Clement*
2 En.	*2 Enoch*
3 En.	*3 Enoch*

Contributors

Michael Allen is the John Dyer Trimble Professor of Systematic Theology and Academic Dean at Reformed Theological Seminary in Orlando. He serves as general editor of Zondervan Academic's New Studies in Dogmatics series and the T&T Clark International Theological Commentary series. He has written numerous books on Christian doctrine and interpretation of Scripture, most recently *Grounded in Heaven* (Eerdmans) and *Sanctification* (Zondervan).

Khaled Anatolios is the John A. O'Brien Professor of Theology at the University of Notre Dame. His writings include *Retrieving Nicaea: The Development and Meaning of Trinitarian Doctrine* (Baker Academic, 2011 & 2018); the *Athanasius* volume of the Routledge Early Church Fathers series (Routledge, 2004); and *Athanasius: The Coherence of his Thought* (Routledge, 1998 & 2004). He is presently completing a manuscript on soteriology from the perspective of the Byzantine Christian tradition.

Harold W. Attridge is the Sterling Professor at the Yale Divinity School. His scholarly interests range from the New Testament to the literature and history of the early Church. His writings include *Hebrews: A Commentary on the Epistle to the Hebrews* in the Hermeneia series and *Essays on John and Hebrews*.

Gabriella Gelardini is Professor of Christianity, Religion, Worldview, and Ethics at Nord University, Norway. Her many publications on New Testament topics and beyond include *Christus militans: Studien zur politisch-militärischen Semantik im Markusevangelium vor dem Hintergrund des ersten jüdisch-römischen Krieges* (NovTSup 165, Brill 2016) and *Verhärtet eure Herzen nicht": Der Hebräer, eine Synagogenhomilie zu Tischa be-Aw* (BINS 83, Brill 2007). She is also the editor of *Hebrews in Contexts* (together with Harold W. Attridge, AJEC 91, Brill 2016) and *Hebrews: Contemporary Methods – New Insights* (BINS 75, Brill 2005).

Mark S. Gignilliat is Professor of Divinity at Beeson Divinity School, Samford University. His writings include *Karl Barth and the Fifth Gospel, A Brief History of Old Testament Criticism, A Commentary on Micah (International Theological Commentary)*, and *Reading Scripture Canonically: Theological Instincts for Old Testament Interpretation*. He also serves as canon theologian at the Cathedral Church of the Advent in Birmingham, Alabama.

George H. Guthrie is Professor of New Testament at Regent College in Vancouver, BC, Canada. His scholarly interests have included the book of Hebrews, selected writings among the Pauline Epistles, use of the Old Testament in the New, and hermeneutics. His publications include *The Structure of Hebrews: A Text-linguistic Analysis*, Supplements to Novum Testamentum (E. J. Brill, 1994), the Hebrews section in the *Commentary on the New Testament Use of the Old* Testament, ed. G. K. Beale and D. A. Carson (Baker, 2007), *2 Corinthians* in the Baker Exegetical Commentary series (Baker, 2015), and the *NIV Application Commentary: Hebrews* (Zondervan, 1998).

Karen H. Jobes is the Gerald F. Hawthorne Professor Emerita of New Testament Greek and Exegesis at Wheaton College and Graduate School (Illinois). Her scholarly interest has focused on the Septuagint, especially as it is used in the New Testament and particularly in Hebrews and the General Epistles. She is the author of *Invitation to the Septuagint* (with Moisés Silva), *Discovering the Septuagint, Letters to the Church: A Survey of Hebrews and the General Epistles, 1, 2, 3 John* (ZECNT), *1 Peter* (BECNT), and *Esther* (NIVAC).

Jon C. Laansma is the Gerald F. Hawthorne Professor of Greek and New Testament at Wheaton College. His publications include, *I Will Give You Rest: The Rest Motif in the New Testament with Special Reference to Mt 11 and Heb 3-4* (1997), *The Letter to the Hebrews: A Commentary for Preaching, Teaching, and Bible Study* (2017), and (coeditor) *Christology, Hermeneutics, and Hebrews: Profiles from the History of Interpretation* (2014).

Matthew Levering holds the James N. and Mary D. Perry Jr. Chair of Theology at Mundelein Seminary. He is the author of over twenty monographs on a wide diversity of subjects, including *Participatory Biblical Exegesis* (Notre Dame), *Ezra and Nehemiah* (Brazos), and *Paul in the Summa Theologiae* (Catholic University of America Press). With Michael Dauphinais, he coauthored *Holy People, Holy Land: A Theological Introduction to the Bible* (Brazos). He has been a participant in Evangelicals and Catholics together since 2004. He serves as the coeditor of two scholarly quarterlies, *Nova et Vetera* and the *International Journal of Systematic Theology*.

David M. Moffitt is Senior Lecturer in New Testament Studies at the University of St Andrews. He is author of *Atonement and the Logic of Resurrection in the Epistle to the Hebrews*, as well as numerous journal articles and essays on Hebrews, early Christian concepts of atonement and sacrifice, and the New Testament's use of the Old Testament.

L. Michael Morales is Professor of Biblical Studies at Greenville Presbyterian Theological Seminary. He is the author of *The Tabernacle Pre-Figured: Cosmic Mountain Ideology in Genesis and Exodus* and *Who Shall Ascend the Mountain of the LORD? A Biblical Theology of the Book of Leviticus*, and editor of *Cult and Cosmos:*

Tilting Toward a Temple-Centered Theology. He has a forthcoming commentary on the Book of Numbers.

Amy Peeler is Associate Professor of New Testament at Wheaton College and Associate Rector at St. Mark's Episcopal Church, Geneva, IL. Author of *"You Are My Son": The Family of God in the Epistle to the Hebrews* (T&T Clark, 2014) she continues to write in the areas of Hebrews and theology of family.

Nicholas Perrin holds the Franklin S. Dyrness Chair of Biblical Studies at Wheaton College. He is the author of numerous articles and books, including most recently *Jesus the Priest* (SPCK; Baker Academic) and *The Kingdom of God* (Zondervan).

Eckhard J. Schnabel is the Mary F. Rockefeller Distinguished Professor of New Testament at Gordon-Conwell Theological Seminary. He is the author of *Law and Wisdom from Ben Sira to Paul* (1985), *Early Christian Mission* (2004), *Der erste Brief des Paulus an die Korinther* (2006), *Paul the Missionary: Realities, Strategies, and Methods* (2008), *The Book of Acts* (2012), *The Trial and Crucifixion of Jesus: Texts and Commentary* (2015, with D. Chapman), *Der Brief an die Römer* (2015/2016), *The Gospel of Mark* (2017), *Jesus in Jerusalem* (2018), and other publications.

Matthew Thiessen is Associate Professor of Religious Studies at McMaster University. He is the author of *Contesting Conversion: Genealogy, Circumcision, and Identity in Ancient Judaism and Christianity* and *Paul and the Gentile Problem*.

Daniel J. Treier is the Knoedler Professor of Theology at Wheaton College Graduate School. He has authored several books including, in the area of theological exegesis, a commentary on *Proverbs and Ecclesiastes* as well as *Introducing Theological Interpretation of Scripture: Recovering a Christian Practice*. He has also coedited several books, including a new edition of the *Evangelical Dictionary of Theology*.

Cynthia L. Westfall is Associate Professor of New Testament at McMaster Divinity College. Her publications include *A Discourse Analysis of the Structure of Hebrews: Relationship between Form and Meaning* (T&T Clark, 2006) and *Paul and Gender: Reclaiming the Apostle's Vision for Men and Women in Christ* (Baker, 2016). She coedited *The Bible and Social Justice* (2016), *The Church Then and Now* (2012), *Christian Mission: Old Testament Foundations and New Testament Developments* (2010), *Empire and the New Testament* (2010) and is the Associate Greek Editor of the Common English Bible.

Preface and Acknowledgments

The present collection of essays devoted to the study of the atonement in Hebrews builds on an earlier volume, *Christology, Hermeneutics, and Hebrews. Profiles from the History of Interpretation*[1] and related works, though the present volume is not structured as a history of interpretation. What was said in the preface to *Christology* about the aims of such work as this applies to the present case. A more complete explanation is provided in the introductory chapter below.

Thanks are due to Stephen Wunrow and Lucia Sanders for their extensive roles in assisting and managing the editorial process, though responsibility for any errors and infelicities is owned by the editors alone. Thanks are also due to Michael Allen for his input in the planning stages, for help with some initial contacts with authors, and for suggested edits. Dan Treier's assistance from the beginning to the very end amounted to the rank of a coeditor. The epigraph was completed with the help of Gregg Okesson, Helen Mui, Simon He, John Monson, Andrew Burlingame, Adam Abate, Enoch Okode, Sharenda Barlar, Christine Kepner, Manoj Varughese, and Yousaf Sadiq.

We are grateful to the Evangelical Theological Society for welcoming non-members into the conversation during their annual meetings, and for their encouragement of this sort of work. Wheaton College provided release time and other aid, including a generous Aldeen Grant, without which much of the work could not have been completed. We are also grateful to Dominic Mattos, Sarah Blake, and T&T Clark for accepting this work into the LNTS series and providing ample support.

A planned background chapter on related issues in Second Temple Judaism was unable to be completed, but the substance of this material will not have been ignored among the thematic chapters.

In the nature of our project, more work and patience was required of the authors than is typically the case. The editors are most appreciative of their willingness to donate this extra time.

On a personal level, we the editors express our love and thanks to our families and friends for their support, patience, and contributions to our understanding of and progress on the Way to which Hebrews witnesses.

Soli Deo gloria
Spring, 2019

---

[1] Laansma, Jon and Daniel J. Treier (eds.), *Christology, Hermeneutics, and Hebrews. Profiles from the History of Interpretation* (LNTS 423; T&T Clark, 2012).

Introduction

Jon C. Laansma

The unnamed author of Hebrews has been regarded as one of the three great theologians of the NT and the book itself has played a significant part in the church's atonement theology. It still has much to offer. A comment made by T. F. Torrance, though with reference to Protestant traditions in particular, might indicate its wider potentials. Torrance for his part distinguished three aspects of the atonement as the "dramatic," "cultic-forensic," and "incarnational," each of which he believed received special attention in different Protestant traditions to the neglect of the other two. He longed for a "biblical wholeness" and commented that "it has long been my conviction that joint study of the *Epistle to the Hebrews* would have an immense part to play in such a rapprochement."[1] In this spirit, the present volume will draw together studies of the atonement in Hebrews that both represent the *status quæstionis* and press forward with fresh proposals. The result, it is hoped, will be of service well beyond the confines of Hebrews' specialists, a collection as important for what it says about the atonement and the twenty-first-century church as for what it says about Hebrews.

Our approach

Our subtitle, *A Dialogue on the Atonement in Hebrews*, works with a broad conception of the word "atonement," covering not only the means of expiation/propitiation but the whole of what Hebrews intends by "the great salvation," which is also the whole of what Israel's combined tabernacle rites encompassed: all that led to the at-one-ment of God's people with the God of creation, and that at-one-ment as such. That this collaborative, interdisciplinary project is, or was, a "dialogue" speaks more to the process of this book's production than to its final form. In the design of the project, dialogue was made *possible* for contributors over a span of several years and it was repeatedly *encouraged*. This was done chiefly in two ways. First, as many papers as possible were read at sessions of annual meeting of the Evangelical Theological Society over the span of 2014–2017. Second, as drafts were submitted they were sent out to all project members in complete batches, providing a wide opportunity to revise and make suggestions. The result is that there is disagreement and agreement contained

---

[1] T. F. Torrance, "Doctrinal Consensus on Holy Communion," *SJT* 15 (1962), pp. 4–21 (9); cited in F. F. Bruce, *The Epistle to the Hebrews*, rev. ed. (NICNT; Grand Rapids, MI: Eerdmans, 1990), pp. 31–32.

herein without an attempt to bring a harmonized master-theory to this particular facet of Hebrews' witness. Hebrews continues to speak for itself. The Lord lives as Lord.

Ultimately, there is disagreement that will have some of the usual characteristics of all collections but that represents at least some effort to bring our voices and minds together over a span of time so as to offer to our colleagues a conversation that they can carry forward.

Limits to such an approach can be readily guessed. Our approach, however, promised some advantages. Our membership was intentionally interdisciplinary: historians, exegetes, theologians, both OT and NT, both Hebrews specialists and those who specialize elsewhere, Protestant, Roman Catholic, and Orthodox. Authors were allowed freedom to be more neutrally descriptive or ideologically argumentative. All wrote from their individual expertise; some dared to address themselves to challenges outside their wheelhouse. The opportunity to learn from each other in the process was already mentioned. As is routinely true of collections, the opportunity for a scholar to mine down into a particular question, rather than attempt something comprehensive, brings its own depth and clarity.

This is, after all, the sort of work that comports with a broader vision of our shared enterprise. No one of us sees the whole. It happens at times that we succumb to the illusion that our own insight is the key to the whole. Moreover—and to make short work of this, since it was the burden of an earlier volume to make this point[2]—the very ontology of Scripture as divine speech requires more than (not less than) sound historically minded exegetical scholarship alone can supply, more than (not less than) sound theologians alone can supply, more than (not less than) sound scholarship as such can supply. Here, at least, a representative cross-section of scholars can have their say. The results for both parts and whole are provisional. We, too, are a community "on the way," not yet arrived.

Overview of contents

The following chapters fall into two main parts: contexts and themes.

The *context* chapters trace the historical, literary, and theological contexts for Hebrews' rhetoric concerning the atonement. These are less discussions of Hebrews' treatment of the atonement than of the surrounding historical and theological context within which it must be understood, both proximate and remote. Naturally they take into view both theological and historical considerations, though, with one exception, they are limited by and large to more narrowly historical questions of investigation stretching from the ANE into earliest Christianity; theology figures in by way of the historical description of movements, influences, and effects. The discussions of these chapters are limited further by the explicit concern with this particular writing, The

---

[2] Jon Laansma and Daniel J. Treier (eds.), *Christology, Hermeneutics, and Hebrews: Profiles from the History of Interpretation* (LNTS 423; London: T&T Clark, 2012). The present collection is not pursuing these hermeneutical questions directly but merely getting on with the work. It was not required and should not be assumed that all contributors to this volume share this editorial perspective in part or whole.

Letter to the Hebrews. No matter how broadly one of these chapters ranges to sketch in the larger context, it finally pivots on Hebrews. The balance between diachronic and synchronic survey was left to the discretion of the respective authors. Among the chapters that are omitted from this unit of the volume, two can be mentioned, namely, Second Temple Judaism (see the preface) and the most immediate context of the book's occasion: the situation of the human author and original readers as these illuminate Hebrews' rhetoric. It is assumed that all contributors to the volume have weighed these contexts and framed their contributions with them in view.

The chapters in the second unit of the book (*themes*) naturally overlap with each other but attempt to view the one "great salvation" of Hebrews distinctively from the angle of a given theme and to highlight the contours (and tensions, problems, etc.) that are focused with special clarity. These chapters are exegetical in nature, answering to "the way the words run." To whatever degree an individual contributor appeals to wider theological contexts of historical and systematic theology and relates them to their grasp of the subject matter, it was asked that these readings explicitly address themselves to first-century historical and literary questions. Beyond this and the general approach of the volume, the editors deliberately held back from stipulating any theology of the text and any hermeneutical theory. Certainly other themes could have received devoted attention: *Christus Victor*; *theosis*; and more. Hopefully, these are present in part or by implication, but without question the work required by our topic is larger than is contained in these covers.

Given the nature and history of this collection, there will be no concluding chapter that draws from these separate studies a unified theory. This is not because we view such an attempt as wrong-headed. Rather than exercise an editorial prerogative in favoring one perspective over others we provide here a summary of the respective chapters and permit readers to distill their own judgments. The following summaries combined with the chapters themselves will make sufficiently clear where there are differences and points of convergence. In this way, too, we allow this to stand as an ongoing *dialogue*. Two of the editors have expressed themselves in part in their own chapters, and the third has indicated his views elsewhere.[3]

The following summaries do not undertake to isolate what might turn out to be the most interesting comments in these chapters—sound bites, if you will—but what seems to represent the overall argument. For some chapters, this main line of argument may be the key contribution, for others it may be little more than the vehicle for an assortment of subsidiary points. Even in the former case, it may turn out that particular claims made along the way, possibly unguarded, attract the most attention. These significant, provocative, and controversial insights will be discovered only by reading the chapters themselves.

---

[3] Jon C. Laansma, *I Will Give You Rest: The "Rest" Motif in the New Testament with Special Reference to Mt. 11 and Heb. 3-4* (Tübingen: Mohr, 1997); idem, "Hebrews and the Mission of the Earliest Church" in *New Testament Theology in Light of the Church's Mission: Essays in Honor of I. Howard Marshall* (ed. Jon Laansma, Grant R. Osborne, and Ray F. Van Neste; Eugene, OR: Cascade, 2001); idem, "The Living and Active Word. A Theological Reading of Hebrews" in *Listen, Understand, Obey: Essays on Hebrews in Honor of Gareth Lee Cockerill* (ed. Caleb T. Friedeman; Eugene OR: Wipf and Stock, 2017); idem, *The Letter to the Hebrews: A Commentary for Preaching, Teaching, and Bible Study* (Eugene, OR: Cascade, 2017).

Contexts[4]

1. Old Testament Israel: Hebrews positions itself in the canonical history and literature of Israel as the culmination of the speech of Israel's God. It challenges us to read those Scriptures attentively and closely. To be sure, this is a reading "in the Son," but insofar as Hebrews purports to represent what these Scriptures themselves say—particularly with respect to the tabernacle and covenant— it behooves us to examine them ourselves (Acts 17:11). Such an effort also contributes to the historical reconstruction of a trajectory from ancient Israel into early Christianity. L. Michael Morales adopts a literary and canonical (*versus* a history of religions) approach to argue for the whole burnt offering as central to Israel's cult. Israel's cult was founded upon the doctrine of atonement, and the whole burnt offering, which Morales prefers to refer to as an ascension offering, serves as the summation of that cult. Viewed as a whole, the Israelite liturgy, which is something of a journey into God's Presence, began with a purification (and/or reparation) offering, proceeded to the ascension offering, accompanied by the tribute offering, and then concluded with the communion offering. Ultimately, the ascension offering may be understood as encompassing the whole ritual movement in itself, with the expiatory offerings being *pre-fixed* to it so as to highlight that aspect of the ascension offering's blood rite, and the communion offering *suffixed* to it so as to underscore the divine acceptance aspect of the soothing aroma's ascent to heaven. In the ascension offering the *whole* animal underwent burning, conveying the sense of self-denial and utter consecration—a life yielded entirely unto YHWH. In the smoke of this offering, there is a *transfer* of the animal, as a vicarious substitute, from the ordinary earthly plane to the divine heavenly realm, to the ownership of God. Reading Hebrews with this background in mind, the cult's fulfillment cannot be separated from the fulfillment of God's *Torah*; that is, the cult's meaning can only be satisfied and made obsolete through the sacrifice of Christ's will unto God in absolute obedience. As to the ascent aspect of the ascension offering, atonement in its broadest sense is indeed *through* blood but does not stop with blood. The blood rite's *telos* is humanity's restoration to God portrayed in the smoke's ascent to heaven, an ascension theology that comprehends Jesus's own ascent. This ascent was historically traced as an exodus pattern. While Jesus's ascension is sometimes described by the author of Hebrews in terms of the *Yom Kippur* ritual, this exodus pattern of the ascension offering was expressed daily, weekly, monthly, and annually through the cult's ascension offering. Thus, watching the fragrant, billowing column of the ascension offering's smoke ascend into heaven, propitiating and pleasing YHWH God, the ancient Israelite had glimpsed a hint of what Hebrews describes as Jesus entering "into heaven itself, now to appear in the presence of God for us" (Heb. 9:24).

---

[4] In the following summaries quotation marks are dispensed with, though the summaries quote extensively and verbatim from the chapters. This was done with the authors' approval.

2. The LXX: Within the sea of literary remains that represent the cultures of antiquity and the context, near and far, of Hebrews, the Greek translation(s) of Israel's Scriptures is (are) singular for our interests. Hebrews makes sole use of the Greek version of the OT for the purposes of this exposition, raising the questions of its possible influence on Hebrews' expositional argument, how it is appropriated, and the significance of its use. Karen H. Jobes addresses these larger questions through the close examination of the two places where Christ speaks in Hebrews, both of which have him addressing his Father in the words of the LXX. Hebrews' practice represents an advancement on Jesus's use of Scripture in the Gospels, and on the "Christological ventriloquism" that Hays finds in Paul. Attridge's suggestion that these passages in Hebrews function as *examples* for the rest of God's covenant people is good, but might not go far enough in explaining how Hebrews' use of the *Greek* Old Testament amplifies and underscores the mission of atonement that lies at the heart of the Incarnation. A comparison of Heb. 10:5-7 with the Göttingen Old Greek highlights differences from the wording of Ps. 39:7-9 LXX that are finally best attributed to Hebrews' hand, and that are calculated for both rhetorical and theological effect. God spoke in both David and the Son. The quotation signals Christ's continuity with the Davidic monarchy, but the differences introduced by Hebrews signal the discontinuity. Ultimately, giving attention to Hebrews' use of this psalm, what we overhear is nothing less than Jesus Christ agreeing to the terms of the New Covenant in his blood that would be required to bring many sons and daughters to glory (Heb. 2:10; 13:20). From there, Jobes turns to the quotations of Ps. 21:23 LXX and Isaiah 8:17-18 LXX in Heb. 2:12-13. Examination of the differences between both the (Göttingen) LXX and the Hebrew *Vorlage*, on the one hand, and the LXX and Heb. 2:12-13, on the other, sheds light on the way in which the LXX's rendering facilitated Hebrews' appropriation and how Hebrews' own adjustments sharpened the intended point in this context. The net effect is to explain the necessity of the Incarnation, that it was necessary for a human being to conquer suffering and death in order for any human beings to be led to glory.
3. Jesus traditions: Within the NT, Jesus is openly called a priest only in Hebrews. Was this identification as such, apart from the open mention of it, the writer's innovation as many think? Nicholas Perrin argues that in fact we have good reason to believe that when the *auctor Hebraeos* grounds Jesus's priesthood on the convergence of Psalms 2 and 110, the writer is neither introducing a *novum* nor extending a recent notional development; rather the writer is reiterating a very early line of reasoning which may have even struck root in the *Sitz im Leben Jesu*. To arrive at this conclusion, Perrin first demonstrates the foundational role of Psalms 2 and 110 in the thematizing of Jesus's priesthood within Hebrews itself. Along the way, it is argued that Psalm 2, rather than Ps. 110:4 alone, provides support for Jesus's priesthood: In the Judaism of the day, Psalm 2 was most closely associated not so much with ontological claims of royal status but with the anointed figure's envisioned role in restoring the purity of temple space (*4Q174*; *Psalms of Solomon* 17.21-25). When in Hebrews 5 the writer justifies Christ's priesthood with both Psalm 110 *and* Psalm 2, his

argument is not taking an idiosyncratic turn but is in keeping with contemporary reception of both psalms as textual signposts for an eschatological priestly figure. Moreover, the same background prompts us to take Hebrews more seriously as political theology. Secondly, Perrin then examines the Gospel of Mark's use of Psalms 2 and 110, with special attention to Jesus's baptism and the *Davidssohnfrage* debate. Not only Psalm 2 but echoes of the Aqedah (Genesis 22) are noted in connection with the baptism, which echoes suggest that in it Jesus is being anointed not just as the son of David but also as the new Isaac, that is, as one who would one day sacrifice his life willingly for God's purposes; he is marked off both as the sacrificing royal-priest and as the sacrifice. The Baptist was essentially establishing a new priesthood for the newly emerging eschatological temple. Further evidence along these lines is drawn in from the transfiguration, Gethsemane, and cross narratives. Psalm 110, for its part, features in Mk 12:35-37 and 14:53-65, where Perrin argues that the Melchizedekian reference is significant: Jesus is identifying himself as Melchizedek *redivivus*, which amounts to a direct challenge to Caiaphas and opens Jesus to the charge of blasphemy. Thirdly and finally, Perrin marshals evidence that both these gospel traditions stand in good stead as authentic reminiscences of Jesus, an argument corroborated by observing the strategic role those remembered events would have had in the liturgical life of the early church. Thus, he argues that not only is the event of Jesus's baptism well-established historically, but that the connection with Psalm 2 goes back to the event itself; further, we may regard Heb. 5:5 as evidence that the *auctor Hebraeos* was familiar with the story of Jesus's baptism complete with its reference to Ps. 2:7. Moreover, the case for Psalm 110, as it occurs in Mk 12:35-37, reaching back to Jesus is all the stronger, and the likelihood that the earliest church associated that psalm with the memory of Jesus self-identifying with the Melchizedekian high priest is confirmed by its eucharistic connections. As a result, in his identification of Jesus as our Great High Priest, the author of Hebrews is situated along an interpretive thoroughfare originating in the Palestinian movement.

4. Greco-Roman polytheism: The writer of Hebrews wrote and, we can be confident, thought in Greek. It is arguable that the audience was partially (if not entirely, in some estimations) Gentile in derivation; the writing's argument would seem to depend on a Hellenistic strain in its audience, whatever their religious or philosophical background. It is possible (given time, almost certain) that this text would have been read by those with no acquaintance with either Judaism or Christianity. For all these reasons, it is of value to isolate the language and rites of Hebrews and consider them in their Greco-Roman context, for the sake of marking both continuities and discontinuities. As well, the question of what Hebrews seems to assume and not assume in its readers is better estimated by such a comparison. Eckhard J. Schnabel, in tackling this sizeable task, begins by noting that, since there was no limit to the variety of gods among the Greeks, there was no limit to the number of gods and no limit to the number of stories that were told about the gods. This stands in stark contrast to the comparative agreement about the story of Israel's God as seen in Jewish and early Christian

history. This lack of unity in the polytheist setting is manifested in the disparate scholarly theories—summarized in turn by Schnabel—that compete to account for the significance(s) of sacrifice in Greek and Roman belief and practice. Among the more confident results: Both Greek and Roman sacrifices had multiple purposes, but forgiveness of transgressions is not a relevant category. Punishment by the god was not much talked about or counted on. The terms "sin" or "transgression" are virtually absent from this literature. Even this has contradictory evidence in Hesiod, inconsistency which may have to be accepted as pluralistic and opportunistic eclecticism on the part of the Greeks. In attempting to understand expiation and propitiation among polytheists, it is noted that a worshiper rarely knew for which deity the expiatory rite was performed. Outside of Aristotle, none of the other philosophical schools showed much interest in forgiveness; by the middle of the first century CE, the main gods were mostly seen as passionless and benevolent, so that seeking divine forgiveness came to appear almost countercultural. Again, mishap in daily life was not predominantly interpreted as a divine penalty in this period. After additional discussion of vicarious death in Greek and Roman tradition and the unique case of the Lydian-Phrygian confession inscriptions, Schnabel turns to a point-by-point comparison between Hebrews and polytheists touching sacrifice, blood, expiation and purification, and vicarious death—noting overlap where it existed, whether substantive or superficial, but stressing repeatedly how mystified and perplexed polytheists, untutored in Christian or Jewish traditions, would be if they encountered Hebrews' language and argument, and how fundamentally they differed from Hebrews' vision.

5. Early Christianity: In conventional biblical scholarship, the term "backgrounds" is generally limited to an empiricist's perspective on the historical and cultural context of a writing—the temporally immediate, developing material-social-conceptual world from which, in which, and to which a writing is composed. It is a matter of the "background" of the human author and "original readers." It is common to restrict this perspective to convictions about reality with which the writer of Hebrews—depending on one's interpretation of Hebrews—would not have agreed, let alone the many heirs of its witness. If, however, the "people of God" in which and for which the letter was written embraces its many believing readers into the present, then a wider lens is called for. Moreover, there is more to be said about "background" than what was going on (politically, linguistically, etc.) or believed in Italy or Palestine in the mid-first century, and we may learn much from the Church Fathers who were preoccupied with the divine world behind, in, and in front of the text. The God who speaks is not a mere textual product or effect, and the Fathers did not believe that their doctrines were anything other than accounts of the realities from which and to which the Scriptures, including Hebrews, spoke. Finally, from the usual perspective of a biblical critic there is good reason to carry the study of the historical trajectory into the post-history of our letter. Thus, Khaled Anatolios has undertaken to elucidate some highlights of the impact of Hebrews in the development of Trinitarian and Christological doctrine, especially in regard to its understanding

of Christ's salvific work as priestly sacrifice, while also indicating how this development constituted a hermeneutical background that determined the understanding of this biblical text. For this undertaking to be manageable, four figures are selected for treatment: Athanasius, Cyril of Alexandria, Maximus the Confessor, and Augustine. The Christological and soteriological developments Anatolios traces through these Fathers are demonstrably and crucially dependent on Hebrews, illustrating the strategic influence of this text on the church's teaching. In sum, Athanasius applied to this text the hermeneutical rule that the Scriptures presented a "double account of the Savior" in order to substantiate both the full divinity of the Son, as the coessential "radiance" of the Father's glory, and his humanity, in which he offered himself to the Father. Athanasius's classic text, *On the Incarnation*, presents the sacrificial self-offering of Christ as the synthesizing motif by which it integrates the salvific efficacy of the Incarnation of the Word, as well as Christ's death and resurrection. Following in the footsteps of Athanasius, Cyril of Alexandria insisted on the hypostatic union of Christ's humanity with the Word, according to which it is the Word himself who makes the sacrificial offering of his humanity to the Father and thereby makes efficacious intercession for human sin. For Maximus the Confessor, the priesthood of Christ encompasses his entire life in which he allowed his humanity to be the target of demonic powers and was thereby "tested in every respect as we are, yet without sin," thus granting humanity the power to overcome disordered "passions" which are contrary to nature. Augustine envisioned Christ's priestly self-offering as the origin and ultimate substance of the Church's self-offering, which is manifested in the Eucharist. Common to all these early theologians is the premise that Christ's sacrificial self-offering is both a divine and a human work and the presupposition that humanity's incorporation into Christ's self-offering is constitutive of salvation.

Themes

6. Christology: Daniel J. Treier approaches the reading of Hebrews as a systematic theologian, exploring what dogmatic Christology might contribute to understanding Hebrews, particularly with respect to the neglected, yet climactic and crucial, motif of Christ as *mediator* of a New Covenant. A preliminary survey of key Christological texts yields the conclusion that as to *names*, Christ is presented preeminently as the Son of God and so as superior to other OT figures. He is also High Priest, requiring full identity with humanity; that priesthood's superiority lies in its unique sacrifice, its heavenly presentation, and its everlasting implementation. Christ's *benefits* are summarized as salvation from sin; the inheritance of eternal rest; a holy pilgrimage from deliverance to glory; ongoing divine presence and help; participation in Christ's approach to God; and perfection for humanity. Asking how all this intersects with dogmatic theology involves the ecumenical creeds' claims of full divinity, full humanity, and the

union of these two natures in the one Person of Christ; secondly, the traditions of the threefold office of prophet, priest, and king; thirdly, the Reformed tradition of Christ as the one Mediator between God and humanity. The remainder of Treier's argument appeals to Christ's mediation to unify the threefold office and undergird the full divinity at stake in the creeds but disputed by moderns. After a survey of texts using mediator terminology he concludes that we see from their location—at hinge points of the central argument and the pastoral climax of its application—the importance of this designation of Mediator. It does not compete with the prevalence of Son and Priest, but it is climactic in unfolding the unified significance of those titles. Considering the meaning of μεσίτης along with its use in Gal. 3:19-20 and 1 Tim. 2:5 yields the conclusion that the term focuses upon what is somehow in the middle of a collectively plural entity or between multiple entities. The term does not preclude a measure of identity with one or more of the entities themselves, so long as the middle place is filled. Adding Hebrews' understanding of the New Covenant in Jeremiah 31 leads to the insight that the fundamentally new form of covenant mediation in Christ is not external but internal, in which believers deal with God directly yet without the expected terror. The concept of priesthood covers much of this, but the broader concept of mediation ties that together with Christ's divine sonship. To establish the basis and result of this distinctive mediation requires appreciation of the full humanity of Jesus but also the indications in Hebrews of full divinity. Ultimately, the basis of the believer's confidence is that no merely external self-offering has been made: God has offered himself to take away sin, taking it upon himself to provide the requisite human faithfulness. The basis of this mediation is the divine Son's perfection as High Priest. A closing step establishes how Christ's identity as Mediator implies the unity of Prophet and Priest and King and much else. Treier's conclusion goes on to propose how both Athanasian and classically Protestant accounts of salvation can be instructed by Hebrews' Mediator Christology, and, if so, how they can learn from each other.

7. Blood, Death, and Sacrifice: Matthew Levering allows us to see Hebrews through the eyes of Thomas Aquinas with a view to understanding both: Aquinas has been accused of a sinister supersessionism of which he deserves to be absolved. This is done through a careful documentation of Thomas's discussion of blood, death, and sacrifice in Hebrews, which, in turn proves to be an illuminating exposition of these motifs in its own right. Noting Soulen's argument that Irenaeus of Lyons was the originator of this supersessionist reading and its (for Soulen) inimical effects, Levering asks whether the "Irenaean solution" may in certain respects be biblical rather than simply "Irenaean," and whether Aquinas is justifiably blamed for theological readings that are almost wholly without reference to God's way with Israel. Aquinas, in fact, has been instructed by Hebrews itself in his approach. He pays deep attention to Torah in his theology of the cross, and repeatedly goes out of his way to cite the Old Testament and to underscore the goodness and relevance of the Torah for Christians of his own day. Thus, commenting on Heb. 2:9, Aquinas notes that Jesus's death goes to the farthest extreme of human death; his death was the bitterest and most

shameful. These claims are illuminated from Wisdom of Solomon 2:10-11, 20, and, following the medieval Gloss on Scripture, from Isaiah 52–53's description of the Servant. Contemplating what it means for Jesus merely to have "tasted" death leads Aquinas to observe both that Jesus rose quickly and discerned the flavor of death rather than merely drank it; for biblical testimony he turns to Lam. 1:12; Mt. 26:39; Isa. 24:9 (in context); Ps. 16:10 (Levering is careful to note where Aquinas's Parisian version of the Vulgate differs from modern translations represented by the RSV). Hebrews 2:10 for Aquinas places Jesus's death in the framework of divine providence, comparing Rev. 1:8; Rom. 11:36; Prov. 16:4; Ps. 146:6; and Wis. 6:7. Hebrews 2:14-15 prompts Aquinas to ask why Hebrews teaches that the devil has the power of death in light of 1 Sam. 2:6 and Deut. 32:39. He turns to 2 Pet. 2:18; Rev. 5:5; Lk. 11:21; Jn 14:30, along with the patristic theme of Jesus's overcoming the devil by means of justice, and Ps. 69:4. In short, in these and numerous other particulars, Aquinas is interrogating Hebrews closely in the expectation that insight can be gained into the realities to which it speaks from other canonical witnesses to the same realities, particularly from the OT, and with the assistance of other interpreters in the tradition. An example of a "mystical interpretation" attaches to Heb. 9:6, which Levering uses to elaborate on Aquinas's larger hermeneutical approach and his general focus upon the "literal sense." When discussing 9:9, Aquinas cites 10:4 and argues that this teaching regarding the inefficacy of animal sacrifices in themselves does not rest solely on the New Testament; cf. Isa. 1:13 and Mic. 6:7. Indeed, Levering observes, throughout this section, Aquinas is concerned to ward off attacks upon the Old Testament. He sets Hebrews 9 against the heretics who say that the Old Testament was not from the Holy Spirit, but from an evil god. Aquinas observes as well that there were many holy persons under Moses's law, who were perfected not by the animal sacrifices per se, but by the faith (implicitly a faith in Christ) with which they performed the sacrifices. Commenting on Heb. 9:19-22 and its use of Exodus 24, Aquinas explains Moses's actions by observing that Jesus's free sacrificial death for our salvation involved the shedding of blood, and therefore Moses was justified in his use of the blood of animal sacrifices, which prefigured Jesus's. Aquinas notes that the reasons of the figurative sacrifices of the Old Law should be taken from the true sacrifice of Christ, rather than vice versa. Yet Aquinas also points out that there were "literal" reasons for the animal sacrifices, including preventing idolatry and signifying the right ordering of man's mind to God. Related to Heb. 9:23, Aquinas decisively refutes negative judgments of the Mosaic law's animal sacrifices. He points out that if "better sacrifices" were needed, the Mosaic law's sacrifices must have been good: for something is called better in relation to something good. Space forbids even a summary of the many other expositions Levering surveys. In short, Aquinas's consistent appeal to the Old Testament in interpreting Hebrews and his insistence upon the goodness of the Mosaic law and upon the spiritual depth of the psalms and prophets enable him to show the beauty and wisdom, rather than contradiction, of God's plan of salvation. It is the Old Testament itself that leads to an appreciation of the relationship of sacrifice to faith and love, a relationship present already in

Israel and evident in Jesus Christ's fulfillment of sacrifice and in the Church's sacramental representation of Christ's sacrifice. Thus, Aquinas uses the Old Testament to interpret itself and to interpret Hebrews' understanding of what Israel's Scriptures say about death, sacrifice, and blood.

8. Resurrection, Ascension, Heavenly Session: Michael Allen approaches the complex of resurrection, ascension, and session by giving particular attention to the somewhat overlooked *prophetic* aspects of Christ's heavenly session; how the exalted Christ continues to send forth the Word of God in living and active form. First, in appreciative, albeit critical engagement with the work of David Moffitt, Allen highlights the exaltation as a context for continued activity rather than merely the sign of Christ's finished work. Giving due notice to the significance of Christ's bodily resurrection for Hebrews' argument, it is noted that resurrection fits within the theo-logic of exaltation, which is of primary interest for Hebrews: The exalted Christ serves as minister unto his people from the throne room on high. Allen notes here how Question 49 of the Heidelberg Catechism expressed the same emphasis on the benefits we receive from Christ's ascension. Secondly, Allen explores how the exaltation of the Son is linked to the ministry of the Word of God, such that the teaching of Hebrews regarding Scripture can be appreciated as being more tightly tethered to the present action of the great prophet, even Jesus. Here he gives attention to several passages that indicate the continued speech of the exalted Son, speech directed not only in his priestly role to the Father (e.g., 7:25) but in both his prophetic and priestly roles to his household (especially 1:1-4; 2:12; 3:1-6, 7, 14). More extended attention is then given to 12:25, where the exalted Son warns and speaks and in so doing shakes not only the earth but also the heavens. In particular, Hebrews 12:25 prompts our communicative imagination to be alert to the exalted Son's warning amidst and through the words of his emissaries. This apostle proves faithful over his household oftentimes (3:1, 6)—perhaps we must say ordinarily—through the delegated agency of his own apostles. Finally, Allen frames a particular question, regarding what light the attestation of the exalted Son as an active prophet might shed upon the doctrine of Scripture taught by Hebrews—a deductive question to be distinguished from the usual inductive attempt to infer a doctrine of Scripture from the author's use of the OT. In this, he wishes to avoid the methodological imposition of categories of peripheral disciplines or later eras, and to attend to claims internal to and overt within the text itself. He concentrates this discussion on 4:12 and 13:8. Zwingli attested the power of the Word (4:12) by describing it as the glove, not the fist; the scriptural Word has significant impact because the force of the mighty hand and outstretched arm of the Almighty stands behind its collision course with sinners. It is Christ's resurrection life and activity that is at work in his own Word. The Spirit also is at work in the Word's piercing and discerning power. It is divine discipline that is in view in this activity: judgment takes not only punitive but also paternally restorative and thus pedagogical intonations here. The divisions it highlights are not wheat and tares but the true and false within God's people; it is a disciplining and forming activity, the ascended Son's ongoing sanctification of his own company. Thus, the exalted

prophecy of the Son provides the lens through which we ought to view the teaching of Hebrews regarding the nature and power of the Word of God. In summarizing and concluding, Allen contemplates 13:8. The "sameness" of Jesus Christ preserves the integrity of each historical era, both the goodness of the old and the greater glory of the new, while attesting the ongoing exalted agency of the Son in the present proclamation of his Word. Reviewing 12:18-29 with the aid of Michael Kibbe's work leads to the insight that what Deuteronomy portrays as well and good is viewed by Hebrews as actually being a good state for that prior era but is seen now as a negative step backward. This judgment about the unity and varied administrations of the divine economy stems from a further awareness regarding the new mediator and the greater glory he has communicated. The steady service of the Son undergirds our confidence and boldness. In just this way does the "great shepherd of the sheep" exercise his pastoral oversight and equip his disciples for that which is pleasing in God's sight. In short, Hebrews presents an exalted Christology that heralds the prophetic work of the Son, and it ties this ever so closely to his living and active Word. Thus, bibliology and soteriology are bound up together, not conflated but coordinated Christologically for the sake of hearkening God's people onward in their journey today while it is yet today.

9. Priesthood: David M. Moffitt corrects an imbalanced emphasis on the completeness of Christ's offering in his death and entrance into his Father's presence by highlighting the ongoing atoning work of his heavenly session. The latter work implies the need of ongoing forgiveness for the duration of the present age, it entails the incompleteness of Christ's work in the cross and ascension, and it consists in the maintenance of the New Covenant relationship between God and his people. All of this corresponds closely to the ministry of the Old Covenant priesthood, to which Christ's priestly ministry organically relates. En route to his argument, Moffitt enumerates several of his working assumptions relating to Hebrews' careful thinking out of the problem of Jesus's tribal lineage for his priestly role; to the bodily resurrection of Jesus as the solution to this problem; to Jesus's ascension to the highest heaven and entrance into the inner sanctum of the heavenly tabernacle; to Hebrews' dialogical manner of reading the OT in light of Christ, and Christ in light of the OT; to the irreducible ritual process of sacrifice, the incongruence of suffering and a fitting Levitical sacrifice, and the properly priestly and ritually weightier acts touching the altars themselves in the presence of God; and to the sustained, Pentateuchally shaped narrative with which the argument works throughout (a story that moves from exodus to inheritance). Moffitt also notes that in his use of the theological word, "atonement," he works with a narrower notion of sacrificial or Levitical atonement; sacrificial atonement primarily aims to effect forgiveness and purification in order to maintain the covenant relationship, not least by enabling impure and guilty humans to approach God's presence, and by fulfilling the terms God himself has given whereby he condescends to be in covenant relationship with and to dwell among his people. Given all this, Moffitt argues in light of 7:25 that Jesus's followers are in need of ongoing atonement. The very work that the

high priests on earth could do only once a year is done by Jesus perpetually; by virtue of his resurrection he can do this work without interruption, bringing a level of purity and forgiveness that exceeds that of the Old Covenant. This pattern conforms exactly to the ministry of the late-second temple high priest in the Holy of Holies on Yom Kippur, in which supplication for the people and the offering of blood were inseparable. It also offers a historically plausible explanation of the development of early Christian reflection that deduced aspects of Christological and soteriological reflection from the very Jewish scriptures and practices it cherished. Moreover, all this assumes that Jesus has not stepped out of space and time, for he continues to be an embodied human being in a particular place, the place of God's right hand, and one who will at a future day no longer be absent from his *waiting* (not "wandering") brothers and sisters (9:28)—who are pictured as waiting as did the exodus generation at Kadesh Barnea, prior to their subsequent wanderings which came as the result of judgment. Thus, the work of salvation is presently ongoing. Jesus is appealing to God for his brothers and sisters. This intercession ensures their full salvation. His intercession is making God's people perfect, as the Old Covenant ministry could not. In closing, Moffitt anticipates and resolves the apparent tension of his argument with the "once-for-all" language of Hebrews, showing how these in reality cohere. He also observes that Hebrews differs from Paul's idea (Rom. 8:34) that those for whom Christ intercedes cannot be condemned. While Hebrews would not envision God condemning any who remain partakers of Christ, the people of the New Covenant can effectively remove themselves from the covenant relationship; when this happens, they can no more reenter the covenant than Christ can repeat his once-for-all work.

10. Plight and Solution: In his biblical-theological approach to the reading of Hebrews, Mark S. Gignilliat pursues the triune subject matter of the Christian bible. This sort of biblical theology, which he contrasts with the approach of Vos, exists for the sake of exploring the inner-canonical conversation of the Bible's two testaments and constitutive parts in light of Scripture's subject matter. The topic of "plight and solution" admits of several points of entry, one of which has been adequately treated by David Moffitt's monograph. The point of entry selected by Gignilliat is that of the promised rest (chs. 3–4). The warning against the danger of forfeiting this rest stands at a signal moment in the sermon's movement. The priesthood of Jesus as intimated in the first three chapters peppers the sermonic flow and highlights a central motif awaiting further elaboration. This further elaboration begins at the end of chapter four, immediately following the warning against forfeiting God's promise of entering his place of rest. Rest in 4:1 is conceived of as eschatological; the Numbers account to which it alludes is figural; faith is eschatological with the plight emanating from 3:14. Gignilliat observes the employment of Jewish exegetical strategies applied by Hebrews to the LXX, the logical flow of Hebrews 3–4, Hebrews' use of Psalm 95 as an interpretive lens for understanding God's promise, and the eschatological understanding of the whole in terms of the person and work of Jesus Christ. The connection drawn with Gen. 2:2 reveals that God's seventh day of rest is itself

an anticipation of a future reality; God's own space is a perpetual seventh day of rest. God's rest is the crowning achievement of creation, as von Rad saw, and God's rest or cessation exists now, alongside and in human history. It is this that awaits the pilgrim people addressed by Hebrews if they heed the warning and persevere in faith. An examination of both the Greek and underlying Hebrew terminology for "rest" and "cessation" leads to an appreciation of the thematic development of God's promise in the Deuteronomistic history. The resulting insight is that God's Sabbath rest, a rest promised as an eschatological hope, is a location; it is the promised land where God dwells as he attends providentially and redemptively to the created world, the work from which God has ceased. This leads to a discussion of the distinction between creation and providence with the help of Jn 5:17, and the conclusion that God can cease and work at the same time because a distinction is made between the creative activity of God and his providential/redemptive attendance to his finished creation. O'Donovan provides assistance in probing the problems of the modern notion of *creatio continua*, which handles poorly the distinction between creation and providence. A solid understanding of the creation Sabbath, argues O'Donovan, would have circumvented this problem. O'Donovan himself points to Hebrews 3–4 and comments that for Hebrews the completion of creation, so far from being put in doubt by the thought of a yet-to-be completed history, is the only ground on which we can take the latter seriously. Moreover, looking at Genesis 2 itself, eschatological hope or teleology is built into the very fabric of God's seven-day work of creation. When we are armed with these insights we can better appreciate (and sympathize with) Martin Luther's exposition of the seventh day of creation in his Genesis commentary, which Gignilliat summarizes. Augustine's literal commentary on Genesis, though differing from the later Luther at points, provides substantial support for Luther's understanding. Karl Barth provides an exclamation point: "On the seventh day God was well pleased with His Son. He saw creation perfect through Christ; He saw it restored again through Christ; and He therefore declared it to be finished and rested." Gignilliat concludes that such a Trinitarian conception of creation and the seventh day as the apex of the created order resides at the very core of the Book of Hebrews' inner logic regarding the Father's creation of the world by the effective and personal agency of the Son (Heb. 1:1-4). Creation is framed Christologically and so too is Creation's eschatological rest. All this coheres with both the OT's own development and Hebrews' explicit argument. The challenge from Israel's history remains: do not harden your hearts. Herein lies the perennial threat, the real human plight. And the solution remains a clinging to the future, saving promises of God in Jesus Christ.

11. Law: Matthew Thiessen argues that Hebrews does not intend to dismiss the relevance of the Jerusalem temple and tabernacle cult, and does not conclude that the legislation of the cultic system is no longer valid. Rather, it argues that Christ's death and resurrection are rituals that belong to a different cultic system in the heavenly realm. It is not comparing two different religions but two different cultic centers, earthly and heavenly, both of which are in force for the present

age. The earthly is inferior, as any ancient Jew would have agreed. The readers are not tempted to return to Jerusalem as if this is something to be opposed; they are taken to be members of Israel. They have not abandoned observance of the Jewish law and so are not now thinking of returning to it. It is taken for granted that they are concerned about the Jewish law and issues pertaining to Jewish ritual and cult, and wish to know how Christ's high priesthood can be in accordance with the Jewish law. The writer approves of this facet of his implied readers' theology. The author envisages two realms—the mortal and immortal—coexisting. The mortal realm pertains to the earth and has an earthly sanctuary, while the immortal realm is heavenly and has a heavenly sanctuary. Though they coexist for now, the author believes that only the immortal will remain at some point in the future. Looking at Heb. 8:10 and 10:16, Thiessen concludes that there simply is no evidence in Hebrews that the author rejects the ritual and cultic aspects of the Jewish law. Rather, there is strong evidence that he thinks these aspects of the law remain in effect at the time of his writing. Heb. 10:28, alluding to Deut. 17:6; 19:5, signals that Hebrews believes in the continuing applicability of *this* particular law; it hints at the enduring significance of ritual categories. Considering Hebrews 7–10, it is taken for granted that the laws of proper genealogical descent of Jewish priests are still in effect. It is not true that there can only be one priesthood at a time in Jewish thinking; the idea that there would be two priestly lines, one for the earthly and another for the heavenly cultic places was known elsewhere (Wis. 9:8; *1 En.* 9.1; Philo *Spec.* 1.67; 4Q400 frag. 1 1.1-4; *Test of Levi* 3:4-6; *2 Bar.* 4:2-6; *Num. Rab.* 12.12; *b. Hag.* 12b; *Gen. Rab.* 69.7; *Song. Rab.* 48.8; *Pesiq. Rab.* 40.6), and none of these authors intend to undermine or abolish the earthly priesthood in general. Heb. 7:12 does not refer to abrogation but to the transformation that must occur when one moves from the terrestrial cult to the heavenly realm. There is a hierarchy but this hierarchy does not abolish the Levitical priesthood or speak to its obsolescence. The earthly ritual purity system addresses the problem of mortality (to which is connected immorality) coming into contact with the God in their midst but does not address the root problem of mortality itself. This earthly Jewish system is not abolished but coexists with the heavenly which always ran in parallel with it while hoping for deliverance of not only Israel but the entire cosmos from bondage to death, sin, and demonic forces.

12. Covenant: Amy Peeler argues that access to and continuing relationship with God—atonement broadly conceived—is for our author covenantal. Hence, attending to the nuances of this author's view of covenant is vital to his understanding of atonement. In sum, the question that this chapter seeks to answer is this: "*How* does covenant shed light on atonement in Hebrews?" The relationship between covenant and atonement is this: When humans receive the full promises of the covenant they experience full atonement with God, and therefore the author discusses God's covenantal keeping of promises to help the audience trust that God will continue to keep his promises and if they trust they will remain in the covenant by which they have relationship with God and hence at-one-ment, now and forever. Peeler gets there by discussing God's

promises to the Son of sovereignty and priesthood (in the exordium; Pss. 2, 8, 110; and so on), indicating how the fulfillment of these promises, duly registered by Hebrews, should engender trust in the Promise-Giver, as well as how that fulfillment accomplishes salvation itself. The latter leads into an explication of the atoning nature of the New Covenant which comes about because of the kept promises to the Son. If God's promise/oath to the Son brought a better covenant as seen in chs. 7–8, we can see the elements the author highlights that make this covenant, this atonement with God, in his estimation, better. There are three prominent elements: perfection, access to God, and the covenant's enduring nature, which Peeler treats in turn. Finally, she turns to a presentation of the author's encouragements and exhortations to trust in the promises of God based on the texts of the people of Israel. There is a sense in which the Christian readers of Hebrews have been given the New Covenant, and there are ways in which its promises remain to be fulfilled: they still need instruction; they are still susceptible to sin; they are not yet fully in God's heavenly presence. Their hearts must therefore remain faithful if they are to arrive at the fullness of what was promised, as the exposition of Psalm 95 also reinforces. By way of bolstering further their confidence, Hebrews devotes considerable attention to a retelling of God's faithfulness to previous generations of Israelites, especially Abraham and Moses. In the case of Abraham, God had sworn a promised inheritance to him. He received a part of it, and after much patience he obtained residence in the heavenly city and the vision of his many descendants. Abraham's story shows that God keeps his promises, sometimes in life and sometimes past life, because death is no barrier to the faithfulness of God. Abraham is lifted up as an example. The audience has an inheritance waiting for them and have attained some of its promises, yet until they possess it in full Hebrews wants them to demonstrate the same patience. A final section reprises these arguments by a reflection on Hebrews' exposition of Psalm 8, within the larger context of the book.

13. Time: George H. Guthrie devotes most of his chapter to issues of the *timing* of atonement in conversation with David Moffitt's work (*Atonement and the Logic of Resurrection*), but also attempts to indicate a presupposed understanding of *time* and to contextualize the former within the latter. He proceeds in three steps: Hebrews' approach to Levitical cult language; Hebrews' prioritizing of the Christ event over the cultic imagery, such that the latter is filtered through the former more than the other way around; the way in which a presupposed concept of time might shape our thinking about the timing of the atonement. He wishes to push the conversation about cultic language back a step to consider how the author of Hebrews uses such language. First, then, in light of the way that Hebrews' vision of the atonement corresponds to the liturgical timing of Yom Kippur, Guthrie argues that the author of Hebrews builds the Christological movements of his discourse using a complex interplay of general (not limited to Yom Kippur) Levitical language and imagery. Here Guthrie registers reasons to be cautious about making Yom Kippur imagery all-controlling for Hebrews' conception. He observes that Hebrews in fact rarely uses overt atonement terminology. Further, in the Pentateuch the language of atonement is used

generally in relation to a wide range of offerings and sacrifices, not just those made on Yom Kippur, and *atonement is a multifaceted concept even on Yom Kippur*. The upshot is that it is at least possible that atonement was conceived by Hebrews as a broader dynamic than what occurred in the heavenly holiest place. Again, at key points, Hebrews uses general language related to sacrifice and offering not tightly bound to Yom Kippur in the OT. Jesus's priestly ministry is presented as parallel to and fulfilling the whole of the priestly ministry of offering gifts and sacrifices under the Old Covenant, not just a particular offering on Yom Kippur. Finally, in this connection, Guthrie focuses allusions or direct references in Hebrews to various kinds of sacrifices beyond Yom Kippur. Thus, we must allow all of the sacrificial language and imagery (not merely the blood ceremony of Yom Kippur) to speak and inform our understanding of the atonement in Hebrews. Secondly, then, the author of Hebrews refracts OT sacrificial language through the Christ event, not the other way around. Guthrie observes here that though Moffitt is critical of approaches that filter the Christ event through the OT's sacrificial imagery rather than the other way around, he, Moffitt, reverses the refraction at points, so that the Christ event is refracted primarily through the Yom Kippur word picture. Though Moffitt assigns significance to Christ's death, when the event of Christ's death is refracted through Yom Kippur certain theological conclusions about the death are read onto the text of Hebrews, leading to inadequate attention to the death-impregnated unit found at 9:11-28, a vitally important unit as the author moves toward the culmination of his great Christological treatise on the Son's high priesthood. In fact, Hebrews accesses a wide array of images from the Levitical cult, refracting them for various theological and rhetorical ends through various aspects of the Christ event. Moreover, the death of Christ particularly holds great significance in Heb. 9:11-28. The grounding reality for Hebrews' entire approach is the Christ event, rather than any OT rite or package of rites. Bringing the first two parts of his argument to their conclusion, Guthrie agrees with Moffitt that Jesus's death is the first element in the larger process of blood sacrifice, which should not be collapsed or conflated with the offering in heaven. Yet, in agreement with Jamieson, Guthrie holds that Moffitt fails to note adequately the role that the death of Christ plays as atoning. Thus, Christ's death stands as of vital significance in the Christology of Hebrews, accomplishing multiple effects. This takes nothing away from Yom Kippur's imagery and the heavenly ministry of Christ, but it does elevate the death of Christ as of central significance in the book. Thirdly and finally, Guthrie notes what might be called "a wrinkle in time" in our nice, sequential conceptions of atonement in Hebrews. Heb. 9:25-26 corresponds to other NT texts that relate Christ's work to "the foundation of the world" in some way, taking it out of a neatly developing, linear history. The verbal connection of that passage with Heb. 4:3, coupled with larger structural features of Hebrews, hints that Hebrews may be tying the Christ event back to God's rest established at the foundation of the world. Thus, the atonement would extend beyond the constraints of time as we know it, working backward to cover all the ages of the world. Further support for this is noted in the work of Ben Ribbens and the thought is correlated with the reflections of Augustine,

Aquinas, Pannenberg, Barth, and others. Guthrie closes by asking whether the work of Christ can be considered temporally from two vantage points: As a logical sequence, as it appears to temporally linear creatures, with all of the events (death, resurrection, ascension) playing a role in the atonement, and with the atonement inaugurated on the cross and consummated in the exaltation. From another vantage point, however, the author of Hebrews is both "anticipating the past" and "remembering the future," as the Christ event wrinkles time as we experience it. It is possible, then, that in asking the exact "time" of the Atonement, we may be focusing on the wrong question, for we are dealing with the Christ, who is both in and out of time.

14. Space: Drawing on critical spatial theory, distinguishing place from space, and noting the modern domination of space and place by time, Cynthia Long Westfall's thesis is that the interpretation of the Hebrews author of the heavenly tabernacle and its use in the LXX are based on the meaning of place in the continuity and contrast between the past Mosaic tabernacle and what is true in the present of the heavenly tabernacle in the light of Jesus's sacrificial death. A carry-over from largely outdated Platonic readings of Hebrews is that images of space/place are construed as abstract symbols, while modern, scientifically informed conceptions of geography and place can lead us to misinterpret Hebrews' spatial motifs. Moreover, besides importing Pauline categories and making selective use of Hebrews' teachings, interpreters frequently seem to assume a dualism that pits "Christian-heavenly-spiritual-true" against "Jewish-earthly-unspiritual-false," whereas Hebrews operates with a stronger notion of continuity between the earthly and heavenly tabernacles and with deep running ties to Judaism. After summarizing and applying Soja's critical space concepts of Firstspace (in Hebrews = what is "real" or "true" about the place of atonement), Secondspace (copy or map of the real place of atonement), and Thirdspace (the ways Hebrews urges the recipients to occupy and use Firstspace), she states that the central argument of her chapter is that the author of Hebrews was interpreting the atonement of Christ by correlating, disambiguating, and applying a form of spatial interpretation to the place of atonement in the LXX. The concept of "place" as opposed to "space" can help clarify what is important to Hebrews' conception of the High Priesthood and atonement, while showing that questions of timing may not be primary. Having prepared the ground, Westfall proceeds: the author of Hebrews makes the Firstspace of the heavenly tabernacle concrete through the descriptive detail given it. The locality of Jesus on the divine throne, presupposing a bodily resurrection, gives him a physicality that prevents abstraction. Taking careful note of invisibility of Hebrews' Firstspace and the language used of it (e.g., 11:1-3; 10:1), and, further, discounting references to the eschatological future, she comments that Firstspace is not Platonic imagery—the heavenly tabernacle is so concrete that it casts a shadow. The author of Hebrews claims that its invisibility is consistent with a biblical understanding of reality. The once-visible Mosaic, earthly tabernacle is Secondspace, a symbol that points to the reality and a map from which the heavenly space can be described. More precisely, the earthly tabernacle was two stages removed from the original as

a copy of the divinely revealed map drawn from the original construction; the Jerusalem temple was three stages removed. In spite of the language of 10:1 this is not a Platonic vindication of the temple's destruction and a supersessionist theology. Firstspace and Secondspace exist in a symbiotic relationship; the former does not eliminate the existence, function, and importance of Secondspace. The author's choice of the Mosaic tabernacle rather than the Herodian temple sidesteps the problematic meaning of the latter for first-century Jews and articulates a belief that the institutions of Judaism are enduring, accurate maps of heaven itself. Moving on, Thirdspace is how the space is actually used. Both non-Christian Jews and Christian Jews would regard the heavenly temple and its service as superior, but would disagree over whether Jesus is bodily present there as High Priest. Based on a literal reading of Ps. 110:1, Hebrews locates Jesus there and adds the culturally distinctive argument that Jesus's followers may occupy and use that space. Hebrews' argument challenges both Jewish and Greek "illusions" of reality, not through imaginative projection but through faith's literal reading of the biblical witness. It emerges that the readers are not marginalized—per the viewpoint of Second Temple Judaism—but are in line with and literally in the company of the ancestors (11:2) who were commended for their faith. In the light, however, of Hebrews' portrayal of these Christian Jews as marginalized in their earthly Jewish and Roman context—a portrayal that parallels the social situation of Christian Jews in the time of the Jewish revolt begun in 66 CE (here Westfall pauses to note three problems that make it difficult to recognize the context of Hebrews as one of marginalization and have led in fact to anti-Semitic uses of Hebrews' argument)—the exhortations in Hebrews are a form of "collective resistance." Jesus's work had revealed a new teaching of a use of the heavenly tabernacle that was not accepted by non-Christian Jews; it was a subversion of the dominant Jewish understanding of the "use" of the heavenly tabernacle that had implications for the use of the earthly temple. Armed with the foregoing, and taking note of Hebrews' interpretations of the LXX (esp. Exodus 25–30, 35–40; Leviticus 16), Westfall proposes that Hebrews' claims are characterized by literal *correlations* between the Secondspace intended use of the earthly tabernacle which is described/mapped in the Torah and what occurs in Firstspace. However, the person, life, death, and resurrection of Jesus provides an interpretive grid for *disambiguation*. What cannot be applied to Jesus cannot be applied to the heavenly tabernacle. On this basis, Hebrews is able to make *applications* to the recipients that enable them to find the face of God, live in his presence, and find grace in their time of crisis. From this perspective, and noting David Moffitt's arguments, Westfall takes up the question of where Hebrews locates the atonement. Drawing together theories of place, Jesus's bodily existence, the rites of Leviticus 16, and Hebrews' portrayal of Christ's work leads to the conclusion that the heavenly temple is the literal place where Christ obtained redemption; the information does not correspond well with confining the location of the offering for the atonement on the cross. In the final section, Westfall takes up the challenge of bringing the ancient and modern worlds into meaningful dialogue, moving moderns beyond the relegation of Hebrews' portrayals of Firstspace as metaphor, allegory, or eschatology. Hebrews does recognize the essential atoning importance of Jesus's *death*, albeit as synecdoche for the process of the atonement that was completed with the offering in the heavenly tabernacle. In conclusion: Westfall suggests that in the current debate about the place and timing of the atonement, the interpreter of Hebrews stands at crossroads: we can either take the author's spatial description of the atonement literally or we can spiritualize it. If our objective is discovering authorial intent, we should lean toward a literal reading.

15. Faith: Gabriella Gelardini highlights Hebrews' concept of salvation over against Rome's imperial "salvation," as this comes to light through an examination of Hebrews' faith-concept. She develops the empire-critical undertones of Hebrews' πίστις rhetoric while observing the failure of earlier studies to appreciate the complexities of bilingualism, biculturalism, and code-switching relating to Hebrews' use of the Greek language. She begins by noting Martin Buber's distinction between Judaism's (and Jesus's) historically grounded and immediate trust in God (*emunah*), and Christianity's (Paul's) Greek πίστις, born not in history but in the souls of individuals and centering in the acceptance of the truth of certain tenets of faith. For Buber, in Heb. 11:1 these two aspects—assurance and conviction, as he translates the two words—stand unconnected beside each other. Recent research has also been convinced that Hebrews introduces a certain Greek rationalization to his OT concept of *emunah* (compare Käsemann, Grässer, Schliesser). Making reference to 11:6, however, Gelardini finds evidence that while the Greek way of thinking certainly has a persuasive function, the work of persuasion is carried out on those in whom the confessional tradition is already alive, or at least still awake, in whom faith lives and breathes; the author has addressees in mind whose thinking is already at home with religious beliefs from the Old Testament/Jewish understanding of trust in God's faithfulness. Pausing to note recent work on bilingualism, biculturalism, and code-switching in relation to Greek-speaking Judaism and Christianity, Gelardini asserts that against the backdrop of a long-established tradition of bicultural interactions in the Hellenistic-Roman Mediterranean, we need to take due account of this—constant—process of negotiating identity. Noting that these cultural anthropological studies have already been applied to the idea of faith in Paul and in the Roman world, Gelardini wishes to apply them to Hebrews. Classical and philological studies have highlighted the importance of the πίστις or *fides* culture for the Roman empire, particularly the function of *fides* for relations in society, within the state and between states. Among the differences between the Greek πίστις concept and the Roman/Latin one, reciprocity is crucial for the Roman concept of *fides*. It marks a reciprocal, albeit hierarchically structured, relationship between the patron and his client in public, private, and also official contracts, as in alliances. Faithfulness and covenant belong together, as also justice and salvation; this is manifest in the fact that *fides* is a deity symbolizing Roman respect for international law. From this observation Gelardini turns to note how in Hebrews both God and Christ are πιστός (10:23; 2:17; 3:2). The noun πίστις is used for the attitude of the wandering people of God and

is associated with the keyword διαθήκη, Latin *foedus*. Πίστις is a means of salvation, for instance in 11:7. And 10:37-39, a kind of "*skopos* of Hebrews," presents salvation through faithfulness, that is, the "acquisition" or "production" of (eternal) life—the word [περιποίησις] does indeed have the basic meaning of the manufacture of commodities. At this point Gelardini notes that the theme of empire, important to the Roman conception, also belongs in this context, for the empire celebrated covenants and friendships in the temple of *Fides* on the Capitol. Thus also in Hebrews, empire-critical undertones may well also resonate (12:22; 13:14; cf. 11:14, 16). Unlike Augustan court poets, Hebrews hardly considers Rome to be the empire without borders in space and time, nor Rome the lasting and eternal πόλις. That sort of description is reserved for the "unshakable kingdom" in heaven, to which hope, patience, perseverance, and πίστις are directed (cf. 11:10). Christ is the leader of the salvation (*salus* and σωτηρία being the theme of empire). It is this empire-critical subtext that also underlines the capacity for bilingual or bicultural identity politics. Borrowing and rejection belong together in code-switching. In closing, Gelardini turns to 11:1 and 12:1. Ὑπόστασις indicates that πίστις is indeed a reality, but precisely the substrate of something else. Ἔλεγχος denotes an objective proof: faithfulness is proof or evidence of invisible things. The examples of faith that follow 11:1 are characterized in 12:1 as a νέφος μαρτύρων: the forensic idea of μάρτυς suits both the force of ἔλεγχος in 11:1 and the fact that πίστις can certainly mean credible witness in legal language. In the light of 11:3, πίστις does have an "intellectual" element. But Hebrews' use of Koine rhetoric, especially with the emphasized contextual link with the comprehensive Greco-Roman concept of πίστις/*fides*, is also of importance. There might be irony that *fides*—an identity marker of Roman culture and domination—was used by Hebrews to culturally strengthen allegiance to the celestial empire.

16. The Church: Harold W. Attridge begins with the comment that the Epistle to the Hebrews offers the most comprehensive and complex treatment of the effects of Christ's death in the New Testament. It does so within the context of a symbolic presentation of the life of the Church, developed through two intersecting metaphors: the wandering people of God and the family or household of God. The homilist frames the treatment of Christ's death as an atoning sacrifice that works precisely as a covenant inaugurating event that creates the Church by proclaiming God's forgiveness of sin and offering the model by which a faithful life is to be led. This carefully worded comment is unpacked in the remainder of Attridge's argument. After a brief statement of what Attridge presupposes about the setting and genre of the book, he provides support from throughout Hebrews for the twin characterization of the church as the wandering people and as God's household, noting already the motif of imitating the Son as central for Hebrews' vision of salvation. The culminating vision of 12:24 shows that what created this people is the voice of the "mediator" whose blood created a New Covenant. To answer *how* this is done it is necessary to explore sacrifice and atonement in Hebrews. Preliminary to this, Attridge surveys contemporary scholarship on the ancient practice of sacrifice, noting among other things the need to

appreciate the complexity of sacrificial practices in antiquity, and the language games that used sacrificial categories for various purposes. He cautions against both wanting the sacred texts to make some sense that accords with a (Church) theological system deemed rational and coherent, and oversimplifying what an ancient author can do with multivalent terms such as "sacrifice." As a further preliminary Attridge surveys the ideas of sacrifice and atonement in the NT tradition behind Hebrews, especially in John and Paul. In Hebrews' argument as we have it, the importance of the Day of Atonement ritual, onto which Hebrews maps Christ's death, is obvious, but Attridge also gives attention to the various other rites and sacrifices that contribute to the argument (daily sacrifices, the *Aqedah*, Passover, the covenant inauguration), as well as the ways in which people of the time criticized sacrifice and used it as a metaphor for something else, as far back as the OT prophets (Hos. 6:6; 8:13; Amos 4:4-6) but including Hellenistic philosophers. The ground cleared, he proceeds to Hebrews' argument in 7:1–10:18 and its surprising twists. The argument begins by asserting that Christ is a priest of an eternal order (7:1-28). What follows (8:1-10:18) is a well-defined homily, similar in form to 3:1–4:13, and structured around several antitheses (heaven-earth, new-old, exterior-interior). Attridge considers the way the heavenly ideal and earthly realities could have been construed—whether or not as in Philo—and notes the "tensive structure" created by the idea of literal blood being brought into the heavenly realm. This tensive structure, we discover, is held together by the transformation of the vertical dichotomy into the antithesis of old and new, particularly via Jer. 31:31-34 in Heb. 8:8-13. How Jeremiah comes into a discussion of Christ as high priest is shown in part by the way the old-new antithesis is deployed in ch. 9, and then in ch. 10. As to how blood gets into heaven, Hebrews teaches that the realities to be cleansed are not in some transcendent heavenly space but within us; the space the Christ enters as high priest is, in fact, the hearts and minds of his followers. This becomes most clear in 10:1-10, with Christ's body casting the shadow of the Mosaic law. The body that casts the shadow is the "will" or "intent" embodied in the action of Jesus who conforms himself in fidelity to God's will and that will is the source of sanctification for his followers as they imitate him. According to the same passage (10:1-10), the principle of "doing your will, O God," takes away the principle of sacrifice (v. 9). The essential component of at least the "ultimate" sacrifice is a personal commitment of one's self to do God's will, an idea that is paralleled in Philo (Spec. 1.271-272). Hebrews has more work to do, however, to show how the sacrificial death of Christ had its effect on his followers, as the inherited tradition of the readers taught them it did. The solution, which probably explains the writer's citation of Jeremiah 31 in the first place, was the by-then traditional notion of the New Covenant (cf. 2 Cor. 3:1-11). Wherein is the connection between Christ's death and this New Covenant? This is answered by the word play, covenant-will (9:15-17), and the citation of Exod. 24:8. The inheritance bestowed in the will involves union with God and fellowship with others, but it also involves the way to attain that union; it includes an example for the present. The exemplary act of dedication and commitment of Jesus stands at the heart of the inheritance left by Jesus. But, Attridge hears the readers asking, "What about the blood?" The answer comes by linking the blood to the inauguration of the New Covenant. The "blood" that inaugurates a covenant and provides "forgiveness for sin" is that life which he lived and in which his followers now participate. But, they ask, "How does the blood do the atoning thing?" The argument surrounding Exod. 24:8 answers this by indicating that what is sprinkled with the blood is not a heavenly altar or mercy seat, but a people whose lives are now marked by the life for which that blood stands. When the people of the wandering household stand before God in that covenant relationship, listening to Jeremiah's voice, they hear the promise of what the covenant entails (10:16-17). The "law written on their heart" is the acceptance of the example of Christ's dedication and the covenantal life lived in faith, hope, and love. The covenantal promise that God would remember their sins no more is not given in view of a debt paid or ransom delivered, but is gracious divine amnesia pure and simple. As to how this impacts the life of the church, they have been "perfected" in the sense of being "qualified" for their entry into sacred space, and "sanctified," made eligible to serve at the place where the true altar resides. This sanctification continues as they move in the footsteps of Jesus. They also engage in acts of worship, in which the writer himself leads them (13:6; cf. 13:15).

Part One

Contexts

1

Atonement in Ancient Israel: The Whole Burnt Offering as Central to Israel's Cult

L. Michael Morales

Toward understanding the theology of atonement in Hebrews more deeply, this chapter will explore atonement in the Old Testament (OT), narrowing the focus primarily to that of the whole burnt offering within the Pentateuch. Various scholars have remarked that the epistle's author was saturated in the OT, knowing the scriptures intimately and quoting them extensively.[1] Others have noted, moreover, that the treatment of cultic ritual within Hebrews appears bookish or literary, relying more upon the OT rather than demonstrating firsthand knowledge of current Temple practice.[2] These observations encourage a renewed appreciation for the OT as the fundamental background to the theology of Christ's atoning work expressed in Hebrews. This same point also supports a literary and canonical study *versus* taking a history of religions approach; seeking to surmise the evolution of sacrifice or cultic ritual in the ancient Near East (ANE), for example, would prove less relevant for understanding Hebrews since its arguments make use of the literature and theology of the OT. Nevertheless, the historical point made by Watts is relevant, that at least by the Second Temple period, though likely much earlier, the whole burnt offering had become representative of Israel's worship, shaping the religious imaginations of Jews and Christians, so that, for the latter, the crucifixion was understood as the ultimate whole burnt offering.[3]

Broadly, atonement in the OT functions as a means to an end,[4] that of reconciliation with YHWH God—itself a prerequisite for the life with God originally purposed in

---

[1] See, for example, Paul Ellingworth, *The Epistle to the Hebrews: A Commentary on the Greek Text* (NIGTC; Grand Rapids, MI/Carlisle, PA: Eerdmans/Paternoster, 1993), pp. 37–42; Luke T. Johnson, *Hebrews: A Commentary* (NTL; Louisville, KY: Westminster John Knox, 2006), pp. 21–24; George H. Guthrie, *Hebrews* (NIVAC; Grand Rapids, MI: Zondervan, 1998), p. 19.

[2] P. W. L. Walker, *Jesus and the Holy City: New Testament Perspectives on Jerusalem* (Grand Rapids, MI: Eerdmans, 1996), p. 202; F. F. Bruce, *The Epistle to the Hebrews* (NICNT; Grand Rapids, MI: Eerdmans, 1990), p. 5; Johnson, *Hebrews*, p. 25.

[3] James W. Watts, "ʻōlāh: The Rhetoric of Burnt Offerings," *VT* 56.1 (2006), pp. 125–37 (134–37); see also Jon D. Levenson, *The Death and Resurrection of the Beloved Son: The Transformation of Child Sacrifice in Judaism and Christianity* (New Haven, CT: Yale University Press, 1993).

[4] Regarding the Hebrew verb כִּפֶּר: given a now widely rejected Arabic cognate, the meaning would be "to cover" or "hide," while an Akkadian and Aramaic root suggests "to wipe off," and the Hebrew noun כֹּפֶר signifies "ransom"; see R. Laird Harris, "Exegetical Notes: Meaning of Kipper," *JETS* 4.1 (1961), p. 3; Yitzhaq Feder, "On *Kuppuru*, *Kippēr* and Etymological Sins That Cannot Be Wiped

creation and, after humanity's descent into the guilt and pollution of sin, promised in redemption.[5] This chapter's focus on the whole burnt offering may be justified by a two-pronged reflection. First, as Harmut Gese observed, "The whole sacrificial system serves to atone and finds its meaning in the atoning function of the sacrifice itself."[6] Secondly, "Hebrew ritual was," as McCarthy put it, "essentially of the burnt-offering type,"[7] that is, the whole burnt offering was the center of Israel's sacrificial system—"the paradigmatic offering" holding "pride of place" in the Hebrew Bible.[8] In other words, Israel's cult was founded upon the doctrine of atonement, and the whole burnt offering serves as a summation of that cult.[9] Accordingly, this study will begin by considering (1) the prominent role of the whole burnt offering within the Pentateuch, and then proceed to probe (2) the significance of the whole burnt offering within Israel's cult, (3) closing with remarks applicatory to Hebrews.

Finally, while typically translated as whole burnt offering, the עֹלָה will from this point onward (with few exceptions, such as in quotations) be designated as "ascension offering," a name which reflects not only its root meaning but also a significant aspect of the offering's theology.

The prominent role of the ascension offering in the Pentateuch

Though perhaps not especially obvious in a cursory reading of the OT, yet when approached with deliberate attention, the prominent role of the ascension offering in scripture is impressive. To begin with, this offering occurs twice in Genesis, in the book's two literary (and literal) mountain peaks: Noah's post-deluge sacrifice on an Ararat mountain in Genesis 8 and Abraham's near-sacrifice (or *Akedah*) of Isaac on Mount Moriah in Genesis 22. In the first account, Noah, at the dawn of a new creation, builds an altar and offers ascension offerings unto YHWH, a priestly act that brings the

---

Away," *VT* 60.4 (2010), pp. 535–45. Scriptural usage typically refers to the outcome or effect ("purify," "atone," "expiate") of *kipper* rather than the manner ("wipe," "rub," "cover"), and implies a twofold meaning (by varying degrees according to context) of ransom from death and purification from pollution, as per Jay Sklar, *Sin, Impurity, Sacrifice, Atonement: The Priestly Conceptions* (Sheffield: Sheffield Phoenix, 2005).

[5] See L. Michael Morales, *Who Shall Ascend the Mountain of the Lord? A Theology of the Book of Leviticus* (Downers Grove, IL: IVP Academic, 2015), pp. 39–49.
[6] H. Gese, "The Atonement," in *Essays on Biblical Theology* (trans. K. Crim; Minneapolis: Augsburg, 1981), pp. 93–116; see also Bernard Low, "The Logic of Atonement in Israel's Cult," *Scripture and Interpretation* 3.1 (2009), pp. 5–32.
[7] Dennis J. McCarthy, "The Symbolism of Blood and Sacrifice," *JBL* 88.2 (1969), pp. 166–76 (175).
[8] Watts, "ʿōlāh," p. 125.
[9] Moreover, the place of the *Yom Kippur* ritual and the cult's use of blood in Hebrews are paths already well trodden, while the whole burnt offering has generally been neglected, though it is more foundational within Israel's cult. On the function of blood in the sacrificial system, see McCarthy, "The Symbolism of Blood and Sacrifice"; Stephen A. Geller, "Blood Cult: Toward a Literary Theology of the Priestly Work of the Pentateuch," *Prooftexts* 12.2 (1992), pp. 97–124; Stanislas Lyonnet and Leopold Sabourin, *Sin, Redemption, and Sacrifice: A Biblical and Patristic Study* (Rome: Biblical Institute, 1970), pp. 167–81. Some caution about over-emphasis on *Yom Kippur* in Hebrews has been expressed; for example, W. Loader, *Sohn und Hoherpriester: Eine traditionsgeschichtliche Untersuchung zur Christologie des Hebraerbriefes* (WMANT 53; Neukirchen-Vluyn: Neukirchener Verlag, 1981), p. 172; James P. Scullion, "A Traditio-Historical Study of the Day of Atonement" (unpublished doctoral dissertation, Catholic University of America, 1990), p. 252.

narrative to its resolution, as a comparison between Gen. 6:5-7 and 8:21 demonstrates.[10] "Restful aroma" (רֵיחַ הַנִּיחֹחַ) in 8:21, the Pentateuch's first use of this technical cultic designation, anticipates the inauguration of the sacrificial cult as one of its major aims, namely, to propitiate the divine wrath by atonement.[11] The second occurrence of the ascension offering is no less intense, as YHWH bids Abraham to "take now your son, your only one whom you love, Isaac, and get yourself to the land of Moriah, and offer him up [or, 'cause him to ascend' (וְהַעֲלֵהוּ)] there as an ascension offering upon one of the mountains which I will tell you" (Gen. 22:2). The ensuing substitution for Isaac (and therefore of Israel) marked the entire sacrificial system of the Temple, even while soliciting from Israel the self-sacrifice implicit in the symbolism of the cult.[12]

Turning to the book of Exodus, the ascension offering is noted as essential to the worship for which Moses calls on Pharaoh to release Israel (10:25), and then forms the central means of engagement in Exodus 24, as Israel enters into covenant with YHWH at Mount Sinai—note here that the sprinkled blood of the covenant was collected from ascension offerings (24:5-8). An even weightier role for this offering is established later in Exod. 29:38-46, where God legislates the daily divine service for the tabernacle, the תָּמִיד ascension offerings.[13] Every day, in the morning and at twilight, Aaron's priesthood was to offer up a yearling lamb (two on the Sabbath) as an ascension offering, these morning and evening sacrifices bookending and, therefore, subsuming all of the day's other sacrifices—along with all Israel—within the ascending smoke of their soothing aroma. Thereby the daily life of Israel was lived out within the context of the flames of these ascension offerings. Whether plowing a field or weaving a basket, all of Israelite life was offered up to God—by the priesthood on behalf of Israel—through the soothing aroma that, morning and evening, ascended continually to God from the altar. The same aroma that had in the primeval era quelled the wrath of God, allowing for the continuance of the cosmos, now served to preserve Israel—daily or "continually" (תָּמִיד). Furthermore, inasmuch as the legislation for daily offerings belongs properly in Numbers 28, where it is duplicated, here the focus is not on the laws for which offerings need to be brought on a particular day, but remains on the altar's consecration, which precedes the תָּמִיד in Exod. 29:35-37. As Ezra Bick explains, the Torah is teaching Israel that the תָּמִיד ascension offering fulfills the purpose of the altar, even as the altar establishes the purpose of the tabernacle.[14] This understanding comports with the majestic summary statement by YHWH concerning the daily ascension offering:

> This will be a continual ascension offering throughout your generations at the door of the Tent of Meeting before YHWH, where I will meet with you and speak

---

[10] For further development of this account, see L. Michael Morales, *The Tabernacle Pre-Figured: Cosmic Mountain Ideology in Genesis and Exodus* (Leuven: Peeters, 2012), pp. 121–92.

[11] Parallels to ANE literature cannot be taken up here; see H. P. Müller, "Das Motiv Für Die Sintflut. Die Hermeneutische Funktion Des Mythos Und Seine Analyse," *ZAW* 97.3 (1985), pp. 295–316; Morales, *The Tabernacle Pre-Figured*, pp. 181–85.

[12] On this latter point, see Leigh M. Trevaskis, *Holiness, Ethics and Ritual in Leviticus* (Sheffield: Sheffield Phoenix, 2011).

[13] On the daily divine service, see Kleinig, *Leviticus* (Concordia Commentary; Saint Louis: Concordia, 2003), pp. 39, 218–20; Morales, *Who Shall Ascend the Mountain of the Lord?*, pp. 141–43.

[14] Ezra Bick, "Tamid" (etzion.org.il/en; Yeshivat Har Etzion—Virtual Beit Midrash, 1997), pp. 1–8 (5–7).

with you there.... And I will dwell among the sons of Israel and I will be their God. (29:42, 45)

As God's Presence among Israel through the Dwelling is meant to be permanent, the altar, as the basis for that presence, must also be in a state of continual offering,[15] and that of the ascension offering.

Given the dominant role of the תָּמִיד as fulfilling the purpose of the altar, what is perhaps the most honorific detail concerning the ascension offering is rendered unremarkable, namely, that the altar itself derives its name from it—the altar is, more fully, called "the altar of the ascension offering" (מִזְבַּח הָעֹלָה).[16] Even when other sacrifices are being legislated, this title for the altar ensures that the ascension offering "upstages" them. A case in point is found in relation to the purification offering:

> And he [a ruler who has sinned] will lay his hand on the head of the goat, and kill it at the place where they kill *the ascension offering* before YHWH—it is a purification offering. The priest will take some of the blood of the purification offering with his finger, put it on the horns of *the altar of the ascension offering*, and pour out its blood to the base of *the altar of the ascension offering*. (Lev. 4:24-25; emphasis added)

Also, since every other offering was simply added to the morning תָּמִיד, and was afterward enclosed by the evening תָּמִיד, all sacrifices were "virtually incorporated into it," making the ascension offering "the fundamental sacrifice."[17] Israel was defined by the altar and that altar was itself defined by one sacrifice, the ascension offering.

Turning to another example, the opening verses of Leviticus mark a momentous and historic event, as YHWH God, from the newly constructed Dwelling patterned after his heavenly abode (Exod. 25:9), delivers his first speech. Remarkably, the chief order of business and concern revealed by YHWH is legislation for the ascension offering, comprising the book's first chapter (Lev. 1:1-17). Actually, the ascension offering opens the delineation of sacrifices both in the lay-oriented legislation (Lev. 1:1-6:7 [MT 5:26]) as well as in the priestly (6:8 [MT 6:1]-7:38), and, furthermore, does so as a matter of course in nearly all the lists of offerings spread throughout the Hebrew Bible, across genres, periods, and authors.[18]

Restricting this survey to a few more examples, the legislation in Numbers 28-29 is especially relevant. Whereas the similar cultic laws found in Leviticus 23-25 evince calendric concerns (see 23:2), the corresponding material in Numbers displays an emphasis upon the particular offerings required throughout Israel's calendar.[19] Delineated according to daily, weekly (Sabbath), monthly, and annual feast offerings,

---

[15] Ibid., p. 7.
[16] So designated seven times in Exodus (30:28; 31:9; 35:16; 38:1; 40:6, 10, 29), seven times in Leviticus 4 (vv. 7, 10, 18, 25 [x2], 30, 34), and four times in Chronicles (1 Chron. 6:34; 16:40; 21:26, 29; 2 Chron. 29:18).
[17] Kleinig, *Leviticus*, p. 40.
[18] Watts, "'ōlāh," p. 126.
[19] Cf. Baruch A. Levine, *Va-Yikra/Leviticus* (JPS Torah Commentary; Philadelphia, PA: Jewish Publication Society, 1989), pp. 153-54.

even a peripheral reading of Numbers 28–29 proves striking in relation to the utter centrality of the ascension offering, not only for marking and consecrating every single day of Israel's life but also for being the principal event of virtually every sacred occasion, regardless of seasonal cycle or theological point of stress. As Watts observes, Numbers 28–29 portray "regular priestly services as consisting mostly of *ʿōlôt* offerings"[20]—indeed, and incredibly, the first day of Tabernacles required no less than thirty-one ascension offerings. Also apparent, the ascension offerings served as cultic markers of sacred time on the cosmic level, coordinated with the (Gen. 1:1–2:3) creation account's movement from day 1 (period of a day, the תָּמִיד) to day 4 (the lights marking out monthly and annual cultic festivals, the מוֹעֲדִים), to day 7 (the blessed and holy Sabbath day).[21] Finally, and more briefly, the ascension offering is central to the worship envisioned in Deuteronomy, with the place YHWH chooses defined as where "you will offer your ascension offerings" (12:6, 11-14), and with the liturgical role of the priesthood summarized as "They will put incense before you, and whole burnt sacrifice (*kālîl*) upon your altar" (33:10).

Clearly, then, the Pentateuch portrays the ascension offering as highly cherished by YHWH God, and is not averse to using anthropomorphic language to convey its prominent role (cf. also Lev. 26:31). He smells its restful aroma and his grieving heart is pacified, so that he turns away from a posture of wrath toward humanity. Given these contexts, translations of רֵיחַ הַנִּיחֹחַ as a propitiating, pacifying, or soothing savor are fully justified.[22] Such a uniquely prominent role, of appeasing and pleasing the Maker of heaven and earth, cannot but lead to the question of the meaning of the ascension offering, to which the next section turns.

The significance of the ascension offering within Israel's cult

When considering the meaning of sacrificial ritual it must be admitted that discerning the symbolism of various rites, given the sparseness of explanation in scripture, can often be a subjective and arbitrary matter. In the case of the ascension offering, however, there is wide consensus as to its fundamental significance, and adequate exegetical support. Moreover, it is possible to offer a constraint on supposed meaning by positioning this offering within the complex of Israel's cultus. Because the procedural order of sacrifices reflects actual cultic practice, opening a window into Israel's liturgy, it is key for understanding the theology of sacrifice.[23] Accordingly, we will probe the theology of the ascension offering within its place in the procedural order of sacrifices,

---

[20] Watts, "'ōlāh," p. 133.
[21] Cf. Morales, *The Tabernacle Pre-Figured*, pp. 85–86; idem, *Who Shall Ascend the Mountain of the Lord?*, pp. 44–45, 198–200; Frank H. Gorman, "Priestly Rituals of Founding: Time, Space, and Status," in *History and Interpretation: Essays in Honour of John H. Hayes* (ed. M. Patrick Graham, William P. Brown, and Jeffrey K. Kuan; Sheffield: JSOT, 1993), pp. 47–64 (52–53); Edward L. Greenstein, "Presenting Genesis 1, Constructively and Deconstructively," *Prooftexts* 21.1 (2001), p. 4.
[22] Geller, "Blood Cult," p. 100; Derek Kidner, "Sacrifice: Metaphors and Meaning," *TynBul* 33 (1982), pp. 119–36 (123).
[23] A. F. Rainey, "The Order of Sacrifices in Old Testament Ritual Texts," *Bib* 51.4 (1970), pp. 485–98; Baruch A. Levine, "The Descriptive Tabernacle Texts of the Pentateuch," *JAOS* 85.3 (1965), pp. 307–18.

and by observing its distinguishing feature in comparison with the other sacrifices of the cult.

The legislation for Israel's basic sacrifices is found in Lev. 1:1-6:7[MT 5:25], which covers laws for the ascension (עֹלָה), tribute (מִנְחָה), communion (שְׁלָמִים), purification (חַטָּאת), and reparation (אָשָׁם) offerings, respectively. The first three offerings (ascension, tribute, and communion), taken together and in order, form an ideal worship scenario, each being voluntary and dubbed an אִשֶּׁה (gift by fire) and a restful aroma to YHWH, while the next two (the purification and reparation offerings) were expiatory in nature, required as a remedy for particular sins. In practice, one or both of these expiatory sacrifices would precede the triad of ascension, tribute, and communion offerings, as described in the cult's inaugural ceremony (Leviticus 9). The liturgy, therefore, begins with the purification (and/or reparation) offering, proceeds to the ascension offering, accompanied by the tribute offering, and then concludes with the communion offering.

While there is substantial overlap in the rituals for each of these sacrifices, it is possible nevertheless to isolate their primary significance. What is emphatic for the purification and reparation offerings is the blood manipulation, which underscores expiation, cleansing from sin. The ascension offering was unique in that the entire animal (apart from its skin), rather than just a portion of its meat and fat, was consumed on the altar's fire and transformed into a pleasing aroma, conveying the idea of full consecration. The communion offering was the only offering in which the Israelite worshiper partook of the sacrificial meat, along with family and friends, in a meal of communion and fellowship in the Presence of God. The overall logic of the order, then, is expiation → consecration → fellowship.[24]

Name of Offering:	**Purification**	**Ascension**	**Communion**
Ritual Emphasis:	Blood manipulation	Completely burned up, transformed into smoke	Eating a meal
Meaning:	*Expiation →*	*Consecration →*	*Fellowship*

Communion and fellowship with God, as expressed in the communion-offering meal, required therefore utter and complete consecration, as expressed in the ascension offering. Yet even before consecration to God can become a possibility, sins must be dealt with, expiated—only a cleansed humanity may belong to YHWH. This threefold movement presents "atonement" in the fullest sense. Moreover, as the offering "most representative of Israel's worship" and "the purest form of divine service," which "exemplifies the temple cult of the priests,"[25] the ascension offering may be understood as encompassing the whole ritual movement in itself, with the expiatory offerings being *pre-fixed* to it so as to highlight that aspect of the ascension offering's blood rite,

---

[24] Johann Kurtz has it as: justification, sanctification, and union (*Offerings, Sacrifices and Worship in the Old Testament* [trans. James Martin; Peabody, MA: Hendrickson, 1863], pp. 160–63).
[25] Watts, "'ōlāh," p. 132.

and the communion offering *suffixed* to it so as to underscore the divine acceptance aspect of the soothing aroma's ascent to heaven.[26]

More deeply, the theological categories of expiation, consecration, and fellowship are positioned within a cultic ritual of drawing near to YHWH, as evident in the term "offering" (קָרְבָּן) itself, the root of which is used four times in Lev. 1:2. The liturgy of sacrifice may be understood, then, as something of a journey into God's Presence, a rite of passage involving transformation and consecration.[27] The liturgical journey involved six major rites (apart from the priestly benediction), in the following order (though some were repeated): (1) the presentation rite, (2) the hand-leaning rite, (3) the slaughter rite, (4) the blood manipulation rite, (5) the burning rite, and (6) the communion rite. Space precludes development of each of these rites here,[28] so two points must suffice before turning to the burning rite. First, as evident in passages like Lev. 1:3, the animal presented, beyond falling within the category of clean, was to be תָּמִים. Unfortunately, the typical translation "unblemished" misses the symbolic import; used of human beings, the term is translated "blameless" or "whole-hearted,"[29] and is set forth in scripture as a prerequisite for drawing near the abode of YHWH, whether at his tabernacle/temple or the summit of his holy mountain (Ps. 15:2; cf. Gen. 6:9; 17:1). Secondly, as such, the animal represents the blameless life able to draw near to YHWH's Presence, consecrated on behalf of the worshiper, so that the Israelite approaches YHWH vicariously—likely, the hand-leaning rite established this substitutionary function.[30]

Performed after the blood manipulation rite, wherein the priest collected the animal's blood and dashed, tossed, scattered, sprinkled, daubed, or poured it out, the burning rite is particularly relevant for our purpose since the ascension offering, in which the whole animal (again, apart from its skin) was turned into smoke on the altar, was the burning rite par excellence. The Hebrew verb used for this process of burning, הִקְטִיר, is a technical term for cultic burning, signifying the transformation of the sacrifice into smoke. Whereas שָׂרַף is used as the general word for burning to destroy in

---

[26] For the purification and reparation sacrifices usurping the expiatory aspect of the ascension offering, see Jacob Milgrom, *Leviticus 1-16* (New York: Doubleday, 1991), p. 176.

[27] Cf. Edmund Leach, "The Logic of Sacrifice," in *Anthropological Approaches to the Old Testament* (ed. Bernhard Lang; Issues in Religion and Theology 8; Philadelphia, PA: Fortress, 1985), pp. 136–50; Richard D. Nelson, *Raising Up a Faithful Priest: Community and Priesthood in Biblical Theology* (Louisville: Westminster John Knox, 1993), pp. 55–56.

[28] See Morales, *Who Shall Ascend the Mountain of the Lord?*, pp. 124–41; Raymond Abba, "The Origin and Significance of Hebrew Sacrifice," *BTB* 7.3 (1977), pp. 134–35; Joshua Berman, *The Temple: Its Symbolism and Meaning Then and Now* (Northvale: J. Aronson, 1995), pp. 116–24; Low, "Logic of Atonement."

[29] Trevaskis, *Holiness, Ethics and Ritual*, pp. 202–07.

[30] See, for example, discussions in Roy E. Gane, *Cult and Character: Purification Offerings, Day of Atonement, and Theodicy* (Winona Lake, IN: Eisenbrauns, 2005), pp. 53–59; Bernd Janowski, "Schöpferische Erinnerung: zum 'Gedenken Gottes' in der biblischen Fluterzählung," in *Sprachliche Tiefe—Theologische Weite* (ed. Oliver Dyma and Andreas Michel; Biblisch-Theologische Studien, 4; Neukirchen-Vluyn: Neukirchener, 2008), pp. 220–21; N. Kiuchi, *The Purification Offering in the Priestly Literature: Its Meaning and Function* (JSOTSup, 56; Sheffield: Sheffield Academic, 1987), pp. 112–19; Gordon J. Wenham, "The Theology of Old Testament Sacrifice," in *Sacrifice in the Bible* (ed. Roger T. Beckwith and Martin J. Selman; Carlisle, PA: Paternoster, 1995), pp. 77–80; David P. Wright, "The Gesture of Hand Placement in the Hebrew Bible and in Hittite Literature," *JAOS* 106.3 (1986), pp. 433–46.

the common spheres of life,³¹ הִקְטִיר refers to the burning that takes place specifically upon the altar fire and focuses upon the particular aspect of "sending up in smoke" (to use Kleinig's translation),³² a purpose intimately connected to the offering's designation as an ʿōlâ. The word for incense, קְטֹרֶת, which properly means "that which goes up in smoke (to the Deity),"³³ is built off of the same root, highlighting its emphasis on transformation into smoke. In an insightful study, Eberhart noted that all five sacrifices of Israel's cult share this similar הִקְטִיר rite of burning sacrificial material on the altar, a ritual, he suggests, which not only serves to define each sacrifice as an "approach to God" (קָרְבָּן), a "gift by fire" (אִשֶּׁה), and a "restful aroma" (רֵיחַ־נִיחוֹחַ), but which consequently serves as the climactic rite in worship.³⁴ How, we might ask, does the הִקְטִיר rite cause an approach to God? The burning on the altar transforms the animal's flesh into a "restful aroma," transporting the sacrifice to God's heavenly abode as the smoke *ascends* from the altar. Sacrifices may, thereby, be summarized in scripture according to the burning rite (see Deut. 33:10; Ezra 6:10).

Accordingly, to understand the significance of the ascension offering, we will examine two aspects of the הִקְטִיר rite, which contribute to its meaning. First, once more, the *whole* animal underwent the burning, not merely a part of it, thus conveying the sense of self-denial and utter consecration—a life yielded entirely unto YHWH, in full submission to his will and in complete obedience to his law. There is, then, an essential element of absolute surrender and total self-dedication involved in the ascension offering, which, however vicarious, must contribute to our understanding of its peculiar influence upon God. It is this gesture of utter consecration, including the fundamental element of atonement underlying it, that alone explains its profound worth in the divine estimation—indeed, as instituted and solicited by YHWH God himself. Berman captures well how the *Akedah* (Genesis 22) in particular relates to this significance of the ascension offering:

> The word *olah* means "one that rises," meaning, within a sacral context, toward God above.... Our entire being—even our very lives—should be selflessly devoted to God. When an animal is offered as a *korban olah*, it functions in the same way as the ram that was offered in the place of Isaac. It symbolizes our willingness to devote our entire existence to the service of God.³⁵

It is this cost—not the animal's value, but the utter devotion the offering signifies—that leads David to declare that he would not "cause-to-ascend (אַעֲלֶה) to YHWH my God ascension offerings that cost me nothing" (2 Sam. 24:24). Similarly, Samuel had earlier admonished Saul, asking, "Does YHWH delight in ascension offerings and sacrifices as much as in obeying the voice of YHWH? Look, to obey is better than sacrifice, and to

---

[31] Sometimes שָׂרַף describes the burning of offering remains after the ritual is completed, without any cultic significance, while הִקְטִיר always describes the burning rite on the altar—cf. Christian A. Eberhart, "A Neglected Feature of Sacrifice in the Hebrew Bible: Remarks on the Burning Rite on the Altar," *HTR* 97.4 (2004), pp. 485–93 (489n15).

[32] Kleinig, *Leviticus*, 41.

[33] Cf. Norman H. Snaith, "Sacrifices in the Old Testament," *VT* 7.3 (1957), pp. 308–17 (314–15).

[34] Eberhart, "A Neglected Feature of Sacrifice."

[35] Berman, *The Temple*, p. 123; see also Kidner, "Sacrifice," pp. 131–32; Watts, "ʿōlāh," pp. 132–33.

heed than the fat of rams" (1 Sam. 15:22). Indeed, this understanding of the cult's relationship to obedience appears uniform throughout the Hebrew Bible, as evident in passages like Ps. 40:6-7[MT 39:7-8], quoted by the author of Hebrews, and others (e.g., Ps. 51:16-17[MT 18-19]; Prov. 21:3; Hos. 6:6; Mic. 6:6-8). It follows, then, that simplistic notions of Israel's cult being merely expiatory—that is, as primarily a system of negation in the removal of sin's guilt and pollution—are severely in error, since its defining sacrifice solicits nothing less than the positive fulfillment of the Torah to "love YHWH your God with all your heart, with all your soul, and with all your strength" (Deut. 6:5) and to "love your neighbor as yourself" (Lev. 19:18). The ascension offering, in other words, is about selfless submission to the will of God, a life of absolute surrender and consecration unto God. Israel's cult formed, thereby, a divine solicitation to, and profound exposition of, Israel's *will*—a point in full accord with one of the major emphases in Deuteronomic theology, namely, Israel's need for circumcision of the heart (cf. Deut. 30:6).[36]

The second aspect of the הַקְטִיר rite is that of ascension. As the fire transforms the animal parts into an aroma pleasing to God, the offering—by that transformation into smoke—is caused to ascend to God's heavenly abode, thus fulfilling the name עֹלָה. In the burning rite, therefore, "the offering is not destroyed but transformed, sublimated, etherealized, so that it can ascend in smoke to the heaven above, the dwelling-place of God."[37] Through this rite, the ascending smoke becomes a visible presentation of humanity's return to God:

> The holocaust, therefore, was considered as "the most perfect sacrifice," because it expressed perfectly that oblation inasmuch as the whole victim, apparently transformed into the vapor of smoke (but not destroyed or reduced to nothing), could ascend unto God "in fragrant odor" (see Eph. 5:2) and thus represent in a visible manner, as it were, the return of man to God.[38]

Stated differently, the transformational burning was for the sake of *transferring* the animal, as a vicarious substitute, from the ordinary earthly plane to the divine heavenly realm, to the ownership of God. The theology, to be clear, is based not merely on the aromatic smoke's ascent, but rather on the substitute's ascent through the smoke, as transformed into smoke. Nelson writes that "the altar fire was a pipeline into the other world, vaporizing a burnt offering, the fat of a communion sacrifice, some grain, or even wine (Num. 15:7), up to Yahweh's domain."[39] Similarly, Leach states that the "fire of the altar is the gateway to the other world, the channel through which offerings can

---

[36] For the unity between Leviticus 1–16 and the so-called ethical dimensions of chs. 17–27, see Trevaskis, *Holiness, Ethics and Ritual*.

[37] Frederick C. N. Hicks, *The Fullness of Sacrifice: An Essay in Reconciliation* (3rd ed.; London: SPCK, 1953), p. 13; on this notable point, see also Kurtz, *Offerings, Sacrifices and Worship in the Old Testament*, pp. 154–55; S. C. Gayford, *Sacrifice and Priesthood: Jewish and Christian* (2nd ed.; London: Methuen, 1953), p. 79; Hugh Blenkin, *Immortal Sacrifice* (London: Darton, Longman and Todd, 1964), p. 29; Milgrom, *Leviticus 1–16*, pp. 160–61; Low, "Logic of Atonement," pp. 27–29.

[38] Lyonnet and Sabourin, *Sin, Redemption, and Sacrifice*, p. 169; "the most perfect sacrifice" is quoted from Ceslas Spicq, *L'Épître aux Hébreux: Commentaire* (vol. II; Paris: Gabalda, 1953), p. 276.

[39] Nelson, *Raising Up a Faithful Priest*, p. 60.

be transmitted to God."[40] A similar idea of ascending to heaven *via the sacrificial fire* of the ascension offering is found in a curious incident in Judges 13 where the messenger of YHWH announces Samson's birth. After Manoah offered up an ascension offering, we read in verse 20 that "as the flame ascended heavenward from the altar, the messenger of YHWH ascended in the flame of the altar!" (This scene is of no little significance for understanding the ascension of Jesus within the theology of the ascension offering.) Kidner is, therefore, correct in declaring that this Godward ascent is the offering's leading thought, as brought out by its name.[41] As the fundamental offering of Israel's cultus, the עֹלָה thus underscores what one might call the ascension theology at the heart of Israel's understanding of atonement. Through the הִקְטִיר rite, the Israelite ascends, as it were, ushered into YHWH's Presence with the clouds.[42] The altar "of the ascension offering" thus existed for Israel's cultic ascent to God.

This vicarious entrance into God's Presence through the ascending smoke of a pleasing aroma explains the logic of the tribute offering, which always accompanied the ascension offering, as well as that of the final communion-offering meal, where, having entered the abode of God, one then enjoys his unsurpassed hospitality. In the custom of the ANE, Israel is amply sated by the abundance of YHWH's house (Ps. 36:8-9), who prepares a table for them and anoints their head with oil (Ps. 23:5).

Ancient Israel's cult and the epistle to the Hebrews

The use of Israel's cult within Hebrews, and in the New Testament (NT) more generally, will be approached, first, with a definition of atonement as *broadly conceived*, as salvation, humanity's restoration to the life and fellowship of God; and, second, with a *holistic* understanding of the Levitical cult. Even as Israel's calendar emphasized Passover on one day and *Yom Kippur* on another, without contradiction, so, too, the NT authors are apt to refer to one part of the whole, without losing sight of the reality that Christ's person and work have rendered the entire temple system itself, including its priesthood, obsolete.[43] These points, again, make a study of the ascension offering ideal, as it both sums up Israel's cult and unifies Israel's calendar by its daily offering— it even closed the *Yom Kippur* ceremony, its ascension offerings being said to "make atonement" for Aaron and for the people (Lev. 16:24).[44] Indeed, in a reference oft neglected in studies on the Day of Atonement, Lev. 23:27 sums up part of Israel's duty on this convocation with: "You will . . . offer an אִשֶּׁה ('fire offering') to YHWH."

---

[40] Leach, "The Logic of Sacrifice," p. 144.

[41] Kidner, "Sacrifice," p. 130.

[42] The entrance of the high priest into the holy of holies with the clouds of incense in Leviticus 16 may be compared to the son of man's approach to God in Daniel 7; ascension offering imagery may underlie both accounts.

[43] Hebrews explains the transition from the Old Covenant to the new primarily in terms of a change in priesthood, from the Levitical way of approaching God to the "new and living" way after the order of Melchizedek (cf. 7:11-28; 10:19-22).

[44] Geller's attempt to disconnect these offerings from the *Yom Kippur* ritual ("Blood Cult," p. 107) remains unconvincing since the concluding rites (vv. 25-28) are related *after* the ascension offerings (v. 24).

Beginning first with the consecration aspect of the ascension offering, the cult's fulfillment cannot be separated from the fulfillment of God's *Torah*; that is, the cult's meaning—its function and quest—can only be satisfied and made obsolete through the sacrifice of Christ's will unto God in absolute obedience. Jesus's tormented night of prayer in Gethsemane's garden, therefore, was not only the counter to Adam's self-willed failure in Eden's garden, but also the fulfillment of the Levitical cult, as out of his deep sorrow and distress he cried, "Nevertheless not as I will, but as you will—your will be done" (Mt. 26:36-46). The cross, then, was but the capstone and culmination of his entire life of consecration, the last act of obedience that through the Spirit would become the blameless life offered up finally and fully unto the Father upon Jesus's entrance into heaven. As an obedient Son his daily life, morning and evening, conformed to the ascension offering. The author of Hebrews has this obedience in mind, not only in 5:7-9, but especially as fulfilling the cultic system in 10:1-10.[45] After addressing the imperfect nature of the Levitical cult, he writes that, *therefore*, when Jesus came into the world it was to offer more than whole burnt offerings and sacrifices for sin. Rather, the Son says (quoting Ps. 40 [MT 39]): "Behold, I have come ... to do your will, O God!"[46] This fulfillment and transfiguration of the cult is explained by the author as follows:

> He [Jesus] takes away the first [the Levitical sacrifices] so that he may establish the second [obedience to God's will]. By that will we have been sanctified through the offering of the body of Jesus Christ once and for all. (10:9b-10)

Surrendering himself wholly to the will of God, as offering up his "body," Jesus satisfies the significance of the whole burnt offering. In doing so, Jesus not only fulfills humanity's role as solicited by the sacrificial system, but he replaces the sacrificial cult in the lives of God's people (see 7:24-27; 8:1-6; 9:11-15; 10:19-22)—and, as a result, induces New Covenant obedience whereby the law is set within their hearts (see the ensuing quotations of Jeremiah 31 in 10:16-17). Within the central section of the epistle (8:1–10:18),[47] moreover, 10:1-10 comprises a key argument and is in parallel with 9:1-14, both units beginning with the deficiency of the Levitical cult (9:1-10; 10:1-4) and ending with the efficaciousness of Christ's bodily sacrifice (9:11-14; 10:5-10).[48] This parallel progresses by expanding from the annual *Yom Kippur* ritual to that of the

---

[45] Cf. Simon Kistemaker, *Psalm Citations in the Epistle to the Hebrews* (Eugene: Wipf & Stock, 1961), pp. 124–30; Harold W. Attridge, *Hebrews: A Commentary on the Epistle to the Hebrews* (Hermeneia; Philadelphia: Fortress, 1989), p. 275; David M. Moffitt, *Atonement and the Logic of Resurrection in the Epistle to the Hebrews* (Leiden: Brill, 2011), pp. 244–46; Gert J. Steyn, *A Quest for the Assumed LXX Vorlage of the Explicit Quotations in Hebrews* (Göttingen: Vandenhoeck & Ruprecht, 2011), p. 296; Guthrie, *Hebrews*, pp. 326–28.

[46] This is the second and last time Christ himself speaks in Hebrews; cf. Mary Healy, *Hebrews* (Catholic Commentary on Sacred Scripture; Grand Rapids, MI: Baker Academic, 2016), p. 196.

[47] This section culminates the expositional units, cf. George H. Guthrie, *The Structure of Hebrews: A Text-Linguistic Analysis* (Grand Rapids, MI: Baker, 1998), pp. 84–85, 106–08, 125–27; R. J. McKelvey, *Pioneer and Priest: Jesus Christ in the Epistle to the Hebrews* (Eugene, OR: Pickwick, 2013), p. 99.

[48] Scullion, "Day of Atonement," pp. 242–46.

Levitical cult as a whole, as expressed in its daily service (cf. 10:11; 7:27).[49] That daily service, founded upon the *tāmîd 'ōlōt*, with their emphasis on the entire consecration, is where the author of Hebrews turns, citing Psalm 40, to explain the logic of how indeed Christ has put an end to the Levitical cult.[50]

Turning now to the ascent aspect of the ascension offering, it is important to recall that the soothing aroma's ascent to heaven formed merely the epitome of a broader movement, involving various rites. The pattern of a blood rite followed by the burning rite's ascent to God was historically traced as an *exodus pattern*: the blood of the Passover lamb was followed by the ascent of Israel, God's firstborn son, out of Egypt to God at Mount Sinai (and, eventually, up to the promised land/Zion). As such, this exodus pattern constitutes a reversal of humanity's exile from God, and its ritual silhouette may be discerned on *Yom Kippur* as the high priest, representing Israel, ascends into the cultic counterpart to God's heavenly abode and paradise, the holy of holies—and he enters with the "cloud of incense" (עֲנַן הַקְּטֹרֶת, Lev. 16:12-13), an act that embodies, as it were, the ascension offering.[51] The exodus pattern of sacrifice is, therefore, a movement of restoration to communion and fellowship with God. Atonement, then, in its broadest sense, is indeed *through* blood (and, again, this point was enlarged by prefixing the expiatory sacrifices to the ascension offering's blood rite), but does not stop with blood—there is no blood rite in the Hebrew cultus outside the context of a burning rite. The blood rite's *telos* is humanity's restoration to God—true "at-one-ment"—portrayed in the smoke's ascent to heaven. The following quote by Wyatt elucidates the vertical axis of Israel's cultic theology, which fits remarkably well as an exodus pattern:

> Egypt serves as a symbolic location in many biblical passages, as a cipher for exile, a "land of the dead." Consequently, one always "goes down (*yārad*) to Egypt," as though entering the underworld. The supreme sacrifice, the burnt offering, or holocaust, is in Hebrew *'ōlâ*, "a going up."[52]

Here, once more, the author of Hebrews elucidates a profound understanding of the cult's inner meaning, particularly with reference to his focus upon Christ's ascension—beginning already with Lane's correct interpretation of Heb. 1:6 as the Son's entrance into the heavenly realm following his sacrificial death, which Andriessen connected to Israel's entry into the promised land (cf. LXX Deut. 6:10; 11:29), and which Ellingworth further connects to the high priest's entry into the sanctuary (LXX

---

[49] 10:1-18 refers broadly to the law of sacrifices, cf. Cynthia L. Westfall, *A Discourse Analysis of the Letter to the Hebrews: The Relationship Between Form and Meaning* (London: T&T Clark, 2005), pp. 219–30.

[50] This not by an obedience *versus* sacrifice dichotomy, but by Christ's bodily sacrifice as the ultimate expression and consummation of his obedient life of utter consecration. Cf. Benjamin J. Ribbens, *Levitical Sacrifice and Heavenly Cult in Hebrews* (BZNW 222; Berlin: De Gruyter, 2016), p. 147.

[51] Given the probable analogy between the altar and the tent (with its incense altar), the possibility that *Yom Kippur* itself was an enactment and expansion of the ascension offering merits exploration.

[52] Nicolas Wyatt, *Space and Time in the Religious Life of the Near East* (Sheffield: Sheffield Academic, 2001), p. 40.

Exod. 28:30, 43)[53]—all three ascents are analogous,[54] and Adam Christology is likely present as well (cf. Hebrews 2).[55] These observations, each of which conforms to the exodus pattern, are in keeping with understanding Jesus's resurrection and ascension as the *new exodus*, his death as that of the Passover lamb. Therefore, the cross without the ascension is a cause without an effect. By his ascension into heaven, the Son lifts humanity itself—first, though his own human nature, then through his Spirit-wrought union with God's people—into the heavenly paradise of God.[56] While Jesus's ascension, visibly manifesting humanity's restoration unto God, is sometimes described by the author of Hebrews in terms of the *Yom Kippur* ritual, this exodus pattern, as already observed, was expressed daily, weekly, monthly, and annually through the cult's ascension offering. As comparison with the standard OT formula (see Exod. 20:2; Lev. 11:45; cf. Gen. 15:7; Neh. 9:7) demonstrates, the author of Hebrews understands Jesus's resurrection out of the grave and ascension into heaven as the NT exodus: ultimately, God is the God "who brought up our Lord Jesus from the dead" (Heb. 13:20).

To conclude, watching the fragrant, billowing column of the ascension offering's smoke ascend into heaven, propitiating and pleasing YHWH God, the ancient Israelite had glimpsed a hint of what Hebrews describes as Jesus entering "into heaven itself, now to appear in the presence of God for us" (Heb. 9:24).

---

[53] William L. Lane, *Hebrews 1-8* (WBC; Nashville: Nelson, 2009), p. 27; P. C. B. Andriessen, "La Teneur Judéo-Chrétienne de He I 6 et II 14b-III 2," *NovT* 18.4 (1976), pp. 293-313; Ellingworth, *The Epistle to the Hebrews*, pp. 116-17.
[54] See Morales, *Who Shall Ascend the Mountain of the Lord?*, pp. 265-67; James McCaffrey, *The House with Many Rooms: The Temple Theme of Jn. 14,2-3* (Rome: Pontifical Biblical Institute, 1987), p. 129.
[55] Moffitt, *Atonement*, pp. 110-16, 130-44; Sarah S. Musser, "Sacrifice, Sabbath, and the Restoration of Creation" (unpublished doctoral dissertation, Duke University, 2015), pp. 177-81.
[56] In Hebrews, the New Covenant is associated with (heavenly) Zion, *versus* the Old Covenant's association with (earthly) Sinai; see Kiwoong Son, *Zion Symbolism in Hebrews: Hebrews 12:18-24 as a Hermeneutical Key to the Epistle* (Milton Keynes: Paternoster, 2007).

2

Putting Words in His Mouth: The Son Speaks in Hebrews

Karen H. Jobes

The book of Hebrews and its inner-trinitarian dialogue

The book of Hebrews is well known for its opening statement: "In the past God spoke to our ancestors through the prophets at many times and in various ways, but in these last days he has spoken to us by his Son" (NIV). It is therefore all the more intriguing that there is not one parable, beatitude, or other teaching of Jesus in this book. For the author of Hebrews, the *mission* of Jesus Christ in the event of the Incarnation itself is the mode in which God has spoken to us in these last days. Rather than reporting the teachings and miracles of Jesus as the gospels do, the writer of Hebrews is theologically focused on the event of the Incarnation, what it achieves, and what God reveals about himself through it, particularly with respect to the covenant and promises of the OT.

Although we find no parables, beatitudes, or teachings from the earthly ministry of Jesus, he does speak twice in the book of Hebrews, in Heb. 2:11-13 (quoting from Psalm 21 LXX and Isaiah 8 LXX), and in Heb. 10:5-7 quoting from Psalm 39 LXX. In Hebrews, Jesus Christ speaks *only* words of the OT—and the *Greek* OT (LXX) at that—and in both places they are words that reveal and clarify the mission of his Incarnation. Although some interpreters consider this similar to when Jesus quotes the OT in the gospels, Hebrews is doing something quite different. For starters, Jesus is not quoting Scripture while he teaches his disciples or the crowds on a Galilean hillside, but in Hebrews Christ addresses God the Father in response to what God has said in Hebrews 1 to and about the Son. Despite the statement that God has spoken to us by his Son (Heb. 1:2), the Son does not address *us* in Hebrews, but is responding to the Father.

Secondly, there are no conventional formulae used to introduce the Scripture which Christ quotes in Hebrews—no "it is written" or "as the prophet has said" as found in the gospels. Instead the very words of the OT text are attributed directly to Christ, as if the psalmist and the prophet had not penned them many centuries prior. The author of Hebrews presents these words from Psalms and Isaiah as if they were Jesus Christ's own words.

The third reason Christ's words in Hebrews are different from his quotations of the OT in the gospels is that when Christ speaks in Hebrews, he is not giving instruction for his hearers as he most often does in the gospels, for instance in his ethical instructions in the Sermon on the Mount. Instead, he is making declarations about himself to God the Father concerning his incarnational mission.

Richard Hays points out that the tradition of putting the words of the Psalms into Christ's mouth had been established early in Christian tradition. For example, in Rom. 15:8-9 Paul reads the first person pronoun "I" in the quotation of Ps. 18:49 to be the voice of Christ.[1] Hays explains this phenomenon, which he charmingly calls "Christological ventriloquism," to have resulted from early Christian exegesis that fused the past King David with the future Messiah, by understanding that "the Messiah embodies Israel's destiny in such a way that David's songs can be read retrospectively as a prefiguration of the Messiah's sufferings and glorification."[2] But in Romans 15 the OT quotations applied to Christ are nevertheless introduced with the phrase, "as it is written" (Rom. 15:3, 9), acknowledging a source text. That is quite different than introducing an OT quotation in Hebrews with "[Jesus] says" (Heb. 2:12) or "Christ ... said" (Heb. 10:5), which seems to reflect a further development beyond reading the Psalms Christologically.

Harold Attridge considers the words of the Son in Hebrews to be exemplary for Christian discipleship. He observes that the words of Christ in Hebrews are part of a dialogue in which Christ responds to what the Father has said. Attridge argues that "the dialogue of the first two chapters inaugurates a recurring pattern" where the response of the Son models a behavior of fidelity expected of all God's sons and daughters.[3] He considers that "a particularly telling indication of that exemplary function is the emphasis on the *incarnate* character of the Son's response to God" (italics added).[4] And so Attridge concludes, God's covenant people "have heard in the person of God's Son a model for their own dialogue with God, a paradigm for words of faith lived out in action."[5]

While not disagreeing with either Hays's biblical-theological model or Attridge's exemplary reading, this chapter will consider how Hebrews' use of the *Greek* OT amplifies and underscores the mission of atonement that lies at the heart of the Incarnation.

When Christ speaks in Hebrews it is part of a dialogue with the Father, which Hebrews presents for readers to overhear, thereby allowing God to speak to us by the Son. The dialogue begins in ch. 1 with God's identification of himself as the Father of the Son (Heb. 1:5). God commands the angels to worship the Son when he comes into the οἰκουμένη (Heb. 1:6), which David Moffitt has demonstrated is most likely the Son's entrance into the eschatological realm rather than a reference to the Incarnation or *parousia*.[6] God continues to reveal the Son by declaring the eternal reign of the Son in righteousness (Heb. 1:8, 9), the Son's role in creation (Heb. 1:10-12), and a promise of the Son's victory over his enemies (Heb. 1:13). This overview of the Son's eternal roles functions as a prologue to the role of the earthly Jesus. It is composed of

---

[1] Richard B. Hays, "Christ Prays the Psalms: Paul's Use of an Early Christian Exegetical Convention," in *The Future of Christology: Essays in Honor of Leander E. Keck* (ed. Abraham J. Malherbe and Wayne A. Meeks; Minneapolis: Augsberg, 1993), pp. 122–36 (125).
[2] Ibid., pp. 125, 134, 135.
[3] Harold W. Attridge, "God in Hebrews," in *The Epistle to the Hebrews and Christian Theology* (ed. Richard Bauckham, Daniel Driver, Trevor Hart, and Nathan MacDonald; Grand Rapids, MI: Eerdmans, 2009), pp. 95–110 (105).
[4] Ibid., p. 107.
[5] Ibid., p. 110.
[6] David M. Moffitt, *Atonement and the Logic of Resurrection in the Epistles to the Hebrews* (NovTSup 141; Leiden: Brill, 2011), pp. 53–119.

God speaking various excerpts of the OT, re-appropriating them from their original historical context to describe the work of the Son by whom God has spoken once and for all.

In ch. 2 of Hebrews, the perspective is brought down to earth by bringing the human race into the picture with the quotation from Psalm 8, "what is mankind . . . ?" It is interesting—and odd—that this quotation is introduced by the statement, "there is a place where someone has testified," an oblique way of referring to Scripture. I believe this oblique statement functions to remove this quotation from the otherwise ongoing conversation between God and Jesus comprised of the other OT quotations throughout chapters 1 and 2. Psalm 8 points out that God crowned humanity "with glory and honor and put everything under their feet," and then observes that we do not at present see everything put under their feet, apparently because sin and death's victory ends even the most stellar of human achievement. But "we do see Jesus," who by the grace of God tastes death for everyone and brings many sons and daughters to glory (2:5-10). By switching from "the Son" to the name of the man "Jesus," Hebrews is introducing the Incarnation by bringing the Son down to earth as a member of the human race of which Psalm 8 speaks.

Hebrews also reports what Jesus Christ says in response to God, which are the only two places in the book where Christ speaks, in Heb. 2:12, 13 (quoting Psalm 21 LXX and Isaiah 8) and in Heb. 10:5-7 (quoting Psalm 39 LXX). Remarkably, in this dialogue we overhear the agreement between God the Father and the Son to establish the New Covenant! As Attridge observes, "the most creative theological work" of Hebrews resides in the development of this conversation between God and the Son.[7] While it is true that we should not think of the Father and the Son conversing in Greek words, or words of any human language, any belief in divine revelation through Scripture attributes divine illocutionary purposes to God that are capable of being achieved by human locutions.[8] Hebrews presents this as a dialogue between two members of the Trinity which readers are allowed to overhear.

Hebrews 10:5-7 quoting Psalm 39:7-9 LXX

Turning first to Christ's words in Heb. 10:5-7, we read, "when Christ came into the world, he said:

Heb. 10:5   'Sacrifice and offering you did not desire,
            but **a body you prepared for me**;

Heb. 10:6   with burnt offerings and sin offerings
            you were not pleased.'

Heb. 10:7   Then I said, 'Here I am—it is written about me in the scroll—
            I have come to do your will, my God.'"(NIV)

---

[7] Attridge, "God in Hebrews," p. 104.
[8] Richard S. Briggs, "Speech-Act Theory," in *Dictionary for Theological Interpretation of the Bible* (ed. Kevin J. Vanhoozer, Craig G. Bartholomew, Daniel J. Treier, and N.T. Wright; Grand Rapids, MI: Baker Academic, 2005), p. 765.

This is a quotation from Ps. 39:7-9 LXX (Eng. 40:6-8). Hebrews follows the critically reconstructed Göttingen Old Greek text closely,⁹ but presents four small and exegetically significant variations:

1. Instead of ὠτία δὲ κατηρτίσω μοι ("ears you have fashioned for me"; Ps. 39:7 LXX), Hebrews writes, σῶμα δὲ κατηρτίσω μοι ("a body you prepared for me"; Heb. 10:5).
2. The plural ὁλοκαυτώματα ("burnt offerings"; Heb. 10:6) replaces the singular ὁλοκαύτωμα ("burnt offering"; Ps. 39:7 LXX).
3. The negated verb οὐκ εὐδόκησας ("you were not pleased"; Heb. 10:6) is substituted for οὐκ ᾔτησας ("you did not demand"; Ps. 39:7 LXX).
4. The vocative, ὁ θεὸς ("my God"; Heb. 10:7), is transposed with the noun phrase τὸ θέλημά σου ("your will"; Heb. 10:7) and the remainder of the verse as it appears in the Greek psalm is omitted (τοῦ ποιῆσαι τὸ θέλημά σου, ὁ θεός μου, ἐβουλήθην; Ps. 39:9 LXX).

There is significant debate as to whether the wording of the OT quotations found in Hebrews in general, and in this quotation in particular, was already in the Greek OT text used by the author or whether they were introduced by him.¹⁰ I have argued elsewhere that the author of Hebrews introduces them into the text because when these four differences are viewed together, rather than as four independent elements, together they achieve *paronomasia*, a rhetorical ornamentation of the Greek conventionally used at that time by Greek orators.¹¹ Given the high rhetorical style of Hebrews it is not surprising that its author would employ recognized rhetorical devices such as *paronomasia*, and therefore, that the variations of the citations from their sources texts should be examined together rather than in isolation. Quintilian (*Inst.* 9.3.66) explains *paronomasia* as:

- a technique based on the phonetic resemblance, equality, or contrast of words;
- a technique that employs a selection of words of equal length which have similar terminations, producing a pleasing cadence and alliteration when read aloud;
- a technique that concludes clauses alike, the same syllables being placed at the end of each.

If this achievement of *paronomasia* in the citation of Heb. 10:5-7 was already in a Greek version of Psalm 39 used by the author of Hebrews, it reflects a very different translation technique than encountered elsewhere in the extant Greek Psalms, and one would have to consider what might have motivated a Jewish translator to introduce

---

⁹ *Psalmi cum Odis*, Septuaginta Vetus Testamentum Graecum 10 (ed. Alfred Rahlfs; Göttingen: Vandenhoeck & Ruprecht, 1979).
¹⁰ See Gert J. Steyn, *A Quest for the Assumed LXX Vorlage of the Explicit Quotations in Hebrews* (FRLANT 235; Göttingen: Vandenhoeck & Ruprecht, 2011); Susan E. Docherty, *The Use of the Old Testament in Hebrews* (WUNT 260; Tübingen: Mohr Siebeck, 2009).
¹¹ Karen H. Jobes, "Rhetorical Achievement in the Hebrews 10 'Misquote' of Psalm 40," *Bib* 72 (1991), pp. 387-96; Karen H. Jobes, "The Function of Paronomasia in Hebrews 10:5-7," *TJ* 13 (1992), pp. 181-91.

these particular four variations. But because they are so apt to the argument of the context in which they appear in Hebrews 10, it seems more probable the NT author has introduced them to highlight and embellish his theological point, and therefore they are exegetically significant as an interpretation of Psalm 39 LXX in light of Christ's Incarnation.[12]

The phrase "a body you prepared for me" in Heb. 10:5 is especially intriguing because the Hebrew psalm reads, "my ears you have dug," an idiom expressing the ability to hear and obey God. Rahlfs reconstructed Ps. 39:7 LXX as "ears you fashioned for me" (ὠτία δὲ κατηρτίσω μοι), likely because of the translation technique of the rest of the Psalms which follows the Hebrew *Vorlage* closely. But according to Hatch and Redpath, the rendering of the Hebrew verb כרה (dig) with καταρτίζω is unexpected, as this is the only place this Greek verb renders this Hebrew verb, suggesting that either a different Hebrew verb was found in the *Vorlage* or that this is an interpretive rendering, perhaps a metonymy, where the digging or hollowing out of the ears was understood to be part of the work of fashioning a human body.[13]

Moreover, there is a perplexing textual problem in the manuscripts of this verse of the Greek psalm concerning which noun, ὠτία or σῶμα, was in the psalm text used by the author of Hebrews. Susan Docherty has recently argued that the author of Hebrews was quite faithful to his source text, and that most if not all variations from the extant OT manuscripts should be read as variant readings that were already in the Greek OT source text even if they are no longer extant.[14] She bases this conclusion on the fact that there were multiple versions of the Greek Jewish Scriptures at the time Hebrews was written and that the Hebrew Judean Desert materials support Greek readings that differ from the MT.[15] But one cannot so easily generalize or extend her generalization to Heb. 10:5-7; each potential difference must be judged in light of both the translation technique of the given OT book and then how the citation functions in the NT context. Moreover, Docherty does not at all consider the citations being discussed here.

More recently, Moffitt applied Docherty's generalization in his discussion of the Psalm 39 LXX citation in Hebrews 10, but adds the additional significant argument that σῶμα was already in the source text because it does not occur previously in Hebrews until it appears in this citation and then appears twice more to refer to Jesus (Heb. 10:10, 22).[16] He further argues that had the writer of Hebrews replaced ὠτία it would make more sense, in his opinion, for αἷμα or σάρξ to have been chosen, as these words have both been previously used of Jesus in Hebrews (2:14; 5:7; 9:12, 14).[17] However, the choice (if it was a choice) of σῶμα with its long –o sound creates phonetic assonance with -τώματα which would not be achieved with αἷμα or σάρξ. Furthermore, σῶμα is a more apt word emphasizing Jesus's embodiment in the Incarnation as the single sacrifice in contrast to the many animal sacrifices of the past, which is the major reason

---

[12] Jobes, "Function of Paronomasia," pp. 181–91.
[13] F. F. Bruce, *The Epistle to the Hebrews* (NICNT; Grand Rapids, MI: Eerdmans, 1964), p. 232.
[14] Docherty, *Use of the Old Testament*.
[15] Ibid., pp. 140–42.
[16] Moffitt, *Atonement and the Logic of Resurrection*, pp. 236 n.45.
[17] Ibid.

the citation is introduced (v. 5, "when Christ came into the world, he said ... "). Both Docherty and Moffitt examine the variations from the OT source texts in the Hebrews citations as individual elements, overlooking the rhetorical eloquence they achieve when considered together.

Alfred Rahlfs critically reconstructed the original text as "ears you fashioned for me" (ὠτία δὲ κατηρτίσω μοι) despite the fact that *all* extant Greek manuscripts of Psalm 39 LXX actually read σῶμα (body) instead of ὠτία (ears).[18] As Steyn points out, this could have resulted from a scribal misreading in the transmission of the Greek manuscript (ΗΘΕΛΗΣΑΣΣΩΜΑΔΕ for ΗΘΕΛΗΣΑΣΣΩΤΙΑΔΕ), but if so, it would have had to happen quite early in the transmission for no variant readings to survive in any extant Greek manuscript.[19] And this textual error would have been what the author of Hebrews found in his source text.

Alternatively, if ὠτία was in the source text and the author of Hebrews introduced σῶμα, then *every* extant Greek manuscript of the psalm was revised to read σῶμα, under the influence of Hebrews. The problem is that we do not see any similar overwhelming influence of the NT reading on the transmission of any other Greek OT text, suggesting that the author of Hebrews may have found "a body you prepared" already in his source text. And if that is so, then this is a remarkable example of F. F. Bruce's point that "the Septuagint translators used a form of words which (without their being able to foresee it, naturally) lent itself to the purposes of the New Testament writers better than the Hebrew text would have done."[20] Even if the Old Greek text of Psalm 39 already read σῶμα, the author of Hebrews combined that reading with the other three changes to achieve a rhetorical eloquence that underscored his theological point about the significance of the Incarnation.[21]

Whether or not Hebrews changed his source text from ὠτία to σῶμα —a question that probably cannot be resolved with certainty without further discovery of early manuscripts—this quotation in Heb. 10:5-7 provides an excellent example of the two "speakings" mentioned in Heb. 1:1. A thousand years after David spoke the psalm, Christ the Son—both Son of God and son of David—spoke it. God spoke in both times and ways, first in Hebrew Psalm 40 (and its translations) and secondly, in the Son's Incarnation. The quotation signals Christ's continuity with the Davidic monarchy, but the differences introduced by Hebrews signal the discontinuity.

In Heb. 10:6, the plural form ὁλοκαυτώματα refers to the many sacrificial offerings of animals, repeated endlessly year after year, which were insufficient to deal once-for-all with sin. The plural form achieves paronomasia with **σῶμα δέ** (cf. ὁλοκαυτώματα), and contrasts the many burnt offerings with the one body of Christ which God prepared for him in order to achieve the atoning mission of the Incarnation. The entire point of

---

[18] Only two Latin mss., including the Gallican Psalter, have a translation that supports ὠτία. (The Greek versions of Aquila, Symmachus, and Theodotion read ὠτία, as one would expect.) This, and the fact that the Psalm is elsewhere translated very word-for-word, led Rahlfs to conjecture that the original reading of the LXX must have been ὠτία.

[19] Steyn, *Quest*, p. 285.

[20] F. F. Bruce, *The Canon of Scripture* (Downers Grove, IL: IVP, 1988), p. 53.

[21] The textual situation for these three is different from that of σῶμα, as they occur in only a few late Latin and Bohairic manuscripts and more obviously under the influence of the Hebrews quotation.

Hebrews 10 is to show that the many sacrificial offerings of animals, repeated endlessly year after year, were insufficient to deal once-for-all with sin (Heb. 10:1), and the rhetorical flourish of *paronomasia* underscores that point eloquently and memorably.

The change of the three-syllable verb ᾔτησας to the four-syllable εὐδό**κησας** (with all its redemptive connotations in NT usage elsewhere) achieves paronomasia with ἠθέ**λησας**, contrasting the demand of the OT sacrificial law with the redemptive good pleasure of God in Christ. The sacrifice of the body God had prepared for the Son, Christ Jesus, when he entered the world, and not the many animal sacrifices, was what "pleased" God.

The change involving transposition of ὁ θεός and τὸ θέλημά σου in Heb. 10:7 is especially powerful. It achieves paronomasia between μοῦ and σου while at the same time making the articular infinitive τοῦ ποιῆσαι the purpose for the coming (I have come to do ...) instead of the complementary object of ἐβουλήθην (I desire to do ...). David says, "To do your will, my God, I desire." But David's desire exceeded David's ability. When the words are put in Christ's mouth, the transposition and truncation of the quotation locates the accomplishment of God's will as the purpose for the preceding "I have come." When Christ comes into the world he says, "I have come to do, O God, your will." What David could only desire, Christ accomplished. The transposition and truncation introduces an efficacy and finality to Christ's words that are appropriately lacking in David's.

Moffitt has argued that this quotation of Ps. 39:7-9 LXX focuses not on Incarnation but on the obedient suffering and endurance of Jesus as exemplary for Christian life.[22] While the internalization of the law and the call to perseverance are prominent in the rest of the chapter following v. 15, vv. 1-14 center on the sacrifice of the New Covenant that replaces those of the old, the final sacrifice that makes Jeremiah's New Covenant promises possible (Heb. 10:16). Hebrews 10:14 concludes the discussion of the efficacy of Christ's sacrifice, and v. 15 introduces the subsequent work of the Holy Spirit who puts the laws in hearts and minds. Therefore, the sacrifice of Christ's human body for atonement is both theologically and temporally prior to the application of atonement to his followers.

It is poignantly apt that Christ spoke this quotation of Scripture *coming into the world* (εἰσερχόμενος εἰς τὸν κόσμον; Heb. 10:5), a reference to the Incarnation.[23] Although most English Bibles translate, "when he came into the world," suggesting a temporal reference, perhaps it should be understood as expressing means, "*by* coming into the world Christ said." Christ's Incarnation is a statement. This construal of the participle coheres nicely with the Incarnation as the mode of God speaking to us in these last days (Heb. 1:2). What Christ says by coming into the world is addressed to God (Heb. 10:7), declaring, "I have come (into the world) to do your will." Therefore, what we overhear in this is nothing less than Jesus Christ agreeing to the terms of the New Covenant in his blood that would be required to bring many sons and daughters

---

[22] Moffitt, *Atonement and the Logic of Resurrection*, pp. 238–56.
[23] The use of κόσμος distinguishes this verse from 1:6, in which the word typically translated "world" is οἰκουμένη, and there possibly refers to Christ's entrance into the coming eschatological world after passing from his earthly life. See Moffitt, *Atonement and the Logic of Resurrection*, pp. 63–118, 230.

to glory (Heb. 2:10; 13:20)! With this we return to the one other place in Hebrews where Christ speaks: Heb. 2:12, 13.

Hebrews 2:12, 13 quoting Psalm 22:22 and Isaiah 8:17, 18

The first time Jesus is mentioned in Heb. 2:9, it is in victorious retrospect of his death and suffering that brings many sons and daughters to glory, subjecting even death itself to the victorious pioneer of human salvation. The major point made about Jesus here is of his solidarity with the human race: he shares their identity and they are one (ἐξ ἑνός). It is here that Hebrews states that the Incarnation of the Son as a human being was *necessary* for the atonement on which the New Covenant was established.

When Jesus speaks in Heb. 2:12-13, the words of three different OT verses are put in his mouth. The first is from Ps. 21:23 LXX (Eng. 22:22), the other two are from Isa. 8:17 LXX and 18. The first thing Jesus says in Hebrews is, "I will declare your name to my brothers and sisters; in the assembly I will sing your praises." Here also Jesus addresses God (note the second person pronoun σου), not his brothers and sisters, even while declaring his role as revealer *to* his brothers and sisters. This is a quotation from Ps. 21:23 LXX (Eng. 22:22), from which Jesus, in another address to God from the cross, cries out the first verse of the lament psalm, "My God, my God, why have you forsaken me?" (Mt. 27:46; Mk 15:34). Although not a messianic psalm of Judaism, the opening verse of the psalm in the mouth of Jesus while on the cross made this a prominent Christological psalm in early Christian tradition.[24] But in keeping with the perspective that Jesus is now crowned with glory and honor because he tasted death for everyone, Heb. 2:12 quotes from the victorious half of Ps. 21:23 LXX of the lament that acknowledges that God did indeed hear the cry of the Davidic king for deliverance. Because God delivered his king, all Israel should praise the LORD (Ps. 21:24 LXX). When applied to Christ, this appears to be an allusion to his victorious afterlife—which is the vindication of Jesus's sacrifice of himself and the basis for singing God's praise.[25]

When the critically reconstructed Göttingen text of Ps. 21:23 LXX is compared to its corresponding Hebrew *Vorlage* (Ps. 22:22 MT), the translation is conventional and no noteworthy differences are found. But when the quotation in Heb. 2:12 is compared with its presumed Greek source text, the change of the verb from διηγήσομαι ("I shall describe, explain") to ἀπαγγελῶ ("I shall proclaim") both achieves *paronomasia* and makes the statement more apt in the mouth of Christ.[26] Furthermore, with this small change "each of the four quoted lines in Heb. 2:12-13 opens strikingly with an *o-sound*" (italics original), achieving phonetic assonance that highlights the author's point.[27]

---

[24] It is worth making the distinction between Messianic texts of the OT, which would have been recognized as such by Judaism in the Second Temple period and Christological texts which had no such Messianic connotation until the NT writers applied them to Jesus.
[25] See Moffitt, *Atonement and the Logic of Resurrection*, esp. pp. 27–40.
[26] There are no textual variants listed for this verse in the critically reconstructed psalm in the Göttingen edition.
[27] Steyn, *Quest*, p. 154.

Hebrews 2:13a quoting Isaiah 8:17 LXX, 18

When we move to the second of the three OT texts put in Jesus's mouth in Heb. 2:12-13, we find the adverbial phrase καὶ πάλιν joins it to the first, a citation formula that frequently introduces quotations from Scripture throughout Hebrews (1:6; 2:13; 4:5, 7; 10:30), in other NT books (e.g., Jn 19:37; Rom. 15:10; 1 Cor. 3:20), and in other contemporaneous authors such as Philo.[28] Although it is often translated "and again"—suitable for narrative contexts—its adverbial sense here may be better translated "furthermore" (i.e., "he said furthermore").

The source of this second quotation is either Isa. 8:17 LXX, Isa. 12:2 LXX, or 2 Kgdms 22:3 LXX (Eng. 2 Sam.), all of which read identically, πεποιθὼς ἔσομαι ἐπ᾽ αὐτῷ (it may also echo the very similar Ps. 2:12 LXX (μακάριοι πάντες οἱ πεποιθότες ἐπ᾽ αὐτῷ) the psalm put in God's mouth in reference to the Son in the opening quotation in Heb. 1:5.) Because the third and final text immediately following this in Heb. 2:13b is unambiguously from OG Isa. 8:18, most interpreters believe it is likely that Hebrews had in mind Isa. 8:17 here.[29]

Although that identification is likely correct, there are nevertheless meaningful metaleptic resonances with the Isa. 12:2 passage, which opens the chapter following immediately after the reference to the messianic "root of Jesse" in Isa. 11:1, 10.[30] Isaiah 12:1 speaks of the wrath of God turned away, the Lord's salvation for the one who will trust in him in Isa. 12:2, and then mentions a hymn fest to the Lord in Isa. 12:4. These thoughts in Isaiah 12 are similar to those found in the immediately preceding context of the quotation in Heb. 2:12 (Ps. 21:23 LXX).

However, the same phrase, πεποιθὼς ἔσομαι ἐπ᾽ αὐτῷ, also appears in 2 Kgdms 22:3 LXX (Eng. 2 Samuel) in a Davidic hymn titled "Song of Deliverance," which is the entirety of Psalm 17 LXX (Eng. Psalm 18) embedded in the narrative. Psalm 17 LXX carries the superscription that it was sung on the day the Lord delivered David from all his enemies. As Steyn points out, this is a very striking nexus of texts to be represented in Heb. 2:13 when the submission of enemies under Christ's feet was explicitly mentioned in the immediately preceding context of Heb. 1:13 and Heb. 2:5-8.[31]

Although the phrase πεποιθὼς ἔσομαι ἐπ᾽ αὐτῷ occurs in all three of these OT books, the author of Hebrews is most likely quoting the phrase from Isa. 8:17. In that context we find one of the "stone" passages ("The LORD . . . will be a stone that causes people to stumble . . . ," Isa. 8:14). Following that, Isaiah declares, "Here am I, and the children the LORD has given me," pointing to himself, and to the child that had been prophesized in Isa. 7:14 ("behold, the virgin will conceive . . .") as "signs and symbols

---

[28] For example, Philo, *Opif.* 41, 70; *Her.* 2.122; *Conf.* 169; *Somn.* 1.166; 2.19; *Leg.* 3.4; *Sobr.* 8; *Plant.* 171; *1 Clem.* 10:4, 6; 14:5; 15:3, 4; *Barn.* 6:2, 4.

[29] For example, Attridge, *Hebrews*, p. 90; also Steyn, *Quest*, pp. 164–65; George H. Guthrie, "Hebrews," in *Commentary on the New Testament Use of the Old Testament* (ed. G. K. Beale and D. A. Carson; Grand Rapids, MI: Baker Academic, 2007), pp. 919–95 (949).

[30] Richard Hays explains metalepsis as the effect of a literary echo that lies in the unstated or suppressed points of resonance between the two texts. (*Echoes of Scripture in the Letters of Paul* [New Haven, CT: Yale University Press, 1989], p. 20). It is one of the primary mechanisms through which intertextual references between biblical texts carry meaning.

[31] Steyn, *Quest*, p. 159.

in Israel from the LORD." That statement precedes the messianic passage in Isa. 9:6-7, "For unto us a child is born . . . . And he will be called 'Wonderful Counselor.'" Clearly there are messianic associations all around the verse from Isaiah that Hebrews has put in Christ's mouth.

When the Hebrew Isa. 8:17 was translated into Greek, the words καὶ ἐρεῖ ("and he shall say") were added, resulting in, καὶ ἐρεῖ Μενῶ τὸν θεὸν . . . ("And he shall say, 'I will wait for God, who has turned away his face from the house of Jacob, and I will trust in him'"). Although the LXX translator probably intended it to be a clarification that smoothed the otherwise abrupt shift to first person singular, "I will wait" (וְחִכִּיתִי), this small addition may have opened the way for Hebrews to read Isa. 8:17 as a messianic text, and therefore applicable to Jesus.

When Hebrews put the text of Isa. 8:17 LXX into the mouth of Jesus, two small changes apparently were made:[32]

Isa. 8:17 . . . καὶ πεποιθὼς ἔσομαι ἐπ' αὐτῷ.

Heb. 2:13 . . . ἐγὼ ἔσομαι πεποιθὼς ἐπ' αὐτῷ . . .

The καί was dropped and the emphatic pronoun ἐγώ was added, emphasizing Jesus's trust in God even through the experience of death. The addition of the pronoun ἐγώ probably then motivated the change in word order of the periphrastic participle from πεποιθὼς ἔσομαι in the LXX (because there the translator followed even the order of the Hebrew pronominal suffix) to ἔσομαι πεποιθὼς, a more conventional Greek word order for this construction.

Whereas the first two quoted verses in Heb. 2:12-13a deals with the relationship between God and Jesus, the focus of the third in v. 13b shifts to the solidarity of Jesus with those sons and daughters he leads to glory through his suffering (cf. Heb. 2:10). The separation of the source text by the second occurrence of the adverbial phrase καὶ πάλιν apparently is meaningful, as Hebrews could have continued the quotation from Isa. 8:17 to v. 18 without interruption. However, there is a difference between the Hebrew MT and the LXX rendering that may have invited Hebrews to separate them with the adverbial prepositional phrase καὶ πάλιν. In the MT, Isa. 8:18a and b form one sentence,

הִנֵּה אָנֹכִי וְהַיְלָדִים אֲשֶׁר נָתַן־לִי יְהוָה לְאֹתוֹת וּלְמוֹפְתִים בְּיִשְׂרָאֵל מֵעִם יְהוָה צְבָאוֹת

("Behold, I and the children whom the LORD has given me are signs and portents in Israel from the LORD of hosts" [ESV]). But in the LXX, that sentence becomes two clauses, with the words of Isa. 8:18a LXX forming a separate clause:

ἰδοὺ ἐγὼ καὶ τὰ παιδία, ἅ μοι ἔδωκεν ὁ θεός, καὶ ἔσται εἰς σημεῖα καὶ τέρατα ἐν τῷ Ισραηλ παρὰ κυρίου σαβαωθ, ("Here am I and the children whom God has given me, and *they* shall become signs and portents in Israel from the Lord Sabaoth . . . "). This difference between the MT and LXX allows the author of Heb. 2:13a to put only the first of the two clauses in Jesus's mouth.[33] Readers are allowed to hear a victorious Jesus

---

[32] The Greek text of Isa. 8:17 does not have these variant readings.
[33] Docherty notes that Hebrews often divides a Scripture text into two, citing in addition to this example Deut. 32:35-36 in Heb. 10:30, Ps. 94:7-11 in Hebrews 3-4, and Ps. 39:7-9 in Hebrews 10 as exegeted in two separate sections. Docherty, *Use of the Old Testament*, p. 165.

proclaiming his identification with humanity before God and providing a Scriptural basis for the claim that follows in Heb. 2:11 that "both the one who makes people holy and those who are made holy are of the same family."[34] Jesus's atoning death has resulted in many sons and daughters in the same family as Jesus, who are not ashamed to share their humanity so they can share in his resurrected life, consequently freeing them from their fear of death (Heb. 2:15).

The echoes of King David's "Song of Deliverance" that was sung to the Lord on the day he was delivered from all his enemies is quite apt in the mouth of Jesus. It provides another example of Hays's observation that early Christian exegesis of the OT fused the past King David with the future Messiah, because the apostles understood the Messiah to embody "Israel's destiny in such a way that David's songs can be read retrospectively as a prefiguration of the Messiah's sufferings and glorification."[35] The resurrection and ascension of Jesus Christ's human body from the grave was the final and eternal victory of a Davidic king. Not only was it Jesus's own vindication but also the day of deliverance for the human race, led by the pioneer of their salvation, the true Davidic king (Heb. 2:10). It is only in the victory of Jesus over death that we finally see "everything put under their feet" as referenced in the quotation of Ps. 8:4-6 in Heb. 2:8.

The placement of these three OT quotations in the mouth of Jesus as the first thing he says in Hebrews explains the necessity of the Incarnation, that it was necessary for a human being to conquer suffering and death in order for any human beings to be led to glory. But that was something no human being except the incarnate God could achieve. Establishing the necessity of the Incarnation prefaces the introduction of the role of the Son as high priest who makes atonement (Heb. 2:17), a concept that Hebrews will more fully develop in Heb. 7:1–10:18.

Concluding thoughts

Remarkably, when the Son speaks in Hebrews we overhear him accepting his atoning role in the New Covenant. It is notable that for this divine illocutionary purpose, a *translation* of the Hebrew source texts was used, and that the differences between the LXX translation and the MT were exploited to develop the theology of atonement in Hebrews. In overhearing the Son address the Father, God has spoken to us by his Son, whom we hear consenting to be the one, final sacrifice for sin through a translation of OT words put directly in his mouth.

In the book of Hebrews Jesus is described as "the guarantor of a better covenant" (7:22), the mediator of a better covenant (8:6), and the mediator of a New Covenant (9:15; 12:24), whose blood established the eternal covenant (13:20). God, through the locutions of the author of Hebrews, allows us to overhear an inner-Trinitarian conversation between the Father and Jesus Christ that establishes the eternal covenant. God has indeed spoken to us by the Son!

---

[34] See Attridge, *Hebrews*, pp. 90–91; Steyn, *Quest*, p. 156.
[35] Hays, "Christ Prays the Psalms," pp. 125, 134, 135.

3

The Origins of Hebrews' High Priest Christology: A Conundrum Revisited

Nicholas Perrin

In the Epistle to the Hebrews, Jesus's role as priest surfaces as a leading theme. For reasons that cannot be explored here fully, Hebrews scholarship has generally assumed that the historical origins of this concept were traceable either to the *auctor Hebraeos* himself or to his immediate precursor tradition.[1] On this line of thinking, the writer's assertion of Jesus as "high priest in the order of Melchizedek" (Heb. 7:17), demonstrated not least on the basis of Psalms 2 and 110, constitutes a more or less novel advance on earlier messianism and/or Christological reflection. The original impetus for Jesus's priestly aspect lies with not so much any event or set of events associated with the life of Jesus, but rather an ecclesial linkage between post-Easter atonement theology and

---

[1] J. T. Sanders, *The New Testament Christological Hymns* (SNTSMS 15; Cambridge: Cambridge University Press, 1971), pp. 19–20, for example, contemplates the possibility of previous liturgical traditions. Similarly, according to Harold W. Attridge, *The Epistle to the Hebrews: A Commentary on the Epistle to the Hebrews* (Hermeneia; Philadelphia: Fortress, 1989), pp. 97–103, "the understanding of Christ as High Priest is probably based on Jewish notions of priestly angels and was already a part of the Christian liturgical or exegetical tradition on which our authors draws" (p. 103). Others have traced a trail back to Hasmonean ideology (George W. Buchanan, *To the Hebrews: Translation, Comment and Conclusion* [AB 36; Garden City, NY: Doubleday, 1972], pp. 38–51) or Qumran-style messianism (e.g., Joseph Coppens, "Les affinités qumraniennes de l'Épître aux Hébreux," *NRTh* 84 [1962], pp. 128–41). Earlier scholars have generally credited Hebrews' sacerdotal imagery to the *auctor Hebraeos* himself, even if he was shaped by one or more influences. See James Moffatt, *A Critical and Exegetical Commentary on The Epistle to the Hebrews* (ICC; Edinburgh: T&T Clark, 1924), pp. xlvi–lii; Hans Windisch, *Die Hebräerbrief* (2nd ed.; NTG 14; Tübingen: Mohr [Siebeck], 1931), p. 13; Albert Vanhoye, *Situation du Christ: Hébreux 1–2* (LD 58; Paris: Cerf, 1969), p. 372; Graham Hughes, *Hebrews and Hermeneutics: The Epistle to the Hebrews as a New Testament Example of Biblical Interpretation* (SNTSMS 36; Cambridge: Cambridge University Press, 1979), pp. 29–31; M. E. Clarkson, "The Antecedents of the High-Priest Them in Hebrews," *ATR* 29 (1947), pp. 89–95. But the same view is also current enough in more recent scholarship; see, for example, Udo Schnelle, *Theology of the New Testament* (trans. M. E. Boring; ET Grand Rapids, MI: Baker Academic, 2009), p. 637. To my knowledge, Jon C. Laansma (in *The Letter to the Hebrews: A Commentary for Preaching, Teaching, and Bible Study* [Eugene, OR: Cascade, 2017] p. 130) is the only commentator who takes this possibility seriously. See also his crisp discussion of the relevant sacerdotal backgrounds to Hebrews (pp. 128–30).

messianic *testimonia*. This assumption has been so well ensconced in the literature that it has virtually achieved the status of inexpungable fact.[2]

Yet, as I hope to show in this chapter, it is an assumption that is open to serious question. Indeed, we have good reason to believe that when the *auctor Hebraeos* grounds Jesus's priesthood on the convergence of Psalms 2 and 110, he is neither introducing a *novum* nor extending a notional development, but rather reiterating an early conviction which may have even struck root in the *Sitz im Leben Jesu*. My argument proceeds in three parts. In the first part, I will explore the relevant passages of Hebrews with a view to demonstrating the foundational role of Psalms 2 and 110 in the thematizing of Jesus's priesthood. Then, in part two, I will examine the Gospel of Mark's use of Psalms 2 and 110, with special attention to Jesus's baptism (Mk 1:9-11) and the *Davidssohnfrage* debate (Mk 12:35-37). Third and finally, I will marshal evidence that both these gospel traditions (together with their supporting scriptural citations) stand in good stead as authentic reminiscences of Jesus, even as I will also maintain—as corroborating evidence—the strategic role those remembered events would have had in the liturgical life of the early church. The reconstruction of an exegetical trajectory from the *Sitz im Leben Jesu* to the writing of Hebrews decades later, if viable, promises not only to shed light on the antiquity of the *auctor Hebraeos*'s working concepts but also to situate the same author along an interpretative thoroughfare originating in the Palestinian movement.

Psalms 2 and 110 in Hebrews

Traces of Psalms 2 and 110 appear as early as the homily's exordium. In Heb. 1:2 readers are introduced to "a son" (υἱῷ) who, as a revelatory agent, is superior to the prophets. While the filial term has often been understood as an otherwise indeterminate Christological title, its theological density comes into fuller view once we recognize its derivation from Ps. 2:7. This derivation is confirmed on at least two observations.[3] First, the son of Hebrews' exordium has been "appointed" (ἔθηκεν) (Heb. 1:2), much as the messianic son of Psalm 2 has also been "appointed" (LXX: κατεστάθην; MT: *nāsaktî*) (Ps. 2:6).[4] Second, the son is identified as the universal heir (Heb. 1:2), a role also reserved

---

[2] This of course has entailments for dogmatics, as shown Wolfhart Pannenburg's (in *Jesus—God and Man* [2nd ed.; Philadelphia: Westminster, 1977], pp. 219-20) judgment: "A tradition of the church that reaches back into the early Christian period designates Jesus' vicarious suffering by the concept of his priesthood.... Here, too, the picture of Jesus as the acting agent results only from transferring the Messianic office of the exalted Lord back into the path of Jesus to the cross. This interpretation may be well founded in and of itself. It does not, however, agree with the character of Jesus' pre-Easter life.... Hence, one probably cannot speak here of an office Jesus, at least not in the same sense as with reference to his pre-Easter activity." (My gratitude to Jon Laansma for this reference.)

[3] On these points, see David Wallace "The Use of Psalms in the Shaping of a Text: Psalm 2:7 and Psalm 110:1 in Hebrews 1," *ResQ* 45 (2003), pp. 41-50 (45-46).

[4] The absence of complete lexical agreement with the LXX is no argument against no dependence. Notwithstanding his failure to reproduce the exact verbiage of the LXX, Paul is undoubtedly drawing on the same subtext of Psalm 2 when he describes Jesus as being "declared to be Son of God" (τοῦ ὁρισθέντος υἱοῦ θεοῦ) by virtue of his resurrection (Rom. 1:4); cf. Christopher G. Whitsett, "Son of God, Seed of David: Paul's Messianic Exegesis in Romans 1:3-4," *JBL* 119 (2000), pp. 661-81 (676-77); Robert M. Calhoun, *Paul's Definitions of the Gospel in Romans 1* (vol. 2; WUNT 2.316; Tübingen: Mohr Siebeck, 2011), p. 103.

for the psalmist's messianic son (Ps. 2:8). At the same time, in describing this figure as having made purification of sins and having "sat down at the right hand" of majesty (Heb. 1:3b), the writer drops hints that he is also trading on the enthroned Melchizedekian priest of Psalm 110, who likewise is made to "sit at my right hand" (Ps. 110:1). If such parallels by themselves are not compelling evidence of the exordium's reliance on Psalms 2 and 110, the explicit citation of Ps. 2:7 ("You are my Son, today I have become your father") at Heb. 1:5a and of Ps. 110:1 ("Sit at my right hand until I make your enemies a footstool for your feet") at Heb. 1:13 renders the intertextual connections beyond doubt.

Whereas the exordium affirms the revelatory superiority of Christ in respect to the prophets, the subsequent catena (Heb. 1:5-13) upholds the Risen Jesus's preeminence over the angels. It does so through seven tightly packed quotations. The first of these is the aforementioned text of Ps. 2:7 (Heb. 1:5a); the seventh and final, the (also aforementioned) text of Ps. 110:1 (Heb. 1:13).[5] However the reader structures this chain of seven links, there's little doubting that Ps. 2:7 and Ps. 110:1 together function as bookends, presumably subsuming the intervening series of scriptural proofs under the broader claim shared by the two psalms. The *inclusio* forged by citations of Psalms 2 and 110 is programmatic. Likewise, Hebrews' early and strident gestures toward the two psalms anticipate their prominence in the epistle's larger argument.[6]

Having treated Jesus's superiority over both the angels (Hebrews 2) and Moses (Heb. 3:1-4:13), the *auctor Hebraeos* now takes up an extended discussion of Jesus's highpriesthood (Heb. 4:14-10:18). Introducing the topic with an exhortation to persevere, the writer assumes (without argument) that Jesus is "a great high priest who has passed through the heavens" (Heb. 4:14; cf. 3:1). While Hebrews will later seek to contrast the priesthoods of Aaron and Jesus, for now their shared similarities are emphasized. One key comparison is the elective nature of their respective callings:

> And one does not presume to take this honor, but takes it only when called by God, just as Aaron was. So also Christ did not glorify himself in becoming a high priest, but was appointed by the one who said to him: "You are my Son, today I have begotten you" [Ps. 2:7b]; as he says also in another place, "You are a priest forever after the order of Melchizedek" [Ps. 110:4b].[7]

Two remarks are in order. First, in the lead-up to the cited Ps. 2:7 (Heb. 5:5a), the choice of verb (λαλέω) in the phrase "was appointed by the *one who said* to him" (γενηθῆναι ἀρχιερέα, ἀλλ' ὁ λαλήσας πρὸς αὐτόν) seems to presuppose an oral exchange, perhaps suggesting God addressing Jesus in his preexistent state (through the scriptural utterance of Ps. 2:7) or the event of Jesus's baptism, where according to the synoptic witness, a divine voice appoints Jesus to ministry (also through the terms of Ps. 2:7).[8] Second, the writer seeks to establish Jesus's divine ordination on

---

[5] See the thorough analysis of the catena in J. P. Meier, "Symmetry and Theology in the Old Testament Citations of Heb. 1:5-14," *Biblica* 66 (1985), pp. 504-33.
[6] As David Wallace ("Use of Psalms," p. 43) summarizes, "The first chapter of Hebrews is an exceptional example of the literary and theological significance of both Psalms 2 and 110 for the entire document."
[7] Heb. 5:4-6.
[8] Mt. 3:13-17//Mk 1:9-11//Lk. 3:21-22.

scriptural grounds by (re-)appealing to the paired Psalms 2 and 110 (more exactly, by repeating Ps. 2:7b and now citing v. 4 of Psalm 110 rather than v. 1). Apparently, from the writer's point of view, when Jesus fulfills Psalms 2 and 110, he does so precisely as a priest.

This line of reasoning with reference to Psalm 110 is neither unsurprising nor illogical. Even if pre-Christian Judaism did not necessarily discern a messianic figure in the text of Psalm 110, the early church quickly recognized the same text as a convenient map on which to plot Jesus's atoning death, resurrection, and ascension.[9] Of course, the psalm also allowed the early Christians to locate Jesus's priestly atoning activity within the matrix of Jewish apocalyptic belief, which, in at least some circles, expected the return of an exalted Melchizedekian figure. Similarly, Psalm 110 also proves crucial for the writer's distinctive agenda of presenting Jesus as the eschatological Melchizedek (Heb. 6:13–8). But quite apart from this specific concern, even if the writer were only interested in proving Jesus's priesthood in the most general terms, he could have hardly settled on a more strategic proof-text.

Whereas Ps. 110:4 provides obvious support for Jesus's priesthood, it may not be immediately evident how Ps. 2:7 sustains the same point.[10] Faced with this problem, I suggest, it is important that we first get our hermeneutical bearings. Though modern scholarship has consistently categorized Psalm 2 as a "royal psalm," with putative origins in some coronation ritual now lost to history, this identification is potentially misleading both on a general level and for our specific purposes. In the first place, we must remind ourselves that such classifications depend on certain form-critical judgments that in turn are the offspring of an increasingly uneasy marriage between *Gattung* (form) and *Sitz im Leben* (sociohistorical context).[11] Whatever heuristic value "royal psalm" or "messianic psalm" may have for us, such constructs would have been largely foreign to the ancient readers. In the second place, even if it *were* granted that the psalm originated in a coronation setting, to assume that this reconstructed origin was material to its significance in its first-century (CE) reception or to the writer of Hebrews would simply be to succumb to a genetic fallacy. All to say, in seeking to grasp the writer's pre-understanding of Psalm 2, we are best served not by defaulting to inevitably distortive categories borne out of our historical-critical reconstruction of origins, but by examining the way in which the psalm was understood by the (near) contemporaries of the *auctor Hebraeos*.

On this approach, the evidence suggests that while Second-Temple Jewish readers may have recognized Psalm 2 as a guarantee for a future restoration of the Davidic

---

[9] For studies of Psalm 110 in early Christianity, see Martin Hengel, *Studies in Early Christology* (Edinburgh: T&T Clark, 1995), pp. 119–226; Gerhard Dautzenberg, "Psalm 110 im Neuen Testament," in *Liturgie und Dichtung. Ein Interdisziplinäres Kompendium 1* (ed. Hansjakob Becker and Riener Kaczynski; Pietas Liturgica 1-2; Sankt Ottilien: EOS, 1983), 1: pp. 141–71; William R. G. Loader, "Christ at the Right Hand: Ps. 110:1 in the New Testament," *NTS* 24 (1978), pp. 199–217.

[10] Along these lines, Gert J. Steyn (in "Psalm 2 in Hebrews," *Neotestamentica* 37 [2003], pp. 262–82 [264]) calls this a "strange application" of Psalm 2.

[11] The long-standing paradigm associated with such heavies as von Rad and Alt seems to be showing signs of erosion; see, for example, Bob Becking, "Nehemiah 9 and the Problematic Concept of Context (*Sitz im Leben*)," in *The Changing Face of Form Criticism for the Twenty-First Century* (ed. Marvin A. Sweeney and Ehud Ben Zvi, Grand Rapids, MI: Eerdmans, 2003), pp. 253–65; J. J. M. Roberts, *The Bible and the Ancient Near East: Collected Essays* (Winona Lake, IN: Eisenbrauns: 2002), *passim*.

royal line, the same readers would have also regarded this significance as ancillary to the psalm's cultic implications. More exactly, in the Judaism of the day, Psalm 2 was most closely associated not so much with ontological claims of royal status but with the anointed figure's envisioned role in restoring the purity of the temple space. To demonstrate this point, I provide two examples, beginning with the Qumran text 4Q174:

> [I will appoint a place for my people Israel and will plant them in order that they may dwell there and no more be troubled by their] enemies. No son of iniquity [will afflict them again] as before, from the day that [I set judges] over my people Israel [2 Sam. 7:10]. This is the house which [in the] last days according as it is written in the book 3 [the sanctuary, O Lord,] which your hands have established, Yahweh shall reign for ever and ever [Exod. 15:17-18]. This is the house in which [ ] shall not enter there 4 [f]orever, nor the Ammonite, the Moabite, nor the bastard, nor the foreigner, nor the stranger forever because there shall be the ones who bear the holy name 5 [f]orever. Continually it will appear above it. And strangers will no longer destroy it as they previously destroyed 6 the sanctuary of Israel because of its sins. He commanded that a sanctuary of men, be built for himself in order to offer up to him like the smoke of incense.... 17 These are the sons of Zadok and the m[e]n of his cou[ns]el [ ] after them to the council of the community. 18 [Why] do the nations [rag]e and the people im[agine] a vain thing? [Kings of the earth] ris[e up] and [and p]rinces conspire together against Yahweh and against [his anointed] (Ps. 2:1-2). 19 [In]terpretation of the saying [concerns na]tions and th[ey] the chosen of Israel in the last days.[12]

Rounding off a series of midrashim with a focus on Psalm 2, the writer demonstrates a palpable interest in sacred space. On the interpretation offered here, the Qumran community itself is the sacred "house" prophesied by Moses (Exod. 15:17-18), "the sanctuary of Israel." Those who constitute the living temple are "the sons of Zadok," the "men of his counsel," and the "council of the community" (4Q174 17); meanwhile, those who opposed this community are the pagan nations of Psalm 2. Thus, the "Anointed One" of Psalm 2 represents the corporate community of Qumran. Its main task is not to rule but to stake out sacred space over and against the illegitimate temple space occupied by the Jerusalem scribal elite.

As far as we can tell, the *Psalms of Solomon* utilizes Psalm 2 in a similar manner. Composed sometime after Pompey's profaning incursion into the temple, the *Psalms* are a lament over the sorry spiritual state of Jerusalem. Yet the text culminates on a note of eschatological hope, a hope centered around the messiah:

> See, Lord, and raise up for them their king, the son for David, to rule over your servant Israel in the time known to you, O God.
> Undergird him with the strength to destroy the unrighteous rulers, to purge Jerusalem from gentiles who trample her to destruction; in wisdom and in

---

[12] 4Q174 1-6, 17-18.

righteousness to drive out the sinners from the inheritance; to smash the arrogance of sinners like a potter's jar;

To shatter all their substance with an iron rod; to destroy the unlawful nations with the word of his mouth;

At his warning the nations will flee from his presence; and he will condemn sinners by the thoughts of their hearts.[13]

In filling out the eschatological scenario, a carefully chosen constellation of words ("nations," "king," "son," "iron rod," "potter's jar") invokes the messianic figure of Psalm 2.[14] From the psalmist's point of view, the coming messiah would do battle with not so much the nations as an ethnic category but all those outside the lines of the covenant, including the false priests who had insinuated themselves in the temple hierarchy. Such a messiah would "purge Jerusalem (and make it) holy as it was from the beginning" (*Pss. Sol.* 17.30). Moreover, the same figure would "gather together a holy people" (*Pss. Sol.* 17.26). What is remarkable in all this is that even while the Romans are fully entrenched in Jerusalem, the *Psalms'* author defines Israel's basic problem not in political but in cultic terms. In other words, the fundamental problem was not *essentially* geo-political but cultic in nature.[15] For all intents and purposes, then, the Qumran community and the community behind the *Psalms of Solomon* looked to the anointed son of Psalm 2 not so much in his capacity as ruler but in his capacity as cleansing priest.

When we allow the *auctor Hebraeos's* citation of Psalm 2 to bear the same payload that we find in *Q174* and the *Psalms of Solomon*, it actually leads to a more satisfying reading of both Hebrews 1 and Heb. 5:5-10. To begin with the latter text, we now realize that when the writer justifies Jesus's priesthood on the grounds of Psalm 110 *and* Psalm 2, his argument is not taking an idiosyncratic turn but is in keeping with contemporary reception of both psalms as textual signposts for an eschatological priestly figure. Moreover, whereas hints of Jesus's priesthood in the exordium (Heb. 1:1-4) have often been understood as a harbinger of the writer's atonement theology, the religio-political implications of Psalm 2, along with Psalm 110 (with their shared vision of a royal-priestly figure judging God's enemies), force us to take more seriously the introduction's implicit political claim. More exactly, for an audience familiar with persecution, the writer's reliance on Psalms 2 and 110 would have held out the eschatological hope of God dealing with such evil precisely through Jesus's exercise of priestly duties.

---

[13] *Pss. Sol.* 17.21-25. Translation is from *OTP*.

[14] The eschatological and messianic interpretation of Psalm 2 is also characteristic of rabbinic interpretation; see Michael A. Signer, "King/messiah: Rashi's Exegesis of Psalm 2," *Proof* 3 (1983), pp. 273-78.

[15] Brad Embry (in "The *Psalms of Solomon* and the New Testament: Intertextuality and the Need for a Re-Evaluation," *JSP* 13 [2002], pp. 99-136 [110]) makes the same point: "While it is undeniable that the Messiah of *Pss. Sol.* 17 is a political figure, the more central issue for the author is purity, not polity"; similarly, Rikki E. Watts, "The Lord's House and David's Lord: The Psalms and Mark's Perspective on Jesus and the Temple," *BibInt* 15 (2007), pp. 307-22 (311).

Psalms 2 and 110 in the Gospel of Mark

If Psalms 2 and 110 occupy a prominent place in the thinking of the writer of Hebrews, the same is no less true for the gospel-writer Mark. This becomes clear as early as the baptism scene (Mk 1:9-11), where Jesus is singled out with wording clearly drawn from Ps. 2:7: "You are my Son, the Beloved; with you I am well pleased" (v. 11).[16] Though commentators are assuredly correct in noting the messianic denotations of the "son" of Ps. 2:7 and therefore the messianic import of the baptism as a whole, I would maintain that the nature of that messiahship cannot be properly understood apart from another subtextual layer: the heavenly voice's invocation of Genesis 22. Here our attention is drawn to Mk 1:11's key terms. As both the "son" (υἱός) and "the beloved" (ὁ ἀγαπητός), the baptized Jesus resembles the figure of Isaac, whose father was commanded as follows: "Take your son (λαβὲ τὸν υἱόν), your only (τὸν ἀγαπητόν) son Isaac, whom you love (ὃν ἠγάπησας" (Gen. 22:2). The same language in fact recurs in Gen. 22:2, 12, and 16, giving Mark ample opportunity to correlate Jesus and Isaac.[17] Along the same lines, it is not insignificant that the voice hails "from heaven" (ἐκ τῶν οὐρανῶν) (Mk 1:11), just as according to Gen. 22:11, 15 a voice also issues from heaven.[18] While Mark's intimations of the Aqedah (Genesis 22) have been widely overlooked in the past, more recent scholarship has shown an increasing willingness to discern this event in the baptism's substructure.[19]

The combination of Psalm 2 and Genesis 22, as tributaries to the heavenly voice's meaning, implies that when Jesus is baptized, he is being anointed not just as the son of David but also the new Isaac, that is, as one who would one day sacrifice his life willingly for God's purposes. I have already noted two lines of evidence that Second-Temple Judaism interpreted the Anointed One of Psalm 2 as a figure who would restore Jerusalem's defiled sacred space. Now by fusing Isaac with Psalm 2's "Anointed One" at Mk 1:11, the evangelist shows that Jesus is not just the restorer of sacred space (in the manner of David), but also the sacrificial basis (in the mode of Isaac) on which said sacred space is made possible. At this baptism, then, Jesus is marked off both as the sacrificing royal-priest and as the sacrifice.

The sacerdotal significance of Jesus's baptism is consistent with the symbolic thrust of John's baptism *qua* water ritual. To be sure, in light of Mk 1:1-3 (with its reference to

---

[16] Mark 1:11's reliance on Ps 2:7 is granted by the vast majority of commentators. See, for example, Adela Yarbro Collins, *Mark: A Commentary* (Hermeneia; Minneapolis: Fortress, 2007), p. 150; R. T. France, *The Gospel of Mark* (NIGTC; Grand Rapids, MI: Eerdmans; Carlisle, PA: Paternoster Press, 2002), p. 80.

[17] Leroy A. Huizenga, *The New Isaac: Tradition and Intertextuality in the Gospel of Matthew* (NovTSup 131; Leiden/Boston: Brill, 2009), p. 153.

[18] Huizenga, *New Isaac*, p. 154.

[19] In addition to Huizenga (*New Isaac*), see C. H. Turner, "Ο ΥΙΟΣ ΜΟΥ ΑΓΑΠΗΤΟΣ," *JTS* 27 (1926), pp. 113–29; Wisse Dekker, "De 'Geliefde Zoon' in de Synoptische Evangelien," *NedTTs* 16 (1961), pp. 94–106; Jon D. Levenson, *The Death and Resurrection of the Beloved Son: The Transformation of Child Sacrifice in Judaism and Christianity* (New Haven, CT: Yale University Press, 1993), pp. 30–31; M. E. Boring, *Mark: A Commentary* (NTL; Louisville: Westminster John Knox, 2006), p. 45; and Matthew S. Rindge, "Reconfiguring the Akedah and Recasting God: Lament and Divine Abandonment in Mark," *JBL* 131 (2011), pp. 755–74.

the Isaianic way) John's baptism must be understood in part as signifying the promised national cleansing (Isa. 1:16; 4:4; Mic. 7:19; Zech. 13:1), especially associated with the return from exile (Ezek. 36:25-33). But at the same time, water was designated as the medium of priestly ordination (Lev. 8:6; Numbers 19), and thus indicates John's priestly function (cf. Lk. 1:5-25), that is, as one who administers forgiveness outside the traditional temple cultus. In baptizing the emerging return-from-exile movement, John was essentially establishing a new priesthood for the newly emerging eschatological temple. The unique basis of that coalescing priesthood, in Mark's mind, was Jesus himself.

Although we cannot be certain on text-critical grounds whether Mk 1:1 originally included the phrase "Son of God," the baptism's identification of Jesus as the divine son certainly forges a gospel-length *inclusio* with Mk 15:38 where the centurion identifies Jesus with the same title. From this it can be inferred that Mark's use of the term, here and elsewhere in the gospel, is highly intentional. This certainly holds true for Mark's transfiguration account (9:1-18), which ties back to the baptism scene through the heavenly voice's identification of Jesus as "son": Mk 9:7 reads "This is my son, the Beloved" (Οὗτός ἐστιν ὁ υἱός μου ὁ ἀγαπητός); Mk 1:11 has "You are my son, the Beloved" (Σὺ εἶ ὁ υἱός μου ὁ ἀγαπητός). Given this connection, we might expect the transfiguration to circle back to the baptism's implicit sacerdotal claims. In this vein, we note a fascinating essay by Crispin Fletcher-Louis, who maintains that when the transfiguration scene is understood alongside Peter's confession (Mk 8:27-38), it serves to sharpen Peter's affirmation into an acknowledgment of Jesus's high priesthood.[20] This follows in part, according to Fletcher-Louis, from Jesus's transformation. For not only is Jesus's transfiguration characteristic of what many ancient Jews would have expected of the high priest's appearance at the supreme cultic moment, but other details in the scene—Peter's bumbling bid to construct booths, Jesus's illuminated clothes, among other factors—also come together to repurpose the mount of transfiguration as a kind of temple mount, with Jesus the would-be high priest taking his rightful place.[21] Nor does this reading of Mark's transfiguration compete with standard readings that tease out a Mosaic typology. After all, Moses himself is designated a priest (Ps. 99:6) and arguably carried out a priestly role on Sinai.

Jesus's filial status resurfaces in Mark's account of Gethsemane (Mk 14:32-42). In this scene, the gospel-writer is concerned to interpret Jesus's imminent death once again with reference to the Aqedah of Genesis 22. Several considerations point in this direction. First, if Jesus incurs his test (πειρασμός) (14:38) on Passover, the same is

---

[20] Crispin Fletcher-Louis, "The Revelation of the Sacral Son of Man: The Genre, History of Religions Context and the Meaning of the Transfiguration," in *Auferstehung—Resurrection. The Fourth Durham-Tübingen Research Symposium. Resurrection, Transfiguration and Exaltation in Old Testament, Ancient Judaism and Early Christianity (Tübingen, September 1999)* (ed. F. Avemarie and H. Lichtenberger, WUNT 135; Tübingen: Mohr Siebeck: 2001), pp. 247–98.

[21] For a discussion of the Feast of Tabernacles as background to Peter's request (Mk 9:5) and the six-day period (9:2) (granted by a number of commentators), see Fletcher-Louis, "Sacral Son of Man," pp. 293–96. For examples of the priest's radiating garments in the primary literature, see *2 En.* 22.8-10; *3 En.* 12; *Let. Aris.* 97; Josephus, *Ant.* 3.216-17.

true of Abraham who according to tradition was also tested on Passover.²² Second, although Jesus has already been put to the test at several points in the gospel (Mk 8:11; 10:2; 12:15), Gethsemane proves to be Jesus's climactic test. Likewise, whatever various challenges faced Abraham during the course of his life, ancient Jewish interpretation regarded these as preparation for the supreme test of the Aqedah.²³ Third, whereas Jesus cries out Abba (α ὁ πτέρ) in Mk 14:36, his antitype, on facing the prospect of being sacrificed, calls out, "Father!" (MT: *'ābî*; LXX: πάτερ; Targums: (#18'*abbā*') (Gen. 22:8). Given these textual moorings in the Aqedah, the complementarity between Jesus's baptism and Gethsemane in the Gospel of Mark can hardly be overemphasized. If Mark's Jesus initiates his ministry as the sacrificial Isaac who would provide the basis for a new system of atonement (much as Isaac provided the notional basis for the Second Temple), then Gethsemane is the point at which that same vocation is first actualized through the great πειρασμός.

Finally, in Mark 15, just as Jesus expires on the cross, a strange turn of events unfolds: "And the curtain of the temple was torn in two, from top to bottom. Now when the centurion, who stood facing him, saw that in this way he breathed his last, he said, 'Truly this man was God's Son!'" (15:38-39). On the face of it, the rending of the temple veil in 15:38, anticipated by the rending of the heavens at Jesus's baptism (Mk 1:10), represents the heavenly access now provided through Jesus's death. Providing the first commentary on Jesus's death, a Roman centurion declares Jesus "Son of God" (Mk 15:39), just as the heavenly voice had done in Mk 1:11. The point is all too clear: the tearing of the temple veil through Jesus's death demonstrates that he (and not Caiaphas) is the true "Son of the Blessed One" (Mk 14:61). At the last, Jesus as the "son" of Psalm 2 proves that he is the true high priest.

Whereas Psalm 2 is clearly cited once in Mark and that in his programmatic baptism scene, Psalm 110 shows up twice—and that in almost equally significant narrative spaces. First and fundamentally, as part of a line of disputes with the scribal leaders, Jesus poses a question about David's son, drawing directly from Psalm 110:

35 While Jesus was teaching in the temple, he said, "How can the scribes say that the Messiah is the son of David? 36 David himself, by the Holy Spirit, declared,

'The Lord said to my Lord,

Sit at my right hand,

until I put your enemies under your feet.'

37 David himself calls him Lord; so how can he be his son?" And the large crowd was listening to him with delight.²⁴

---

[22] According to Gen. 22:1, "God tested (LXX: ἐπείραζεν) Abraham . . . ." On the Passover setting of this test, see *Jub*. 17.15–18.19, as well as references in Roger Le Déaut, *La nuit pascale: Essai sur la signification de la Pâque juive à partir du Targum d'Exode XII 42* (Rome: Institut biblique pontifical: 1963), p. 179.

[23] *Jub*. 17.16; 18.19. See also Joseph A. Grassi, "Abba, Father (Mark 14:36): Another Approach," *JAAR* 50 (1982), pp. 449–58; Mary Andrews, M., "*Peirasmos*: A Study in Form-Criticism," *AThR* 24 (1942), pp. 229–44 (232–36).

[24] Mark 12:35-37.

Though interpreters differ as to whether Jesus is affirming his messianic sonship or denying it, the former option seems far stronger in light of Jesus's confession before Caiaphas, which also draws on Psalm 110.[25] Jesus's point, in short, is to underscore the superiority of the Son of David to David himself, while also explaining himself with reference to the order of the high priest Melchizedek mentioned in Psalm 110. That is to say, if Psalm 110 defines both David and Solomon as priests in the order of Melchizedek, the thrust of Jesus's scriptural lesson may be to suggest that he himself does not belong to the order of Melchizedek but is in fact Melchizedek *redivivus*. When we appreciate this dialogue as one of a long series of anti-priestly disputes (Mk 11:17–12:40), laying the groundwork for Jesus's announcement of the destruction of the temple (Mark 13), the *Davidssohnfrage* makes excellent sense as a veiled assertion of Jesus's identity as the eschatological high priest.

The polemical point is only confirmed at Jesus's trial (Mk 14:53-65). Here after the various false witnesses have failed to produce a convincing case against Jesus, Caiaphas steps forward to ask Jesus if he is "the Messiah, the Son of the Blessed One" (14:61). Jesus replies in terms which can be traced right back to Daniel 7 and Psalm 110: "Jesus said, 'I am'; and 'you will see the Son of Man seated at the right hand of the Power,' and 'coming with the clouds of heaven.'"[26] Drawing on a pair of subtexts, Jesus's response to Caiaphas amounts to a double claim: on the one hand, he is in fact the Son of Man spoken of in Daniel 7; on the other hand, he is the rightful holder of the royal-priestly throne in the terms of Psalm 110. Jesus's audacious double claim explains Caiaphas's counter pronouncement of blasphemy, for in arrogating to himself the priesthood, Jesus had directly challenged Caiaphas's very right to rule—a challenge which was itself legally vulnerable to charges of blasphemy.[27] Jesus's climactic confession in Mk 14:62 resolves the puzzle of Mk 12:35-37: Jesus is at once the Son of David and the exalted Lord of Daniel 7 and Psalm 110. In the evangelist's hands, then, Psalm 2 and 110 are summoned in order to register complementary points: Jesus rules as the eschatological Davidic/Melchizedekian high priest.

Historical Jesus traditions and the emergence of Psalms 2 and 110 in early Christianity

On this reading of Hebrews and Mark, we discover solid evidence that when both writers asserted Jesus's priesthood, they fell back on a shared cache of proof-texts, including not least Psalms 2 and 110. All this suggests that the pairing of these two psalms for this particular argument was not original to the writer of Hebrews.[28] Rather,

---

[25] For a review of this discussion, see Max Botner, "What Has Mark's Christ to Do with David's Son?: A History of Interpretation," *CBR* 16 (2017), pp. 50–70.

[26] Mark 14:62.

[27] Exod. 22:27, cf. Lev. 24:10-23; Num. 15:30-31. For references in Philo and Josephus, see references in A. Y. Collins, "The Charge of Blasphemy in Mark 14:64," *JSNT* 26 (2004), pp. 379–401 (389–94).

[28] *Pace* Steyn, "Psalm 2," pp. 264–65. Without assuming that Mark was written before Hebrews or vice versa, I do presuppose the author of the second Gospel represented a different swathe of early Christianity. That both authors availed themselves to the psalms in a similar way points to a tradition antecedent to both.

the *auctor Hebraeos* like Mark, was appealing to preexisting interpretative traditions. Neither Jesus's priesthood nor its justification *per* Psalms 2 and 110 was a theological innovation by the time Hebrews was composed. The roots for this notion and its scriptural basis lie much deeper in early Christianity.

How much deeper? While the point is perhaps impossible to prove, I would suggest that the origins for this trajectory begin with Jesus's own ministry. As for the connection between Psalm 2 and the historical Jesus's baptism, we can begin with the most basic, agreed-upon fact: Jesus's baptism by John. On the so-called criterion of embarrassment, which prefers to ascribe authentic standing to sayings and actions that potentially reflect poorly on Jesus, Jesus's baptism *under* John stands as a regular parade example. The consistency of the triple tradition, not to mention the consistency of this record with the remarks of John the Baptizer in the fourth gospel, fulfills the criterion of multiple attestation and further cinches the baptism's place in history.

The connection between the historical baptism event and the utterance of Psalm 2 has, not surprisingly, been more disputed. From a historical-critical point of view, the reasons for this judgment may appear weighty. In the first place, some find the stylized parallel between the rending of heaven in Mk 1:10 and the rending of the veil in Mk 15:38 as grounds for doubting Mark's description of the event, including the audible articulation of Psalm 2. Second, some scholars regard the very presence of scriptural language at Mk 1:11 as *prima facie* evidence that this detail was inserted as a post-Easter reflection.[29] Third, and along the same lines, the fact that the voice identifies Jesus as "son" is alleged to be evidence that Mark's notice of the voice was a clumsy attempt to retroject Jesus's status as risen son back into the baptism scene. For reasons like these, many are reluctant to associate Psalm 2 with the historical baptism scene.

Despite the seeming merits of these points, each is subject to some significant weaknesses. First, Mark's positioning of the baptismal voice within a broader and somewhat complex literary parallelism is no grounds for doubting its historicity. After all, if we take this approach consistently, we would be forced to hack away large swathes of critically assured dominical material within the gospel tradition, leaving us with next to nothing related to the historical Jesus. The practical entailments of such a move would amount to a reductio ad absurdum. Second, if the mere use of scriptural language at the baptism scene causes historical offense, then historical Jesus scholars also need to be prepared to be offended at countless other passages where scriptures are either explicitly cited or alluded to. While this approach may have passed muster several generations ago, the rise of the so-called Third Quest renders unviable any principled commitment to eradicate scripture from the mouth of the historical Jesus. Third, we should also disabuse ourselves of the assumption that the heavenly voice's declaration of Jesus's sonship (in the setting of Jesus) must have meant more or less the same thing as Jesus's sonship did to the post-Easter church. In antiquity, the phrase "son of God" meant a lot of different things to a lot of different people. It need not have conveyed in the first instance the full-blown Christology which we have come to associate with certain NT writers and the later church.

---

[29] So J. P. Meier, *A Marginal Jew: Rethinking the Historical Jesus: Vol. 2: Mentor, Message, and Miracles* (ABRL; New York: Doubleday, 1994), pp. 106–08.

Finally, while disagreements over what is and what is not possible (what was and what was not possible in the time of Jesus) will continue to dog discussions like these, it is not for our purposes entirely necessary to reconstruct a "what you would have seen and heard if you had been there" account. The synoptic writers are unanimous that the baptism was an event witnessed by John and Jesus, and this becomes part of the basis of Jesus's public appeal to John's supporting testimony (Mk 11:27-33). For these reasons, we are best off concluding (1) that an extraordinary event occurred on that day by the Jordan River, at least in the perceptions of John and Jesus; (2) that that event, imposing as it was, demanded to be interpreted within the framework of scriptural categories; and (3) that both men interpreted that event with reference to Psalm 2, which in turn lay the basis not only for John's speculation regarding Jesus's messiahship, but also the social memory of a correlation between the baptism and Psalm 2.

In this light, we are inclined to regard Heb. 5:5 ("So also Christ did not glorify himself in becoming a high priest, but was appointed by the one who said to him, 'You are my Son'") as evidence that the *auctor Hebraeos* was familiar with the story of Jesus's baptism, complete with its reference to Ps. 2:7—not necessarily in its synoptic form but as the reported event circulated in pre-Markan oral tradition. Indeed, given the fact that the writer hopes to move his hearers beyond basic "instruction about washings" (Heb. 6:2), it would be short of incredible if the same writer claimed expert knowledge of such washings without also being familiar with the foundational event for Christian baptismal practices.[30] Moreover, the writer's almost certain knowledge of Jesus's testing as a son at Gethsemane (Heb. 5:7-8) would have been virtually unintelligible apart from some prior knowledge that Jesus had already been anointed as a son precisely in the terms of Psalm 2. All said, it is more likely than not that when the writer of Hebrews appropriates Psalm 2 as a proof of Jesus's priesthood, he is tapping into a long-standing oral tradition rooted in the earliest Jesus movement.

The case for Psalm 110, as it occurs in Mk 12:35-37, reaching back to Jesus is stronger still.[31] All three synoptic gospels record that following his celebrated entry into Jerusalem, Jesus—whether as part of a friendly teaching session (Mark) or when surrounded by retractors (Matthew/Luke)—teaches on Psalm 110 (Mk 12:35-37 par.) in order to support the messianic claim implied by the entry itself. On the heels of his triumphal entry, Jesus indirectly styles himself as a priest on the pattern of

---

[30] Modern Hebrews scholarship has tended to see the washing of Heb. 6:2 as including Christian baptism; see Anthony R. Cross, "The Meaning of 'Baptisms' in Hebrews 6.2," in *Dimensions of Baptism: Biblical and Theological Studies* (ed. Stanley E. Porter and Anthony R. Cross; London/New York: Sheffield Academic, 2002), pp. 163–86. On the significance of Jesus's baptism for Christian baptism, see Nicholas Perrin, "Sacraments and Sacramentality in the New Testament," in *The Oxford Handbook of Sacramental Theology* (ed. Hans Boersma and Matthew Levering; Oxford: Oxford University Press, 2015), pp. 52–67 (60–61).

[31] As N. T. Wright (in *Christian Origins and the Question of God: Vol. 2: Jesus and the Victory of God* [London: SPCK; Minneapolis: Fortress, 1996], p. 644) sees it, the passage retains "a total coherence whose historical force is compelling." More than a few scholars agree: C. H. Dodd, *According to the Scriptures: The Sub-Structure of New Testament Theology* (London: Nisbet, 1952), pp. 110, 126; G. R. Beasley-Murray, *Jesus and the Kingdom of God* (Grand Rapids, MI: Eerdmans, 1986), p. 299; James D. G. Dunn, *Jesus Remembered: Vol. 1: Christianity in the Making* (Grand Rapids, MI: Eerdmans, 2003), pp. 634–35; Craig S. Keener, *The Historical Jesus of the Gospels* (Grand Rapids, MI: Eerdmans, 2009), p. 270.

Melchizedek in direct competition with local priesthood. Moreover, given the psalm's vision of enthronement and subjugation, we may also surmise that Jesus expected the plotline of Psalm 110 to be played out through his enemies' demise and own imminent exaltation. That he cited the same psalm with the same force at his trial is likewise probable.[32]

If the story of Jesus's baptism *à la* Psalm 2 would have reimpressed itself on the first-century church's consciousness as it ritually rehearsed the founding narrative behind Christian baptism, Psalm 110 would have likely had an analogous role in the early church's administration of the Eucharist. In providing the full range of scriptural narratives and recollections underwriting the Eucharist, at any rate, the early church would have likely recalled the memory of Jesus self-identifying with the Melchizedekian high priest. This is "likely" the case, because when Jesus appeals to Psalm 110 in one of his last recorded public statements prior to the Last Supper (Mk 14:22-25), he implies his own kinship with the one who served a covenantal meal of bread and wine (Gen. 14:18). When the early church partook in the Eucharist, it almost certainly did so on the understanding that they were reenacting the meal commanded by the eschatological Melchizedek, precisely as the full account of the *Davidssohnfrage* would suggest. Memories of Jesus the soi-disant high priest in connection with these two psalms, along with their accompanying narratives, would have likely been passed down regularly and systematically.

Conclusion

Under the pervasive influence of the History of Religions School, contemporary investigation of early Christology has tended to foreclose on the possibility that at least some of the fundamental tenets of early Christological reflection were of pre-Easter origins—this is a fortiori the case when it comes to the study of Hebrews. The unfortunate consequence of this trend, so far as Hebrews scholarship is concerned, has been a certain lack of historical curiosity in getting behind (historically speaking) the Christology of Hebrews. I hope this chapter serves to challenge such a trend. As prominently as Jesus's baptism and the *Davidssohnfrage* may have been in the social memory of the early church, these traditions and their supporting texts, Psalms 2 and 110, respectively, would have likely acquired an enhanced status. Of such texts and traditions the writer of Hebrews could hardly have been unaware.

In any case, given evidence that both Psalm 2 and Psalm 110 had become self-defining texts for the historical Jesus in the course of his lifetime, and given ample evidence, too, that both these psalms played an important role in post-Easter reflection on Jesus's priesthood (as attested at least in Hebrews and Mark), it follows that Hebrews' sacerdotal Christology belonged to a well-established and broad-ranging trajectory. In

---

[32] See the incisive comments of J. D. G. Dunn ("'Are You the Messiah?': Is the Crux of Mark 14:61-62 Resolvable?," in *Christology, Controversy, and Community: New Testament Essays in Honour of David R. Catchpole* [ed. David Catchpole, David Horrell, Christopher M. Tuckett; Leiden: Brill: 2000], pp. 1–22 [14]).

a separate writing, I have argued that the historical Jesus nurtured certain objectives that were fundamentally sacerdotal in character.[33] If this thesis can be sustained, then it would only underscore the judgment that the *auctor Hebraeos*'s interest in these twinned psalms is neither exegetically innovative nor *mal à propos* within the first-century setting. In explicating Jesus's eternal priesthood in the terms of Psalms 2 and 110, the writer of Hebrews is treading on well-traveled exegetical ground.

---

[33] See Nicholas Perrin, *Jesus the Priest* (London: SPCK; Grand Rapids, MI: Baker Academic, 2018).

4

Jesus's Atoning Sacrifice in Hebrews and Atonement of Sin in the Greco-Roman World

Eckhard J. Schnabel

The soteriological teaching of the Letter to the Hebrews is in broad agreement with the other NT texts[1] and in partial agreement with the OT and Jewish tradition—the relationship between the one true God and human beings, whom God created, has been ruptured by man's and woman's rebellion against God and his revealed will; human transgression of God's will constitutes sin; sinners face God's judgment resulting in death, either physical death or eternal death, or both; sin can be atoned as a result of an initiative of God; according to OT and Jewish tradition, God's salvific initiative has taken place in Israel, and it is tied exclusively to the tabernacle and then to the Jerusalem Temple and to the guilt and sin offerings that are sacrificed there; according to early Christian tradition, Jesus's death is God's new salvific initiative which has taken place on the cross outside of Jerusalem, and it is tied exclusively to Jesus and his death which atoned for sin once and for all and to faith in Jesus as the messianic Son of God which is open to both Jews and Gentiles.

As far as Greek religion is concerned, Robin Osborne has recently reminded us, "The Greeks knew that different people worshipped different gods and did so in different ways. They also knew that worship of different gods or use of different names for the gods tended to correlate with different cult organization and practice."[2] Since there was no limit to the variety of gods, there was no limit to the number of gods and no limit to the number of stories that were told about the gods. Roman religion is diverse, especially when "Roman" is taken to refer to the provinces, regions, and cities that comprised the Roman Empire. We will first survey Greek and Roman views on sacrifice and forgiveness of sin, before we relate our findings to relevant statements in Hebrews.

---

[1] I. Howard Marshall, "Soteriology in Hebrews," in *The Epistle to the Hebrews and Christian Theology* (ed. R. J. Bauckham, Daniel Driver, Trevor Hart, and Nathan MacDonald; Grand Rapids, MI: Eerdmans, 2009), pp. 253–77 (253).

[2] Robin Osborne, "Unity vs. Diversity," in *The Oxford Handbook of Ancient Greek Religion* (ed. E. Eidinow and J. Kindt; Oxford: Oxford University Press, 2015), pp. 11–20 (11); the following point ibid.

Sacrifices in Greek and Roman religion

Sacrifice in Greek and Roman belief and practice

In Greek religion, the essence of the sacred act is, according to Walter Burkert, "the slaughter and consumption of a domestic animal for a god."[3] The fact that sacrifice is a festive occasion for the community is seen in the rituals of washing, dressing in clean clothes, and wearing adornments such as a garland. The sacrificial animal had to be perfect and was adorned as well, with ribbons, its horns gilded. Processions escorted the animals to the altar, accompanied by one or more flute-players. The sacrificial basket with the knife for the sacrifice, concealed beneath grains of barley or cakes, was passed around the circle, at the center of which was the altar—the sacred was delimited from the profane. When the fatal blow kills the animal, the women had to cry out in high, shrill tones, as "life screams over death." As the animal was slaughtered, the blood was collected and then splashed over the altar and against the sides of the altar. The entrails of the sacrificial animal were eaten by the innermost circle of the participants; then the actual meat meal began. The variety of local customs, according to Walter Burkert, do not change the fact that the fundamental structure is identical: "Animal sacrifice is ritualized slaughter followed by a meat meal."[4] The sacrifice creates a relationship between the participants and the god: "Poets recount how the god remembers the sacrifice with pleasure or how he rages dangerously if sacrifices fail to be performed."[5] The shedding of human blood in some cults is traced by the Greeks to some barbaric origin. The first of the three details of the initiation ritual into the mysteries of the Kabeiroi in Samothrace that we know requires the priest to ask the initiand what is the worst deed that he has ever committed. This question was intended "not so much to elicit a confession of sins as to establish complicity, thereby securing unbreakable solidarity."[6]

The problem with composite pictures of animal sacrifice, which Burkert largely derives from Homer, is the fact that there is no paradigmatic sacrificial ritual.[7] Jan Bremmer emphasizes that "not every sacrifice ended with the consumption of meat," and he asserts, against Burkert who stressed the role of bloodshed in the evocation of *angst* and guilt, the "virtually total lack of testimonies of actual fear and guilt among the Greeks."[8] Attic vases associate sacrifice with festivity, celebration, and blessing. As

---

[3] Walter Burkert, *Greek Religion* (trans. J. Raffan; 1977 repr., Cambridge, MA: Harvard University Press, 1985), p. 55; the following summary ibid., pp. 56–66.
[4] Ibid., p. 56.
[5] Ibid., p. 57.
[6] Ibid., p. 283; cf. Plutarch, *Apoph. lac.* 217d, 229d, 236d.
[7] Osborne, "Unity vs. Diversity," p. 14. For a critique of Burkert's grand theory of sacrifice, cf. Fritz Graf, "One Generation after Burkert and Girard: Where are the Great Theories?" in *Greek and Roman Animal Sacrifice: Ancient Victims, Modern Observers* (ed. C. A. Faraone and F. S. Naiden; Cambridge: Cambridge University Press, 2012), pp. 32–51 (43–51). See Jonathan Z. Smith, "The Domestication of Sacrifice," in *Violent Origins: Ritual Killing and Cultural Formation* (ed. R. G. Hamerton-Kelly; Stanford: Stanford University Press, 1987), pp. 191–205, who reject the quest for origins by Burkert, Girard, and others; cf. Graf, "One Generation," pp. 43–47.
[8] Jan N. Bremmer, "Greek Normative Animal Sacrifice," in *A Companion to Greek Religion* (ed. D. Ogden; Malden/Oxford: Wiley-Blackwell, 2007), pp. 132–44 (139, 142); the following points ibid., pp. 139–40; quotation p. 140, commenting on Hesiod, *Theog.* 535–61.

regards the function of sacrifice, in early epic the gods liked the smoke of the fat and they shared the dinners of the mortals. Yet the archaic Greeks felt uneasy about the gods eating in the same manner as mortals; Homer says that only Athena "beheld the offering" (*Od.* 3.435; Murray; LCL 104, p. 101). Hesiod locates the origin of sacrifice at the moment when gods and mortals parted their common ways, which indicates that "sacrifice was *the* pre-eminent act of the 'condition humaine,' which definitively established and continued the present world order, in which men die and immortals have to be worshiped." Theophrastus (ca. 371–287 BC), Aristotle's successor, no longer mentions divine food in his discussion of sacrifice. He gives "three reasons one ought to sacrifice to the gods: either on account of honor or on account of gratitude or on account of a want of things. For just as with good men, so also with these (the gods) . . . . We honour the gods either because we seek to deflect evils or to acquire goods for ourselves, or because we have first been treated well or simply to do great honour to their good character" (Frag. 584A).[9] These three reasons can be found in earlier Greek texts, with honoring the god being the most important factor in sacrifice.

Leaving behind the psychological and sociological approaches to animal sacrifice promoted by Walter Burkert and by Marcel Detienne and Jean-Pierre Vernant,[10] Fred Naiden analyzes Greek sacrifice from the earliest periods into Roman times without a particular typology or strict categorization. He treats the complex details of Greek sacrifice in terms of modes of communication: by offering a sacrifice, the worshiper makes an appeal to the god by means of proper procedure and attitude.[11] Naiden asserts, "No matter the factors, the god's disposition was unpredictable. Accepting a sacrifice was a matter of choice. Sometimes the god declined to be gracious. Sometimes he said no."[12] The reasons why the gods did not accept sacrifices varied: aesthetic reasons concerned the animal, the worshipers' handling of the animal, and other features of the sacrificial ceremony; moral reasons concerned unwritten laws, meaning that the sacrifice was repugnant because of the nature of the request or the character of the worshiper; systemic reasons concerned laws or dispensations affecting the gods, meaning that the sacrifice was ungodly, violating some divine dispensation, for example, the allotment of the world to Zeus and his brothers.[13] Naiden emphasizes that ancient Greek sources do not speak of redemptive bloodshed: "To the offering that must be destroyed, or slain, they add offerings that must be put on tables, called *trapezōmata*, and substitutes for sacrifices not limited to votive tablets."[14] The Greek language does not have a word that designates animal sacrifice as opposed to other

---

[9] William W. Fortenbaugh, Pamela Huby, Robert Sharples, and Dimitri Gutas, *Theophrastus of Eresus. Sources for His Life, Writings, Thought and Influence* (2 vols; Leiden: Brill, 1992).
[10] Marcel Detienne and Jean-Pierre Vernant, *The Cuisine of Sacrifice among the Greeks* (trans. P. Wissing; 1979 repr., Chicago: University of Chicago Press, 1989).
[11] Fred S. Naiden, *Smoke Signals for the Gods: Ancient Greek Sacrifice from the Archaic through Roman Periods* (New York: Oxford University Press, 2013), pp. 39–81. Cf. Fred S. Naiden, "Blessèd are the Parasites," in *Greek and Roman Animal Sacrifice: Ancient Victims, Modern Observers* (ed. C. A. Faraone and F. S. Naiden; Cambridge: Cambridge University Press, 2012), pp. 55–83 (82): sacrifice was both a gift to the gods and an act of thanksgiving or atonement.
[12] Naiden, *Smoke Signals*, p. 130.
[13] Ibid., pp. 131–82, especially pp. 131, 147–48.
[14] Naiden, *Smoke Signals*, pp. 276–77; the following point ibid., p. 278.

kinds of sacrifices: the word for θύειν was also used to refer to offerings of food or incense.

Cult practices imply both the perceived transcendence and the immanence of the gods which were believed to be visible in the images of the gods. This is one main reason why the term *religio* designates "the sum total of current cult practice."[15] Since there were many gods, with varying competencies, their immanence in the world varied. Libanius of Antioch asserts in his Oration to Emperor Theodosius:

> And the most crucial point of all—those who appear to have been our chief opponents in this particular have honoured the gods even against their will. And who might these be? Why, those who have not dared rob Rome of its sacrifices. Yet, if all this business of sacrifice is nonsense (μάταιον), then why has not the nonsense been stopped? If it is harmful, then isn't this all the more reason? But if the stability of empire depends on the sacrifices performed there, we must consider that sacrifice is everywhere to our advantage (ἀπανταχοῦ δεῖ νομίζειν λυσιτελεῖν τὸ θύειν); the gods in Rome (ἐν Ῥώμῃ δαίμονας) grant greater blessings (τὰ μείζω), those in the countryside and the other cities, lesser ones (ἐλάττω), but any sensible man would welcome even such as these. (*Or.* 30.33; Norman; LCL 452, pp. 128-31)

The following survey of classical scholars who have studied Roman sacrifice shows the challenges that a description of Roman religion presents. Georg Wissowa thought of sacrifice in Roman cults as an offering of a group or an individual, a spontaneous gift or a sacrifice that the deity demanded.[16] Kurt Latte regards sacrifice as a gift to the gods which was meant to reinforce their power; the sacrifice in Roman religion had the character of a meal which was offered to the gods and in which the mortals participate.[17] Robert Turcan describes the different stages of the killing of the bull in the Mithras cult but does not analyze the meaning of the ritual.[18] He repeatedly refers to "atonement" in his introductory book on the gods of Rome,[19] but he never defines the term. In their survey of Roman sacrificial rituals, Mary Beard, John North, and Simon Price argue that the forms of animal sacrifice were complex and varied and "carried a range of symbolic meanings that extended far beyond merely 'honoring the gods," but they do not elaborate what these meanings may be.[20] For general theories of sacrifice,

---

[15] Clifford Ando, *The Matter of the Gods: Religion and the Roman Empire* (Transformation of the Classical Heritage, 44; Berkeley: University of California Press, 2008), p. 2, with reference to Cicero, *Dom.* 121.

[16] Georg Wissowa, *Religion und Kultus der Römer* (Zweite Auflage; 1902 repr., München: Beck, 1912), p. 409.

[17] Kurt Latte, *Römische Religionsgeschichte* (Handbuch der Altumswissenschaft, 4; 1960 repr., München: Beck, 1992), pp. 375, 391; for a description of Roman sacrifices, with a focus on ritual, see ibid., pp. 379-93.

[18] Robert Turcan, *The Gods of Ancient Rome: Religion in Everyday Life from Archaic to Imperial Times* (Edinburgh: Edinburgh University Press, 2000), pp. 131-34.

[19] Turcan, *Gods*, pp. 10, 36, 45, 56, 63, 70, 87, 91, 101, 159.

[20] Mary Beard, John North, and Simon Price, *Religions of Rome. Vol. 1: A History. Vol. 2: A Sourcebook* (Cambridge: Cambridge University Press, 1998), 2:148-65, quotation 148. The issues of the new journal *Religion in the Roman Empire*, which appears since 2015, do not yet include an essay on sacrifice, sin, forgiveness, or atonement in non-Jewish and non-Christian religious cults in the Roman Empire; although see now Jörg Rüpke, "Gifts, Votives, and Sacred Things: Strategies, not Entities," *Religion in the Roman Empire* 4 (2018), pp. 207-36.

largely focused on Greek material, they refer to Walter Burkert, Marcel Detienne and Jean-Pierre Vernant, and John Price.[21] Jörg Rüpke, in his introduction to the religion of the Romans, treats sacrifices as "religion in action" under the main heading "social rules."[22] He distinguishes the following layers of meaning: sacrifice defines hierarchies (between gods and humans, and between human beings, for example, between the principals who participate in Roman rites and who officiate *capite velato*); sacrifice creates obligations (the sacrificant offers something to the deity so that the deity gives something in return); sacrifice creates systems (particular gods are given particular animals; male animals are sacrificed to male gods).[23] According to Michael Lipka, Roman sacrifices can be divided into three groups: supplicatory sacrifices in which the worshipers petition the deity for their future well-being; expiatory sacrifices which are demanded as punishment for unfulfilled, neglected, obligations toward the god; lustrations which atone for unfavorable omens or portents.[24]

John Scheid has written extensively on Roman religion.[25] He defines "piety" as "the correct relations with parents, friends and fellow-citizens as well as the correct attitude with regard to the gods." Impiety then consists in "denying the gods the honours and rank that were rightfully theirs, or in damaging their property by theft (sacrilege, in the strict sense of the term) or by neglect."[26] Accidental impiety happened, for example, if one accidentally disturbed the correct performance of a ritual, which could be expiated by sacrifices and perhaps by making reparation. As regards sacrifices, one needs to distinguish between sacrifices in public cults, private sacrifices, and sacrifices connected with divination and magic. The rituals, especially in public cults, were complex and time-consuming. Roman sacrifice was first and foremost a banquet: "To sacrifice was to eat with the gods"—the division of the food derived from the sacrificial animal and the vegetable offerings and libations into food for the deities and food for the sacrificers "established and represented the superiority and immortality of the former, and the mortal condition and pious submission of the latter"; the occasion of the sacrifice and the subsequent banquet "was not placed under the sign of the terror inspired and exercised by the gods."[27] The exceptional human sacrifices—sacrifices of Gauls and Greeks in the Forum Boarium—shifted the emphasis in the relationship between the deities and human beings "by granting the immortals absolute power over mortals other than the Romans themselves."[28] Traditional sacrifice "did not commemorate any particular event," it did "not symbolise total abandonment to the

---

[21] For Burkert, Detienne, and Vernant see above. Cf. Simon R. F. Price, *Rituals and Power: The Roman Imperial Cult in Asia Minor* (1984 repr., Oxford: Oxford University Press, 1998), pp. 272–31.

[22] Jörg Rüpke, *The Religion of the Romans* (trans. and ed. R. Gordon; 2001 repr., Cambridge/Malden: Polity, 2007), pp. 137–54.

[23] Rüpke, *Religion*, pp. 145–52.

[24] Michael Lipka, *Roman Gods: A Conceptual Approach* (Religions in the Graeco-Roman World, 167; Leiden: Brill, 2009), pp. 156–57.

[25] John Scheid, *Romulus et ses frères. Le collège des frères arvales, modèle du culte public dans la Rome des empereurs* (Bibliothèque des Écoles françaises d'Athènes et de Rome, 275; Rome: École française, 1990), pp. 441–666; John Scheid, *An Introduction to Roman Religion* (trans. J. Lloyd; 1998 repr., Edinburgh: Edinburgh University Press, 2003), pp. 79–110; John Scheid, *Quand faire c'est croire: les rites sacrifiels des Romains* (Paris: Aubier, 2005).

[26] Scheid, *Roman Religion*, pp. 26–27.

[27] Ibid., p. 94.

[28] Ibid., p. 95.

deity"—it was a banquet which offered to people "the possibility of meeting their divine partners, of defining their respective qualities and status, and of dealing with business that needed to be done," for example, to compensate for "any deliberate or unavoidable infringement of the deity's property or dignity" through an expiatory sacrifice, or to make a request or convey thanks through prayer, or to conclude contracts with vows.[29] The symbolism of the distinction between immortal gods and mortal man expressed in sacrificial ritual continued to be important in the early imperial period.[30]

Both Greek and Roman sacrifices had multiple purposes, but forgiveness of transgressions is not a relevant category. Punishment by the god was not much talked about or counted on, as Ramsay MacMullen asserts: "Expectation of punishment—that is, guilt—attached to no one cult in any significant manner, rather little talked about or counted on, and generally felt in regard only to basic tabus: parricide, for instance, and incest."[31] In Versnel's magisterial study *Coping with the Gods*, in which he describes the ancient Greek experience of the multiplicity of the gods, the relationship between mortals and the gods, between different gods, and between different versions of a god, the terms "sin" or "transgression" are virtually absent.[32] The word occurs, tellingly, in Theognis's famous complaint about the enigmatic ways of Zeus's justice:

> Dear Zeus, I'm surprised at you. You are lord over all, you alone have great power and prestige, you know well the mind and heart of every man, and your rule, king, is the highest of all. How then, son of Cronus [i.e., Zeus], does your mind bear to hold sinners (ἄνδρας ἀλιτροὺς) and the just man (τόν δίκαιον) in the same esteem, whether the mind of men is disposed to prudent discretion or to wanton outrage, when they yield to unjust acts (ἀδίκοις ἔργμασι)? Have no rules been set by divinity for mortals, is there no path along which one can go and please the immortals? Some people rob and steal quite shamelessly, but for all that they have a prosperity free from harm, while others who refrain from wicked deeds nevertheless get poverty, the mother of helplessness, despite their love of justice, poverty which leads men's hearts astray to sinful action, impairing their wits under the force of necessity.... But now the perpetrator (τὸ κακόν) escapes and another then suffers misery. Also, king of the immortals, how is it right that a man who keeps from unjust deeds and does not commit transgressions and perjury (ἀνὴρ ἐκτὸς ἐὼν ἀδίκων, μήτιν' ὑπερβασίην κατέχων μήθ' ὅρκον ἀλιτρόν), but is just, suffers unjustly? What other mortal, looking upon him, would then be in awe of the immortals? (Theognis, 373-82, 743-46; Gerber; LCL 258, pp. 228-29, 280-81)

---

[29] Ibid., pp. 96-97; see ibid., pp. 79-93 for a description of sacrifices and rituals.
[30] John Scheid, "Roman Animal Sacrifice and the System of Being," in *Greek and Roman Animal Sacrifice: Ancient Victims, Modern Observers* (ed. C. A. Faraone and F. S. Naiden; Cambridge: Cambridge University Press, 2003), pp. 84-98.
[31] Ramsay MacMullen, *Paganism in the Roman Empire* (1981 repr., New Haven, CT: Yale University Press, 1983), p. 58.
[32] For "transgression of boundaries" cf. Hendrik S. Versnel, *Coping with the Gods: Wayward Readings in Greek Theology* (Religions in the Graeco-Roman World, 173; Leiden: Brill, 2011), p. 316.

On the other hand, seemingly contradicting Theognis, Hesiod writes,

> But to those who care only for evil outrageousness and cruel deeds (μέμηλε κακὴ καὶ σχέτλια ἔργα), far-seeing Zeus, Cronus' son, marks out justice. Often even a whole city suffers because of an evil man (κακοῦ ἀνδρός) who sins and devises wicked deeds (ὅστις ἀλιτραίνει καὶ ἀτάσθαλα μηχανάαται). Upon them, Cronus' son brings forth woe from the sky, famine together with pestilence, and the people die away; the women do not give birth, and the households are diminished by the plans of Olympian Zeus. And at another time Cronus' son destroys their broad army or their wall, or he takes vengeance upon their ships on the sea. (*Op.* 238–47; Evelyn-White; LCL 57, pp. 20–21)

Eric Dodds tried to explain the seeming inconsistency with change in Greek beliefs, arguing for a gradual evolution from an arbitrary (a-moral) toward a more ethical attitude in the conduct of the gods,[33] while Hugh Lloyd-Jones sought to save the ethics of the Greek gods by emphasizing divine justice.[34] Henk Versnel explains the two different stances, which he calls "luxuriant multiplicity," as "a corollary of an endemic gnomic type of wisdom sayings characterized by an often asyndetic paratactic style" which "belongs to the most characteristic traits of Greek theological expression."[35] Versnel concludes that the Greeks were "undogmatic in the elasticity of their representations, undaunted in accommodating the incompatible, desperate and hopeful, *polytropic*," a stance which should not be dissolved by our "late-modern quest for unity" but accepted as pluralistic and opportunistic eclecticism.

Atonement and propitiation

In the Roman world, expiatory rites were used to restore divine favor.[36] A worshiper rarely knew for which deity the expiatory rite was performed. Cato suggested that before pruning trees a pig should be sacrificed to the deity thought to be present at the location, with the phrase *si deus si dea es* ("whether you be god or goddess"; Cato, *Agr.* 139); in this case the expiatory rite was performed before any fault was committed (*piaculum*, or "piacular sacrifice," described in the *commentarii* of the Arvales Fratres). In the official cult, expiatory rites at the beginning of the new year expiated the prodigies of the previous year, restoring the violated boundaries. Expiatory rites consisted of sacrifices and processions.

Propitiation, placating a god's wrath, could take many forms. As regards forgiveness, David Konstan points to Aristotle, who argues that συγγνώμη, or pardon, is owed to people who acted involuntarily—when someone acts under external compulsion, for

---

[33] Eric R. Dodds, *The Greeks and the Irrational* (Sather Classical Lectures; Berkeley: University of California Press, 1951).
[34] Hugh Lloyd-Jones, *The Justice of Zeus* (Sather Classical Lectures; Berkeley: University of California Press, 1971).
[35] Versnel, *Gods*, p. 7; see the discussion ibid., pp. 151–237, the following ibid., pp. 234, 235.
[36] Veit Rosenberger, "Expiatory Rites," in *Brill's New Pauly: Encyclopedia of the Ancient World* (ed. Hubert Cancik, Helmuth Schneider, and Manfred Landfester; 22 vols; Leiden: Brill, 2002–2012), 5:275; for the following see ibid., pp. 275–76.

example, surrendering to desires that are natural and common to all, and presumably irresistible, resulting from conditions that he does not have the strength to resist, or when someone acts out of excusable ignorance of facts and circumstances. Since these cases belong to the category of involuntary acts they "do not involve guilt or exoneration."[37] In pleading for συγγνώμη, the objective was not to extenuate responsibility for a crime but to seek exoneration for an involuntary, or unavoidable, act for which responsibility is denied. None of the other philosophical schools showed much interest in forgiveness, including Plato who "never sees it as a virtue or commendable quality."[38] Since a good person is invulnerable to harm, he has nothing to forgive, and because he will not hurt others, he will not be in need of forgiveness. Since the Stoics regarded anger, like the other passions, as unworthy of a wise man, the latter will only have disdain for a fool, understood as a person who does not behave in a virtuous manner; he will not forgive the fool who offended him because forgiveness would ignore the claims of justice and effectually condone the crime.[39] Seneca agrees that a wise man might spare an offender and might even try to improve him, which means that "he will do the same that would do if he pardoned, and yet he will not pardon, since he who pardons admits that he has omitted to do something which he ought to have done"—since the wise man acts according to what must be done, he will not waive the penalty for an intentional wrong (Seneca, *Clem.* 2.7.1-2; Basore; LCL 214, pp. 444-45). In other words, the Stoics believe that "forgiveness is incompatible with justice."[40] In Roman society, the only kind of "forgiveness" that the extant texts discuss, focused on the term *clementia*, "is one that reinforces absolute and arbitrary authority."[41] Zsuzsanna Várhelyi argues that by the middle of the first century AD, the main gods were mostly seen as passionless and benevolent, so that "seeking divine forgiveness came to appear almost countercultural"—something Nero would do to appease the Furies and the Manes of his murdered mother (Suetonius, *Nero* 34.4); angry gods were restricted to literature, "and they were unlikely to be open to practicing forgiveness"—the value of *clementia* was its capacity to limit the anger and revenge of an offended party and its "potential for educating the wrongdoer when exacting punishment."[42]

---

[37] David Konstan, "Assuaging Rage: Remorse, Repentance, and Forgiveness in the Ancient World," in *Ancient Forgiveness: Classical, Judaic, and Christian* (ed. C. L. Griswold and D. Konstan; Cambridge: Cambridge University Press, 2012), pp. 17-30 (19). With reference to Aristotle, *Eth. nic.* 1.6, 1110a24-26, 1109b18-1111a2, 1109b30-32, 1149b4-6; the following point ibid.

[38] Charles L. Griswold, "Plato and Forgiveness," *Ancient Philosophy* 27 (2007), pp. 269-87 (279). On the term συγγνώμη, see Karin Metzler, *Der griechische Begriff des Verzeihens. Untersucht am Wortstamm συγγνώμη von den ersten Belegen bis zum vierten Jahrhundert n.Chr.* (WUNT, 2.44; Tübingen: Mohr Siebeck, 1991).

[39] Konstan, "Assuaging Rage," pp. 20-21; for the example of Seneca cf. ibid., p. 21 and David Konstan, *Before Forgiveness: The Origins of a Moral Idea* (Cambridge: Cambridge University Press, 2010), pp. 32-33.

[40] Konstan, "Assuaging Rage," p. 21.

[41] Susanna Morton Braund, "The Anger of Tyrants and the Forgiveness of Kings," in *Ancient Forgiveness: Classical, Judaic, and Christian* (ed. C. L. Griswold and D. Konstan; Cambridge: Cambridge University Press, 2012), pp. 79-96 (96).

[42] Zsuzsanna Várhelyi, "'To Forgive is Divine': Gods as Models of Forgiveness in Late Republican and Early Imperial Rome," in *Ancient Forgiveness: Classical, Judaic, and Christian* (ed. C. L. Griswold and D. Konstan; Cambridge: Cambridge University Press, 2012), pp. 115-33 (130-31).

The vocabulary of atonement, in particular the verb ἱλάσκεσθαι, which means "to appease" (the gods), "conciliate" (people), or "reverence" (sacred things),[43] is used in classical texts to describe the propitiation of the gods; the noun ἱλασμός describes various acts such as prayers, sacrifices, purifying dances, and games. When Achilles tells his mother of the quarrel he had with Agamemnon after the Achaeans began to die "thick and fast," he tells her, "At once I was the first to urge them to propitiate the god (θεὸν ἱλάσκεσθαι) but then wrath laid hold of the son of Atreus, and quickly he stood up and made a threat which has now come to pass" (Homer, *Il.* 1.386; Murray; LCL 170, pp. 40–43). Homer then relates that the Achaeans "the whole day long . . . sought to appease the god (θεὸν ἱλάσκοντο) with song, singing the beautiful paean, hymning the god who works from afar; and his heart was glad as he heard" (*Il.* 1.472; Murray; LCL 170, pp. 48–49). In the Hymn to Demeter, the goddess says,

> For I am Demeter the honored one, who is the greatest boon and joy to immortals and mortals. Now, let the whole people build me a great temple with an altar below it, under the citadel's sheer wall, above Kallichoron, where the hill juts out. As to the rites, I myself will instruct you on how in future you can propitiate me with holy performance (εὐαγέως ἔρδοντες ἐμὸν νόον ἱλάσκοισθε). (*Hymn. Cer.* 268–74; West; LCL 496, pp. 52–55)[44]

When Demeter leaves Metaneira and her only son starts to gasp, mother, sisters, and nurses tried all night "to appease the dread goddess, shaking with fear" (αἱ μὲν παννύχιαι κυδρὴν θεὸν ἱλάσκοντο δείματι παλλόμεναι, 292–93; ibid.). Hades promises three things to Persephone: that she will rule over all living things on earth, that she will be honored among the gods, and that vengeance would be exacted against those who wrong her or who fail to propitiate her with sacrifices and gifts (οἵ κεν μὴ θυσίαισι τεὸν μένος ἱλάσκωνται εὐαγέως ἔρδοντες ἐναίσιμα δῶρα τελοῦντες, 368–69; ibid.). Foley comments that Demeter's cult at Eleusis seems at first "to have been founded only to propitiate the angry goddess, not to open new opportunities for humankind."[45]

Herodotus relates that Croesus "tried to win the favor of the Delphian god (τὸν ἐν Δελφοῖσι θεὸν ἱλάσκετο) with great sacrifices. He offered up three thousand beasts from all the kinds fit for sacrifice, and he burnt on a great pyre couches covered with gold and silver, golden goblets, and purple cloaks and tunics; by these means he hoped the better to win the aid of the god, to whom he also commanded that every Lydian sacrifice what he could" (*Hist.* 1.50; Godley, LCL 117, pp. 56–57). The verb ἱλάσκεσθαι occurs in a few oracles from Delphi.[46] Strabo, in his description of Gallia,

---

[43] LSJ s.v. ἱλάσκομαι I.1–2; for the meaning "expiate sins" only Heb. 2:17 is given as a reference. The noun ἱλασμα means "propitiation," ἱλασμός "a means of appeasing," ἱλαστής "propitiator," ἱλατήριον "expiatory or propitiatory offering." BDAG s.v. ἱλάσκομαι gives two meanings: (1) to cause to be favorably inclined or disposed, *propitiate, conciliate*, with Lk. 18:13 as the one NT example; (2) to eliminate impediments that alienate the deity, *expiate, wipe out*, with Heb. 2:17 with the one NT example.

[44] Helen P. Foley, *The Homeric Hymn to Demeter: Translation, Commentary, and Interpretive Essays* (Princeton: Princeton University Press, 1994), pp. 16–17.

[45] Ibid., p. 100.

[46] Herbert W. Parke and Donald E.W. Wormell, *The Delphic Oracle* (Oxford: Oxford University Press, 1956), Nos. 32, 326, 335.

relates that the women of the Samnitae who live on a small island situated off the outlet of the Liger River (Loire) "are possessed by Dionysus and make this god propitious by appeasing him with mystic initiations as well as other sacred performances" (Διονύσῳ κατεχομένας καὶ ἱλασκομένας τὸν θεὸν τοῦτον τελεταῖς τε καὶ ἄλλαις ἱεροποιίαις ἐξηλλαγμέ; Strabo, *Geogr.* 4.4.6.4; Jones; LCL 50, pp. 248–49).

Private individuals ask, "Which gods am I to appease to fare better?" (τίνας θεῶν ἱλασκομένου αὐτοῦ καρποὶ καλοι),[47] or "To which god must I sacrifice and which god must I appease to become healthier as to my eyes?"[48] The dossier of Poseidonios from Halicarnassus says in Part I:

> When Poseidonios sent away to make an oracular enquiry to Apollo, (asking) what would be better and more good for him and his descendants who are and who will be born, both from male and female offspring, to do and to attempt, the god replied that it would be better and more good for them to propitiate and to honour (ἱλασκομένοις καὶ τιμῶσιν), as their ancestors did, Paternal Zeus, and Apollo who rules over Telemessos, and the Fates and the Mother of the Gods. And they are also to honour and propitiate (τιμᾶν δὲ καὶ ἱλάσκεσθαι) the Good Daemon of Poseidonios and of Gorgis. And may it be better for those who maintain and enact these (commands).[49]

The subsequent text speaks of sacrifices of a field, courtyard, garden, tillage rights, and serving as priest. The people of Kaunos inquire of the oracle of Grynion which gods they must appease (ἱλασκομένου) in order to secure a good harvest, and receive the answer, "Phoebus son of Leto and Zeus Patroos."[50] A person asked the oracle of Didyma "what god he should propitiate in order to recall his wife from Christianity" (*interroganti . . . quem deum placando revocare possit uxorem suam a Christianismo*).[51] Henk Versnel comments that according to the available evidence, "mishap in daily life was not predominantly interpreted as a divine penalty in this period."[52]

Vicarious death

Since atonement in Hebrews concerns Jesus's sacrificial death, it is necessary to briefly survey the evidence for the notion of "vicarious death" in Greek and Roman

---

[47] Herbert W. Parke, *The Oracles of Zeus: Dodona, Olympia, Amman* (Oxford: Blackwell, 1967), p. 267 (no. 12); Éric Lhôte, *Les lamelles oraculaires de Dodone* (École Pratique des Hautes Etudes, Sciences historiques et philologiques III; Geneva: Droz, 2006), No. 65.

[48] Parke, *Oracles*, p. 267 (no. 12); Lhôte, *Lamelles oraculaires*, No. 72.

[49] Jan-Mathieu Carbon, "The Stele of Poseidonius," in Jan-Mathieu Carbon and Vinciane Pirenne-Delforge, "Priests and Cult Personnel in Three Hellenistic Families," in *Cities and Priests: Cult Personnel in Asia Minor and the Aegean Islands from the Hellenistic to the Imperial Period* (ed. M. Horster and A. Klöckner; Religionsgeschichtliche Versuche und Vorarbeiten, 64; Berlin: De Gruyter, 2013), pp. 65–120 (99–120) (text ibid., pp. 102–03, translation pp. 104–05). Cf. Parke and Wormell, *The Delphic Oracle*, II, p. 136 (no. 335) assume that the oracle comes from Delphi, which is possible but not proven.

[50] SEG XL 1109; cf. Versnel, *Gods*, p. 44 n. 76.

[51] Augustine, *Civ.* 19.23 (trans. from *NPNF1* 2:415), after Porphyry, Frag. 343; cf. Versnel, *Gods*, pp. 44–45 n. 76.

[52] Versnel, *Gods*, p. 45.

tradition.[53] Henk Versnel distinguishes dying for a creed (*exempla virtutis*), with Zenon, Anaxarchos, and Socrates as an example,[54] and "effective death" (dying for or instead), which can be divided into patriotic death (*dulce et decorum est pro patria mori*), in the military sense of dying in defense of (ὑπέρ) the πόλις, one's country, family, or friends,[55] and vicarious death (*unum pro multis dabitur caput*), that is, the idea that the death of one person may save others from impending or actual disaster. Euripides had a keen interest in the theme of vicarious death, particularly explicit in the *Alcestis* in which the protagonist is willing to die voluntarily in order to save her husband from death: "How could any woman give greater proof that she gives her husband the place of honor than by being willing to die for him? (θέλουσ᾽ ὑπερθανεῖν) . . . I am dying. I need not have died in your place (θνῄσκω, παρόν μοι μὴ θανεῖν ὑπὲρ σέθεν)" (*Alc.* 155, 284; Kovacs; LCL 12, pp. 170-71, 182-83). Vicarious death is a frequent theme in Greek tragedy, as it is in myths and legends (e.g., Heracles can free Prometheus only after Cheiron, the centaur, has offered to take his place and die in his stead).[56] Herodotus says that the motive of Leonidas, king of the Spartans, to defend Thermopylae with 300 men was due to an oracle who had predicted that the Persians would destroy Sparta unless one of the kings would die (Herodotus, *Hist.* 7.220). According to Seneca, stories about mythical and historical heroes who voluntarily sacrificed their own lives were studied in the curriculum of Roman schools (Seneca, *Ep.* 24.6). Cicero gives a list of Greek protagonists of noble death (*mortes pro patria*): the Erechthides, Codros, Menoiceus, Iphigenia, Harmodios, Aristogniton, Leonidas, Epaminondas (*Tusc.* 1.116-17), and, as Roman examples, L. Brutus, the Decii, the Scipiones, Paulus and Geminus, Marcellus, Albinus, Gracchus (*Tusc.* 1.89). Authors of the first centuries BC and AD revive the praises of the death of Alcestis,[57] who also is mentioned in funerary epigrams during this period. In sixteen inscriptions in Greek and Latin dating to the first century AD, the devotion of Atilia L.f Pomptilla to her husband is praised since she followed her husband to Sardinia, probably into exile, offering her own life in order to save her sick husband from death; she is praised as "greater than Alcestis" (IG IV 607, 7577; line 7568 uses the term λύτρον). Aelius Aristides boasts that his life was saved three times through the vicarious death of another person (*Or.* 48.44; 51.24-25). Antoninus Liberalis (ca. AD 150, collecting material from earlier authors) tells the story of the self-sacrifice of Menippe and Metioche, the daughters of Orion, who responded to

---

[53] Cf. Hendrik S. Versnel, "Self-Sacrifice, Compensation and the Anonymous Gods," in *Le sacrifice dans l'antiquité* (ed. J. Rudhardt and O. Reverdin; Entretiens sur l'antiquité classique, 27; Vandoeuvres/Geneva: Fondation Hardt, 1981), pp. 135-85; Hendrik S. Versnel, "Quid Athenis et Hierosolymis? Bemerkungen über die Herkunft von Aspekten des 'effective death,'" in *Die Entstehung der jüdischen Martyrologie* (ed. J. W. Van Henten; SPB, 38; Leiden: Brill, 1989), pp. 162-96; Hendrik S. Versnel, "Making Sense of Jesus' Death: The Pagan Contribution," in *Deutungen des Todes Jesu im Neuen Testament* (ed. J. Frey and J. Schröter; WUNT, 181; Tübingen: Mohr Siebeck, 2005), pp. 213-94 (227-53); Christina Eschner, *Gestorben und hingegeben "für" die Sünder. Die griechische Konzeption des Unheil abwendenden Sterbens und deren paulinische Aufnahme für die Deutung des Todes Jesu Christi* (WMANT, 122; 2 vols; Neukirchen-Vluyn: Neukirchener Verlag, 2010), 2:9-317.
[54] Cicero, *Tusc.* 2.52; Philo, *Prob.* 106. Cf. David Seeley, *The Noble Death: Graeco-Roman Martyrology and Paul's Concept of Salvation* (JSNTSup, 28; Sheffield: JSOT Press, 1990), pp. 113-41.
[55] Cf. Homer, *Il.* 15.496-97; Epictetus, *Diatr.* 2.7.3; Philostratos, *Vit. Apoll.* 7.12.
[56] Aeschylus, *Prom.* 1026-29; Hesiod, *Theog.* 526-532; Apollodorus, *Bibl.* 2.5.11,10.
[57] Dionysius Halicarnassus, *Rhet.* 2.5; Musonius Rufus 14; Ps. Apollodoros, *Bibl.* 1.106; Plutarch, *Am.* 761E.

an oracle given in response to the Boetians, stating that the devastating pestilence would end if they sacrificed two willing virgins which would placate the gods of the underworld (ἱλάσσασθαι δύο τοὺς ἐριο[υνίους θεούς) and bring their wrath to an end (καταπαύσειν αὐτοὺς τὴν μῆνιν) (*Metam.* 25.2).[58]

Atonement in the Lydian-Phrygian confession inscriptions

The religiosity of the so-called confession inscriptions from Lydia and Phrygia in western Asia Minor,[59] also called atonement inscriptions,[60] propitiatory inscriptions,[61] expiation texts,[62] or reconciliation inscriptions,[63] have no parallels anywhere else. The question of the origins of these inscriptions continues to be debated. Franz Steinleitner argued that they are the products of a Lydian-Phrygian popular religion which modeled the relationship between gods and mortals on the relationship between master and slave that characterized oriental religion.[64] Raffaele Pettazzoni linked the confession inscriptions with the cults of oriental goddesses such as Isis, Magna Mater, and Dea

---

[58] Cf. Eschner, *Gestorben*, 2:252. This self-sacrifice is a form of human sacrifice, on which see Dennis D. Hughes, *Human Sacrifice in Ancient Greece* (London: Routledge, 1991); Henning Dohrmann, *Anerkennung und Bekämpfung von Menschenopfern im römischen Strafrecht der Kaiserzeit* (Europäische Hochschulschriften, 2.185; Frankfurt: Lang, 1995); Jan N. Bremmer, ed., *The Strange World of Human Sacrifice* (Studies in the History and Anthropology of Religion; Leuven: Peeters, 2006).

[59] Cf. Hasan Malay, "New Confession-Inscriptions in the Manisa and Bergama Museums," *EA* 12 (1988), pp. 147–52; Georg Petzl, *Die Beichtinschriften Westkleinasiens* (Epigraphica Anatolica, 22; Bonn: Habelt, 1994); Marijana Ricl, "The Appeal to Divine Justice in the Lydian Confession-Inscriptions," in *Forschungen in Lydien* (ed. E. Schwertheim; Asia Minor Studien, 17; Bonn: Habelt, 1995), pp. 67–73; Hans-Josef Klauck, "Die kleinasiatischen Beichtinschriften und das Neue Testament," in *Geschichte – Tradition – Reflexion* (Festschrift M. Hengel; ed. H. Lichtenberger; Tübingen: Mohr Siebeck, 1996), pp. 64–87; Georg Petzl, *Die Beichtinschriften im römischen Kleinasien und der Fromme und Gerechte Gott* (Nordrhein-Westfälische Akademie der Wissenschaften: Geisteswissenschaften; Vorträge, G 355; Opladen/Wiesbaden: Westdeutscher Verlag, 1998); Eckhard J. Schnabel, "Divine Tyranny and Public Humiliation: A Suggestion for the Interpretation of the Lydian and Phrygian Confession Inscriptions," *NovT* 45 (2003), pp. 160–88; Richard Gordon, "Raising a Sceptre: Confession-Narratives from Lydia and Phrygia," *JRA* 17 (2004), pp. 177–96; Lochlan Shelfer, "The Temple as Courtroom: The Confession Stelai of Imperial Lydia" (unpublished doctoral dissertation; Baltimore: Johns Hopkins University, 2010); Marijana Ricl, "Observations on a New Corpus of Inscriptions from Lydia," *EA* 44 (2011), pp. 143–52.

[60] Franz S. Steinleitner, *Die Beicht im Zusammenhange mit der sakralen Rechtspflege in der Antike. Ein Beitrag zur näheren Kenntnis kleinasiatisch-orientalischer Kulte der Kaiserzeit* (Leipzig: Dieterich'sche Verlagsbuchhandlung, 1913) *passim*; Otto Eger, "Eid und Fluch in den maionischen und phrygischen Sühne-Inschriften," in *Festschrift Paul Koschaker*. Vol. *III* (Weimar: Böhlau, 1939), pp. 281-93; Peter Frisch, "Über die lydisch-phrygischen Sühneinschriften und die 'Confessiones' des Augustinus," *EA* 2 (1983), pp. 41–45; Ender Varinlioğlu, "Eine Gruppe von Sühneinschriften aus dem Museum von Uşak," *EA* 13 (1989), pp. 37–50.

[61] Angelos Chaniotis, "Illness and Cures in the Greek Propitiatory Inscriptions and Dedications of Lydia and Phrygia," in *Ancient Medicine in its Socio-Cultural Context II* (ed. P. J. van der Eiik, H. F. J. Horstmanshoff, and P. H. Schrijvers; Papers read at the Congress held at Leiden University, April 13–15, 1992; Amsterdam: Rodopi, 1995), pp. 323–43.

[62] Price, *Imperial Cult*, pp. 95–96.

[63] Aslak Rostad, "Human Transgression – Divine Retribution: A Study of Religious Transgressions and Punishments in Greek Cultic Regulations and Lydian-Phrygian Reconciliation Inscriptions" (unpublished doctoral dissertation; Bergen, Norway: University of Bergen, 2006).

[64] Steinleitner, *Beicht*, pp. 76–77.

Syria.⁶⁵ Marijana Ricl sees reminiscences of the religion of the Hittites whose temples, a thousand years earlier, ruled large areas of Anatolia and the people living there.⁶⁶ Hans-Josef Klauck traces some common terms to possible Jewish influence.⁶⁷ Aslak Rostad suggests the meeting and intermingling of Greek and Anatolian traditions,⁶⁸ while Lochlan Shelfer emphasizes the influence of Roman legal language and norms accepted by the local Lydian population, who created a "legal-religious patois."⁶⁹ I have suggested that the confession inscriptions might perhaps be the result of the expansion of the Christian faith in western Asia Minor prompting the priests of local cults to consolidate their power by forcing transgressors to confess their allegiance to the local gods on stelai.⁷⁰

The structure of these texts can be described in terms of nine elements, although not all are necessarily present in a given inscription. (1) Name of the person who has committed (ἁμαρτάνειν) a transgression (ἁμαρτία, ἁμάρτημα). (2) Specific offense of the individual, either violations of cultic purity rules (consumption of forbidden food, entering the sanctuary with unclean clothes, sexual intercourse with a married woman or an unmarried slave belonging to another family) or of sacred property (groves, trees, objects), neglect of religious duties (paying the honor due to the god, neglect of religious offices), or civil conflicts (e.g., perjury). (3) Reaction of the god, sometimes an epiphany in a dream (ὕπνος, ὄνειρος) or through a messenger (ἄγγελος). The gods mentioned in the confession inscriptions are the Anatolian gods Men and Meter as well as Zeus and Apollon. (4) Punishment by the god (κολάζειν, κόλασις). Most inscriptions specify the punishment which affected, most often, the eyes, but also the ability to speak, breasts, legs, the backside. Some reliefs portray the affected part of the body. Sometimes the delinquent became deranged, insane, unconscious, or died. Sometimes the perpetrator is detained in the temple of the god. Sometimes the duration of the punishment is specified: the afflictions described lasted for three months, a year and ten months, four years, or a long period of time. (5) Redressal of the crime by paying a ransom (λύειν) in order to propitiate the god and atone for the misdeed (ἱλάσκεσθαι, ἐξιλάσκεσθαι), which might involve the offering of a sacrifice or erecting a stele. (6) Public confession (ὁμολογεῖν, ἐξομολογεῖν), sometimes inscribed on the stele. (7) Acknowledgment of the power (δύναμις) of the god. (8) Erection of a stele on which the story of the delinquent is inscribed (στηλογραφεῖν), often explicitly demanded by the god. (9) Profession of faith in the god by the sinner who commits to praise the god "from now on" and warning others not to disdain the god.

---

⁶⁵ Raffaele Pettazzoni, *La confessione dei peccati* (Bologna: Zanichelli, 1937), pp. 54–162; idem, *Essays on the History of Religions* (Studies in the History of Religions, 1; Leiden: Brill, 1954), pp. 55–67.
⁶⁶ Ricl, "Appeal"; idem, "CIG 4142 – A Forgotten Confession-Inscription from North-West Phrygia," *EA* 29 (1997), pp. 35–43 (36); idem, "Society and Economy of Rural Sanctuaries in Roman Lydia and Phrygia," *EA* 35 (2003), pp. 77–101.
⁶⁷ Klauck, "Beichtinschriften," p. 69 n. 37: the term ἄγγελος, with reference to Anne R.R. Sheppard, "Pagan Cults of Angels in Roman Asia Minor," *Talanta* 12–13 (1980–81), pp. 77–101 (77).
⁶⁸ Rostad, "Transgression," pp. 242–45.
⁶⁹ Shelfer, "Confession Stelai," p. 209; he calls the process not "Romanization" but "non-reactionary form of Crealization" (205).
⁷⁰ Schnabel, "Divine Tyranny," pp. 182–88; hence Versnel, "Jesus' Death," p. 292; Rostad, "Transgression," p. 31.

The propitiation that the god demands is sometimes described in elaborate detail. For example, in the case of Theodoros from Nonou, a sexual predator who had committed three transgressions of sexual misconduct: after the first transgression he had to offer a sheep, a partridge, and a mole; after the second, a piglet and a tuna fish; after the third a chicken (or rooster), a sparrow, a pigeon, as well as a kypros of wheat mixed with barley and a prochos of wine; then the god says, "behold, I had blinded him in consequence of his actions, but now he has made good his mistakes (κατὰ τὰ πυήματα πεπηρώκιν) by propitiating the gods (εἰλαζομένου αὐτοῦ τοὺς θεούς) and by erecting an inscribed stele (στηλογραφοῦντος)."[71]

Jesus's death as atoning sacrifice in Hebrews in Greek-Roman contexts

The language of sacrifices, blood, expiation, propitiation, purification, sacred, and profane which figures prominently in Greek and Roman cults is present in Hebrews as well. Space allows only a survey of relevant passages, each of which deserves detailed analysis.

Sacrifice

Greek and Roman listeners who were not followers of Jesus—henceforth called "polytheists"—would have understood the references to "gifts" (δῶρα) and "sacrifices" (θυσίας) for sins that the high priest had to offer for his own sins and for the sins of the people (Heb. 5:1, 3; 8:3). But they would have had difficulties understanding that God appointed the high priest, rather than a city of civic institution, and they would have wondered why the author needs to emphasize that the high priest had to offer sacrifices for himself (5:3), and they might have wondered why Israel's priests offered sacrifices every day (10:11). They would have been discombobulated by the statement that Jesus has no need to "offer sacrifices" (θυσίας ἀναφέρειν) for himself (7:27)—this makes sense if he is a divine being sitting next to God (1:3, 13) and if he is the radiance of God's glory (1:2), but seems absurd if he was a human being of flesh and blood who suffered, who was tempted, who had to learn obedience (2:8-18; 4:15; 5:8; 9:15, 25-26).

Polytheists would have agreed with the assertion in 9:9 that "gifts and sacrifices" which are offered (δῶρά τε καὶ θυσίαι προσφέρονται) cannot perfect the conscience of the worshiper, but they would have been mystified by the comment in 9:23 that the heavenly things themselves need "better sacrifices" (κρείττοσιν θυσίαις) than animal sacrifices. They would have had difficulties understanding the statement in 9:26-28 and 10:14 that Jesus's sacrifice was his own death and that by the single sacrifice (μιᾷ προσφορᾷ) of Jesus's death the sin of the many people who believe in him is removed. They would have been mystified by the assertion in 10:10: how could the offering of the body of

---

[71] Petzl, *Beichtinschriften*, no. 5, lines 7–18, 19–21. The verb εἰλαζομένου probably stands for ἱλασαμένου, cf. ibid., p. 10, with reference to H. Brixhe and K. A. Panayotou, *Bulletin épigraphique* 1991, p. 571.

Jesus make other people holy? They would have been perplexed by the statement in 10:18: what has sacrifice to do with the forgiveness of transgressions, and why would one sacrifice make all other sacrifices redundant? Polytheists would concur with the notion expressed in 10:26 that people who willfully persist in sin find that there is no longer a sacrifice (θυσία) for sins but only the prospect of judgment, but they would be baffled to hear that the prospect of judgment is not essentially limited to the violation of basic taboos such as parricide or incest but is said of everyday offenses. They would have understood the notion that some sacrifices are better than others, as Abel's offering was a more acceptable sacrifice (πλείονα θυσίαν) than Cain's (11:4), but not why this was connected with faith (πίστις) rather than with more elaborate or superior ritual. Absent a clear understanding of faith, the statement in 11:4 reinforces the sense that the gods are arbitrary and that they sometimes decline to be gracious.[72] The statement in 12:2 that Jesus endured crucifixion and disregarded its shame "for the sake of joy" (ἀντὶ τῆς προκειμένης αὐτῷ χαρᾶς) would leave polytheists nonplussed. The command to join Jesus who died outside the city (13:12) and bear the abuse he endured (13:13) and thus share in the consequences of his sin offering (13:11), offering a "sacrifice of praise" (θυσία αἰνέσεως) to God (13:15) for Jesus's atoning death, flew in the face of the notion that sacrifice is a banquet of the community in the presence of the gods.

Even though the early Christians saw Greek or Romans sacrifice all around them, "they ignored it, not only as a parallel for the death of Christ but as an antitype," as Naiden argues.[73] Similarity in language and concepts might have resonated with a non-Jewish audience when Hebrews was read, but the specific descriptions of Jesus's sacrifice of atonement and the references to basic Jewish concepts such as sin being rebellion against God the Creator, traditions such as those of Abel and Cain, Moses and the Sinaitic Covenant, places such as the Holy Place and the Holy of Holies, and practices such as the Day of Atonement and the Levitical sacrifices would have sounded rather foreign. Sure, the Roman notion that the sacrifice as gift to a god creates obligations[74] can be compared with the Christian conviction that Jesus's sacrifice demands and implies obedience from those who benefit from it—Hebrews repeatedly warns against disobedience (2:2-3; 3:18; 4:6, 11). On the other hand, the notion that sacrifice defines hierarchies[75] is undermined when we read that Jesus Messiah entered into heaven and appears in the presence of God "on our behalf" (9:24) and that those who benefit from Jesus's sacrifice are sons (12:5-11) of God as Jesus is Son (1:1, 5, 8; 3:6; 4:14; 5:5; 7:28). The systems that sacrifice creates in Roman religion[76] are undermined by Jesus's sacrifice—the particular Roman gods that demand particular animals are regarded as nonexistent, and the demand for particular animals is countermanded: there is only one true God, the Father of Jesus Messiah; there is only one sacrifice, Jesus's voluntary death on the cross; there are no rituals since it is faith in God's provision of Jesus's sacrifice which procures forgiveness (9:23-28; 10:1-18) leading to joyful obedience (13:15, 17, 21).

---

[72] Cf. Naiden, *Smoke Signals*, p. 130.
[73] Ibid., p. 286, with regard to the Gospels.
[74] Rüpke, *Religion*, pp. 149-50.
[75] Ibid., pp. 145-49.
[76] Ibid., pp. 151-52.

Blood

The author asserts in 9:7, 25 that the high priest offers blood (αἵματος ὃ προσφέρει) for himself and for unintentional sins, in 9:12 that Jesus entered the heavenly temple not with the blood of goats and calves (οὐδὲ δι᾿ αἵματος τράγων καὶ μόσχων) but with his own blood (διὰ δὲ τοῦ ἰδίου αἵματος), in 9:13 that the blood of goats and bulls (τὸ αἷμα τράγων καὶ ταύρων) purifies the flesh of people who were defiled, in 9:18-20 that the first covenant was inaugurated with blood (αἵματος), specifically with the blood of calves and goats (τὸ αἷμα τῶν μόσχων καὶ τῶν τράγων), which was "the blood of the covenant" (τὸ αἷμα τῆς διαθήκης). Polytheists would not have regarded these statements as alien. The assertion in 9:14 that the blood of the Messiah (τὸ αἷμα τοῦ Χριστοῦ) purifies the conscience, which the blood of goats and bulls could not do, would leave them perplexed, however: while the concept of vicarious death was not strange, the concept of a pure conscience unattainable through animal sacrifices would be regarded as eccentric if not bizarre. The statement in 9:21-22 that Moses sprinkled the tabernacle and the sacred vessels with blood (τῷ αἵματι), because almost everything is purified with blood (ἐν αἵματι) since "without the shedding of blood" (αἱματεκχυσίας) there is no forgiveness of sins, would have been essentially intelligible, although the reference to the forgiveness of sins would be seen as strange: if forgiveness reinforces absolute and arbitrary authority, and if the gods were seen in the first century as mostly passionless,[77] the absolute necessity of complete forgiveness would hardly have been a "felt need" by Gentile listeners. The statement in 10:4 that the blood of bulls and goats (αἷμα ταύρων καὶ τράγων) cannot take away sins would be met with disbelief, at least outside of Epicurean circles. The statement in 10:29 that the blood of Jesus is "the blood of the covenant" (τὸ αἷμα τῆς διαθήκης) by which believers in Jesus are purified; the statement in 13:20 that Jesus's blood is "the blood of the eternal covenant" (αἵματι διαθήκης αἰωνίου); and the statement in 12:24 that Christians have come to Jesus, the mediator of a New Covenant and "to the sprinkled blood" (αἵματι ῥαντισμοῦ), that is to Jesus's blood shed at the cross which inaugurated the New Covenant, could be linked with the tutelary deities that protected a particular city, but the concept of a covenant between God and individuals and communities of believers implied the historical dimension of the revelation of the one true God in Israel and now in Jesus Messiah which, and the implication that those who belong to this covenant do not actually bring bloody offerings, was foreign.

The identity of the sacrifice that the author of Hebrews describes repeatedly marks a fundamental difference from Greek and Roman sacrificial thinking and praxis. The sacrifice that atones for sin is Jesus's self-sacrifice as the sacrifice of the Son of God who is preexistent (1:2), who assumed a human body (2:11-15; 10:5, 10), whose suffering (2:9, 10, 18; 5:8-9; 13:12), death on the cross (6:6; 12:2), resurrection, and exaltation to the right hand of God (10:5-14; 12:23-24) constitutes the one sacrifice that atones for the sins of all people, and who will one day return again to save those who are eagerly waiting for him (9:28; 10:13, 36-39).[78] Jesus's identity as preexistent, human, crucified,

---

[77] See Braund, "Anger," p. 96, and Várhelyi, "Forgiveness," p. 130.
[78] Cf. Franz Joseph Schierse, *Verheißung und Heilsvollendung. Zur theologischen Grundfrage des Hebräerbriefes* (Müchener Theologische Studien.; München: Zink, 1955), p. 54, on the reference

and exalted Savior has no parallels in either Greek or Jewish tradition, so much so that Paul asserts in the context of a discussion of the effectiveness of the proclamation of the good news that the proclamation of Jesus as crucified Messiah (Χριστὸς ἐσταυρωμένος) is "a stumbling block to Jews and foolishness to Gentiles" (1 Cor. 1:23) and that the acceptance of the gospel message by faith is the result not of polished rhetoric or brilliant arguments but the result of the power of God (1 Cor. 2:2-5). Worshiping a crucified man as a Savior was beyond the hermeneutical parameters of Jews, Greeks, and Romans, whatever terminological overlap and notional similarities may have been perceived. This is demonstrated by the graffito from the Palatine which shows a certain Alexamenos worshiping a figure with a donkey's head in a Jesus-like pose on a cross.[79]

What Fred Naiden says about Paul's view of Jesus's death as sacrifice and sacrifice in relation to Greek sacrifice applies *mutadis mutandis* to the view of Jesus's death as sacrifice in Hebrews as well.[80] The sacrifice of Jesus was neither an animal nor a vegetal sacrifice. Jesus's sacrifice is not a sacrifice in a literal sense: it is not compared with the slaughtering of an animal, burning of incense or any other sacrifice that a pagan would have known. Significantly, Julian Apostata planned to rebuild the Temple of Jerusalem as part of his anti-Christian campaign not only in order to falsify Jesus's prediction that the Temple would not be rebuilt but also in order to revive the animal sacrifices that had ceased in AD 70 and thus prove that the Christians' claim that they worship the God of Abraham, Isaac, and Jacob was false.[81] Jesus's sacrifice consists not only of Jesus's death, but included his life (2:17-18; 5:7-9; 10:10, 20)[82]—a sinless life (4:15; 7:26-28)—as well as his resurrection and ascension (4:14; 8:1; 9:11-12, 24; 10:12). There are no multiple acts of sacrifice: Jesus's sacrifice of atonement happened once-and-for-all (ἐφάπαξ: 7:27; 9:12; 10:10; ἅπαξ: 9:26, 28) and thus has eternal efficacy. There are no multiple forms of sacrifice: there is only Jesus's sacrifice. Jesus's sacrifice is the only genuine sacrifice since no sinner can sacrifice successfully. Jesus's sacrifice is uniquely redemptive because it made redemption by killing animals impossible (9:22-23).

Jesus's sacrifice was the choice of a willing victim, unlike the killing of an animal: "It lacked burning, dismemberment, and a subsequent meal, but it featured crucifixion, disfigurement, and an antecedent meal."[83] What Naiden asserts regarding Paul is true for Hebrews as well: "Paul valued sacrifice more than the Greeks had. For them, it

---

to Jesus's incarnation, crucifixion, exaltation, and parousia in 10:5-14: "Das ganze Christus-Drama ist in dem einen und einmaligen Akt der προσφορὰ τοῦ σώματος Ἰησοῦ Χριστοῦ [10,10] zusammengeschaut."

[79] Cf. David W. Chapman and Eckhard J. Schnabel, *The Trial and Crucifixion of Jesus: Texts and Commentary* (WUNT, 344; Tübingen: Mohr Siebeck, 2015), pp. 753–54 (no. 462); Mika Kajava, "Religion in Rome and Italy," in *The Oxford Handbook of Roman Epigraphy* (ed. C. Bruun and J. Edmonson; Oxford: Oxford University Press, 2015), pp. 397–419 (412).

[80] Cf. Naiden, *Smoke Signals*, pp. 284–87.

[81] Christopher P. Jones, *Between Pagan and Christian* (Cambridge, MA: Harvard University Press, 2014), 64; see ibid., pp. 61–77 for why the Christians rejected bloody animal sacrifices.

[82] Cf. Christian Eberhart, "Characteristics of Sacrificial Metaphors in Hebrews," in *Hebrews: Contemporary Methods – New Insights* (ed. G. Gelardini; Leiden: Brill, 2005), pp. 37–64 (61); also Christian Eberhart, *Kultmetaphorik und Christologie: Opfer- und Sühneterminologie im Neuen Testament* (WUNT, 306; Tübingen: Mohr Siebeck, 2013), p. 152 follows Otfried Hofius, "Inkarnation und Opfertod Jesu nach Hebr 10,19f. [1970]," in *Neutestamentliche Studien* (WUNT, 132; Tübingen: Mohr Siebeck, 2000), pp. 210–19, who interprets the statement about the "veil" which is interpreted in terms of Jesus's "flesh" in 10:20 in terms of the incarnation.

[83] Naiden, *Smoke Signals*, p. 286.

fortified prayers or solemnized oaths. For Paul, the singular sacrifice of Christ was the chief sacrament"; Jesus's sacrifice gave sacrifice a new dignity: "Rather than trafficking in food, drink, and water, the rite had needed only the body of Christ."[84] The relation between sacrifice and prayer is different: whereas in Greek and Roman religion sacrifice built upon prayer, with both of these being either retrospective (giving thanks) or prospective (making requests), Jesus's sacrifice owed nothing to prayer; prayer in which Jesus's death is mentioned is retrospective only.

The efficacy of Jesus's sacrifice does not depend on ritual, nor on any action of a person, but on faith alone (4:2; 6:1, 12; 10:22, 38, 39). Pagan Roman critics denunciated the centrality of and the reliance on faith as credulity, implying and asserting that the traditional *religio* was based on historical evidence, as Clifford Ando explains, "The Romans' famed rectitude and rigor in the performance of cult should be understood in this context: in light of the terrifying superiority of the gods, and knowing what had worked before, one had an overwhelming obligation scrupulously to recreate precisely that earlier performance. For the gods' part, their willingness to abide by this *ius*, by this body of law, was the highest expression of both their *fides*, their norm-based loyalty to the other members of their community, and their goodwill."[85] For the author of Hebrews, Israel's sacrificial cult was "only a matter of food and drink and various ceremonial washings—external regulations (δικαιώματα σαρκός) applying until the time of the new order (9:10 NIV), a mere 'shadow' (σκιά) which can never (οὐδέποτε) make perfect those who draw near to worship (οἱ προσερχόμενοι; 10:1). The life, death, and exaltation of Jesus Messiah constitute the end of sacrificial cult as path to salvation."[86]

While "blood" had expiatory efficacy in Greek and Roman concepts of sacrifice, the author of Hebrews does not connect his explanation of Jesus's "blood"[87] with general notions of the salvific significance of blood but with the cultic realities of the Day of Atonement in Leviticus 16 and the significance of the sprinkling of blood in the context of the Sinai Covenant according to Exod. 24:1-11.[88] The phrase διὰ δὲ τοῦ ἰδίου αἵματος, rather than ἐν αἵματι in 9:12 clarifies that Jesus's blood is not a means of salvation that is distinct from the meditator of salvation: Jesus is

---

[84] Ibid., p. 285.
[85] Ando, *Gods*, p, 14, with reference to Julian the Apostate, quoted by Gregory of Nazianzus, *Or. Bas.* 4.102, and Q. Aurelius Symmachus, *Relatio* 3.8: "For insofar as all reason lies in darkness [where the gods are concerned], whence more properly can knowledge of the gods (*cognitio numinum*) come than from recollection and the evidence supplied by things that turned out well?" (). Cf. Pierre Boyancé, "Les Romains, peuple de la *fides* [1964]," in *Études sur la religion romaine* (Collection de l'École française de Rome 11; Rome/Paris: École française de Rome, 1972), pp. 135–52; John Scheid, *Religion et piété à Rome* (Paris: Découverte, 1985), pp. 128–37.
[86] Erich Gräßer, *An die Hebräer* (EKKNT XVII; 3 vols; Zürich/Neukirchen-Vluyn: Benziger/Neukirchener Verlag, 1990–97) 2:236, formulates: "Christ is the end of the cult as path to salvation" ("Christus ist das Ende des Kultes als Heilsweg").
[87] Reference to "blood": 2:14; 9:7, 12(2x), 13, 14, 18, 19, 20, 21, 22, 24; 10:4, 19, 29; 11:28; 12:4, 24; 13:11, 12, 20, and the *hapax legomonon* αἱματεκχυσία in 9:22.
[88] Eberhart, *Kultmetaphorik*, p. 144 n. 50, with reference to Angela Rascher, *Schriftauslegung und Christologie im Hebräerbrief* (BZNW, 153; Berlin: De Gruyter, 2007), p. 172; Harold W. Attridge, *The Epistle to the Hebrews* (Hermeneia; Philadelphia: Fortress, 1989), pp. 257–58; Guido Telscher, *Opfer aus Barmherzigkeit. Hebr 9,11-28 im Kontext biblischer Sühnetheologie* (FzB, 112; Würzburg: Echter, 2007), pp. 264–66.

both mediator and means of salvation on account of his vicarious sacrifice of his life.[89]

In contrast to Greek, Roman, Israelite, and Jewish priests who officiate during sacrifices standing, signifying their honorable priestly status and signaling their solemn albeit bustling activity, Jesus is described as priest who is "sitting" (ἐκάθισεν; 1:3; 8:1; 10:12; cf. 12:2), signifying his divine dignity and signaling that nothing more needs to be done for the atonement for sins.[90] While Jesus's status as "high priest" (ἀρχιερεύς; 2:17; 3:1; 4:14, 15; 5:5, 10; 6:20; 7:26; 8:1; 9:11) could be compared with the status of the Roman emperor as *pontifex maximus*, usually rendered ἀρχιερεύς in Greek, and Jesus's divine status with the emperors' claim to divinity, emperors did not sacrifice themselves in order to achieve divine blessings for others but, rather, needed prayers for their own safety, as evidenced in the private and public vows on behalf of the well-being of the emperor.[91] Pliny writes, "We have made our annual vows, Sir, to ensure your safety (*vota pro incolumitate tua*) and thereby that of the State" (*Ep.* 10.35; Radice; LCL 59, pp. 208-9); and,

> I call on the gods, the guardians and defenders of our empire, speaking as consul on behalf of all humanity: and to you in particular, Capitoline Jupiter, I address my prayer that you shall continue your benefits, and augment the great gifts you have bestowed by making them perpetual. You heard our prayers under a bad prince; now give ear to our wishes on behalf of his opposite. We are not burdening you with vows—we do not pray for peace, concord, and serenity, nor for wealth and honors: our desire is simple, all-embracing, and unanimous: the safety of our prince. (*salus principis*) (*Pan.* 94.1-2; Radice; LCL 59, pp. 542-43)

Bruce Winter interprets the description of Jesus as high priest as a challenge to the emperors' critical high-priestly office regarded as essential for the welfare of the *pax romana*, so much so that the author encourages the Hebrew Christians, who had already been punished by the authorities (10:32-34), to be prepared for the pending punishment of exile (13:12).[92] Jesus's divine identity is not only connected with his being the Son of God (as in the case of the emperors' claims) but also to his being high priest (unlike in the case of the emperors), as 7:3, 16 asserts, as his atoning sacrifice is both final and permanent.[93]

---

[89] Gräßer, *Hebräer*, 2:151.
[90] Cf. Herbert Braun, *An die Hebräer* (HNT, 14; Tübingen: Mohr Siebeck, 1984), p. 300: in Hebrews, "standing" is "eine rangmindernde Geschäftigkeit, des Opferns ist ja kein Ende."
[91] Cf. Peter Herrmann, *Der römische Kaisereid. Untersuchungen zu seiner Herkunft und Entwicklung* (Hypomnemata, 20; Göttingen: Vandenhoeck & Ruprecht, 1968). Cf. Versnel, "Jesus' Death," pp. 244-48: the devotion to the emperor (*devotio pro principe*) is one of the forms of vicarious death.
[92] Bruce W. Winter, *Divine Honours for the Caesars: The First Christians' Responses* (Grand Rapids, MI: Eerdmans, 2015), pp. 266-85.
[93] Cf. Richard J. Bauckham, "The Divinity of Jesus Christ in the Epistle to the Hebrews," in *The Epistle to the Hebrews and Christian Theology* (ed. R. Bauckham, Daniel Driver, Trevor Hart, and Nathan MacDonald; Grand Rapids, MI: Eerdmans, 2009), pp. 15-36 (27-33).

Expiation and purification

The conviction that God "expiates" the sins of the people (2:17)[94] was intelligible. But the notion that there is a high priest in the service of God who is a human being and at the same time the divine Son of God through whom God expiates sins presupposes OT categories of God, of God's people, and of God atoning his people's sins in the tabernacle (9:5), as well as the early Christian conviction of Jesus's messianic divine identity that polytheists would have to learn. The reference to God's promise of complete forgiveness and his promise to no longer remember their sins (8:12, with quotation of Jer. 31:34) and the notion that this promise was fulfilled in Jesus's shedding of his blood which effected an eternal redemption (9:11-28) was difficult to understand for polytheists. The reference in 9:5 to the "place of atonement" (τὸ ἱλαστήριον; NLT) in the Holy of Holies of the Tabernacle[95] would have been intelligible for Greek and Roman readers.

Both expiation, the removal of sin, and propitiation, the averting of divine wrath, are relevant notions in Hebrews,[96] as they were in the Greek and Roman world. Even though the author does not use the word ὀργή, he asserts that God's wrath threatens his hearers and readers, just as it threatened the people at the time of Moses (3:7–4:13; 10:26-31; 12:29). The notion of expiation is more dominant, indicated by the programmatic statement in 1:3 that Jesus "provided purification for sins" (1:3) and that he made "a sacrifice of atonement for the sins of the people" (2:17). However, the "angry god" was no longer restricted to a particular temple where he could be appeased: he appears as a frightful reality in terms of a literal judgment at the end of time. God's judgment is not linked with a potential for education[97] but with total destruction (10:27; 12:29). And for Jesus's followers God's anger was not merely limited but abrogated. The statement in 8:12 that God promised he would "forgive" (ἵλεως ἔσομαι) his people's wickedness and never again remember their sins (quoting Jer. 31:34) is utterly surprising.

While the language of purification was used in connection with Greek and Roman cults, the repeated references to purification connected with blood (9:13, 22, 22) and sacrifices (10:2) in Hebrews are distinctly Jewish. The emphasis on the purification of the conscience (10:22) and on the once-and-for-all character of the purification effected by Jesus (10:2) was distinctly Christian, as was the foundational statement in 1:3 that Jesus "made purification (καθαρισμόν) for sins"[98] and the exhortation in 12:22, "let us approach with a true heart in full assurance of faith, with our hearts sprinkled clean from an evil conscience and our bodies washed with pure water."

Parallels with the confession inscriptions include the notions of divine punishment for sinners, the necessity of removing the wrath of God, atonement for sin, the power

---

[94] ESV, NASB "make propitiation"; NIV "make atonement"; NRSV "make a sacrifice of atonement"; RSV "make expiation"; GNB "would be forgiven"; NLT "take away."
[95] BDAG "place of propitiation"; NIV "atonement cover"; GNB "the place where sins are forgiven"; ESV, NASB, NRSV, RSV "mercy seat."
[96] Cf. Craig R. Koester, *Hebrews* (AB, 36; New York: Doubleday, 2001), pp. 121–22, 241.
[97] Várhelyi, "Forgivenesss," p. 131.
[98] Cf. Marshall, "Soteriology," pp. 254–55, on the centrality and importance of "salvation by cleansing" in Hebrews. Also Gräßer, *Hebräer*, 1:64.

of God (1:3: God sustains all things "by his powerful word," τῷ ῥήματι τῆς δυνάμεως), the need for the confession of sins (3:1: Jesus is ἀρχιερεὺς τῆς ὁμολογίας ἡμῶν; 4:14: "let us hold fast to our confession," κρατῶμεν τῆς ὁμολογίας; 10:23: "let us hold fast to the confession of our hope without wavering"; 13:15: praise to God is "the fruit of lips that confess his name"), and the praise of God (2:12; 13:15).

For Henk Versnel, the most obvious difference between Greek religiosity and Christian belief and practice is "the disparity between purely physical salvation through the vicarious death of another in the pagan evidence, and the more theological perspective of Jesus's self-sacrifice for many, as transparent in the occasional specification that it is for their/our sins and thus—implicitly and consequently— intended as a salvation from the wrath of God."[99] Versnel adds, "The element 'sin' is in my view a definitely non-pagan conception."

Vicarious death

The concept of self-sacrifice and vicarious death which has a not insignificant role in Greek and Roman tradition can be compared to the references in Hebrews which speak of Jesus offering himself as sacrifice, and to passages that state that Jesus died on behalf of (ὑπέρ) others. In 9:12, 14 the author asserts that Jesus "entered the Most Holy Place" not by means of the blood of goats and calves but "by his own blood (διὰ δὲ τοῦ ἰδίου αἵματος εἰσῆλθεν ἐφάπαξ εἰς τὰ ἅγια), thus obtaining eternal redemption": Jesus "offered himself (ἑαυτὸν προσήνεγκεν) unblemished to God." When Jesus died, he "offered (προσενέγκας) for all time one sacrifice for sins" (10:12).[100] As regards references to the effect that Jesus died on behalf of (ὑπέρ) others, the author asserts that Jesus suffered death "so that by the grace of God he might taste death "for everyone" (ὑπὲρ παντός; 2:9). He is a "forerunner on our behalf" (πρόδρομος ὑπὲρ ἡμῶν; 6:20). He is "able for all time so save those who approach God through him (δι᾽ αὐτοῦ), since he always lives to make intercession for them (ὑπὲρ αὐτῶν)" (7:25). He entered heaven "to appear in the presence of God on our behalf (ὑπὲρ ἡμῶν)" (9:24). Jesus's death is exemplary since "glory" and "honor" with which Jesus was crowned "because of the suffering of death" (2:9) are connected with Jesus's faithfulness in hardship and with his humility in identifying with humankind (2:11), which in turn are expected of the believers who must lay sin aside and persevere (12:1-2) and endure the reproach that Jesus endured (13:12-13), and since Jesus suffered and was exalted to God's right hand (1:3), the believers in Jesus who suffer will receive a kingdom that cannot be shaken (12:28).[101] And Jesus's death is salvific since it is grounded in "the grace of God" and since his death is "for everyone" (2:9)—a death that constitutes "a sacrifice of atonement for the sins of the people" (εἰς τὸ ἱλάσκεσθαι τὰς ἁμαρτίας τοῦ λαοῦ), as Jesus, like the high priest of Leviticus 16, made atonement for others (2:17), a death that constituted a sacrifice for human

---

[99] Versnel, "Jesus' Death," p. 280; the following quotation ibid.
[100] Cf. Hermut Löhr, "Wahrnehmung und Bedeutung des Todes Jesu nach dem Hebräerbrief. Ein Versuch," in *Deutungen des Todes Jesu im Neuen Testament* (ed. J. Frey and J. Schröter; WUNT, 181; Tübingen: Mohr Siebeck, 2005), pp. 455–76 (470).
[101] Koester, *Hebrews*, p. 222; the following point ibid., pp. 222–23.

sin resembling the sacrifices of the Day of Atonement but surpassing the Levitical sacrifices because it needed to be offered only once, because it cleanses not only the body but the conscience, and because it inaugurates the New Covenant with its new relationship between God and his people promised in Jer. 31:31-34 (7:1–10:25).

The most fundamental difference between Greek and Roman sacrifice and the appropriation of Jesus's death as sacrifice is the "location" of the initiative to find salvation in early Christian theology. This is asserted right at the beginning of the homily in 1:1-4 and repeatedly emphasized throughout: it is God himself who takes the initiative in sending his Son who, at the end of his time on earth, died in order that the human sin problem could be dealt with once and for all (2:10-11; 2:17; 3:1-2; 5:5-6, 10; 7:25; 10:10; 13:20).[102] This was "a radical departure from the idea" in Greek and Roman religion "that a human could escape divine wrath only by sacrifice and other means of appeasement."[103] It is this difference that accounts for the fact that both Greeks and Romans believed that political communities had the right to legislate on the gods and the sacrifices they required,[104] while Israelites and Jews believed that it was only the one true God himself who could legislate on the proper ways of worshiping him, while Christians believed that as a result of God's revelation in Jesus, God can be properly and effectively worshipped only through faith in Jesus, the crucified Messiah and Savior.

Conclusion

The expiatory or propitiatory sacrifices of the Greeks removed sin and averted the wrath of a particular god. Jesus's death is a singular act that not only removes sin and averts divine judgment but also brings about a right relationship with God which requires no further sacrifices (10:11-18), a relationship with the God who speaks (12:25), with God the Father who disciplines his children for their good, to consolidate their holiness and to give them the harvest of righteousness and peace (12:4-11), a relationship with God who gives to the believers in Jesus a kingdom that cannot be shaken (12:28), who is a God of peace who makes them "complete in everything good" so that they do his will as he himself works among believers "that which is pleasing in his sight, through Jesus Christ, to whom be the glory forever and ever" (13:20-21).

---

[102] The assertion of Löhr, "Wahrnehmung," p. 470, that Hebrews nowhere states explicitly that God sacrificed his son is technically correct but misses the author's emphasis on God's initiative which front-loads his homily in 1:1–4.
[103] Jones, *Between*, p. 104.
[104] Cf. Ando, *Gods*, pp. 95–119 for Roman cults and their expansion into the provinces where they required oversight from Rome.

5

The Epistle to the Hebrews in Patristic Trinitarian and Christological Doctrine

Khaled Anatolios

Introduction

The goal of this chapter is to outline some key moments in the reception of the *Epistle to the Hebrews* against the background of the development of Trinitarian and Christological doctrine in the early Church. The intelligibility and coherence of an essay on the Patristic reception of the Epistle to the Hebrews is likely to be inversely proportionate to the quantity of material forced under survey. Consequently, the aim of this chapter cannot be to attempt to gather together the different interpretations of different verses of this biblical book which were penned during roughly the first millennium of the Church.[1] In lieu of such a quixotic aspiration, the goal of this chapter is both more ambitious and more modest than that of providing a highly condensed summary of an ideal anthology of Patristic comments on Hebrews. The more ambitious aspect of this chapter is that it will seek to present a sketch of some of the key trajectories by which this biblical book informed the development of Trinitarian and Christological doctrine in the early Church and was itself interpreted in light of Trinitarian and Christological doctrinal presuppositions. In keeping with the focus of this collection, particular attention will be paid to the Patristic reception of the notions of sacrifice and atonement in this biblical text. The task of showing how the reading of Hebrews, especially with respect to its soteriology, was integral to the formation of the early Church's Trinitarian and Christological doctrine is best served by tracing the reception of this text within particular theological texts and its constructive integration with the theological frameworks of these particular texts. Hence arises the more modest material scope of this chapter, which will jettison a survey approach in favor of a limited selection of key authors and texts. First, I will analyze the impact of Hebrews

---

[1] For such an anthology of selected Patristic commentary on Hebrews, see Erik M. Heen and Philip D. W. Krey, *Hebrews* (Ancient Christian Commentary on Scripture, New Testament 10; Downers Grove: Intervarsity Press, 2005). For a more thematic survey, see Rowan A. Greer, *The Captain of Our Salvation. A Study in the Patristic Exegesis of Hebrews*. (Beiträge zur Geschichte der Biblischen Exegese; Tübingen: J.C.B. Mohr, 1975). For a more condensed survey, see Luke Timothy Johnson, *Hebrews: A Commentary* (NTL; Louisville: Westminster John Knox, 2006), pp. 3–8.

on the Trinitarian theology and Christology of Athanasius in his *On the Incarnation* and *Orations against the Arians*. Secondly, I will turn to the role of Hebrews in Cyril of Alexandria's Christology of hypostatic union, as gleaned from his mature work, *On the Unity of Christ*, as well as from his fragments from a commentary on Hebrews. Thirdly, I will focus on Maximus the Confessor's integration into his soteriology of the characterization in Hebrews of Christ as a High Priest "tested in every respect as we are, yet without sin" (Heb. 4:15). I will conclude with Augustine's understanding of the High-Priestly sacrifice of Christ.

Athanasius

The fifth-century theologian, Theodoret of Cyrus, tells us that the Arians rejected Hebrews as part of the canon.[2] If that is true, this rejection likely postdates the early phases of the controversy and would be a reaction to the pro-Nicene use of this biblical text in defense of Nicene theology of the consubstantiality of the Father and the Son. Writing in the early 340s, Athanasius does not mention a rejection of the canonicity of Hebrews by the anti-Nicene defenders of Arius. Instead, he reports their use of this biblical book to argue against the full divinity of the Son. The two key Arian proof-texts he cites are Heb. 1:4, which speaks of Christ "having become as much superior to angels as the name he has inherited is more excellent than theirs" and Heb. 3:1, which describes Christ as "faithful to the one who appointed him" (πιστὸν ὄντα τῷ ποιήσαντι αὐτὸν) (Heb. 3:2). Both these texts lend themselves readily to an Arian interpretation. For Arius, the key descriptor for God was ἀγέννητος, which is best translated as "the one without becoming."[3] This descriptor served to differentiate the one unique entity whose being was underived, and was thus fully God, from any other whose being was derived and thus came into being, including the Son. Since Heb. 1:4 speaks of Christ's "becoming" (γενόμενος) superior to the angels, it was used to align the Son with the realm of creatures who "come into being" (γίγνεσθαι), and whose ontological status was altogether other than the one true and Unoriginated God. Hebrews 3:1, which describes Jesus Christ as "faithful to the one who appointed him," according to the RSV translation, uses the verb "ποιέω" in Greek, which usually means "to make," and was so read by the Arians as scriptural proof that the Son was "made" from nothing, as were other creatures. According to this reading, Heb. 1:3 neatly complemented another Arian proof-text, Prov. 8:22, in which the preexistent Christ, as Wisdom, says, "He created me as the beginning of his ways, for his works." (Prov. 8:22). Aside from these semantic proofs, the references to the weakness and suffering of Christ in Hebrews were also easily read in support of Arius's doctrine and posed a challenge for the Nicene affirmation of the full divinity of the Son. This challenge is

---

[2] Theodoret complains of "those who give admittance to the Arian disease . . . separating the letter to the Hebrews from the others and calling it 'spurious.'" Theodoret of Cyrus, *Commentary on the Letters of St. Paul.* (vol. 2; trans. by Robert Charles Hill; Brookline, MA: Holy Cross Orthodox Press, 2001), p. 136.

[3] On Arius's doctrine, see my *Retrieving Nicaea. The Meaning and Development of Trinitarian Doctrine* (Grand Rapids, MI: Baker Academic, 2011), pp. 42–52.

indicated by a letter from the Alexandrian bishop, Alexander, written at the eve of the Nicene Council which Athanasius attended as Alexander's secretary. Bishop Alexander complains of the Arians: "They extract every passage which refers to the economy of the Savior, and to his humiliation for our sake . . . while they evade all those which proclaim his divinity which is from the beginning and the unceasing glory which he possesses with the Father."[4]

The hermeneutical foundation for Athanasius's reply to the Arian reading of Hebrews is the stipulation that the Scriptures present a two-act emplotment of the identification of Christ, with the Incarnation as the point of transition from the first to the second act. Given this premise, the proper interpretation of any scriptural description of Christ depends on its proper alignment with its corresponding phase or time (καιρός) of this two-act emplotment. We find a condensed articulation of this hermeneutical rule in the Alexandrian bishop's third oration against the Arians:

> Now the scope and character of Holy Scripture, as we have often said, is this— it contains a double account of the Savior; that he was always God, and is the Son, being the Father's Word and Radiance and Wisdom; and that afterwards, for our sake, He took flesh from a Virgin, Mary, Mother of God (*Theotokos*), and was made man. This scope is to be found throughout the inspired Scripture as the Lord himself said, "Search the Scriptures for they are what testify to me" (Jn 5:30).[5]

In order to substantiate this hermeneutical approach on the basis of Scripture itself, Athanasius finds the two aspects of this "double account of the Savior" not only in different parts of Scripture but simultaneously bound together and distinguished from each other within specific self-contained texts. Thus, the Prologue to the Gospel of John describes Christ both as the "Word" who "was with God and was God" and as the one "who became flesh and dwelt among us," while Philippians distributes its description of Christ in the twofold "forms" of God and servant. Hebrews is one of the texts in which Athanasius finds this "double account," inasmuch as it distinguishes between the "former times" in which God spoke to the fathers through the prophets and "these last days" in which God speaks directly through his Son. Since the scriptural writer, whom Athanasius presumes to be the Apostle Paul, further describes "these last days" in which God speaks through the Son as including Christ's making purification for sin, and since Christ's "becoming" superior to the angels is also correlated with this work of purification, Athanasius concludes that the designation of Christ's "becoming" clearly applies to the "last days" in which the Son became incarnate. Similarly, the description of Christ as "faithful to the one who made him" (Heb. 3:1) is aligned in the biblical text with that of Christ as "the apostle and high priest of our confession," thereby indicating that Christ's being "made" refers to the economy of his humanity, in which he became apostle and high priest by "offering a faithful sacrifice," and not to his divine essence.[6] As to the latter, the biblical text offers a description of Christ in

---

[4] Theodoret, "Letter of Alexander to Alexander of Byzantium" 1.4.1–61 in *Ecclesiastical History* (*NPNF*² 3:35; Peabody, MA: Hendrickson, 1995); altered.
[5] C. Ar. 3.29. *NPNF*² 4:409; slightly altered.
[6] C. Ar. 2.9, *NPNF*² 4:353.

his divinity when it speaks of the Son "through whom [God] created the world," and who is "the radiance (ἀπαύγασμα) of God's glory and the exact imprint of God's very being." This description of Christ's divinity is repeatedly put to service by Athanasius as a biblical basis for the doctrine of the consubstantiality of the Father and the Son. Just as radiance is inseparable from light and coexistent with it, so is the Son inseparable and coexistent with the Father. Conversely, to posit the Father's existence apart from and prior to the Son is tantamount to the absurd effort to imagine a light without radiance![7]

It is far from the case, however, that Athanasius's use of the soteriological material of Hebrews is confined only to the defensive maneuver of referring this material to Christ's humanity in order to safeguard the consubstantiality of Christ's divinity with that of the Father. Indeed, the present occasion of a volume on the soteriology of Hebrews is the appropriate venue for introducing the claim that it is this scriptural text, more than any other, which is the cornerstone for Athanasius's own conception of Christian salvation. Moreover, the recognition of Athanasius's use of the soteriological material of Hebrews is the most potent antidote to a prevalent modern interpretation of Athanasius's soteriology which reduces this soteriology to the efficacy of the Incarnation in uniting the divine and human natures without positing any efficacy to the atoning death of Christ.[8] In order to discern the inadequacy of this distorted reading, it is necessary to pay sufficient attention to the way in which Athanasius makes pervasive use of the Hebrews motifs of Christ's priesthood, sacrifice, and self-offering in constructing his account of Christian salvation. The Alexandrian bishop gives a condensed exposition of this account in the course of explicating how Christ's being "made" apostle and high priest should be referred to the human phase of the scriptural two-act emplotment of the identity of Christ:

> Now the Apostle is not discussing things before the creation when he speaks in this way, but rather when "the Word became flesh." For thus it is written: "Therefore, holy brothers, partakers of the heavenly calling, consider the Apostle and high priest of our confession Jesus, who was faithful to the one who made him." Now when did he become "apostle" except when he put on flesh? And when did he become "high priest" of our confession except when, offering himself for us (προσενέγκας ἑαυτὸν ὑπὲρ ἡμῶν), He raised his body from the dead and, as now,

---

[7] For a more detailed exposition of this "shared names, shared essence," exegetical procedure, see *Retrieving Niceae*, pp. 110–14.

[8] The most notorious recent example of the assessment that Athanasius has a narrowly Incarnational soteriology that abstracts from atonement is that of R. P. C. Hanson, *The Search for the Christian Doctrine of God: The Arian Controversy 318-381 AD.* (New York: T&T Clark, 1988), pp. 450–51: "One of the curious results of this theology of the Incarnation is that it almost does away with a doctrine of the Atonement. Of course Athanasius believes in the Atonement, in Christ's death as saving, but he cannot really explain why Christ should have died. When in chapters 19 and following of the *De Incarnatione* he begins trying to explain the necessity of Christ's death, he can only present a series of puerile reasons unworthy of the rest of the treatise. The fact is that his doctrine of the Incarnation has almost swallowed up any doctrine of the Atonement, rendered it unnecessary. Once the *Logos* has taken human flesh on himself, in a sense, certainly in principle, redemption is accomplished . . . . Sometimes he gives the impression that our redemption is a kind of sacred blood-transfusion, or an affair of mass-transference almost independent of our act of faith."

Himself brings near and offers to the Father (προσάγει καὶ προσφέρει τῷ πατρὶ) those who approach him in faith .... When the Father willed that ransom should be paid for all and grace given to all, then did the Word truly take earthly flesh ... having Mary, like untilled earth, as the mother of his body, so that, having an offering as high priest, he might offer himself to the Father (ἑαυτὸν προσενέγκῃ τῷ πατρὶ), and cleanse us all from sins in His own blood, and might rise from the dead."[9]

The above quotation clearly demonstrates how far off the mark is the claim that Athanasius holds to a narrowly incarnational soteriology in which there is no room for an atonement accomplished through the cross and the death of Christ. Indeed, the aspiration of T. F. Torrance that the epistle to the Hebrews might provide the basis for a "biblical wholeness" in our conception of Christ's salvific work, as encompassing incarnational, dramatic, and cultic-forensic elements, finds an exemplary realization in Athanasius's own use of Hebrews.[10] As indicated in the passage quoted above, Athanasius's use of the notion of Christ's "offering" orients the salvific efficacy of the Incarnation with a view to his sacrificial self-offering which encompasses both his death and Resurrection. The divine Word becomes human precisely in order to have something to offer (his own body) to the Father as high priest; he makes this sacrificial offering through his death; and the consummation and result of this offering is the Resurrection.

Nor is it the case that this conception of Christ's salvific work as sacrificial offering occurs only when Athanasius is forced to give an alternative positive content to an Arian proof-text. It is a little-noted fact that his classic treatise, *On the Incarnation*, which does not explicitly deal with Arian proof-texts nor does it in fact make any mention of Arius, quotes Hebrews more than it does any other biblical text.[11] These quotations do not congregate around any focused treatment of Hebrews as a whole but are interspersed throughout the treatise. Moreover, the centrality of Hebrews to the explication of Christ's salvific work in *On the Incarnation* is discerned less by focusing on quotations of phrases and sentences than on noting, here also as in the *Orations against the Arians,* the centrality of the Hebrews motifs of Christ's priesthood, sacrifice, and offering. Whereas these motifs are explicitly embedded in quotations from Hebrews in the *Orations against the Arians*, which are responding directly to Arian proof-texts, that is not always the case in *On the Incarnation*. Nevertheless, in the latter text, which is chronologically earlier, we see the same integrated approach we saw in the *Orations,* in which these motifs are associated with the Incarnation and death, as well as the Resurrection of Christ.[12] Contrary to the prevalent misreading we noted earlier, Athanasius does not here present the mere fact of the Incarnation as

---

[9] *C. Ar.* 2.7; *NPNF*², 4:351–52; slightly altered. Greek text in K. Metzler and K. Savvidis, *Athanasius: Werke, Band I. Die dogmatischen Schriften, Erster Teil, 2.Lieferung* (Berlin: De Gruyter, 1998), pp. 177–260.

[10] As quoted in Introduction by Jon Laansma.

[11] An exception to this neglect is James D. Ernest, *The Bible in Athanasius of Alexandria*. (Boston and Leiden: Brill, 2004). Ernest notes: "In sum, Hebrews is the most heavily quoted New Testament book in *On the Incarnation*, and virtually every verse of Hebrews used in this treatise also functions in the later anti-Arian writings," p. 96.

[12] There is scholarly debate as to whether *On the Incarnation* was written before or after the outbreak of the Arian controversy but the preponderance of recent scholarship places it after that event.

itself constituting salvation, but rather says explicitly that the primary reason for the Incarnation is so that Christ may die and thus pay the "debt" for human sin.[13] In his divinity, the Word could not die and thus had to become human precisely in order to be capable of suffering death:

> For the Word, realizing that in no other way would the corruption of human beings be undone except, simply, by dying, yet being immortal and the Son of the Father the Word was not able to die, for this reason he takes to himself a body capable of death, in order that it, participating in the Word who is above all, might be sufficient for death on behalf of all, and through the indwelling Word would remain incorruptible, and so corruption might henceforth cease from all by the grace of the resurrection. Whence, by offering to death the body he had taken to himself, as an offering holy and free of all spot, he immediately abolished death from all like him, by the offering of a like.[14]

We see in the passage above the same integrative use of the motif of Christ's self-offering which was deployed by Athanasius in the *Orations against the Arians*. The Incarnation provides the material for Christ's self-offering, his death is the performance of that offering, and the resurrection is the manifestation of Christ's overcoming of death through this sacrificial offering. In the following passage, Athanasius explicitly reinserts the Hebrews motifs of Christ's sacrificial self-offering back into the biblical text, aligning key sentences from Hebrews with 2 Cor. 5:14-15, which speaks of Christ's dying for all. Note once again how the motif of Christ's offering is integrated with affirmations of the salvific efficacy of Christ's Incarnation, death, and Resurrection:

> One may be convinced of these things by the theologians of the Savior himself [i.e., the Scriptural authors], taking their writings, which say, "For the love of Christ constrains us, as we judge this, that if one died for all then all died; and he died for all that we should no longer live for ourselves but for him who died and rose from the dead, our Lord Jesus Christ" (2 Cor. 5:14-15). And again, "We see Jesus who, for a little while, was made lower than the angels, crowned with glory and honor because of the suffering of death, that by the grace of God he might taste death on behalf of all" (Heb. 2:9). Then, he also points out the reason why it was necessary for none other than the Word God to be incarnate, saying, "For it was fitting that he, for whom are all things and through whom are all things, in bringing many sons to glory, should make the pioneer of their salvation perfect through suffering" (Heb. 2:10) . . . . And that the Word himself also took to himself a body as a sacrifice for similar bodies, this they indicated, saying, "Since, therefore, the children share in flesh and blood, he himself likewise partook of them, that through them he might

---

Elsewhere, I have argued for a dating between 328–33. The *Orations against the Arians* were written between 339–43. See *Retrieving Nicaea*, pp. 100–01; 108–09.

[13] *Inc.* 9, St. Athanasius the Great of Alexandria, *On the Incarnation. Greek Original and English Translation* (Preface by C.S. Lewis; Translation and Introduction by John Behr; Yonkers, NY: St. Vladimir's Seminary Press, 2011).

[14] *Inc.* 9, pp. 68–69.

destroy him who has the power of death, that is the devil, and might deliver all those who through fear of death were subject to lifelong bondage" (Heb. 2:14-15). For by the sacrifice of his own body, he both put an end to the law that was against us and renewed for us the source of life, giving hope for the resurrection . . . . This, therefore, is the first cause of the Incarnation of the Savior.[15]

If the preceding exposition of the centrality of a Hebrews soteriology of the sacrificial death of Christ in Athanasius's own conception of the salvific work of Christ should be more than sufficient to discredit any imputation to him of a merely "Incarnational" or "physical" notion of redemption, it should also deter us from any attempts to enlist Athanasius in defense of later "penal substitution" conceptions. Though substitutionary language may be found in Athanasius, he does not use penal language and it would be gratuitous to insinuate any penal signification to his language of "debt." Rather, both his "debt" language and his appropriation of the language of sacrificial offering from Hebrews need to be interpreted in light of the ontological framework that is laid out in the beginning of *On the Incarnation*. According to this framework, humanity's being is constituted by its participation in divine being. Sin is the willful withdrawal from such participation and thus intrinsically consists in a diminishment of being, which Athanasius calls "corruption," and which is manifest in death. Christ's self-offering to the Father is a reversal of that withdrawal and thus simultaneously fulfills the sentence and debt of death, by undergoing death, and dispenses the "grace of resurrection" which manifests humanity's reintegration into participation in divine life.[16]

Cyril of Alexandria and the Nestorian controversy

We have already noted that a key exegetical maneuver of those who held to the creatureliness of the Son at the time of the Nicene controversy was the deployment of texts which spoke of the suffering of Christ as evidence of his attenuated divinity. The declaration at the Council of Nicaea that the Son was "consubstantial (*homoousios*)" with the Father implicitly rejected this exegetical logic but did not provide any intimations of just how the suffering of Christ was to be integrated into the confession of his full divinity. In his defense of the Nicene doctrine, in the *Orations against the Arians*, Athanasius had dealt with this problem by setting up the exegetical rule, derived from Scripture itself, that the descriptions of Jesus's human career should not be directly ascribed to his divine nature. At the same time, Athanasius insisted that human salvation was accomplished only because it was the divine Word and Son who himself "appropriated" the suffering and weakness of the human condition. This positive soteriological emphasis on the divine ownership of Jesus's suffering did not, however, directly address the vexing issue of how such ownership did not compromise

---

[15] *Inc.* 10; Behr, pp. 70–73; slightly altered.
[16] For a further exposition of the ontological presuppositions that inform Athanasius's soteriology, see my "Creation and Salvation in St. Athanasius of Alexandria" in *On the Tree of the Cross. George Florovsky and the Patristic Doctrine of Atonement* (ed. Matthew Baker, Seraphim Danckaert, and Nicholas Marinides; Jordanville, NY: Holy Trinity Seminary Press, 2016), pp. 59–72.

divine transcendence.[17] This question was foundational to the controversy that erupted between Cyril of Alexandria and the Patriarch of Constantinople, Nestorius, in the fifth century, and which set the stage for the series of ecumenical councils after Nicaea, stretching from Ephesus in 431 to Constantinople III in 680–681, which dealt with the definition of the person of Christ.

It is well known that the issue which ignited the Nestorian controversy was Nestorius's opposition to the application to Mary of the title of "*Theotokos*," or "God-bearer." It is also universally recognized that what was directly at stake was not the status of Mary, but rather the proper designation of Christ. The question was not whether Mary gave birth but whether the one to whom she gave birth is properly called "God." Yet again, the question is not really about whether Christ is divine or merely human. Both Nestorius and Cyril acknowledged the full divinity of Christ in explicitly Nicene terms, and they both likewise confessed the full humanity of Christ. The point at issue, rather, was how to conceive and articulate the *unity* of Christ's humanity and divinity. Nestorius's conception of this unity was determined by the prescription that the human attributes cannot be predicated of Christ's divinity. Therefore, the child who was born of Mary cannot be called "God," and consequently Mary cannot be called "God-bearer." Nor can it be properly said that God suffers and dies on the cross. Cyril, for his part, acknowledged that the human attributes of Christ can be distinguished from the divine attributes. But, following Athanasius, he insisted that the whole mystery of Christian salvation depends on the divine Word's "ownership" of the humanity, albeit in a mode that does not compromise divine transcendence but rather elevates and divinizes the human condition. It is only because God became a child and suffered and died, without injury to his immutability, that human beings are healed of sin and death and are enabled to share in the divine glory.

The epistle to the Hebrews proved to be fertile ground for both Nestorius and Cyril, both in their positive expositions of their respective Christological positions and in attacking each other's views. The one substantive point of agreement between them is the use of the description of Christ as the radiance of God's glory, in Heb. 1:3, in substantiation of the full divinity of Christ.[18] On the other hand, the descriptions of Christ's priesthood and self-offering, as well as his suffering and learning obedience were divergently interpreted by Nestorious and Cyril, in keeping with their opposing Christological positions and the distinctive soteriologies that correlated with these Christological views. In Nestorius's case, it has been said that it is in the epistle to the Hebrews that he found the texts that appeared to be most favorable to his Christology.[19] It was self-evident to him that the designation of "high priest" attributed to Christ

---

[17] However, I have argued elsewhere that the "reconstruction of divine transcendence" was an important element in the theological elaboration and defense of Nicene doctrine. See *Retrieving Nicaea*, esp. pp. 104–06; 182–204.

[18] For Nestorius, see his *First Sermon against the Theotokos* (trans. Richard A. Norris, *The Christological Controversy*; Sources of Early Christian Thought; Philadelphia: Fortress Press, 1980) p. 125. For Cyril, see his *Fragments on Hebrews* (of which there is at present no English translation) in *Sancti patris nostri Cyrilli archiepiscopi Alexandrini in D. Joannis evangelium* (ed. P. E. Pusey; vol. 3; Oxford: Clarendon Press, 1872) pp. 362–423 (367–70).

[19] M. Jugie, *Nestorius et la controverse nestorienne* (Paris: Beauchesne, 1912), p. 234.

referred to the man, and could not be attributed to the divine Word.[20] As High Priest, Christ made the sacrificial offering of his own body to God, while it was absurd to suppose that God himself would make an offering to himself, not to mention that the divine nature has no body to offer. For exegetical support of this position, Nestorius refers to passages in Hebrews that underline Jesus's humanity; he was of "the seed of Abraham" (2:16) and "chosen among men" (5:1). To ascribe Jesus's sacrificial offering and his suffering exclusively to his humanity also allows one to accept the descriptions of Jesus's development and his "learning" of obedience without compromising divine transcendence. There can be no conflation or confusion between the impassible Word and the passible High Priest.[21]

The soteriology that correlates with Nestorius's Christological exegesis of Hebrews is straightforwardly transactional. Christ the man offers to God the sacrifice of his own body, accompanied by the submission of his will, and thereby gains salvation for the human race and an exalted status for himself. This is how Nestorius explains the salvific efficacy of Christ's sacrificial offering, synthesizing the sacrificial language of Hebrews with the humiliation-exaltation framework of Philippians 2:

> He indeed has been sent to us of the seed of Abraham, through the blessing which was promised, that he might offer his body as a sacrifice on his behalf and on behalf of his kin . . . . I have said that all the chief priests have need of sacrifices for their sins, except Christ; whereas I have also said that Christ has offered the sacrifice of himself for himself and for his race, that he may release them from the condemnation of the signed bond of sin [cf. Col. 2:14]. While he was free from sin, he yet offered himself for himself that there might be given to him a name which is more excellent than all names, and he was obedient unto death, and while free from sin, he accepted death on the cross.[22]

Cyril also parsed the high priesthood of Christ into distinct human and divine aspects. He assigned the performance of Christ's sacrificial offering to his humanity, and the "authority" that made it efficacious and transformative to his divinity.[23] Christ's priesthood thus is not an attribute of the divine essence but a feature of the *kenosis* of the Word, a point that Cyril made by aligning Hebrews with Philippians 2, just as Nestorius had. Cyril dealt in a similar way with the proclamation in Hebrews that "the one who sanctifies and those who are sanctified all have one Father." (Heb. 2:11) Nestorius had used this verse in support of his contention that Christ's sacrificial priesthood, which brings about the sanctification, must be ascribed simply to the person of the man, Jesus. Otherwise, protested Nestorius, how can God himself be sanctified? In retort, Cyril explained that the self-same Incarnate Word was sanctified in his humanity but

---

[20] Nestorius, *On Heb 3.1*, in F. Loofs, *Nestoriana* (Halle A. S.: Niemeyer, 1990), pp. 232–42. See the discussion of Nestorius's exegesis of Hebrews in Greer, pp. 328–32.
[21] Loofs, *Nestoriana*, p. 236.
[22] Nestorius, *The Bazaar of Heraclides* (trans. G. R. Driver and Leonard Hodgson; Oxford: Oxford University Press, 1925; Reprinted in Eugene, OR: Wipf & Stock, 2002), pp. 251–52.
[23] Pusey, *Fragments on Hebrews*, p. 468.

sanctifies in his divinity.[24] The essential difference between Cyril and Nestorius, on this as on other points, was not that Cyril denied the fullness of Christ's humanity or that he denied a distinction between the humanity and the divinity, but that he insisted that the very core of the gospel message depended on taking the further step of affirming that it was the divine Word himself who was the ultimate subject of all of Christ's human actions and suffering. Therefore, it was the divine Word who is the high priest and the offerer of sacrifice to the Father, even if this offering took place in the humanity.

The intelligibility of Cyril's position is as elusive to some modern readers as it was to Nestorious. While it is beyond the bounds of this chapter to explore all the nuances of its perplexity and possible intelligibility, what we can profitably do within the confines of our present concern is note how Cyril applies his logic to the crucial passage from Hebrews in which it is said of Christ that "in the days of his flesh he offered prayers and supplications with loud cries and tears, to the one who was able to save him from death, and he was heard because of his reverent submission. Although he was a Son, he learned obedience through what he suffered; and having been made perfect, he became the source of eternal salvation for all who obey him, having been designated by God a high priest according to the order of Melchizedek." (Heb. 5:7-9). While Cyril concedes that this description does not befit the divine nature of the Word considered apart from the Incarnation, he insists that it nevertheless indicates the "profundity of the economy" of the self-abasement of the Word. It is as if, says Cyril, the scriptural writer "was almost astonished at the mystery, that he who was truly and naturally the Son, and eminent in the glories of the Godhead, should bring himself to such abasement as to undergo the abject poverty of the human state."[25] In order to plumb even more deeply this mystery of the Word's self-abasement, Cyril aligns this description from Hebrews with Jesus's cry of forsakenness from the cross: "My God, my God, why have you forsaken me?" (Mt. 27:26). While in other places, Cyril strains to find imagery to sustain the paradox that such self-abasement is appropriated by the Word while not harming his impassible divinity, such as the interpenetration of fire and iron in which the iron is not harmed by the fire, in this case he deals with this paradox by letting it take the form of a soliloquy delivered by the Son to the Father:

> It was as if he were saying this: "The first man has transgressed. He slipped into disobedience and neglected the commandment he received and he was brought to this state of willfulness by the wiles of the devil and then it was entirely right that he became subject to corruption and fell under judgment. But you Lord have made me a second beginning for all on the earth, and I am called the Second Adam. In me you see the nature of man made clean, its faults corrected, made holy and pure. Now give me the good things of your kindness, undo the abandonment, rebuke corruption and set a limit on your anger. I have conquered Satan himself who ruled of old, for he found in me absolutely nothing of what was his." In my opinion this is the sense of the Savior's words.... The effects of God's anger passed into the

---

[24] John Anthony McGuckin, *St. Cyril of Alexandria. On the Unity of Christ* (Crestwood, NY: St. Vladimir's Seminary Press, 1995), p. 100.

[25] Ibid., p. 103.

whole of human nature as from the original rootstock, that is Adam: "For death has had dominion from Adam up to Moses, even on those who committed no sin in the manner of Adam's transgression" (Rom. 5:14). In the same way, however, the effects of our new first-fruits, that is Christ, shall again pass into the entire human race. The all-wise Paul confirms this for us when he says: "For if many died because of the transgression of one, how much more" (Rom. 5:15) shall many come to life because of the righteousness of one. And again: "As all men die in Adam, so shall all be made alive in Christ." (1 Cor. 15:22)[26]

Cyril's portrayal of the self-abasement of the Word in the form of a dramatic intercession made by the Son to the Father is a performative reverberation of Hebrews' description of the eternal priesthood of Christ in which "he always lives to make intercession" for human beings. (Heb. 7:9), though Cyril himself does not explicitly refer to this verse in this context. Nevertheless, this soliloquy of salvific intercession which Cyril attributes to Christ serves at least to coordinate, if not altogether demystify, the various elements of his understanding of Christ's sacrificial self-offering and priesthood. The suffering and abasement involved in this offering pertain to the humanity and not to the divine nature. Nevertheless, the subject of these sufferings is still the divine Word, who is personally the intercessor for humanity, while the transformative suffering of his humanity supplies the content of his intercession.

Maximus Confessor and the temptations of Christ

In 431, the Council of Ephesus accepted Cyril's understanding that the person of the Word is the subject of all of Christ's human actions and sufferings and rejected Nestorius's proscription against attributing these human actions and suffering to the Word. In 451, the Council of Chalcedon clarified that the single person of Jesus Christ fully joined a complete human nature with the whole divine nature. In 553, in a kind of reprise of the doctrine of Ephesus, the Second Council of Constantinople reiterated that it was the person of the Word who was the single subject of both the human and divine natures in Christ. These three ecumenical councils, taken together, dogmatized the Cyrillian conception as normative Christological doctrine.[27] One of the modern criticisms of this tradition is that its emphasis on the Word's ownership of the human nature implicitly denies the full humanity of Christ, despite any explicit protestations to the contrary, inasmuch as it does not allow for the real possibility that Christ may be genuinely tempted.[28] The import of the letter to the Hebrews once again comes

---

[26] Ibid., pp. 105–06.
[27] For a fuller exposition of the soteriological underpinnings of the doctrines of these councils, see my "The Soteriological Grammar of Patristic Christology," *The Thomist* 78.2 (2014), pp. 165–88. See now also the excellent treatment of Brian Daley, *God Visible. Patristic Christology Reconsidered* (Oxford: Oxford University Press, 2018), esp. pp. 174–231.
[28] Frances Young, in the context of a critique of Cyril, contends, "It must be regarded as a form of Docetism to say: the Logos cannot have suffered; the flesh suffered but it was so united to the Logos that the possibility of its giving way or succumbing to temptation and sin is not a real one. It is generally agreed that this alternative is not open to us today" from "Christological Ideas in the

to the fore, in regard to this issue, inasmuch as it stipulates that an essential element of Christ's priesthood on humanity's behalf is that he has been tempted, or "tested," just as we are: "Since, then, we have a great high priest who has passed through the heavens, Jesus, the Son of God, let us hold fast to our confession. For we do not have a high priest who is unable to sympathize with our weaknesses, but we have one who in every respect has been tested as we are, yet without sin." (Heb. 4:14-15). For a witness to the understanding of this text which follows the Cyrillian and conciliar conception of the impassible Word's ownership of the human nature and yet endeavors to give an intelligible account of the authenticity and soteriological value of Christ's temptations, we can now turn to the seventh-century theologian, Maximus the Confessor.

Maximus gained the appellation of "Confessor" for insisting, against imperial orders prohibiting the discussion of the number of wills in Christ, that Christ has a fully operative human will alongside his divine will. This confession earned him the cutting off of his tongue and right hand, though it was confirmed as normative in the Third Council of Constantinople in 680–81. About fifty years earlier, Maximus had penned a compendium of responses to questions about scriptural conundrums, ostensibly raised by his friend, Thalassius.[29] This compendium seems to predate the controversy about the number of wills of Christ, though Maximus's later insistence on the fully operational human will of Christ is arguably already implicit in this work. The issue of the nature and salvific efficacy of Christ's temptation comes up in this work not in direct reference to Hebrews, but to Col. 2:15, which says of Christ that "he stripped off (ἀπεκδυσάμενος) the principalities and authorities" and triumphed over them. The conundrum posed to Maximus arises because the Greek verb, ἀπεκδύομαι, "to strip off" connotes a previous putting on. Therefore, in speaking of Christ stripping off the principalities and powers, this text seems to imply that Christ had originally put them on. But how did Christ put on these principalities and powers, asks Thalassius, if he was without sin. Maximus's response to this question about the proper interpretation of Col. 2:15 is framed by the use of Heb. 4:15, which is referenced at the beginning and end of this response. In essence, Maximus's response is that Christ "put on" the principalities and authorities when he allowed them to test him and he "put them off" when he sinlessly overcame this testing and thereby transformed the human condition. A key premise in Maximus's reasoning is that the sin of Adam introduced into the human condition a distortion of humanity's natural creaturely receptivity into a propensity for "passions" that are contrary to nature. This liability to passions, τὸ παθητὸν, made human beings subject to the assaults and exploitation of the principalities and powers: "Through the unnatural passions, and by exploiting nature's possibility, every evil power is actively at work, driving the inclination of the will by means of the natural passions into the corruption of unnatural passions."[30] In assuming

---

Greek Commentaries on the Epistle to the Hebrews" in *Christology, Hermeneutics, and Hebrews. Profiles from the History of Interpretations* (The Library of New Testament Studies; ed. Jon Laansma and Daniel Trier; London: T&T Clark, 2014), p. 45.

[29] For an excellent introduction to this work, see now Maximos Constas's introduction from Maximus the Confessor, *St. Maximos the Confessor. On Difficulties in Sacred Scripture. The Response to Thalassios* (trans. Maximos Constas; Fathers of the Church. A New Translation, Washington, DC: Catholic University of America Press, 2018), pp. 3–60.

[30] *To Thalasssius* 21, Constans, p. 145.

our liability to passions, Christ therefore made himself the target of the assaults of these evil powers and, in that sense, he was "tested" by them. But, throughout this testing, he remained without sin and did not allow his natural human possibility to become deformed into actual sin. In this way, Christ disarmed the principalities and powers by defeating them through the overcoming of the temptations to which he allowed himself to be subjected:

> He remained inaccessible and beyond their grasp, clearly winning victory over them not for His sake but for ours, because it was for us that He became man and, in his goodness, offered to us the whole of what He accomplished. For He himself had no need to be tested by experience since He is God and Master and by nature free from all passions. Instead, He provoked, by means of our temptations, the wicked power, thwarting it by His own attack, and putting to death the very power that expected to thwart Him just as it had thwarted Adam in the beginning.[31]

It might seem that Maximus's exposition of Christ's temptation merely gives further credence to the supposition that the conciliar trajectory of Patristic Christology did not allow for his genuine humanity. But, for Maximus, Christ's humanity is salvific and transformative of our humanity not because it was ever in danger of succumbing to sin but because it gained the victory over sin in the realm of the weakness of the flesh. By assuming human possibility, Christ allowed his sinlessness to be put to the test in the weakness of the flesh and thus "freed . . . the whole of human nature from the wicked power that had been mixed into its condition of passibility."[32] This understanding of Christ's temptations coheres with Maximus's contention, stated elsewhere, that the priesthood of Christ is not restricted only to his physical death but encompasses "the inner principles of his actions," in the participation of which human beings also become victorious over sin and the tyranny of evil.[33]

Augustine on Christ's sacrifice in the Church

As Harold Attridge points out in his contribution to this collection, the epistle to the Hebrews presents an account of the salvific effects of the death of Christ "within the context of a symbolic presentation of the life of the Church" and indeed "as a covenant inaugurating event that creates the Church."[34] Hebrews' understanding of Christ's high-priestly sacrifice as the founding event of the Church is implicitly evoked by various theologians of the early Church, as when Athanasius aligns Christ's self-offering with his offering of humanity to the Father.[35] But this notion achieves the most explicit and thematic treatment in Augustine, and especially in his celebrated sixth chapter on sacrifice in Book 10 of his *City of God*. It is true that Augustine does not explicitly

---

[31] Ibid.
[32] *To Thalassius* 21, Constans, pp. 147–48.
[33] *To Thalassius* 36; Constans, p. 215.
[34] See chapter by Attridge.
[35] See the section on Athanasius above in the present chapter.

quote the text of Hebrews in this chapter but it is nevertheless pertinent to our present inquiry into the Patristic reception of this biblical text, inasmuch as the foundation of its understanding of sacrifice is the notion of Christ's high priesthood, which is only found in Hebrews.[36] In the course of his denunciation of pagan cults and his defense of the unique validity and authenticity of Christian worship in Book 10 of *City of God*, Augustine begins the sixth chapter of this book with a definition of "true sacrifice": "The true sacrifice, then, is every act done in order that we might cling to God in holy fellowship, that is, every act which is referred to the final good in which we can be truly blessed."[37] This definition of sacrifice is meant to encompass the entirety of human existence in both its corporeal and incorporeal aspects, a point that Augustine makes by weaving into his exposition excerpts from Rom. 12:1-2. In the latter text, Paul first admonishes his readers to "offer your bodies as a living sacrifice" which constitutes a "rational worship" (*rationabile obsequium*) and then exhorts them to "be transformed by the renewal of your mind." Augustine takes this mind-body sequence as validating the application of the character of "sacrifice" to both the body and the soul: "And so, if the body, which, because it is inferior, the soul uses as a servant or instrument, is a sacrifice when its good and right use is directed to God, how much more does the soul itself become a sacrifice when it directs itself to God."[38] However, such an integral sacrifice, which alone constitutes true worship is not independently accomplished by human agency but can only occur as a participation in the high priesthood of Christ, and it is this participation which constitutes the Church: "It obviously follows that the whole redeemed city, that is, the congregation and fellowship of the saints, is offered to God as a universal sacrifice through the great priest who, in his passion, offered himself for us in the form of a servant."[39] In a fateful conclusion to this line of thought, one whose precise interpretation and application has been much contested in the post-Reformation history of the Churches, Augustine then aligns this ongoing participation of the Church in Christ's high-priestly sacrificial self-offering with the regular celebration of the Eucharist: "And this is the sacrifice that the Church continually celebrates in the sacrament of the altar (which is well known to the faithful) where it is made plain to her that, in the offering she makes, she herself is offered."[40]

Conclusion

This chapter has tried to elucidate some highlights of the impact of Hebrews in the development of Trinitarian and Christological doctrine, especially in regard to its understanding of Christ's salvific work as priestly sacrifice, while also indicating

---

[36] This point is made by Bernard Quinot, who also provides an excellent overview of Augustine's use of Hebrews, in his "L' influence de l'Épître aux Hébreux dans la notion augustinienne du vrai sacrifice," *Revue d' Etudes Augustiniennes et Patristiques* 8.1 (1962), pp. 129–68.

[37] *City of God* 10.6., Saint Augustine, *The City of God. De civitate dei* (trans. William Babcock; *The Works of Saint Augustine: A Translation for the 21st Century*; Hyde Park: NY; New City Press), p. 311.

[38] *City of God* 10.6; Babcock, p. 311.

[39] Ibid.

[40] Ibid., p. 312.

how this development constituted a hermeneutical background that determined the understanding of this biblical text. We saw that Athanasius applied to this text the hermeneutical rule that the Scriptures presented a "double account of the Savior" in order to substantiate both the full divinity of the Son, as the coessential "radiance" of the Father's glory, and his humanity, in which he offered himself to the Father. We also saw that Athanasius's classic text, *On the Incarnation*, presents the sacrificial self-offering of Christ as the synthesizing motif by which it integrates the salvific efficacy of the Incarnation of the Word, as well as Christ's death and Resurrection. Following in the footsteps of Athanasius, Cyril of Alexandria insisted on the hypostatic union of Christ's humanity with the Word, according to which it is the Word himself who makes the sacrificial offering of his humanity to the Father and thereby makes efficacious intercession for human sin. For Maximus the Confessor, the priesthood of Christ encompasses his entire life in which he allowed his humanity to be the target of demonic powers and was thereby "tested in every respect as we are, yet without sin," thus granting humanity the power to overcome disordered "passions" which are contrary to nature. Augustine envisioned Christ's priestly self-offering as the origin and ultimate substance of the Church's self-offering, which is manifested in the Eucharist. Common to all these early theologians is the premise that Christ's sacrificial self-offering is both a divine and a human work and the presupposition that humanity's incorporation into Christ's self-offering is constitutive of salvation.

Part Two

Themes

6

"Mediator of a New Covenant": Atonement and Christology in Hebrews

Daniel J. Treier

Both Christology and atonement pulsate near the heart of Hebrews; correspondingly, they capture scholarly attention despite the epistle's relative neglect. For a systematic theologian to engage all of the specialist literature would therefore be a fool's errand. Instead, while remaining accountable to what the biblical text actually says, and aware of scholarly trends, here I explore what dogmatic Christology might contribute to understanding Hebrews. My core thesis is that "Mediator of a New Covenant"[1] is a neglected, yet climactic and crucial, motif by which Hebrews helps believers to know Jesus Christ by knowing his benefits.

Immediately, of course, we must clarify the meaning of "atonement" in such dogmatic contexts. The concept can narrow to a term and its cognates (Heb. כפר; Grk. καταλλάσσω; in Hebrews, ἱλάσκομαι in 2:17). But it can also broaden, seemingly beyond soteriology, as theologians increasingly speak of "reconciliation" in very general senses. Traditional dogmatics' concept of "atonement" is neither simply equivalent to biblical word usage nor extended beyond the soteriological sphere—which, indeed, it helps to delimit. In dogmatic terms, then, our exploratory interest will be the saving "benefits of Christ," whether personal or communal.

This exploration proceeds in two major steps: first, a brief, broad overview of how the epistle names Jesus Christ and summarizes his benefits; second, comparison of the epistle's Christology with three sets of dogmatic concepts. The most specific concept, Reformed emphasis upon One Mediator, combines with more widely shared categories—Christ's threefold office of prophet and priest and king—to support the claim that is most ecumenically shared yet most contested in modern scholarship: that Hebrews affirms with Chalcedonian Christology the full divinity of the Son. The epistle's two preeminent Christological concepts—Son and High Priest—are mutually reinforcing in Jesus's mediation of the New Covenant. If that covenant is "better" because it brings believers to know God directly, then this benefit implies the identification of Jesus Christ as fully divine: he is High Priest *as* God's Son—by whom, to whom, and of

---

[1] I dedicate this chapter to the memory of Carl B. Hoch, Jr., whose teaching (and book *All Things New: The Significance of Newness for Biblical Theology* [Grand Rapids, MI: Baker, 1996]) continually reminds me of the significance of the New Covenant.

whom God speaks to lead believers into an eternal inheritance. Hearing personally of forgiveness keeps pilgrims moving toward their heavenly home.

Christ and his benefits

Setting the stage for that argument, the following overview of Christ and his benefits in Hebrews contains two aspects: first, a brief survey of how the epistle names Christ; second, a summary of how the epistle categorizes his benefits.

Naming Christ

Hebrews' first Christological passage is the exordium in 1:1-4, containing *the protagonist's introduction as none other than God's Son*—preeminent in divine revelation and providence as well as redemptive purification, now present (again?!) at God's right hand. Thus the exordium introduces the crucial theme of 1:5–2:9 if not the entire epistle.

The crucial theme of the ensuing, second passage is *the Son's superiority over angels*. Historical appeals to angelomorphic Christologies to explain later developments need to account for such early emphasis on the Son's qualitative uniqueness. Here angels serve the God whose eschatological rule the Son shares. If the exordium does not already establish the Son's full divinity, then the application of "God" and "Lord" from the Psalms (Ps. 45:6 in 1:8; Ps. 102:25 in 1:10) certainly raises him beyond mere humanity. Although humans are created a little lower than angels, that beginning is not their end—as Hebrews establishes with its first explicit reference to the earthly Jesus in 2:9. Meanwhile such a created beginning does not seem to be the Son's starting point in the event Hebrews describes.

A third key passage follows in 2:10-18, focusing on *the Son's full humanity*. He identifies with Abraham's heirs as brothers and sisters in two roles introduced here—as Pioneer, ἀρχηγός, and High Priest, who both suffered under temptation and serves God by having atoned for his people.

A fourth relevant passage, 3:1-6, insists on *the Son's superiority over Moses*, Jesus's chief rival as a covenant leader. Jesus is both Apostle and High Priest, unifying in himself Mosaic and Aaronic offices—having been sent both to lead the people on earth and to lead them into the heavenly presence. Moses was a faithful servant, noteworthy for the immediacy of his encounters with God according to Num. 12:8. But as the faithful Son Christ shares all the more fully in God's household reconstruction and rule.

The paraenesis of 3:7–4:13 adds little directly to our subject; however, at its end a fifth important text emerges in 4:14-16, identifying Jesus as the Son of God and asserting *this Son Jesus's great High Priesthood*. After his sinless empathy with human temptation and weakness are underscored, the ensuing heart of the book's argument will characterize this great High Priest at length—as we shall explore later.

Around the conclusion of that large central argument, a sixth set of passages focuses on *Christ's redemptive self-offering*. Hebrews 10:5-7 sees Ps. 40:6-8 anticipating his earthly arrival in terms of that self-offering. Later, after the transition beginning in 10:19, focus rests on Jesus's blood sanctifying the covenant people.

A seventh relevant passage appears in Heb. 12:2, recapitulating prior themes: *Jesus's pioneering and perfecting of faith*. The shame of the cross lay at the heart of his incarnate mission, with this orienting joy now realized in his rest at God's right hand. What he suffered was not discipline for his own sin but opposition to his sacrificial love.

An eighth noteworthy text is Heb. 13:8, affirming *Jesus Christ's eternity in some sense*. For the moment such eternity minimally suggests the basis for the strange narration of texts like 11:26. Moses was not seeing Jesus directly in his mind's eye when forsaking Egyptian treasures, but, trusting in God's reward for diligent seekers, he was already treasuring Christ above all else. For Christ was already present in and as the unchanging divine promise.

Finally, a ninth Christological text, 13:20, refers more directly to *the Lord Jesus's identity as the Resurrected Messiah*. While the great Shepherd of the sheep is the God of peace, this pastoral work occurs "through" Jesus Christ, making it reasonable to wonder if the eternal glory of 13:21 belongs to him as well.

To summarize, in Hebrews Jesus Christ is preeminently the Son of God, therefore superior to angels, Moses, and any other OT figure. His second major identity as High Priest indisputably requires full identification with humanity—although this emphasis may indicate that it was more controversial or neglected in Hebrews' context than ours.[2] That priesthood's superiority lies in its unique sacrifice, the faithful Son's once-for-all self-offering; in its heavenly presentation and divine approval following the resurrection; and in its everlasting implementation, through the Ascended One's leadership of his people.

Summarizing benefits

Having broadly followed the order of Hebrews' Christological presentation, we can now suggest the chief categories with which the epistle summarizes Christ's benefits.[3]

The first basic category is salvation *from sin*. Its major subcategory is cleansing (1:3), especially of the conscience (9:14; 10:2, 19-22; 12:14; 13:12). Another is freedom from slavery (2:15), and a third is forgiveness (9:22; 10:17-18; presumably depending on the "atonement" referenced in 2:17). General references to gifts and sacrifices for sins appear in 5:1ff., 8:3ff., 9:7-9, and 10:26ff, with expiation in 9:26-28; 10:4, 11-12.

Such a great salvation, however, does not solely fixate on sin. A second category of benefits positively construes salvation *as inheriting eternal rest*, celebrated variously in 1:14 and 2:3; 5:9; 6:9, 12ff.; 7:19, 22, 25; 9:12, 15, 26-28; 10:14, 23, 34-36, 39; and in the way chapter 11 leads to 12:22-29 and 13:14. The promised life in the

---

[2] So Larry W. Hurtado, *Lord Jesus Christ: Devotion to Jesus in Earliest Christianity* (Grand Rapids, MI: Eerdmans, 2003), p. 650: "Amid the diversity of earliest Christianity, belief in Jesus' divine status was amazingly common. The 'heresies' of earliest Christianity largely presuppose the view that Jesus is divine. That is not the issue. The problematic issue, in fact, was whether a genuinely *human* Jesus could be accommodated" (emphasis his).

[3] For an extensive survey of Christ's beneficent actions, see Brian C. Small, *The Characterization of Jesus in the Book of Hebrews* (Biblical Interpretation, 128; Leiden: Brill, 2014). Beginning on p. 3 Small provides a contemporary survey of scholarship on Hebrews' Christology.

eternal city-kingdom will be glorious (2:9-10). Fear that the devil will deny it to us through death has already been overcome (2:14-15). Rest (3:18ff.) becomes a crucial motif through which Hebrews celebrates this eternal salvation, already anticipated in Christian worship though not yet realized in enduring eschatological fullness.

If salvation cleanses from sin and leads to eternal rest in divine glory, then in between—thirdly—salvation involves *holy pilgrimage*. Sanctification appears as early as 2:11 and then in 10:10, 14, and 29 (as well as, by implication, being the fruit of faith in chapter 11), plus 13:12. Being sanctified is the virtual equivalent of being enlightened (6:4; 10:32), with God initially setting apart the covenant people—from which particular persons may later fall away. That no one sees the Lord without holiness (12:14) indicates expected progress for those on pilgrimage, toward doing what pleases God (13:21).

Thus, fourthly, Christ's benefits include *ongoing divine presence and help* for pilgrims. The context for such grace may primarily involve temptation as in 2:18, or times of need more generally (4:15-16). This divine promise is decidedly Christological, as 13:5-8 climactically indicates.

A fifth soteriological benefit, already enjoyed on pilgrimage, is *participation in Christ's approach to God*. The theme begins in 3:1, 14, and leads to Christ entering the heavenly sanctuary (9:24), perfecting those who draw near (10:1), and gaining for them confidence to enter God's presence through his cleansing blood (10:19-22). Such benefits indicate that while Christ is obviously an exemplary human, as our Pioneer he provides more than a merely extrinsic example: he accompanies pilgrims on the trail he has blazed.

Hence, finally, a sixth benefit is *perfection of our humanity*. Τελείωσις language first appears in 5:14, introducing the Melchizedek exposition in which it is most prominent. There maturity contrasts with infancy. Hebrews 7, though, more emphatically references perfection that could not be attained through the Levitical priesthood (7:11) yet is available through the indestructible Melchizedek (7:16). The law made nothing perfect, but believers now draw near with a better hope (7:19), even the guarantee of a better covenant (7:22), complete salvation through Christ's eternal intercession (7:25). Perfection is now possible (10:1), even a present perfect reality (10:14), though also eschatologically deferred (12:23). Perhaps Heb. 6:11 configures this inaugurated eschatology: Christian maturity lies in urgently pursuing full assurance of hope until pilgrims are at rest in their perfect end.

The benefits of Christ, the High Priest who is Son, are therefore positive in emphasis. Salvation is from sin, yes, but ultimately offers eternal rest. Here and now Christ offers the redemptive help and hope that humans need to reach their created end.

The divine mediator of the New Covenant

How does Hebrews' presentation of Christ and his benefits, just sketched, intersect with dogmatic theology? The following argument involves three points of comparison. First, the consensus of the ecumenical creeds—with "Chalcedonian Christology" as convenient shorthand—stakes a threefold claim: the Incarnate Son's full divinity, Jesus's full humanity, and the union of these two natures in the one Person of Christ. Second, intermediately, various Christian traditions speak of the *munus triplex* or threefold office of Christ as prophet, priest, and king.[4] Third, most particularly, the Reformed confessional tradition emphasizes Jesus Christ being the one Mediator between God and humanity. The following argument concerning Hebrews appeals to the third dogmatic commitment, Jesus Christ's mediation, to unify the threefold office of the second and preeminently to undergird the full divinity at stake in the first.

Ecumenical consensus: Chalcedonian Christology

When initially weighing Chalcedonian Christology on the scales of Hebrews, what results? First, least controversial and most celebrated in modern contexts, *the Christ of Hebrews must be fully human*. This necessity arises on account of not just his sacrifice but also his priesthood: this unique Priest—himself—is the offering. In patristic language, "What is not assumed is not healed."

This once-for-all offering points, secondly, to the mutual determination of Son and High Priest, so that *Jesus Christ must be one unified (albeit dyothelite) personal subject*. The Pioneer must perfect the faith of human pilgrims. Accordingly sonship, whatever its exact divine nature still to be discerned, already moves beyond qualitative uniqueness as a form of divine speech to include familial identification with other humans. Simultaneously, though, however human this faithful son must be, his priestly self-sacrifice's eternal character and heavenly venue dominate the central argument (see the summary of 8:1-5 plus 9:11, 24-28; 10:5-14): priesthood is interwoven with sonship by the once-for-all offering, which refuses to allow either to reduce neatly to divinity or humanity.

Thus we grapple, thirdly, with the sense in which *the Jesus of Hebrews is divine—and whether he must be so fully*. Given his aforementioned human identity, for the sake of his vocation as sacrifice, the Son cannot simply be equated with "God"—although he receives this designation. Indeed his vocation already points somehow to eternity, raising the question of how, precisely as *both* Son and High Priest, Jesus Christ must be divine. Hence classic "proof texts"—1:1-4, appeals to the Psalter in 1:5–2:9, 13:8, and so forth—may well merit traditional claims regarding the Son's full divinity.[5] However, the present context of biblical scholarship invites an argument here that would strengthen

---

[4] For exposition of the *munus triplex* reaching beyond the Reformed tradition, see Geoffrey Wainwright, *For Our Salvation: Two Approaches to the Work of Christ* (Grand Rapids, MI: Eerdmans, 1997), pp. 99–120.

[5] For a representative argument from modern biblical scholarship against traditional readings of 1:1-4, see Kenneth Schenck, "Keeping His Appointment: Creation and Enthronement in Hebrews," *JSNT* 66 (1997), pp. 91–117. For a contrary argument favoring the Son's full divinity, see Richard Bauckham, "The Divinity of Jesus Christ in the Epistle to the Hebrews," in *The Epistle to the Hebrews and Christian Theology* (ed. Richard Bauckham, Daniel Driver, Trevor Hart, and Nathan MacDonald; Grand Rapids, MI: Eerdmans, 2009), pp. 15–37. In that volume a more traditional dogmatic reading of 1:1-4 comes from John Webster, "One Who is Son: Theological Reflections on the Exordium to the Epistle to the Hebrews," pp. 69–95. For the dogmatic difference that an approach like Schenck's might make, see the critique of Webster by Bruce L. McCormack, "The Identity of the Son: Karl Barth's Exegesis of Hebrews 1.1-4 (and Similar Passages)," in *Christology, Hermeneutics, and Hebrews: Profiles from the History of Interpretation* (ed. Jon C. Laansma and Daniel J. Treier; Library of New Testament Studies; London: T&T Clark, 2012), pp. 155–72.

the case further—demonstrating that Christ's benefits in Hebrews depend on the self-offering High Priest being the fully divine Son.

Widespread categories: The threefold office

When, next, weighing the *munus triplex* on the scales of Hebrews, what results? These OT offices belonged to anointed human figures. As expected, Hebrews appeals to them in their humanity and with special attention to priesthood. Yet in Christ the three offices become unified in a way that hints at new fulfillment in his qualitative uniqueness as the divine Son.

Admittedly the OT offices and officeholders functionally overlapped: priests taught, kings sacrificed, and either might prophesy, as Moses hoped that all of God's people might do. Ancient background also tempts scholars to marginalize the prophetic office in favor of a unified, binary concept of royal priesthood.[6] Initially these two points might suggest some unity of these offices prior to Christ, mitigating his uniqueness. Yet, to address the first point, periodic functional overlap is not the same as formal anointing to multiple offices. To address the second, there is no simple unity of royal priesthood: although prophets frequently confronted priests and kings, prophecy also shared in the periodic functional overlap. For example, King David was involved in revelation while being juxtaposed with Saul's arrogation of priesthood; Moses, the prior leader and paradigmatic revealer, only made inaugural sacrifices while being distinguished from Aaron's ongoing priesthood. Thus, arguably, Near Eastern associations of priesthood and kingship provide background for biblical hesitation about unifying these offices, rather than a tight OT notion of royal priesthood. Despite the periodic functional overlap, the Bible resists definitively unifying these offices until it does so in Jesus Christ, only anticipating this unity partially or proleptically in figures that typify him. The persistent prophetic critique of the establishment involving the other two—and even coopting other "prophets"—underscores and explains this biblical resistance.

In Hebrews, then, each office presumes Christ's humanity in continuity with the OT. But the offices overlap and develop discontinuities in light of their fulfillment in the Son Jesus. That claim requires detailed exploration of his priestly mediation. But first notice his outworking of prophecy and rule in Hebrews. Prophetic revelation appears from the beginning, underlying the contrast with angels in 1:1–2:4. Here the Son does not direct others as prophets or serve as a human prophet. Instead, he radiates divine glory; the Son's own word powerfully rules. He both speaks and is spoken about because of what his priesthood has fulfilled. Still this divinity does not so overshadow his prophetic office as to deny its humanity: though the Son's humanity is not a primary theme until Heb. 2:4, the Son is compared with creaturely forms of divine speech as early as 1:1. Emphasis on his humanity in 2:5-9 recalls the "glory" already mentioned: the Son is now named Jesus and crowned with glory because he suffered death. While Hebrews seemingly associates the Son's prophetic ministry most

---

[6] Uche Anizor, *Kings and Priests: Scripture's Theological Account of Its Readers* (Eugene, OR: Pickwick, 2014), especially pp. 103–16, addresses the reasons why biblical theologians might head in this direction, and finds variety in the dogmatic tradition, without utterly rejecting the threefold office.

with divinity, nevertheless both divinity and humanity are integral to God's speech in the Son—unifying creation and redemption as witnesses to divine glory.

Putting everything under humanity's feet in Christ, Heb. 2:5-9 recalls the royal emphases already appearing: from the beginning, participation in divine rule establishes from the Psalter the Son's uniqueness. Hints of rule in 3:1-6 pertain to this faithful Son who is qualitatively different from servant Moses. Addressing this contrast merely by attaching Jesus to later, official Davidic kings—as divine "sons"—runs aground in 3:7–4:13: those kings could not provide lasting rest for God's people either. Again, Moses was the preeminent OT mediator in the pertinent sense (Num. 12:8). Near the end of the central section in 4:14–10:18, 10:12-13 indicates the crucial issue: how does Christ's Melchizedekian priesthood count as royal, and become definitively so in an eschatological, unshakable kingdom? That depends finally on the nature of the Melchizedekian Priest-King's eternity—on how the priestly office functions in relation to the fact that God speaks most powerfully in the person of the Son. For now, anyway, it hardly seems right to place the ruling followers on the same level as the Pioneer.

So initially the *munus triplex* correlates with Hebrews largely as expected: less emphasis on prophecy than the Gospels narrate in early encounters with Jesus, less emphasis on rule than the Gospels present overall, and overwhelming emphasis on Christ's unique priesthood. That Hebrews integrates priesthood with the other two, however, hints at the Son's uniqueness as their unified bearer. For Christ's priestly cleansing is the means of their fulfillment, reclaiming divine rule over the cosmos, from Hebrews 1 to Hebrews 12 (and beyond). As further exploration of his covenant mediation will establish, bringing that cleansing to bear on the conscience is now his prophetic focus.

A particular concept: One mediator

Ultimately, when weighing the particular emphasis of Reformed confessions and catechisms concerning Christ as Mediator on the scales of Hebrews, what results?[7] The extended argument to follow suggests that this unifying, climactic vocation implies the Son's full divinity in Hebrews.

The first step of this argument is to establish *the importance of the designation "Mediator" in Hebrews*. This importance will not be obvious simply from word usage. Son and High Priest are the two most prominent Christological titles for the One in Hebrews who is also properly named Jesus and designated the Messiah. Pioneering is another prominent vocation and perfecting its result. Even so, "Mediator" of the New Covenant appears at crucial and climactic points.

We can stipulate the widespread consensus that 4:14–10:18 (or 5:1–10:18, with 4:14-16 transitional) contains the central argument (1:1–4:13 clears comparative ground and builds a hortatory foundation; 10:19–13:25 brings the main structure to its paraenetic apex). We can further stipulate that after 4:14–5:10 introduces the forthcoming argument from Psalm 110 about Christ's Melchizedekian priesthood,

---

[7] To substantiate this emphasis, see Joel R. Beeke and Sinclair B. Ferguson, eds., *Reformed Confessions Harmonized* (Grand Rapids, MI: Baker, 1999), pp. 68–74.

5:11–6:20 digresses with more exhortation (both to remain stable in Christian hope and to move past Christian infancy). So the central argument takes detailed shape beginning in 7:1.

The first appearance of a title that explicitly refers to covenant mediation occurs soon thereafter, in 7:22, where Jesus has become the Guarantor (ἔγγυος) of a better covenant. Exposition of Ps. 110:4 in light of the Melchizedek narrative, in contrast with the Levitical priesthood, comprises the surrounding context. Covenantal change emerges, not just with the law change accompanying the priesthood change (7:12) but also with the ultimate priesthood grounded in an indestructible life (7:16), appeal to a better hope (7:19), repetition now involving intercession rather than sacrifice (7:25), and no necessary sacrifice for the perfect High Priest himself (7:26–28). These contrasts emerge from exposition of the Psalm: an eternal oath regarding a priestly order.

The phrase in 7:22 picks up the surrounding "better" language, integration of "priesthood" and "law" in terms of "covenant," and the importance of the divine oath; in other words, it draws together the expository threads in anticipation of 8:1 summarizing the section's main initial point. The ἔγγυος is not merely impersonal or passive: although the divine oath is its prior basis, Jesus's perfect sonship and ever-living intercession ensue. Both God's appointment and the Priest's actual ministry establish the guarantee. The audience has already been prepared for this Guarantor by μεσιτεύω in 6:17, where God confirms his unchanging promise with an oath—the content of which unfolds in the eternal priesthood of Hebrews 7.

The next relevant title, the first occurrence of the key phrase "Mediator of a (better) covenant," appears shortly after 7:22, in 8:6. The central application of Ps. 110:4 to the Son's priesthood having been established, that argument takes a new turn in 8:1–10:18, focusing on the heavenly sphere of his ministry. Early in that context, 8:6 correlates the title of Mediator with a superior ministry involving better promises.[8] The rest of Hebrews 8 establishes another OT basis for covenantal change by quoting Jeremiah 31. Hebrews 9:1-10 rehearses the symbolic function of Old Covenant regulations, again highlighting the temporary character of the old order. When 9:11-14 resumes the broader argument about the heavenly sanctuary, it emphasizes Christ's blood as that which purifies consciences through his heavenly self-presentation.

On that basis the Mediator title makes a third appearance in 9:15, where Christ's New Covenant makes it possible for the people actually to enjoy their promised inheritance. So in 8:6 this key phrase arises in the context of Jesus's priesthood and in 9:15 the context is Christ's sacrifice. The former helps in fairly general terms to set the stage for the detail of the latter.

---

[8] Space prevents doing much more than acknowledging the thorny issues of "supersessionism" here. Racially anti-Semitic, and religiously anti-Judaic, forms of supersessionism leave Christians much to repent for. When we try to understand what Hebrews actually says, though, some connotations frequently attached to this broadly used term may not pertain. Hebrews argues about covenantal change from what the Old Testament itself anticipates. However much the author's reading is shaped by commitment to Jesus Christ, it does not replace the Scriptures' authority with something else. Rather, Hebrews attempts to understand Jesus Christ in terms of the Old Testament; the aim is not another religion but fidelity to Israel's hope. See further the brief discussion in Michael J. Gorman, *The Death of the Messiah and the Birth of the New Covenant: A (Not So) New Model of the Atonement* (Eugene, OR: Cascade, 2014), pp. 71–72; Gorman's book, albeit differently than here, aligns with the present emphasis upon inauguration of the New Covenant.

Of course, surrounding 9:15 wordplay treats διαθήκη as last will and testament, so that Christ's death and priestly presentation of his blood inaugurate a new situation—both purifying the heavenly sanctuary itself (the controlling thought down through 9:28) and perfecting the human worshipers who follow him (10:1-10). Then the major moves of the central argument have been made.

"Mediator" appears once more in 12:24. Pastoral exhortation in the meantime leads to 12:18-29 climactically recalling earlier warnings: response to Christ makes people accountable to God himself—a God associated with fiery judgment. But not all is gloom and doom: although dealing with the same God whose Sinai theophany terrified the earlier covenant people, believers approach God in Jesus, the reality of the New Covenant having come. On that basis they anticipate an unshakable kingdom rather than shaking in fear.

Again the vocation of Mediator appears in the middle of a particularly important passage: the text's climactic warning, on one hand, and celebration of eschatological hope, on the other, before the concluding paraenesis in ch. 13. Within that climactic context, at the climactic point of the climactic litany regarding salvation—there Jesus is named Mediator of the New Covenant, recalling the central argument. Hebrews 12:18-29 does not merely summarize; it draws together key threads with signal hortatory and celebratory force. Hence, in surveying these texts identifying Christ as covenant Mediator, we see from their location—at hinge points of the central argument and the pastoral climax of its application—the importance of this designation. It does not compete with the prevalence of Son and Priest, but it is climactic in unfolding the unified significance of those titles.

The second step of this argument then follows: to establish *the distinctive nature of this mediation*. That will require treating the word itself, as well as the New Covenant in light of the key OT text cited by Hebrews.

To begin with, μεσίτης deals with what is between, among, in the midst or middle of. In addition to texts already mentioned—6:17, 8:6, 9:15, 12:24—the word "family" appears in 2:12, quoting Ps. 22:22: "In the midst of the assembly I will praise you [ἐν μέσῳ ἐκκλησίας ὑμνήσω σε]." Outside Hebrews there are only two relevant NT texts.

In Gal. 3:19-20 the involvement of an intermediary establishes that the Sinaitic Covenant was bidirectional, in contrast with the promise depending on God alone. Here the intermediary refers to a human being, tied to what Hebrews would call the Old Covenant, operating between God and the people. The larger context, like Hebrews including a reference to angels, draws a contrast with the mediation of Christ. In him, as God's children by faith, we inherit the promise—thus dealing with God directly, enjoying full status as adult children (3:21-4:7) and as such knowing God (4:9).

In 1 Tim. 2:5 the man Christ Jesus is the one mediator between the one God and humanity. He fulfills this vocation by ransoming humanity. While the text does not immediately specify that from which people are ransomed, the immediate reference to salvation (2:3-4) and the prior, near reference to sin (1:15-16) clarify at least the proximate entity from which humans need to be reclaimed. Alongside Christ's humanity as mediator being made explicit, emphasis upon oneness—with the *Shema* lurking in the background—resists relegating Christ's mediation to humanity alone.

Reference to God as our Savior and Christ as our one mediator suggests that this mediator is unique, no mere human.

In any case, the term focuses upon what is somehow in the middle of a collectively plural entity or between multiple entities.[9] The term does not preclude a measure of identity with one or more of the entities themselves, so long as the middle place is filled. As with the Hebrews texts in the context of priesthood, so in the Pauline texts: Christ's humanity is most explicit, albeit in superior contrast to other creaturely mediators.

Next, understanding the Mediator's distinctive ministry requires engaging the New Covenant as Hebrews understands Jeremiah 31 presenting it. Indeed, Jeremiah 31 resonates with Hebrews at numerous points. In 31:1 (plus vv. 20, 28) the Lord makes a promissory oath about restoring Israel as his people. In 31:2 they are on a wilderness pilgrimage. In 31:4 (plus v. 28) they will be built up. In 31:6 they will be called to Zion for worship. In 31:9 God and Israel have a father-son relationship. In 31:11 God ransoms or redeems the people. In 31:12 their joy (already referenced) will be such that they no longer grow faint or weary (see also v. 25). In 31:14 priests will be granted abundant provisions. In 31:17 there is hope for weeping Rachel's posterity. In 31:18 Israel has learned from divine discipline. In 31:22 the Lord promises something new while asking how long the people will vacillate. In 31:23 restoration will make Jerusalem a holy mountain. In 31:26 rest appears. In 31:30 people will die for their own sins; within the covenant community personal responsibility emerges more clearly. In 31:35-37 Israel has a promise of remaining divine descendants. In 31:38-40 Jerusalem will be rebuilt as God's special city.

The point of this litany is not to suggest linguistic or intentional thematic connections with Hebrews in every case, but to establish that Jer. 31:31-34 is not cited on a narrow basis. Its broader context anticipates Israel's covenant restoration with themes that are prominent in Hebrews' understanding: promise, pilgrimage, worship, filial relationship and discipline, joy and redemption, with all of these serving and served by Jerusalem's restoration.[10]

What then does Hebrews take Jer. 31:31-34 to contribute? Most of the several differences between Hebrews' quotation and the Masoretic Text are understandable either in homiletical context or in light of a Greek original, as suggested by relative proximity to the Septuagint. Hebrews makes no explicit reference to restoration in the land, while more emphatically negating the need for teaching others to know God. Hebrews takes the former covenant to involve divinely planned obsolescence: it did not ensure that the people would keep faith. In the New Covenant, with God placing his law inside the people's hearts, no one will teach neighbors or siblings to know God.

---

[9] Directly following the article in *BDAG*, p. 634b, Craig R. Koester, *Hebrews: A New Translation with Introduction and Commentary* (AB; New York: Doubleday, 2001), pp. 378-79, suggests that the term has two facets: an intermediary helping to resolve a dispute or reach a goal, and a guarantor or surety. Both of these facets certainly are convenient for Hebrews' argument. The term itself does not preclude the theologically implicit need argued for here: someone mediating as surety between God and humanity, in the relevant sense, must be fully divine and not just human or (if it were possible) partially divine.

[10] Without embracing the thesis of Gabriella Gelardini, "Hebrews, An Ancient Synagogue Homily for *Tisha Be-Av*: Its Function, Its Basis, Its Theological Interpretation," in *Hebrews: Contemporary Methods—New Insights* (ed. Gabriella Gelardini; Leiden: Brill, 2005), pp. 107-27, its evidence is telling for the importance of 8:7-13 and the Jeremiah text in Hebrews' argument.

Now the Christological contrast with angels and Moses comes into its own. These external mediators of the Old Covenant law must leave the picture since internalization of knowing God lies at the heart of the New Covenant. The point is not simply, as softer translations have it, that there is no longer need for teaching: when it comes to knowing God *in the sense addressed here*, there will be no external, merely human teaching. Teachers can acknowledge the strength of this claim without panic since Hebrews obviously affirms, accomplishes, and appeals for teaching in other senses. Such teaching offers important theological resources and pastoral incentives for Christian maturity. Yet its outcome remains dependent upon faithful responses, so only its participation in God's New Covenant self-communicating Word by the Spirit renders it effective. Presumably such participation is the author's own hope for the epistle's effectiveness.

The end of this New Covenant passage adds another way in which the form of covenant mediation is fundamentally new: God will be merciful, remembering their sins no more. God promises to do this himself, yet according to Hebrews the means is the mediation of Christ—his priestly presentation of his self-sacrifice. This forgiveness is comprehensive, direct, and eternal, in a way that can actually be internalized by the conscience. Such is the reassurance that people can truly know God, trusting his promise and obeying his instruction. Jeremiah 31:31-34 has the fundamentally new character of this covenant consist in the absence of former forms of mediation. Hebrews has the fundamentally new character of this covenant consist in Christ's mediation. Therefore this fundamentally new form of covenant mediation in Christ is not external but internal, in which believers deal with God directly yet without the expected terror. Hebrews makes much of this argument in terms of priesthood, but the broader concept of mediation ties that together with Christ's divine sonship: in him believers hear from God directly, hearing chiefly that they are forgiven.

Having established the importance of the designation "Mediator" and the distinctive nature of this mediation, the argument now takes its third step, to establish *the basis and result of this distinctive mediation*. This step requires examining the perfection that this New Covenant Mediator attains as well as the eternity upon which this attainment depends. As already apparent regarding priesthood and sacrifice, so here dogmatic theology must begin with Jesus's full humanity. Christ was perfected in human suffering (2:10) and obedience (5:8). Since he endured temptation without sin (4:15), the perfecting runs not from unrighteousness to righteousness but from infancy to maturity. Christ perfects pilgrims by taking them on a path he himself walked—without wandering.

On this basis, in part, he is the Pioneer of their pilgrimage. But he offers more than an expiatory sacrifice or exemplary humanity before God. In contrast with the law and its imperfect priesthood (7:19), the Guarantor (7:22) is himself perfect not only in needing no sacrifice for sin but also in having an indestructible life and saving people completely via continual intercession (7:23–28). The next Mediator text, 8:6, bases the New Covenant's superiority on better promises that cluster around this reassurance: God will not—cannot—find fault with the New Covenant people perfected in Christ. The Old Covenant sacrifices could not clear the worshiper's conscience (9:9) but Christ has entered the more perfect, heavenly tabernacle with his self-offering:

thereby he can cleanse the conscience (9:11-14). That introduces the third Mediator text, 9:15, wherein all who are called receive the promised eternal inheritance—as the ensuing treatment of Christ's once-for-all sacrifice explains in terms of cleansed, confident consciences freeing believers to approach God, encourage each other, and hold fast to hope. Chapters 11 and 12 continue this focus on pilgrims following in the steps of their perfect Pioneer, proleptically drawing near to God in anticipation of finally reaching their eternal home. Such is the context of the fourth Mediator text, the climax of 12:24.

Granted that the Priest's perfection must be human, can it be merely human? We encounter a bevy of references to eternity. Can they all be a function of a special, resurrected human—merely an everlasting and not a fully divine figure?

If Hebrews' affirmation of the Son's full divinity were completely explicit and conceptually tidy, perhaps modern scholarship would enjoy more consensus and this present argument would be unnecessary. Presumably such a clear affirmation would have rendered some of the early church's struggles unnecessary, so those struggles limit what we could realistically ask of Hebrews. We cannot ask for indisputable exegetical evidence that Hebrews intentionally affirmed Christ's full divinity with the conceptual apparatus of Chalcedonian Christology. Nevertheless, we can ask if Christ's priestly ministry and covenant mediation require that he be the eternal divine Son, not just an everlasting (because resurrected) messianic figure. In short, we can ask whether Hebrews speaks of Christ's New Covenant benefits in ways that implicitly—perhaps without the author's full recognition—require the Son's full divinity. The function of exegetical evidence—here concerning eternity—is to signal that presuppositions, implications, and entailments of the text's argument head in this direction.

Thus, from the beginning, the Son's cleansing of sin precedes returning to the Creator's right hand (1:2-3)—establishing a preliminary, not just eventually everlasting, context for the eternal high priesthood. The indestructible life of 7:16, when contrasted with earthly ancestry, becomes more than just everlasting. The Incarnation appears in 9:11 and 9:26: Christ has come from somewhere, and his second appearance in 9:28 will come from the heavenly sanctuary. His once-for-all sacrifice at the culmination of the ages has retrospective, not just prospective, force, dealing with all of the sin that the former covenant could only address in its temporary and symbolic or partial way. The heavenly tabernacle's transcendence of the earthly creation also hints at the qualitatively distinct perfection of this Christ, putting the myriad other references to eternity within this central argument in a glorious light.

So in 10:5 Christ's first coming into our cosmos again has an implicitly heavenly origin. This One knows the true meaning of Psalm 40 regarding human self-offering from the very beginning and with authority. When he perfects people forever, his one sacrifice affects the past as well as the future—as 11:26 suggests. Once 13:8 insists that Jesus Christ is the same yesterday and today and forever, we have been well prepared—not to ignore his first and second comings but to recognize the significance of the eternal true God-language.

If this Mediator's priestly ministry involves a unique sacrifice and enduring intercession, how can troubled consciences be confident that this self-offering is acceptable—that they are really cleansed? The basis of such confidence is that no merely external self-offering has been made: God has offered himself to take away sin, taking it upon himself to provide the requisite human faithfulness. Accordingly, this covenant mediation perfects consciences so that the people reach the end of their pilgrimage. The basis of this mediation is the divine Son's perfection as High Priest: the perfection is human, yes, but Jesus does not merely pioneer a path to follow; he also presents in God's presence, himself, by the eternal Spirit (9:14), perfect worship in which his people participate. Furthermore, his perfect self-offering enacts God's eternally loving plan.

We can draw out more clearly the implications of the appeal to eternity by taking a final, fourth step in the argument: to establish the *unifying uniqueness of this mediation*. Notice the union of eternal priesthood with kingship: the Melchizedekian High Priest who goes ahead to salvation's unshakable kingdom is the King of peace. Entering God's resting place involves human sharing in Christ's rule, but sitting at God's right hand is the divine Son whose saving work has reclaimed—himself (1:8)—God's rightful rule over the cosmos (1:2-3). This unity of kingship with priesthood simultaneously signals the unity of creation with redemption.

How does God administer this reclaimed rule? Hebrews repeatedly has God exercising power through his Word, by speaking. God creates, promises, invites, commands, warns, testifies, reassures, exhorts, commends, disciplines, shakes, stabilizes, and through it all teaches: in the New Covenant the people do not teach each other to know God because God himself does so. Who is the Mediator of that teaching? The Son, himself the ultimate form of the divine Word. Kingship and prophecy unite, and again creation and redemption unite. Prophecy and priesthood unite too, given God's chief New Covenant declaration in Christ: he will remember our sins no more. The Son perfects his people not just by pioneering and presenting perfect humanity before God but also by personally proclaiming God's forgiving Word to humanity.

"Mediator of a New Covenant," then, implies the unity of Prophet and Priest and King, and of Pioneer and Perfecter of faith, while explaining the unity and prominence of Son and High Priest. Christ's mediation is climactic, integrating all of covenant history—creation and redemption and consummation. Furthermore, Christ's mediation unifies not just the prior mediating offices that it replaces, and the epochs of salvation history, but also the life histories of the covenant people.

Whether particularly Jewish or not, Hebrews' audience faced a problem of confidence, struggling to persevere toward the heavenly city and to help each other along the way. But their problems were not merely moral or spiritual in the sense of laziness or isolation. Their sluggishness was also theological in the sense of hard-hearted hearing and complacent understanding of the Word. What Word must they particularly heed? Jeremiah 31:31-34, combined with repeated emphasis on Christ cleansing the conscience, reassured the audience of forgiveness and clarified how it became so completely unshakable. What enables God's people really to know God without external mediation is the internal Word of forgiveness they encounter in Christ—the One Mediator who replaces other intermediaries and presents to them God himself.

Can believers really have confidence enough to encounter God boldly? Not if sins remain between them and God. Perhaps a particularly Jewish audience worried over post-baptismal sin,[11] thinking that the Messiah removed the former apostasy but ongoing sins linger. Or perhaps the problem was pastoral and not so conceptual; absent the sacrificial repetition of the old system, consciences lacked ongoing reassurance. In any case, Hebrews makes a virtue out of necessity: the singularity of Christ's self-offering *is* God's reassuring invitation to draw near once believers realize that not only is the High Priest himself the sacrifice but he is also the divine Son who continually intercedes. He intercedes as the One who sympathetically and securely blazed the trail he now helps pilgrims to walk by faith. This powerful Word goes beyond initially declaring people forgiven and continually exhorting them; this powerful Word upholds, intercedes for, and reassures them.

This Word does not replace external mediation with disembodied abstractions; this Mediator took on embodied human weakness without sin and eventually a bloody death. Now this Mediator fosters a new form of bodily sacrifices—praise and good works (13:15). This Word teaches believers to know God gratefully and approach God boldly because in him there is no gap between humans and God himself: the same Word promises in person that God will remember our sins no more.

Conclusion

Ecumenically orthodox Christology came to insist, like Hebrews, on Christ's full humanity: "What is not assumed is not healed." This bedrock principle was apparently harder won for those forebears than for modern people to whom it seems natural. Conversely, for contemporary scholars another bedrock principle is much harder won: "The law of prayer is the law of faith." Yet ecumenically orthodox Christology came to insist that worshiping Jesus as the Son of God entailed his fully divine identity.

The logic of approaching God in Hebrews, I suggest, portrays Christ as not just a middleman but the Mediator—God Incarnate. If we formulate the principle in less worship- and more New Covenant-oriented terms, then Athanasius-like arguments emerge: salvation means knowing God. Salvation does not involve humans reaching upward; God reaches downward. What's more, if Christ's work is to save then in him we must encounter God himself—not just to reassure us of God's benevolence but ultimately to realize salvation's very meaning and aim. "Son" and "Word" are so integral to NT Christology and so integrated in Athanasian Christology because Christ's chief benefit is renewing human communion with God. In fact, the distinction shaping the first section of this chapter—that between Christ and his benefits—can be artificial and misleading. The statement "To know Christ is to know his benefits," is true, but it is not fully reversible: on Hebrews' terms we could not know his benefits in some transactional sense apart from knowing the Living God in Christ—the One who says, "I will remember your sins no more."

Prompted by Hebrews itself and Reformed theological interests, this argument adds a priestly dimension to the broadly Athanasian pattern. Or, in other words,

---

[11] Barnabas Lindars, SSF, *The Theology of the Letter to the Hebrews* (New Testament Theology; Cambridge: Cambridge University Press, 1991), pp. 10–15.

this argument develops a broadly Athanasian version of priestly mediation—both the earthly sacrifice and the heavenly session. Protestant accounts focusing on penal substitution can fall into distortions from a surface reading of sacrifice and priesthood: for atonement nothing is necessary except the death of a sinless human, expiating sin and perhaps propitiating God. These distorted accounts stammer to explain why Christ must be fully divine: the exaltation of his resurrection and ascension signals God's approval of the sacrifice, but the Incarnation seems rather preparatory—largely ensuring that the sinless sacrifice makes it to the altar. At most, Christ's divinity explains why one can substitute for many, suffering for a seemingly infinite number of sins. Such distorted accounts must learn from the Athanasian pattern: atonement involves not just a sacrifice but a Priest who is God's Son.

In return, however, Athanasian accounts often fail to address Scripture's sacrificial and priestly dimensions adequately. Neither revelation nor the Incarnation accomplishes atonement per se. Hebrews works out priesthood and sacrifice in ways that not only require but even emphasize Jesus's full humanity. Moreover, Christ's perfecting work follows from his pioneering path of perfect human faith. Patristic and medieval accounts typically struggle to uphold these truths. Yet Hebrews will not let Christian dogmatics off the hook regarding either Christ's priestly sacrifice or his full humanity: Athanasian accounts can learn from classically Protestant concerns too.

In Job 9:33-35, the protagonist laments, "If only there were someone to mediate between us, someone to bring us together, someone to remove God's rod from me, so that his terror would frighten me no more. Then I would speak up without fear of him, but as it now stands with me, I cannot." These words, speaking far beyond what Job knew, find fulfillment in the Christ of Hebrews. Job needed no mere middleman but an encounter with God himself—an encounter that first silenced yet then reassured him, even establishing him as a kind of priest. Referencing this appearance of *mesitēs* in the LXX, Herman Bavinck notes that the NT reserves the name for Moses and Christ. Moses bears the name provisionally whereas, Bavinck says, Christ "does not stand between the two parties: he *is* those two parties in his own person."[12] That is the intersection of Christology and atonement in Hebrews: as Mediator of the New Covenant, Christ Jesus is the fully divine Son teaching fellow humans to know God, reassuring them of forgiveness in light of his own self-offering and ongoing intercession.

---

[12] Herman Bavinck, *Sin and Salvation in Christ* (ed. John Bolt; trans. John Vriend; Reformed Dogmatics, 3; Grand Rapids, MI: Baker Academic, 2006), p. 363.

Blood, Death, and Sacrifice in the Epistle to the Hebrews According to Thomas Aquinas

Matthew Levering

When hearing the words blood, sacrifice, and death, a Christian unacquainted with the epistle to the Hebrews might assume that these words simply refer to Jesus's death on the Cross. But in fact most of Hebrews' references to blood, sacrifice, and death, while certainly not lacking application to Jesus's Cross, have to do first and foremost with the animal sacrifices of the Mosaic law. Carefully examining the references to blood, sacrifice, and death in Hebrews therefore enables one to do two things: to gain an understanding of the Mosaic law's rituals and to see how Hebrews relates those rituals to the Cross of Jesus Christ in light of the whole OT. The common denominator is the fact that just as the animals spilled their blood and died as sacrificial victims, so also did Jesus on the Cross. But what it means to say that Jesus's death was a sacrifice is much less clear, since unlike animals Jesus had free will (love) and since God expressly forbids human sacrifice. In light of these challenges, Hebrews offers an interpretation of blood, sacrifice, and death that helps to make sense of Jesus's Cross in light of the Mosaic law as interpreted via the psalms and prophets.[1]

---

[1] For Hebrews, as Harold W. Attridge has observed, "The key to understanding the word of God of old is the conviction that the God who spoke through the prophets has finally and decisively spoken in one who is not mere prophet but Son" (*The Epistle to the Hebrews: A Commentary on the Epistle to the Hebrews* [Minneapolis: Fortress, 1989], p. 24). This produces a reading of the Mosaic law's rituals that insists upon Christology, and thus upon the present "eschatologically oriented context," as "the hermeneutical framework within which the interpretation of the Old Testament proceeds" (ibid.). Within this hermeneutical framework, Attridge explains, Christ's sacrifice, blood, and death have both earthly and heavenly dimensions, both of which are figured by the "once-yearly Yom Kippur or Day of Atonement offering" (ibid., p. 26). On the one hand, the requirement of covenant sacrifice that blood be shed points to Christ's earthly sacrifice, while on the other hand the ability of this covenant sacrifice to attain an enduring heavenly dimension and to inaugurate a new interior covenant (see Jer. 31:31-34) comes from Christ's free obedience and "conformity to God's will" (ibid., p. 27). See also Benjamin J. Ribbens, *Levitical Sacrifice and Heavenly Cult in Hebrews* (Berlin: Walter de Gruyter, 2016). Reviewing a wide range of late Second Temple Jewish texts, Ribbens finds that "by the first century CE, consistent depictions of a heavenly cult are found in Jewish literature. An ornate heavenly temple is populated by angels of the presence who are tasked with offering sacrifices and, in so doing, propitiating God" (ibid., p. 80). He shows that for many Jewish texts, "The legitimacy of Levitical sacrifices . . . was based on their correspondence with the heavenly sacrifice," so that the efficacy of the sacrifice was derived from the heavenly sacrifice (ibid., p. 237). Ribbens

In the standard biblical commentaries on Hebrews, which are naturally focused on the Second Temple context before the definitive split between Christians (including Jewish Christians) and Jews, the issue of Christian "supersessionism" often receives little or no explicit attention. Theologically, however, the issue is an important one. Kendall Soulen defines "supersessionism" as the view that "Israel corresponds to Christ in a merely prefigurative and carnal way, whereas the church corresponds to Jesus Christ in a definitive and spiritual way. Hence Christ's advent brings about the obsolescence of carnal Israel."[2] Within this supersessionist framework of obsolescence, Soulen adds, Christian practices and symbols literally replace Jewish ones: "Everything that characterized the economy of salvation in its Israelite form becomes obsolete and is replaced by its ecclesial equivalent. The written law of Moses is replaced by the spiritual law of Christ, circumcision by baptism, natural descent by faith as criterion of membership in the people of God, and so forth."[3] Soulen goes on to identify Irenaeus of Lyons as a key figure in the development of a supersessionist reading of the two Testaments, one that displaces the history of Israel. He explains, "Irenaeus' solution to the unity of the canon reinforces the logic of economic supersessionism at the same time that it underscores the continuity of divine purpose that unites Israel and the church, Old Covenant and New . . . . The Old Covenant is fulfilled by the New Covenant according to its inner christological substance but superseded and displaced according to its outer carnal form."[4]

For Soulen, therefore, supersessionism involves a twofold movement with respect to the OT: "Fulfillment and cancellation."[5] He faults Irenaeus for establishing this enduring supersessionist model in Christian theology and for thereby rendering "the Hebrew Scriptures largely irrelevant for shaping conclusions about God's *enduring* purposes for creation."[6] With regard to the effects of the "Irenaean solution" upon Christian theology, Soulen argues that Christian doctrines have been formulated without sustained attention to the history of Israel and with an "emphasis upon the cosmic and universal dimensions of salvation history."[7] As an example of this unfortunate result, he observes that "the Western debate about sin and salvation received its patristic resolution in Augustine's doctrine of nature and grace. In each case, the dominant categories are those of divine and human natures. By contrast, the Scriptures' testimony to God's history with the Jewish people is almost wholly absent from view."[8] He goes on to make this complaint even clearer by arguing more broadly that the dominant Irenaean (supersessionist) model has an inevitable "tendency to render the bulk of Israel's Scriptures indecisive for the formation of Christian doctrine. Nothing testifies to this more eloquently than the classical edifice of Christian dogmatic theology. Following the structure of the creeds, countless works of Christian theology

---

concludes that for Hebrews, Christ's earthly sacrifice is in fact the true, once-for-all efficacious and atoning heavenly sacrifice, which was symbolized by the Old Testament sacrifices.
[2] R. Kendall Soulen, *The God of Israel and Christian Theology* (Minneapolis: Fortress, 1996), p. 29.
[3] Ibid.
[4] Ibid., p. 47.
[5] Ibid.
[6] Ibid., p. 49.
[7] Ibid., pp. 49–50.
[8] Ibid., p. 50.

set forth the dogmatic content of Christian belief almost wholly without reference to God's way with Israel."[9]

This background is relevant to the present chapter for two main reasons. First, certain passages from Hebrews raise the question of whether the "Irenaean solution" of the Old Covenant being "fulfilled by the New Covenant according to its inner christological substance but superseded and displaced according to its outer carnal form" may in certain respects be biblical rather than simply "Irenaean."[10] It is noteworthy that Soulen discusses the epistle to the Romans but not the epistle to the Hebrews, which (with Jer. 31:31-34 in view) teaches that "in speaking of a new covenant he [the Lord] treats the first as obsolete. And what is becoming obsolete and growing old is ready to vanish away" (Heb. 8:13). Hebrews 3:5-6 observes that "Moses was faithful in all God's house as a servant, to testify to the things that were to be spoken later, but Christ was faithful over God's house as a son"; and Heb. 7:12 argues that "when there is a change in the priesthood [from the Levitical priesthood to Jesus's priesthood after the order of Melchizedek], there is necessarily a change in the law as well." Some form of supersessionism, no doubt, is implied by Heb.7:18's conclusion: "On the one hand, a former commandment is set aside because of its weakness and uselessness (for the law made nothing perfect); on the other hand, a better hope is introduced, through which we draw near to God." If all aspects of the "Irenaean solution" are rejected, it will become impossible to assent to Heb. 10:1's affirmation that "the law has but a shadow of the good things to come instead of the true form of these realities." To put it simply: we should expect Aquinas's reading of Hebrews on blood, death, and sacrifice to operate within a fulfillment model like that of Irenaeus.[11]

---

[9] Ibid.

[10] Scott W. Hahn indicates the complexities of this problem, given that both Rabbinic Judaism and Christianity "are, in a sense, post-Levitical" (Hahn, *Kinship by Covenant: A Canonical Approach to the Fulfillment of God's Saving Promises* [New Haven, CT: Yale University Press, 2009], p. 327). Hahn recognizes that "due to the consistently negative analysis of the Sinai covenant throughout the Epistle to the Hebrews, many scholars express the view that the author leans toward anti-Semitism and advocates a Christian supersessionism. In light of our research, we would suggest that such a view is in need of revision. To be precise, *the author is not anti-Semitic but post-Levitical*. The author grounds the salvation available in Christ in the pre-Levitical form of the (royal) priesthood which existed in the patriarchal period and was promised by covenant oath to David and his heirs. It is not the people of Israel, the Hebrew Scriptures, or covenants that stand in need of replacement—it is the Levitical priesthood and its liturgical economy" (ibid.). For Hahn, the covenant that God made with the people at Moab in Deuteronomy 29 (after the covenant at Sinai and the primal sin of the Golden Calf) is responsible for "the Levitical priesthood and its liturgical economy," which are not meant to be enduring. The key point for our purposes is Hahn's emphasis that "the author of Hebrews is attempting, through his Epistle, to explain theologically how God's people may continue to live in fidelity to the Abrahamic covenant in the absence of the Levitical covenant, that is, the features of its economy: animal sacrifice, the earthly sanctuary, and its liturgy, etc. In doing so, the author addresses questions that lie at the heart of the development of Christianity and Rabbinic Judaism. In the aftermath of 70 CE, both religious traditions had to redefine their faith and practice in such a way as to remain faithful to the promises of God to Abraham and David, while taking into account the absence of any Levitical ministry" (ibid.).

[11] For constructive engagement with Soulen and others, see my "Aquinas and Supersessionism One More Time: A Response to Matthew A. Tapie's *Israel and the Church*," *Pro Ecclesia* 25 (2016), 395–412. See also the perspective of Gregory W. Lee in his study on the Old and New Covenants (or Testaments) in Augustine, Calvin, and the Letter to the Hebrews: "Neither Augustine nor Calvin adopts an unqualified supersessionism that understands the church entirely to have replaced Israel, rendering the covenant with the Jews totally null and void. Both respect the literal sense too much to allegorize

Second, however, we should be deeply instructed by Soulen's point that the *sour fruits* of supersessionism are that "countless works of Christian theology set forth the dogmatic content of Christian belief almost wholly without reference to God's way with Israel." Emphatically, this is not Aquinas's approach to the doctrine of Christ's Cross or to reading Hebrews on blood, death, and sacrifice. Recall that Soulen expresses the concern that due to the legacy of "Irenaean" supersessionism, "Western debate about sin and salvation" leaves out almost wholly "the Scriptures' testimony to God's history with the Jewish people." Again, the opposite is the case with Aquinas's theology of the Cross, which pays deep attention to the Torah.[12] His reading of Hebrews on blood, death, and sacrifice helps us to understand why. In interpreting Hebrews on blood, death, and sacrifice, Aquinas repeatedly goes out of his way to cite the OT and to underscore the goodness and relevance of the Torah for Christians of his own day. I submit that this indicates that the problem of supersessionism, at least in Aquinas's theology, is more complex than Soulen's argument about the legacy of the "Irenaean model" would suggest.

In what follows, I focus upon carefully expositing Aquinas's interpretation of Hebrews' central texts about blood, sacrifice, and death.[13] In the context of contemporary engagements with the problem of supersessionism, Aquinas's reading of these passages of Hebrews might be considered to be particularly baneful due to his acceptance of Hebrews' teaching that the definitive "New Covenant" in Jesus Christ has rendered "obsolete" the "First Covenant" and "what is becoming obsolete and growing old is ready to vanish away" (Heb. 8:13–9:1).[14] Aquinas affirms that

---

God's promises to Israel completely away, and thus retain some place for ethnic Israel's restoration at the end of times. Yet Israel also presents a stumbling block for both figures, each of whom struggles to provide a satisfactory account of God's people across the testaments, or the grounds for God's plan to restore the Jewish people. Hebrews provides a singular contribution to the canonical witness by insisting that the new covenant begins with and cannot bypass Israel" (*Today When You Hear His Voice: Scripture, the Covenants, and the People of God* [Grand Rapids, MI: Eerdmans, 2016], p. 265). Lee argues that in Hebrews, God employs Old Testament Scripture to address his people (Israel) directly in the present moment, in light of Christ.

[12] See my *Christ's Fulfillment of Torah and Temple: Salvation according to Thomas Aquinas* (Notre Dame: University of Notre Dame Press, 2002).

[13] Whenever possible, I cite scriptural texts using the Revised Standard Version (Catholic Edition); the present chapter is intended for contemporary theological readers of Scripture who employ modern translations. When Aquinas's Parisian version of the Vulgate differs significantly from the RSV, I alert the reader. For helpful insights into Aquinas's perspective on Hebrews, see also such works as Antoine Guggenheim, *Jésus Christ, grand prêtre de l'ancienne et de la nouvelle Alliance. Étude du* Commentaire *de saint Thomas d'Aquin sur l'Épître aux Hébreux* (Paris: Parole et Silence, 2004); Thomas G. Weinandy, O. F. M. Cap., "The Supremacy of Christ: Aquinas' *Commentary on Hebrews*," in *Aquinas on Scripture: An Introduction to His Biblical Commentaries* (ed. Thomas G. Weinandy, O. F. M. Cap., Daniel A. Keating, and John P. Yocum; London: T&T Clark International, 2005), pp. 223–44; O. P. Romanus Cessario, *The Godly Image: Christ and Salvation in Catholic Thought from Anselm to Aquinas* (Petersham, MA: St. Bede's, 1990), pp. 35–36.

[14] Considering Hebrews to be a baneful influence upon Aquinas, Matthew A. Tapie argues that "there exist rival versions of Christ's fulfillment of the ceremonial law in Aquinas's thought. This study shows that this tension is most pronounced when comparing, on the one hand, the teaching from the commentaries on Galatians and Hebrews, and the *Summa theologiae*, which states that the ceremonial law is dead and deadly after the passion of Christ, and, on the other hand, the teaching from the Romans commentary, which states that the ceremonial law is a present spiritual benefit that retains a theological value as a prerogative of the Jewish people that cannot be declared superfluous without compromising the faithfulness of God" (*Aquinas on Israel and the Church: The Question of Supersessionism in the Theology of Thomas Aquinas* [Eugene, OR: Pickwick, 2014], p. 183).

Christians now fulfill the ceremonial precepts of the law in Christ rather than through the Mosaic law's sacrificial cult. Yet in his *Commentary on Hebrews* he works to show that the Mosaic law and the OT are utterly indispensable for understanding Christ. He uses the psalms and prophets to make clear that Hebrews' understanding of blood, sacrifice, and death does not displace the OT, but rather expresses the very fulfillment for which OT itself prepares. For Aquinas, if Jesus Christ's blood, sacrifice, and death fulfill and, within the Christian dispensation, bring to an end the cultic animal sacrifices of the Mosaic law, it is the OT that will *today* show us how and why this is so within the unity of God's plan of salvation. As Thomas Weinandy remarks, "Aquinas perceives the whole biblical narrative, Old and New Testaments together, as proclaiming the one complete gospel," so that "it is only in the interrelationship, and so the interweaving, of the whole biblical content that one is able to come to a full understanding of that gospel."[15]

My exposition of Aquinas's interpretation of Hebrews on blood, sacrifice, and death has three sections, divided according to Aquinas's treatment of specific texts of Hebrews that address these themes. The first section treats blood and death in Hebrews 2, followed by a second section on blood, death, and sacrifice in Hebrews 9–10 and a third section on other places where blood, death, or sacrifice appear: Heb. 5:1, 5:7, 7:23, 11:4-5, 11:28, 12:4, 12:24, 13:11-16, and 13:20. My exposition shows the complex significance of the OT both in Hebrews itself and for the task of understanding Hebrews.

Although my chapter is expository in nature, I hope that it assists Christians today in recognizing that Hebrews does not in any way justify the vanishing of the OT, a temptation that Friedrich Schleiermacher exemplifies in his claim that the OT does not "share the normative dignity or the inspiration of the New."[16] By comparison to Aquinas, Catholic theologians today often have a positive theology of Judaism but exhibit little engagement with the OT in their own theology. Aquinas is the opposite: his reading of Hebrews is focused on Christianity rather than on a theology of Judaism, but he draws heavily upon the OT for his theological understanding of Christ. Without needing to follow Aquinas in all aspects of his interpretation, let alone in all aspects of his theology of Judaism, we should allow his reading of Hebrews to complicate and enrich our understanding of Christ and the problem of supersessionism.[17]

---

[15] Weinandy, "The Supremacy of Christ," p. 224.

[16] Friedrich Schleiermacher, *The Christian Faith* (ed. H. R. Mackintosh and J. S. Stewart; trans. D. M. Baillie, W. R. Matthews, Edith Sandbach-Marshall, A. B. Macualay, Alexander Grieve, J. Y. Campbell, R. W. Stewart, and H. R. Mackintosh; Edinburgh: T&T Clark, 1989), p. 608. Schleiermacher adds that "a strong inclination to the use of Old Testament texts in expressing pious feeling is almost invariably accompanied by a legalistic style of thought or a slavish worship of the letter" (ibid., p. 609).

[17] After all, as Jon C. Laansma observes, because the message of Hebrews has "worked itself so fully into the church's reading of all of Scripture, a theological understanding of the whole of the canon is impossible to imagine without this brief word of exhortation [i.e., Hebrews]" (Laansma, *The Letter to the Hebrews: A Commentary for Preaching, Teaching, and Bible Study* [Eugene, OR: Cascade Books, 2017], p. 3). Laansma's point is not only that it is impossible to read Christian Scripture without Hebrews, but that we would not (or certainly should not) want to try, because Hebrews helps us to perceive how "the *history* of God's covenantal speech . . . attained its goal and revealed to center in the *Son*" (ibid., pp. 12–13; cf. 19–20). Laansma makes clear what I would term the deeply "participatory" understanding of history that characterizes Christian Scripture as a whole, and Hebrews in particular. He notes that for Hebrews, "real history is the history of the Son, and

Hebrews 2: Jesus's death

Aquinas's first comments on our topic occur in discussing Heb. 2:9: "But we see Jesus, who for a little while was made lower than the angels, crowned with glory and honor because of the suffering of death, so that by the grace of God he might taste death for every one." He notes that the phrase "crowned with glory and honor because of the suffering of death" indicates that Jesus's death, as such, was not "just any death."[18] Instead, Jesus's death goes to the farthest extreme of human death. Aquinas states that Jesus's death was "the bitterest and most shameful."[19] All death is bitter and (in a sense) humiliating to the one who dies, but Jesus's was more bitter and more shameful than any other, and therefore—although Aquinas does not say this explicitly—it was human death in its deepest sense.

In defense of the claim that Jesus's death was "the bitterest and most shameful," Aquinas seeks insight into Jesus's death from the OT. He thinks first of Wisdom of Solomon's account of the slaying of the righteous man by wicked men. These wicked men reason that death means everlasting annihilation, as well as being forgotten on Earth, and they conclude that the only sensible thing to do is to seek as much pleasure as possible. Given that those who chastise sinners get in the way of such pleasure, they determine to "oppress the righteous poor man" and to "let our might be our law of right, for what is weak proves itself to be useless" (Wis. 2:10-11). This text cannot but strike the reader as prefiguring Jesus's death. No wonder, then, that Aquinas reads, Heb. 2:9 in light of Wis. 2:20 ("Let us condemn him to a shameful death").[20]

The other OT text that Aquinas cites with respect to Jesus's death is Isaiah 53. Hebrews 2:9 states that Jesus "for a little while was made lower than the angels." Following the lead of the medieval Gloss on Scripture, Aquinas suggests that this phrase implies that Jesus was "made lower than the angels" precisely in his "suffering of

---

from it we understand Israel's history. If that seems too abstract and therefore unlikely we should remind ourselves of the comparison of the tabernacles—the true tabernacle preceded Moses's (8:5), casting its shadow down from heaven and back from the Son, and its history overarched the whole of time (9:12, 14, 26)—and then repeat that the rest of the cosmos is understood from this. The universe itself was made "through" the Son and he is the heir of all things; he bears all things by his own powerful word. This applies not only to the history that preceded Jesus but the history that follows" (ibid., 14; cf. 18). For Laansma, both the structures of Rabbinic Judaism and the structures of Catholic Christianity are put into question by Hebrews, insofar as according to Laansma Hebrews' gospel brings "the person of faith straight into God's presence on the power of Jesus' atonement alone" (ibid., 16). From a Catholic perspective, Hebrews does not rule out participatory modes (such as Scripture itself, or the Eucharist or the offices of the Church) that enable us to share in the Mediator who brings us into God's presence. I approach Rabbinic Judaism through an understanding of modes and degrees of participation (which can be implicit) that enables us to affirm, rather than negate, the value of the covenantal election and religious practices of the ongoing Jewish people without thereby denying the call of all peoples to unity in Christ. For background, see my *Participatory Biblical Exegesis: A Theology of Biblical Interpretation* (Notre Dame: University of Notre Dame Press, 2008) and my "Aquinas and Supersessionism One More Time." See also Gavin D'Costa's *Vatican II: Catholic Doctrines on Jews and Muslims* (Oxford: Oxford University Press, 2014).

[18] Thomas Aquinas, *Commentary on the Letter of Saint Paul to the Hebrews* (ed. J. Mortensen and E. Alarcón; trans. F. R. Larcher, O.P.; Lander, WY: The Aquinas Institute for the Study of Sacred Doctrine, 2012), §122, p. 58.
[19] Ibid.
[20] Cited in ibid.

death."²¹ Aquinas adds that in his death Jesus was not only lower than angels, but also lower than all men. He finds this explicitly in Isa. 53:3, which in his Parisian version of the Vulgate states that the Servant will be "despised and the most abject of men." Indeed, Heb. 2:9's combination of Jesus's humiliation with his exaltation fits well with Isa. 52–53's description of the Servant. The lowest human, the human who endures the misery of death most fully, is the one who will be exalted, "crowned with glory and honor" (Heb. 2:9).

Aquinas next asks why Jesus is said to "taste death." Why only "taste," given the depths of Jesus's suffering and humiliation? Aquinas reasons that "a person who has not eaten or drunk much is said to have tasted."²² This point seems to suggest that Jesus did not experience the fullness of death. In response, Aquinas observes that Jesus rose quickly, and so in this sense Jesus only "tasted" death, whereas other humans still await the resurrection of their bodies. Lest this seem to imply that Jesus endured death less than others, Aquinas adds that "taste is a discerner of flavor; hence, one who tastes discerns more than one who drinks."²³ In this sense, Jesus tasted depth more deeply than anyone else, because he freely experienced the fullest misery of death. Aquinas fills out Hebrews' portrait of Jesus tasting death by means of another OT text, Lam. 1:12: "O, all you that pass by the way, attend and see if there be any sorrow like to my sorrow."²⁴ Israel's uniquely profound sorrow at the Babylonian exile here prefigures Jesus's suffering and death.

Aquinas goes on to observe that the image of tasting is suggested by Jesus himself, when in the Garden of Gethsemane Jesus compares his approaching death to a "chalice" or cup from which he would rather not drink (Mt. 26:39). Aquinas states that Jesus's purpose in using the image of tasting is to convey the bitterness of death, by comparing it to a bitter flavor. In this regard, Aquinas once more quotes Lam. 1:12, to which he adds Isa. 24:9, which in its context is about God's cursing of the earth for the sins of its people, an event that will occur on the eschatological Day of the Lord: "The drink shall be bitter to those who drink it."²⁵ Jesus's death—as the eschatological judgment of sin—is preeminently sorrowful and bitter, but unlike us, Jesus freely chooses when to die (cf. Jn. 10:18) and Jesus does not remain dead for long. With respect to Jesus's

---

[21] See ibid. On the Gloss, see Gilles Berceville, O. P., "Le sacerdoce du Christ dans le *Commentaire de l'épître aux Hébreux* de saint Thomas d'Aquin'd," *RevThom* 99 (1999), pp. 143–58 (144): "Thomas interprets the epistle [to the Hebrews] by referring constantly to the Gloss composed in the previous century by Lombard (*Magna glosatura*) that comes to us in two versions, and that itself reprised and amplified the Gloss of Anselm of Laon, enriched by the additions of his disciple Gilbert de la Porrée (*Media glosatura*). Thomas appears to cite the Fathers (Ambrose, Chrysostom, Jerome, Augustine) and other commentators only indirectly, through the Gloss." Berceville's essay is valuable for understanding both Christ's priesthood according to Aquinas's *Commentary on Hebrews* and, indeed, the way in which Aquinas conceives of Christ's priesthood in his whole corpus. Berceville notes that for Aquinas, "To affirm that Christ is priest, is therefore first of all to refer to his humiliated condition in the mystery of his Passion" (ibid., p. 147).

[22] Aquinas, *Commentary on Hebrews*, §126, p. 59. Referred to by section and page number only in the following.

[23] Ibid.

[24] See ibid. The RSV reads, "Is it nothing to you, all you who pass by? Look and see if there is any sorrow like my sorrow."

[25] See ibid. The RSV reads, "Strong drink is bitter to those who drink it."

resurrection from the dead, Aquinas quotes Ps. 16:10, which in his version reads, "You will not leave my soul in hell."[26]

Commenting on Heb. 2:10 ("For it was fitting that he, for whom and by whom all things exist, in bringing many sons to glory, should make the pioneer of their salvation perfect through suffering"), Aquinas places Jesus's death in the framework of divine providence. Alongside two NT texts (Rev. 1:8 and Rom. 11:36), he cites three OT texts that indicate that nothing happens without God's causality, since from eternity God acts to accomplish his purpose of "communicating his goodness."[27] Jesus's death belongs to the work of the God who "has made all things for himself" (Prov. 16:4); "who made heaven and earth, the sea, and all that is in them" (Ps. 146:6); and who "takes thought for all alike" (Wis. 6:7).[28] God's plan from the beginning involves the vast humility of his own shameful death in Jesus Christ.[29] This perfect suffering out of love enables Jesus to bring "many sons to glory." Aquinas explains that Jesus tasted death so that "he might lead the sons to glory, just as a doctor tastes a medicine lest the sick man shrink back from it."[30]

Reflection upon Heb. 2:14-15 extends Aquinas's study of Jesus's death according to Hebrews 2. Hebrews 2:14-15 states, "Since therefore the children share in flesh and blood, he himself likewise partook of the same nature, that through death he might destroy him who has the power of death, that is, the devil, and deliver all those who through fear of death were subject to lifelong bondage." After commenting on the ways in which "flesh and blood" can be interpreted—including its Eucharistic application (cf. Jn. 6:55)—Aquinas inquires into why Hebrews teaches that the devil "has the power of death."[31] He contrasts this claim with 1 Sam. 2:6 ("The Lord kills and brings

---

[26] See ibid.
[27] §127, p. 60.
[28] The RSV for Prov. 16:4 is "the Lord has made everything for its purpose."
[29] Aquinas's teaching here, of course, presumes the Incarnation of the Son of God, which Aquinas discusses in detail in §§17-44. Thomas Weinandy insightfully observes that Aquinas's *Commentary on Hebrews* "clearly articulates two interrelated aspects that are essential to the Letter's argument: first, the fulfilment of Old Testament revelation as found in the supremacy of the Incarnation and, secondly, the ensuing fulfilment and supremacy of Christ's priestly sacrifice" (Weinandy, "The Supremacy of Christ," p. 225).
[30] §128, pp. 60-61. Aquinas gives other similar reasons for the fittingness of the Incarnation of the Word for the salvation of sinners. See also §39, p. 19: "It should be noted that in sin is involved, first of all, a transgression of the eternal law and of God's rights, since all sin is an iniquity which transgresses the law: *they have transgressed the law, they have changed the ordinance, they have broken the everlasting covenant* (Isa. 24:5). Therefore, since the eternal law and divine right stem from the eternal Word, it is clear that cleansing from sins is Christ's prerogative, inasmuch as he is the Word: *he sent his word and healed them* (Ps. 107:20)." For discussion, see Adam Johnson, "A Fuller Account: The Role of 'Fittingness' in Thomas Aquinas' Doctrine of the Atonement," *International Journal of Systematic Theology* 12 (2010), pp. 302-18, as well as Aidan Nichols, O.P., "St. Thomas Aquinas on the Passion of Christ: A Reading of *Summa Theologiae* IIIa, q. 46," *SJT* 43 (1990), pp. 447-59.
[31] Aquinas's biblical commentaries frequently contain theological inquiries of this kind, quite similar to those found in his *Summa theologiae*. For discussion, see John F. Boyle, "On the Relation of St. Thomas' Commentary on Romans to the *Summa theologiae*," in *Reading Romans with St. Thomas Aquinas* (ed. Matthew Levering and Michael Dauphinais; Washington, DC: Catholic University of America Press, 2012), pp. 75-82; Gilles Emery, O.P., "Biblical Exegesis and the Speculative Doctrine of the Trinity in St. Thomas Aquinas's *Commentary on John*," in *Reading John With St. Thomas Aquinas: Theological Exegesis and Speculative Theology* (ed. Michael Dauphinais and Matthew Levering; Washington, DC: Catholic University of America Press, 2005), pp. 23-61. See also Daniel

to life") and with Deut. 32:39 ("I [the Lord] kill and I make alive"). He explains that the devil "has the power of death" only in the sense that he can persuade humans to sin, which he did at the outset of the human race, thus enslaving the whole race to sin and death. On this view, the contention that Jesus's death "destroy[ed] him who has the power of death" refers to Jesus's victory on the Cross over the devil. Referring to 2 Pet. 2:18, Rev. 5:5, Lk. 11:21, and Jn 14:30, Aquinas commends the patristic theme of Jesus's overcoming of the devil by means of justice: the devil put an innocent man to death, and thereby lost his power over the guilty. Aquinas also speaks of Jesus paying "the price for our sin."[32] In this regard, he cites an OT text that he also employs in the *Summa theologiae*'s discussion of Jesus's death, namely Ps. 69:4 (Vulgate 68:5), which in the Vulgate reads, "then did I pay that which I took not away."[33]

With respect to Heb. 2:15's recounting of the "lifelong bondage" to "fear of death" from which Jesus liberates us, the OT again provides a foundation for Aquinas's interpretation. He comments upon the way that fear works to restrain human action, and he observes that "the fear of death is the greatest" of all fears.[34] He confirms this point by citing Sir. 41:1: "O death, how bitter is the reminder of you."[35] Jesus Christ removes this bitter fear and enables his followers no longer to "fear those who kill the body" (Mt. 10:28). Demonstrating the truth of Heb. 2:15, Paul even expresses desire for death (cf. Phil. 1:23).[36]

Hebrews 9–10: Blood, death, and sacrifice

Hebrews 9–10 contains numerous references to the Mosaic law's cultic animal sacrifices. Aquinas's comments on blood begin with Heb. 9:7: "Into the second [the second tent, the Holy of Holies] only the high priest goes, and he but once a year, and not without taking blood which he offers for himself and for the errors of the people." Commenting on the phrase "into the second," Aquinas recalls Lev. 16:29-30, where the Lord commands Moses to institute the Day of Atonement. On this Day, as Aquinas says, "the high priest offered a calf for himself and for his whole house, and a goat for the sin of the people. When these were immolated, he took some of their blood and filled the thurible with the burning coals from the altar of holocausts."[37] Aquinas explains what the high priest did with this blood: he "entered into the holy of holies to

---

A. Keating and Matthew Levering, "Introduction" to St. Thomas Aquinas, *Commentary on the Gospel of John: Chapters 1-5* (ed. Daniel A. Keating and Matthew Levering; trans. Fabian Larcher, O.P. and James A. Weisheipl, O.P.; Washington, DC: Catholic University of America Press, 2010), pp. ix–xxx.

[32] §142, p. 66. For an extensive discussion of Aquinas's account of Jesus's satisfaction for sin, with reference to the range of scholarship on this topic, see my *Engaging the Doctrine of Creation: The Wise and Good Creator and His Theophanic, Fallen, and Redeemed Creatures* (Grand Rapids, MI: Baker Academic, 2017), ch. 7.

[33] See ibid. The RSV reads, "What I did not steal must I now restore?" See also III, q. 47, a. 2, ad 1.

[34] §144, p. 67.

[35] See ibid.

[36] Mt. 10:28 and Phil. 1:23 are cited in ibid.

[37] §426, p. 188.

expiate the tabernacle with blood, sprinkling some of the blood on the veil. After he came out, he used the same blood to anoint the altar of incense."[38]

Moving on to comment on the phrase "for himself and for the errors of the people" (which in Aquinas's version is "for his own and the people's ignorance"), Aquinas states that what Heb. 9:7 means here is "for our sins."[39] He cites Prov. 14:22, which in his version reads, "they err that work evil."[40] The sins that the high priest sought to expiate on the Day of Atonement were all the ways in which Israelites had done evil in the past year.

Aquinas notes that since only the high priest could enter the Holy of Holies and then only once a year, the animal sacrifices did not take place in the Holy of Holies (the second tent) but rather in the "outer tent" (the first tent).[41] On this basis, referring to Heb. 9:6's statement that "the priests go continually into the outer tent," Aquinas proposes a mystical interpretation. Namely, the "outer tent" mystically signifies the Church, which awaits full entrance into eternal life and the presence of the ascended Lord.[42] Mystically, Aquinas observes that instead of sacrificing animals in the "outer tent" (the Church), Christians should sacrifice themselves by acts of holiness, repentance, and almsgiving.

---

[38] Ibid. Aquinas is obviously aware, as Mayjee Philip observes, that "the central themes of Hebrews, though not identical, clearly are similar to those of Leviticus. The centrality of holiness representing God's presence in Israel and its implications in relation to the covenant, the tabernacle, the sacrifices and offerings, and the priesthood, clearly hold Leviticus together . . . . In Hebrews, the context and meaning of the text are undergirded by Jesus as the high priest, as well as the fulfilment of the covenant, the priesthood, and the sacrifices in relation to the heavenly tabernacle" (Philip, *Leviticus in Hebrews: A Transtextual Analysis of the Tabernacle Theme in the Letter to the Hebrews* [Bern: Peter Lang, 2011], p. 60).

[39] §427, p. 188.

[40] Cited in ibid. The RSV reads, "Do they not err that devise evil?"

[41] See §§429-30, p. 189.

[42] For Aquinas's mystical or spiritual (as distinct from literal) interpretation of Scripture, see Thomas Prügl, "Thomas Aquinas as Interpreter of Scripture," in *The Theology of Thomas Aquinas* (ed. Rik Van Nieuwenhove and Joseph Wawrykow; trans. Albert K. Wimmer; Notre Dame: University of Notre Dame Press, 2005), pp. 386–415 (392–94). Prügl explains that for Aquinas, as for the Fathers and Aquinas's medieval contemporaries, "God's 'language' has at its disposal more possibilities than are available to human beings. While the language of humans depends upon words with which to designate things, God is able to transcend words by turning things, events, indeed even the entire course of history, into possible ways of expressing Himself . . . . These two levels of signification are the reason for a second level of scriptural meaning of the Bible. The first important level of signification on which the divine truth is expressed by words corresponds to the *sensus litteralis*, while the designated reality of the literal meaning itself becomes a reference to something different, and then the text is understood in its *sensus spiritualis* . . . . The spiritual sense is further divided according to its contents. Its three variations are informed by the three epochs of salvation history. Allegorically speaking, the facts of the Old Testament are interpreted as *figurae* for the events in the New Testament. Morally speaking, the acts of Christ in the New Testament signify the conduct required of Christians; while the anagogic meaning reveals the life of the Church, especially that of the early Church, as foreshadowing future glory. Thus, all three spiritual meanings interpret the objects of a certain *status* in salvation history as a sign of a subsequent *status*, revealing in fact a uniform direction of salvific activity" (ibid., pp. 393–94). Without denigrating the mystical or spiritual sense, Aquinas generally focuses upon the literal sense. For discussion of the spiritual sense and insistence upon its value today, see Francis Martin, "The Spiritual Sense (*Sensus Spiritualis*) of Sacred Scripture: Its Essential Insight," in his *Sacred Scripture: The Disclosure of the Word* (Naples, FL: Sapientia Press, 2006), pp. 249–75; Karlfried Froehlich (with Mark S. Burrows), *Sensing the Scriptures: Aminadab's Chariot and the Predicament of Biblical Interpretation* (Grand Rapids, MI: Eerdmans, 2014); and Henri de Lubac, S. J.'s classic *Medieval Exegesis*, especially volume 2: *The Four Senses of Scripture* (trans. E. M. Macierowski; Grand Rapids, MI: Eerdmans, 2000).

Thus Paul exhorts in Rom. 12:1 (cited by Aquinas), "present your bodies as a living sacrifice, holy and acceptable to God, which is your spiritual worship."[43] In support of this mystical interpretation, Aquinas also quotes Ps. 51:17: "The sacrifice acceptable to God is a broken spirit; a broken and contrite heart, O God, thou wilt not despise."[44] Psalm 51:17 should be read in the context of the psalm's preceding two verses: "O Lord, open thou my lips, and my mouth shall show forth thy praise. For thou hast no delight in sacrifice; were I to give a burnt offering, thou wouldst not be pleased" (Ps. 51:15-16).

Commenting on Heb. 9:8-11, Aquinas remarks that because Jesus Christ is "the way into the sanctuary" (Heb. 9:8)—the heavenly Holy of Holies—"the Old Testament was unable to make perfect those who served it because the sacrifice had not yet been offered that would satisfy for the sin of the whole human race."[45] Aquinas supports this claim by means of a quotation from the prophet Isaiah: "And a highway shall be there, and it shall be called the Holy Way; the unclean shall not pass over it" (Isa. 35:8).[46] Similarly, when—in discussing Heb. 9:9—he cites Heb. 10:4 ("For it is impossible that the blood of bulls and goats should take away sins"), he suggests that this teaching regarding the inefficacy of animal sacrifices in themselves does not rest solely on the NT. He quotes Isa. 1:13 ("Bring no more vain offerings") and Mic. 6:7 ("Will the Lord be pleased with thousands of rams?").[47]

Indeed, throughout this section, Aquinas is concerned to ward off attacks upon the OT. For example, in commenting on the phrase "the Holy Spirit indicates" (Heb.

---

[43] §427, p. 188.
[44] See ibid.
[45] §430, p. 189.
[46] The "unclean" here should be read in light of Isaiah 59's discussion of the injustice and violence of the wicked (i.e., the sinners for whom Christ died). For reflection upon Aquinas's approach to Isaiah, see Brevard S. Childs, *The Struggle to Understand Isaiah as Christian Scripture* (Grand Rapids, MI: Eerdmans, 2004), pp. 148–66. Drawing upon James Samuel Preus, *From Shadow to Promise: Old Testament Interpretation from Augustine to the Young Luther* (Cambridge, MA: Harvard University Press, 1969), pp. 46-60, Childs suggests that although Aquinas "acknowledges the theological substance of the Old Testament, his great emphasis on the New Testament as the goal of the Old Testament promise is such that its [the OT's] theological role can become blurred or even concealed. For example, there is little emphasis on the voice of the faithful Jewish remnant of Isa. 7 and 8 that confesses in its plight that 'God is with us.' In his reading of Isa. 12 one hears little of the responding answer of a historic Israel professing 'God is my salvation . . . . I will trust . . . he has become my salvation'" (*The Struggle to Understand*, p. 163). In my view, although no doubt Aquinas's commentary on Isaiah could be improved via historical-critical insights, much depends upon whether one conceives historic Israel's effort to obey God's commandments (including the "ceremonial" laws) as intrinsically related to its yearning for a Redeemer and a New Covenant. Childs notes that there is a "widespread acknowledgment in today's Christian church that a true interpretation of the Old Testament as an abiding testimony to God's faithfulness to his people of the covenant is an absolute desideratum for Christian theology" (ibid.). I would add that this insistence upon "God's faithfulness to his people of the covenant" as the central "abiding testimony" of the Old Testament corresponds with Aquinas's own perspective, although Aquinas thinks about this faithfulness in terms of God's faithfulness in Christ. Aquinas thus develops a valuable theology of Old Testament Israel, but not a Christian theology of ongoing Judaism—although Aquinas's principles, in my view, can be helpfully applied to the latter task. For different perspectives on this task, see Henk Schoot and Pim Valkenberg, "Thomas Aquinas and Judaism," in *Aquinas in Dialogue: Thomas for the Twenty-First Century* (ed. Jim Fodor and Frederick Christian Bauerschmidt; Oxford: Blackwell, 2004), pp. 47–66; David B. Burrell, C. S. C., *Towards a Jewish-Christian-Muslim Theology* (Oxford: Wiley-Blackwell, 2011); and my *Jewish-Christian Dialogue and the Life of Wisdom: Engagements with the Theology of David Novak* (London: Continuum, 2010).
[47] §430, p. 190.

9:8), Aquinas states that Hebrews 9 sets itself "against the heretics who say that the Old Testament was not from the Holy Spirit, but from an evil god."[48] Similarly, he asks whether there were no holy persons under the Mosaic law, if its sacrifices could not "perfect the conscience of the worshiper" (Heb. 9:9). His reply is that there certainly "were many holy and perfect persons then," even though they were perfected not by the animal sacrifices per se, but by the faith (implicitly a faith in Christ) with which they performed the sacrifices.[49]

Hebrews 9:12 states that Jesus "entered once for all into the Holy Place, taking not the blood of goats and calves but his own blood, thus securing an eternal redemption." Hebrews 9:13-14 then compares Jesus's blood to the blood of the animal sacrifices: "For if the sprinkling of defiled persons with the blood of goats and bulls and with the ashes of a heifer sanctifies for the purification of the flesh, how much more shall the blood of Christ, who through the eternal Spirit offered himself without blemish to God, purify your conscience from dead works to serve the living God." In the spiritual sense, Aquinas suggests that the bulls here figuratively signify Christ not only because of their courage, but also because Christ "uses the two testaments as two horns."[50] This image of "two horns" shows how Aquinas envisions Hebrews 9's treatment of blood; namely, in Hebrews 9, the strength of the NT is aided by the strength of the OT. With respect to the image of the "two horns," Aquinas cites Hab. 3:4, part of a prophecy of God's coming victory for the salvation of his people, which in Aquinas's Parisian Vulgate proclaims that "horns are in his hands."[51]

Reflecting upon the power of Jesus's blood, Aquinas comments that Jesus's "power is infinite," that Jesus "entered heaven," and that Jesus "wrought eternal salvation by his own blood."[52] Yet, he does not explain the power of Jesus's blood by repeating his earlier comments (on Hebrews 2) about Jesus's paying our debt. Instead, in light of Heb. 9:13's reference to "the sprinkling of defiled persons with the blood of goats and bulls and with the ashes of a heifer," he augments his earlier discussion of the Day of Atonement (Leviticus 16) by now examining Numbers 19. In Numbers 19, the Lord gives instructions for a variety of cleansings, including cleansing oneself after touching

---

[48] §429, p. 189.
[49] §431, p. 190; cf. *Summa theologiae* III, q. 49, a. 5, ad 1; I–II, q. 102, a. 5, ad 4. Aquinas's view of historic Israel is largely a positive one of people obeying God, worshiping God alone, and yearning for the divine redemptive work by which God would fulfill what the law promised—communion with God, forgiveness of sins, the fullness of the people of God. He recognizes, of course, that historic Israel also disobeyed God's precepts. In his view, a careful reading of the Old Testament indicates that "the common weal of the people prospered under the Law as long as they obeyed it; and as soon as they departed from the precepts of the Law they were overtaken by many calamities. But certain individuals, though they observed the justice of the Law, met with misfortunes—either because they had already become spiritual (so that misfortune might withdraw them all the more from attachment to temporal things, and that their virtue might be tried)—or because, while outwardly fulfilling the works of the Law, their heart was altogether fixed on temporal goods, and far removed from God, according to Isa. 29:13 (Mt. 15:8): *This people honoreth me with their lips; but their heart is far from me*" (I–II, q. 99, a. 6, ad 3).
[50] §439, p. 194.
[51] Cited in ibid. The RSV reads, "rays flashed from his hand." The connection of horns with strength, though developed by Aquinas in a figurative sense here (using a mistranslated passage from Habbakuk), is found in a number of psalms as well as in Daniel 7–8, Zechariah 1, Rev. 5:6, and (in a negative way) Revelation 13 and 17.
[52] §440, p. 194; §441, p. 194; §442, p. 195.

a dead body, cleansing a tent in which a person has died, and so forth. These cleansings require water that is obtained by the following process. Aquinas explains that "the Lord commanded Eleazar to take from Moses a red cow without blemish, of full age and which has not carried the yoke, and bring her forth outside the camp and immolate her in the sight of all."[53] After sacrificially killing the red cow, the high priest sprinkled the blood of the cow upon the door of the tent of meeting seven times, and then burned every part of the cow. The ashes were gathered, deposited outside the camp, and "kept for the congregation of the people of Israel for the water for impurity, for the removal of sin" (Num. 19:9).

Following the interpretation of Augustine, Aquinas supposes that Heb. 9:13's claim that the red cow's ashes can accomplish "the purification of the flesh" means that leprosy might in fact be able to be cleansed in this way. By comparison, Jesus's blood is much more powerful. First of all, says Aquinas (interpreting Heb. 9:14), it is the blood of the Christ, the one who "will save his people from their sins" (Mt. 1:21). Second, given Heb. 9:14's statement that Jesus offered himself for our sins "through the eternal Spirit," not only the Son but also the Spirit is behind the cleansing power of Christ's blood.[54] This enables Aquinas to tie in striking statements from the prophet Isaiah about the Spirit. From Isaiah 59, which depicts the Lord coming "to Zion as Redeemer" to overcome the injustice of the people, Aquinas draws the prophetic teaching that the Lord "will come like a rushing stream, which the wind [Spirit] drives on" (Isa. 59:19). From Isaiah 4, which foresees the triumphant Day of the Lord, Aquinas quotes the prophetic teaching that the people will be holy "when the Lord shall have washed away the filth of the daughters of Zion and cleansed the bloodstains of Jerusalem from its midst by a spirit of judgment and by a spirit of burning" (Isa. 4:4). In both cases, Christ's coming as Redeemer is joined to the power of the Spirit. Aquinas offers a third reason for the power of Jesus's blood, namely that Jesus was "without blemish" (Heb. 9:14), and here again he makes positive connections with the OT. He cites Exod. 12:5 (about the Passover lamb: "Your lamb shall be without blemish, a male a year old") and Sir. 34:4 ("From an unclean thing what will be made clean?").

Aquinas adds a brief note regarding the difference between outward and inward cleansing. Jesus's blood is able to "purify your conscience from dead works to serve the living God" (Heb. 9:9) because we are united to the saving power of Jesus's blood interiorly, by faith.[55] Furthermore, "dead works" does not mean, Aquinas considers, the works of the law (such as animal sacrifices) that may at best serve "the purification of the flesh" (Heb. 9:13). Rather, Aquinas holds that "dead works" means "sins."[56] He also makes clear that the insistence upon the purification of the conscience is found often in the OT, for example, in Ps. 101:6: "He who walks in the way that is blameless shall minister to me."[57] Even the phrase "living God" (Heb. 9:14) spurs Aquinas to a positive link with the OT, encapsulated in Sir. 10:2: "Like the magistrate of the people, so are his

---

[53] §443, p. 195.
[54] On the Spirit's work, see Guggenheim, *Jésus Christ*, pp. 297–300, 306–08.
[55] Berceville comments that for Aquinas, "The exterior sacrifice is thus the cause of the salvation of man, first of all because, as a sign, it gives rise to the interior act of faith" (Berceville, "Le sacerdoce du Christ," p. 154).
[56] §446, p. 196.
[57] Cited in ibid.

officials." Since God's life is holy, so must be the lives of all who serve God (the divine "magistrate").

Hebrews 9:15-17 shifts Aquinas's attention from Jesus's blood to his death. Commenting on Heb. 9:15 ("He is the mediator of a new covenant, so that those who are called may receive the promised eternal inheritance"), Aquinas observes that "in every testament [i.e., covenant] there is something promised and something by which that testament is confirmed."[58] In the NT, God promises eternal life or "eternal glory."[59] While citing various NT texts about our eternal inheritance, Aquinas also shows that the OT (specifically the psalms) backs up this promise. He cites Ps. 16:5, which in his version reads, "the Lord is the portion of my inheritance." Hebrews 9:15 observes that "those who are called may receive the promised eternal inheritance" precisely because "a death has occurred which redeems them from the transgressions under the first covenant." Without this death, the first covenant and its covenantal curses would still be in effect. Thus Aquinas concludes that the "promise was confirmed by the death of Christ."[60]

Interpreting Heb. 9:16 ("For where a will [or covenant/testament] is involved, the death of the one who made it must be established"), Aquinas observes that the reason for this stipulation comes in v. 17: "For a will takes effect only at death, since it is not in force as long as the one who made it is alive." After all, if a man is still alive, then one cannot be sure that a particular testament is his final one; he may still change its terms. Moreover, although a testament parcels out the inheritance, the actual inheritance cannot be enjoyed until the testator has died: as Aquinas says, "No one can seek anything, nor an heir his inheritance by reason of the testament, till after the death of the testator."[61] Understood in this way, the testament of Jesus could only go into effect upon Jesus's death. Turning to v. 18, "Hence even the first covenant was not ratified without blood," Aquinas remarks that the first covenant was ratified by the sprinkling of (animal) blood; the second covenant too involved blood, in this case Jesus's, which the animal blood had prefigured.

But if God wishes to give us an eternal inheritance, surely he could do so without blood and death? Aquinas, following Hebrews, calls upon the OT for insight. Hebrews 9:19-22 recounts how Moses, in Exodus 24, ratified the first covenant by blood. In Exodus 24, having read the law to the people and secured the people's promise to be obedient, Moses sprinkled the blood of sacrificial animals upon the book of the altar and upon the people, and Moses then proclaimed, "Behold the blood of the covenant which the Lord has made with you in accordance with all these words" (Exod. 24:8). Aquinas accepts Hebrews' teaching that Moses's ratification of the covenant in this way was good. He explains Moses's actions by observing that Jesus's free sacrificial death for our salvation involved the shedding of blood, and therefore Moses was justified in his use of the blood of the animal sacrifices, which prefigured Jesus.[62] According to

---

[58] §448, p. 198.
[59] Ibid.
[60] Ibid. As Berceville observes, Aquinas holds that "the death of Christ enables the testament to be irrevocable and to take effect" (Berceville, "Le sacerdoce du Christ," p. 154).
[61] §451, p. 199.
[62] See §460, p. 201. In I–II, q. 102, a. 3, Aquinas notes that "the reasons of the figurative sacrifices of the Old Law should be taken from the true sacrifice of Christ," rather than vice versa. Yet Aquinas

Aquinas—in accordance with the perspective of Hebrews—the blood used by Moses "was a figure of Christ's blood, by whom the New Testament is confirmed; therefore, Christ used the words in Matthew: *this is the blood of the New Testament* (Mt. 26:28)."[63] Jesus's death and blood are not to be despised, due to our need for his payment of the penalty of our sin, and so Moses's liberal use of the blood of sacrificial animals should also not be despised.

Aquinas shows additional respect for the OT by asking why the OT seems to conflict with what Hebrews teaches about it. For example, Heb. 9:19 describes Moses as using "the blood of calves and goats," whereas in fact Exodus 24 says nothing of goats. Similarly, Heb. 9:19 depicts Moses as adding to the blood "water and scarlet wool and hyssop," but these things are not mentioned in Exodus 24. Again, Heb. 9:21 portrays Moses as sprinkling the tent or tabernacle with the blood, but as Aquinas observes, "the command to consecrate the tabernacle was not given until Exodus 25."[64]

Are there theological reasons for these apparent oversights, reasons that would help us to better understand the use of blood? Aquinas answers first that we should recall that Paul was a Jew. Paul would have known "what the usages were in cleansing according to the law," and therefore Paul (as the author of Hebrews) might have filled in some details left out in Exodus 24.[65] Second, Aquinas points out that Leviticus 16's instructions for the Day of Atonement include the use of the blood of both bulls (or calves) and goats, and Numbers 19's instructions for cleansing from sin involve water and scarlet wool and hyssop. When Hebrews unhistorically asserts the presence of these elements already in Exodus 24, Aquinas suggests that this claim may flow from a praiseworthy theological sense that "the first consecration [Exod. 24] . . . virtually contained the other sanctifications to come," since God acts with the end in view.[66] With similar faith in the interior unity of God's plan of salvation, Aquinas considers Moses's sprinkling of the book of the law with blood (recorded in Heb. 9:19) to be connected with Jesus's fulfilling of the law by his spilling of his blood on the Cross.[67]

What about the fact that in Exodus 24 the tent or tabernacle had not yet been constructed and consecrated? Aquinas does not consider it a cause for concern, since when the tent was constructed, surely it was sprinkled with the blood of sacrificial animals. Against this interpretation, however, he finds in Lev. 8:10 that, at the ordination of Aaron and his sons, the tent was anointed with oil rather than with blood. Aquinas

---

also points out that there were also "literal" reasons for the animal sacrifices, including preventing idolatry and signifying "the right ordering of man's mind to God" (I–II, q. 102, a. 3, ad 1; cf. ad 2). On "the centrality of blood" for the understanding of atonement in Hebrews, see Philip, *Leviticus in Hebrews*, pp. 71, 74. Philip remarks that "the author [of Hebrews] exercises extreme care in maintaining the sacrificial metaphors related to the Levitical system as the primary signifiers that point to the new signified, which is the sacrifice of Jesus on the cross" (ibid., p. 77).

[63] §457, p. 200. In Berceville's words, "The Passion, a priestly work at once spiritual and corporeal, causes, as final cause, the sacramental act that prefigured it in the Old Law, and, as efficient cause, the sacramental act that will apply its effects in the New Law. Both before and after the Passion, the sacrament only justifies if it is received in faith" (Berceville, "Le sacerdoce du Christ," p. 155).

[64] §458, p. 201.
[65] §456, p. 200.
[66] Ibid.
[67] §457, p. 201.

supposes that perhaps "there he anointed it with oil and later sprinkled it with blood."[68] Drawing the two covenants together via a spiritual or mystical interpretation, Aquinas observes that "these two things are necessary for sanctification, namely, the power of Christ's blood and the oil of mercy, by which the tabernacle, i.e., the Church, and the vessels, i.e., the saints, are sanctified."[69] The point is to insist upon the spiritual unity of the two Testaments, by contrast to readings of Hebrews that would devalue the things of the OT.

Hebrews 9:22's insistence that "without the shedding of blood there is no forgiveness of sins" generally accords with the perspective of the OT. Aquinas notes, however, that the animal sacrifices were fundamentally figurative since, in fact, sins are forgiven only "by the blood of Christ."[70] Although this point may seem to undermine the OT, Aquinas considers that already under the OT, faith was the standard way of receiving the forgiveness of sins. In this regard he cites Lev. 5:10, which in his version reads, "the priest shall pray for him and for his sin, and it shall be forgiven him."[71] Although "pray for" should be "make atonement for" (RSV), Aquinas takes Lev. 5:10 to indicate that it is the priest's prayers for the sinner during the sacrificial act, not the animal sacrifices themselves except insofar as they prefigure Christ's sacrifice, that bring about the forgiveness. Aquinas's approach aims to uphold the significance of the OT priesthood and ritual even while affirming the figurative nature of the animal sacrifices.

Commenting on Heb. 9:23 ("it was necessary for the copies of the heavenly things to be purified with these rites, but the heavenly things themselves with better sacrifices than these"), Aquinas enunciates a principle: "Better things are always cleansed with better things. But they [the tent or tabernacle, the altar] were heavenly things, that is, the figures of heavenly things. If therefore they were cleansed with blood, these heavenly things ought to be cleansed with better blood."[72] What does it mean, however, for the tent or the altar to be "cleansed"? Aquinas holds that these physical things were not unclean in themselves, since all physical things, as such, are good. Even so, people could be "hindered from coming to the sanctuary" by "irregularities" that had occurred there.[73] In this sense, the cleansing of the tent and altar could restore the tent or tabernacle to its proper status. For our purposes, the key aspect is Aquinas's

---

[68] §459, p. 201.
[69] Ibid.
[70] §460, p. 202.
[71] Cited in ibid. The RSV reads, "The priest shall make atonement for him for the sin which he has committed, and he shall be forgiven." In Leviticus 5, one who sins comes to the priest and brings either a lamb or two turtledoves (or pigeons), and the priest kills the animal and sprinkles "the blood of the sin offering on the side of the altar" (Lev. 5:9). Certainly the priest must have prayed for the sinner during the ritual, but the difference between Aquinas's version and the RSV is nonetheless significant.
[72] §462, p. 204. See Mayjee Philip's observation: "The author's preoccupation with dualities, such as earthly-heavenly and pattern-real, together with his method of argumentation, have led earlier Hebrews scholars to conclude that the author was influenced by Platonic and Philonic modes of argumentation and interpretation . . . . However, though there is sufficient reason to arrive at the conclusion that Hebrews is a Christian-Platonic text, with the normal, expected background level of Platonism which was common to early Christian writings, evidence in this study [i.e., *Leviticus in Hebrews*] has shown that the author's use and emphasis of the earthly and heavenly tabernacle, besides other such dualities, are clearly influenced by the OT; apart from them his discourse is incoherent and therefore meaningless" (Philip, *Leviticus in Hebrews*, p. 85).
[73] §463, p. 204.

connection of "better sacrifices" with "better blood." This connection arises from Hebrews itself, and yet the notion of "better blood" seems an awkward one: why would God want "better blood"? Aquinas's answer is found already in his discussion of Hebrews 2; namely, God willed that Jesus pay our penalty, the penalty of death, out of supreme love. It is not that God is bloodthirsty and desires blood per se, but rather God wants for us that human nature be restored in justice, precisely as an act of divine mercy. In this sense, it was according to the divine will that Jesus Christ entered heaven—the true tent or tabernacle—"with blood."[74]

Aquinas inquires about why Heb. 9:23 speaks of "better sacrifices" in the plural. Given that Hebrews itself affirms the singleness of Jesus's sacrifice, why does Hebrews here refer to plural sacrifices? Aquinas answers that Hebrews thereby indicates the way in which the one sacrifice of Jesus contains within itself that which it fulfills; namely, the many animal sacrifices of the OT. Although Jesus's one sacrifice accords with the psalmist's teaching that "burnt offering and sin offering thou hast not required" (Ps. 40:6) and that "thou hast no delight in sacrifice; were I to give a burnt offering, thou wouldst not be pleased" (Ps. 51:16), Aquinas decisively refutes negative judgments of the Mosaic law's animal sacrifices. He points out that if "better sacrifices" were needed, the Mosaic law's sacrifices must have been good: "the sacrifices of the old law were good, for something is called better in relation to something good."[75]

After commenting very briefly on Heb. 9:26 ("he has appeared once for all at the end of the age to put away sin by the sacrifice of himself"), Aquinas asks why Heb. 9:27 states that "it is appointed for men to die once." As he observes, the question is whether death belongs to the necessities of nature, or whether death comes about from sin. Wisdom of Solomon 1:13 (quoted here by Aquinas) states bluntly that "God did not make death, and he does not delight in the death of the living . . . . But ungodly men by their words and deeds summoned death."[76] Aquinas pauses here, therefore, to offer a short discourse on death. It is fully natural in its "material cause," since matter decays. But God bestowed upon the first humans the gift of original justice, by which the soul governed the body so perfectly that death (as the rupture of soul and body) would not have occurred. Thus human death came about due to the loss of original justice, a loss occasioned by the first sin. Since Jesus was not subject to original sin, he *freely* willed to die for our salvation, rather than being compelled to die. Aquinas cites a passage from his version of Isa. 53:7 that is absent from the RSV: "He was offered because it was his own will."[77] He emphasizes the difference between Jesus's death and ours, both because Jesus is not enslaved by sin to death, and because Jesus "was offered once to bear the sins of many" (Heb. 9:28). Our death results from sin, but "Christ's death destroys sin."[78]

---

[74] §468, p. 205; cf. §470, p. 206.
[75] §464, p. 204.
[76] Cited in §475, p. 207.
[77] Cited in §477, p. 208.
[78] Ibid. Aquinas here cites 1 Pet. 3:18, Rom. 6:23 and 8:3, and 2 Cor. 5:21. Hebrews does not make an explicit connection between sin and the penalty of death, but Hebrews presents Jesus as sinless (Heb. 4:15) and also presents the devil as the one "who has the power of death" (Heb. 2:14).

Returning to the topics of sacrifice and blood in commenting on Heb. 10:1-2, Aquinas observes that Jesus's sacrifice does not need to be repeated because it has "everlasting power" and therefore is sufficient "for sins already committed and sins still to be committed."[79] If this is the case, however, why does the Church offer the Eucharistic sacrifice? Aquinas replies that although the Eucharistic sacrifice might appear to be a different sacrifice from Christ's, it is in fact the same sacrifice, because the same blood is offered.[80] By contrast to this sacrifice, the sacrifices of animals seemingly accomplished nothing, because as Heb. 10:4 says, "It is impossible that the blood of bulls and goats should take away sins." Aquinas grants that the animal sacrifices in themselves did not take away sins, but he argues that since they prefigured Christ's blood, they offered an occasion for an act of faith that would take away sins.[81] Aquinas supports his position by citing the prophet Jeremiah's rhetorical question: "Can vows and sacrificial flesh avert your doom?" (Jer. 11:15). In the OT, it was already clear that animal sacrifices in themselves could not heal humans from sin.

Hebrews 10:5-7 places the words of Ps. 40:6-8, somewhat paraphrased, into the mouth of Christ: "Sacrifices and offerings thou hast not desired, but a body hast thou prepared for me; in burnt offerings and sin offerings thou hast taken no pleasure. Then I said, 'Lo, I have come to do thy will, O God,' as it is written of me in the roll of the book."[82] Aquinas takes the opportunity to survey various kinds of offerings found in the Mosaic law: offerings, holocausts, sacrifices for sin, holocausts of peace. Their differences enable him to conclude that Jesus's one sacrifice combines all of them, by reconciling humans to God, by removing our sin, and by meriting our exaltation. He also examines why the psalmist (or, as Heb. 10:5 says, Christ) argues both that God does not want sacrifices or offerings and that God has prepared a (sacrificial) body for him. The answer is that Jesus's body is perfectly pure, the true Passover lamb: "Your lamb shall be without blemish" (Exod. 12:5).[83] What God desires, then, is Jesus's free offering of himself out of perfect love for sinners. Since Jesus is holy (and free), his bodily life is an acceptable sacrifice in charity. When Jesus comes to do God's will, he does so by offering himself "for the redemption of the human race."[84]

Even so, if the psalmist/Christ is correct that God truly does not desire sacrifices and offerings, why does God command in Lev. 1:9 that "the priest shall offer the whole [animal], and burn it on the altar; it is a burnt offering, an offering by fire, a

---

[79] §482, p. 212.
[80] See Berceville, "Le sacerdoce du Christ," pp. 151–52. See also my *Sacrifice and Community: Jewish Offering and Christian Eucharist* (Oxford: Blackwell, 2005).
[81] See §483, p. 212. For discussion see Guggenheim, *Jésus Christ*, pp. 342–44.
[82] For the significant difference between the Gloss's interpretation of Heb. 10:5-9 and Aquinas, see Berceville, "Le sacerdoce du Christ," p. 149. Berceville notes that by contrast to the Gloss, which reads Heb. 10:5 as about the Incarnation and Heb. 10:7 as about the Passion, Aquinas thinks that Heb. 10:5-6 is about the inadequacy of the Old Covenant's sacrifices and Heb. 10:7 is about the adequacy of the New Covenant's sacrifice (Christ's Passion).
[83] Cited in §487, p. 213.
[84] §490, p. 215. See Weinandy's remark (on Aquinas's *Commentary on Hebrews* 8 [§384]) that "Christ's sacrifice was holy because he offered his own holy life. It was right for him to do so because he was of the same race of Adam as were all. He offered himself to the Father, but equally, as man, he offered himself to himself because he himself is God. Lastly, the causal effect of such a supreme sacrifice is that it forms an everlasting and unbreakable communion with God for those for whom it was offered" (Weinandy, "The Supremacy of Christ," p. 238).

pleasing odor to the Lord"? This seems to be a blatant contradiction, one that is found repeatedly in the OT. Why does God say in Isa. 1:11, "What to me is the multitude of your sacrifices? says the Lord; I have had enough of burnt offerings of rams and the fat of fed beasts; I do not delight in the blood of bulls, or of lambs, or of he-goats"?[85] Aquinas proposes three possible answers, and suggests that the first two provide the framework for the third "toward which [Hebrews] is tending."[86] The first answer is that God desired animal sacrifices in the past but does not desire them once Jesus Christ has arrived. The second is that God does not desire them if they are presumed in themselves to be able to cover sins; here Aquinas cites Isa. 1:15 ("your hands are full of blood"), where God calls for justice rather than merely for cultic sacrifices. Combining these two answers, Aquinas proposes that for Hebrews (and arguably for the biblical witness as a whole), God was never pleased with animal sacrifices per se, but he was pleased by their prefiguring of Christ (cf. 1 Cor. 10:11 on typology) and by their weaning Israel from idolatry after the calamity of the golden calf (cf. Jer. 7:22).[87]

Aquinas comments only briefly on Heb. 10:14: "For by a single offering he has perfected for all time those who are sanctified." Aquinas earlier covered the efficacy of Jesus's single sacrifice, and besides, he finds his main point reiterated by Heb. 10:18: "Where there is forgiveness of these [sins], there is no longer any offering for sin." The efficacy of Jesus's sacrifice explains why Christians no longer need the cultic ritual of the OT, especially since the animal sacrifices could not satisfy for sin in the first place (cf. Heb. 10:11). The overcoming of sin, of course, is not the only theme of this section of Hebrews, which also focuses on the entrance of Jesus Christ and believers into heaven (the true Holy of Holies). Hebrews 10:19 notes that this entrance comes about "by the blood of Jesus," and Heb. 10:22 similarly refers to having "our hearts sprinkled clean," but Aquinas has already covered the topic of Jesus's blood, and does not add anything new here.

Aquinas inquires in some detail into Heb. 10:26 (cf. Heb. 6:4-6): "For if we sin deliberately after receiving the knowledge of the truth, there no longer remains a sacrifice for sins." Are Christians who sin inevitably damned, and is the sacrament of penance a mere delusion? In answer, Aquinas first appeals to the Gloss's distinction between "sinners who are willing" (cf. Jer. 8:6; sins of passion) and sinners "who sin willfully" (cf. Prov. 2:14; sins of contempt).[88] The idea is that Heb. 10:26 may refer only to the latter, because willful sinners are hardened in their sins and do not think of repenting. For such sinners, Jesus's sacrifice cannot do anything, because they never turn to it in repentance. Aquinas finds justification for his interpretation in Isa. 49:4, where God's Servant complains, "I have labored in vain, I have spent my strength for nothing and vanity"; and in Jer. 6:29: "in vain the refining goes on, for the wicked are not removed."[89] But Aquinas casts doubt upon this interpretation, on the grounds that

---

[85] Cited in §492, p. 215.
[86] §488, p. 214.
[87] See ibid.
[88] §515, p. 223. Although Aquinas does not mention it, see also Num. 15:30: "The person who does anything with a high hand, whether he is a native or a sojourner, reviles the Lord, and that person shall be cut off from among his people."
[89] Cited in ibid., p. 224. Aquinas's version of Jer. 6:29 reads, "The founder has melted in vain, for their wicked deeds are not consumed."

a solution proposed by Augustine fits better with Hebrews' emphasis on the diverse states before and after Christ. Augustine holds that if we sin deliberately despite having received Christ, we are fully accountable for the consequences of our sin, as there is no further sacrifice or baptism for which we can wait.[90] In such a situation, we can only be saved by a new infusion of sanctifying grace.

When Heb. 10:28-29 compares someone who has violated the Mosaic law and received the death penalty with someone "who has spurned the Son of God, and profaned the blood of the covenant by which he was sanctified, and outraged the Spirit of grace," Aquinas reflects further upon the two ways of sinning: out of passion and out of contempt. Hebrews 10:29, he thinks, has the latter in view. With regard to "the blood of the covenant by which he was sanctified," Aquinas identifies a further OT text that points to Christ's work: "For from the rising of the sun to its setting my name is great among the nations, and in every place incense is offered to my name, and a pure offering; for my name is great among the nations" (Mal. 1:11).[91] In every place, humans are sanctified by Jesus's blood, and those who repudiate God's gift of sanctification (cf. Eph. 2:8) have "profaned the blood" or, as Aquinas's Vulgate version has it, have "esteemed the blood of the testament unclean."

Other references in Hebrews to blood, sacrifice, and death

Hebrews 5:7 recalls that "Jesus offered up prayers and supplications, with loud cries and tears, to him who was able to save him from death"; Heb. 5:1 states that "every high priest chosen from among men is appointed to act on behalf of men in relation to God, to offer gifts and sacrifices for sins." But if Jesus is the high priest who freely and sacrificially offers his own life for our sins, why did Jesus himself beg to be saved from death? And how can Heb. 5:7 say that Jesus "was heard for his godly fear," as though Jesus's plea to be saved from death was answered, whereas in fact Jesus died?

In response, Aquinas suggests that Jesus's priesthood needs to be assessed not only in terms of his offering of his bodily life, but also in terms of his spiritual sacrifices. Here Aquinas builds upon two OT texts: "He who brings thanksgiving as his sacrifice honors me [God]" (Ps. 50:23) and "we will render the fruit of our lips" (Hos. 14:2).[92] A priest's action involves prayer and praise. Aquinas considers that "two things are necessary in one who prays, namely fervent love along with pain and groans."[93] When Jesus accompanied his prayers with "loud cries and tears," this is entirely what we should expect from the perfect priest, as Aquinas confirms via the psalmist's example: "Lord, all my longing is known to thee, my sighing is not hidden from thee" (Ps. 38:9). With respect to Jesus's pleading with God "who was able to save him from death," Aquinas points out that in terms of "the will acting as a natural appetite," Jesus naturally shrank from death, but "under the influence of the will influenced by reason

---

[90] See §516, p. 224.
[91] Cited in §529, p. 227.
[92] Cited in §255, p. 114.
[93] §256, p. 114.

he willed to die."⁹⁴ God answered his prayer "by raising him up," as Aquinas finds anticipated in the psalms: "For thou dost not give me up to Sheol" (Ps. 16:10) and "do thou, O Lord, be gracious to me, and raise me up" (Ps. 41:10). In this way, unlike Aaron and the high priests of the OT, "who were prevented by death from continuing in office" (Heb. 7:23), Jesus remains high priest forever—again showing, in Aquinas's words, "that the priesthood of Christ has greater efficacy than the priesthood of the Old Testament."⁹⁵

Discussing Heb. 11:28 ("By faith he [Moses] kept the Passover and sprinkled the blood"), Aquinas first describes the commands of Exodus 12—beginning with the command "to immolate a lamb and put its blood on both the side posts and on the upper door posts of the houses"—and then reflects upon the significance of the "Pasch," a word whose etymology he traces to a Hebrew word that, he says, means "passage."⁹⁶ Given the emphasis in Heb. 11:23-28 on Moses's faith in Christ, Aquinas connects the Passover and sprinkled blood figurally to Jesus's Pasch and its effects for those who have faith: Jesus Christ passes "out of this world by his passion," and "in virtue of Christ's blood" we follow him.⁹⁷ Aquinas comments in this vein that "by the merit of his death we have passed from earthly things to heavenly, and from hell to heaven."⁹⁸ We make this passage when our mind and will are transformed by faith and charity, so that we are fully united to Christ.⁹⁹ In accord with the figural faith-meaning of the Passover and sprinkled blood in Heb. 11:28, Aquinas adds that "with the blood of Christ, who is the lamb without blemish, the posts of the faithful should be besmeared, namely, their intellect and affections."¹⁰⁰ He places this discussion of blood and sacrifice under the rubric not only of Exodus but also of Sirach, known for its paean to wisdom: "Come to me, you who desire me" (Sir. 24:19). When we come to Christ, our mind and heart are filled with heavenly things, and we receive strength to resist sin "to the point of shedding [our] blood" (Heb. 12:4).

Hebrews urges believers that "you have come to Mount Zion and to the city of the living God, the heavenly Jerusalem . . . and to Jesus, the mediator of a New Covenant, and to the sprinkled blood that speaks more graciously than the blood of Abel" (Heb. 12:22, 24). Commenting on this passage, Aquinas notes that the "sprinkled blood" is a figural connection of Jesus's blood with the ritual use of blood in the OT, as we have seen earlier in Hebrews. The reference to Abel, says Aquinas, indicates that "the shedding of Christ's blood was prefigured in the shedding of the blood of all the just from the beginning of the world."¹⁰¹ Jesus's blood "speaks more graciously" because

---

⁹⁴ §257, pp. 114–15.
⁹⁵ §367, p. 161. For discussion see Weinandy, "The Supremacy of Christ," pp. 236-38; Guggenheim, *Jésus Christ*, pp. 166–67.
⁹⁶ §621, p. 268.
⁹⁷ Ibid.
⁹⁸ Ibid.
⁹⁹ See Weinandy's observation that "faith . . . is the unqualified response to Christ's supremacy—the fulfilment and perfection of the old covenant through the offering of his own blood as the new and eternal covenant" ("The Supremacy of Christ," p. 241).
¹⁰⁰ §621, p. 268.
¹⁰¹ §712, p. 305. For Hebrews' (and Aquinas's) view of history, see Laansma, *The Letter to the Hebrews*, p. 14. With regard to Heb. 11:4's praise of Abel's sacrifice, Aquinas confirms the primacy of the interior intention in sacrificial offerings: Abel's sacrifice was "a better and more excellent one than Cain's because . . . the external sacrifice was a sign of the faith within" (§568, p. 246).

Jesus died for our pardon, so as to accomplish mercy, whereas Abel's blood cried for vengeance. It also "speaks more graciously" because Jesus is the God-man "making us just," whereas Abel was simply a "just man."[102] Again, Aquinas appeals to the prophet Isaiah for his interpretation of Jesus: the Servant "made intercession for the transgressors" (Isa. 53:12).

Hebrews 13:11-12 teaches, "For the bodies of those animals whose blood is brought into the sanctuary by the high priest as a sacrifice for sin are burned outside the camp. So Jesus also suffered outside the gate in order to sanctify the people through his own blood." The reference here, as Aquinas notes, is to Lev. 16:27, where God gives instructions for the Day of Atonement: "The bull for the sin offering and the goat for the sin offering, whose blood was brought in to make atonement in the holy place, shall be carried forth outside the camp; their skin and their flesh and their dung shall be burned with fire." Earlier in his commentary, of course, Aquinas already discussed the figural meanings of Leviticus 16, including the fact that Jesus's blood brings us into the Holy of Holies (heaven). Now Aquinas adds that the figural meaning of "burned outside the camp" (Heb. 13:11; cf. Lev. 16:27) is twofold: Jesus died outside the gate of Jerusalem, and Jesus died for those who "are outside the camp of ceremonies of the law," because those who continued observing the Mosaic law did not recognize what Jesus had accomplished.[103] Aquinas interprets "the bodies of those animals whose blood is brought into the sanctuary" as being literally about the cow and the goat, but figuratively about Christ and his members. He observes that "the body of Christ, whose blood was brought into the heavenly holies for the sin of the whole world, suffered by fire on the altar of the Cross, and was burned outside the camp, i.e., outside the common society of men, with the fire of charity, with fasts, prayers, and other works of mercy."[104] Extending the figural connection made by Hebrews between the Day of Atonement's burnt offering "outside the camp" and Christ's death "outside the gate" (Heb. 13:11-12), Aquinas figuratively depicts Christ as a burnt offering for our sins, burnt by "the fire of charity."

Hebrews 13:15 urges believers to "continually offer up a sacrifice of praise to God, that is, the fruit of lips that acknowledge his name." In commenting upon this verse, Aquinas observes that this "sacrifice" should include "devotion to God and mercy towards our neighbor."[105] Part of it must consist in praising God, and here Aquinas remarks that "God is praised better by the mouth than by the killing of animals."[106] Aquinas supports this claim, which might seem to tell against his own insistence upon the goodness of the Mosaic law's animal sacrifices, by citing such OT texts as Ps. 50:23, Hos. 14:2, and Isa. 57:18. Without rejecting animal sacrifices, these texts urge that "he who brings thanksgiving as his sacrifice honors me" (Isa. 50:23). Aquinas defends the injunction to offer this sacrifice of praise "continually" by citing Ps. 34:1, "I will bless the Lord at all times; his praise shall continually be in my mouth."[107]

---

[102] §712, p. 306.
[103] §743, p. 320.
[104] §746, p. 321.
[105] §751, p. 322.
[106] §752, p. 322.
[107] Cited in ibid.

As Aquinas points out, Heb. 13:16 augments our understanding of what Hebrews considers proper sacrifices to be on the part of Christian believers. Hebrews 13:16 reads, "Do not neglect to do good and to share what you have, for such sacrifices are pleasing to God." It follows that in addition to the "sacrifice of praise" (Heb. 13:15), we must do works of mercy, since they are meritorious sacrifices for which God will reward us with everlasting life (cf. Heb. 10:35 and 11:6). In this regard Aquinas cites Gen. 15:1, where the Lord tells Abraham—commended in Hebrews 11 for his faith in the heavenly homeland—"I am your shield; your reward shall be very great."[108] Aquinas suggests that such sacrifices (specifically works of mercy) are what the eschatological portrait in Isa. 19:21 figuratively has in view, even if Isa. 19:21 seems to be about animal sacrifices: "And the Lord will make himself known to the Egyptians; and the Egyptians will know the Lord in that day and worship with sacrifice and burnt offering."[109]

Hebrews 13:20 begins, "Now may the God of peace who brought again from the dead our Lord Jesus, the great shepherd of the sheep, by the blood of the eternal covenant . . . ." This is the last mention of blood in Hebrews, and Aquinas comments that "Christ by his passion merited the glory of his resurrection for himself and for us."[110] Jesus's Passion is meritorious, of course, because it involves more than (though not less than) his spilling of his blood; it involves his supreme charity and obedience. It seals the "eternal covenant" because it satisfies for all sins and opens heaven for us. Aquinas cites an OT prophecy about the Day of the Lord that, when applied to Jesus, captures Heb. 13:20's meaning: "Because of the blood of my covenant with you, I will set your captives free from the waterless pit" (Zech. 9:11).

Conclusion

I have examined death, sacrifice, and blood in Aquinas's *Commentary on Hebrews*. Focusing on the relationship of the priesthood of Christ to faith (both before and after Christ's Passion), Gilles Berceville takes note of "the extreme attention given by Thomas [in his *Commentary on Hebrews*] to the details of the ritual described in the Pentateuch."[111] This attentiveness to the OT in Aquinas's *Commentary on Hebrews* has been the focus of the present expository chapter. As we have seen, Aquinas thinks that Hebrews nicely encapsulates both the goodness and purpose of the Mosaic law's animal sacrifices, and the goodness and purpose of Jesus Christ's free sacrificial death for our salvation. Aquinas emphasizes that all the animal sacrifices—and all the blood of innocent humans spilled before Christ—prefigure and are contained in

---

[108] Cited in §754, p. 323. The promise of a reward for works of mercy is strewn throughout the Sermon on the Mount, although Aquinas does not refer to it here. See for example Jesus's commandment: "But when you give alms, do not let your left hand know what your right hand is doing, so that your alms may be in secret; and your Father who sees in secret will reward you" (Mt. 6:3-4; cf. Mt. 6:20 on "treasures in heaven"). For discussion, see Gary Anderson, *Sin: A History* (New Haven, CT: Yale University Press, 2009); idem., *Charity: The Place of the Poor in the Biblical Tradition* (New Haven, CT: Yale University Press, 2013).

[109] Cited in §754, p. 323.

[110] §768, p. 328.

[111] Berceville, "Le sacerdoce du Christ," p. 155.

Jesus's action, which is where we find salvation. God does not will death, but, given humankind's slavery to sin, there is one death that is good, namely Jesus's utterly free death out of supreme love.

To prepare believers to seek spiritual cleansing from Jesus's death, God gives Israel the Mosaic law's sacrificial cult. It is in Jesus's death and Resurrection that God's purpose is definitively revealed, namely God's purpose of mercifully restoring us in justice and opening eternal life to us. Since Christ has redeemed us in love by his sacrificial death, the sacrifices that God requires of his people are not bloody sacrifices. Rather, our sharing by faith and the sacraments in Christ's sacrifice requires that we perform spiritual sacrifices, such as thanksgiving, mercy, and almsgiving; and indeed a careful reading of the OT makes clear that such has always been the case. The Mosaic law's sacrifices were never thought to be salvific in themselves, but neither did they lack goodness and value, as Hebrews makes clear.

Writing about fourteenth- and fifteenth-century piety (which certainly did involve some odd devotions), however, Caroline Walker Bynum remarks: "How can violation—and later miracles that mirror it—represent grace and love? How can death bring life? Such contradictions had lurked at the heart of Christianity from its inception."[112] In reflecting upon blood, death, and sacrifice in Hebrews as interpreted by Aquinas, I have sought to show that the answer to her questions—the resolutions of these "contradictions"—are to be found in Hebrews itself, despite Bynum's negative view of Hebrews' "overlaying" of early Christian teaching about the "life-giving death" of Christ "with the template of Levitical sacrifice."[113] Aquinas's consistent appeal to the OT in interpreting Hebrews, and his insistence upon the goodness of the Mosaic law and upon the spiritual depth of the psalms and prophets, enable him to show the beauty and wisdom, rather than contradiction, of God's plan of salvation. It is the OT itself that leads to an appreciation of the relationship of sacrifice to faith and love, a relationship present already in Israel and evident in Jesus Christ's fulfillment of sacrifice and in the Church's sacramental representation of Christ's sacrifice. The "life-giving death" of Jesus, his spilling of his blood for our salvation, must be understood through an OT (Mosaic) lens in order to be recognized as the deeply spiritual, love-filled sacrificial act that in fact it is.

---

[112] Caroline Walker Bynum, *Wonderful Blood: Theology and Practice in Late Medieval Northern Germany and Beyond* (Philadelphia: University of Pennsylvania Press, 2007), p. 254.

[113] Ibid., p. 255. Bynum remarks critically, "To the aporia of Old Testament sacrifice (that is, the destruction of the gift in order to give it), Christians added the further aporias of, on the one hand, a gift exchange in which there is only one party and, on the other, the eternal performance of a historical (that is, temporal) violation that cannot be repeated" (ibid.). In an essay surveying her career, Bynum states that "*Wonderful Blood* focused on the increasing centrality in late-medieval Christianity of an ideology of sacrifice in all its horrific consequences . . . . The killing at the heart of the Eucharistic offering—the sacrifice of God to God by God in the Crucifixion—took its toll as well as on the logic of Scholastic theologians and the hearts of pious laity" (Bynum, "Why Paradox? The Contradictions of My Life as a Scholar," in *Journeys in Church History: Essays from the* Catholic Historical Review [ed. Nelson H. Minnich; Washington, DC: Catholic University of America Press, 2015], pp. 29–51 [48–49]). Obviously, I disagree with Bynum on numerous levels.

8

Living and Active: The Exalted Prophet in the Epistle to the Hebrews

Michael Allen

"In many times and in various ways" the Word attests our God and his instruction through the prophets (Heb. 1:1). Hebrews not only affirms the varied and voluminous character of God's speech but displays its flavor by engaging in myriad exegetical maneuvers. The text rarely argues apart from explicit scriptural analysis, and its argumentative moves range from the exemplarist to the typological to yet more narrow hermeneutical approaches. The catena of texts pulled together in 1:5-14 attest a Christocentric approach to exegesis of the OT to be sure, yet that survey is matched by the later panoramic sketch of that first testament in 11:1-40 where the "great cloud of witnesses" (12:1) provides so many examples of living by faith, examples which are to be imitated.

The danger for theologians today comes in narrowing the contours of what it means for Hebrews to speak of God's prophetic speech of and by his Son (1:2). Too often this can take the form of a myopic focus on a supposedly Christ-centered hermeneutic wherein earlier biblical episodes are meant to point only unto a Christological resolution or fulfillment of something which Christ does outside us and in our place. Such readings are needful, appropriate, and beautiful, and Hebrews offers them aplenty. Such readings are also insufficient as a guide to the full panoply of ways in which the Word of God dwells richly in this sermon. We do well to note that speech of and by the Son also comes in a number of forms; even the seemingly exemplarist is no less Christological, at least not when considered in the light of 12:1-2. For Hebrews, Scripture charts many exegetical ways to and from the Christ.

Exegetical myopia can be matched by Christological narrowness and, I suggest, this can easily happen in Christian proclamation as well as in Christian theology and biblical interpretation. In this chapter I hope to prompt reflection on the broader scope and sequence of Christological teaching in Hebrews, so that we might be alerted to the varied ways in which the Son acts to make atonement for his people. While problems can settle in by failing to attend to the states of Christ's work as in the revisionary approach of Karl Barth, much more common is the danger of fixing one's eye upon too narrow a span of his history of redemption.[1] In that regard, I will seek to bring into

---

[1] Karl Barth, *Church Dogmatics*, Volume Four: *The Doctrine of Reconciliation*, Part One (ed. G. W. Bromiley and T. F. Torrance; London: T&T Clark, 1956), pp. 132–35. Barth's revision shifts the

relief the significance of the exalted Christ's ongoing work not only as a priest serving like unto Melchizedek but also as a prophet who continues to send forth the Word of God in living and active form. My argument will first draw out some of the most salient ways in which Hebrews attests the place of the exaltation of Christ as a context for further agency and not merely an acknowledgment of accomplished activity. Then I will focus upon ways in which the exaltation of Christ is linked to the ministry of the Word of God, such that the teaching of Hebrews regarding Scripture can be appreciated as being more tightly tethered to the present action of the great prophet, even Jesus. Like a three-stranded cord, the threefold office of Christ serves to alert us to the ways he fills up all the needs for delivering a sure salvation; that being the case, to depend solely on one strand (the cultic) in developing an atonement theology apart from the other two (the royal and the prophetic) will fail to affirm the wholeness and completeness of his salvific work. Hopefully this analysis will show the significance of the prophetic task of the exalted Christ for the saving of his people.

"Into heaven itself, now" (9:24): The exaltation of the son in the Epistle to the Hebrews

"After making purification for sins, he sat down at the right hand of the Majesty on high" (1:3). With all its talk of sacrifice and of blood offered, Hebrews shouts a word of finality. "Once for all" (9:26; 10:11) hangs over that central section (in chs 5–10) as a profound summary statement attesting the reality that there is now "no longer any offering for sin" (10:18). The immediate prompt for the sermon itself involves a need to understand the singularity of Christ's sacrifice which need not be repeated, lest the Hebrews fall back into the rhythms of Jewish cultic worship again. Not surprisingly, then, the rhetoric of completion and finality lands so strongly. Yet Hebrews attests more, noting also the "again and again" character of the good news of this Son. He has gone "into heaven itself, now" on our behalf "to appear in the presence of God" (9:24).

The exaltation of Christ has been shown renewed attention in the work of David Moffitt, whose book *Atonement and the Logic of Resurrection in the Epistle to the Hebrews* has gestured toward the significance of resurrected life for the sake of Christ's ongoing priesthood.[2] He has presented four arguments in this vein. First, Heb. 6:2 and 11:19 attest a confession that the resurrection of the dead is part and parcel of the Christian's hope: Abraham could expect a resurrection of the soon-to-be-slain child of the promise (11:19) and, likewise, "the elementary doctrine of Christ" includes, among other things, "the resurrection of the dead" (6:2).[3] Second, Heb. 12:2 presents

---

distinction of humiliation and exaltation away from a chronological sequence and toward dual aspects of the divine being understood dialectically.

[2] David M. Moffitt, *Atonement and the Logic of Resurrection in the Epistle to the Hebrews* (Supplements to Novum Testamentum 141; Leiden: Brill, 2011); see also idem, "Blood, Life, and Atonement: Reassessing Hebrews" Christological Appropriation of Yom Kippur," in *The Day of Atonement: Its Interpretations in Early Jewish and Christian Traditions* (ed. Thomas Hieke and Tobias Nicklas; Leiden: Koninklijke Brill, 2012), pp. 211–24.

[3] Moffitt notes that 11:35 confirms the place of the resurrection of the dead in the Christian faith: here the "better resurrection" or "better life" (ἀναστάσεως) speaks of resurrection, while the term

Jesus as the "author and perfector" of this faith. If Abraham and the others looked to resurrection, how much more the perfectly faithful one?[4] Third, Heb. 5:7 identifies Jesus as one who prayed to him "who was able to save him from death, and he was heard."[5] Fourth, Heb. 7:16 says that Jesus has become a high priest "by the power of an indestructible life" rather than by bodily descent from Aaron or the Levites. The argument of chapter 7 turns to Melchizedek rather than the Israelite priesthood as a paradigm for Jesus, highlighting, of course, the way in which this mediator from Salem lived forever (7:3, 8). Jesus has "arisen" in the likeness of Melchizedek (7:15): while this term could refer to simple elevation or assumption of office, the wider context points toward genuine resurrection, because chapter 7 emphasizes Melchizedek's service lasting forever, uses the verb "to arise," and references the "indestructible life" of Jesus, a term that seems to connote eternality or immortality.[6]

In light of these four points, the benediction of 13:20 is no mere appellation, but a genuine reference to a discrete and explicit aspect of Hebrews' teaching: the "God of peace" has "brought again from the dead our Lord Jesus." To summarize thus far: Moffitt's first two points strongly show that Hebrews affirms the resurrection of the dead, broadly speaking, and his last two points suggest that Hebrews assumes or implicitly affirms the resurrection of Jesus specifically. Unfortunately, neither is a direct reference, so one wonders how far we are from the recent commentators that Moffitt says he will correct: F. F. Bruce and William Lane, for example.[7] While I can affirm that Moffitt has shown the unlikeliness of what he calls the agnostic, the spiritual ascension, or the no-resurrection approaches,[8] Moffitt seems to offer a lovely return to what Bruce, Lane, and others have argued: Hebrews largely passes over direct reference to the resurrection as a discrete event in the life of Jesus, but implicitly or indirectly notes its importance for his exalted service in the holy of holies.

The presence of resurrection is one thing, but far more interesting is the significance of the resurrection as articulated by Moffitt. He argues that atonement occurs in one place: the throne room of God. Hebrews 7:16 is crucial: Jesus is not a priest until he has the power of an indestructible life. Therefore, Calvary is out as a venue for atoning service: there was no priest present there, Jesus not having been perfected yet with "indestructible [that is, resurrected] life." Recent work on the nature of the Yom Kippur sacrifice by Jewish and Christian interpreters of Leviticus is referenced as a crucial

---

"resurrection" (κρείττονος ἀναστάσεως) probably implies temporary resuscitation (see Moffitt, "Blood, Life, and Atonement," pp. 215–16).

[4] Moffitt, "Blood, Life, and Atonement," p. 216.
[5] "Ibid., pp. 216–17."
[6] Moffitt, "Blood, Life, and Atonement," pp. 217–18. The key term in 7:15 is ἀνίσταται. Moffitt argues this particular point at length in "'If Another Priest Arises': Jesus' Resurrection and the High Priestly Christology of Hebrews," in *A Cloud of Witnesses: The Theology of Hebrews in Its Ancient Contexts* (ed. Richard Bauckham, Daniel Driver, Trevor Hart, and Nathan MacDonald; London: T&T Clark, 2008).
[7] Moffitt, *Atonement and the Logic of Resurrection*, pp. 4–10 (see pp. 4–5 fn. 2 for full bibliography of those holding to what Moffitt terms the "passed over" view); see F. F. Bruce, *The Epistle to the Hebrews* (New International Commentary on the New Testament; Grand Rapids, MI: Eerdmans, 1990), pp. 32–33; William Lane, *Hebrews 1–8* (Word Biblical Commentary 47a; Dallas: Word Books, 1991), p. 16.
[8] For description and criticism of the "agnostic," "spiritual ascension," and "no-resurrection" views, see Moffitt, *Atonement and the Logic of Resurrection*, pp. 10–40.

background for what Hebrews says about the atonement. Jacob Milgrom and others have argued that it is not the death of an animal, but the life of the sacrificial offering that makes atonement. Further, the moment of atonement takes place in the holy of holies when the blood is presented, rather than outside when the animal was slaughtered. I take the rendering of Lev. 17:11 that is argued by Jay Sklar, affirmed by Milgrom and others, and depended upon by Moffitt, to be not only valid but necessary.[9] Atonement is made by blood, that is, "by means of the life" of the blood. Further, when Moffitt argues that this approach allows us to read Heb. 8:4 and a whole slew of texts that speak of Jesus making his offering in the presence of God in heaven (6:19-20; 7:26; 8:2; 9:11; 9:23-25; 10:12) seriously and without manipulation as some spiritual rendering completely restricted to the event of Good Friday, I am in agreement.[10] And yet I'll confess to finding a serious mistake in the argument of Milgrom and, still further, in the presumption that Milgrom's reading of Leviticus would be the foundational presumption of the author of Hebrews.

Leviticus 17:11 does identify atonement with the giving of life, symbolized by blood, "for the life of the flesh is in the blood, and I have given it for you on the altar to make atonement for your souls, for it is the blood that makes atonement by the life." Yet as Hebrews addresses the role of blood in atonement it makes plain that "without the shedding of blood there is no forgiveness of sins" (9:22). Yes, the translation of this phrase might be rendered "the outpouring of blood" rather than the "shedding of blood," but the Levitical background refers not only to the "ritual manipulation" of blood previously shed but also to the ritual shedding of it in the first place (see Leviticus 4; 8:15; 9:9).[11] Blood is not redemptive in the abstract; shed blood—resulting in death—is redemptive when presented in the very holy of holies.[12] I think this has to temper Moffitt's insistence that atonement occurs only in the holy of holies and that the death of Jesus is not atoning.[13] Hebrews certainly looks beyond the death to the presentation of blood on the heavenly ἱλαστήριον, but it in no way suggests that the death is not itself also a part of the full sweep of Christ's service. While we can agree with Moffitt that Christ is not properly a priest after the order of Melchizedek until his resurrection in eternal glory (so Heb. 7:16), this is not the same as saying that his priestly work cannot begin in any fashion before then.[14]

---

[9] See especially Jay Sklar, *Sin, Impurity, Sacrifice, Atonement: The Priestly Conceptions* (Hebrew Bible Monographs 2; Sheffield: Sheffield University Press, 2005), pp. 168-73.

[10] Cf. Jon Laansma, *The Letter to the Hebrews: A Commentary for Preaching, Teaching, and Bible Study* (Eugene, OR: Cascade, 2017), esp. pp. 179-84.

[11] contra Moffitt, *Atonement and the Logic of Resurrection*, p. 291 fn. 157. The closest that Moffitt comes to linking these two ritual acts—the shedding and the presentation of blood—is to say that the latter cannot be "completely abstracted" from the other (p. 269). Surely this understates the ritual nature of *both* acts.

[12] Nobuyoshi Kiuchi, *Leviticus* (Apollos Old Testament Commentary 3; Downers Grove, IL: IVP Academic, 2007), p. 321.

[13] See also Laansma, *The Epistle to the Hebrews*, p. 34 fn. 35.

[14] See further nuances prompted by engagement of early modern Protestant engagement with Socinian readings of Hebrews in this vein, sketched by Benjamin J. Ribbens, "The Ascension and Atonement: The Significance of Post-Reformation, Reformed Responses to Socinians for Contemporary Atonement Debates in Hebrews," (*Westminster Theological Journal*) (forthcoming); as well as more detailed analysis in Michael H. Kibbe, "Is It Finished? When Did It Start? Hebrews, Priesthood, and Atonement in Biblical, Systematic, and Historical Perspective," *Journal of Theological Studies* 651 (2014), pp. 25-61.

In summary, Moffitt has argued for a significant, discrete accent upon the resurrection in Hebrews. He has argued that Hebrews should be read against the backdrop of Jewish apocalypticism rather than Middle Platonism, and he sees the eschatological hope of humans to be an embodied state rather than a mystical flight from the material.[15] In both this book and a recent SBL paper Moffitt has made mention of the distinct phases, noting the various terms: resurrection, ascension, session.[16] It seems to me that his proposal could be clarified. Hebrews presents a robust account of Christ's heavenly session or exalted agency. Hebrews more than any other NT text speaks of the priestly work of Jesus (10:21). He remains the "great shepherd of the sheep" (13:20). Indeed, God's work "in us" is pleasing to God and is "through Jesus Christ" (13:21), suggesting that he remains operative as our cultic mediator. To that end, Hebrews addresses the ascension of Jesus Christ as well. Jesus, having made atonement, has gone into the presence of God (1:3-4; 10:12). His ascended enjoyment of God's presence is a pledge of what shall be ours: he has gone to it now via ascent, before God brings it to us in glory via divine descent. Finally, Hebrews presents the foundation of these exalted actions in the resurrection of the Lord Jesus. The resurrection is only explicit in a couple places (e.g., 13:20), albeit it serves a fundamental role in making sense of so many other explicit teachings. Here Heb. 7:16 is decisive: only one who is resurrected—note: not resuscitated, but glorified and raised anew to "indestructible life"—is fit to serve in this way as a priest forever.[17]

In light of the location of resurrection teaching in the theo-logic of exaltation, dare I suggest that his book might have better been titled *Atonement and the Logic of Exaltation in the Epistle to the Hebrews*? The exalted Christ serves as minister unto his people from the throne room on high. In grasping the precious purpose of his exalted presence, Moffitt has returned our attention to something prized by classical Reformed theology in its alertness not only to the earthly sojourn but also the heavenly service of our Lord. The Heidelberg Catechism inquired not only after the meaning of this exaltation but its significance as well.

> Q. 49 What benefit do we receive from Christ's ascension into heaven?
>
> A. First, that he is our Advocate in the presence of his Father in heaven. Second, that we have our flesh in heaven as a sure pledge that he, as the Head, will also take us, his members, up to himself. Third, that he sends us his Spirit as a counter-pledge by whose power we seek what is above, where Christ is, sitting at the right hand of God, and not things that are on earth.[18]

We do well now to attend to something of the breadth of that exalted beneficence, following the exegetical prompts of Moffitt and tracing out more fully the scope suggested by Heidelberg.

---

[15] See especially David Moffitt, "Serving in Heaven's Temple: Sacred Space, Yom Kippur, and Jesus' Superior Offering in Hebrews," (Presented to the Hebrews Study Group at the National Meeting of the SBL 2012), pp. 3–6; Moffitt, *Atonement and the Logic of Resurrection*, chapter 2.

[16] Moffitt, *Atonement and the Logic of Resurrection*, pp. 42–43; Moffitt, "Serving in Heaven's Temple," pp. 2, 15.

[17] Moffitt, *Atonement and the Logic of Resurrection*, pp. 202–3.

[18] "The Heidelberg Catechism (1563)," in *Reformed Confessions of the Sixteenth Century* (ed. Arthur Cochrane; Louisville: Westminster John Knox, 2003), p. 313.

The son "who is speaking ... warns from heaven" (12:25): The word of the exalted son

Having seen the significance of the exalted work of the Son, we turn now to press still further and consider whether or not his heavenly session also bears significance upon the prophetic ministry of his Word. Does the epistle to the Hebrews attest or suggest that the risen Son also fills his prophetic office from the heavenly throne room? Does the "great shepherd of the sheep" speak even now, so that his flock is equipped and knowledgeable unto his will (13:20-21)? I will argue that the reflections of David Moffitt upon the exalted priestly work of the Messiah may and should be matched by awareness of his ongoing prophetic work. We will consider three elements: the scattered allusions to the speech of the Son throughout the epistle, the significance of Heb. 12:25 for affirming his ongoing speech, and then the implications for the practice of theology. The evidence for an ongoing prophetic ministry seems to be no less explicit and a good bit more widely suggested than is the case made by Moffitt regarding his priestly action.

Christ's speech throughout the epistle

The epistle begins with speech: "Speech to our fathers by the prophets ... long ago, at many times and in many ways" (1:1), and speech "in these last days ... by his Son" (1:2). When identifying the Son through whom this latter-day speech has come, the author goes on to call him "the radiance of the glory of God and the exact imprint of his nature" (1:3). The Son's character is not only an "imprint" (χαρακτήρ) of the Father, suggesting his divinity, but is also a communicative manifestation of that divine, for he is not only glory but also the "radiance" (ἀπαύγασμα) of that transcendent glory.[19] The Son does not become or assume the form of radiant communication; he *is* that resplendent manifestation.

And this exordium does not leave it at just that; the prior attestation of the Son's role in creation now extends into his work of preservation. With respect to creation, we have already read that the Son is the one "through whom also he created the world" (1:2). With respect to preservation, the Son is no less active: "He upholds the universe by the word of his power" (1:3). The two claims are tied together, for 11:3 will eventually remind us that "the universe was created by the Word of God." Luke Timothy Johnson comments that "the same 'power' (δύναμις) has been at work from the beginning and continues now in the 'last of these days,' namely the power of God (see Heb. 2:4; 6:5; 7:16; 11:11)."[20]

The next chapter turns to focus more upon the sufferings of this Son in his incarnate form, and even here his speech continues to be affirmed with a new intonation. "He is

---

[19] "Glory" language will be extended in 2:7, 9, 10, where it is tied to the exaltation of the Son and is shared inclusively with his brothers. Language of "honor" and "exaltation" occurs also in 5:4-5 and of his fullness he shares as "the source of eternal salvation to all who obey him" (5:9). In this context, priestly language conveys the notion not only of distinction from others but also of ministration unto others.

[20] Johnson, *Hebrews*, p. 70.

not ashamed to call them brothers," so the Son's speech takes the form of identification with "his brothers in every respect" (2:11, 17). The author turns to Psalm 22, however, and says, "I will tell of your name to my brothers; in the midst of the congregation I will sing your praise" (2:12, quoting Ps. 22:22). That he will "tell" (ἀπαγγελῶ replacing διηγέομαι from the LXX) takes up the language of the Psalmist not only turning to intra-trinitarian discourse but in witness unto the "congregation." Such witness occurred while on earth; there is no reason, however, to presume that this testimony was concluded therein.

The third chapter identifies the Son with a distinctive title: "Apostle and high priest of our confession" (3:1). While "high priest" comes in for detailed and extended elaboration throughout chs. 5–10, the term "apostle" (ἀπόστολος) also warrants our attention. His sending for the sake of testimony not only relates to past activity but also to ongoing agency: to the earlier affirmation that he "*was* faithful to him who appointed him" (3:2), we see added later that "Christ *is* faithful over God's house as a Son" (3:6). Again, a scriptural quotation expresses the form of this activity. Here the author turns to Psalm 95, which begins with the gripping words, "Today, if you hear his voice, do not harden your hearts" (3:7, citing Ps. 95:7). Notice that the words are said by the Holy Spirit (3:7, "as the Holy Spirit says"), though it goes on likely to attest another's speech ("his" in 3:7b probably referring to the Son and not to the Spirit who speaks).[21] We see this differentiation drawn out more explicitly when Ps. 95:7 reappears several verses later. "We have come to share in Christ, if indeed we hold our original confidence firm to the end. As it is said, 'Today, if you hear his voice . . . '" (3:14-15, quoting Ps. 95:7). Here the identification of "his voice" with the Christ in whom one places one's confidence is all the more explicit. It seems to be the case that the apostolic mission of the Son continues even now over his house.

Hebrews will go on to speak of the mediatory work (μεσίτης) of the Son in various contexts (8:6; 9:15; 12:24).[22] It fixes upon the priestly role of the Son, as noted earlier in our reflections on the work of Moffitt, and thus focuses on words rendered by the Son unto our Father in intercession (e.g., 7:25). These three passages, however, suggest that Hebrews presents an account of the Son speaking unto his household as well, wherein he fills the office of a prophet as well as a royal priest (7:1). One later passage extends this exalted speech more fully, and so we turn now to consider Heb. 12:25 at slightly greater length before finally asking how this affirmation of Christ as an exalted prophet shapes the doctrine of Scripture found within Hebrews.

Hebrews 12:25

Zion and Sinai come in for comparison in Hebrews 12, and communication proves to be fundamental to each in its own way. "So terrifying was the sight" (12:21), and the author depicts various facets of the overwhelming vista: "Blazing fire" and "darkness and gloom and a tempest" on the one side, and "innumerable angels in festal gathering" and "the assembly of the firstborn who are enrolled in heaven" on the other side (12:18,

---

[21] Thomas Aquinas, *Commentary on the Epistle to the Hebrews* (trans. Chrysostom Baer; South Bend, IN: St. Augustine's, 2006), p. 83.
[22] See Chapter 6 by Daniel J. Treier in the present volume.

22-23). Yet amidst all that whirling dervish and redolent brilliance, the author comes back to the vocal: "And a voice whose words made the hearers beg that no further messages be spoken to them" (12:19) on the one hand, and "Jesus" and "the sprinkled blood that speaks a better word than the blood of Abel" (12:24) on the other hand. Like Sinai, with its characterization of a promised sight of God from the rear and around the cleft of a rock, so here vision of God takes the form of hearing from God (see Exod. 34:6-7).[23]

A moral summons draws out the reality of this speech explicitly: "See that you do not refuse him who is speaking" (12:25). The God who reigns may be identified as the speaking one here (τὸν λαλοῦντα); his character takes the form of communicative presence. The language of warning (τὸν χρηματίζοντα) expands and clarifies on this claim regarding divine speech. The exalted Son—this Jesus whose blood was sprinkled in the heavenlies (9:14; 10:22)[24]—warns and speaks and in so doing shakes not only the earth but also the heavens. This warning arises "from heaven" (ἀπ' οὐρανῶν). Divine agency and initiative comes to the fore with the language of heaven employed here: not so much a geographic or spatial term in this context as an agential and operative appellation. Hebrews takes up the categories of Platonic philosophy and puts them to covenantal and active use, turning what might be perceived as solely metaphysical demarcations and throwing them in both a temporal and an ethical framework (albeit no less ontological a lens).[25]

Edward Adams and James Thompson have thereby noted that this is "the main eschatological passage of the epistle."[26] Indeed, Adams suggests that while this voice comes from heaven, its effects are felt tangibly upon this earth. To this end, Adams points to the physical and meteorological impress of "shaking" in the Sinai event (12:18-21, 26a read that occurrence as involving what he deems a "global earthquake").[27] Irrespective of one's judgment regarding the best interpretation of the "shaking" language, whether metaphorical or directly meteorological, the vocabulary and conceptuality surely speaks to divine agency and its vivid effect (whether catastrophic materially or in other registers).

Again, mediation and identification are not juxtaposed or at least not mutually exclusive. Just as God spoke through and to prophets (1:1-2), so now Christ speaks (12:25) even when others speak in his name. "There is a general rule in the words, namely, that we are diligently to attend unto, and not to refuse any that speak unto

---

[23] For reflections on the epistemology of Sinai, see especially Gregory Nyssa, *Life of Moses* (trans. Abraham Malherbe and Everett Ferguson; Classics of Western Spirituality; New York: Paulist, 1978), esp. pp. 91-93; see also Nathan Eubank, "Ineffably Effable: The Pinnacle of Mystical Ascent in Gregory of Nyssa's *De vita Moysis*," *International Journal of Systematic Theology* 16.1 (2014), pp. 25-41.

[24] The Christological focus manifests itself in reading 12:25 against the backdrop of Jesus's speech in 12:24.

[25] Further analysis of the relation of Platonic language in Hebrews exceeds the bounds of this chapter. See the sketch of the issues so well portrayed by Luke Timothy Johnson, *Hebrews: A Commentary* (NTL; Louisville: Westminster John Knox, 2006), pp. 18–21.

[26] Edward Adams, *The Stars Will Fall from Heaven: "Cosmic Catastrophe" in the New Testament and its World* (LNTS 347; London: T&T Clark, 2007), p. 185; see also James W. Thompson, *The Beginnings of Christian Philosophy: The Epistle to the Hebrews* (CBQMS 13; Washington, DC: Catholic Biblical Association of America, 1982), pp. 42–43.

[27] Adams, *Stars Will Fall From Heaven*, p. 189; *contra* Anton Vögtle, *Das Neue Testament und Die Zukunft des Kosmos* (KBNT; Düsseldorff: Patmos, 1970), p. 88.

us in the name and authority of Christ. And so it may be applied unto all the faithful preachers of the gospel, however they may be despised in this world. But it is here the person of Christ himself that is immediately intended."[28] Hebrews 12:25 prompts our communicative imagination to be alert to the exalted Son's warning amidst and through the words of his emissaries. This apostle proves faithful over his household oftentimes (3:1, 6)—perhaps we must say ordinarily—through the delegated agency of his own apostles.[29] We turn finally then to ask how this exalted Christology and its distinctively prophetic aspect flavors the way in which Hebrews speaks of the Word of God in written form.

Word of God: Hebrews 4:12-13 and 13:8 and the doctrine of Scripture

The epistle to the Hebrews has much to commend regarding the doctrine of Scripture, and recent studies have offered analysis of its contribution to a Christian theology of Holy Scripture, both its being and the appropriate ethic of its recipients. The leading studies—as in the recent essays of Treier and Schenk or the earlier monographs of Graham Hughes and F. Synge—analyze what may be called the "doctrine of Scripture practiced in Hebrews."[30] Much can be gleaned inductively from watching an apostolic emissary refract the witness of earlier prophetic testimony. We do well to ask another question, however, regarding what light the attestation of the exalted Son as an active prophet might shed upon the doctrine of Scripture taught by Hebrews. May we work

---

[28] John Owen, *Exposition of Hebrews 11:1-13:25* (Edinburgh: Banner of Truth Trust, 1991), p. 354.

[29] See D. Johanne Polyandro, "Disputation 42: On the Calling of those who Minister to the Church, and on Their Duties," in *Synopsis Purioris Theologiae*, volume 2: *Disputations 24–42* (ed. Henk van den Belt; trans. Riemer Faber; Studies in Medieval and Reformation Traditions 204; Leiden: Brill, 2016), pp. 620–21 (Thesis 1).

[30] The language comes from Treier's subtitle. See Daniel J. Treier, "Speech Acts, Hearing Hearts, and Other Senses: The Doctrine of Scripture Practiced in Hebrews," in *The Epistle to the Hebrews and Christian Theology* (ed. Richard Bauckham, Daniel Driver, Trevor Hart, and Nathan MacDonald; Grand Rapids, MI: Eerdmans, 2009), pp. 337–50; cf. Ken Schenck, "God Has Spoken: Hebrews' Theology of the Scriptures," in *The Epistle to the Hebrews and Christian Theology* (ed. Richard Bauckham, Daniel Driver, Trevor Hart, and Nathan MacDonald; Grand Rapids, MI: Eerdmans, 2009), pp. 321–36; Luke Timothy Johnson, "The Scriptural World of Hebrews," (*Interpretation* 57, 2003), pp. 237–50; T. Lewicki, "*Weist nicht ab den Sprechenden!*": *Wort Gottes und Paraklese im Hebräerbrief* (Padorborner Theologische Studien 41; Paderborn: Schöningh, 2004); Graham Hughes, *Hebrews and Hermeneutics: The Epistle to the Hebrews as a New Testament Example of Biblical Interpretation* (SNTSMS 36; Cambridge: Cambridge University Press, 1979); see also the comments on what might be termed prosopological exegesis found in Karen Jobes's Chapter 2, "Putting Words In His Mouth: The Son Speaks in Hebrews," in the present volume. Many additional studies could be culled from the literature that address portions of the text as readings of prior scripture (e.g., the catena of texts cited in 1:5-13 or the narrative allusions in ch. 11), much of which was summarized well in George H. Guthrie, "Hebrews' Use of the Old Testament: Recent Trends in Research," *Currents in Biblical Research* 1 (2003), pp. 271–94. The literature focusing on specific case studies has grown exponentially since 2003. Only the rare study manages to move beyond its immediate focus to range more widely regarding the canonical, covenantal, and theological shape of Hebrews more broadly; such an example can be found in David M. Allen, *Deuteronomy and Exhortation in Hebrews: A Study in Narrative Re-Presentation* (WUNT 2:238; Tübingen: Mohr Siebeck, 2008).

deductively as well to glean further insight into its implications for a Christian theology of Holy Scripture and of theological knowledge?

Oftentimes discussions of hermeneutics and of bibliology move too much in the categories of peripheral disciplines or later (and perhaps misleadingly anachronistic) eras.[31] While such comparative and conversational approaches may open up new angles by which we might see more within the witness of Scripture itself, we do well nonetheless to attend to claims internal to and overt within the text itself. A recent example of much benefit in this regard can be found in the way that Uche Anizor uses the biblical-theological category of "royal priesthood" to describe the ideal reader of Scripture in its own terms.[32] In the space that remains, I wish to explore a similar approach regarding our account of scripture's voice that seeks to honor the claims of that scripture itself. In so doing, we will remain focused upon the Christological claims of Hebrews, especially as we find them in 4:12 and then in 13:8.

"For the word of God is living and active, sharper than any two-edged sword, piercing to the division of soul and of spirit, of joints and of marrow, and discerning the thoughts and intentions of the heart" (4:12). The oft-benighted sixteenth-century reformer Huldrych Zwingli riffs on this language in testifying to what he deems the clarity and the certainty of the Word. To Hebrews' "living and active," Zwingli resounds with the pairings of "sure and strong," "alive and strong," and "alive and sure."[33] In expounding the certainty or power of the Word in 1522, Zwingli attests not its literary or syntactical simplicity but its theological nature. The Word packs a punch because it is a glove, not itself a fist; the scriptural Word has significant impact because the force of the mighty hand and outstretched arm of the Almighty stands behind its collision course with sinners.[34] We must tend to several elaborations found herein.

God's Son lives and acts with the life and agency of one raised into glorified existence in God's own presence. His being now is not merely his own, but he lives for us and we exist in him. Hebrews employs the language of Platonism here also in its deployment of covenantal agency and identity. We have talked now at some length about this exalted existence of God's own Son and also about his verbal agency, which prompts us to say that not only does Jesus live and act but his own Word is "living and active" as well

---

[31] Such analyses find their way even into case studies focused on portions of Hebrews, such as Dale Leschert, *Hermeneutical Foundations of Hebrews: A Study in the Validity of the Epistle's Interpretation of Some Core Citations from the Psalms* (Lewiston, NY: Edwin Mellon, 1994); to a lesser extent, one can observe similar valuation arising from anachronistic principles in A. T. Hanson, *The Living Utterances of God: The New Testament Exegesis of the Old* (London: Darton, Longman, & Todd, 1983). A case study approach that avoids modern anachronism by gleaning from the history of interpretation (specifically Augustine and Calvin) can be found in Gregory W. Lee, *Today When You Hear His Voice: Scripture, Covenants, and the People of God* (Grand Rapids, MI: Eerdmans, 2017).

[32] Uche Anizor, *Kings and Priests: Scripture's Theological Account of Its Readers* (Eugene, OR: Pickwick, 2014).

[33] Huldrych Zwingli, "The Clarity and Certainty of the Word of God," in *Zwingli and Bullinger* (ed. G. W. Bromiley; Library of Christian Classics; Louisville: Westminster John Knox, 2006), pp. 68, 70, 72.

[34] See especially W. P. Stephens, *The Theology of Huldrych Zwingli* (Oxford: Clarendon, 1986), pp. 51–52; Gottfried W. Locher, *Die Theologie Huldrych Zwingli sim Lichte seiner Christologie, Erster Teil: Die Gotteslehre* (Zürich: Zwingli Verlag, 1952), pp. 93–95.

(Heb. 4:12). We do well now to consider the purpose and the object of that active speech. Unto whom does it speak? And to what ends?

God's Word pierces. Zwingli finds the Word of God to pack a powerful punch in as much as it serves as a tool in the Spirit's agency. As Daniël Timmermann says, "Just like Luther's principle of the general priesthood, Zwingli's emphasis on the inner illumination of believers primarily bears a soteriological connotation."[35] Hebrews uses a term here—μερισμός—which speaks to division of that which is most fundamental and internal to the person. The divided pair—πνεῦμα and ψυχή—are not natural opposites (cf. 1 Thess. 5:23), and that is precisely the point. The Spirit's Word not only sorts that which is overtly distinct and obviously contradictory but even divides that which is seemingly woven together in the fabric of our sinful form.

God's Word discerns. "As with 'soul and spirit, joints and marrow,' the discernment between thought and conception is the more impressive because the difference between them is so slight and unavailable to human perception."[36] The paragraph will crescendo with the cryptic line πρὸς ὃν ἡμῖν ὁ λόγος (4:13), often translated "To him is our account directed," and likely meaning something more relational and less formally tied to a household servant's accounting unto his or her master, as might be rendered "with whom we have to do" (RSV).[37]

In so doing, God's Word cuts "sharper than any two-edged sword." A theology of divine discipline lays beneath this imagery—judgment takes not only punitive but also paternally restorative and thus pedagogical intonations here. True enough, Hebrews speaks of that which shall be judged: "If it bears thorns and thistles, it is worthless and near to being cursed, and its end is to be burned" (6:8). But the sword attests not only, and perhaps not even primarily, the division of wheat and tares, and sheep and goats, but more fundamentally the division within the people of God which can better be termed true and false. Hebrews 12:5-13 speaks to this fatherly discipline (drawing on Prov. 3:11,12) which marks legitimate sons (13:7).[38] The living and active Word of the great shepherd of the sheep disciplines and forms his own, extending grace by addressing them with life and confronting them with his own active presence. The category of "discipline" proves fundamental here to speak of the purposive character of Scripture in Christ's own hands, in as much as it speaks to the continual conversion or ongoing sanctification of his own company. His apostolic embassy serves to trumpet and to transform with his vocal pronouncement. And in so doing he does not allow us to wallow in our self-enclosed spiritual echo chambers; he pierces and discerns and, as needs be, cuts so as to bring us into the life and action which are his own. Hebrews presents an exalted Christology that heralds the prophetic work of the Son, and it ties this ever so closely to his living and active Word. Thus, bibliology and soteriology are bound up together, not conflated but

---

[35] Daniël Zimmermann, *Heinrich Bullinger on Prophecy and the Prophetic Office (1523–1538)* (Reformed Historical Theology 33; Göttingen: Vandenhoeck & Ruprecht, 2015), p. 85.

[36] Johnson, *Hebrews*, p. 135.

[37] See E.-M. Becker, "'Gottes Wort' und 'Unser Wort': Bemerkungen zu Heb. 4,12-13," *BZ* 44 (2000), pp. 254–62.

[38] On the background to this discussion, see Matthew Thiessen, "Hebrews 12.5-13, the Wilderness Period, and Israel's Discipline," *New Testament Studies* 55.3 (2009), pp. 366–79.

coordinated Christologically for the sake of hearkening God's people onward in their journey today while it is yet today.

Conclusion

We have seen in this chapter that Hebrews does draw out the exalted mediation of the Son, in so doing relying on, adjusting, and furthering the arguments of David Moffitt. Then we have pointed to an even more prevalent emphasis on the speech of this exalted Son, culminating in the attestation of 12:25. Finally we have seen that the exalted prophecy of the Son provides the lens through which we ought to view the teaching of Hebrews regarding the nature and power of the Word of God, and we have found the polemical ruminations of Huldrych Zwingli to be a useful prompt in drawing out the shape of this "living and active" speech of the Son. Before concluding, we do well to attend to one further Christological confession of this sermon.

"Jesus Christ is the same yesterday and today and forever" (13:8). Such words do not undercut the integrity of each era. They do not negate the events of any epoch by placing them in relief with the vivid activity of any other season. They certainly do not demean the present amidst the palpable gravity of the past or the pressing hope of the future. Rather, they attest the ongoing agency and being of the Son who was before all things, through whom all things perdure, and to whom all things aim (cf. Rom. 11:33). The "pastoral eschatology" offered in Hebrews manifests an alert eye to the goodness of the old and yet the greater glory of the new. There is truly and only "a better hope" (7:19).[39] Appreciating the significance of the exalted agency of the Son helps attune us to the present proclamation of his Word, whereby he ministers unto his own that which is "living and active" (4:12).

The invariable integrity of the Word throughout all generations relates rather directly to a seeming shift in textual observation here. Michael Kibbe has noted that Heb. 12:18–29 suggests a rather negative judgment regarding Israel at Sinai when compared to the prior judgment suggested by Deut. 5:28. In that Pentateuch text, we read Moses saying: "And the LORD heard your words, when you spoke to me. And the LORD said to me, 'I have heard the words of this people, which they have spoken to you. They are right in all that they have spoken.'" Kibbe notes that Zion exceeds Sinai in as much as the mediator has enacted a greater ministry in two ways. First, we are summoned into the holy place of heaven to find rest, rather than summoning us in and out and in and out. Second, the mediator not only enters for others but also with others.[40] We have an unbreakable union and we all may enjoy a personal communion with God. Therefore, Hebrews again and again speaks of the "better" and the "great," not the merely well and good.

---

[39] See John Webster, "One Who Is Son: Theological Reflections on the Exordium to the Epistle to the Hebrews," in *The Epistle to the Hebrews and Christian Theology* (ed. Richard Bauckham, Daniel Driver, Trevor Hart, and Nathan MacDonald; Grand Rapids, MI: Eerdmans, 2009), p. 72.

[40] Michael Kibbe, *Godly Fear or Ungodly Failure? Hebrews 12 and the Sinai Theophanies* (BZNW 216; Berlin: De Gruyter, 2016), esp. p. 183. See also Benjamin J. Ribbens, *Levitical Sacrifice and Heavenly Cult in Hebrews* (BZNW 222; Berlin: De Gruyter, 2016), esp. pp. 109–226 (comparing Old and New Covenant sacrifices in terms of their perfection[s]).

What Deuteronomy portrays as well and good is viewed by Hebrews as actually being a good state for that prior era but now as a negative step backward. This judgment about the unity and varied administrations of the divine economy stems from a further awareness regarding the new mediator and the greater glory that he has communicated. "Jesus Christ is the same yesterday and today and forever" (13:8). In and through him, we too enter into the heavenly places boldly. The steady service of the Son—who stands "the same" in the very presence of God—undergirds our confidence and boldness. In just this way does the "great shepherd of the sheep" exercise his pastoral oversight and equip his disciples for "that which is pleasing in [God's] sight" (13:20, 21).

It Is Not Finished: Jesus's Perpetual Atoning Work as the Heavenly High Priest in Hebrews

David M. Moffitt

"Even at this moment, as a human being, [Jesus] is making intercession for my salvation, for he continues to wear the body that he assumed."

Gregory of Nazianzus, *Oration* 30.14

Introduction

The ongoing high-priestly ministry of Jesus in the heavenly tabernacle stands among the more neglected aspects of NT Christology and soteriology in much modern biblical and theological reflection. Jesus's cry in John's Gospel, "It is finished," has taken on a life of its own, becoming a prooftext in certain circles for the view that the full and final completion of Jesus's sacrificial and salvific work occurred as he expired on the cross. Alan Stibbs makes this case particularly clearly in the introductory paragraph to his book, *The Finished Work of Christ*. Stibbs claims, "The idea that Christ's atoning work is 'finished' is Scriptural in origin: it is indeed based on a word uttered by our Lord Himself before His death on the cross."[1] This word is, of course, Jesus's cry in Jn 19:30—Τετέλεσται ("It is finished!"). Stibbs continues, "Clearly, therefore, when Jesus at last reached the point of departure from this present earthly life, the work to which this word τετέλεσται referred was already fully accomplished."[2] Whether or not this is

---

[1] Alan M. Stibbs, *The Finished Work of Christ* (London: The Tyndale Press, 1954), p. 5.
[2] Ibid. Stibbs states the thesis of his book as follows: "Christ's work of offering Himself for men's salvation is unmistakably represented in Scripture as *exclusively* earthly and historical, the purpose of the incarnation, wrought out in flesh and blood, in time and space, under Pontius Pilate; that by this once-for-all finished happening the necessary and intended atoning work was completely accomplished . . . " (p. 8, emphasis added). It is worth pointing out here that such an account of Jesus's death as the sum total of his atoning sacrifice cannot be made to square with the actual scriptural depictions of atoning sacrifices detailed in Leviticus. Stibbs may be aware of this issue. He tellingly labels approaches that emphasize Jesus's heavenly presentation of his atoning sacrifice to the Father as "more Jewish than fully Christian" (*Finished Work*, p. 22). One of the problems Stibbs does not engage, however, is the very real historical one of how the first Christians, who were Jews, could have thought about sacrifice in such new and different "fully Christian" categories rather than the "Jewish" ones that they believed God gave them in scripture.

the proper interpretation of Jn 19:30,[3] the witness of Hebrews differs in kind from such an account of Jesus's priestly and sacrificial work precisely because Hebrews stresses more emphatically and explicitly than any other NT text that Jesus is currently the great high priest who now ministers for his people in the heavenly holy of holies (Heb. 8:1-4; see also 7:25).

But what comprises Jesus's heavenly ministry? Hebrews suggests that upon his passing through the heavens as the one appointed by God to the position of high priest in Melchizedek's order, Jesus drew near to the Father in order to appear in his presence (see esp. 4:14-16; 5:8-10; 9:24-26). There, as the great high priest, he presented to God nothing less than himself as the ultimate atoning sacrifice on behalf of his brothers and sisters. He thereby made purification for sins and sat down at the Father's right hand where he waits for all his enemies to be made his footstool (esp. Heb. 1:3; 10:12-14). His once-for-all offering has been presented and accepted. He has no need to re-present or re-offer himself to the Father.[4]

But is this the sum total of Jesus's heavenly ministry? Moreover, does the once-for-all-ness of his sacrifice mean that his atoning work is fully and finally finished even now? If this were the case, one might wonder why Hebrews emphasizes the need to have a high priest who presently serves as a minister in the heavenly holy of holies (8:1), particularly one who continually intercedes for his people (7:25). If all sin and impurity is fully and finally taken care of by the singular entry of Jesus into the Father's presence, why is his ongoing intercession, presumably a constituent element of his high-priestly ministry, still necessary?[5]

This study reexamines these questions and offers the following three conclusions: 1) Jesus's work of high-priestly intercession implies the need for ongoing forgiveness and purification—some kind of ongoing work of sacrificial atonement[6]—for his followers; 2) if this is correct, Hebrews does not conceive of Jesus's atoning, high-priestly work as completed on the cross or even upon his ascension, though his singular act of presenting himself to the Father is clearly unrepeatable;[7] 3) the atoning work that

---

[3] For a few examples of commentators who argue the case, see R. V. G. Tasker, *The Gospel According to St. John* (TNTC; Grand Rapids, MI: Eerdmans, 1960), p. 211; Leon Morris, *The Gospel According to John* (rev. ed.; NICNT; Grand Rapids, MI: Eerdmans, 1995), p. 720 n. 77; cf. pp. 130–31.

[4] I detail the case for this interpretation of Hebrews' understanding of Jesus' sacrifice in David M. Moffitt, *Atonement and the Logic of Resurrection in the Epistle to the Hebrews* (NovTSup 141; Leiden: Brill, 2011).

[5] As one might guess from the quotation of Gregory of Nazianzus in the header to this chapter, a rich history of reflection on this question can be found in Patristic literature (I survey some of this literature here: David M. Moffitt, "Jesus' Heavenly Sacrifice in Early Christian Reception of Hebrews: A Survey", *JTS* 68 [2017]: pp. 46–71). See also the fascinating late-nineteenth-century study of William Milligan, *The Ascension and Heavenly Priesthood of Our Lord: The Baird Lecture 1891* (London: Macmillan, 1892), esp. pp. 113–65. Though my own account of Hebrews differs in significant ways from Milligan's, our questions and interpretations of Hebrews are similar at many points. (I am grateful to Michael Kibbe for bringing Milligan's volume to my attention.)

[6] I define this term later in this chapter. See also, David M. Moffitt, "Hebrews," in *T&T Clark Companion to Atonement* (ed. Adam J. Johnson; London: Bloomsbury T&T Clark, 2017), pp. 533–36.

[7] This does not mean that Jesus's death/work on the cross is not salvific. The point rather is that Jesus does more to effect salvation than simply die. The tendency to speak of the atonement as if it were equal to a systematic account of Christian soteriology creates confusion when the wide variety of problems that early Christians believed Jesus solved in order to save humanity are lumped together into one concept and event. I discuss this issue more later in this chapter.

Jesus continues to perform now is that of maintaining the New Covenant relationship between God and his people, work that is necessary while the covenant people are still in the process of being sanctified and have not yet been perfected.

In short, the author reflects on Jesus's ongoing work of sacrificial atonement in ways that are remarkably analogous to the ministry of the Old Covenant priesthood, especially the high priests, and the Levitical-sacrificial system. As the high priest of the New Covenant, Jesus now ministers in the heavenly tabernacle by offering to the Father the ongoing worship that maintains God's new covenant relationship with his people and mediates the blessings and promises associated with that relationship. This act of ongoing offering consists in the very presence of the interceding Son, Jesus, with the Father. The author of Hebrews, in other words, has neither embraced a logic of sacrifice that stands against that of the Levitical system, which God ordained, nor does he work with a New Covenant logic that differs radically from that of the Mosaic Covenant. Instead, as one might expect given that the earliest Christians were Jews, he draws insights about who Jesus is and how Jesus saves his followers from the very scriptures and practices he takes to be inspired and revealed by God (cf. Heb. 1:1-2). The logic of the New Covenant and the sacrificial and high-priestly ministry Jesus performs within it relate organically for this author to those of the Old Covenant.

Some key assumptions

The arguments advanced here depend in part upon six working assumptions and one caveat concerning Jesus's high priesthood, sacrifice, and atonement in Hebrews. I have explored and defended these conclusions in other publications, but some acknowledgment and elaboration of my working conclusions are necessary for the sake of the case being advanced here.

First, I assume that the author of Hebrews has thought carefully through the problem of Jesus's tribal lineage for the legitimacy of the claim that Jesus is a high priest. The author and the original audience likely shared a confession that identifies Jesus as a high priest. This identification may be a central element of the confession that some have begun to call into question.[8] The writer presents his apologetic reflection on the validity of Jesus's high priesthood in Heb. 5:1–7:28, and especially in Hebrews 7.

---

[8] George H. Guthrie demonstrates conclusively the structural links between Heb. 4:14-16 and 10:19-23, arguing that these verses form an *inclusio* (*The Structure of Hebrews: A Text-Linguistic Analysis* [NovTSup 73; Leiden: Brill, 1994], pp. 79–80). This is relevant for reflecting on the confession the author urges the congregation to maintain. While he never gives the content of the shared confession he wants his intended readers to continue to affirm, the fact that the bulk of the material that stands between his two explicit calls to hold fast to this confession (4:14; 10:23) revolves around the topic of Jesus's high priesthood (with the author first defending the legitimacy of Jesus's high priesthood in Heb. 5:1–7:28, and, second discussing the covenantal context, location, and nature of Jesus's high-priestly ministry in 8:1–10:20) implies that the affirmation of Jesus's high-priestly status is one of the central elements of the common confession that he thinks his readers are in danger of surrendering (see also the explicit reference to Jesus's high priesthood in the author's first reference to a shared confession in Heb. 3:1). A similar conclusion, though via a different route, was advanced by Ernst Käsemann, who located the confession of Jesus's high priesthood in early Christian liturgy that predates Hebrews (*Das wandernde Gottesvolk: Eine Untersuchung zum Hebräerbrief* [4th ed.; Göttingen: Vandenhoeck & Ruprecht, 1961], pp. 108–10).

His main goal in Hebrews 7 is to show how Jesus, a Judahite by birth, can legitimately be the high priest he is confessed to be. The problem the author faces concerns Jesus's humanity.[9] This latter point has at times not been properly explored in the commentary literature due to the misguided assumption that Hebrews derives Jesus's high-priestly status from the fact of his divine Sonship.[10] Thus, it bears repeating that the issue of Jesus's priestly status is in Hebrews chiefly a question of his humanity, not one of his status as divine Son per se.

A few observations help to clarify the point. If the author thought that Jesus's high priesthood was a function of Jesus's divine nature rather than one of Jesus's humanity, he has done a particularly poor job laying out his case. One could well imagine him reducing the complex argument of Hebrews 7 to a simple statement that Jesus is high priest *because* he is the Son. Instead, however, the logic of the author's argument aims to show that, *although* Jesus is the Son, he suffered, died, and, after being made perfect (τελειωθείς), *became* (ἐγένετο) the source of eternal salvation (Heb. 5:8–10). That is to say, although Jesus is the royal and divine Son, he nevertheless became the high priest that he is confessed to be. This logic implies that simply being the Son does not qualify Jesus to be a high priest.

Unpacking this concessive logic requires sustained and careful argumentation on the part of the author precisely because he knows that as the Son Jesus lacks the proper qualification to be a priest at all, at least on earth where the Mosaic law has authority (compare Heb. 7:14 and 8:4). To put the point differently, when the divine Son took up the blood and flesh of Abraham's seed, he took up the blood and flesh of the line of Judah. The Son came into the world in the tribe and lineage of Judah. While this coheres well with the Son's royal role as the Christ, the reigning messiah, the fact of the incarnation creates a problem for Jesus's elevation to service in the priesthood. According to the Mosaic law no one from the tribe of Judah can legitimately serve as a priest. To be a priest of God who serves in the earthly sanctuary, one must belong to the tribe of Levi (esp. Deut. 18:1-5). Thus, even though Jesus is the Son and, like Aaron, God called him to the office of high priest, his elevation to that office faces a problem created by the incarnation itself, precisely because the incarnation placed the Son in the wrong tribe for priestly service. The issue the author therefore has to solve when looking at both the confession of Jesus's high-priestly status and God's revelation through Moses revolves around his status as the incarnate Son in Judah's tribe.[11]

---

[9] For my detailed arguments on this subject, see Moffitt, *Atonement and the Logic of Resurrection*, esp. pp. 200–14.

[10] See, for example, B. F. Westcott, *The Epistle to the Hebrews: The Greek Text with Notes and Essays* (3rd ed.; London: MacMillan and Co., 1903), p. 124; James Moffatt, *A Critical and Exegetical Commentary on The Epistle to the Hebrews* (ICC; Edinburgh: T&T Clark, 1924), p. 64. Other accounts that do not look to Jesus's divinity but nevertheless think Jesus's priesthood is a function of his sonship are present in the secondary literature (e.g., Käsemann, *Das wandernde Gottesvolk*, p. 141). Deborah W. Rooke suggests that Hebrews draws on the ancient Israelite notion of sacral kingship ("Jesus as Royal Priest: Reflections on the Interpretation of the Melchizedek Tradition in Heb 7", *Biblica* 81 [2000]: pp. 81–94). Among other considerations, the fact that Hebrews does so little to develop the royal office of Melchizedek works against Rooke's thesis.

[11] One wonders if this difficulty with confessing Jesus as both royal Son from Judah's tribe and high priest may be one of the points under contention among those who might be tempted to abandon the community and its confession.

The author must have seen a number of possible solutions to this issue. He has already ruled out a simple deduction from the Son's divine preexistence, taking seriously the need for high priests to be human beings (Heb. 5:1). Still, he could have merely reasserted in Hebrews 7 God's call of Jesus to the role (Heb. 5:5-6), a fact he obviously thinks is fundamental for Jesus's elevation to high-priestly status. Divine fiat would seem to offer sufficient warrant to allow for an exception to the Mosaic law. The writer does not, however, center his argument in Hebrews 7 on the fact of Jesus's divine appointment. He could have simply appealed to Melchizedek, the priest-king, as offering a model from Psalm 110 that justifies the application of both roles to Jesus. Here, too, he is clearly aware of Melchizedek's dual offices (Heb. 7:2-3) and his passing comment on Melchizedek's kingship seems designed to highlight the fact that this figure holds both royal and priestly offices. Yet after pointing this out, he surprisingly does not develop Melchizedek's royal role as his argument in Hebrews 7 unfolds.

The author adopts instead a different solution, one that takes Jesus's death, bodily resurrection, and ascension into account. In the process, he highlights his respect for the authority of the Mosaic law. Rather than appealing to the Son's divinity as something that simply trumped the particularity of Jesus's humanity; rather than playing out the mention of God's call of the Son to the high priesthood in terms of divine fiat that simply supersedes the law; rather than developing Melchizedek's royal status and explaining how this is a model for Jesus, the tack he takes both (1) recognizes that the law forbids Jesus to serve as a priest on earth (Heb. 7:14; 8:4), and (2) develops the claims that Jesus's high-priestly office is heavenly and that the high-priestly service he performs occurs in the heavenly tabernacle (Heb. 8:1-4).

Second, I assume that the bodily resurrection of Jesus from the dead, which Hebrews correlates with the Son's perfection and which also pertains to the incarnate Son's humanity, provides the author with the solution to the Mosaic problem of Jesus's tribal descent barring him from priestly ministry. The bodily resurrection of Jesus perfects his Judahite humanity. As a perfected Jew from the tribe of Judah, Jesus's humanity is now immortal, no longer corruptible and no longer subject to death, as it clearly was when he died on the cross. The indestructible life he now has as a human being qualifies him to serve in another legitimate priesthood, the heavenly one to which the ministering spirits belong.[12] As noted above, the author does not resolve the problem of the Mosaic law's stipulations on tribal descent by dismissing the law *tout court*. Indeed, the law's authority regarding priestly legitimation appears to be the presupposition that necessitates his defense of the legitimacy of Jesus's high priesthood. The logic of the argument in Hebrews 7 seizes on the transformation of Jesus's particular Judahite humanity in the resurrection such that, as a human being, Jesus now has life that is like that of Melchizedek. This indestructible life into which he arose qualifies him to serve as the priest of Melchizedek's order spoken of in Psalm 110 (see esp. Heb. 7:15-16).[13] Further, this implies that Jesus became the high priest he

[12] For additional argumentation, see David M. Moffitt, "'If Another Priest Arises': Jesus' Resurrection and the High Priestly Christology of Hebrews," in *A Cloud of Witnesses: The Theology of Hebrews in it Ancient Contexts* (ed. Richard Bauckham, Daniel Driver, Trevor Hart, and Nathan MacDonald; LNTS 387; London: T&T Clark, 2008), pp. 68–79.

[13] In an excellent essay Georg Gäbel has recently argued against this conclusion ("'[. . .] inmitten der Gemeinde werde ich dir lobsingnen' Hebr 2,12: Engel und Menschen, himmlischer und irdischer

now is at the resurrection, when his human lineage no longer barred him from priestly service.[14] The author has, then, constructed a careful and precise argument that takes seriously both the particularity of the heavenly Son's incarnation and the authority of the divinely given law of Moses.

Third, I work with the assumption that this author believes that the resurrected Jesus ascended through the heavens into the highest heaven where he entered the inner sanctum of the heavenly tabernacle. This is the location where he serves as high priest.

Gottesdienst nach dem Hebräerbrief", in *Gottesdienst und Engel im antiken Judentum und frühen Christentum* [ed. Jörg Frey and Michael R. Jost; WUNT 2/446; Tübingen: Mohr Siebeck, 2017], pp. 185–239 [212–15]). I continue, however, to be persuaded that the writer assumes that Melchizedek is an angelic priest, one of the ministering, that is, priestly, spirits (see Heb. 1:7, 14), above whom Jesus has been elevated in his resurrected humanity. This means, contra Gäbel, that Hebrews is interested in Melchizedek himself, particularly because of the kind of life this mysterious figure possesses, and how Jesus relates to him (as well as how Melchizedek relates to the eternal Son). The conclusion that Melchizedek is an angel not only explains why the author can identify him in immortal terms, which is surely the most straightforward reading of the language about him in Heb. 7:3 and 7:8, but also coheres well with the writer's identification of Jesus as the great *high* priest even though this fact (that is, his *high* priesthood) cannot be deduced from Ps. 110:4, which speaks only of a priest. Gäbel is right to note that the priestly order to which Jesus belongs has only one high priest—Jesus himself. But why is the Son the high priest of an order named after Melchizedek? In my view, the Son has become the sole high priest of Melchizedek's order because the Son, unlike any of the other priests currently serving in the heavenly priesthood, is the first perfected human being elevated to serve in this priestly order. As such, he has been exalted above *all* the angels/ministering spirits and taken his place at God's right hand, just as the argument of Hebrews 1–2 demonstrates. Melchizedek is *priest* of God most high (the author follows the language of Genesis, which speaks of Melchizedek only as a priest), but the perfected Jesus, who has been elevated above all the angels (including on this hypothesis Melchizedek), is the *high* priest of God most high. For more detailed argumentation, see Moffitt, *Atonement and the Logic of Resurrection*, pp. 204–07.

[14] It is common in the secondary literature to read that Hebrews does not identify a moment when Jesus became high priest (e.g., Harold W. Attridge, *The Epistle to the Hebrews: A Commentary on the Epistle to the Hebrews* [Hermeneia; Philadelphia: Fortress, 1989], pp. 146–47). David Peterson (*Hebrews and Perfection: An Examination of the Concept of Perfection in the "Epistle to the Hebrews"* [SNTSMS 47; Cambridge: Cambridge University Press, 1982], pp. 191–95), in arguing for this view, provides an excellent discussion of some of the main issues that are at stake. Interestingly, Peterson himself notes, "[Jesus's] death on the cross must be included in our view of his priestly work, *though our writer nowhere explicitly states this*" (*Perfection*, p. 193, emphasis added). What the literature shows is that the twinned assumptions (1) that the death of Jesus must be the locus of his high-priestly sacrifice, and (2) that Hebrews has little concern for Jesus's resurrection, bodily or otherwise, are among the major drivers of this conclusion. Thus, in spite of the facts that Hebrews (1) predicates Jesus becoming a high priest (ἵνα ... γένηται ... ἀρχιερεύς) on his full participation in the human condition, something which must include his suffering and death (Heb. 2:17); (2) locates Jesus becoming the source of eternal salvation after (or upon) his being made perfect (τελειωθεὶς ἐγένετο ... αἴτιος σωτηρίας αἰωνίου, Heb. 5:9); (3) implies that Jesus entered the heavenly holy of holies after having become a high priest (ἀρχιερεὺς γενόμενος, Heb. 6:20); (4) says Jesus arose in the likeness of Melchizedek and has become a priest (ὃς ... [ἱερεὺς] γέγονεν) by the power of his indestructible life (Heb. 7:15–16); and, (5) states clearly that Jesus could not be even a priest on earth (εἰ ... ἦν ἐπὶ γῆς, οὐδ᾽ ἂν ἦν ἱερεύς), let alone a high priest (Heb. 8:4), many continue to assume that the author of Hebrews did not think with precision about when Jesus became a high priest. If, however, the author did think carefully about this and did not, like so many of his interpreters, assume that Jesus had to be a high priest on the cross, but concluded instead that Jesus became a high priest at his resurrection in order to pass through the heavens and serve in this capacity in the heavenly holy of holies, then the data from Heb. 2:17, 5:9, 6:20, 7:15-16 and 8:4 fall neatly and consistently into place. If this interpretation is correct, it is not the author of Hebrews who is confused and imprecise on when Jesus became a high priest. Rather, interpreters create confusion by continuing (1) to assume that that author of Hebrews must identify the cross as the primary if not exclusive place and time of Jesus's atoning, high-priestly sacrifice, and (2) to downplay or deny the importance of Jesus's bodily resurrection for the argument of Hebrews.

Moses saw this heavenly structure while he was on Sinai and therefore patterned the earthly tabernacle on the heavenly exemplar he saw. For the author of Hebrews, the priority of the heavenly tabernacle implies that the structure of and worship within the earthly tabernacle brim with analogies to their heavenly counterparts. Analogies of structure, activity, and function naturally hold between the earthly and heavenly realities because Moses obeyed God and made everything according to the pattern that was shown to him on the mountain (see Exod. 25:40; Heb. 8:5). These analogies imply a hermeneutical corollary: one can learn something of the heavenly structure and its cultic service, and so also about where Jesus is and what Jesus is presently doing, by looking at its earthly model.[15]

Fourth, this last assumption implies further that Hebrews not only reads Jewish scripture/the OT in the light of Christ, but also learns about Christ by reading him in the light of scripture. The relationship between Christology and scripture in Hebrews is dynamic and dialogical. The author even suggests that given space and time he could have said more about the significance of the earthly tabernacle for understanding the realities that Christ entered and the service that he performs there (Heb. 9:5).

Fifth, a note on my working assumptions about Jewish sacrifice is in order. I assume that a sacrifice consists of an irreducible ritual process. Roy Gane has compellingly argued that the rituals that constitute the process of sacrifice as presented in Leviticus relate to each other hierarchically.[16] This means that some elements of the process hold more importance or weight than do others relative to achieving the goals of a given sacrifice. This also implies that a sequence of ritual elements is necessary, but not one of these elements is alone sufficient for the sacrifice. That is to say, a sacrifice involves several ritual events and cannot, therefore, be reduced simply to one element within the sequence. Contrary to the assumption of many today, therefore, neither the verb nor the noun *sacrifice* is, in biblical terms, self-evidently synonymous with the ritual act of slaughtering a victim.[17] The word *sacrifice* does not mean to *slaughter* or *kill* something. If one only slaughtered a victim, even at the temple, but did not bring the body and blood of the victim to the altars and offer them to God, no sacrifice has occurred.

This last point partly explains why killing the victim is an essential element of some, but not of all, sacrifices.[18] Additionally, slaughter is a constitutive part of some sacrifices, such as Passover and peace offerings, that are not offered for the purpose of

---

[15] I argue this point at length in David M. Moffitt, "Serving in the Tabernacle in Heaven: Sacred Space, Jesus's High-Priestly Sacrifice, and Hebrews' Analogical "Theology", in *Hebrews in Contexts* (ed. Gabriella Gelardini and Harold W. Attridge; Ancient Judaism and Early Christianity, 91; Leiden: Brill, 2016), pp. 259–79.

[16] Roy E. Gane, *Cult and Character: Purification Offerings, Day of Atonement, and Theodicy* (Winona Lake, IN: Eisenbrauns, 2005), esp. pp. 3–24.

[17] The point can be shown from another angle. In, for example, Lev. 2:1-15 LXX, flour, loaves, and the first-fruits of the grain are all identified with the noun θυσία. Plainly the noun *sacrifice* cannot here denote a slaughtered thing. The term is used because the basic elements of a priest bringing something to an altar on behalf of a supplicant are in play. The logic of *sacrifice*, in other words, revolves around giving a gift to God, not around the act of slaughter, which may or may not be a constitutive part of a particular θυσία.

[18] On this issue, see esp. Christian A. Eberhart, *The Sacrifice of Jesus: Understanding Atonement Biblically* (Minneapolis: Fortress, 2011), pp. 60–101.

sacrificial atonement. There are also examples of ritual acts that can atone but do not entail any act of slaughter (e.g., Num. 16:46-50 MT). These facts suggest that death is not central to the logic of atonement in the Levitical system. Moreover, in those cases where an animal is slaughtered as part of a sacrifice, including but not limited to atoning sacrifices, there is no hint that the animal is made to suffer, nor that the victim is an object of abuse or wrath. Inflicting suffering on the sacrificial victim is not a part of the biblical sacrificial system, and, while sacrifices can serve in part to protect the people from the danger of God's wrath breaking out against the guilt they have incurred (e.g., Num. 18:5; cf. Sir. 34:19), the items offered to God are never themselves depicted as objects of that wrath. The common assumption that suffering and dying for someone else is an act of sacrifice, which clearly is a denotation of the term *sacrifice* in contemporary English, leads to a category mistake when read back into the biblical accounts of Levitical sacrifice. To maltreat a sacrificial animal would be to render it ineligible to be offered to God, since a sacrificial victim that suffered physical damage from abuse would no longer be ἄμωμος ("without blemish").[19]

Rather than being abused or made to suffer, the requirement that sacrificial animals be unblemished implies that they were treated with care prior to their being handed over to God. Further, the supplicant is the one who "pays" for the sacrifice by supplying the actual gift that is offered. It hardly seems a stretch to imagine the cost being borne joyfully when the gift offered is given in thanks; solemnly, even gratefully, when offered to make atonement for an impurity; or sorrowfully and as a penalty when, with repentance, the gift is given to atone for a moral infraction.

Be that as it may, within the series of elements that constitute an atoning sacrifice, the priestly work of applying blood to the various altars and burning portions of the victim on the outer altar (the acts whereby the sacrifice is ultimately offered or given over to God) are weightier than other elements for effecting atonement—they are higher up, as it were, in the hierarchically structured process. This conclusion follows from the fact that these elements of the process, in contrast to that of slaughtering the victim, (1) occur at and upon the various altars, and (2) can only be performed by priests.[20] To reduce Levitical sacrifice to the act of slaughtering a victim, which is not done on any of the altars, is a mistake.[21]

---

[19] It is interesting to note that the author of Hebrews locates Jesus's perfection after the completion of his suffering and death. If, as I have argued, the author correlates Jesus's perfection with his resurrection (*Atonement and the Logic of Resurrection*, esp. pp. 198–200), then it makes good sense to interpret him as speaking of Jesus as the one who offered himself without blemish (ἄμωμος, Heb. 9:14). Such language should not be reduced simply to moral categories. What is needed for Jesus, who is the high priest and the sacrifice, to approach God and offer himself is for him to be not only morally pure, but also ritually pure—to have a purified body. The resurrection, which on this reading of Heb. 9:14 would be the work of the eternal spirit (cf. Rom. 8:11), renders Jesus's humanity perfect so that he can ascend to the Father and offer himself "without blemish." By virtue of his resurrection the morally pure Jesus, who was without sin (Heb. 4:15), now has ritually pure humanity.

[20] So, for example, Eberhart, *Sacrifice of Jesus*, p. 85; Gane, *Cult and Character*, p. 67.

[21] In an attempt to avoid confusion, I try to speak consistently of "slaughter" or "sacrificial death/slaughter" when referring to the act of killing the victim, reserving the term *sacrifice* either for the larger process as a whole, or to identify either the acts of presentation, or the actual materials offered.

These points imply that one can speak about a sacrificial death/slaughter as an essential, constituent part of much Levitical sacrifice. To speak, however, of a sacrificial death is not to identify the death or slaughter itself as the sum total of a sacrifice.[22] Furthermore, the data of Leviticus suggest that the central aspects of the sacrificial process, the weightier elements in the hierarchy, have to do with the priest moving through progressively more sacred space in the tabernacle/temple precinct in order to approach the various altars and thereby bring the material of the sacrifice into God's presence. Bringing the blood and parts or all of the body of the victim, depending on the sacrifice, into the presence of God by doing things with these elements at altars is at the center of the process. Sacrifice, in other words, is about giving the material of an offering, that is, the required elements of a particular offering, over to God. God's willingness to accept the gift stands at the conceptual and effectual core of the process.[23] When the biblical data about sacrifice are so understood, Hebrews' emphasis on Jesus's entrance into the heavenly tabernacle where he appears before the Father in the heavenly holy of holies and presents himself as a sacrifice—that is, offers the Father himself, his living blood and flesh—coheres remarkably well with the accounts and logic of sacrifice as depicted in Leviticus. As modern people we may balk at such ideas, but that is hardly a concern of the author of Hebrews.

Sixth, I assume that the author works with a sustained, Pentateuchally shaped narrative throughout his homily. The narrative singles out the death of Jesus as the event that frees the seed of Abraham from slavery. Like Moses's use of the blood at the first Passover, Jesus's death liberates the people of God from the one who enslaved them.[24] This is clearly a salvific act, one of the necessary events that constitute the people's salvation. In Pentateuchal terms, however, the act of liberation/exodus itself is neither the sum total of salvation for God's people, nor is Passover a Levitical offering for sacrificial atonement. The story of salvation, if one may put it that way, moves forward from the exodus to the inheritance. Thus, the basic outline of the Pentateuchal narrative in Hebrews involves a new Passover-like event in which Jesus defeats the devil, liberates his people, and inaugurates the New Covenant for them.[25] These are

---

[22] It seems reasonable to assume that one could speak metonymically about sacrifice, taking one of the various elements of the process to stand in for the whole, but such utterances would not ultimately abstract the named element from or set it against the process as a whole.

[23] The real problems with the sacrificial system occur when God refuses to receive or accept sacrifices that are offered to him (e.g., Lev. 26:31; Jer. 14:10-12; Hos. 8:13-14; Amos 5:20-27). This is a curious datum if the center or effective mechanism of sacrifice has to do with a penalty being borne by a substitute victim by way of its death. To point this out is not necessarily to suggest that some notion of penal substitution should therefore be removed from Christian accounts of Jesus's suffering and death, but rather to highlight that such a notion is not likely, in historical terms, to have developed out of or to have been assumed to function within the sphere of Jewish blood sacrifice. To attempt to read suffering and the centrality of death back into Jewish sacrifice leads to all manner of misunderstanding about sacrifice as Leviticus portrays it.

[24] I develop this argument in David M. Moffitt, "Modelled on Moses: Jesus' Death, Passover, and the Defeat of the Devil in the Epistle to the Hebrews," in *Mosebilder: Gedanken zur Rezeption einer literarischen Figur im Frühjudentum, frühen Chrsitentum und der römisch-hellenistischen Literatur* (ed. M. Sommer, et al.; WUNT 1/390; Tübingen: Mohr Siebeck, 2017), pp. 279-97.

[25] For more detailed argumentation for this claim, see David M. Moffitt, "Wilderness Identity and Pentateuchal Narrative: Distinguishing between Jesus' Inauguration and Maintenance of the New Covenant in Hebrews," in *Muted Voices of the New Testament: Readings in the Catholic Epistles and*

the primary salvific functions of Jesus's death in Hebrews.[26] In keeping with these past events, the original readers have become members of the New Covenant who find themselves in a new wilderness-like period, simultaneously gathered around Mount Zion and waiting at the edge of their promised inheritance for their new Joshua to return to them. When Jesus appears again, he will bring salvation to his people (Heb. 9:28) and they will receive the fullness of the inheritance and rest God has promised them (cf. Heb. 1:14).

These six assumptions provide the stepping off point for the current study. Before proceeding, however, one caveat is in order about the word *atonement*. Atonement is a theological term, not a biblical one. As such, the word encapsulates a number of biblical terms and concepts relating to how Jesus brings God and humanity back into full fellowship (e.g., ransom, redemption, reconciliation, forgiveness, purification, propitiation). I work with a narrower notion of sacrificial or Levitical atonement, a qualification I make for the cultic language in Hebrews because the author himself so often highlights the high-priestly and sacrificial person and work of Jesus.[27] Sacrificial atonement has to do with offering God a gift in order to effect purification and/or obtain forgiveness for sins.[28]

Hebrews (ed. Katherine M. Hockey, Madison N. Pierce and Francis Watson; LNTS 565; London: Bloomsbury T&T Clark, 2017), pp. 153–71.

[26] Jared Compton has characterized my accounts of Jesus's elevation to his priestly office and of the function of Jesus's death in Hebrews as "reductive" and "overcooked" ("Review of *Atonement and the Logic of Resurrection in the Epistle to the Hebrews*," *TJ* 36 [2015], pp. 133–35). Compton repeatedly intimates that I "reduce" Jesus's death "simply" to an act of preparation for Jesus's atoning work. In fact, while I focus on Jesus's resurrection and entrance into the heavens, I state clearly in the book that "the death of Jesus can be seen as an event that accomplishes more than one thing in the argument [of Hebrews]" (Moffitt, *Atonement*, p. 285, see also the subsequent discussion of pp. 285–95).

[27] I speak explicitly in *Atonement and the Logic of Resurrection* about "Levitical atonement" (see esp. pp. 256–57). I intentionally sought to avoid speaking in the book about "*the* atonement." I did this in order to focus attention on Hebrews' engagement with the Levitical logic, pattern of atoning sacrifice and priestly work when explaining when and where Jesus offers his high-priestly sacrifice and why, on Levitical-sacrificial terms, this offering correlates with his entrance into the heavenly holy of holies and appearance in God's presence. This is not to say that Jesus's high-priestly sacrifice is the sum total of the author's soteriology (as if everything he says about salvation revolves solely around Jesus's high-priestly work), but to point out that the author is not working with a broad, synthetic/systematic-theological account of *the* atonement when he explains Jesus's high-priestly and sacrificial ministry. I reemphasize the point here because some reviewers appear to think that highlighting Hebrews' attention to Jesus's act of bringing the elements of his sacrifice, that is, himself, into God's presence is a reductive account of atonement easily disproven by pointing to non-sacrificial occurrences of the language of atonement (e.g., Compton, "Review," p. 134).

[28] To limit atonement only to what was accomplished when Jesus suffered and died leads to a reduction of the significance of the incarnation to the crucifixion (see, e.g., Stibbs, who identifies Jesus's death as *the* purpose of the incarnation [*Finished Work*, esp. p. 28]). This reduction also leads to a confusion of biblical categories. The wide array of problems identified in scripture that prevent fellowship between God and humanity are, on such an account, all imagined as being solved solely by means of Jesus's suffering and death. Reconciliation, redemption, propitiation, purification, and forgiveness, to name some of the major biblical categories, basically become indistinguishable (if not in terms of the problems they address, then in terms of the solutions given in scripture to those problems). If, instead of trying to load everything onto the cross, we allow that Jesus is in himself the center of atonement (Jesus is the solution to all the problems that separate God and humanity, not the death of Jesus), then the entirety of the incarnation—Jesus's birth, life, suffering, death, resurrection, ascension, session, and return—can be seen to contribute in particular ways to *the* atonement. Importantly, such an account would allow for distinct biblical problems to be solved

Purification and forgiveness needed to occur in order for God's people to enter into covenant with him and, importantly, for them to remain in covenant relationship with him.[29] Central to the cultic system of the Mosaic Covenant were those who crossed the boundaries between God and his people, that is, the priests, and drew near to God's presence to present the gifts and offerings they brought on behalf of the supplicants. The one who came closest to God was the high priest who, on Yom Kippur, entered the most holy place and thereby came more fully into God's earthly presence than any other human being. These elements are central to sacrificial atonement, which primarily aims to effect forgiveness and purification in order to maintain the covenant relationship, not least by enabling impure and guilty humans to approach God's presence, and by fulfilling the terms God himself has given whereby he condescends to be in covenant relationship with and to dwell among his people.

Jesus's high-priestly maintenance of the New Covenant

As just noted, the Levitical priests and sacrifices were essential to the maintenance of the covenant relationship between God and his people. They are key elements of the mechanism, as it were, that helps to ensure the continued health of the relationship between God and his people such that the people can dwell close to God and God condescends to remain in the midst of his people. So long as God accepts these sacrifices, the covenant relationship remains healthy.

Hebrews, I suggest, understands these Levitical concepts and reflects on the New Covenant and its high priest and sacrifice in terms that cohere with, are even informed by, the Old Covenant and its priests and sacrifices. Because Jesus ascended into the heavenly holy of holies and remains there, it follows for the author that Jesus is *the* high priest who can guarantee that the New Covenant relationship is perpetually maintained, something no earthly high priest could do because of death and because the law never brought about perfection. The law, in other words, never made it possible for someone to enter the earthly holy of holies and remain there in God's presence, to say nothing of making it possible for a high priest to pass through the heavens and remain in the heavenly holy of holies. Moreover, as Heb. 7:25 states, because Jesus is the high priest who always lives and is always at God's right hand, he is always able to intercede for his people and so is able to save them completely (εἰς τὸ παντελές).[30]

---

by distinct aspects of the larger sweep of the incarnation. In the case of atoning sacrifice, rather than forcing this to be fundamentally about suffering and death, which Leviticus simply does not support (something that should matter if one wishes to avoid theologies that are essentially Gnostic and/or Marcionite), one could identify ways in which the logics of Jewish sacrifice and high-priestly ministry resolve particular problems that hinder divine-human relations without assuming that these solve all the problems.

[29] In keeping with Leviticus, these problems would particularly relate to the ongoing maintenance of the covenant relationship between God and his people. This appears to be Yom Kippur's *raison d'être*.

[30] Given that Hebrews views salvation not as something one presently possesses, but as something one receives in the future (e.g., 1:14; 9:28), Jesus's continual intercession appears to be an essential part of his work that ensures that his people will be fully saved—they will successfully enter the

The logic of Heb. 7:25 implies that, were it the case that Jesus were not actively interceding for his people, their complete salvation would not be possible. Yet this implication suggests another: Jesus's followers are in need of ongoing atonement. The very work that the high priests on earth could do only once a year is done by Jesus perpetually. In contrast to the Old Covenant high priests, who were prevented by death from remaining in their office, Jesus's resurrection not only enables him to serve as the heavenly high priest, but also means he can do so *without interruption*. Thus, Jesus's high-priestly ministry brings a level of purity and forgiveness that exceeds that of the Old Covenant. Jesus's ministry ensures that the New Covenant relationship is fully maintained. As the one who is in himself both high priest and sacrificial offering, his very presence in the Father's presence secures the covenant relationship and ensures the salvation of its members.

This kind of activity is, it should also be noted, the sort of thing one might expect of a high priest in the holy of holies on Yom Kippur, at least in the late-second-temple period.[31] This is where and when the high priest makes annual supplication for the people as he offers the sacrificial blood on Yom Kippur. Indeed, supplication on behalf of the people and the other ritual acts performed in the holy of holies, including the offering of the blood, would be inseparable on Yom Kippur. The author of Hebrews conceives of the ongoing high-priestly work of Jesus along remarkably analogous lines. Jesus's ongoing high-priestly intercession works in ways that follow the pattern and logic of the annual work of the high priest in the earthly holy of holies.[32] Insofar as the author reflects on Jesus in light of this Jewish holy day, he does so by highlighting both Jesus's presentation of himself to the Father in the heavens, where there is presumably an altar (cf. Heb. 13:10) and where his ongoing work of intercession occurs (compare Heb. 7:25 and 8:1-4). This also makes good sense of the metaphor in Heb. 12:24 of Jesus sprinkling his blood. Here Jesus's role as covenant mediator is correlated with the act

---

promised inheritance. In all probability, this full salvation has to do with all God's people being resurrected when they are all made perfect together (Heb. 11:39-40).

[31] Philo identifies offering sacrifices and prayers on behalf of the people as the main responsibilities of the priest and especially of the high priest (see the evidence and discussion in Jutta, Leonhardt, *Jewish Worship in Philo of Alexandria* [Texts and Studies in Ancient Judaism, 84; Tübingen: Mohr Siebeck, 2001], pp. 228–33). Thus, Philo assumes that the high priest offers prayers when he goes into the holy of holies on Yom Kippur (*Leg. Gai.* 306; see also Leonhardt, *Jewish Worship*, pp. 128–29). For additional evidence that the ministry of the high priest included offering sacrifices and prayers on behalf of the covenant people see Josephus, *Ant.* 3.189-191.

[32] Milligan recognized this, too, writing with respect to Jesus's heavenly session: "What is [Jesus] about [i.e., doing]? He is not simply interceding on the strength of a past gift or sacrifice. He is presenting an offering on which his intercession is based, and in which it is involved. The idea of offering . . . cannot be separated from the action of our Lord after His Ascension, unless we also separate the thought of offering from what was done by the high-priest of Israel in the innermost sanctuary of his people. Such a separation the ceremonial of the law does not permit. The Jewish high-priest ministered in that sanctuary with more than the recollection or the merit of an offering already made. He had to sprinkle on the mercy-seat and before the veil the blood which he carried in along with him; he had to complete the reconciliation of Israel to God. . . . And all of this was part of the offering, not merely something done after the offering was ended. . . . As, therefore, the Jewish priest continued his work of offering after he had gone within the veil, so, in similar circumstances, we must connect with [Jesus] in whom the economy of Judaism is fulfilled the idea of offering" (*The Ascension and Heavenly Priesthood of Our Lord*, pp. 122–23).

of offering his blood by way of sprinkling, an act which the author says "is speaking" (λαλοῦντι) a better word than Abel.³³

The preceding account of Hebrews' sacrificial and high-priestly reflection on Jesus's entrance into the heavenly holy of holies has the benefit of offering a historically plausible explanation of the development of early Christian reflection that deduced aspects of Christological and soteriological reflection from the very Jewish scriptures and practices it cherished.³⁴ On this sort of reading, in other words, the confession of Jesus's ascension into the heavens and the identification of Jesus as high priest has real content that would make sense to the earliest Christians in terms of their Jewish background. To assume that new and different conceptions of a high priest and of the way in which sacrifice functioned are at the roots of the earliest reflection on Jesus is not impossible, but such an account is much harder to explain historically.³⁵

Additionally, the work of covenant maintenance by Jesus the heavenly high priest assumes, at least from the perspective of the author of Hebrews, that Jesus has not stepped outside of space and time, even if these are not precisely the same in the heavens as they are on earth. The central points to note here are (1) the reality and ongoing nature of the incarnation, which the resurrection guarantees; and, (2) the

---

[33] The comparison and contrast with Abel in this verse probably does not intend to highlight Abel's death, as if Abel's death were somehow compared to the sacrificial act of sprinkling blood in God's presence. Rather, the parallel intends to recall Abel's actual act of offering a sacrifice to God. Abel, in contrast to Cain, was the first one to offer a blood sacrifice to God. In Jewish terms, Abel was the first one to sprinkle sacrificial blood as an offering to God. God looked favorably on Abel and the sacrifices he offered (Gen. 4:4; compare Heb. 11:4). The point of Heb. 12:24, in other words, is that God is more pleased by the better offering of Jesus than he was with the blood offering made by Abel (and by implication, with the Levitical sacrifices). Abel's offering from the firstborn of his flocks was good, was motivated by faith, and God looked upon it with favor, but Jesus's act of presenting himself to God is even better.

[34] Stibbs appears not to see the historical problem with an interpretation of Jesus's sacrifice and high-priestly ministry that bifurcates his high-priestly intercession from the act of presenting his sacrifice. Against those who highlight the need to hold the two together he argues that Jesus's sacrifice "is unmistakably represented in Scripture as exclusively earthly and historical, the purpose of the incarnation . . .; [so] that by this once-for-all finished happening the necessary and intended atoning work was completely accomplished" (*Finished Work*, p. 8). He later adds that the idea that Jewish concepts of sacrifice and high-priestly ministry in the holy of holies suggest that offering and intercession belong together fails "to give due consideration to certain new facts in the New Testament fulfilment of the Old Testament figure, which completely alter the situation. Such a view is, indeed more Jewish than fully Christian, because it fails properly to appreciate the true . . . perfection, and the consequent surpassing glory, of the priesthood of Christ compared with that of the Levitical system" (*Finished Work*, p. 22). Hebrews, he later affirms, demands the separation of offering and intercession in the case of Jesus (*Finished Work*, p. 32). In historical terms (to say nothing of the potential theological problems such a view raises), Stibbs' account is highly implausible. He places the cart of a certain kind of later soteriological reflection before the horse of the actual appeal on the part of the earliest Christians to biblical and second-temple sacrificial practice as they sought to understand and explain the saving work of Jesus in terms of God's prior revelation.

[35] One needs, too, to take seriously the possibility that the self-evidence of a reduction of all of Jesus's sacrificial and atoning work to the cross is both anachronistic and potentially leads to a kind of diminution of the importance of Jewish scripture and practices for early Christian understandings of Jesus. This is still a long way from Marcion, but there are nevertheless real theological concerns that need to be borne in mind if one wants to confess that the God who revealed the tabernacle, priesthood, and sacrificial system to Moses is the same God who appointed Jesus to the status of sacrifice and high priest according to the order of Melchizedek, but meant something entirely different by the terms *sacrifice* and *high priest* than what he revealed to his people in the Mosaic law.

confession in Hebrews that Jesus will return to bring salvation to those who are waiting for him (Heb. 9:28). To take seriously the bodily resurrection and ascension of Jesus, as I have argued the author of Hebrews does, allows the inference that Jesus continues to be an embodied human being located in a particular place. For the author of Hebrews this place is the heavenly holy of holies at God's right hand. Furthermore, Hebrews looks ahead to a future time and place when Jesus is no longer absent from his brothers and sisters but will return to them, bringing their salvation with him.

This last point is worthy of more reflection. There has been a tendency in Hebrews' scholarship, especially after Ernst Käsemann's influential book, *Das wandernde Gottesvolk: Eine Untersuchung zum Hebräerbrief*, to assume that Hebrews is about pilgrimage, forward motion that leads one out of the world and into God's presence where Jesus is. God's people wander through this life but are ultimately headed toward their inheritance. The goal is for God's people to endure their earthly suffering and be released into the salvation of the heavenly inheritance. They will one day join Jesus where he sits in the heavenly world to come.

But such a conception struggles to incorporate Heb. 9:28, where the author does not say that Jesus will bring his people to himself by leading them out of the wilderness and through the heavens to where he is, but rather that Jesus will appear again to be present with his people who are waiting for him, ready to receive him back (ἀποδέχομαι). Hebrews does not envision the wandering people of God but the waiting people of God.[36] This coheres with the directional metaphor in the writer's admonition for the readers to exhort each other as they see the day "drawing near" (ἐγγίζουσαν, 10:25), and with his reminder that in just a little while, the one for whom they wait "will come" (ὁ ἐρχόμενος ἥξει, 10:37). In Heb. 11:10 the author even describes Abraham as "waiting" (ἐξεδέχετο) for the city without foundations. The English translation tradition mutes the point, tending to render the verb ἐκδέχομαι in terms of "looking for/forward to" (KJV, RSV, NIV, ESV). The notion of expectation is plainly present, but as several commentators note, the Jewish apocalyptic idea of waiting for the heavenly Jerusalem is the chief point in play here (see Heb. 11:16; 12:22).[37] This does not prove that Hebrews envisioned the descent of the heavenly Jerusalem as in, for example, Rev. 21:2, 10. The idea is hardly implausible, however, when considered in light of Heb. 9:28, particularly given the close collocation in Hebrews of salvation and obtaining the promised inheritance (e.g., 1:14). If the promised inheritance includes receiving the heavenly city, and if receiving this inheritance is at least part of what the writer

---

[36] Otfried Hofius made this point forcefully in his volume entitled *Katapausis: Die Vorstellung vom endzeitlichen Ruheort im Hebräerbrief* (WUNT 1/11; Tübingen: Mohr Siebeck, 1970). With respect to this very point he writes, "[D]ie Gemeinde [ist] nicht als das zum Himmel wandernde, wohl aber als das auf die Heilsvollendung *wartende* Gottesvolk gesehen, und der Verfasser will dieses Volk ... mit aller Dringlichkeit dazu aufrufen, die Erwartung nicht preiszugeben, der allein die Erfüllung verheißen ist" (*Katapausis*, p. 150, emphasis original).

[37] For example, Attridge, *Hebrews*, pp. 323-24; Craig R. Koester, *Hebrews: A New Translation with Introduction and Commentary* (AB 36; New York: Doubleday, 2001), p. 486. Erich Grässer agrees that Abraham is here depicted as waiting for the heavenly city, but argues that the city's ultimate transcendence in Hebrews means that even here the idea of wandering rather than waiting is primary (*An die Hebräer* [EKKNT 17; vol. 3; Zurich: Benziger; Neukirchen-Vluyn: Neukirchener, 1997], p. 127; see also Erich Grässer, "Das wandernde Gottesvolk Zum Basismotiv des Hebräerbriefes," in *Aufbruch und Verheißung: Gesammelte Aufsätze zum Hebräerbrief* [ed. Martin Evang and Otto Merk; Berlin: De Gruyter, 1992], pp. 231-50).

considers to be constitutive of salvation, then it seems plausible to interpret the idea of Jesus appearing a second time for the salvation of those who wait for him in terms of his bringing the heavenly city to his waiting people. All of this coheres well with the author's claim that the audience does not have a permanent city here, but seeks instead the one that is coming (τὴν μέλλουσαν, Heb. 13:14).

Furthermore, it is unclear why the idea of a final shaking of the earth and heavens and the removal of created things (Heb. 12:27) cannot cohere with the idea of Jesus returning to his people and bringing them their inheritance. The very fact that author says in 12:27 that the removal of the shakable things is done in order to allow the unshakable things to remain (ἵνα μείνῃ) implies that these unshakable things are not Platonic, eternal realities. If the author meant something like the latter idea his statement is nonsensical. How can the removal of the present creation impinge in any way on the ability of the unshakable things to remain?[38] A more satisfying account of the verse would seem to be foreshadowed in Heb. 1:12, where the citation of Ps. 102:26 implies that the present created things will be changed, like a garment. The image is not one of simple removal, but of replacement (cf. Rev. 21:1).

Be that as it may, the waiting motif of 9:28 correlates well with the Pentateuchal narrative the author develops in his epistle. It may be tempting to assume that being in the wilderness must imply the forty years of wandering. The author, however, locates his audience in a time and place in the wilderness narrative prior to the failure of the exodus generation at Kadesh Barnea.[39] Even as he discusses that generation as a negative example in Heb. 3:15–4:7, he focuses not on their wandering but on their failure to obtain the promised inheritance,[40] a failure that resulted in the forty years of wandering and that generation's loss of the inheritance. The equivalent act of unbelief for the contemporary audience would be falling away from the community of the faithful and its confession about Jesus. For this author, to wander in the wilderness would appear to be tantamount to having lost already the opportunity of the "today" of Psalm 95.[41]

---

[38] Most commentators recognize that Hebrews, if it works with a version of a Platonic dualism, does not do so in a thoroughgoing way (e.g., Attridge, *Hebrews*, p, 383; James W. Thompson, *Hebrews* [Paideia; Grand Rapids, MI: Baker, 2008], pp. 268–69). I continue, however, to maintain that Hebrews' confession of Jesus's bodily resurrection and ascension suggests that the author does not work with an earthly material/flesh versus heavenly/spiritual dualism (see Moffitt, *Atonement and the Logic of Resurrection*, esp. pp. 300–3).

[39] Albert Vanhoye places more emphasis on Hebrews' call to enter the promised rest than on the motif of waiting for salvation ("Longue marche ou accès tout proche?: Le contexte biblique de Hébreux 3,7–4,11," *Biblica* 49 [1968]: pp. 9–26). Nevertheless, he recognizes that wandering is not the right conceptual category for Hebrews. In his words, "La situation religieuse des chrétiens est comparée à celle des Israélites arrivés aux portes du pays. Il n'est plus question d'un chemin interminable, mais des derniers pas à franchir: le moment est venu de passer du désert au royaume de Dieu" ("Longue marche", p. 17).

[40] Hofius notes that the author's use of Psalm 94 LXX does not even emphasize the journey from Egypt to the edge of the promised land, but rather the actions and judgment of the people at Kadesh Barnea: "Ihn beschäftigt im Hinblick auf die Wüstengeneration einzig und allein das Geschehen bei Kades-Barnea, während die vorausgegangene Wüstenwanderung als solche für ihn gänzlich außerhalb des Interesses liegt. Auch an den beiden Stellen 3,9 und 3,16, wo an die Zeit des Exodus erinnert wird, ist auf die Wanderung selbst kein Bezug genommen" (*Katapausis*, p. 144).

[41] Again, Hofius saw the point clearly commenting that the wilderness generation "ist ... dem auctor ad Hebraeos ein eindringlichen Beispiel für die *Unmöglichkeit der zweiten Buße*. Für den, der von Gott abgefallen ist, gibt es keine Möglichkeit der Umkehr mehr" (*Katapausis*, p. 137, emphasis

None of this is to suggest a neat one-to-one correspondence between the broad narrative of the Pentateuch and the wilderness metaphor the author of Hebrews develops. Hebrews works more freely with the Pentateuchal narrative than that and does not have trouble conflating elements from these texts and from other scriptural passages. But there is a macro-level structure here. As stated above, the broad Pentateuchal narrative of liberation from the enslavement, inauguration of the covenant and the tabernacle, establishment and inauguration of the means and practices of ongoing worship, and waiting in the wilderness to receive the promised inheritance forms the structure the author uses to locate followers of Jesus in relation to their past, present, and eschatological hope.

Just here, however, in the waiting in the wilderness, the notion of covenant maintenance and ongoing high-priestly intercession makes so much sense. In the wilderness, even before the forty years of wandering, God's people experienced tests and trials.[42] The readers of Hebrews continue to face the problems of sin, death, and persecution. What is needed above all else in this wilderness moment is ongoing intercession, some way in which they are being made perfect and being sanctified while they wait for their inheritance.[43] This is part of the hermeneutical dynamic in play in Hebrews. Hebrews, more than any other NT text, shows how the high-priestly work of Jesus is now keeping God's people safe in the wilderness, ensuring that they can approach their exalted high priest boldly in times of need, and how Jesus now intercedes for them such that they will be saved completely and will be able to enjoy the inheritance God has promised his people.

To summarize thus far, the affirmation in Heb. 9:28 that Jesus will appear again to bring salvation to those waiting for him implies, as one can also deduce from Heb. 7:25, that aspects of Jesus's work of salvation are presently ongoing. Jesus is appealing to God for his brothers and sisters. This intercession ensures their full salvation. Not only can this be inferred from 7:25, but the language in 2:11 that speaks of Jesus as the one who sanctifies those who are being sanctified (οἱ ἁγιαζόμενοι) appears to hint at this dynamic too. I suspect further that this offers the best interpretation of Heb. 13:20-21 where, unlike the NIV's incomprehensible translation to the effect that the blood of the covenant brought Jesus back from the dead, the point is more likely to be that the blood of the covenant is the means by which God's people are being equipped to please God by doing his will. Jesus's ongoing high-priestly intercession is making God's people perfect—doing what the sacrifices and ministry of the priests in the Old

---

original). Vanhoye similarly observes that the wandering Israelites "loin d'être proposées en exemple aux fidèles, elles constituent le châtiment des incrédules, de ceux qui refusent l'invitation divine à entrer. Ceux-là sont renvoyés dans le désert pour y errer indéfiniment jusqu'à y mourir. . . . Leur sort ne représente pas la vie chrétienne, mais la damnation" ("Longue marche", pp. 17–18).

[42] See Exod. 15:25; 16:4; 20:20; Num. 14:22.

[43] If this is correct, it suggests that Jesus's continuing absence from his people was not primarily a problem to be solved, but an opportunity for creative Christological reflection. If one knows where Jesus has gone—to God's right hand in the highest heaven, that is, into the heavenly holy of holies—then one can deduce things about who he is and what he is doing: he must be a high priest and he must be performing priestly service on behalf of his people. All of this deduction was in dialogue with scripture. Texts like Psalm 110 would naturally rise to the foreground, but, at least for the author of Hebrews, so did biblical notions of priestly service and priestly legitimation as one places the confession of Jesus's high-priestly status up against God's past revelation in the Mosaic law.

Covenant aimed to do, but ultimately could not do in such a way as to bring perfection (see Heb. 7:11, 19; 9:9; 10:1).

The once-for-all-ness of Jesus's sacrifice and the inability to return to the covenant

The preceding discussion is likely to raise a number of questions, but two are especially obvious. First, how does this account cohere with the "once-for-all" language in Hebrews and the language of Jesus sitting at God's right hand *after* having accomplished purification and forgiveness for sins? Texts like Heb. 1:3 and 10:10-18 might appear, prima facie, to disallow the arguments made above. Second, if Jesus is interceding for his people and thereby maintaining the covenant, how is it that the author can envision the possibility of some falling away from this relationship without any means for restoration?

To take the initial question first, two points can be made. The failure of the Old Covenant fully to remove sin implies that there are numerous sins of the past that need to be dealt with in order for the New Covenant to be made with the house of Israel and the house of Judah. The Jeremiah 31 text cited in Hebrews makes this very point—in the New Covenant, the sins and lawless deeds of the past are no longer remembered. At the very least, Jesus's act of sacrificial presentation aimed at dealing fully with certain past sins.[44]

More, however, seems to be implied in the unqualified language of 1:3 and 10:10ff. I suggest that the resolution of the apparent tension between these texts and 7:25 is to be found in the recognition that Jesus is, in his resurrected self, both the high priest and the sacrifice of the New Covenant. Given that the covenant people are continuing to be sanctified (2:11; 10:14), continue to wait for their perfection (11:39-40), and will ultimately be saved completely, Hebrews assumes that there continues to be a need for their ongoing forgiveness and purification even after their initial purification upon entering the covenant.[45] This is part of the dynamic of their present status as those who wait in the wilderness for Jesus to return to them.

Jesus performs this ongoing ministry by being in himself both the high priest and the sacrifice who sits at the Father's right hand. Because he remains in the Father's presence and intercedes for his people, his sacrificial, atoning work is perpetual. This is partly why there can be no repetition of Jesus's sacrifice—he never has to leave the presence of the Father and then return again in order to present himself again. The once-for-all-ness of Jesus's presentation of himself is correlated with the once-for-all-ness of his death, resurrection, and ascension. There can be no repetition of the process of his sacrifice within the once-for-all-ness of the incarnation, for the risen Jesus cannot leave the Father in order to again take up blood and flesh, die, rise again, and return again to the heavenly holy of holies.

---

[44] One wonders if this may be one of the aspects of Jesus's sacrificial work that is implied in the author's comment in 9:23 that the heavenly things themselves required purification.

[45] This initial purification may well be what the author has in mind in 10:29 when he speaks of apostates in terms of counting the blood of the covenant by which they were sanctified as profane.

Further, the idea in Heb. 10:14 that Jesus makes perfect those who are being sanctified appears to restate the claim made in 2:11. Jesus is the one who, by means of his one sacrifice, perfects those who are in the process of being sanctified. If this is right, then the point of 10:14 is not, as in many English translations, that this work of perfection is fully completed for all time, but rather that Jesus is now in the state of making his people perfect. This would correlate perfectly with the idea that he is the high priest who now intercedes for his people. Similarly, in 10:10, his people are said to be in the state of being sanctified by means of his one offering. The idea that his brothers and sisters are being sanctified coheres well with the interpretations of 2:11, 7:25, 12:24, and 13:20-21 offered above. If, as I have argued elsewhere, the author of Hebrews thinks the perfection of humanity lies ultimately in the eschatological resurrection of the body and reception of the eternal inheritance, as is also the case with Jesus's own perfection,[46] this again coheres with the resolution of the apparent tensions between these texts. Jesus is the sanctifier who is making his people perfect. His people are being sanctified while they wait for him to perfect them and bring them the inheritance of their salvation. This ongoing work of making his people holy and perfect follows directly from Jesus's ongoing work of interceding for them as their high priest. This high-priestly work is the means by which they will be saved completely such that they will receive the fullness of the inheritance promised to them. Jesus's high-priestly ministry, in other words, ensures that the great narrative of salvation in the Pentateuch will come to its intended denouement and God and his people will dwell together in the unshakable inheritance.

As for the impossibility of restoring those who fall away, Hebrews appears to take a different approach than does Paul, for example, on the question of being able to be removed from the covenant relationship. Paul also seems to have a concept of Jesus performing high-priestly work at God's right hand. He says in Rom. 8:34 that Christ Jesus who died, but even more who was raised, is now at the right hand of God interceding for his people. On the basis of this intercession, those who follow Jesus, presumably those who confess that Jesus is Lord and believe that God raised him from the dead (Rom. 10:9), cannot be condemned. Paul goes on to affirm in Rom. 8:35-39 that nothing therefore is able to separate those whom Christ loves from God. Jesus's ongoing intercession means that the saving relationship between God and his people cannot be broken. This looks like a concept of covenant maintenance, the mechanism of which is nothing less than Jesus's ongoing intercession. Hebrews, however, seems

---

[46] Hebrews is not a unique witness in the New Testament to Jesus's ongoing work of forgiveness and purification for his people in the Father's presence. The idea appears in 1 Jn 1:7–2:2 as well. The collocation of Jesus's blood, confession of sin, forgiveness of sins, and purification in 1 Jn 1:7-9 suggests that the author reflects on Jesus's ongoing work of forgiveness and purification in terms of Jewish sacrificial categories. That the author thinks believers need ongoing forgiveness and purification from sins becomes particularly clear in 2:1. He states there that he is writing to believers ("my little children") in order to encourage them not to sin, the obvious aim or ideal. If, however, they do sin, their sins can be dealt with by means of Jesus's ongoing advocacy for them before the Father. This ongoing advocacy is possible because, the author suggests in 2:2, Jesus is the atoning sacrifice (ἱλασμός) for their sins. The point appears to be that Jesus is the advocate who can intercede for his people when they sin because he is the atoning sacrifice for their sins who is alive and with the Father right now. This looks remarkably like the notions of Jesus's high-priestly ministry and ongoing work of covenant maintenance that one finds in Hebrews.

to argue that the people of the New Covenant can effectively remove themselves from the covenant relationship. They can repudiate their confession (4:14; 10:23). They can give up meeting together with the rest of the community (Heb. 10:25). They can go on sinning willfully (Heb. 10:26). Should these things happen, they could find themselves in a position like the generation of Israelites after their failure at Kadesh Barnea—wandering in the wilderness without hope of receiving the promised inheritance. It appears to be the case in Hebrews that just as Jesus's work of liberating his people, inaugurating the New Covenant, and entering into the Father's presence is unrepeatable, so also one's entrance into this covenant and community cannot be repeated.

Conclusion

If the preceding arguments are correct, Hebrews assumes that the new and living way to God opened by Jesus consists in a life of ongoing cultic relationship within the context of the New Covenant. This relationship revolves around worship that involves and is made possible by the perpetual ministry of the great high priest Jesus, the Son of God, in the heavenly tabernacle. This high priest, who is always also in his crucified and resurrected body the sacrifice offered to God, intercedes on behalf of his brothers and sisters. Because of his resurrection and passing through the heavens, Jesus, who is always the crucified one, is interceding for his brothers and sisters. He, as Gregory of Nazianzus puts it, continues even now to wear that body that died and was resurrected. This is why even now he can intercede for his people's salvation. In this sense, the sacrificial work of Jesus is not finished. The fact of his ongoing presence with the Father and physical absence from his people means that he is working on their behalf as their high priest mediating and maintaining the New Covenant relationship. So long as Jesus remains in the heavenly holy of holies and so long as his people are waiting in their own new-wilderness state for their perfection and are in the process of being sanctified, Jesus's high-priestly intercession continues. For the author of Hebrews, the return of the high priest to his waiting people will mark the point at which they finally obtain the salvation that all of Jesus's incarnate work guarantees them.

10

Plight and Solution: Hebrews and the Invitation to Rest

Mark S. Gignilliat

Introduction

I come into the scholarly discussion of Hebrews as an interloper, fascinated as I am by the subject matter. My instincts are to think about the book of Hebrews as presenting a set of interesting biblical-theological opportunities. And by biblical theological, I mean an attendance to the triune subject matter of the Christian bible, composed of OT and NT in dialectical relation the one to the other. I do not necessarily mean by biblical theology, in the Vosian tradition, a reordering of the biblical material for the sake of coming to terms with the historical development of biblical themes or redemptive history per se. Such attempts can be helpful but often fall under the ruse of being more "biblical" than Christian dogmatics or systematic theology. Even Vos himself admitted in the preface to his famed Biblical Theology that "Biblical" theology reorders the biblical material as much as "systematic" theology.[1] The organizing principles differ from each other; nonetheless, reorganization exists in both. In my estimation, biblical theology, where and if it can be properly distinguished from Christian dogmatics, exists for the sake of exploring the inner-canonical conversation of the Bible's two testaments and constitutive parts in light of Scripture's subject matter. Hebrews is especially fruitful in this regard.

My assigned topic for this chapter is "Plight and Solution" in the witness of Hebrews. The points of entry for this subject matter are manifold, the most obvious as the priestly character of Jesus Christ's person and work and the attendant atonement theology emerging from this *realia*. David Moffitt's monograph on the Atonement and the Logic of the Resurrection in Hebrews stimulates on several accounts, the least of which is the necessity of Jesus's corporal resurrection and presentation of his life/body to the father as the crowning achievement of Christ's atoning work. So, from one angle, the issue of Plight and Solution can be addressed by Moffitt's close exegetical analysis. The plight of human existence emerges from the impurity of the ritual and worshiping relationship between God and his people, a relationship requiring the sacrificial

---

[1] Geerhardus Vos, *Biblical Theology: Old and New Testaments* (Edinburgh: Banner of Truth, 1948), p. 14.

purging and cleansing of blood, a blood made eternally efficacious by the continued high priestly role of Jesus in the very life of God.

Notwithstanding the preceding comments, I remain intrigued by the theme of rest in Hebrews 4 and wish to pursue this theme in light of Hebrew's conception of plight and solution.[2] The promised rest in chapter 4 and the danger of not entering that rest because of unbelief stand at a signal moment in the sermon's movement. Focusing on these themes within a biblical-theological frame and in conversation with key voices from the Christian interpretive tradition may prove fruitful. Why? Because it appears that the priesthood of Jesus as intimated in the first three chapters—with reference to Jesus's priesthood, his learned obedience in the school of suffering, and his attendant "fittingness" as high priest because of his faithful suffering—peppers the sermonic flow and highlights a central motif awaiting further elaboration. This further elaboration begins at the end of chapter 4 after the exhortation to believing obedience or the obedience of faith and the danger of failing to enter into God's rest. In other words, the inner logic of the first four chapters of Hebrews presents the failure to enter into rest as a potential plight of the highest order.

I make no pretense of exhausting the subject of plight and solution in the following chapter but wish to offer a modest attempt to understand these conceptions by engaging the theology of rest in chapters 3:17–4:13. This theme will remain this chapter's focal point for the duration because it provides an important entry point to the subject matter at hand: plight and solution.

Rest in biblical and theological frame

Rest in Heb. 4:1 is an eschatological promise. The Numbers account of entering into the land is a proleptic or figural picture of the eschatological rest awaiting those in Christ. Faith is understood as a confident expectation for future security based on the gospel promises of God. Faith is conceived of in this eschatological vein, with the warning, the perpetual plight threatening God's people, emanating from chapter 3:14: "For we share in Christ, if we hold on to our initial confidence/faith until the end."

One does not read far in the secondary literature before stumbling across terms like *midrashic* interpretation or the associative reading practice of *gezerah shewa* on the basis of the shared lexemes in Gen. 2:2 and Ps. 95:11 (94 MT), shared lexemes unavailable in the Masoretic tradition but made available in the Greek translation stream. The parenetic section introduced in 3:7-19 is brought to its completion in chapter 4, culminating in the searching character of God's word and moving into an elaborate exploration of the high priesthood of Jesus Christ.

Psalm 95 functions as an interpretive lens for the author to the Hebrews. The author tells us as much in the recognition of the Psalm as eschatologically reorienting our conception of rest. The promised rest of God for his people could not have been achieved in the conquest of the land, or else Psalm 95 would become superfluous. However,

---

[2] For a thorough treatment of *rest* in Hebrews, as well as a tradition-historical account of the theme, see Jon Laansma, *I Will Give You Rest: The "Rest" Motif in the New Testament with Special Reference to Mt. 11 and Heb. 3-4* (Tübingen: Mohr, 1997).

Psalm 95's rereading of the Numbers narrative highlights the symbolic/figural role this episode plays as an eschatological adumbration of a future day of coming rest. For the author to the Hebrews, Psalm 95's promised "Today" is in fact the eschatological "Today" shaped by the person and work of Jesus Christ, God's final word.

Genesis 2:2 and Ps 95:11 merge horizons so that God's seventh day of rest is itself an anticipation of a future reality, a reality made available Today because God's own space is a perpetual seventh day of rest. It is worth remembering the seventh day of creation is the crowning achievement of creation, not the sixth day. As von Rad reminds, "God's desisting from a continuation of his work of Creation and his resting are obviously to be taken and pondered as things in themselves."[3] God's rest or cessation exists now, alongside and in human history. We will press into this subject matter in due course.

God's own Sabbath rest, therefore, is the space prepared for those whose pilgrim existence awaits a future consummation and this awaiting takes place from the perspective of Today's assured promises. Thus, the warning, do not let the disobedience of unbelief keep you from entering into the space of God's own cessation from his creative labors. The warning is real, as real for the first-century Christians as it was for those under the auspice of Psalm 95's backward look and future warning. The struggle, the pilgrimage, the holding fast with confidence to the saving promises of God entails the burden of faith and the promise of eventual cessation or rest.

"Cessation" is an important term here because our linguistic conceptuality of "rest" runs into trouble upon close analysis of the term's lexical field in Hebrew and the Greek equivalent καταπαύω. Gerhard von Rad's influential article "Es ist noch eine Ruhe vorhanden dem Volke Gottes" identifies the rest theme of the OT as of central importance.[4] The problem, however, is whether the term "rest" or *Ruhe* does connotative justice to the *shabbat* and *navach* verbs in the Hebrew Bible. Upon second glance the answer seems to be no; "rest" in the sense of an overcoming of physical depletion for the sake of renewed energy does not do justice to the "rest" concept of the OT for either humanity or God.[5]

In most instances, the use of *navach* emphasizes the cessation of wandering and the settling down in the Promised Land. Deuteronomy conceptually links the verbal form of *navach* with the nominal *menuchah* or the promised land (cf. Deut. 25:19). Promised "Rest" is a cessation from wandering and an alleviation of threat from the surrounding enemies. This theme is picked up in the Deuteronomistic history as well with David in 1 Sam. 26:19: "Rest/*navach*" is the possibility of living in the promised land undisturbed. The Lord himself identifies Zion as his habitation with *menuchah* or the promised land as in parallel to his habitation, (cf. Ps. 132:13f). Here, God's *menuchah* is understood locally, as a place he inhabits. These linguistic insights have

---

[3] Gerhard Von Rad, *Old Testament Theology* (2 vols; New York: Harper and Row, 1962), p. 147, n. 23.
[4] Idem, "Es ist noch eine Ruhe vorhanden dem Volke Gottes," In Zwischen den Zeiten 11 (1933), pp. 104–11.
[5] As an aside, see Barth's misgivings about Gunkel's religious-historical account of rest. "Gunkel connects the idea of tiredness and compensating recuperation with the divine rest. He concludes that it is a 'strong anthropomorphism,' and criticizes those expositors who (like Delitzsch) appeal to Is. 40.28 ('God, the Lord, the Creator of the ends of the earth, fainteth not, neither is weary') in their anxiety to escape something which is offensive to the modern religious consciousness. But it is not our business to make concessions to the modern religious consciousness." Karl Barth, *Church Dogmatics III.1* (trans. J. W. Edwards, O. Bussey, H. Knight; Edinburgh: T&T Clark, 1958), p. 221.

much to do with the texts of Psalm 95 and Gen. 2:2-3 as deployed in Hebrews 4. God's Sabbath rest, a rest promised as an eschatological hope, is a location; it is the promised land where God dwells as he attends providentially and redemptively to the created world, the work from which God has ceased.

This distinction between creation and providence remains instructive for the matter at hand.[6] One does not have to read far in the tradition before the juxtaposition of God's cessation from the work of creation as expressed in Gen. 2:2-3 and Jesus's claim in Jn. 5:17 regarding his and the Father's continued work comes to the fore. How can God have ceased and still be working? Such internal canonical matters are the stuff of Christian theology and provide a green light for theological reflection on the subject matter at hand, along with a striving to provide a theological grammar that is consonant with the biblical material. God can cease and work at the same time because a distinction is made between the creative activity of God and his providential/redemptive attendance to his finished creation. Or in Karl Barth's terms, "God does not retire. As the Creator He now begins to confront the completed world-totality, and to be active towards it and in it."[7]

Oliver O'Donovan's learned work *Resurrection and Moral Order* draws attention to the theological significance of the creation/providence distinction for the sake of coming to terms with the relation between eschatology and history. O'Donovan playfully refers to Anglican hymns of the more broad church stripe where the collapsing of this distinction becomes problematic. "Creation's Lord, we give you thanks That this your world is incomplete." O'Donova quips, "God's loose ends, it appears, are man's opportunity!"[8] All humor aside, O'Donovan points out the problems of a modern

---

[6] "Divine providence is to be understood not as continuing or perpetuating the original act of creation as if the act of creation were still incomplete, but as the continuation of God's creation through his disposing and ordering presence within it through the incarnate Word. We must think of this, however, as conditioned by his redemptive activity. There is, and cannot but be, an inseparable relation between divine creation and divine providence, for God does not withdraw his activity from the world which he has once for all brought into being, but correlates the creation with himself in a new way by embodying his creative Word and redemptive activity within the created order." Thomas F. Torrance, *The Christian Doctrine of God: One Being, Three Persons* (London: T&T Clark, 2001), p. 223.

[7] Barth, *CD III.1*, p. 220. See the following from Barth as well: "Without ceasing to be God, He has made Himself a worldly, human, temporal God in relation to this work of His. He is now free to act as this kind of God, and as such He now celebrates and rejoices . . . . Time was intended for this day: Lord of creation and Lord of humanity. This is the day toward which time was moving." Karl Barth, *Church Dogmatics III.2* (trans. H. Knight, G. W. Bromiley, J. K. S. Reid, R. H. Fuller; Edinburgh: T&T Clark, 1960), p. 457. "It is not a question of recuperation after a toilsome and well-done job. Even the Sabbath rest of man corresponding to the divine rest does not have this sense in the Old Testament, but means negatively a simple cessation and abstention from further work. The freedom, rest and joy of the Sabbath consist in the face that on this day man is released from his daily work. On the Sabbath he does not belong to his work." Barth continues, "The fact that God rested means quite simply, and significantly, that He did not continue His work of creation, i.e., that he was content with the creation of the world and man. He was satisfied to enter into *this* relationship with *this* reality distinct from Himself, to be the Creator of *this* creature, to find in *these* works of His Word the external sphere of His power and grace and the place of His revealed glory. A limit was revealed. God Himself had fixed it for Himself and had now reached it. His creative will was divine from the very outset just because it was not infinite but had this specific content and no other" (Barth, *CD III.1*, pp. 214–15). For Barth, God's Sabbath rest reveals his (1) freedom and (2) love for His creatures and creation.

[8] Oliver O'Donovan, *Resurrection and Moral Order: An Outline for Evangelical Ethics* (Grand Rapids, MI: Eerdmans, 1994), p. 61.

understanding of *creatio continua* as poorly handling the distinction between creation and providence. For O'Donovan, an adequate understanding of the Sabbath would have circumvented this problem. "The sign," he clarifies, "which celebrates the completeness of creation looks forward also to the fulfillment of history. Does this eschatological meaning replace, or annul, the reference to creation?"[9]

In light of the previous insights, O'Donovan points to Hebrews 3–4 and its appeal to Psalm 95. "God's works," O'Donovan continues, "have been completed since the beginning of the world, he [author to the Hebrews] tells us. What remains is for us to *enter* that sabbath rest which has been waiting for us all this time, as it were, unoccupied."[10] Disobedience kept them out formerly, so God appointed another day. "For the author to the Hebrews, then, the completion of creation, so far from being put in doubt by the thought of a yet-to-be completed history, is the only ground on which we can take the latter seriously. Historical fulfillment means our entry into a completeness which is already present in the universe. Our sabbath rest is, as it were, a catching up with God's."[11] O'Donovan's comments offer a perspicacious insight into the eschatological and salvific dynamic of Hebrews 4. Protology and eschatology mutually inform one another regarding the space of creative cessation wherein God resides now in his salvific mission *ad extra*. Moreover, this seventh-day existence of God is located at the apex of the creative week, attesting to creation's necessary movement into this particular space of cessation. In brief, eschatological hope or teleology is built into the very fabric of God's seven-day work of creation.

Such an understanding of the interplay of eschatology and protology helps make some sense of Martin Luther's rather fascinating reading of the seventh day of creation in his Genesis commentary. Luther understands God's rest as eternal, with the seventh day of creation as humanity's end as well.[12] The seventh day brings the creative work of God to an end from a temporal/creative standpoint and opens before creation God's perpetual mode of Sabbath being. God sanctified the seventh day, setting it apart from the other six by means of its relation to the preceding six days—the seventh day comes after the first six—and by means of its discontinuity with the preceding six days, God sanctifies this day and inhabits its space. It is from God's inhabition of the seventh day where God attends to and orders the first six days toward their creative end.

Luther speculates, and not without good reason, that if Adam had not sinned, then the goal of Adam's existence in his state of innocence was not paradise per se but was the Sabbath rest of God, eschatologically conceived as the seventh day. Luther clarifies, "Adam would have lived a definite time in Paradise, according to God's pleasure; then he would have been carried off to that rest of God which God, through the sanctifying of the Sabbath, wished not only to symbolize for men but also to grant them."[13] God's state of creative cessation in the seventh day is the location from which his continued providential and redemptive oversight of the first six days occurs and thus remains the teleological goal of all being. Disorienting as his reading might be, Luther is on to

---

[9] Ibid.
[10] Ibid., pp. 61–62.
[11] Ibid.
[12] Martin Luther, *Lectures on Genesis: Chapters 1-5* (*Luther's Works*; American Edition 1; Saint Louis: Concordia Publishing House), pp. 79–82.
[13] Ibid., p. 80.

something about Adam's pre-lapsarian existence or even his hypothetical non-lapsarian existence as not yet inhabiting God's own moment of cessation in the seventh day. Even non-fallen Adam, blissful as his existence might have been, would await something more, something fuller, something eschatological, namely, God's sanctified seventh day.

If I might stay in the tradition for a bit longer, Luther's quite interesting reading has substantial support from Augustine's literal commentary on Genesis. Admittedly, Luther and Augustine frame the conversation in their own ways, and I have hunted in vain to discover Augustine hinting in a similar direction as Luther's conception of Adam's telos. Nevertheless, Augustine conceives of the seventh day as the teleological end of creation. He provides material support for his reading by attending closely to the creation account in Genesis 1. The first six days of creation are constituted by morning and evening. The days have a beginning and an ending, and from the perspective of the day's evening or ending, God deems the creative content of each of the first six days as good. But the seventh day intimates a beginning—God finishes his work; the day is identified as the seventh day—but there is no ending. Put succinctly, the seventh day has a morning but no evening. And Augustine being Augustine thinks this exegetical insight important and presses into it in a way that only he can.

Augustine can be hard to track through this section—he can be hard to track period!—but what Augustine recognizes is the tension present in the seven-day account. On the one hand, you have the creative activity ending on the sixth day. Six is an important number signaling the perfection of the nature of creation. So why does perfection need a seventh day? Because, for Augustine, the perfection of the six days is a perfection of the created beings in accord with their *nature*. But the seventh day opens the possibility of the perfected nature of created beings finding rest by "abiding in God himself."[14] The perfection of the created nature cannot be bested. Thus, God ceases his creative activity in the merism of evening and morning. But even perfected creaturely being has opened before it the promise of perpetual resting in God and, crucially, *the integrity of the created nature is only preserved in the seventh day rest of God*. Augustine elaborates in the following: "And for this reason, while God abides in himself, like a boomerang [not in Latin text], so that every creature might find in him the terminus and goal for its nature, not to be what he is [preserving the Creator/creature distinction], but to find in him the place of rest in which to preserve what by nature it is in itself."[15] The preservation of creaturely identity in accord with its nature is brought to its *telos* when created beings enter the space of God's seventh-day Shabbat. (Augustine carefully maneuvers here in his preservation of the Creator/creature distinction protecting the integrity of both.)

Augustine concludes, "So then, what the morning that was made after the evening of the sixth day represents is, in my judgment, the start of creation's sharing in the quiet rest of the creator; after all it could not rest in him unless it had been perfected."[16] So while Augustine does not speculate about Adam's end if he had not fallen into sin, the material rationale for Luther's reading finds support in Augustine's understanding of the seventh day's relation to the preceding six. For in the seventh day, perfected nature

---

[14] Saint Augustine, *On Genesis* (trans. E. Hill; New York: New City Press, 2002), IV.34.
[15] Ibid.
[16] Ibid., IV.35.

finds its perpetual rest in the shared and quiet rest of the Creator. The seventh day is the eschatological telos of created being even in the perfection of its creaturely nature.

Or in Karl Barth's accent, "There is no avoiding an eschatological explanation of this rest. God does not only look upon the present of His creation, nor does He only look back to that which He did in creating it. God knows its future." And in what way does he know it? "But as God created heaven and earth through Christ or in Christ, so He has created all things with a view to Christ. On the seventh day God was well pleased with His Son. He saw creation perfect through Christ; He saw it restored again through Christ; and He therefore declared it to be finished and rested."[17]

Conclusion

Such a Trinitarian conception of creation and the seventh day as the apex of the created order resides at the very core of the book of Hebrew's inner logic regarding the Father's creation of the world by the effective and personal agency of the Son (Heb. 1:1-4). Creation is framed Christologically and so too is Creation's eschatological rest. We may seem far afield from Hebrews at this point—off in some abstract theology land—but in point of fact we are not. The Sabbath commandment, in the preceding light, functions as an adumbration of humanity's existence in God's perpetual rest. Moreover, as the theme of rest develops on the far side of the fall, the relation of creation and redemption become inextricably linked. Exodus 33:14: my presence will go with you and I will give you rest (*navach*). The entry of God's people into the promised land figures the promise of cessation from wandering: a proleptic, even if imperfect, look forward to that which constitutes the people of God in their future existence in God's seventh day.

Thus the challenge from Israel's history remains: do not harden your hearts. As the good news was announced to the wilderness generation, so too, yet in exponentially more abundant fashion as the first three chapters of Hebrews reveals, has the gospel of Jesus Christ been declared to you. Do not harden your hearts; do not fall prey to the sin of disobedience, which, according to Lane, is almost exclusively conceived of as the disobedience of faith. Faith, herein, connotes the forward-looking trust in the saving promises of God declared unto humankind in Christ Jesus our Lord. Do not shrink back. The gift of the promised land anticipates something greater and you run the risk, like the wilderness generation, of coming to the door's edge but not entering God's perpetual rest, his eschatological space awaiting us in the future yet fully existent and operative in the Today—the place from which God governs the world and moves it toward its redemptive end as God gives himself to a temporal relation with his people.

Do not harden your hearts; herein lies the perennial threat, the real human plight. And the solution remains a clinging to the future, saving promises of God in Christ Jesus: the solution remains perpetual for Today and Tomorrow because what *is* Today if not yesterday's Tomorrow.

---

[17] Barth, *CD III.1*, p. 222.

11

Hebrews and the Jewish Law

Matthew Thiessen

Although modern interpreters no longer believe that Paul wrote Hebrews, too often they continue to read its treatment of the Jewish law through the lens of what scholars commonly refer to as the "Lutheran" reading of Paul: Christ has abolished the Jewish law, the observance of which was deeply problematic because it (1) required perfect obedience in order to merit salvation, (2) could not be kept perfectly, and, therefore, (3) led to either (a) self-despair or (b) deluded self-pride.[1] For example, in a brief treatment of the law and Hebrews, Harold Attridge aligns Hebrews with Paul, concluding that "both argue against the continuing religious validity of the Torah."[2]

In this chapter, I seek to challenge this understanding of Hebrews, arguing that, while the author of the letter attempts to provide a theological account of Jesus in light of the Jerusalem temple and wilderness tabernacle cult, he does not intend to dismiss the relevance of this cult. In fact, all but three of the author's references to νόμος pertain quite clearly to the laws regulating this cultic system. Further, the author does not conclude that the legislation of the cultic system is no longer valid; rather, he argues that Christ's death and resurrection are rituals that belong to a different cultic system in the heavenly realm where, given the markedly different reality of that sphere, distinct laws apply. Before turning to these occurrences of νόμος, though, I shall briefly treat the three outlying instances.

The New Covenant in Hebrews 8:10 and 10:16

In Heb. 8:10 and 10:16 the author quotes Jer. 38:33 LXX (31:33 MT): "This is the covenant that I will make between the house of Israel after those days, says the LORD:

---

[1] See, for instance, Rudolf Bultmann, *Theology of the New Testament* (trans. Kendrick Grobel; 2 vols.; London: SCM, 1952), 1:242–44.

[2] Harold Attridge, *Hebrews: A Commentary on the Epistle to the Hebrews* (Hermeneia; Minneapolis: Fortress, 1989), p. 204. For similar readings of the law in Hebrews, see Erich Grässer, *An die Hebräer* (EKKNT, 17; 3 vols.; Neukirchen-Vluyn: Neukirchener, 1990), 2:49–52, and Hans-Friedrich Weiss, *Der Brief an die Hebräer: Übersetzt und Erklärt* (KEK, 13; Göttingen: Vandenhoeck & Ruprecht, 1991), pp. 403–07.

I will place my laws[3] into their mind, and upon their hearts I will write them. And I will be their God, and they will be my people." The New Covenant that God promises Israel through the prophet Jeremiah does not consist in new covenantal stipulations; rather, the newness of the covenant consists in the fact that it will not be something external—a written legal code—but an internal disposition that God gives to his people.[4] Jeremiah, then, envisages a future time when Israel would undergo an ontological change that would enable them to obey and worship God naturally, without requiring the external compulsion of written laws. Of this passage, and similar passages in Ezekiel (e.g., 36:25-26), Christine Hayes states:

> For both of these prophets, it is not the law that will change in the messianic future. The same laws and rules will continue to function as residency requirements for those who would live in Yahweh's land. What will change is *human nature*. Israel will be hardwired to obey Yahweh's will without effort or struggle. The *elimination of human moral freedom* is nothing less than a utopian redesign of human nature, in which the difficulties associated with the exercise of moral freedom are obviated. With perfect knowledge of Yahweh's teaching, obedience to the divine law is automatic, a state we may refer to as "robo-righteousness."[5]

Nonetheless, in his effort to understand how the author of Hebrews employs this prophecy from Jeremiah, Barry Joslin states, "If the chief purpose of internalization is to produce obedience, and there is no alteration in content to what is inwardly written, then it logically follows that the [New Covenant] people are to obey the [Old Covenant] law with no change of content (including keeping the cultus)."[6] For Joslin, this conclusion is self-evidently absurd because he thinks it incomprehensible that one could internalize the ritual and cultic laws of the Mosaic Covenant. He thus concludes that Hebrews cannot possibly mean that the Mosaic Law is internalized: the newness of the New Covenant in Hebrews is not merely an internalization of the Jewish law, but a law with new content stripped of ritual and cultic laws.[7] What Joslin fails to consider is that if it is a priori unthinkable that Hebrews' use of Jer. 38:33 LXX could include the entirety of the Jewish law, then it must be just as unthinkable that the prophet

---

[3] Hebrews, following the LXX, reads νόμους μου, "my laws." The Hebrew reads תורתי, which, depending on how one points this phrase, could mean either "my law" [as in the MT] or "my laws" which is how the LXX translator of Jeremiah interpreted it.

[4] So too Moshe Weinfeld, "Jeremiah and the Spiritual Metamorphosis of Israel," *ZAW* 88 (1976), pp. 17–56 (28).

[5] Christine Hayes, *What's Divine about Divine Law? Early Perspectives* (Princeton: Princeton University Press, 2015), p. 48 (emphasis original). Hayes (p. 49) draws a compelling conclusion from such texts: "Insofar as Jeremiah and Ezekiel assume that perfect Torah observance will require a future redesign of human nature and elimination of moral freedom that only God can effect, they reinforce the general biblical narrative—perfect Torah obedience is neither expected nor required of human beings as they are."

[6] Barry Joslin, *Hebrews, Christ, and the Law: The Theology of the Mosaic Law in Hebrews 7:1–10:18* (Paternoster Biblical Monographs; Exeter: Paternoster, 2008), p. 217.

[7] Similarly, Stefan Nordaard Svendsen (*Allegory Transformed: The Appropriation of Philonic Hermeneutics in the Letter to the Hebrews* [WUNT 2, 269; Tübingen: Mohr Siebeck, 2009], p. 170) claims that the author "had to muster a significant amount of revisionary creativity in order to turn the text into an oracle about the abolition of the Law."

Jeremiah could have intended his prophecy to refer to the entirety of the Jewish law, rituals included. But we have no evidence either that Jeremiah thought that such a New Covenant entailed the obsolescence of ritual and cultic laws or that other early Jews understood this passage to hint at such an obsolescence of the law. So how, apart from certain Christian presuppositions, can we conclude that Hebrews does? In fact, as I shall show shortly, there simply is no evidence in Hebrews that the author rejects the ritual and cultic aspects of the Jewish law. Rather, there is strong evidence that he thinks these aspects of the law remain in effect at the time of his writing.

The one who annuls the law in Hebrews 10:28

In Heb. 10:28, the author cites scripture regarding what is to happen to one who does away with the law: "Anyone who annuls the law of Moses" (ἀθετήσας τις νόμον Μωϋσέως) dies without compassion "upon the testimony of two or three witnesses." Here he refers to the legal requirement that one cannot be put to death unless the testimonies of more than one person support the accusation (Deut. 17:6; 19:5). The author's quotation of this passage demonstrates, at the very least, that he believes in the continuing applicability of *this* particular law. In terms of the judicial requirement for more than one witness, Hebrews is not alone among early Christ followers (cf. Mk 14:55-59; Mt. 18:16; Jn 8:17; 2 Cor. 13:1; 1 Tim. 5:19).[8] But the author's commitment to the Jewish law goes further: he continues to believe that the person who annuls the law of Moses ought to be put to death.[9] For the author, Jewish law observance is so important that the rejection of it merits death. None of this thinking does the author undermine or dismiss. In fact, using a *qal wahomer* argument, he bolsters his own declarations about the seriousness of rejecting the son of God (v. 29). If breaking the law of Moses merits the death of the transgressor, how much worse must the punishment be for the one who spurns the son of God? If the author believes that the Jewish law no longer remains valid, then Deut. 17:6 and 19:5 no longer apply: that is, no longer must one be put to death for breaking the law of Moses. And, if this is the case, his claims about a greater punishment for the one who rejects Christ unravels.

In fact, this passage hints at the enduring significance of ritual categories for the author's thinking. Those who reject the son of God after having received the knowledge of truth (10:26) become guilty of profaning the blood of the covenant (τὸ αἷμα τῆς διαθήκης κοινὸν ἡγησάμενος) by which they had been sanctified (10:29). To treat as profane something that sanctifies, and is therefore itself sacred, is to confuse a central priestly binary. According to Lev. 10:10: "You are to distinguish between

---

[8] See Hendrik van Vliet, *No Single Testimony: A Study on the Adoption of the Law of Deut. 19:15 par. into the New Testament* (Utrecht: Kemink & Zoon, 1958).

[9] Readers might wonder whether the author himself is guilty of the very thing that he here asserts makes one worthy of death, for in Heb. 7:18 he argues that there is an annulment (ἀθέτησις) of the legal requirement that earthly priests must descend from Levi. If the majority of interpreters is right in claiming that the author dismisses the ritual and cultic law, then the author would indeed stand condemned by his own words. As I shall argue, and as one can see from Heb. 8:4, the author does not intend to suggest that this law (or any other) is annulled per se, only that it does not hold once one moves into a different cultic sphere.

the holy and the profane, and the impure and the pure (διαστεῖλαι ἀνὰ μέσον τῶν ἁγίων καὶ τῶν βεβήλων)" (see also Ezek. 22:26 and 44:23). Although Hebrews does not follow the LXX in referring to profane things with the word βέβηλος, instead using the adjective κοινός, it is clear that the author shares the priestly aversion to mixing these categories. To profane the sacred, life-giving blood of this New Covenant is to court divine punishment because the author believes that God continues to be deeply concerned about these ritual categories.

Cultic Νόμος in Hebrews 7–10

The ten remaining references to νόμος occur in Hebrews 7–10. Unlike Paul, the author of Hebrews does not concern himself with questions of circumcision (e.g., Rom. 2:17-29; Gal. 5:2-3), Sabbath (e.g. Gal. 4:10), or dietary laws (e.g., Romans 14). Nor does he contrast works or works of the law to faith. Hebrews' treatment of the law has very little in common, at least on the surface, with the questions Paul faced with regard to the Jewish law. No doubt a large part of this difference is the result of the fact that Paul, as the apostle to the gentiles, wrote his letters predominantly, if not exclusively, to gentile believers in Jesus and had to address the question of whether or not gentiles ought to observe the Jewish law. In contrast, the author of Hebrews appears to address Jewish believers in Jesus.[10] Consequently, he focuses on the priesthood and cult.

What does the author think about the laws that pertain to priesthood and the temple/tabernacle complex? In the only monograph devoted to the study of the law in Hebrews, Joslin repeatedly claims that Christ "abrogates," "cancels," renders "obsolete,"[11] and causes the "cessation" and "annulment" of the commandments related to the Levitical priesthood. Consequently, he concludes that, for the author of Hebrews, "to follow the same priesthood and to sacrifice animals for sin is now to go against the work of God and not to hear his speaking in the son."[12] Such claims are far from unique in scholarship on Hebrews, yet they fail to take account of the evidence from Hebrews 7–10.[13]

---

[10] David M. Moffitt ("Jesus the High Priest and the Mosaic Law: Reassessing the Appeal to the Heavenly Realm in the Letter 'To the Hebrews,'" in *Problems in Translating Texts About Jesus: Proceedings from the International Society of Biblical Literature Annual Meeting, 2008* [ed. Mishael Caspi and John T. Greene; Lewiston, NY: Mellen, 2011], pp. 187–224 [188]) also notes this considerable difference. Clement of Alexandria (according to Eusebius, *Hist. eccl.* 6.14.4) already recognized this difference between Paul's letters and Hebrews, although he believed that Paul penned the letter.

[11] Joslin, *Hebrews, Christ, and the Law*: cancelled, p. 142; obsolete, p. 144; cessation, p. 133; annulment, p. 152.

[12] Joslin, *Hebrews, Christ, and the Law*, p. 133. Later (*Hebrews, Christ, and the Law*, p. 171), he avers, "Since Christ is the new high priest, the commands that regulated the priesthood are no longer to be kept. To keep them would assert that the Christ event did not fulfill the old priesthood's cultic duties. Such commandments within the law have been cancelled." Similarly, Svendsen (*Allegory Transformed*, p. 94): "In the author's view, submission to the Torah after the inauguration of the new covenant would imply a disregard of the new and efficient means of salvation brought about through the sacrifice of Jesus."

[13] For example, Morna D. Hooker, "Christ, the 'End' of the Cult," in *The Epistle to the Hebrews and Christian Theology* (ed. Richard Bauckham, Daniel Driver, Trevor Hart, and Nathan MacDonald Grand Rapids, MI: Eerdmans, 2009), pp. 188–212 (204–05): "The author of Hebrews, by spelling

First, the author assumes that the law concerning the proper genealogical descent of Israel's priests—they must descend from the tribe of Levi—is still in effect.[14] The letter concedes that Christ was descended from the tribe of Judah, not from the tribe of Levi. The author admits that Moses did not connect the tribe of Judah to the priesthood (7:14). How, then, can he claim that Christ is a high priest? This fact is a real problem facing the author of Hebrews and his readers, as he acknowledges in Heb. 8:4: if Jesus were on earth, "he would not be a priest at all," for there already are priests who offer gifts "in accordance with the law."[15] In other words, Jesus is not qualified to be a priest on earth *precisely because* the law has already established an earthly priesthood and, in stipulating a genealogically determined priesthood, precluded Jesus of the tribe of Judah from ever becoming a priest in the temple in Jerusalem. For the author, the law regarding priestly descent from Levi remains valid and permanently disqualifies Jesus from being a priest on earth.[16] This fact confirms the author's argument that, if Jesus is a high priest, then he must be one in the celestial realm,[17] a realm that does not require priests to be descendants of Levi.

To say, as does Craig R. Koester, then, that there can only be one priesthood at a time in Jewish thinking is inaccurate. Relatedly, Marie Isaacs concludes, "For the author of Hebrews, the cult place has not been replaced by the church, but superseded altogether, and re-located in heaven."[18] Again, such claims fail to take account of the author's argument that Jesus is a high priest within the line of Melchizedek. In other words, this cultic place has always coexisted with the tabernacle and temple, so no relocation or replacement occurs. In fact, not only did this celestial cult coexist with

---

out Christ's work as high priest, shows how he has not only fulfilled the purpose of the cult, but has at one and the same time done away with the whole system."

[14] Joslin, *Hebrews, Christ, and the Law*, p. 143.

[15] Moffitt ("Jesus the High Priest," p. 201) rightly concludes that "the consistent emphasis on genealogy in the argument allows the inference that this issue is of central importance for the author."

[16] So too Moffitt, "Jesus the High Priest," p. 194. As early as Origen (*Commentary on the Gospel of John* 1.11), Christian interpreters did not find it inconceivable that there might be more than one legitimate priesthood functioning at the same time.

[17] Kenneth L. Schenck (*Cosmology and Eschatology in Hebrews: The Settings of the Sacrifice* [SNTSMS, 143; Cambridge: Cambridge University Press, 2007], p. 8) argues that "the author is largely playing out a metaphor and thus . . . , as with so many metaphors, we run into difficulties if we press them too far." Cf. idem, "An Archaeology of Hebrews' Tabernacle Imagery," in *Hebrews in Contexts* (ed. Gabriella Gelardini and Harold W. Attridge; Ancient Judaism and Early Christianity, 91; Leiden: Brill, 2016), pp. 238–58. Peterson (*Hebrews and Perfection*, pp. 131–32) likewise argues that the heavenly sanctuary is mythological and metaphorical. Simply put, this is incorrect. As Ithamar Gruenwald ("God the 'Stone/Rock': Myth, Idolatry, and Cultic Fetishism in Ancient Israel," *JR* 76 [1996], pp. 428–48 [432]) argues in regard to the modern interpretation of ancient texts, "Metaphoricism, as a hermeneutic principle, is very likely to do the opposite of what is expected. Instead of making us hear the voice of the text in all its clarity, it may critically distort the issues involved." For a thoroughly convincing case that Hebrews is using analogy, not metaphor, see David M. Moffitt, "Serving in the Tabernacle in Heaven: Sacred Space, Jesus's High-Priestly Sacrifice, and Hebrews' Analogical Theology," in *Hebrews in Contexts* (ed. Gabriella Gelardini and Harold W. Attridge; Ancient Judaism and Early Christianity, 91; Leiden: Brill, 2016), pp. 259–80. Moffitt depends upon the illuminating discussion of Janet Martin Soskice, *Metaphor and Religious Language* (Oxford: Clarendon, 1985).

[18] Craig R. Koester, *Hebrews: A New Translation with Introduction and Commentary* (AB, 36; New York: Doubleday, 2001), p. 359. See also Marie Isaacs, *Sacred Space: An Approach to the Theology of the Epistle to the Hebrews* (JSNTSup, 73; Sheffield: Sheffield Academic Press, 1992), p. 146, and Svendsen, *Allegory Transformed*, p. 144.

the Jerusalem temple (and wilderness tabernacle), it also preceded it: after all, the earthly cult was patterned after the preexisting heavenly cult (Heb. 8:5).[19] Hebrews envisages two priesthoods functioning simultaneously—an earthly priesthood of Levitical descent and a heavenly priesthood in the order of Melchizedek. Christ cannot be priest on earth because there is *already* an earthly priesthood: there are those priests who *currently* offer gifts according to the law (ὄντων τῶν προσφερόντων κατὰ νόμον τὰ δῶρα, 8:3). Apparently, then, the law is not abrogated, cancelled, made obsolete, or annulled. It remains valid, despite the coming of Jesus and the inception of his own high priesthood in the heavenly realm.

In his belief in two distinct, yet simultaneously valid, priesthoods and cultic systems, the author of Hebrews explicitly depends upon Exod. 25:8-9, where God says to Moses, "And let them make me a sanctuary, that I may dwell in their midst. According to all that I show you concerning the pattern of the tabernacle, and of all its furniture, so you shall make it" (cf. 25:40). The earthly structure is a model of that heavenly temple in which God himself dwells. The author of Hebrews is not alone in thinking that two distinct but related cultic centers can function concurrently. Most succinctly, the first century BCE or CE Wisdom of Solomon glosses Exod. 25:8-9 in the following way: "You said to build a temple on your holy mountain, and in the city of your dwelling an altar, a copy of the holy tent that you prepared from the beginning" (9:8 NRSV). Much earlier, *1 Enoch* speaks of the angels who did not sin remaining in heaven and looking out of the heavenly sanctuary (9.1). In the first half of the first century CE, Philo depicts the entire cosmos as a temple, with heaven functioning as the holy of holies. Within this realm, the angels serve as priests—precisely because they are incorporeal souls they can dwell in this sacred space. Like Hebrews, Philo says that the earthly temple is built with hands. Clearly, this earthly structure is subordinate to the heavenly one, but it nonetheless serves a useful purpose: "There is also the temple made by hands; for it was right that no check should be given to the forwardness of those who pay their tribute to piety and desire by means of sacrifices either to give thanks for the blessings that befall them or to ask for pardon and forgiveness for their sins" (*Spec.* 1.67; Colson; LCL 320, pp. 138–39).[20]

In a similar vein, the Songs of the Sabbath portrays the angels in priestly terms:

Praise
[the God of . . . ,] you gods of all the most holy ones; and in {his} the divinity;
[of his kingdom, rejoice. Because he has established] the most holy ones, so that
    for him they can be priests
[of the inner sanctum in the temple of his kingship,] the servants of the Presence
    in his glorious sanctuary.
                      (4Q400 frag. 1 1.1–4; Martínez and Tigchelaar; 2:806–809)

---

[19] Similarly, Gabriella Gelardini, "The Inauguration of Yom Kippur according to the LXX and Its Cessation or Perpetuation according to the Book of Hebrews: A Systematic Comparison," in *The Day of Atonement: Its Interpretations in Early Jewish and Christian Traditions* (ed. Thomas Hieke and Tobias Nicklas; Themes in Biblical Narrative, 15; Leiden: Brill, 2011), pp. 225–54.

[20] As Jonathan Klawans (*Purity, Sacrifice, and the Temple: Symbolism and Supersessionism in the Study of Ancient Judaism* [New York: Oxford University Press, 2006], pp. 111–44) stresses, there is an important difference between considering the entire heaven a temple, as does Philo, and believing there to be a temple/tabernacle in heaven, as does Hebrews.

Likewise, the *Testament of Levi* portrays the seven realms of heaven with the angels serving as priests before God: "In the uppermost heaven of all dwells the Great Glory in the Holy of Holies (ἐν ἁγίῳ ἁγίων) superior to all holiness. There with him are the archangels, who serve and offer propitiatory sacrifices (οἱ λειτουργοῦντες καὶ ἐξιλασκόμενοι) to the Lord in behalf of all the sins of ignorance of the righteous ones. They present to the Lord a pleasing odor, a rational and bloodless oblation" (3.4-6; Kee; *OTP* 1:789). At the end of the first century CE, *2 Baruch* refers to a temple and city that God showed both Adam before he sinned and Moses on Mount Sinai (4:2-6). Much later than Hebrews, *Num. Rab.* claims that at the same time that God commanded Moses to erect a tabernacle in the wilderness, he instructed the angels to do so in heaven (12.12; cf. *b. Hag.* 12b; *Gen. Rab.* 69.7; *Song Rab.* 48.8; *Pesiq. Rab.* 40.6).[21]

These texts, stemming from diverse periods, locations, and forms of Judaism, show that belief in a celestial priesthood and temple was widespread around the time that the author of Hebrews wrote.[22] Most significantly, it is clear that none of these authors intend to undermine or abolish the earthly priesthood in general.[23] Rather, the earthly priesthood mimics and derives its authority from the heavenly priesthood.[24] These parallels in Jewish literature that originates outside of the early Jesus movement raise the question: why do so many scholars interpret Hebrews' portrayal of Jesus as a high priest to signify the annulment of the Levitical priesthood and earthly cult? That scholars do not come to this conclusion with regard to these texts, but do so when discussing Hebrews is a rather telling sign of the continuing inability of NT scholars to read texts written by early Christ followers as Jewish textual productions.

Interpreters who believe that the author concludes that Christ abolishes the law point to Heb. 7:12, which states that "when there is a change in the priesthood, there is, of necessity, also a change in the law" (μετατιθεμένης γὰρ τῆς ἱερωσύνης ἐξ ἀνάγκης καὶ νόμου μετάθεσις γίνεται). Does this passage imply "l'abrogation de la Loi," as Ceslas Spicq suggests?[25] The noun μετάθεσις means "transformation" or "translation," while the verb μετατίθημι means "to transfer" or "to translate." Most relevant, though, for the use of this word within the discussion of an earthly and a celestial priesthood is the author's use of μετατίθημι and μετάθεσις in his treatment of the faithful Enoch: in dependence upon Gen. 6:24 LXX, he interprets it, as was customary, as evidence that

---

[21] See Klawans, *Purity, Sacrifice, and the Temple*, pp. 128-38.
[22] This Jewish thinking belongs within a much larger temple ideology in the ancient world. See Deena Ragavan, ed., *Heaven on Earth: Temples, Ritual, and Cosmic Symbolism in the Ancient World* (Oriental Institute Seminars, 9; Chicago: Oriental Institute of the University of Chicago, 2013).
[23] To be sure, the Qumran Community could point to the heavenly cult to criticize contemporary practices in the Jerusalem temple, but this was not intended as a final dismissal of the Jerusalem temple, only a condemnation of its current misuse. In fact, such a condemnation of, for instance, the calendar used at the temple, shows how committed the Qumran Community was to the Jerusalem temple: so important were the rituals performed there that priests needed to ensure their proper observance.
[24] As Mircea Eliade (*The Myth of the Eternal Return: Cosmos and History* [trans. William R. Trask; Princeton: Princeton University Press, 1954], pp. 3-4) states, "Objects or acts acquire a value, and in so doing become real, because they participate, after one fashion or another, in a reality that transcends them."
[25] Ceslas Spicq, *L'Épître aux Hébreux* (2 vols.; Paris: Gabalda, 1952-1953), 2:225.

God translated or transformed Enoch so that he could move from the terrestrial realm to the heavenly realm without experiencing death.[26]

It is this same transformation or change that the author envisages with regard to the laws of priesthood. That is to say, the laws of the earthly priesthood do not apply just as they are to the celestial cult—they must be transformed. What qualifies one to be a priest changes when one moves from the terrestrial cult, where mortals become priests through genealogical descent, to the celestial realm, where the mortal simply cannot exist. Rather, in this celestial cult, only the power of an indestructible life qualifies one to serve as priest.[27] To serve in this cult requires that one have a life appropriate to the heavenly habitat in the presence of a holy God who cannot exist in close proximity to death and mortality. This contrast between the qualifications of the earthly priesthood and the celestial priesthood hinges on the mortality of the former and the immortality of the latter. The former, in depending upon a genealogical requirement, underlines the significance of the mortality of the Levitical priesthood: this priesthood must be genealogical because the priests are mortal. There are many of them because of death (7:23). The celestial priesthood, though, requires only one high priest because this priesthood has overcome the power of death and participates in everlasting life (2:14-15; 7:24).

Upon what basis does the author of Hebrews claim that the celestial priesthood depends upon the requirement of an indestructible life? Psalm 109:4 LXX (110:4 MT), which states, "You are a priest forever, according to the order of Melchizedek" (Σὺ εἶ ἱερεὺς εἰς τὸν αἰῶνα κατὰ τὴν τάξιν Μελχισέδεκ). The centrality of this Psalm to the author's argument again confirms the continuing significance of the Jewish law: it is the author's authoritative text for making theological arguments about Jesus.[28]

But is this the only aspect of the Jewish law that changes with this new celestial priesthood? Mary Schmitt avers, "Whereas most commentators assume that, in Hebrews, νόμος is equivalent to Torah, I argue that νόμος in 7:12 refers only to the cultic laws pertaining to priesthood."[29] Schmitt is right to conclude that νόμος here refers, at least in the first instance, to the requirement that priests be of Levitical descent, although context suggests that it refers also to the complex of laws pertaining to the Jerusalem cult and Levitical priesthood. Far beyond the stipulations of who can serve as a priest, Hebrews envisages numerous transformations of the law as one moves from the earthly to the heavenly. The terrestrial cult, for instance, uses the blood of animals—goats and calves—in many of its sacrifices. In contrast, in the celestial cult the high priest uses his own blood to provide purification (9:12-14). The idea

---

[26] On Enoch, see James C. VanderKam, *Enoch: A Man for All Generations* (Studies on Personalities of the Old Testament; Columbia: University of South Carolina Press, 1995). On heavenly ascents, see Martha Himmelfarb, *Ascent to Heaven in Jewish and Christian Apocalypses* (New York: Oxford University Press, 1993), and, with regard to Moses in Exod. 25:40, David M. Moffitt, *Atonement and the Logic of Resurrection in the Epistle to the Hebrews* (NovTSup, 151; Leiden: Brill, 2011), pp. 150-62.

[27] See Moffitt, *Atonement and the Logic of Resurrection*, pp. 200-08.

[28] So too Moffitt, "Jesus the High Priest," p. 205. Contrary to Isaacs (*Sacred Space*, p. 116), though, Psalm 110 does not serve as "Hebrews' mandate for abrogating pentateuchal priestly Law"; rather, it serves as scriptural evidence for the existence of another priesthood.

[29] Mary Schmitt, "Restructuring Views on the Law in Hebrews 7:12," *JBL* 128 (2009), pp. 189-201 (189).

that a Levitical priest might bring in the blood of a human to provide purification for the tabernacle would have caused great consternation, but in the heavenly realm such a ritual detergent is not only permissible but also required. Further, according to Hebrews, while the blood of animals purifies the bodies, specifically the flesh, of humans, the celestial offering purifies the consciences of those who believe in Christ (9:13-14).[30]

To be sure, the author sees a hierarchy here: the Levitical priesthood and earthly cult are inferior to Christ's priesthood and the celestial cult. But such a hierarchy does not abolish the Levitical priesthood or speak to its obsolescence. As David Peterson contends, "We are told that the Law [pertaining to the Levitical priesthood] provided some measure of cleansing and sanctification (9:13, 19ff), but our writer denies absolutely that perfection was available under the former system ('for the law made nothing perfect', 7:19)."[31] To participate in the earthly cult, one needs to have the flesh purified. As long as this cult remains, and as long as both priests and lay people remain mortal, these purifications are neither cancelled nor obsolete. Were one to think that such purificatory rites are sufficient to participate in the celestial cult, though, one would be gravely mistaken. So too Isaacs rightly notes, "In claiming that Christ cleanses the conscience, unlike the cult which made no such provision, our author goes further. Jesus does far more than the Levitical system was ever intended to do."[32]

Hebrews claims that the cultic regulations have changed because there has been a change in location—from terrestrial to celestial. The earthly cult, both tabernacle and temple, were made with human hands (9:11, 24). The celestial realm contains an ontologically different—and better—tent, not made by human hands and not of this creation. It is heavenly, consisting of better materials and therefore in need of a different detergent than the blood of animals that the priests use on earth. And the detergent used in the celestial realm not only purifies a heavenly tent, but it also treats the deep-set stains that penetrate to the very inner part of the human—the conscience (9:14),[33] and not the ritual impurities that stain human flesh (9:13). Only Christ's blood—the blood of one who has overcome death—has the purificatory power to deal with the heavenly cultic apparatus. Consequently, both Otto Michel and Peterson are incorrect to interpret the author's reference to Christ's blood here in nonmaterial ways.[34]

---

[30] Since Heb. 9:13 explicitly claims that earthly sacrifices purify the flesh, it is exegetically indefensible to suggest, as do R. V. G. Tasker (*Gospel in the Epistle to the Hebrews* [2nd ed.; London: Tyndale Press, 1956], p. 21) and Hermann V. A. Kuma (*The Centrality of Αἷμα [Blood] in the Theology of the Epistle to the Hebrews: An Exegetical and Philological Study* [Lewiston, NY: Mellen, 2010], p. 283), that the author intends to condemn Jewish law observance as "dead works."

[31] Peterson, *Hebrews and Perfection: An Examination of the Concept of Perfection in the "Epistle to the Hebrews"* (SNTSMS 47; Cambridge: Cambridge University Press, 1982), p. 128. Similarly, Kuma (*Centrality of Αἷμα*, p. 291) asserts that "the sacrificial role of blood presented in the OT is strongly affirmed by the author of Hebrews," and Isaacs (*Sacred Space*, p. 92) claims that "the author of Hebrews shares with his Jewish contemporaries a belief in sacrifice as the divinely appointed means of dealing with sin."

[32] Isaacs, *Sacred Space*, p. 101.

[33] On the question of the relationship between conscience and the tabernacle/temple cult, see Jacob Milgrom, *Cult and Conscience: The Asham and the Priestly Doctrine of Repentance* (SJLA, 18; Leiden: Brill, 1976), and idem, "On the Origins of Philo's Doctrine of Conscience," *Studia Philonica* 3 (1974-1975), pp. 41-44.

[34] Michel, *Der Brief an die Hebräer: Übersetzt und Erklärt* (KEK, 13; Göttingen: Vandenhoeck and Ruprecht, 1966), p. 314, and Peterson, *Hebrews and Perfection*, p. 138.

An earthly cultic system for mortals

In his fascinating book *The Bodies of God*, Benjamin Sommer argues that "a central theme of priestly tradition—perhaps, the central theme of priestly tradition—is the desire of the transcendent God to become immanent on the earth this God had created."[35] How can the immortal and perfect God dwell in the midst sinful and mortal people? In the priestly worldview, the ritual purity system addresses the latter condition of people—their mortality—by prohibiting people who experience ritual impurities, which represent death or mortality, stemming from corpses, *lepra* (which is *not* leprosy), and genital emissions, from entering into sacred space where God dwells.[36] Consequently, according to priestly thought, the wilderness tabernacle and later Jerusalem temple are shaped by and intended to function in a world governed by mortality. The system excludes from God's dwelling those most proximately connected to mortality, but it does not and is not intended to address the root problem of human mortality itself.

Connected to human mortality is human immorality. The cultic system again expects that Israelites will sin—that is, commit moral impurities—and at the same time provides the means of atonement for such sins, most especially in the Day of Atonement rituals. As Joshua M. Vis has recently argued,

> The motivation for the [purification] offering was not for the maintenance of a good, well-ordered cosmos inhabited by a people made in the image of God. It was nearly the opposite, in fact. It was a ritual that assumed the repetitious creation of material substances that resulted from wrongdoing and that clung to individuals and to the sanctuary. This cosmos was constantly under threat of losing the divine presence due to the unavoidable uncleanness and sinfulness of the people in it.[37]

When we situate the letter to the Hebrews within this worldview, we see that the author envisages two realms—the mortal and the immortal—coexisting. The mortal realm pertains to the earth and has an earthly sanctuary, while the immortal realm is heavenly and has a heavenly sanctuary. Whatever the limitations of the earthly sanctuary and the laws pertaining to the sanctuary, priesthood, and cult, they are inexorably tied to the *nature* of this realm—since this realm is mortal all aspects of its cult have built-in limitations. In contrast to this earthly, mortal realm, "the coming οἰκουμένη represents the yet-to-be-realized hopes for immortality in the presence of God for the audience (2:8)."[38] Although these two realms currently coexist, the author believes that only the

---

[35] Sommer, *The Bodies of God and the World of Ancient Israel* (Cambridge: Cambridge University Press, 2011), p. 74 (original emphasis removed).

[36] See, for instance, Jacob Milgrom, *Leviticus 1–16: A New Translation with Introduction and Commentary* (AB, 3; New York: Doubleday, 1991), pp. 742–1009.

[37] Joshua M. Vis, "The Purification Offering of Leviticus and the Sacrificial Offering of "Jesus" (PhD diss., Duke University, 2012), p. 54. So too Pamela Eisenbaum, "Ritual and Religion, Sacrifice and Supersessionism: A Utopian Reading of Hebrews," in *Hebrews in Contexts* (ed. Gabriella Gelardini and Harold W. Attridge; Ancient Judaism and Early Christianity, 91; Leiden: Brill, 2016), pp. 343–56 (353).

[38] Jason A. Whitlark, "Cosmology and the Perfection of Humanity in Hebrews," in *Interpretation and the Claims of the Text: Resourcing New Testament Theology* (ed. Jason A. Whitlark, Bruce W.

immortal will remain at some point in the future, as Heb. 12:27 demonstrates: "This phrase, 'yet once more,'" indicates the transformation (μετάθεσιν) of what is shaken, that is, what has been made, so that those things that cannot be shaken remain." The author of Hebrews believes that the time will come when the earthly cult will cease to exist, not because he has a negative view of the Levitical priesthood and earthly sanctuary, but because he believes that the mortal realm will disappear, obviating the need for the earthly cult and the laws that pertain to it. But, although Jesus the high priest has come, that time where mortality no longer exists has not yet arrived and so the two systems function concurrently.

Nehemia Polen contrasts Hebrews to the priestly thinking of Leviticus in the following way: "Hebrews argues for perfection: for the perfect priest offering the perfect sacrifice in the heavenly Temple, once and for all. For its part, Leviticus glories in the endless repetition, the day-by-day regularity of one lamb in the morning, one lamb in the evening."[39] While Leviticus does not explicitly envisage a time when mortality will no longer be the final word, this hardly means that it "glories in the endless repetition" that sin and mortality necessitate. If the priestly theology of Ezekiel is any indication, priestly thinkers longed for the day when God would fully address the mortal and immoral state of his people, creating an ontological change in them. The author of Hebrews fits within a larger stream of Jewish thinking that hoped for and expected God to deliver not only Israel but also the entire *kosmos* from bondage to death, sin, and demonic forces. Such a hope seems to be a natural corollary to the belief that Israel's God is holy and cannot abide impurity in any form. Sooner or later God would have to destroy impurity. For the author of Hebrews, such a destruction of impurity and perfection of humanity was in the process of coming about through Christ's resurrection from the dead and subsequent inauguration as high priest in the celestial realm.[40]

Conclusion: The intended audience and the Jewish law

It has been a remarkably persistent trope in literature on Hebrews to conclude that the author writes to Jewish believers in Christ who, in the words of Barnabas Lindars, are tempted to "return to Judaism," a possibility that the author supposedly considers "virtual apostasy."[41] Such claims are problematic for a number of reasons. First, as Hooker notes, this reading "assumes that Christianity was already understood as 'another' religion, separate from Judaism. It treats faith in Jesus as incompatible with

---

Longenecker, Lidija Novakovic, and Mikeal C. Parsons; Waco, TX: Baylor University Press, 2014), pp. 117-28 (120).

[39] Polen, "Leviticus and Hebrews . . . and Leviticus," in *The Epistle to the Hebrews and Christian Theology* (ed. Richard Bauckham, Daniel Driver, Trevor Hart, and Nathan MacDonald; Grand Rapids, MI: Eerdmans, 2009), pp. 213-25 (224-25).

[40] Moffitt "(Jesus the High Priest," p. 207) again rightly connects the author's emphasis on perfection to resurrection: resurrection to eternal life entails the perpetual ritual and moral purity of those who experience it. See further, Moffitt, *Atonement and the Logic of Resurrection*, pp. 194-208.

[41] Barnabas Lindars, *The Theology of the Letter to the Hebrews* (New Testament Theology; Cambridge: Cambridge University Press, 1991), p. 11. Slightly different is Svendsen's (*Allegory Transformed*) argument that the author addresses gentile believers who are tempted to judaize.

Jewish beliefs."[42] Nothing in the letter suggests that the author envisages his community as anything other than belonging to Israel.

Second, nothing within the letter indicates that the implied readers previously abandoned observance of the Jewish law and now are thinking of returning to it. In fact, the author's focus on priesthood and tabernacle cult implies precisely the opposite: the intended readers are both deeply knowledgeable and concerned about the Jewish law and issues pertaining to Jewish ritual and cult. They want to understand how Christ's high priesthood can be in accordance with the Jewish law. The author's detailed and sustained explanation of Christ's high priesthood and cultic service in relation to the Levitical priesthood suggests that he approves of this facet of his implied readers' theology.

To be sure, the author makes numerous arguments about the superiority of the high priesthood of Jesus and the heavenly cult. Such arguments have been used as support by those Christian interpreters who have sought evidence for the superiority of Christianity to Judaism. But the author of Hebrews does not intend to compare and contrast two different religions. Instead, the author intends to compare two different cultic centers. Of course the earthly priesthood and cultic system is inferior to the heavenly priesthood and cultic system. Would any ancient Jew who held to a similar cosmology have disagreed with the author of Hebrews on this hierarchical ordering? Likewise, would any ancient reader have considered the author's claim regarding the limitations and inferiority of the earthly cultic system vis-à-vis the heavenly cultic system to be a derogation of the earthly system? What is new and unique about the author's theology is not his claim about the existence of a heavenly cult, or its superiority in relation to Israel's earthly cult; rather, it is his placement of Jesus at the center, both in front of *and* on the altar, of this heavenly cult.

---

[42] Hooker, "Christ, the 'End' of the Cult," p. 190.

Promises to the Son: Covenant and Atonement in Hebrews

Amy Peeler

Introduction

What has covenant to do with atonement? Were the author of Hebrews to answer this question, the answer, I surmise, would be, "everything." Atonement, broadly conceived in this volume as the restored and continuing relationship between God and God's people, now exists because of the covenant God established with the people of Israel.[1] Although the answer to this initial question might be simple,[2] the nuances of covenant in Hebrews are, conversely, quite complex. The author focuses upon the *New* Covenant, and thereby suggests a certain relationship with the previous. Moreover, he connects the covenant closely with the theme of promise, and also establishes a connection between covenant and the concept of legislation. Because of these anything-but-simple connotations of covenant and its relationship to atonement, to parse out the details of covenant grants a more lucid and rich understanding this author's concept of the divine-human relationship.

I suggest that the logic proceeds in this way: the author sees Psalm 110 (Psalm 109 LXX) as God's promises, oaths even, to the Son. Because this promise included priesthood, that indicates to him that the different priesthood brings with it a different covenant with different administration of God's laws (7:11-12). He connects this change in priesthood and change in legislated relationship with the New Covenant promised by Jeremiah, and the author can call it better because, in his view, it brings internal, heavenly, and eternal access to God, in other words full atonement. This kind of relationship with God, however, neither he nor his readers presently experience. For

---

[1] The author of Hebrews refers to the covenant explicitly at 7:22; 8:6; 8:8-10; 9:4, 15, 16-17, 20; 10:16, 29; 12:24; 13:20.
[2] At the beginning of her monograph, Susanne Lehne makes this broad association: "The author of Heb. associates a whole symbolic universe with the idea [of covenant], a particular relationship of God with his people," Susanne Lehne, *New Covenant in Hebrews* (JSNTSup; Sheffield: JSOT, 1990), pp. 11–12. Mary Ann Beavis and Hye-Ran Kim Cragg state, "For the homilist the new covenant heralds a new quality of relationship between God and God's people," Mary Ann Beavis and Hye-Ran Kim Cragg, *Hebrews* (ed. Barbara E. Reid and Linda Maloney; Wisdom Commentary Series, 54; Collegeville, MN: Liturgical Press, 2015), p. 77.

this community to receive all the promises included in and resulting from this New Covenant (full atonement), they must trust that God is a God who keeps promises. Therefore, the author reminds them of how God has kept his promises to the Son, to them, and to the ancestors. By demonstrating the trustworthiness of God, the author seeks to strengthen the faith of the listeners so that they can endure and then inherit the full promises—the full atonement—of the New Covenant.

This chapter then, proceeds in three movements: first, an analysis of God's promises to the Son; second, an explication of the atoning nature of the New Covenant which comes about because of the kept promises to the Son; and finally, a presentation of the author's encouragements and exhortations based on the texts of Israel so that his audience will trust in the promises of God. The author asserts that some promises have been fulfilled and others remain to be fully realized, hence the structure of the explication is this: Promise, Covenant, Promise, all in the service of understanding Hebrews' view of atonement.

God's promises to the son: Kingship and priesthood

Sovereignty

Hebrews begins, one might say,[3] with a promise from God to the Son. The author opens his letter by recalling that the promise between God and Israel, that they would be joined,[4] includes a parallel promise to Israel's king, that God and he would be in relationship as father and son. The author draws from this Davidic covenant (2 Sam. 23:5) by his use of the term "Son" and his citation of such promises to Israel's king (Heb. 1:2, 5/Ps. 2:7; 2 Sam. 7:14; Heb. 1:8/Ps. 44:7-8; Heb. 1:13/Ps. 109:1). With the introduction of a υἱός as God's new vehicle of speech in v. 2, the author says first that God appointed him as heir of all things. In other words, God has promised to give to the Son τὰ πάντα. Within the schema of wills and inheritance (9:15-16), the author portrays the Son as a beneficiary of a testament, an heir. The only difference, and a striking one at that, is that God is not a human father, so if Jesus is God's heir, he is an heir like no other. He takes an inheritance from a Father who will never die, and therefore never ceases to administer the inheritance himself.

Other promises resound in the following texts in the catena of the first chapter. God says to the Son: "Your throne is forever and forever" (Ps. 44:7 LXX/ Heb. 1:8), and with the words of Psalm 101 LXX, "You will remain (1:11), and your years will not come to an end (1:12)." The catena concludes with a promise as well, a promise that God will subject the enemies under the feet of the Son (Ps. 110:1; Heb. 1:13).[5] The theme of subjugation continues into the next citation (Psalm 8) where the Son, here named as Jesus, has not just enemies but everything subjected under his feet (2:8-9).

---

[3] My turn of phrase seeks to mimic Hebrews who, in 7:9 and 9:22, acknowledges his use of a bold statement.
[4] Exod. 6:7; Deut. 6:7.
[5] The promise of the Davidic Messiah's sovereignty comprises the majority of Psalm 109 LXX. Not only will his enemies be a footstool for his feet (1), but he will have a rod of power (2), other kings will be shattered (5), nations judged (6), and heads crushed (6) while his head is lifted high (7).

The language of the last claim of sovereignty, that from Psalm 8, underscored by the author in his following comments seems not like a promise but the assertion of a reality, a claim that everything has already been subjected, that the promised sovereignty already exists. The line of the Psalm puts God's subjection in the aorist tense (ὑπέταξας), and, clearly in the original context of the Psalm, humanity is sovereign over the animals of creation. In the author's explanation as well, with the use of an aorist infinitive, "in subjecting to him everything," God left (aorist, ἀφῆκεν) nothing that is not subject to him. It is a painful reality for them that he and his readers do not yet see everything that has been subjected to him (perfect tense, ὑποτεταγμένα), but is his sovereignty a reality they cannot see or not yet a reality at all?

Such assertions that God has subjected all things to him, lead to a reevaluation of the assertions of ch. 1. Has he already inherited all things? Has God already put the enemies under his feet? Have the promises already been kept? The strong assertions of ch. 2 seem to point in this direction, and find some confirmation in the rest of the letter. Specifically pertaining to enemies, the author asserts in 2:14 that the Son, through his death nullifies, makes nothing (καταργέω), the devil, who has the power of death. Pertaining to family, the author claims that God has put the Son over his house (3:6). He is present as mediator of the festal gathering of God's angels and children (12:24). He is seated at the right hand of the majesty of God (Heb. 1:3, 13; 7:26; 8:1; 10:12; 12:2). Consequently, after his death and exaltation, He is supreme over some enemies and those who participate in God's people. Consequently, Jesus is already fulfilling the messianic hopes that a descendant of David (Heb. 7:14) would stand in the relationship with God and reign as king (2 Sam. 7:11-16; 1 Chron. 17:11-14; 2 Chron. 6:16; Ps. 2:7-9; Ps. 89:3-4). One key subtext of Hebrews 1 then is that God has been faithful to keep these promises of the covenant with David. This is *not* the only thing to be said about the supremacy of Christ as promised to him by God—there are enemies yet to be subjected (10:13)—but it also needs to be stated that the author displays that God has already kept some grand promises to the Son.

Priesthood

The author also alludes to a second promise to the Son in the opening sentence of Hebrews. The Son takes his place of supremacy next to the right hand of God after he has made purification for sins (1:3c). At the end of ch. 2, the echo of this promise becomes more precise—the Son has become a merciful and faithful high priest by virtue of God making him like his human brothers and sisters (2:17). The author does not articulate the promise that brought this priesthood of the Son to reality, though, until he turns to explicate this vocation in earnest, beginning in 4:14. Having described the particular priesthood of the Son (as heavenly and compassionate), and the general dynamics of priests, the author asserts that the Messiah did not glorify himself, but God chose him for this role. Just as God declared him to be his Son—the author quotes Ps. 2:7 again, and thereby, I argue, alludes to the promise of comprehensive inheritance that God has made to his Son—God also declared him to be a priest forever in the order of Melchizedek, citing Ps. 109:4 LXX. The priesthood that Christ now exercises has come about because God made a promise to him and kept that promise. He is, the author states again at the end of this section, designated (προσαγορευθείς) *by God* as high priest.

The author's foray into the promise made to Abraham prepares the audience to hear about the promise made to the Son. There, in ch. 6, the author emphasizes that God both made a promise and an oath to Abraham. Certainly God did not need to do so since there is nothing greater than Godself upon which God can swear (Heb. 6:16), but God employed both a promise and an oath to underline the unchanging quality of his will (6:17).

God's interactions with Abraham provide the example to God's exchange with the Son because, as the author will explain in ch. 7, not only did God promise that the Son would be a priest, he swore it as well. Whereas in Hebrews 5, the author cites only the claim that "you are priest forever according to the order of Melchizedek," in Hebrews 7, after the story of Abraham, the author quotes more from the beginning of Ps. 110:4, where he states, *The Lord swore* (Heb. 7:21). Jesus is priest because God promised and swore this would be so—and then brought it to fruition.

The process of this kept promise unfolds in this way. First, God gave him a body so that he could offer a sacrifice, a reality the author affirms beginning in ch. 2 (2:14, 17) and for which he provides Scriptural support from Psalm 40 in ch. 10 (Heb. 10:5, "a body you have prepared for me"). Second, God accepted that sacrifice (2:17; 6:20; 8:3, 6; 9:12-14, 24, 28) which brought purification for humanity (Heb. 1:3, 2:17; 9:14, 28; 10:10, 12, 22) and raised that body (7:11; 13:20; 7:23, 24) so that he could sit at the right hand of God, and there make sympathetic intercession for his brothers and sisters (Heb. 2:17; 4:15; 7:25).

God has kept two promises to his Son: that he would be the sovereign King, and that he would be the everlasting High Priest. In discussing God's relationship with the Son, the author makes this point clear: God keeps promises.

The New Covenant atonement brought by the promises

The Story of the Son, though, functions not just as example of God's trustworthiness. "Look what God did for the Son, he will also be faithful to you." It does that, but in good Hebrews fashion, where the author deals in syncrisis—not equality but comparison—the affirmations of God's kept promises to the Son do this and even more. God's faithfulness to fulfill these two vocational roles of the Son, King and Priest, is also the means through which God fulfills promises made to humanity. The author states in ch. 8, the second time he mentions the covenant brought by Christ, that this covenant has been legislated, given a legal standing, upon better promises. The mention of promises here likely alludes to God's Psalm 110 promises to the Son, for sovereignty and an eternal, perfect, singular, and heavenly priesthood as well as the promises found in Jeremiah's prophecy of the coming New Covenant. Before getting to those promises the author finds in the New Covenant, however, I must give attention to the author's comments about the law, because they establish the link between Christ's priesthood and the atoning promises of the New Covenant.

After telling the story of Melchizedek's interaction with Abraham from Genesis 14, thereby establishing Melchizedek's superiority over Abraham, and consequently his descendant Levi (7:9), the author makes this statement, "if perfection was through the Levitical priesthood—for upon it (the priesthood) the people have been given the law[6]—what need is there for another priest to be raised according to the order of Melchizedek and not to be spoken according to the order of Aaron?" (7:11). Although the grammar seems complex, the author's assertion is clear that since God did raise a priest in the order of Melchizedek, that indicates that there was a need for a priest from a line other than that of Aaron. Then he explicates his parenthetical about the people receiving the law: "For when there is a change of the priesthood, there is by necessity a change of the law" (Heb. 7:12). He has two law changes in mind. First, now there is a priest from a tribe, Judah, about whom Moses had said nothing about serving the altar (7:13-16). Second, the commandment pertaining to the people served by the priest, namely the commandment for animal sacrifice, has been removed (ἀθέτησις), because it was weak and ineffective (Heb. 7:18). The author pulls no punches, as he states boldly that law perfected nothing (Heb. 7:19). He does not end though, with a negative critique, but moves to a positive affirmation. There is also the ushering in of a better hope by which we draw near to God (7:19).

It is at this point (7:20) that the author highlights the oath aspect of Ps. 110:4, so I will restate the previous points to make clear my argument about the way in which his logic works. The author starts with God's promise/oath to the Son. The different priesthood promised there must mean there was something insufficient in the previous priesthood, and the author locates that insufficiency in the commandment, the law which regulates the previous priesthood.[7] He proclaims the weak and ineffective nature of the commandment as the law's inability to perfect and relates that lack of perfection to one's proximity to God. Now that there is a different priesthood, there is a different, and better, way for the people of God to be perfected and to approach God. The author, for the first time in 7:22, names this relationship as a διαθήκη, a covenant.[8]

If God's promise/oath to the Son brought a better Covenant, a better way of being in relationship with God, we can see the elements the author highlights that makes this covenant, this atonement with God, in his estimation, better. Through both his comments and his citation of Jeremiah 31 (38 LXX),[9] three elements are most prominent: perfection, access to God, and the covenant's enduring nature.

---

[6] This is a contested phrase and could denote either that the people received the law from the priesthood or that the law given to the people established the priesthood. This second reading rests upon two factors. First, the grammatical likelihood that αὐτῆς refers back to ἱερωσύνης and the contextual indication that the author focuses upon the law pertaining to the priesthood. Johnson states the connection in this way: "[Hebrews 7:11 is] based upon the assumption that the entire purpose of the law has to do with the relations between God and people expressed through the priestly cult," Johnson, Luke T., *Hebrews: A Commentary* (NTL; Louisville: Westminster John Knox, 2006), p. 185.

[7] J. F. Bayes, *The Weakness of the Law: God's Law and the Christian in New Testament Perspective* (Paternoster Biblical Monographs; Eugene, OR: Wipf & Stock, Publishers, 2006), "One commandment is a reflection upon, and an expression of the character of, the entire law," p. 178.

[8] Lehne states, "What is most distinctive and original about the writer's reworking of the covenant motif is his *cultic perspective*," *New Covenant*, p. 93.

[9] With this text, he articulates the shape of the New Covenant God promises to bring. It seems little surprise that this author is attracted to this text because it too conveys the spoken first-person speech of God, as have so many of the texts which he has cited.

The author begins his focus on the state of the covenant member with his appeal to the previous administration of the law as a foil: it perfected nothing (7:19). There in ch. 7, it seems that he assumes the new administration of law under the New Covenant does in fact perfect, and this becomes clear in following statements. As the guarantor of this New Covenant, Jesus is able to save to the utmost (παντελές) those who are approaching God through him. The word παντελές speaks to the completeness or the perfection of the salvation that he offers. Jeremiah's articulation of the New Covenant also includes its ability to perfect. The covenant brings about an internal change. God will place his laws in the members of the New Covenant and write them on their hearts (Heb. 8:10). Because of the author's interest in complete cleansing, bodily and conscience (9:13-14), the change of hearts and minds points toward a complete perfection. Moreover, the New Covenant will deal with the problem of sin. God says, "I will have mercy on their unrighteousness, and their sins I will never still remember" (Heb. 8:12). The author alludes to these statements in his affirmations that the previous sacrificial system could not perfect (the conscience of those who served in 9:9 and generally in 10:1), but Christ's offering of his blood cleanses the conscience (9:14), makes holy (10:10), and perfects those who are being sanctified (10:14). He immediately follows this statement in 10:14 with the second citation of Jeremiah 31, jumping to v. 33, "This is the covenant I will make with them after those days says the Lord, giving my laws upon their hearts and writing them upon their minds." Then skipping to a summary of v. 34, "Their sins and their lawless deeds I will remember no more." Finally, when the author paints the picture of the Mountain of God, those who are gathered there come to Jesus the mediator of the New Covenant, and he describes them as the spirits of the righteous made perfect (12:23-24). Since Jesus's sacrifice finally deals with sin, this is how God can forget sins and lawless deeds forever. Since Jesus's blood cleanses the conscience, God can write the laws on the inside of the people and begin the sanctifying process. This different priest and his New Covenant is better because it makes perfection possible.

With the possibility of perfection secured, the New Covenant also changes the level of access humanity has to God. As mentioned, in his statements in ch. 7, the author asserted that in contrast with the previous administration of the law, there exists a better hope that people can draw near to God (7:19). In the words of Jeremiah, the New Covenant, like the first, will be relational. God will be their God, and they will be his people. Moreover, it will be equally immediately accessible to all. No one will need to teach her fellow citizen or sibling because all will know the Lord, from the least to the greatest. Therefore, after his two citations of the New Covenant passage, he can repeat the invitation he issued at the beginning of his discussion of priesthood, "Let us approach" (4:14; 10:22). Now everyone who participates in Christ gets to do what a high priest would do, go into the holy of holies past the veil, having been washed and sprinkled (Heb. 10:19-20). This approach, in distinction from its predecessor, is not a posture of distance, as he recounts the Israelites before Mount Sinai (12:18-21; alluded to in 9:18-20), but an approach of boldness because they have been cleansed internally, sanctified, perfected, forgiven.

Finally, with the fourth presentation of God's promise from Ps. 110:4, the author highlights the eternal quality of the priesthood by including, ὤμοσεν κύριος καὶ οὐ μεταμεληθήσεται ("the Lord swore and will not change his mind"), and also, according to the earliest manuscripts, ends the citation with the word "forever" (Heb. 7:21). After making the link between this priesthood and the covenant in 7:22, the author returns again to the enduring quality of this priesthood. Other priests couldn't remain because of death, but this one, the Son, remains forever, and so he has an unchangeable priesthood. Since he is always there at God's right hand, he is always living. Since he is always living, he can always make intercession. Since he can always make intercession, he can save to the utmost (παντελές, denoting both the quality of perfection and the quantity of time until the end), those who approach God through him (7:25). When this author quotes vv. 31-34 of Jeremiah 38 LXX (Heb. 8:8), he begins with, "The Lord says, behold days are coming, I will complete (συντελέω)." The author has been proclaiming the complete (παντελές) salvation (7:25) and the unchangeable priesthood (7:24) which brings a New Covenant (7:22; 8:6), and Jeremiah's prophecy corroborates this hope for finality. Christ's priesthood secures eternal redemption (9:12), and an eternal inheritance (9:15). Christ's one offering removed sin and does not have to be dealt with again (9:28). It is a once-for-all (10:10) singular (10:14) offering, the fulfillment of the New Covenant promise (10:17), securing such forgiveness that no other offerings are necessary (10:18). This is, he can say in his final appeal to the covenant, an eternal one (13:20).

This covenant, though, very important for a non-supercessionist reading of Hebrews, will be, Jeremiah promises (and the author of Hebrews includes twice), with the house of Israel and the house of Judah. In the author's own words in ch. 2, God's work is directed to the seed of Abraham (2:16). The new covenant is not different because it brings a relationship with God; previously God took them by the hand (Jer. 38:32/Heb. 8:9). It is not better because it sets Israel into a direct relationship with God. The covenant formula, "I will be their God and they will be my people" appears earlier (Exod. 6:7; Deut. 6:7). The previous also was a covenant of deliverance where God led them out of the land of Egypt. Moreover, just as all the people agreed to the covenant (Exod. 24:3, 7), here the covenant is for all. Nevertheless, this author asserts that God's kept promise of a new priest has brought a new *lasting* covenant for God's people that *completely* removes sin and thereby makes possible a *closer* relationship between God and all God's people.

Promises reprieve

Promises remaining for the audience

The New Covenant makes a perfect, close, and lasting relationship with God—again full atonement—possible, but not automatic. Put another way: does the author of Hebrews assert that he and this congregation have been given the New Covenant? Yes, and no. Yes, first and foremost because they are in relationship with God. They are encouraged to come to God's throne (4:16; 10:19-22); they are members of God's household (3:6); they are children of God (12:5-11). Yes, in that their hearts have been sprinkled (10:22). Yes, also because they have experienced the forgiveness of which this New Covenant speaks. Where there is forgiveness such as that promised by the New

Covenant, there no longer remains the necessity for an offering for sin (10:18). Finally, yes because they can approach God with boldness. The author says, let us go boldly into the inside of the holies by the blood of Jesus (10:19).

The answer is "No" however on three accounts. First, they do not live in a situation in which they need no instruction about God. It is not the case that no one needs to teach them about the Lord (Heb. 8:11/Jer. 38:34 LXX). In ch. 5, the author states clearly that they have much they still need to learn (5:12) and, in truth, the entirety of the letter is a vehicle for that teaching. Their moral instruction is a way they are living out their membership in the New Covenant, but also demonstrates that their membership has not been fulfilled. Second, though their hearts have been sprinkled, their hearts are still susceptible to sin (3–4; 13). This faithfulness of heart is the focal exhortation of the author's exposition of Psalm 95 in chs. 3–4. The wilderness generation disclosed the fact that they did not know God as fully as the knowledge described in the New Covenant (8:11), and that their hearts were deceived and hardened, surely then without the lasting inscription of God's laws (8:10). The author is worried that his congregation might follow the same example. Finally, they have relationship with God, but they are not yet fully in God's heavenly presence. They are being led into glory (2:10), but a Sabbath rest remains (4:9), or put another way, they still have a race to run (12:1), and a mountain to ascend (12:22). God has shown himself faithful to bring the forgiving relationship of the New Covenant to all, but elements/promises of the New Covenant remain, namely for a heart so inscribed with God's laws that it need not be instructed anymore. They still need that enduring quality of holiness, the state in which they would need to be in to be able to ascend to God's presence (12:14).

Herein lies the link between unattained covenantal promises and full atonement: their hearts must stay faithful so that they *can* come to experience their relationship with God forever in the unshakable kingdom (12:28) of rest and celebration.

Another way to approach this yes and no of the covenant lies in another oath of God discussed in Hebrews which I have not mentioned yet. The author's citation of Psalm 95 mentions God's swearing, this time not for intimacy and blessing, but for distance and punishment. Because of the Israelite's hardness of heart and lack of knowledge, because they put God to the test, doubting that he was faithful to do what he had promised, God swore that they would not enter his rest, they would not obtain the covenant promises to their father Abraham (Heb. 3:11; 4:3; Num. 14:1–10; Ps. 95:11 LXX).[10] Afterward, though, God issued a call to enter this rest through David even after the Israelites went into the land under Joshua. The Spirit urged those who heard the message of the Psalm not to follow the example of the generation of Israelites in the wilderness. The author's particular concern with a hardened heart is that it would be unfaithful (3:12, 19; 4:2) or untrusting (4:6). If they, however, refrain from hardening their heart, if they join the good news with faith (4:2), then in our author's reading that means that the invitation to go into a restful place where God himself rests (4:4, 10) remains. If God's covenantal promises to David's heir have been brought to fruition in Jesus Christ as He reigns at God's right hand, and God's covenantal promises of a restful place remain open to the descendants of Abraham (Heb. 2:14) whose hearts

---

[10] See Michael Harrison Kibbe, *Godly Fear or Ungodly Failure? Hebrews 12 and the Sinai Theophanies* (BZNTW 216; DeGruyter, 2016).

are not hardened, then the audience stands in a place where they are participants in the New Covenant. Nevertheless, if they want to have the kind of relationship with God it promises—forever—they must continue to trust that God will keep all of the covenantal promises.

Promises kept for the ancestors

Hence, having displayed God's faithfulness to keep promises to the Son and faithfulness to keep aspects of the New Covenant promises to himself and his readers, the author also devotes considerable attention to a retelling of God's faithfulness to previous generations of Israelites as further encouragement that God himself is faithful and worthy of trust. Most prominent among them is Abraham. In chapters 6, 7, and 11 of Hebrews the author asks his listeners to consider the patriarch, the one who had faith and patience to inherit the promise.[11] The tectonic shift that is Genesis 12 begins with God's simple yet profound promise to bless Abraham. Specifically, he will have many children, he will possess a good land, and his good fortune will overflow to all the families of the earth (Gen. 12:1-3). The summary of the story is simply that God swore to him that he would be blessed and multiplied, and after waiting, he was. Clearly Abraham functions as exemplar. The exhortation, "Imitate those who through faith and patience are inheritors of the promises" leads to the story of Abraham. The author's point being: "Be patient and faithful as was he."

Abraham as exemplar shifts to a more foundational point for the author. In this exchange, if Abraham was patient (and the implication for members of his audience is that they should be also), then his story shows ultimately that God was faithful. God promised to him, undergirded that promise with an oath, and brought it to fruition (Heb. 6:17-18). Abraham's story shows the trustworthiness of God to keep his oaths. That is where the author has been heading for some time, because, as discussed, only at this point does he return to the peculiar oath God made to the heir of David: God

---

[11] Convinced by those who argue that Hebrews functions with a narrative substructure, such as: Kenneth L. Schenck, *Cosmology and Eschatology in Hebrews: The Settings of the Sacrifice* (SNTSMS, 143; Cambridge: Cambridge University Press, 2007), p. 10; idem, *Understanding the Book of Hebrews: The Story Behind the Sermon* (Louisville: Westminster John Knox Press, 2003), pp. 5, 23; N. T. Wright, *New Testament and the People of God* (London: SPCK, 1992), p. 10; James Miller, "Paul and Hebrews: A Comparison of Narrative Worlds" in *Hebrews: Contemporary Methods—New Insights* (ed. Gabriella Gelardini; Leiden: Brill, 2005); I find it helpful to reconstruct the story of God's covenant with Abraham in sequence to which the author refers throughout the letter, from which we can notice which promises are kept and when. If I were to imagine the author of Hebrews retelling the story of God's covenant with his people from Israel's Scriptures, it might go something like this:

> Long ago God spoke to the fathers (Heb. 1:1), including our patriarch Abraham (Heb. 7:4; Gen. 12:1-3). God's speech to Abraham began with a call to go out to a place he would inherit (Heb. 11:8; Gen. 12:1) and a promise that he would become a great nation (Heb. 11:12; Gen. 12:2). In sum, God pledges that he would be blessed. Abraham obeyed God's call by going out, even though he didn't know exactly where he was going (Heb. 11:8; Gen. 12:4). As he sojourned in the land (Gen. 14:13; Heb. 11:9, 13), he encountered a priest of the most high God, Melchizedek, who blessed him (Heb. 7:1, 6; Gen 14:17-20). After this, God confirmed the covenant to Abraham with the shedding of blood, that of animals (Gen. 15:11) and that of Abraham (Gen. 17:11; Heb. 9:17). Abraham was faithful to conceive Isaac the promised descendant, with the elderly Sarah (Heb. 11:11-12; Gen. 21:2), and also to offer him up when God tested him (Heb. 11:17; Gen. 22:1-19).

swore that he would be a priest forever in the line of Melchizedek. Abraham's story corroborates God's faithfulness to the Son upon which the atoning New Covenant promises rest.

This is not all the author has to say about Abraham, however. In ch. 11, the author acknowledged that he died without having attained the promises (Heb. 11:13). Which leads to the question, what promise did he obtain and when? If timing matters to our author, and it often does (1:1; 4:7), it is good to note that in ch. 6, the author cites a passage from Genesis 22 that focuses on God's promise of blessing and multiplication. If the context of Gen. 22:17 is in view, at this point in Abraham's story, he has already been blessed by the enigmatic persona Melchizedek (Gen. 14:19, cited in Heb. 7:6). Abraham is blessed and his blessing serves to point to the faithfulness and therefore greatness of God, as it does in Melchizedek's uncited benediction (Gen. 14:19-20). In addition, he has been multiplied. He and Sarah have conceived Isaac, and moreover Abraham, who was willing to offer him, has received him back (Gen. 22:12-14; Heb. 11:19). It seems not a happenstance for the author of Hebrews to say in ch. 6, quoting from Genesis 22, Abraham is promised blessing and multiplication. The context of this promise indicates that after events of being blessed and multiplied, and after he had already showed patience and obtained some promises, then *again* in Gen. 22:17, he is blessed and multiplied and he shows patience and obtains the promise. The implication is that there is a promise/obtaining pair that happens another time in Abraham's relationship with God.

The author is, I think, beginning to make his argument that Abraham was patient his entire life and even after until he obtained more of God's promises to him. This exhortation for extended patience and trust becomes clear when the story of Abraham resumes in ch. 11. There, as I've stated, the author acknowledged that Abraham died without having attained the promises (Heb. 11:13). He did not really possess any kind of land. In the earthly land of promise he dwelt in tents as a foreigner along with his son and grandson. Besides, our author adds, he was really looking forward to a heavenly city anyhow, and he certainly did not dwell there during his life (Heb. 11:14-15). Second, he did not live to see descendants as numerous as the sand and the stars. He and Sarah had a son of promise, but only one. Therefore, he died with a down payment on his promises, but not the full reality. Even so, he remained faithful, looking forward to what he could not see because he regarded God as faithful to keep his promises even beyond the pale of death (Heb. 11:19). This was the definitive nature of his faith. One that believed God could bring life and blessing even past the reality of death, and so he was faithful to conceive Isaac the promised descendant, with his equally necrotic wife (Heb. 11:11–12). He was faithful to offer him up when God tested him (Heb. 11:17), knowing that God could raise the dead. He and his son and grandson faithfully looked forward to the true land of blessing, the many descendants, and the blessing that would come to them even though they did not possess it at the end of their lives.

Was God faithful, then, to keep the promises of blessing and multiplication uttered in the latter part of Genesis 22 (Gen. 22:16-17; Heb. 6:13-14). Near the end of the sermon, the author reveals how faithful God has been to Abraham. Since Abraham was faithful, it seems fully appropriate to include him in that group of saints who dwell in the city he was anticipating, the heavenly Jerusalem (Heb. 12:22-24). He is now in the heavenly country he was anticipating. From that location he sees his many descendants (Heb. 2:14), the saints who celebrate along with him and those who are being sanctified (Heb. 10:14), who are still running the race (Heb. 12:1), including the members of the audience themselves. Their very existence and journey is evidence of the patience of Abraham and the faithfulness of God.[12]

God had sworn a promised inheritance to him (Heb. 1:14; 6:12). He received a part of it, and after much patience he obtained residence city and the vision of his many descendants. Abraham's story shows that God keeps his promises, sometimes in life and sometimes past life, because death is no barrier to the faithfulness of God. He demonstrates to them that lasting faith that is willing to trust God throughout the entirety of one's life, because even as death approaches, God can be trusted to keep his promises beyond it. He lifts up Abraham as someone in the position of the audience. They have an inheritance waiting for them (Heb. 1:14) and have attained some of its promises, yet until they possess it in full, he wants them to demonstrate the same patience.

Although Abraham serves as the primary example, the author's presentation of Moses's story also supports the theme of God's faithfulness.[13] Moses, the faithful servant (Heb. 3:5), who knew that the deliverance from death into life came at a price, the giving up of pride and place and suffering with the less esteemed. Now, too, is participating in the reward to which he looked forward (Heb. 11:26). No longer a servant but a son (Heb. 2:10), he dwells in the land of promise, entrance into whose earthly reflection he was denied. There with the Messiah and his people, no longer suffering but celebrating, and no longer afraid, he is confident in the presence of God who is the judge of all.

When Moses ratified God's covenant with the people at Sinai, after that, sadly, they did disobey. They did not trust that God would bring them into the land of Canaan

---

[12] Even for Abraham and the other saints, the fullness of the promise might remain. Are they yet living in the unshakable kingdom (12:27-28)? They certainly are not yet dwelling with their many descendants even though they can see them. Hebrews does not give evidence of a fully developed explicit eschatology of a resurrected body and a new heavens and new earth, so these faithful departed might still have promises to which they look forward. Thank you to Erhard Gallos for his provoking questions in this regard.

[13] Were I to continue the covenant story with which the author seems to be working, it would proceed thus: God was faithful to multiply Abraham's progeny to the degree that they raised the concern of the King of Egypt who enslaved them all (Exod. 1:8-10). Joseph foresaw that they would be delivered from that land (Heb. 11:22; Gen. 50:25), and it was under the leadership of Moses that they were. Moses was a faithful servant to God (Heb. 3:2, 4) worthy of glory (Heb. 3:3) and approval (Heb. 11:2). Raised in a faithful household with parents who defied a bloodthirsty king, Moses himself did not fear the king either (Heb. 11:27). He chose to associate with the shames of the Messiah's people rather than enjoy the pleasures of Egypt (Heb. 11:25-26). Under the cover of red blood (Exod. 12:42-51) and through the walls of the Red Sea (Exod. 14:21-31) he obeyed God in order to protect his people from destroyers angelic and human. Once the people of Israel came out of the land of Egypt, it was Moses who led them to the mountain where God revealed himself in mighty and fearful signs (Exodus 19). The sights and sounds served to underscore and emphasize the commandment that if anyone or anything approached it would mean certain death (Exod. 19:12-13). The people were terrified, and even Moses who had a track record of boldness, trembled (Heb. 12:21). In this setting, Moses conveyed the commandments of the law and then applied blood to the book that held the laws and the people who had committed to them (Heb. 9:19-20; Exod. 24:3-8). By this, the covenant was established with these descendants of Abraham. Then God showed Moses in a vision on the mountain how this covenant was to be maintained, how gifts and sacrifices were to function in the tabernacle on earth (Heb. 8:5; Exod. 25–31).

(Heb. 3:7-4:10; Num. 14:1-10). Once they got there, they worshipped foreign gods, so that ultimately God had to discipline by removing them from the land (2 Kgs 18:11-12; 2 Kgs 25:4-7). This covenant ratified with the blood of animals could not prevent the sin of the people and the just anger of God (Heb. 8:8). Then, Heb. 9:15 raises the possibility that Jesus's inauguration of the New Covenant affects those who came before him, the members of the previous covenant because his death results in redemption of the transgressions of the first covenant. Those who have been called now can receive the promise of the eternal inheritance. This could indicate that all the Israelites who committed sins under the first covenant no longer have to remain distant from God, as was the case at Sinai (12:20), but can experience the closeness to God they hoped the blood of the first covenant would have afforded them.[14] In these last days in which the readers of Hebrews live, Abraham, Moses, and possibly even the previous generation of Israelites are living in God's presence for which they hoped.[15]

Promises that remain for all

The fulfillment of relationship with God for the members of the first covenant suggests that this New Covenant, made possible through the priestly work of Jesus, might bring to fulfillment some very ancient promises indeed, including the initial promises given to humanity for sovereignty over creation. Psalm 8 does not have explicit covenant language but it does promise a particular relationship with God where humans are cared for by God, glorified by God, and reign in sovereignty at God's behest.

Psalm 8 allows then a return to the first topic of this chapter, God's promises to the Son. While God has fulfilled many of the promises to Jesus, some remain outstanding. He is priest, and he sits at God's right hand. Nonetheless, the author holds together seemingly paradoxical affirmations of settled sovereignty with expectant waiting.[16] The author asserts that he still waits until the time that enemies are under his feet (1:13). The author repeats this statement in Heb. 10:13 where he adds the phrase: "the rest [of the time] he is eagerly awaiting" (10:13) until his enemies are put under his feet. The author stated in ch. 2 that his death happens so that he might nullify the one who has the power of death. The author seems not to doubt that this will happen, his death has guaranteed this, but the subjunctive of nullify (καταργήσῃ, 2:14) leaves open the unsettled nature of this destruction. His death happened so that he might destroy the one who has the power of death, but that has not yet occurred (Paul in 1 Cor. 15:24-26 provides a parallel idea). Thereby Jesus becomes both a testimony to God's faithfulness and an example of waiting with assured hope. He will come a second time

---

[14] See Peeler, "Desiring God: The Blood of the Covenant in Exod. 24," *BBR* 23 (2013), 187–205.

[15] Paul Ellingworth entertains this possibility as well, "The author does not specify whether or not οι κεκλημένοι include those called to be members of God's people in OT times. This is possible, in the light of 11:40; 12:23, and the author's general tendency to emphasize continuity in the chosen people under both dispensations," Paul Ellingworth, *The Epistle to the Hebrews: A Commentary on the Greek Text* (NIGTC; Grand Rapids, MI/Carlisle, PA: Eerdmans/Paternoster, 1993) p. 462.

[16] Mackie speaks of the "eschatological ambiguity . . . with regard to nature and extent of the Son's rule," Scott D. Mackie, *Eschatology and Exhortation in the Epistle to the Hebrews* (WUNT, 223; Tübingen: Mohr Siebeck, 2007), p. 44. Johnson states it this way, "Jesus' Lordship is actual but it has not yet been extended to all reality," *Hebrews*, p. 91.

(9:28) when he brings salvation and hence deals completely with the enemies who still cause difficulty for his followers.

For the readers too do not yet see all things subjected to Jesus (Heb. 2:8). They long for their struggle with sin to be over, and their place of sovereignty, promised to them in Psalm 8, to be secured. As his following exegesis will reveal, the anticipated comprehensive authority of humanity as described in Psalm 8 is telescoped into and inaugurated by the sovereignty of this heir of David (Heb. 1:13/Ps. 109:1 LXX). As it is true that elements of the New Covenant remain unfulfilled, it is also true that God's design of creation in which humans are sovereign (2:8) and are at rest in God's presence (4:3-10) remain an unfulfilled hope. If this author, like many other Jews of the first century,[17] look toward this kind of restitution of the original creation, then God, by keeping promises to the Son, has begun the process by which the creation-restoring covenantal promises will come to fruition. They who see Jesus but do not yet dwell with him know one set of promises has been fulfilled and the fulfillment of another remains to be seen. For the audience to have this kind of relationship, this kind of unity with God, they must hold fast to their confession by trusting that the One who promised is faithful (10:23).

Conclusion

You have come, concludes the author of Hebrews, to the mediator of the New Covenant (12:24). This, the penultimate in a series of comments about the covenant, draws together the whole. His audience has come to Jesus and the New Covenant is enacted in him. The previous covenant shows God to be a promise keeper, but could not on its own, in this author's view, achieve full atonement. The previous covenant, however, serves not just the role of foil. The author actually has a great deal to say about the members of that covenant and explicates their story to show God's trustworthiness and therefore shore up this community's ability to enter into the full at-one-ment of the New Covenant. The New Covenant also shows God to be one who keeps promises; this New Covenant is legislated upon the promises of God. The trustworthiness does not rest on promises alone, but also on oaths. God has kept the promise to his Son to become a High Priest, and through that vocation, kept his promise to bring the New Covenant, the difference being it can achieve full salvation. The audience has come to him the mediator of the New Covenant and as member of him they will reap the promises only if they endure. Endure they can because their hearts have been changed. The New Covenant arrived, their hearts and minds cleansed, they can abide in the covenant in a way impossible before the sacrificial presentation of Jesus. God has restored them in every good thing so they can do God's will and please him (Heb. 13:21).

Even in the New Covenant, however, some promises of full atonement remain, namely, God's first promises to his human creation, for sovereignty in God's presence.

---

[17] "The renewed creation will be the full and complete inheritance to Abraham regarding the land is taken ultimately to be a promise to inherit the world as it will be in the coming age—incorruptible, pure, and consisting of the entire created realm . . . there is also an echo of the restoration of the human being to the place that Adam was created to hold (cf. Ps. 8)." David Moffitt, *Atonement and the Logic of Resurrection in Hebrews* (NovTSup 141; Leiden, Brill, 2011), p. 117.

God who has kept his promises and oaths to bring the New Covenant will fulfill the promises of it that remain. Promise, in other words, both undergirds and flows out of the Covenant. God's priestly oath to Christ has brought it to be and God's promise of sovereignty to Christ will bring all of its blessings. Because these promises remain for the Son and for the audience, the readers need to be reminded of the story of God's kept covenant promises—old and new—to shore up their faith in God's trustworthy promise-keeping so that they can endure in faith and eventually experience the New Covenant's full atonement.

Note well that although some promises have been fulfilled and some remain, the author discusses no promises of God that have not even been inaugurated. No promises are completely unfulfilled, so this audience has already begun on a path where promises are being brought to fruition. They've already begun; he just wants them to endure. Covenant promises made with Abraham, sacralized through Moses, promised to David, prophesied by Jeremiah, are now begun through the mediation of the blood and intercession of Jesus Christ. This covenant restores the vision of creation—unites God with his people. In other words, atones.

The question then, that this chapter seeks to answer is this, "*How* does covenant shed light on atonement in Hebrews?" The relationship between covenant and atonement is this: When humans receive the full promises of the covenant they experience full atonement with God, and therefore the author discusses God's keeping of covenant promises to help the audience trust that God will continue to keep his promises. If they trust, they will remain in the covenant by which they have relationship with God and hence continue to abide in at-one-ment, now and forever.

13

Time and Atonement in Hebrews

George H. Guthrie

Introduction

In his famous statement on time, Augustine writes,

> What is time? Who can explain this easily and briefly? Who can comprehend this even in thought so as to articulate the answer in words? Yet what do we speak of, in our familiar everyday conversation, more than of time? We surely know what we mean when we speak of it. We also know what is meant when we hear someone else talking about it. What then is time? Provided that no one asks me, I know. If I want to explain it to an inquirer, I do not know.[1]

As noted by Henri Blocher, when we begin to think theologically about time, we are out of our depth, presented with "exceptional difficulties," paradoxes on every hand.[2] The question concerning the way time works in relation to God and the works of God is worth asking.

More particularly, however, we might reflect on how the Son's work, as depicted in Hebrews, fits into our conception of time. Is it always to be considered sequentially, for instance? And, even more particularly, how does the work of Christ work in terms of *timing*,[3] for the *timing* of atonement within the Christ event has become a matter of considerable debate since David Moffitt threw the proverbial rock at the

---

[1] Augustine, *Confessions* 11.14.17; Augustine, *Saint Augustine Confessions: A New Translation by Henry Chadwick* (trans. Henry Chadwick; Oxford World's Classics; Oxford: Oxford University Press, 2008), p. 230.
[2] Henri Blocher, "Yesterday, Today, Forever: Time, Times, Eternity in Biblical Perspective," *Tyndale Bulletin* 52 (2001), pp. 183–202 (183–85).
[3] The chapter focuses a great deal on "timing" rather than "time" generally. The framework of "time and atonement" was set by an invitation to present on that topic, but the focus of recent discussions has had to do more with "timing." It may be suggested that the two are interrelated, for the topic of "timing" of the atonement presupposes certain understandings of time. Thus, although the former constitutes the focus of this chapter, setting it within thoughts about time as a topic is meant to stimulate and push our thinking on the topic of "timing" as it relates to the work of Christ. This will become more clear in the final movement of the chapter.

hornet's nest with his 2011 monograph, *Atonement and the Logic of Resurrection in the Epistle to the Hebrews*.[4] The flurry of responses, in the form of reviews, articles, dissertations, and conference papers bears witness to the importance of Moffitt's lucid, beautifully written work, and I believe he has advanced the discussion considerably, focusing fresh attention on Christ's high-priestly work in the heavenly holy of holies. Let me make clear that both in terms of Hebrews' cosmology[5] and in his understanding of Hebrews' high-priestly work as culminating dynamically in the heavenly holy of holies, there is a great deal on which Moffitt and I agree. Yet, partly in response to Moffitt, I wish to raise questions about timing and the atonement in Hebrews from the vantage point of both methodology and theology, agreeing with Moffitt at points and pushing back at others, especially in terms of approach or method. My suggestion is that while focusing on the Yom Kippur imagery in the book is vital, standing as it does at the center of Hebrews' soteriology, as Moffitt has demonstrated, that motif must be read contextually in Hebrews as a significant component, profoundly integrated within a very complex tapestry of sacrificial/Levitical language.

This chapter proceeds in three primary movements. The first two offer proposals concerning Hebrews' approach to handling Levitical cult language and word pictures, an approach that must rightly be discerned if we are to assess the author's perspective on the timing of the atonement. In the first movement I propose that we grapple deeply with the interplay of Levitical cult imagery in the book.

In the second movement I propose that our author filters this OT language and imagery through the Christ event, rather than filtering the Christ event through particular aspects of the Levitical imagery. This movement argues that the author's own methodology in utilizing OT imagery must be rigorously followed to understand the significance or theological payoff he offers. If we fail in this matter, the message of Hebrews becomes skewed as a dominant word picture which begins to control, rather than aid, that process of communication.

The chapter's third movement concludes the chapter by offering a cautionary note, putting the timing of the atonement in the broader framework of the issue of time, addressing briefly what might be called "a wrinkle in time" in Hebrews' reflections on atonement. This final movement is only meant to be suggestive, stimulating reflections that might lead to further research.

In an article entitled "When and Where Did Jesus Offer Himself? A Taxonomy of Recent Scholarship on Hebrews," published in *Currents in Biblical Research*, R. B. Jamieson seeks, among other things, to enhance the conversation on the topic by "a more fine-grained analysis of the ways in which scholars have answered the question."[6]

---

[4] David M. Moffitt, *Atonement and the Logic of Resurrection in the Epistle to the Hebrews* (NovTSup, 141; Leiden: Brill, 2011).

[5] See for instance, David M. Moffitt, "Serving in the Tabernacle in Heaven: Sacred Space, Jesus's High-Priestly Sacrifice, and Hebrews' Analogical Theology," in *Hebrews in Contexts* (ed. Gabriella Gelardini and Harold W. Attridge; Ancient Judaism and Early Christianity 91; Leiden: Brill, 2016), pp. 259–79.

[6] R. B. Jamieson, "When and Where Did Jesus Offer Himself? A Taxonomy of Recent Scholarship on Hebrews," *Currents in Biblical Research* 15 (2017), pp. 338–68 (343).

Jamieson delineates five distinct views that align three variables (Christ's death, his entrance to the heavenly sanctuary, and his self-offering). These views are:

1. Jesus's self-offering begins and ends on the cross.
2. Jesus's self-offering is an earthly event with heavenly significance. His sin offering is metaphorically described as his entrance into the heavenly sanctuary.
3. Jesus's self-offering begins with his death and culminates in his immediately subsequent spiritual exaltation to the heavenly sanctuary.
4. Jesus's self-offering begins with his death and culminates in his post-resurrection entrance into the heavenly sanctuary.
5. Jesus offers himself at his post-resurrection entrance into the heavenly sanctuary.

Notice that Jamieson's three elements and each of the five interpretive positions he identifies utilize language related to the Levitical cult, particularly "offering" and "sanctuary," and understandably so. Such language sits at the hermeneutical center of discussions on our topic, since it permeates the main Christological movements of the book to which we are trying to listen. What I wish to do in the chapter's first two movements is push the conversation back a step to consider how the author of Hebrews uses such language. How is the language appropriated and to what theological and rhetorical ends?

Proposal 1

The author of Hebrews builds the Christological movements of his discourse using a complex interplay of general Levitical language and imagery.

There is no doubt that Yom Kippur imagery, with a focus on the superiority of Christ's heavenly offering, stands as a cornerstone for Hebrews' Christology.[7] The danger, however, is that the Yom Kippur imagery in the book—and a reading of "atonement" theology in Hebrews as being tied to one aspect of that imagery—can become an overriding control, muting other important theological nuances in Hebrews that have been taken from the author's store of biblical cult imagery. Consider the following aspects of that imagery.

---

[7] For example, David M. Moffit, "Blood, Life, and Atonement: Reassessing Hebrews' Christological Appropriation of Yom Kippur," in *The Day of Atonement: Its Interpretations in Early Jewish and Christian Traditions* (ed. Thomas Hieke and Tobias Nicklas; Themes in Biblical Narrative, 15; Leiden: Brill, 2012), pp. 211-24; Felix H. Cortez, "From the Holy to the Most Holy Place: The Period of Hebrews 9:6-10 and the Day of Atonement as a Metaphor of Transition," *Journal of Biblical Literature* 125 (2006), pp. 527-47; Hanno Langenhoven, Eliska Nortjé, Annette Potgieter, Yolande Steenkamp, "The Day of Atonement as a Hermeneutical Key to the Understanding of Christology in Hebrews," *Journal of Early Christian History* 1 (2011), pp. 85-97; R. B. Jamieson, "Hebrews 9.23: Cult Inauguration, Yom Kippur and the Cleansing of the Heavenly Tabernacle," *New Testament Studies* 62 (2016), pp. 569-87.

Atonement

Let me begin with the concept of atonement itself. Moffitt has titled his book as having to do with atonement, since he is keen to address particularly dynamics surrounding what he sees as the "atoning moment" at the heart of Hebrews' Christology, understanding that moment to take place in the heavenly holy of holies.[8] Yet, we need to remember two things concerning atonement as it relates to Hebrews.

First, while Yom Kippur imagery looms large in Hebrews' lexicon of scriptural word pictures, and the author evokes other imagery related to atoning sacrifices in the Levitical cult, the book rarely uses overt atonement terminology. We have the use of ἱλάσκομαι at 2:17, which both the NET and the NIV11, for instance, translate as "make atonement."[9] There, in that very important, anticipatory exclamation on high priesthood, we learn that Jesus became human to function as a "merciful and faithful high priest in service to God, and that he might make atonement for the sins of the people" (NIV11). In his 2016 monograph, *Levitical Sacrifice and Heavenly Cult in Hebrews*, Benjamin Ribbens suggests the verb here is roughly synonymous with the common verb for atoning action in the Greek OT, ἐξιλάσχομαι, the ἱλάσκεσθαι τὰς ἁμαρτίας most likely referring to "atonement through Christ's sacrifice."[10] The position is disputed by some, but I think it is sound.

A second thing we need to remember concerning atonement theology as appropriated by Hebrews is that in the Pentateuch the language of atonement is used *generally in relation to a wide range of offerings and sacrifices*, not just those made on Yom Kippur, and *atonement is a multifaceted concept even on Yom Kippur*.[11] For instance, that main verb just mentioned, ἐξιλάσκομαι, occurs seventy-one times in the Greek Pentateuch, forty-nine of these in Leviticus, where a wide variety of atoning actions are described. But, for the sake of time, let me focus attention on the varied ways "atonement" language is used in relation to two key priestly moments in Leviticus, moments that may be said to correspond somewhat to the two great movements of

---

[8] Moffitt, *Atonement and the Logic of Resurrection*, pp. 277, 290, 293. How the author comes to focus on the heavenly, Yom Kippur work of Christ, depends a great deal on Psalm 110 in the development of the discourse, for the author anchors his discourse in the Son's exaltation as prophesied in Ps. 110:1 and extends the traditional appropriation of that messianic psalm to include the oath of appointment for Christ as a Melchizedekian high priest found in 110:4. The event of the exaltation, both in terms of enthronement, as well as high-priestly activity in the heavenly Holy of Holies, frames the book's Christology and provides rhetorical payoff at key turning points in the discourse, on which see George H. Guthrie, *The Structure of Hebrews: A Text-Linguistic Analysis* (Supplements to Novum Testamentum 73; Leiden/New York: E.J. Brill, 1994), pp. 121–26.

[9] The cognate noun ἱλαστήριον occurs at Heb. 9:5, where the author refers to the "propitiatory," the lid on the ark of the covenant (e.g., Exod. 25:16-21; Num. 7:89).

[10] Benjamin J. Ribbens, *Levitical Sacrifice and Heavenly Cult in Hebrews* (BZNW 222; Berlin: De Gruyter, 2016), p. 211.

[11] On pp. 256-71 under the subtitle, "Blood Offering and Atonement in Leviticus," Moffitt focuses on five main offerings in Leviticus, detailed in the first seven chapters of the book. Yet, the verb is used throughout Leviticus forty-nine times (Lev 1:4; 4:20, 26, 31, 35; 5:6, 10, 13, 16, 18, 26; 6:23; 7:7; 8:15, 34; 9:7; 10:17; 12:7-8; 14:18-21, 29, 31, 53; 15:15, 30; 16:6, 10-11, 16-18, 20, 24, 27, 30, 32-34; 17:11; 19:22; 23:28).

high-priestly Christology in Hebrews—the ordination of the priests (along with the worship service that follows; Lev. 8–9) and Yom Kippur (Leviticus 16).[12]

In Lev. 8:15, a passage set in the narrative on ordination or appointment of Aaron and his sons as priests, Moses takes blood from the sin offering bull and applies it to the altar to purify it and "to make atonement on it" (τοῦ ἐξιλάσασθαι ἐπ' αὐτοῦ). Later in that chapter (8:34), in a summary of the ordination process, Moses says to Aaron and his sons that the Lord had commanded the specific details of the ordination service "in order that atonement might be made for you" (ὥστε ἐξιλάσασθαι περὶ ὑμῶν). Finally, as the priests begin their ministry, Moses instructs the priests, "Draw near to the altar, and perform the one for your sin and your whole burnt offering, and make atonement (ἐξίλασαι) for yourself and your house. And deal with the gifts of the people, and make atonement (ἐξίλασαι) for them, as the Lord has commanded Moyses" (Lev 9:7 NETS). Thus "atonement" plays a key role in the ordination of the priests.[13] We deal with this theme of ordination in more detail later in the chapter, but for now we should attend to the fact that *atonement in the Levitical cult is a broad concept*.

Furthermore, if we read Leviticus 16 carefully, there actually are several key moments of atonement in the ceremony. In addition to blood manipulation by the high priest in the holiest place (Lev. 16:16-17 LXX), when the goat for Azazel is sent off into the wilderness as an elimination offering, Lev. 16:10 describes the process as follows: "He shall set it alive (or 'living'; ζῶντα) before the Lord to make atonement over it (ἐξιλάσασθαι ἐπ' αὐτοῦ), to send it away into the place for sending away" (NETS). In the next verse, at 16:11, we read, "And Aaron shall offer the bull calf for sin, which is his, and shall make atonement for himself and for his house (ἐξιλάσεται περὶ αὐτοῦ καὶ τοῦ οἴκου αὐτοῦ), and he shall slaughter the bull calf for sin, which is his own" (Lev. 16:11 NETS). In 16:18, having sprinkled the blood in the Holy of Holies, the High Priest then goes out to the altar in front of the tabernacle "to make atonement on it" (ἐξιλάσεται ἐπ' αὐτοῦ), by putting blood on the horns of the altar. Then, in 16:23-24a Aaron is instructed to enter the tent of witness and change clothes, bathing his body in water in the process. Verse 24b reads: "Then he shall come out and perform his sacrifice and the sacrifice of the people and shall make atonement (ἐξιλάσεται) for himself and his house and for the people as for the priests" (Lev. 16:24 NETS).

---

[12] In my work on *The Structure of Hebrews*, I have argued that the high-priestly Christology in the book develops in two movements, "The Appointment of the Son as a Superior High Priest" (5:1-10, 7:1-28) and "The Superior Offering of the Appointed High Priest" (8:3–10:18). My reason for focusing here on Leviticus 8–9 and Leviticus 16 concerns these two great movements of Hebrews. As demonstrated below, the appointment of the priests, detailed in Leviticus 8 and extended in terms of the resulting worship service in Leviticus 9, also involved atonement, and this section of Leviticus has been given inadequate attention in Hebrews studies. And while Yom Kippur imagery stands as vital to Hebrews' imagery and argument, its relation to the concept of atonement needs probing.

[13] Again, it should be remembered that the author of Hebrews lays the foundation for his high-priestly Christology by focusing on the oath of appointment in Ps. 110:4, unpacking the theme, "the appointment of the Son as High Priest" (5:1-10; 7:1-28), which fits well with the emphasis on ordination proposed here. See George H. Guthrie, *The Structure of Hebrews: A Text-Linguistic Analysis*, 1994, pp. 121–22, 26.

As L. Michael Morales summarizes, "The Day of Atonement includes three main rites that are interwoven as one ceremony: an *entrance rite*, of the high priest into the inner sanctum; a *cleansing rite*, of the tabernacle cultus; and an *elimination rite*, of the people's sins into the wilderness."[14] Consequently, as demonstrated above, even in the instructions concerning Yom Kippur, atonement is a general term used with a variety of sacrifices and actions. Accordingly, the ceremonies of Yom Kippur involve multiple times and places in the process of atonement, all contributing to the atoning of the nation's sins. Thus, while Hebrews, in its orientation to Psalm 110, is keenly interested in the imagery surrounding the heavenly holy of holies—perhaps the most important theological focal point for the author—it is at least possible that atonement was conceived as a broader dynamic than what occurred in the heavenly holiest place.[15] Atonement is a more general term than that in the Pentateuch as a whole and a more general term than that in the Yom Kippur instructions of Leviticus 16.

Other terminology

Further, in framing his discourse and to set up his discussion of Christ's high priesthood, Hebrews utilizes other general language related to sacrifice and offering. For instance, in 5:1 and 8:3 we have "parallel introductions"[16] to the two movements of the Christology found in the book's great, central section, the first introducing the *appointment* of Christ as a superior priest, and the second introducing his superior New Covenant *offering*. These "parallel introductions" may be seen as follows:

Πᾶς γὰρ ἀρχιερεὺς ἐξ ἀνθρώπων λαμβανόμενος ὑπὲρ ἀνθρώπων καθίσταται τὰ πρὸς τὸν θεόν, ἵνα προσφέρῃ δῶρά τε καὶ θυσίας ὑπὲρ ἁμαρτιῶν (5:1)

Πᾶς γὰρ ἀρχιερεὺς εἰς τὸ προσφέρειν δῶρά τε καὶ θυσίας καθίσταται· ὅθεν ἀναγκαῖον ἔχειν τι καὶ τοῦτον ὃ προσενέγκῃ (8:3)

The reference to the "offering," as well as to "gifts and sacrifices" in these verses, utilizes general language from the Levitical cult worship found in the Pentateuch. For instance, the verb προσφέρω is used sixty-nine times in Leviticus and is a general term related to the presenting of sacrifices and offerings.[17] The only time the word occurs

---

[14] L. Michael Morales, *Who Shall Ascend the Mountain of the Lord? A Theology of the Book of Leviticus* (Downers Grove: IVP Academic, 2015), p. 169. In conversation with Daniel Stevens, currently a PhD student working on Hebrews at Cambridge University, he suggested that one might consider the change in this order we see in Hebrews. In Heb. 13:11-12, for instance, "elimination" imagery aligns with Christ's death outside of the city. This is followed by Christ's entrance into the heavenly holy of holies as high priest. Thus, the *sequence* of the Levitical imagery is inverted in the actual Christ event.

[15] For example, Moffitt considers the death of Christ as a pre-step, a sine qua non, for the focal moment of atonement in the heavenly holy of holies (Moffitt, *Atonement and the Logic of Resurrection*, p. 294).

[16] Guthrie, *The Structure of Hebrews*, 1994, pp. 85, 104.

[17] For example, Lev 1:2-3, 5, 13-15; 2:1, 4, 8, 11-14; 3:6, 9; 4:23, 32; 6:13; 7:3, 8-9, 11-13, 18, 29-30, 33, 38; 8:6.

in Leviticus 16, the Yom Kippur instructions, is at 16:9, where the goat is "offered for sins" (καὶ προσοίσει περὶ ἁμαρτίας).

The author of Hebrews most often uses προσφέρω as a general term of offering,[18] only once specifically speaking of the Old Covenant high priest bringing blood into the Holy of Holies (9:7). According to Hebrews, Christ offered "both requests and supplications, with loud cries and tears" (Heb. 5:7 NET); he "offered himself *without blemish*" (9:14), which is not Day of Atonement language; "he did not enter to offer himself again and again" (9:25), which is Day of Atonement language; "Christ was offered once to *bear the sins* of many" (note the passive participle; 9:28), which is not Day of Atonement language; and he "offered one sacrifice for sins for all time" (10:12). Most of the twenty uses of προσφέρω in Hebrews are more general, speaking, for example, of the offering of a sacrifice by Abel in 11:4 or Abraham offering Isaac as a sacrifice at 11:17. The five uses of the noun προσφορά in the book, all in chapter 10, are offered in or flow from the author's use of Psalm 40, which too seems to relate to Levitical offerings and sacrifices in general.[19] Thus the priestly act of offering in Hebrews is much broader than blood manipulation on Yom Kippur.

Further, in the Pentatuech δῶρον, the term for "gift," is used 103 times, 44 of these in Leviticus. Gifts are "brought before the Lord" (ἐναντίον κυρίου) in the sense of bringing them to the priests at the tabernacle (e.g., Lev. 1:3; 3:1), or "offered" (προσφέρω) to the Lord,[20] and the presentation at times also involves a slaughter (see e.g., 3:1-6). Significantly, in twelve places the word is used in tandem with θυσία, "sacrifice."[21] Although between them the two terms occur 122 times in Leviticus, neither is used in Leviticus 16. Thus, in the lexicon of Leviticus, "gifts" or "sacrifices" are never related directly to Yom Kippur instructions. Rather, Jesus's priestly ministry is presented as parallel to and fulfilling the whole of the priestly ministry of offering gifts and sacrifices under the Old Covenant, not just a particular offering on Yom Kippur.

Allusions or references to various sacrifices

To these lexical examples we can add allusions or direct references in Hebrews to various kinds of sacrifices, which Moffitt and others recognize.[22] First, I am now convinced that Heb. 5:1-4 and 7:26-28 allude to passages concerning ordination to priesthood (Leviticus 8) and the priestly ministry following ordination (Leviticus 9), rather than Yom Kippur. The language of appointment, καθίστημι, seen above in the parallel introductions of 5:1 and 8:3,[23] is drawn particularly from ordination

---

[18] Heb. 5:1, 3, 7; 8:3-4; 9:7, 9, 14, 25, 28–10:2; 10:8, 11-12; 11:4, 17; 12:7.
[19] See, for example, Harold W. Attridge, *Hebrews: A Commentary on the Epistle to the Hebrews* (Hermeneia; Philadelphia: Fortress, 1989), p. 274, who notes that the offerings here "allude to the whole cultic system."
[20] Lev. 1:2-3, 14; 2:1, 4, 12-13; 3:6; 4:23, 32; 6:13; 7:13, 29, 38; 9:15; 17:4; 21:6, 8, 17.
[21] Lev. 2:1, 4-5, 7, 13; 3:1, 6; 6:13; 7:13, 16, 29; 21:6, 21.
[22] For example, Moffitt, *Atonement and the Logic of Resurrection*, p. 270.
[23] See Guthrie, *The Structure of Hebrews,*, 1994, pp. 85, 104.

instructions given in Num. 3:10 and 4:19, and it is at Lev. 8:2, at the beginning of the "ordination" section in the book, that Aaron and his sons are said to be "taken" (Λαβὲ Ααρων καὶ τοὺς υἱοὺς αὐτοῦ, "Take Aaron and his sons . . .") from among the Israelites, the exact language at Heb. 5:1 and 8:3; this language is not found in the Yom Kippur instructions of Leviticus 16. The same can be said of the terminology of "being called" (Heb. 5:4; see the heading at Lev. 9:1[24]) and the association of the priestly ministry with "glory" (Heb. 5:5; Lev. 9:6, 23; 10:3).

Furthermore, the idea of "drawing near," found in Heb. 4:16, 7:19, and 10:22, is especially important in the ministry language of Leviticus 9,[25] language not found in the Yom Kippur instructions of Leviticus 16. As with Yom Kippur, the ministry of the priests following their ordination service involved sacrifices made for Aaron and his house, as well as for the people (Heb. 5:3; 7:27; Lev. 9:7). Interestingly, the verb τελειόω (Lev. 4:5; 8:33; 16:32; 21:10) and its cognate noun τελείωσις (Lev. 7:27; 8:22, 26, 28-29, 31, 33) are used eleven times in Leviticus to speak of the validation of a priest in the priestly office. Among other places in Hebrews, 5:9 and 7:28—both of which occur in context alongside of terminology related to "appointment"—speak of the Son being "perfected," "validated" for the office of priest.[26] We might add that in passages like Heb. 2:9-10,17-18, and 5:8-10 the suffering of Christ was prerequisite for him serving as high priest. In 7:28, moreover, the stative aspect of the participle τετελειωμένον might be read as the "perfection" or "ordination" of Christ, and it should be pointed out that in context, then, this perfection can be read as *preceding* the oath of Ps. 110:4.

In fact, we might read the evidence as suggesting the following. Hebrews applies sacrificial language from the ordination section of Leviticus to reflect on the Son's death as accomplishing his ordination—just one of a number of effects of the death. The oath of Ps. 110:4 the author understands as the culmination of the ordination process, the Son declared to all as a high priest in the order of Melchizedek, who by his resurrection is shown to have an indestructible life.

Thus, I would suggest that lexical and conceptual links in Hebrews' section on the appointment of the Son as priest evoke not Yom Kippur imagery, but rather the imagery of ordination/appointment to the priestly ministry. Significantly, in the summary of the section on appointment (7:26-28), the author includes the statement that the Son "offered himself" (ἑαυτὸν ἀνενέγκας) at 7:27. There is no doubt that the

---

[24] "And it happened on the eighth day that Moses called Aaron and his sons and the council of elders of Israel" (Καὶ ἐγήθη τῇ ἡμέρᾳ τῇ ὀγδόῃ ἐκάλεσεν Μωυσῆς Ααρων καὶ τοὺς υἱοὺς αὐτοῦ [Lev 9:1 LXX]).

[25] Leviticus 9:5, 7-8 presents the ministry of Aaron and his sons following their ordination. The passage reads,

> And they took them, as Moses commanded, to the front of the tent of witness, and the whole congregation *drew near* (προσῆλθεν), and they stood before the Lord. And Moses said to Aaron, "*Draw near* (Πρόσελθε) to the altar, and perform the one for your sin and your whole burnt offering, and make atonement for yourself and your house. And deal with the gifts of the people, and make atonement for them, as the Lord has commanded Moses." "And Aaron *drew near* (προσῆλθεν) to the altar and slaughtered the calf for sin. (Lev. 9:5, 7–8 NETS)

Passages later in the book give stipulations for who can and cannot "draw near" to perform the ministry of priest (Lev. 18:6, 19; 19:33; 20:16; 21:17-18, 21, 23; 22:3).

[26] See John M. Scholer, *Proleptic Priests: Priesthood in the Epistle to the Hebrews* (JSNTSup 49; Sheffield: Sheffield Academic Press, 1991), p. 187, who arrives at different conclusions.

controlling topic in context is "appointment to high priesthood." And the language of the earthly high priests offering sacrifices (θυσία) first for their own sins and then the sins of the people (Heb. 7:27), matches the language of the worship service associated with ordination of the priests (Lev. 9:4, 17-18), rather than the language of Yom Kippur. It may be suggested, therefore, that the sacrifice of Christ at 7:27 constitutes a sacrifice related to the ordination of Christ as priest. We will have more to say on this momentarily.

To what other sacrifices does Hebrews allude? Several can be noted briefly. It might be suggested that, as a second example, the author evokes the morning and evening sacrifices in Heb. 7:27 and 10:11.[27] These he uses rhetorically as a foil for the once-for-all offering of Christ. Third, at Heb. 9:13 the author appropriates the imagery of the red heifer offering (cf. Num. 19:1-10) to point to the cleansing effects of Christ's superior offering. Fourth, at 8:7-13 and 10:15-18 the author brackets his section on Christ's superior offering with Jer. 31:31-34, a passage on the New Covenant.[28] He further develops a key moment in his discourse at 9:15-21 by pointing out the role of death in both addressing the defilement of sin under the Old Covenant and establishment of the New Covenant.[29] Fifth, the general reference to "sacrifices and offerings, whole burnt offerings and sin offerings," taken from Psalm 40 and evoked at Heb. 10:5-8, seems to function as a summary of the Levitical-sacrificial system, the rhetorical goal to evoke the replacement of the Old Covenant system as a whole (cf. 10:18).[30]

Thus the allusions to sacrifices vary greatly in Hebrews, and they have various rhetorical payoffs. My point with this brief review of cult language and word pictures is to remind us that Hebrews often uses general language of offerings and sacrifices, language not tied specifically to Yom Kippur, or language used in relation to Yom Kippur but taken from moments in the Yom Kippur ceremony other than the high priest's work in the holy of holies. The way we hear the interplay of these Levitical word pictures and whispers with Yom Kippur language is vital to our assessment of the author's thought on atonement specifically and the sacrificial work of Christ generally. The variety of sacrificial imagery and language in Hebrews, drawn from the Levitical cult generally (rather than just Yom Kippur), suggests that to understand the sacrificial/atoning work of Christ in Hebrews *we must allow all of the sacrificial language and imagery to speak and inform our understanding*. In fairness, Moffitt's task was to bring much-needed attention to the heavenly, high-priestly work of Christ as the culminating moment of atonement in Hebrews, which he accomplishes in his monograph. Yet, such cannot be

---

[27] So Moffitt, *Atonement and the Logic of Resurrection*, p. 270; Craig R. Koester, *Hebrews: A New Translation with Introduction and Commentary* (AB, 36; New York: Doubleday, 2001), p. 368. Most commentators note that the daily offerings represent the general ministry of the priests and are being conflated here with the offering on Yom Kippur. So, for example, Attridge, *The Epistle to the Hebrews: A Commentary on The Epistle to the Hebrews*, p. 213; Lane, William L., *Hebrews 1-8* (WBC; Nashville: Nelson, 2009), p. 193. We suggest that the conflation is with the worship following the ordination service of the priests (Lev. 9:7-21) instead of Yom Kippur.

[28] Guthrie, *The Structure of Hebrews*, 1994, p. 85.

[29] On which, see Jamieson, "Hebrews 9.23: Cult Inauguration, Yom Kippur and the Cleansing of the Heavenly Tabernacle."

[30] For example, Gareth Lee Cockerill, *The Epistle to the Hebrews* (The New International Commentary on the New Testament; Grand Rapids, MI: Wm. B. Eerdmans, 2012), pp. 438-39.

abstracted from the fabric of atoning sacrificial work, which is woven with a variety of nuanced images from the Scriptures. This brings me to a second, related proposal.

Proposal 2

The author of Hebrews primarily refracts OT sacrificial language through the Christ Event, not the other way around.

Does the author, reflecting on the Christ event, filter that event through sacrificial imagery from the Jewish Scriptures, especially Yom Kippur, or is it primarily the other way around, the author taking the Christ event as the grounding prism and filtering various aspects of the sacrificial imagery from the Jewish Scriptures through that event in order to communicate various theological points? This is not meant to set up a strict dichotomy.[31] The question is one of interpretive priority (which is the grounding "reality" and which is the means of communicating the reality?).

One of Moffitt's concerns has to do with the former approach as the grounds of a cross-oriented understanding of atonement in Hebrews. He explains that flawed understanding in this way:

> Yom Kippur allows the author to envision the cross in terms of the slaughter of the sacrificial victim. The cross is the place of Jesus' self-sacrifice (where the noun *sacrifice* is assumed to denote "slaughter/death"). On the other hand, the imagery/metaphor of the high priest's entry into the holy of holies allows him to reflect on the heavenly/spiritual significance of that event—Jesus' death can be likened to the presentation of the blood before God on Yom Kippur as an atoning sacrifice. *In Hebrews, Yom Kippur functions as a theological prism through which the manifold significance of the singular event of the crucifixion can be refracted and seen distinctly.* By way of his creative appeal to Yom Kippur, the author can elucidate the theological/spiritual meaning of the crucifixion (italics mine).[32]

Moffitt's work has demonstrated the fallacy of this approach, and at points in his monograph he models effectively a grasp of the inverse of this reading strategy.

For instance, his treatment of the Greek version of Psalm 40 I find largely convincing as he identifies the use of metalepsis, elements from the broader context of the psalm playing a role in the author's discussion of Christ's obedience and endurance, tying the internalization of the law in the psalm to a key motif in the New Covenant passage of Jeremiah.[33] Moffitt explains "that the psalm is being refracted through a christological lens,"[34] and I think that is exactly the way the process should be understood.

---

[31] Discussion with Moffitt in personal correspondence has been helpful in this regard, and his caution about setting up a dichotomy is heard. Yet, the question is whether any of us can slide into placing interpretive priority wrongly at given moments.

[32] Moffitt, *Atonement and the Logic of Resurrection*, p. 216.

[33] Ibid, p. 246.

[34] Ibid, p. 245.

Yet, with Moffitt's treatment of Heb. 9:11-28, it seems to me that this pattern of refraction is reversed at points, the Christ event now, in particular ways, being refracted *primarily* through the Yom Kippur word picture, rather than the rich, varied Levitical images in the passage being refracted through various moments in the Christ event.

Let me make clear that David Moffitt often is responsible in giving the death of Jesus a certain amount of due, admitting, for instance, that the blood language of 9:15, 22 "is apparently used as a shorthand for death,"[35] and that there is an important link between blood and death at 9:18.[36] He grants that the death of Christ might have some sacrificial significance, and he emphasizes that it plays a vital role in Hebrews' soteriology.[37] But since he argues so forcefully for a particular understanding of the role of Yom Kippur as a controlling image of the author's Christology, that backdrop in the Levitical system affects how the death of Christ is allowed to speak in the reading of Hebrews.[38] In other words, when the event of Christ's death is refracted through Yom Kippur, certain theological conclusions about the death are read onto the text of Hebrews. My concern particularly has to do with what at times may be read as a downplaying of the death of Christ as vitally significant in terms of sacrifice and atonement for sins.[39] This is not suggesting that Moffitt's emphasis on the Son's work as high priest in the heavenly holy of holies is wrong. I long have argued for the importance of the "offering in heaven" as a key to the superiority of the New Covenant offering. Rather, I propose that each stage in the Christ event—death, resurrection, exaltation—has a vital soteriological role to play in Hebrews' theological program. Moffitt's contribution lies in a reconsideration of the resurrection and exaltation in that program. His misstep, perhaps in trying to return appropriate focus to the offering in heaven, has to do with inadequate attention to the death-impregnated unit found at 9:11-28, a vitally important unit as the author moves toward the culmination of his great Christological treatise on the Son's high priesthood.

---

[35] Ibid, p. 291.
[36] Ibid, p. 291.
[37] Ibid, pp. 291-95.
[38] See, for example, his p. 279-80, where Moffitt writes that the allusions to Yom Kippur in 9:12 "indicate that even in the midst of this conflation of rituals, the purification (καθαρότητα, 9:13; καθαριεῖ, 9:14) and redemption (λύτρωσις, 9:12) of the Yom Kippur offerings remain of chief significance." This is true. Yet, what is not addressed adequately is *why* the author shifted his imagery and language at this point. Cleansing language occurs over 150 times in the Greek Pentateuch, three of these occurrences found in Leviticus 16 (Lev. 16:19-20, 30); but other images of cleansing are in play as well in our passage. Further, while "redemption" language occurs 60 times in the Pentateuch, it does not appear at all in Leviticus 16, the noun form only found in Lev. 25:29, 48; Num. 18:16. Why does the author use that language at 9:12? Could it be that the insertion of a complex array of sacrificial and ritual language is brought to bear in Heb. 9:11-28 *so that it might be filtered or refracted through various moments and effects of the Christ Event, including the death of Christ on the cross?*
[39] Moffitt has continued to develop his expression of these dynamics. For instance, in his article "Jesus' Heavenly Sacrifice in Early Christian Reception of Hebrews: A Survey," *JTS* 68 (2017), pp. 46–71, he writes of interpretation of Jesus's atoning work in the Early Church: "Nevertheless, by thinking sequentially through the whole sweep of the incarnational narrative, they are able to work with a broad perspective on Jesus' atoning work. The cross is essential for them, particularly for the defeat of death and the devil, but they do not view it as the sum total of Jesus' atoning sacrifice" (p. 69). Thus, the cross is spoken of as an aspect of the "atoning sacrifice."

For example, Moffitt follows Milgrom and Sklar on the role and function of blood sacrifice in the Pentateuch.[40] Putting aside for a moment whether his assessment of blood sacrifice is correct, his logic moves as follows:

1. *blood offering was primary in the Levitical cult's practice of sacrifice and*
2. *the death of the victim was not of central significance, either in the sacrificial system generally, nor in Yom Kippur specifically,*[41]
3. *therefore, the author was "unlikely to have conflated Jesus' atoning work with his death at the crucifixion."*

The broader context of this last conclusion reads,

> If, however, we assume for the moment that the author of Hebrews understood Yom Kippur along the lines just discussed—that the blood is the life and that the presentation and manipulation of that blood/life in the holy of holies is the central point for atonement on Yom Kippur—then a remarkable conclusion follows: the writer is unlikely to have conflated Jesus' atoning work with his death at the crucifixion. The Levitical description of blood offering described above allows for the possibility that the author of Hebrews could reflect on the cross without that event necessarily functioning as the focal point of Jesus' offering. Rather, an expansion or parsing out of the moments in the process, and in particular, an emphasis on the moment of presentation as the point at which atonement occurs, would allow him to do exactly what he has done—stress the presentation of the blood of Jesus before God in the heavenly holy of holies.[42]

This statement assumes that Hebrews, unlike Leviticus even in the Yom Kippur instructions, limits atonement to the blood manipulation in the heavenly holy of holies, and we have already noted that this is not the case. The statement also refracts the Christ event through a particular part of the Yom Kippur imagery, rather than the other way around. In other words, how Hebrews thinks of and treats the death of Christ and its significance has now been restricted by a particular reading of one aspect of the Yom Kippur imagery. Thus, it may be suggested that with this refraction the "death-impregnated" section of Heb. 9:11-28 becomes skewed in certain parts, or at least muted, in the process, the death of Christ primarily conceived of as a trigger in a sequence that culminates in the real moment of atonement in the heavenly holy of holies.

The death of Christ and variegated Levitical imagery in Hebrews 9:11-28

However, it can be argued that the death of Christ stands as a vitally important dynamic at the heart of the author's soteriological intentions for Heb. 9:11-28, woven with other

---

[40] Ibid, pp. 268–69.
[41] This understanding, as one colleague noted, does raise the question as to why death was necessary at all. If blood was the point, then why not just bleed an animal over and over, rather than committing it to death?
[42] Ibid, p. 273.

cultic images to speak of the sacrificial significance of that death. In 9:11-12, with the reference to Christ entering by his own blood the "most holy place" of the heavenly tabernacle, Yom Kippur imagery clearly is in view. But the source of sacrificial imagery begins to change rather abruptly, and the key question is *why*? The reference to μόσχων at Heb. 9:12 is an image from Yom Kippur (Lev. 16:3, 6, 11) yet also used of priestly ordination at Exod. 29:10; Lev. 8:2, 14, 17; 9:4, 18-19). Further, "the blood of male goats and bulls" (τὸ αἷμα τράγων καὶ ταύρων) at 9:13 is not Yom Kippur language, but rather is taken from a more general cache of sacrificial images in the LXX.[43] This broader orientation is confirmed at 9:13 by the addition of language from the Red heifer ceremony and the reference to Christ offering himself "without blemish" in 9:14. These broader images of sacrifice are being refracted through the Christ event in part to underscore rhetorically the effectiveness of Christ's sacrifice in bringing about the cleansing and forgiveness of persons.[44] Also related to cleansing rituals, with 9:15-22 the author turns to the imagery of covenant inauguration being refracted through the Christ event,[45] and a main point here focuses on the role of death both in dealing with defilement under the Old Covenant and in establishing the New Covenant.[46]

Further, in this section death is associated with the removal of sin by sacrifice in Heb. 9:26, for Christ appeared, Hebrews tells us, "to do away with sin by the sacrifice of himself" (εἰς ἀθέτησιν [τῆς] ἁμαρτίας διὰ τῆς θυσίας αὐτοῦ; Heb. 9:26 NIV11). In fact, aside from the general Levitical material on sacrifices that deal with sin, it is instructive to note how sacrifices done "concerning sin" (περὶ ἁμαρτίας), and at points the death of those sacrifices, play specifically into Yom Kippur itself, for the focus does not rest solely on blood manipulation in the holy of holies. The sacrificial calf is called "a calf for sin" (Lev. 16:3, 6), and both of the two goats are labeled as "for sin" (16:5). Aaron "shall slaughter the bull calf for sin" (16:11), taking its blood into the Holy of Holies, and he "shall slaughter the goat for sin that is for the people before the Lord and bring its blood inside the veil" (16:15). Yes, the high priest cleanses the holy place ritually "concerning all their sins" (16:16), but the narrative does not stop there. Aaron then

---

[43] The one time the two terms are used together in the Pentateuch is at Deut. 32:14; the two are found elsewhere together at 1 Esd. 8:63; Ps. 49:13; Ode. 2:14; Isa. 1:11.

[44] The verb καθαρίζω is used thirty-nine times in Leviticus and thus plays a significant part in cult language: Lev 8:15; 12:7-8; 13:6-7, 13, 17, 23, 28, 34-35, 37, 59; 14:2, 4, 7-8, 11, 14, 17-20, 23, 25, 28-29, 31, 48, 57; 15:13, 28; 16:19-20, 30; 22:4.

[45] One key basis for the author's integration of covenant inauguration with Yom Kippur at this point in the discourse may be related to the rabbinic appropriation move of "building up a 'family' from two or more texts." For example, see Richard N. Longenecker, *Biblical Exegesis in The Apostolic Period* (Grand Rapids, MI: Eerdmans, 1975), p. 34. In the Jewish Scriptures both covenant inauguration and Yom Kippur have to do with sprinkling the tabernacle for cleansing (Exod. 24:8; 40:9; Lev. 8:11-12; Lev. 16:19-20; 30), and we find a mixing of the images in our passage. In fact, the additional language of the "water, scarlet wool, and hyssop" in Heb. 9:19 appropriates other "sprinkling" images in the Levitical cult as well, including those having to do with the Red Heifer ceremony, the cleansing of skin diseases (Num. 19:9, 18-20; Lev. 14:4-6), and the ordination of the priesthood, in which both oil and blood are used (Exod. 29:21). In this way, the sprinkling of water and blood overlap as images of cleansing and dedication, with sprinkling as the integrating image. Accordingly, the "cleansing motif" is drawn from a wide array of sacrificial contexts, not just Yom Kippur.

[46] On the integration of covenant inauguration and ongoing cult operations, including purification, see Jamieson, "Hebrews 9:23: Cult Inauguration, Yom Kippur and the Cleansing of the Heavenly Tabernacle," pp. 576-77.

lays his hands on the head of the live goat, confessing "all their sins and shall put them on the head of the live goat," and send it away, "and the goat shall bear on itself their offences to an untrodden region" (Lev. 16:22 NETS). In 16:25 the fat offered up on the altar is called "the fat for sins." In this chapter something being offered for sin (e.g., 16:6, 9) and slaughtered for sin at times are noted in the same breath:

> And Aaron shall offer the bull calf for sin, which is his, and shall make atonement for himself and for his house, and he shall slaughter the bull calf for sin, which is his own. (Lev. 16:11 NETS)

Thus, rather than focused only on the blood manipulation inside the holiest place, the various offerings "for sin(s)" constitute a more general concept in Leviticus 16, and the ceremony does include death of the animal, ritual slaughter "before the Lord," as a vitally important aspect of the ceremony.

Further, note that at 9:26 Hebrews uses the language of θυσία—language not associated with Yom Kippur in Leviticus 16—to speak of the effectiveness of Christ's death, who appeared "to do away with sin by the *sacrifice* of himself" (εἰς ἀθέτησιν [τῆς] ἁμαρτίας τῆς θυσίας αὐτοῦ). It should be noted that in Leviticus the language of θυσία always has to do with the grain or animal offering itself, *not* the manipulation that follows the sacrifice of an animal.[47] The blood is not the sacrifice.[48]

One more point from this penultimate moment in Hebrews' Christology bolsters this reading of the book. At Heb. 9:28 we read that "Christ was offered once to *bear the sins of many*." As is often recognized, the words πολλῶν ἀνενεγκεῖν ἁμαρτίας form a loud allusion to Isa. 53:12, with only a slight change from aorist indicative to an aorist infinitive in the verb form and a move of ἁμαρτίας to the front of the phrase. In context, of course, the servant who bore the sins of many was given over to death (παρεδόθη εἰς θάνατον ἡ ψυχὴ αὐτοῦ; Isa. 53:12 LXX). In a passage riddled with allusions to Isaiah 53, and also using the words ἀνενεγκεῖν ἁμαρτίας, 1 Pet. 2:24 speaks of Christ as the one "who bore our sins in his body on the tree."

In Leviticus 16, we find that sin bearing lies not with blood manipulation but rather the goat for Azazel: "And the goat shall bear on itself their offences to an untrodden region" (Καὶ λήμψεται ὁ χίμαρος ἐφ᾽ ἑαυτῷ τὰς ἀδικίας αὐτῶν; Lev. 16:22 NETS). The verb in Hebrews, probably under the influence of the Servant passage in Isaiah, is different from the one in Leviticus LXX, the latter being a future indicative form of λαμβάνω, but the Hebrew term underlying both Lev. 16:22 and Isa. 53:12 is the same (נשׂא, *nasa*).

My point in this movement of the chapter is that, in his expression of the significance of Christ's death, Hebrews accesses a wide array of images from the Levitical cult, refracting them for various theological and rhetorical ends through various aspects of the Christ event. Moreover, the death of Christ particularly holds

---

[47] See, for example, Lev. 1:9, 13, 17; 2:2, 14; 3:3, 9; 4:26, 35; 6:14; 7:15; 14:20-21. It could be argued that the use of θυσία at Heb. 9:23 is more directly related to blood manipulation, since it is tied to the cleansing of the heavenly tabernacle. However, in Leviticus sacrifice *always* precedes blood manipulation but is not identical with it. Sacrifices "cleanse" in that they provide the effectual blood. There exists a direct relationship without identity.

[48] In fact, the blood at times is described as the blood "of the sacrifice." For example, Exod. 23:18; 34:25.

great significance in Heb. 9:11-28. If we take the Christ event as the grounding reality that is being explicated by Hebrews, understanding that a wide array of images is used to explicate that event to various theological and rhetorical payoffs, we notice that various aspects of the Christ event are reflected upon by using variegated imagery, as depicted in the Figure below.

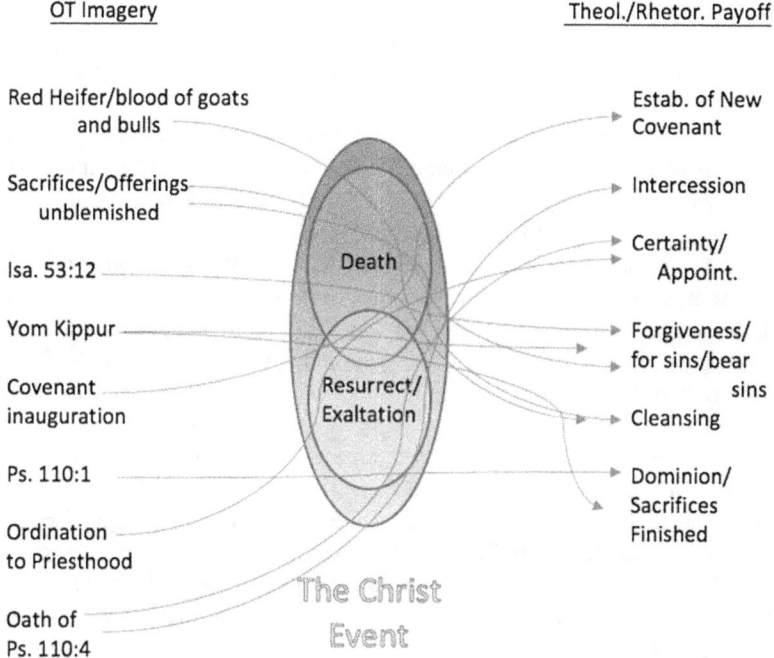

For example, the ashes of the Red Heifer imagery in Heb. 9:13 is refracted through the death of Christ specifically to emphasize cleansing of consciences by Christ's work. The oath of Ps. 110:4, on the other hand, the author refracts particularly through the resurrection/exaltation of Christ. It may be suggested, moreover, that Yom Kippur imagery, as well as imagery related to ordination for priesthood and establishment of the New Covenant, refract through both the death and the resurrection/exaltation of Christ. The grounding of our hermeneutical process in the Christ event itself, with the OT imagery being read in light of various steps in the Event (not the other way around) affords a symphonic hearing of Hebrews' Christology that gives appropriate attention to the soteriological importance of the death, resurrection, and exaltation of Christ.

Death and atonement

Coming full circle in our chapter, how then might this affect our understanding of the "moment of atonement" in Hebrews? David Moffitt argues that Christ's death is the trigger in a sequence that puts the New Covenant in motion and constitutes "Jesus' preparation for making his atoning offering." I agree with him when he describes Jesus's death as "the first element in the larger process of blood sacrifice,"[49] which should not be collapsed or conflated with the offering in heaven. I also agree that the offering in heaven constitutes a key moment of atonement for Hebrews. Yet, as Bobby Jamieson demonstrates in his monograph, Moffitt fails to note adequately the role that the death of Christ plays as atoning. In relation to Heb. 9:22b Jamieson states, "Hebrews presents ritual slaughter as prerequisite to forgiveness because, in order for forgiveness to obtain, a life must be given for the life that is forfeit. In a maxim that underscores the indispensability of blood for atonement, Hebrews puts death center frame."[50] He concludes that the death of Christ is one "locus of atonement" in Hebrews.[51] I agree. Thus, I believe the "time of the atonement" to correspond with the Christ event from death to exaltation, with significant emphasis placed on the exaltation of Christ as vital, as David Moffitt has so compellingly demonstrated.

Further, we must not press Hebrews' use of the Levitical imagery into a neat linear package. For instance, even if we limit ourselves to Yom Kippur imagery for the moment, which the author of Hebrews does not, where in the Levitical system is blood spilled prior to or concurrent to the appointment of the priest who will carry it into the Holy of Holies? It is the steps in the Christ event—death, then resurrection, then exaltation—that are sequential and logically so. As we have shown, OT sacrificial imagery is accessed variously to elucidate aspects of these events, and that imagery itself need not conform to a rigid, logical sequence.

Thus, Christ's death stands as of vital significance in the Christology of Hebrews, accomplishing multiple effects. This does nothing to take away from the importance of the Yom Kippur language in the book, nor from the clear focus on the heavenly *Session* as the consummation of atonement. But it does elevate the death of Christ as of central significance in the book.

A wrinkle in time

Thus, I want to close by noting what might be called "a wrinkle in time" in our nice, sequential conceptions of atonement in Hebrews. One of the more interesting passages in the book, which has to do with time, is found in Heb. 9:25-26. In arguing for the decisive, once-for-all nature of Christ's sacrifice, the author notes that Christ did not enter the heavenly Holy of Holies over and over again, "for then he would have had to suffer again and again since the foundation of the world" (Heb. 9:25-26 NET). Harold Attridge, in his Hermeneia volume on Hebrews, reads the statement as a rhetorically offered absurdity,[52] but I think there may be more going on here, a theological hint, if you will, which corresponds to other places in the NT where Christ's work is related

---

[49] Moffitt, *Atonement and the Logic of Resurrection*, p. 285.
[50] R.B. Jamieson, *Jesus' Death and Heavenly Offerings in Hebrews* (SNTSMS 172; Cambridge: Cambridge University Press, 2018), p. 159.
[51] Ibid. 168.
[52] Attridge, *The Epistle to the Hebrews: A Commentary on The Epistle to the Hebrews*, p. 264.

to "the foundation of the world" in some way (Mt. 13:35; 25:34; Eph. 1:4; Heb. 4:3; 1 Pet. 1:20; Rev. 13:8; 17:8). It may be that this statement means that efficacy of Christ's offering reaches back to the very foundation of the world, taking it out of a neatly developing, linear history.

The only other time that ἀπὸ καταβολῆς κόσμου is used in Hebrews is with reference to the κατάπαυσις, the "rest" of God, in Heb. 4:3: "And yet God's works were accomplished from the foundation of the world." I have suggested in the Hebrews section of *The Commentary on the New Testament Use of the Old Testament* that the rest of Hebrews 4 is a "Day of Atonement," Sabbath of Sabbath's rest.[53] If that is the case, the author of Hebrews at 9:25-26 may be tying the Christ event back to God's rest established at the foundation of the world. Thus the atonement would extend beyond the constraints of time as we know it, working backward to cover all the ages of the world. In his 2013 dissertation, Benjamin Ribbens suggests something like this when he writes,

> The singular sacrifice of Christ is efficacious for all time. The result is that the efficacy that emanates from Christ's sacrifice to the earthly sacrifices must be proleptically applied to old covenant believers. They were accessing salvific goods that were dependent on a future act or development, but for the time being those efficacies were sealed with the promise of God that, when sacrifice was made, there would be atonement and forgiveness.[54]

Or might we say that the work of Christ worked analeptically from the standpoint of linear time? Also, it might be suggested that the statement at 10:14, "by one sacrifice he has perfected forever those being made holy," can be read as working in the other direction, proclaiming that Christ's sacrificial offering has already perfected New Covenant believers who come into New Covenant at various points all the way to the end of the age.[55]

There exists a rich history of interpretation when it comes to Christian reflections on God's relation to time. The classical view of time and eternity in Western theology and philosophy has its foundation in *the Confessions of Augustine*, Book XI (354–430) and the fifth book of Boethius's (480–c.525) *The Consolation of Philosophy*.[56] A certain trajectory can be traced through Aquinas. Eugene Schlesinger points out that for Aquinas, eternity must not be conceived of as a concept apart from God the Trinity. Rather, "'God is his own eternity,' because life and esse are one in him."[57] Schlesinger explains,

> Eternity as a concept is an abstraction from God himself, and while this conceptual abstraction is helpful, it must be remembered that eternity is not

---

[53] George H. Guthrie, "Hebrews," in *Commentary on the New Testament Use of the Old Testament* (ed. G. K. Beale and D. A. Carson; Grand Rapids, MI: Baker Academic, 2007), pp. 919–95 (959–60).
[54] Ribbens, *Levitical Sacrifice and Heavenly Cult in Hebrews*, p. 238.
[55] Note that the verb communicates stative aspect, and the participle is imperfective, perhaps being read as "iterative."
[56] Helm, Paul, "Eternity" in *The Stanford Encyclopedia of Philosophy* (Spring 2014 Edition), Edward N. Zalta (ed.), URL = https://plato.stanford.edu/archives/spr2014/entries/eternity/.
[57] Eugene R. Schlesinger, "Trinity, Incarnation and Time: A Restatement of The Doctrine of God in Conversation with Robert Jenson," *Scottish Journal of Theology* 69 (2016), pp. 189–203 (197).

anything other than God. For were eternity distinct from God, there would be another principle other than God, transcending the universe of space and time, and predicating eternity of God would determine God with reference to this other principle. Therefore, we must posit a positive content of eternity, which is the divine life.[58]

Thus, the life of God the Trinity may be set over against spatio-temporal reality as we know it, which is created, but God's life is not opposite of that reality but rather outside of and can work within that reality. God is not foreign to time, nor time to him. For Aquinas, eternity contains all the moments of time and thus can coincide with temporal history.[59] Further, the coming together of time and eternity may be understood as Trinitarian and specifically Christological in nature. As Wolfhart Pannenberg writes, it is only the triune life of God that allows the Boethian definition of eternity as the full possession of life to be fully realized.[60]

Karl Barth, in a section of his work entitled "Jesus, the Lord of Time," also grounded his understanding of time and eternity in a Christological interpretation, writing, "Because Jesus Christ was himself the relationship between time and eternity, the relation was governed by a pattern of unity, distinction and asymmetry."[61] As a member of the Trinity, the eternal Son, who lived as a human being within time, must be understood as standing over against created time. The past, present, and future are simultaneous to God. In Christ, simultaneity and sequence come together, since Christ in his incarnation lived within time. In fact, Barth structured his section on "Jesus, the Lord of Time" on the basis of Heb. 13:8, "Jesus Christ is the same yesterday and today and forever." The point I wish to emphasize here is the importance of reading the significance of time theologically from a Christological vantage point, one that takes seriously time as an aspect of creation. If we listen to Heb. 1:2, 10-12, the world and its temporal ages have been created by the Son; his first and second comings form the key turning points in history. In Hebrews we have hints and whispers that the creator of time walks and works within linear time in significant ways without being limited by his creation.

Might this mean that when it comes to Christ's work of atonement, we could consider that work temporally from two vantage points:

1. as temporally linear creatures, the that-ness of the events within the Christ event, particularly the death, resurrection, and exaltation, can be considered in a logical sequence, all of the events playing a role in the atonement. I believe that for Hebrews atonement is inaugurated on the cross and consummated in the exaltation—an "inaugurated and consummated soteriology," if you will.

---

[58] Ibid.
[59] Ibid, p. 199.
[60] Wolfhart Pannenberg, "Eternity, Time, and the Trinitarian God," in *Trinity, Time, and Church* (ed. C. E. Gunton; Grand Rapids, MI: William B. Eerdmans, 2000), p. 70.
[61] As quoted in George Hunsinger, "Jesus as the Lord of Time According to Karl Barth," *Zeitschrift für Dialektische Theologie* 4 (2010), pp. 113–27 (117).

From another vantage point,

2. since in the person and work of Christ we have the Christological nexus of past, present, and future, one that seems to step beyond the constraints and logic of linear time, perhaps in 9:26 and 10:14 the author of Hebrews is both "anticipating the past" as well as "remembering the future," as the Christ event wrinkles time as we experience it. From that vantage point, in asking the exact "time" of the atonement, we may be focusing on the wrong question, for we are dealing with the Christ, who is both in and out of time.

14

Space and Atonement in Hebrews

Cynthia L. Westfall

Introduction

David Moffitt's publication of *Atonement and the Logic of Resurrection in the Epistle to the Hebrews*[1] generated a considerable amount of discussion among scholars because of his conclusion that the author of Hebrews places the completion of the atonement after Jesus's resurrection and ascension.[2] Moffitt's thesis was that the resurrection was an assumption in Hebrews that was fundamental to the central argument, but the negative responses to Moffitt's work have reflected an overriding theological concern with the *time* in which he concludes the final act of the atonement took place. Did the atonement in Hebrews take place on the cross at the time of Jesus's crucifixion and death, which is the position of most modern scholars,[3] or was the atonement in Hebrews a process that was completed in the heavenly sanctuary after the resurrection and ascension? Moffitt's observation that heaven is the place in which the author of Hebrews depicts the atonement leads him to deduce that the culmination of the atonement was after the resurrection and ascension.[4]

Place and time are linked without question. As Hermann Minkowski who was Einstein's teacher said, "Nobody ever noticed a place except at a time or a time except at a place."[5] However, interpreters of Hebrews often ascribe metaphorical, symbolic, or

---

[1] David M. Moffitt, *Atonement and the Logic of Resurrection in the Epistle to the Hebrews* (NovTSup 141; Leiden: Brill, 2011).

[2] Moffitt's work was the topic of the invitation session of the Hebrews section of ETS on November 21, 2013. Besides Moffitt, papers were given by Michael Allen, I. Howard Marshall, and Douglas Moo.

[3] See Moffitt, *Atonement*, p. 217, for a discussion of how "blood" in Hebrews is generally taken by modern interpreters as a metaphor for Jesus's death.

[4] Moffitt, *Atonement*, p. 228, concludes, "Attempts to conflate the high-priestly activity of Jesus with his death on the cross may . . . unduly spiritualize the straightforward language of the author." The issue of space and the atonement quickly became a bit of an exegetical, theological, and traditional minefield. Notably, Michael Kibbe, in print and in presentations, has associated Moffitt's view on the time and place of atonement with Socinianism, which denied the deity of Christ and thus the Trinity. See, for example, Michael H. Kibbe, "Is It Finished? When Did It Start? Hebrews, Priesthood, and Atonement in Biblical, Systematic, and Historical Perspective," *Journal of Theological Studies* 65.1 (2014), pp. 25–61 (25–30).

[5] This quotation is from Hermann Minkowski's famous Cologne address in 1908.

otherwise abstract significance to the references to place,[6] treating them as if they were references to time (e.g., most often in eschatological/apocalyptic future)[7] or assigning them to a theological category or idea (e.g., exaltation).[8] Studies on the role of place say that the preference for mapping reality on time is an anachronistic bias of the "characteristically modern domination of space by time," and speak of "recovering" a sense of place on which meaning is mapped which was characteristic of ancient thought.[9] This appears to be confirmed by scholars such as Walter Brueggemann who suggest that the OT "was concerned with *place*, specific real estate that was invested with powerful *promises* and with strategic arrangements for presence in the place as well."[10] Critical spatial theory provides definitions and categories for place and space that are helpful, and allow us to explore the meaning of place as its own category.[11] This study suggests that spatial references and their meaning play an important role in Hebrews' description of the atonement. The study of the atonement and space/place narrows our focus to the heavenly tabernacle and the consideration of how the atonement is related to that place.

---

[6] See Moffit's central argument that the author's conception of heaven and Jesus's high-priestly sacrifice are not metaphor, but analogical in David M. Moffitt, "Serving in the Tabernacle in Heaven: Sacred Space, Jesus's High-Priestly Sacrifice, and Hebrews' Analogical Theology," in *Hebrews in Contexts* (ed. Gabriella Gelardini and Harold W. Attridge; Ancient Judaism and Early Christianity, 91; Leiden: Brill, 2016), pp. 259–80. See also Moffitt's discussion and conclusion on the relationship of οἰκουμένη to the temple in which he deals with these tendencies in *Atonement*, pp. 69–118, cf. p. 118: "When the author speaks of the unseen city, land and heavenly tabernacle, and links the Son's entry into the οἰκουμένη with his ascension into the realm of heaven and God's presence, it need not be the case that he posits the kind of spiritual/material dualism he is often thought to have assumed."

[7] See, for example, G. W. MacRae, "Heavenly Temple and Eschatology in the Letter to the Hebrews," *Semeia* 12 (1978), pp. 179–99. MacRae exemplifies most of these tendencies such as assigning future reference to spatial reference and assuming the use of metaphor. He infers "futurist eschatology" from the reader's relationship to the heavenly sanctuary (he assumes heaven and the effects of Jesus's sacrifice are future for the reader): "The future is anticipated in the sacrifice of Jesus. Christ has already entered the sanctuary, thus inaugurating the end time, which for the believer nevertheless remains future, an object of hope" (p. 188). However, the message of Hebrews depends on readers' present hope and activity while on earth in relationship to the tabernacle, rather than hope for a future heaven (though future might be in view in the entrance to "rest" in ch. 4). He also assumes a relationship between Hebrews and Philo, and assigns a symbolic value to the tabernacle as his first preliminary observation (pp. 180–81), and then assumes "an apocalyptic idea of the temple in heaven" (p. 182). He prioritizes the abstract and believes that place is derived from ideas: spatial references to the heavenly tabernacle are described as "a tendency to 'materialize' or 'hypostatize' ideas in such a way that they became independent realities" (p. 183).

[8] For example, Harold W. Attridge interprets the spatial reference to Jesus taking a seat at God's right hand in 1:3 from Psalm 110 (109 LXX) as "a focus on the exaltation" in *The Epistle to the Hebrews: A Commentary on the Epistle to the Hebrews* (Hermeneia; Philadelphia: Fortress, 1989) p. 46. However, Jesus's location in the heavenly tabernacle is the author's clear focus in his argument. The author's combination of providing purification for sins with his spatial enthronement (sitting down at the right hand of the Majesty on high) is crucial for his spatial description of Jesus's sacrifice in the heavenly tabernacle rather than any kind of focus on his exaltation.

[9] Edward S. Casey, *Getting Back into Place: Toward a Renewed Understanding of the Place-World* (2nd ed.; Bloomington, IN: Indiana University Press, 2009), p. 6.

[10] Walter Brueggemann, *The Land: Place as Gift, Promise, and Challenge in Biblical Faith* (2nd ed.; Minneapolis: Fortress, 2002), p. xi.

[11] Critical Spatial Theory, see Edward W. Soja, *Thirdspace: Journeys to Los Angeles and Other Real-and-Imagined Places* (Cambridge, MA: Blackwell, 1996).

My thesis is that the interpretation of the Hebrews author of the heavenly tabernacle and its use (priesthood and sacrifices) in the LXX is based on the meaning of place in the continuity and contrast between the past Mosaic tabernacle and what is true in the present of the heavenly tabernacle in the light of Jesus's sacrificial death. The author's primary orientation to time was introduced in 1:1-2: time in the past (πάλαι) is contrasted with the apocalyptic phrase "these last days" (ἐπ' ἐσχάτου τῶν ἡμερῶν τούτων), which is the author and recipients' present time. The first sentence of the epistle constrains the interpreter to regard apocalyptic imagery/intertextuality as fulfilled eschatology in the absence of clear temporal indicators of the future. In his description of the heavenly tabernacle, the author not only represents the heavenly tabernacle as a concrete real place, but he assists the recipients in multiple ways to make Jesus real and concrete as high priest. Jesus is not only located in place but also interpreted and encountered by the recipients in and through place. The interpreter's understanding of the meaning of place may then be used to determine the timing of the process of the atonement.

Platonic influence on the interpretation of Hebrews

In the history of interpretation, the heavenly tabernacle has been interpreted in Platonic terms and categories, and those interpretations continue to cast a shadow over how Hebrews is read. As Moffitt asserts, there is a "*Tendenz* among modern interpreters to spiritualize and/or to moralize these terms by appealing to Jesus's death as the event/concept" that holds the three terms body, blood and self together.[12]

There has been a vigorous discussion in scholarship as to whether or how much the author of Hebrews was influenced by Alexandria, Philo, and Platonic philosophy.[13] For most of the twentieth century, it was the scholarly consensus that Alexandria, Philo, and Platonism were the conceptual background, which was thought to be clearly indicated in passages such as 8:5:[14] They offer worship in a sanctuary that is a sketch and shadow of the heavenly one; for Moses, when he was about to erect the tent, was warned, "See that you make everything according to the pattern that was shown you on the mountain" (NRS).

---

[12] Moffitt, *Atonement*, p. 218.

[13] However, William G. Johnson described a tendency among Catholic scholars to focus on cultus and find Platonic influence, and a tendency in Protestant scholars to neglect cultus and find apocalyptic influence in "The Cultus of Hebrews in the Twentieth Century" *ExpTim* 89 (1978), pp. 104–08. However, apocalyptic interpretations often assume a platonic dualism. C. K. Barrett led the way in suggesting a mixture of Platonic language and eschatological events in "The Eschatology of the Epistle to the Hebrews," in *The Background of the New Testament and its Eschatology: Studies in Honour of C. H. Dodd* (ed. W. D. Davies and D. Daule; Cambridge: Cambridge University Press, 1954), pp. 363–93, see p. 385. See William L. Lane's bibliography for "non-Christian" backgrounds, in *Hebrews 1–8* (WBC; Dallas: Word Press, 1991), pp. civ–cvii.

[14] C. Spicq's work was the culmination of the support of a Platonic background which he argued in several journal articles and his influential *L'Épitre aux Hébreux* (2 vols; EBib; Paris: Gabaldo, 1977).

However, with Willamson's critique in *Philo and the Epistle to the Hebrews* in 1970[15] and Hurst's critique in *The Epistle to the Hebrews: Its Background of Thought* in 1990,[16] scholarly consensus shifted to the position that, as Lane's summarizes, the differences between Philo and the writer of Hebrews were "striking and fundamental, both in outlook and exegetical method,"[17] so that subsequently, the consensus has been that the author was not using Platonic categories. Nevertheless, scholars have continued to understand the nature of the tabernacle as Platonic in some sense (in the of assumption spiritual/material dualism), and we have inherited those interpretations for many of the passages by and large uncritically. Hence, in addition to overt or embedded assumptions of Platonic thought in Hebrews, the classification and analysis of spatial references as typology, thought, or metaphor[18] are often applied without consideration of the meaning of space/place apart from their assumed function as abstract symbols. Furthermore, according to Edward Casey, our Western perception of location and geography has developed on a Platonic trajectory fueled in part by the Scientific Revolution, the age of exploration, and even the exploration of space.[19] I argue that we perceive location, geography, and place with so completely different a paradigm than the author of Hebrews, that we are prone to miss or misinterpret the meaning of spatial motifs that permeate the discourse. We generally agree that the author of Hebrews is not Platonic, but fail to recognize that we are Platonic in our understanding of space, or, at least, more a product of Platonism in our worldview in this area than a product of the text and the biblical worldview.

We recognize that that author of Hebrews belonged to the world of Second Temple Judaism, and that world had related quite differently to place, space, and time. If we wish to access the meaning of the text in its contexts it is necessary to negotiate the profound distance between that world and our own in terms of the presuppositions of how we obtain knowledge and make sense of the world.[20] I suggest that spatial theory is a tool that can move us in that direction. It can help us to better identify the role of place in the central argument of Hebrews and throw significant light on aspects of the hermeneutics of the author of Hebrews through which he obtained some of the details of his argument.

---

[15] R. Williamson, *Philo and the Epistle to the Hebrews* (ALGHJ 4; Leiden: Brill, 1970).

[16] L. D. Hurst, *The Epistle to the Hebrews: Its Background of Thought* (SNTSMS 65; Cambridge: Cambridge University Press, 1990).

[17] Lane, *Hebrews 1-8*, pp. cvii-cviii. Williamson concludes that Philo and the author of Hebrews belonged to "two entirely different schools of O.T. exegesis" in *Philo*, p. 79.

[18] See, for example, Kenneth L. Schenck, *Cosmology and Eschatology in Hebrews* (SNTS 143; Cambridge: Cambridge University Press, 2007), p. 8.

[19] See Casey, *Getting Back into Place*, pp. 3–8 for a brief description of the impact of the Scientific Revolution, the age of exploration, and even the exploration of space. But for a full description of how place was assimilated into space by the seventeenth century, see Edward S. Casey, *The Fate of Place: A Philosophical History* (Berkeley: University of California Press, 1997).

[20] See Soja's discussion of epistemology in modernism and postmodernism in *Thirdspace*, pp. 2, 4-6. Soja, following Henri Lefebvre, suggests that the modern human sciences have focused on life's historicality and sociality, but neglected its spatiality. Casey similarly argues that place has been subordinated to time and space (see n. 18). But often, spatial critics speak of "recovering" spatiality, because space arguably was a source of knowledge and meaning in worldviews prior to the seventeenth century.

Historically, Hebrews has been understood as a polemic against Judaism. This goes hand in hand with a Platonic understanding of the heavenly tabernacle: scholars have most often associated "heavenly" with the abstract, universal, and infinite in contrast with a pejorative evaluation of the earthly Jewish institutions. However, the Hebrews author painstakingly constructs a concrete heavenly tabernacle through the assumption of continuity between the earthy tabernacle and the heavenly tabernacle. Nothing ties the book of Hebrews to Judaism more closely than the central argument about priesthood, sacrifice, tabernacle, and covenant. The particular (and [to us] peculiar) nature of the descriptions of the temple and sacrifice in Hebrews in the author's argument has largely been neglected, and more often it is (mis)interpreted with Pauline categories. Theologically, we have been heuristic in what we have mined from this text. We have taken what we wanted and left the rest without due reflection.

Methodology: Theories of place/space

My methodology will utilize Edward W. Soja's critical spatial concepts of Firstspace, Secondspace, and Thirdspace to identify and classify spatial features in the author's representations of the earthly and heavenly tabernacles and how they are utilized and occupied.[21] I will implement the insights of the works of Edward S. Casey to illumine the author's hermeneutics with which he interpreted the atonement of Christ.[22] As is generally the case in my work, spatial methodology will be enhanced by insights from contemporary linguistic theory and my analysis will incorporate additional studies about the role of land and space in the Second Temple Judaic worldview. One of the primary tasks will be to sort out the author's expressed or "literal" representations of the tabernacles and to distinguish them from our own prior assumptions and then conclude what is literal and what is abstract or metaphorical in the text.

Soja's theory of critical spatial analysis is developed from Lefebvre's concept of social space built on a triad of spatial fields: Firstspace is perceived space, Secondspace is conceived space, and Thirdspace is lived space.[23] Firstspace, or perceived space, is "material and materialized 'physical' spatiality that is directly comprehended in empirically measurable configurations: in the absolute and relative locations of things and the activities, sites and situations."[24] Firstspace is measurable and mappable natural and constructed objects (such as rivers and buildings).[25] Secondspace, or conceived space, is the perception, mapping, or representation of physical space. It is the conception of space that explains and influences Firstspace. Architects, urbanists,

---

[21] Soja introduces these three concepts in his introduction of *Thirdspace*, p. 10, as a utilization of LeFebvre's method which balances historicality, sociality, and spatiality. See Henri Lefebvre, *The Production of Space* (Oxford: Blackwell, 1991).

[22] See nn. 10, 20.

[23] See also Andres Ramirez, *Other Spaces, Plural Narratives of Space in Berlin's SO 36* (Berlin: Universitätsverlag der TU Berlin, 2015), pp. 22–25.

[24] Soja, *Thirdspace*, p. 74.

[25] Jon L. Berquist, "Critical Spatiality and the Book of Hebrews," in *Hebrews in Contexts*, pp. 181–93, states on p. 183, "Firstspace refers to what we might otherwise call physical space, that which we might say is objective." However, it is crucial to this study to note that what we might say is objective in the book of Hebrews may well differ from what the author of Hebrews says is objective.

and geographers work in the realm of Secondspace. Thirdspace is lived space, or representational space. It is how a space is actually used. It is "a dominated space that the imagination is constantly playing with, trying to change and appropriate it," creating alternatives and challenging existing illusions of reality.[26] For example, a friend recently described a memorable trip to Ottawa in which his entire junior hockey team skateboarded through the Rideau Centre, successfully dodging and evading the security guards—thus it was a "transgression of the Secondspace intention."[27] For Lefebvre and Soja, Thirdspace is the location of the multitiered struggle and right to be different, which was a space of collective resistance: *le droit à la différence*.[28] On the other hand, Relph calls lived space "existential space" whose meanings are "those of a culture as expressed by an individual" and is "constantly being created and remade by human activities."[29]

Critical spatial theory has been applied to biblical studies in general,[30] and recently to the book of Hebrews.[31] As Berquist explains, scholars cannot fully access Firstspace and Thirdspace of the ancient world. However, he suggests that instead of limiting ourselves to Secondspace information, we can utilize the Secondspace data to reflect "locations that are at once Firstspace, Secondspace, and Thirdspace," by finding the traces of physical space and the transgressions of the physical space, and thus accessing the ancient world.[32] However, in this study the goal will not be the access of the ancient world. The goal is rather to heuristically utilize these three categories to highlight and describe the three ways in which the author of Hebrews does something of the same thing with texts in the LXX. His description of the place(s) of the atonement are uncannily similar to Soja's triad of spatial fields, and yet distinctly different.[33] The author's description of Firstspace will be identified by what he asserts is "real" and "true" about the place of atonement. The author's description of Secondspace will be identified by that which he claims is a copy or map of the real place of atonement. It will be seen that the author of Hebrews subverts and reverses the dominant culture's categories of reality, and, when brought in dialogue with Soja, it subverts Soja's categories as well.

---

[26] Ramirez, *Other Spaces*, p. 24.
[27] Berquist, "Critical Spatiality," p. 183.
[28] Lefebvre introduced the right to be different in *Le Droit à la ville* (Paris: Anthropos, 1968).
[29] E. Relph, *Place and Placelessness* (London: Pion, 1976).
[30] See Berquist, "Critical Spatiality," p. 182 n. 6 for an overview of the initial use of Critical Space Theory in biblical studies.
[31] The application of Critical Spatial Theory to the book of Hebrews is a fairly recent phenomenon. Besides Berquist and my presentation at ETS in 2015 and SBL International in 2018 (n. 1), see Ellen Bradshaw Aitken, "The Body of Jesus Outside the Eternal City: Mapping Ritual Space in the Epistle to the Hebrews," in *Hebrews in Contexts*, pp. 194–209; Gabriella Gelardini, "Charting 'Outside the Camp' with Edward W. Soja: Critical Spatiality and Hebrews 13," *Hebrews in Contexts*, pp. 210–37; idem., "Existence Beyond Borders: The Book of Hebrews and Critical Spatiality" in *The Epistle to the Hebrews: Writing at the Borders* (ed. R. Burnet, D. Luciani and G. Van Oyen; Leuven: Peeters, 2016), pp. 187–204.
[32] Berquist, "Critical Spatiality," p. 184.
[33] There is no need or intention to anachronistically project either postmodern or Marxist presuppositions on the author of Hebrews, nor for the interpreter or reader to assume ideological presuppositions for the sake of this argument. The use of subversive actions and language has been identified in postcolonial criticism as typical of the marginalized in response to issues of control and power by a dominant culture and/or empire. For a brief overview of postcolonial criticism, see Bart Moore-Gilbert, Gareth Stanton, and Willy Maley, *Post-colonial Criticism* (London: Longman, 1997).

However, the author's representation of Thirdspace has a similar purpose as Soja's category, if not the same intention. It will be identified in the ways that the author urges the recipients to occupy and use Firstspace (the "literal" place of atonement), which is indeed subversive to what was assumed to be the intended use of the place of atonement by those who were mapping the space in Second Temple Judaism.

Hebrews is concerned with place. Furthermore, the importance of place permeates OT theology and the culture of Judaism in the Second Temple Period, with two of the three central commitments being to place: the land, the temple, and the Torah.[34] As Brueggemann says, "Land is a central, if not THE central theme of biblical faith. Biblical faith is a pursuit of historical belonging that includes a sense of destiny derived from such belonging."[35] Hebrews 11 interprets the relationship of Jews to the land and their placedness with the grim realities of sojourning, forced migration, and homelessness. Similarly, the temple "is the location plus everything that occupies that location seen as an integrated and meaningful phenomenon."[36] Notably, Hebrews does not have a direct reference to the Temple in Jerusalem, but consistently refers to the Mosaic tabernacle, on which the design for the temple is based.

The central argument of this chapter is that the author of Hebrews was interpreting the atonement of Christ by correlating, disambiguating, and applying a form of spatial interpretation to the description of the place of atonement in the LXX. Casey writes that in modernism "place has come to be not only neglected but actively suppressed" and subordinated to time and space.[37] Space is abstract, universal, and infinite, while place is concrete, local, particular, and finite. Georges Poulet writes "Without places, beings would be only abstractions. It is places that make their image precise and that give them the necessary support thanks to which we can assign them a place in our mental space, dream of them, and remember them."[38] Space is measured by time. Casey's distinction between space and place may place a finger on one of the issues that underlie our current controversy about the location of the atonement in the book of Hebrews. References to place are crucial to Hebrews' presentation of Jesus as high priest and his atoning sacrifice and the message of Hebrews. Perhaps the timing is not a primary consideration in Hebrews.

Hebrews' triad of spatial fields

The sanctuary in heaven is compared to the earthly tabernacle. Contrary to what one would expect, the Hebrews author does not choose to compare the temple in Jerusalem to the heavenly sanctuary. While most scholars believe that Hebrews was written while

---

[34] See N. T. Wright's identification of Land, Temple, and Torah as the "major symbols" of Judaism in *The New Testament and the People of God* (Minneapolis: Fortress Press, 1996), p. 226. However, Wright argues that Christianity appropriated these "symbols" as metaphors, which we will argue against in regards to the temple (tabernacle) in Hebrews.
[35] Brueggemann, *The Land*, p. 3.
[36] E. Relph, *Place and Placelessness*, p. 3.
[37] Edward S. Casey, *Getting Back into Place: Toward a Renewed Understanding of the Place-world* (Bloomington, IN: Indiana University Press, 1993), p. ix.
[38] Georges Poulet, *Proustian Space* (Baltimore: Johns Hopkins University Press, 1977), p. 27.

the temple was still in operation, some believe that the temple was already destroyed and inaccessible.[39] Regardless, it is significant that the author refused to use that which was either present as a concrete and measurable physical object, or that which was vividly part of the shared memory of the Jewish community. Instead, the author chose to painstakingly recover "traces" of physical space in texts that provide information about the prototype of the temple: the tabernacle and the activities associated with it as described in (but not limited to) Num. 24:6 LXX, Exod. 25-30, 35-40 LXX, and Leviticus 16 LXX. Psalm 110:1 holds an important interpretive key: the enthroned/ seated messiah determines place and (as a consequence) time.

Firstspace: The heavenly tabernacle

The descriptive detail and the activity serve to identify the heavenly tabernacle as a concrete place that is occupied. Jesus serves as a priest in the "true" tabernacle in 8:2 (τῆς σκηνῆς τῆς ἀληθινῆς). Since Israel's tents were good "as tents which God pitched" according to Num. 24:6 LXX,[40] the comparison shows that in heaven there is a "true tabernacle" which provides the standard for Israel's tents (8:2). According to Lane, the "'true tabernacle' is used not in contrast to what is false, but to what is symbolic and imperfect."[41] In other words, ἀληθινῆς means that the heavenly tabernacle is Firstspace: it is the concrete reality. As the LXX text says, God himself erected the true tabernacle. This means that the heavenly sanctuary is made by the original designer—he is the master builder and the heavenly tabernacle is his original construction.

Furthermore, the heavenly tabernacle is the location of God's throne where Jesus is seated at his right hand (8:1), which was introduced in 1:3 and repeated in the immediate context of the association of the heavenly tabernacle with a concrete existence.[42] The location of Jesus in Firstspace makes the descriptions of Jesus in Hebrews precise—it gives him a physicality that prevents abstraction.[43] As Moffitt argues, such a description presupposes a physical resurrection[44] consistent with the oral and written traditions of the early church.

The obvious discrepancy between the categorization of the heavenly tabernacle as Firstspace and Soja's description, is that although the heavenly tabernacle was

---

[39] Many are confident that Hebrews could not have been written after 70 CE because the author uses the present tense to refer to ongoing priestly activity (e.g., 7:27-28; 8:3-5; 9:7-8, 25; 10:1-3, 8; 13:10-11). However, verbal aspect theory would indicate that dating cannot be based on tense alone, as argued by Stanley E. Porter, *Verbal Aspect and the Greek New Testament with Reference to Tense and Mood* (SBG; New York: Peter Lang, 1989). On the other hand, Marie E. Isaacs, for example, argued that Hebrews was an attempt to find sacred space after the loss of the temple in *Sacred Space: An Approach to the Theology of the Epistle to the Hebrews* (JSNTSup 73; Sheffield: Sheffield Academic Press, 1992).

[40] Καὶ ὡσεὶ σκηναί ἃς ἔπηξεν κύριος (Num. 24:6 LXX).

[41] Lane, *Hebrews 1-8*, pp. 205-06.

[42] An allusion to Ps. 110:1, but the phrase perhaps was also influenced by Zech. 6:13 LXX.

[43] This is not a Platonic ideal or abstraction, the point of the relationship is not chronological/eschatological, and there is no need to see typology for the covenant relationships as in A. Cody, *Heavenly Sanctuary and Liturgy in the Epistle to the Hebrews: The Achievement of Salvation in the Epistle's Perspectives* (St. Meinrad, IN: Grail, 1960), p. 151.

[44] Moffitt, *Atonement*, p. 41.

supposed to exist in the author's and recipients' present time, it could not be observed and measured by the recipients because it was not visible. This would have been a problem for the original recipients as well as Soja. In 11:1-3, the author of Hebrews explicitly subverts definitions of the physical, concrete, and real as observable: faith is reality (ὑπόστασις) of things hoped for.[45] Faith consists of certainty in the unseen (οὐ βλεπομένων), and in the context, this refers to what is unseen in the past, present, or future (past creation and acts of faith, the present race, the ancestors' hope in what was ahead), so that this is by no means an explicit reference to the eschatological future. That which is seen is derivative from the ὑπόστασις; it is not made from what is visible (μὴ ἐκ φαινομένων).

The unseen "realities" (τῶν πραγμάτων) in 10:1 are the heavenly temple and those actions associated with the ministry of Jesus in the heavenly tabernacle (9:11): the "good things [that are now here]" (τῶν γενομένων ἀγαθῶν/ τῶν μελλόντων ἀγαθῶν) are. Attridge states that Jesus's priesthood, sacrifice, and the temple are in view in 10:1, and says in 10:1, "the futurity of the 'good things' is defined primarily in relationship to the law and not to the present condition of the addressees."[46] In linguistic terms, the deictic center of the future reference is the past. Together with the author's claims in 8:5 that the heavenly tabernacle has provided the design for the earthly one, we see that the author of Hebrews argues that the earthly tabernacle is a sketch and shadow of the original underlying reality and therefore may be treated as a map that represents the heavenly tabernacle. The author's language is evocative of Platonic thought, but as Attridge argues, "The use of that language is . . . playfully rhetorical . . . . Our author indulges to the full his penchant for dramatically exploiting the polyvalence of his language."[47] Firstspace is not Platonic imagery—the heavenly tabernacle is so concrete that it casts a shadow. Therefore, the author describes the heavenly tabernacle as a concrete reality that may be associated with Firstspace. He claims that its invisibility is consistent with a biblical understanding of reality.

Secondspace: The earthly tabernacle

The author describes the earthly tabernacle, which had been visible, as Secondspace. It is a symbol that points to the reality and a map from which the heavenly space can be described. In a sense, the author's description of the earthly tabernacle can be compared to the study of a statue that is labeled by art historians and art museum curators as a "Roman copy of a Greek Original." Experts on ancient art in the nineteenth century were primarily interested in recovering traces of the lost Greek originals through *Kopienkritik*,

---

[45] The definition of ὑπόστασις in 11:1 is therefore constrained by the author's representation of the heavenly tabernacle that was described in Hebrews 8–10 as Firstspace: it corresponds to "substance, actual existence, reality" in *LSJ* III.2. But see Attridge, *Hebrews*, pp. 308–10 for five alternative interpretations of ὑπόστασις. However, Attridge also favors "reality," a metonymy in which "the act or virtue of faith is described in terms of its end or goal," p. 310.

[46] See Attridge, *Hebrews*, p. 269.

[47] Attridge, *Hebrews*, p. 271. Note the similarity to the postmodern theory of intertextuality where meanings of words and texts change when they are used in new contexts, and a new meaning is created. In the case of Hebrews, his language is tied to Platonic and apocalyptic intertexts, but he creates new meaning with them.

reflecting Platonic values in regarding copies as inferior to the original. However, within the last fifty years, experts have argued that Roman "copies" not only preserved the prototype, but were works of art in their own right that served specific religious and civic functions in the Roman culture that the originals did not have in the Greek culture.[48] We shall see that the author of Hebrews similarly uses a methodology that recovers traces of the original that cannot be seen from the narrative of the inauguration of the covenant in Exodus 24: the mapping of the tabernacle in Exodus 25–30, 35–40, and the intention for its function in Leviticus 16. The exegetical payoff comes through his distinction of the *differences* in function between the heavenly tabernacle and the specific religious functions of the copy, which will correspond to Thirdspace.

In a description of the Levitic priesthood, the author of Hebrews quotes Exod. 25:40 LXX in 8:5 to show that the "sanctuary" in which the Levitic priests serve is Secondspace. It is a copy (ὑποδείγματι) and shadow (σκιᾷ) of what is in heaven. The author states that when Moses was about to build the tabernacle, God warns Moses to be sure to "make everything according to the pattern that was shown you on the mountain" (ποιήσεις πάντα κατὰ τὸν τύπον τὸν δειχθέντα σοι ἐν τῷ ὄρει). Therefore, the earthly tabernacle is not the implementation of a blueprint design or a direct copy of the original so much as a copy of a map (τὸν τύπον) which was drawn from the original construction—which makes the earthly tabernacle two stages removed from the original which is accessed through the "traces" in the Mosaic "map" in Exodus 25–30. The temple in Jerusalem was three stages removed from the original.[49] The law (a synecdoche for the Second Temple institutions) is only a shadow (σκιάν) of the realities of the heavenly tabernacle, the ministry of Christ, the once and for all sacrifice and the covenant (10:1).[50]

If read with Platonic categories and values, this would indeed be a pejorative description, and the author's language has been understood as pointing to the inferiority and essential corruption of Judaism, in essence vindicating the Roman destruction of the temple and the ministry of the Levitic priesthood and proving the necessity of the supersession of the institutions of Judaism by Christianity. If the heavenly institutions of Judaism are interpreted as Secondspace, not so much. Firstspace and Secondspace

---

[48] The first to argue the enculturated function of Roman copies of Greek art was Brunilde S. Ridgway, *Roman Copies of Greek Sculpture: The Problem of the Originals* (Ann Arbor: University of Michigan Press, 1984). However, in many ways, the practice of architectural mimicry has a closer correspondence. See, for example, Bianca Basker, *Original Copies: Architectural Mimicry in Contemporary China (Spatial Habitus)* (Honolulu: University of Hawaii Press, 2013).

[49] The Herodian temple is described by Flavius Josephus, *Wars of the Jews*, 5:5, *Apion* 2.8,103-109; and in the Mishna, though there is some discrepancy both between the descriptions and with the archaeological evidence (which has larger dimensions). The Herodian temple allegedly followed the floor dimensions of the Tabernacle and the set up for the Holy Place and the Holy of Holies but it significantly reinterpreted the space of the tabernacle, not only in building materials, elements of style, and its permanent location, but also in features such as height (following Solomon's temple), the addition of side rooms and enormous outer courtyards.

[50] Contra an eschatological understanding of the present participle μελλόντων in the word group τῶν μελλόντων ἀγαθῶν (Heb. 10:1). It appears to be based on a time-based view of tense which finds a contrast with the aorist participle in the word group τῶν γενομένων ἀγαθῶν (Heb. 9:11). Rather, 9:11 constrains 10:1 so that they have the same referent. The change in tense to present highlights the comparison between the law and the things that have now come: the heavenly tabernacle, Jesus's ministry, once-and-for-all sacrifice and the New Covenant.

exist in a symbiotic relationship. The identification of Firstspace does not eliminate the existence, function, and importance of Secondspace.

Instead of reading the authors' representation of the institutions of Judaism as pejorative and secessionist, identifying his representation of the function of the tabernacle and its associated aspects as Secondspace opens up new possibilities. The temple was "dominated space" by the dominant Jewish culture in Palestine and Christian Jews were a minority. Most of scholarship dates the book of Hebrews as being written during the Great Revolt or after. If that is the case, the author's claim in 8:13 that God made the first covenant obsolete and it will soon disappear is either an accurate prediction or an historic evaluation.[51] The temple and the ministry of the Levitic priesthood in the temple were central to the maintenance of the Mosaic Covenant; it was destroyed in 70 CE, but the process began in 66 CE, and the conflicts that led up to the destruction predated Jesus's ministry. The temple and priesthood have remained out of commission for nearly 2,000 years. By going back to the foundations of the Mosaic Covenant and the prototype for the temple and priesthood, the author articulates a belief that the institutions of Judaism are accurate maps of heaven itself, ascribing a value to their representations that outlasts, relativizes, and overcomes their "disappearance." The spatial information is a key, arguably the master key, to the author's hermeneutic in this unique contribution to Christology.

Thirdspace: The presence and participation of Jesus and the recipients

Thirdspace is how the space is actually used. Pious contemporary Jews would agree with the author of Hebrews that any ministry that took place in the heavenly sanctuary in the presence of God on his throne (as in Isaiah 6) is superior to or has priority or precedence over any ministry in the tabernacle or temple on earth. However, whether or not Jesus occupies the heavenly sanctuary and ministers there would be a major point of contention. The author bases his understanding on the messianic reading of Ps. 110 (109):1, in which the author interprets the spatial reference to Jesus's enthronement in heaven literally—as the messiah; Jesus literally sat down at the right hand of the majesty on high, which places him seated in the heavenly temple. Another major point of contention would be the author's conclusion that those who follow Jesus could occupy and use that space, particularly in the way that the author of Hebrews claims. Within the worldview of Second Temple Judaism, the exhortations of Hebrews for the recipients to enter the Holy of Holies (10:19-22) and eat from the heavenly altar (13:10) were absolutely "transgression[s] of the Secondspace intention."[52]

---

[51] It is interesting that the record of the Mosaic tabernacle itself was one of transition and obsolescence, which may provide support for the author's argument. After the location at Shiloh until the time of Eli when the ark was taken by the Philistines, the Mosaic tabernacle was moved to Nob, then placed at Gibeon (1 Chron. 21:29; 2 Chron. 1:3). However, David built a tent for the ark in Jerusalem (1 Chron. 15:1), and then Solomon and the assembly brought the tabernacle and the furnishings to Solomon's temple in Jerusalem and stored the Mosaic tabernacle (2 Chron. 5:4–5).

[52] As mentioned above, "to change and appropriate it," Berquist, "Critical Spatiality," p. 183.

The author of Hebrews treats the heavenly sanctuary as a space dominated by Second Temple Judaism. He claims that the space has been changed and appropriated[53] because of the biblical alternatives caused by Jesus's sacrifice and enthronement. His argument challenges both Jewish and Greek "illusions" of reality. However, the author of Hebrews parts company with Soja and Lefebvre's postmodern relativism and revolutionary subversion. He does not believe that he *creates* alternatives or that his *imagination* is *playing* with the space of the heavenly temple; he attempts to demonstrate that it is faith that is informed and supported by a literal reading of texts such as Exodus 25–30, 35–40 and Leviticus 16, which he interprets with the spatial reference to enthronement in Ps. 110:1 (109 LXX),[54] which was an important messianic Psalm in the early church.[55]

Rather than portraying the recipients as marginalized, he presents them as in line with and literally in the company of the ancestors (11:2) who were commended for their faith—in 12:1, he describes the ancestors as a cloud of witness that surrounded the recipients (περικείμενον ἡμῖν νέφος μαρτύρων). On the other hand, the author places the emphasis on identifying the recipients with faithful ancestors who were marginalized in their earthly context: they were identified with those who were persecuted, forced into migration, homeless, tortured, and killed/murdered (11:35-38): those "of whom the world was not worthy" (11:38). As I said elsewhere, "Chapter 11 constrains both the nature of the race for the recipients in 12:1 (sojourning, reversal, suffering and death) and the scene in heavenly Jerusalem in terms of the existence outside of the city and its inhabitants."[56] The recipients who follow Jesus are told that they have access to the heavenly alter in the heavenly tabernacle, where they are nourished by grace (13:9).[57] But as far as their location on earth, they appear to be on the verge of losing their place like many of the exemplars listed in chapter 11. Therefore, I suggest that there is ample evidence in Hebrews that indicates that the exhortations in Hebrews are a form of "collective resistance," which has much in common with contemporary theory about Thirdspace.

This description poignantly parallels the condition of Christian Jews,[58] particularly following the inception of the Great Revolt in 66 CE. Christian Jews in Palestine,

---

[53] Ramirez, *Other Spaces*, p. 24.
[54] Attridge identifies an allusion to Ps. 110:1 (109 LXX) in 1:3: "Reference to Christ's exaltation is made through allusion to *the key scriptural text*" in *Hebrews*', p. 46. The citations of and allusions to 110:1 occur in 1:13; 8:1; 10:12 and 12:2.
[55] For the importance of Psalm 110 (109 LXX), see George W. E. Nickelsburg, *Glory at the Right Hand: Ps. 110 in Early Christianity* (SBLMS 18; Nashville: Abigndon, 1973).
[56] Cynthia Long Westfall, *A Discourse Analysis of the Letter to the Hebrews: The Relationship between Form and Meaning* (LNTS 297; London: T&T Clark, 2005), p. 262.
[57] But for an alternate reading of 13:9, see Gelardini, who combines Critical Spatial theory with literary criticism (use of chiasm) and the use of "intertexts" in "Critical Spatiality," pp. 221–22. The altar is "determined metaphorically" through a chiastic link with 13:15-16 to mean the sacrifices of the "lips" of the people, so that the food is offered to God.
[58] Daniel Boyarin suggested that the correct term for the faith of Jewish believers in Jesus should be "Christian Judaism" in *Dying for God: Martyrdom and the Making of Christianity and Judaism* (Stanford, CA: Stanford University Press, 1999), p. 20. At the 2007 Annual Meeting of the Society of Biblical Literature in San Diego, in the Jewish Christianity session on November 19, Daniel Boyarin was a panelist in the review of Skarsaune and Hvalvik and delivered a paper: "Definitions, Sources, and Aims." He repeated his suggestion that the correct term should be "Christian Judaism" rather than "Jewish Christianity," which marks a shift in terminology.

Samaria, and numerous other places disrupted by the Jewish-Roman wars literally had to access Jesus "outside of the city" (13:13-14) because they were in the process of being alienated from their homeland, their family/people, the Roman Empire and their local community of faith and forced into migration if they were not killed or enslaved.[59]

Three problems make it difficult to recognize the context of Hebrews as one of marginalization. The first problem is the absence of any explicit information about the identity of the author and recipients and the date of composition.[60] The other two problems involve analyzing and drawing inferences from the information that is available in the text, and being able to distinguish it from the interpretive frames that we have inherited that may influence us unduly. The center of leadership in the early church was moved from Jerusalem and from Christian Jews as a direct result of what can only be described as a series of genocidal military actions by Rome against the Jews. Subsequently, leadership in the early church shifted to churches in cities dominated by Gentile believers, who in turn came into positions of power in the Roman Empire as it became the official religion of the Roman Empire.[61] Subsequently Christendom became established in Western Europe and political power held by Christian leaders was used to persecute the Jews. These historical developments and a multitude of related factors create intertextual layers in the history of the interpretation of the "Jewishness" of Hebrews which are complicated by the absence/loss of information about the author and recipients.

The second problem is the recognition of and empathy for the social location of the author of Hebrews. Regardless of the identity of the recipients, the consensus of scholarship is that the author was a Hellenist Jew, but the contextual dots are seldom connected in a way that adequately impacts the reading of Hebrews. Until recently, not enough has been said about the role of Christian Judaism in the early church.[62] Similarly, little is said about the incredibly difficult position of Christian Jews (either in Palestine or the diaspora), and how that might be reflected in the book of Hebrews: the author portrayed himself and the recipients as the faithful remnants in line with the Jewish ancestors (1:1, 11:2), and there should be no doubt that the author himself

---

[59] For an expanded description of the social location of Christian Jews in the Roman Empire, see Cynthia Long Westfall, "Running the Gamut: The Varied Responses to Empire in Jewish Christianity," in *Empire in the New Testament* (ed. Stanley E. Porter and Cynthia Long Westfall; Bingham Colloquium Series; Eugene, OR: Pickwick, 2010), pp. 230–58.

[60] For an overview of the issues of authorship dating and recipients/addressees, see Attridge, *Hebrews*, pp. 1–13.

[61] The church did not forget that Rome had persecuted the Christians, and yet with political power, the church identified with the Roman Empire rather than its Roman origins and the Roman Empire was evaluated positively by the church and later church historians. Protestants, who may deplore Constantine, would still accentuate the benefits of the Roman Empire for the advancement of Christianity.

[62] For an overview of the discussion of Christian Judaism, see Matt Jackson-McCabe, "What's in a Name? The Problem of Jewish Christianity" in *Jewish Christianity Reconsidered: Rethinking Ancient Groups and Texts* (ed. Matt Jackson-McCabe; Minneapolis: Fortress, 2007), pp. 10–38. Christian Judaism became more of a focus in the beginning of the twenty-first century. See Matt Jackson-McCabe, ed., *Jewish Christianity Reconsidered: Rethinking Ancient Groups and Texts* (Minneapolis: Fortress, 2007), Oskar Skarsaune and Reidar Hvalvik, eds., *Jewish Believers in Jesus: The Early Centuries* (Peabody, MA: Hendrickson, 2007), Skarsaune, *In the Shadow of the Temple: Jewish Influences on Early Christianity* (Downers Grove, IN: IVP Academic, 2008) and Daniel Boyarin, *The Jewish Gospels: The Story of the Jewish Christ* (New York: The New Press, 2012).

was marginalized in his relationship to land, temple, and tribe/family and occupied a difficult social position within the Roman Empire. It is ironic that early Christianity's identification with Judaism has been thought to be a political advantage. This would only be true from the vantage point of Christian gentiles who would not have reaped the consequences of the conflicts between ethnic Jews and the Roman Empire. Christian Jews were persecuted by the Roman Empire as Jews *and* as Christians and marginalized by the Jewish population to a degree that rarely if ever happened to the Christian gentiles from the beginning of the early church (cf. 1 Thess. 2:14).

The third problem is the nature of the history of interpretation: triumphalist readings of Hebrews within Christendom have dominated, utilized by a church and Reformation traditions that yielded political power. That is, those in positions of power appropriated and interpreted a text that was written from a marginalized Jew to the marginalized.[63] This has resulted in a misreading of Hebrews. Interpreting the text from the centers of power of the dominant cultures resulted in a much different alternative reality than that which is described by the author: the text of Hebrews became a "dominated space" (Secondspace) that was used as a weapon against the marginalized Jews, so that the arguably most Jewish book in the NT has been interpreted as anti-Semitic and as discounting the central institutions of Judaism on which its argument depends.[64]

Interpreting the temple with Critical Spatial Theory gives us a tool with which we can identify and highlight certain features that characterize the author's interpretation of the Torah and of the heavenly temple. With the sacrifice of Jesus for sins came a revelation or new teaching of a use of the heavenly tabernacle and a function of priesthood that was not accepted by Jews who did not accept Jesus as their Messiah. Therefore, it was a form of subversion of the dominant Jewish understanding of the "use" of the heavenly tabernacle that had implications for the use of the earthly temple. Furthermore, once the author has established the heavenly tabernacle as Firstspace (concrete and specific), he urges the recipients to "literally" follow Jesus into the

---

[63] Although most Hebrews scholars have assumed that the recipients of Hebrews were Jewish, it has recently become in vogue to argue that the recipients were predominantly Gentiles or a mixed group of Christian Jews and Gentiles, as favored by David A. deSilva, *Perseverance in Gratitude: A Socio-Rhetorical Commentary on the Epistle "to the Hebrews"* (Grand Rapids, MI: Eerdmans, 2000), pp. 2–7. The inclusion of Gentiles as recipients works well with those who assume a Roman destination on the basis of 13:24 (those from Italy greet you). See Koester, *Hebrews*, pp. 49–50, in which the Jewish orientation is explained by the foundation of the church by Jewish Christians, but Paul's epistle to the Romans shows recipients who "would have related to the dominant Greco-Roman culture, Jewish subculture, and Christian community" (p. 48). However, this would apply to a Jewish Christian community, notwithstanding that the author does not address circumcision. It is beyond the purposes of this chapter to extensively argue that the "ideal recipient" was a Christian Jew and to argue against a Roman destination. It is enough to rest on the overwhelming consensus that the author was a Christian Jew. Therefore, the content of Hebrews accurately reflects the context(s) of Christian Jews, and the author believes that his teaching, which assumes and addresses marginalization, is superlatively relevant to marginalized recipients in their time of crisis (4:16).

[64] As J. C. McCollough asserts in "Anti-Semitism in Hebrews?" *IBS* 20 (1978), pp. 30–45, "There has been massive anti-Jewish use made of Hebrews in Christian history (p. 33). The view that Hebrews is a polemic written to prevent the recipients from 'returning to Judaism'" has dominated the study of Hebrews nearly until the twenty-first century. See Lloyd Kim, *Polemic in the Book of Hebrews: Anti-Judaism, Anti-Semitism, Supersessionism?* (PTM 64; Eugene, OR: Wipf & Stock, 2006). It is the position of this chapter that the author does not believe that either he or the community has left Judaism.

heavenly sanctuary (10:19-22). The author's exhortations to the recipients were in many ways comparable to the spatial strategies of the recent "Occupy Movement"[65] as a response to "their time of need" (4:16) which encompasses social and political threats that potentially ranged from social alienation to death.[66] In 13:13 they were exhorted to go to Jesus outside the "camp" (ἔξω τῆς παρεμβολῆς), and in doing so they too were functioning as priests and occupying the true tabernacle.

Correlation, disambiguation, and application

Through an interpretation of the heavenly sanctuary as Firstspace and the earthly tabernacle as Secondspace, we possess helpful critical tools with which we can throw light on how the author is able to arrive at his representation of Jesus as High Priest through basic foundations of the faith (Jesus's life and teaching) passed on though eyewitnesses (2:1-4; 5:11-6:6), including the belief that Jesus provided a sacrifice for our sins, a messianic understanding of Psalm 110, and access to the LXX—he exegetes the spatial references to the tabernacle and its use with Jesus's sacrifice in the heavenly tabernacle.

The author believes that the instructions and description of the earthly tabernacle in Exodus 25-30 and 35-40 have a direct correlation to the heavenly tabernacle and its physicality. In 8:5, the author quotes God's warning from Exod. 25:40, in which Moses is warned to make the tabernacle according to the pattern. The author adds the word "everything" (πάντα) to the LXX text: "Make *everything* according to the pattern."[67] The point is stressed that every detail in the earthly tabernacle corresponded to the heavenly tabernacle. The only exceptions were the differences between Christ's ministry in Firstspace and the Levitical ministry on earth in Secondspace, though there is still analogical continuity, such as the statement in 8:3: "For every high priest is appointed to offer gifts and sacrifices; hence it is necessary for this priest also to have something to offer." So even though the nature of Christ's ministry redefined aspects of service in the heavenly temple, the nature of the earthly ministry still required a general correspondence with the heavenly one.[68] For the author of Hebrews, the features of the earthly tabernacle would require us to find certain features in the heavenly one.

---

[65] For the application of Spatial Theory and Critical Spatial Theory to the Occupy Movement, see Sarah Heck, "Space, Politics and Occupy Wall Street." (MA Thesis, Georgia State University, 2014), http://scholarworks.gsu.edu/geosciences_theses/76.

[66] There is considerable debate about the threats that the recipients of Hebrews were facing. See Bryan R. Dyer's description of the various views and his convincing methodology and argument about the context of suffering in Hebrews in Suffering in the Face of Death: The Epistle to the Hebrews and Its Context of Situation (LNTS 568; London: T&T Clark, 2017).

[67] Compare 8:5, ποιήσεις πάντα κατὰ τὸν τύπον τὸν δειχθέντα σοι ἐν τῷ ὄρει, with Exodus 25:40 LXX, ποιήσεις κατὰ τὸν τύπον τὸν δεδειγμένον σοι ἐν τῷ ὄρει. However, Philo also includes πάντα (*Leg. All.* 3.102; *Quaest. in Exod.* 2.52), so it is possible that they were using the same variant, though Philo does not include πάντα in *Quaest. in Exod.* 2.82, 90. See Craig R. Koester, *Hebrews: A New Translation with Introduction and Commentary* (Anchor; New York: Doubleday, 2001), p. 378.

[68] Koester says, "Details of Levitical ministry correspond in a general rather than an exact way to Jesus's ministry," in *Hebrews*, p. 404.

Similarly, the author saw a direct correlation between the effects of Jesus's sacrifice and the actions associated with Day of Atonement in Leviticus 16. Thus the author's claims are characterized by literal *correlations* between the Secondspace intended use of the earthly tabernacle which is described/mapped in the Torah and what occurs in Firstspace. However, the person, life, death, and resurrection of Jesus provides an interpretive grid for *disambiguation*, because Jesus accounts for the significant differences between the way that the earthly tabernacle was used and the way that the heavenly tabernacle is used in the areas of priesthood, atonement/sacrifice, and covenant: what cannot be applied to Jesus cannot be applied to the heavenly tabernacle.

The author finds both continuity (assumed) and discontinuity inferred from the particular ways that Jesus's person and activity are not the same as that of the priests in the earthly tabernacle. Therefore, on the basis of the effects of the atonement on the followers of Jesus,[69] and the fact that they are partners with Jesus in his holy calling (2:5–3:1), the author is able to make *applications* of Jesus's high priesthood in the heavenly sanctuary to the recipients that enable them to find the face of God, live in his presence, and find his grace in their time of crisis (4:16//10:19-22; 12:1-3, 22-28).[70]

Where did the author of Hebrews locate the atonement?

From a spatial standpoint, there should be no debate as to where Jesus made atonement according to Hebrews. As Moffitt claims, when the author "specifies where Jesus offered his sacrifice, he *always* locates that offering in heaven."[71] The question is, how do we understand the nature of that location and how does that impact our understanding of the timing? We find the author's description of the heavenly tabernacle at various places in 8:1–10:22, but I will focus the discussion on 8:1-5 and 9:1-14.

While the ministry of Jesus, and particularly the once-for-all sacrifice, has a location in past time, the physicality of the heavenly sanctuary itself is not qualified by temporal indicators.[72] The author associates the sanctuary with the eternal throne of God, and according to the prophets of Israel and Second Temple Jewish sources, we can place that throne inside the tabernacle with confidence.

---

[69] The followers of Jesus are those who move forward together in response to God's message through Jesus (4:11-13//10:23), who hold on to the foundations of their faith (4:14–15//10:24-25), and who follow Jesus into the heavenly sanctuary (4:16//10:19-22). The hortatory subjunctive commands to move forward, hold on, and draw near utilize spatial metaphor and are repeated throughout Hebrews, and represent the message of the discourse, which is hortatory/rhetorical. See Westfall, *Discourse Analysis of Hebrews*, pp. 297–98.

[70] The effect of the teaching on the recipients is similar to the commands in Col. 3:2-4, "Think about the things that are above (τὰ ἄνω), and not about the things that are on earth (τὰ ἐπὶ τῆς γῆς), because you died and your life is concealed together with Christ in God." The author of Hebrews is able to utilize the Jewish institutions to represent the realities of τὰ ἄνω (Col. 3:2) in a way that pragmatically reframes the believers' existence so that they can occupy the Firstspace of the heavenly sanctuary and experience the partnership with Christ in his heavenly calling (3:1).

[71] Moffitt, *Atonement*, p. 218.

[72] Some think of aspects or use of the heavenly sanctuary in temporal categories in apocalyptic or eschatological analyses. For example, C. K. Barrett, "The Eschatology of the Epistle to the Hebrews" in *The Background of the New Testament and Its Eschatology* (ed. W. D. Davies and D. Daube (Cambridge: Cambridge University Press, 1954)).

According to theories of place, these spatial expressions make the description of Jesus as high priest precise—it gives him a physicality that prevents abstraction.[73] The author provides the reader with a concrete structure of place in which Jesus's identity as high priest is established and worked out—which is the function of place according to Malpas.[74] Once the author establishes the concrete reality and existence of the heavenly tabernacle, he establishes the reader's self-identity as it relates to that same place in 10:19-22.

In my initial discussion of place, I said that place was finite while space is infinite and universal. At first blush, we might theologically gravitate toward an understanding in which Jesus's attributes are infinite, reflecting the divine attribute. However, in regards to the place of his priesthood, the Hebrews writer states that Jesus is finite in 8:4: "Now if he were on earth, he would not be a priest at all, since there are priests who offer gifts according to the law."

Furthermore, the language about the earthly tabernacle itself is positive rather than pejorative—it is elevated by the association with the heavenly tabernacle. However, the nature of the ministry of the high priest and the sacrifices also indicates the limitation of the high priest and the superficial purification provided by the high priest's sacrifices. According to 9:8, the way into the inner holy place had not been revealed while the first tabernacle was still standing. The inner holy place of the earthly tabernacle represents the presence of God in a literal sense. There is some ambiguity about whether the "first" tabernacle would extend to the temple, but regardless, the people literally could not go into God's presence in the earthly sanctuary—that is, the "way" in the sense of a road or path was not open.

As said above, it is widely agreed that the author is applying a template from the instructions for the Day of Atonement in Leviticus 16 in order to exegete the nature of Jesus's sacrifice. The details of the sacrifice by necessity are different in nature, location, and temporal aspects, but there is continuity in the process. The sacrifice (the death of Jesus) is done outside of the actual tabernacle (outside the camp), and the high priest carries the blood into the holy place to make atonement in both cases.[75] Specifically,

---

[73] This is not a Platonic ideal or abstraction; the point of the relationship is not chronological/eschatological, and there is no compelling necessity to see typology for the covenant relationships as in A. Cody, *Heavenly Sanctuary and Liturgy in the Epistle to the Hebrews: The Achievement of Salvation in the Epistle's Perspectives*, p. 151.

[74] J. E. Malpas states, "Narrative is that which can be seen as structuring . . . both memory and self-identity, as well as the places, the landscapes, in which self identity is itself worked out and established" in *Place and Experience: A Philosophical Topography* (Cambridge: Cambridge University Press, 1999), p. 185.

[75] Contra Moffitt's de-emphasis of the significance of the death of Jesus in Hebrews. The author explicitly states that Christ's death is a ransom (θανάτου γενομένου εἰς ἀπολύτρωσιν) that sets those who are called free from the transgressions committed under the first covenant (9:15). In regards to the New Covenant, he states that it is necessary to *prove* the death of the one who makes a covenant/will to put it into effect (9:16), and concluded in the immediate context that without the shedding of blood which cleanses all things, there is no forgiveness (9:22). Still, the point is well-taken that Jesus's death was one element in the process of atonement, and that (according to Hebrews) it was not complete until he offered the blood in the heavenly sanctuary (9:12; cf. 1:3, 7:27). Also, the point is well-taken that the author did not limit Jesus's sacrifice to his blood—he explicitly offered *himself* (7:27) and his *body* (σώματος Ἰησοῦ Χριστοῦ in 10:10) to perfect believers, and his priestly service during his time on earth is described as offering prayers, petitions, fervent cries, and tears (5:7).

Lev. 16:15-16 says that after the sacrifice is made, the priest was to "bring its blood inside the curtain, and do with its blood as he did with the blood of the bull, sprinkling it upon the mercy seat and before the mercy seat. Thus he shall make atonement" (Lev. 16:15-16). So the process of atonement started with the sacrifice but was not complete until the blood was physically brought into the inner holy place and offered.

In a minor discourse peak in 9:11-14,[76] Christ travels on the corresponding path in the heavenly tabernacle, and the recipients have quite "a visual" for that journey. Christ's ministry in the heavenly tabernacle is described in such a manner that emphasizes the spatial journey through the heavens and the physical context of the tabernacle. It emphatically evokes all the previous literal detail of both the earthly and the heavenly tabernacles (9:1-10): *coming* (παραγενόμενος) through the greater and more perfect tent that was not made by human hands, he went into (εἰσῆλθεν) the inner holy place (9:11).[77] The author has made an effort to render the heavenly tabernacle as physical and concrete and to make Christ's person and presence real and tangible/physical. Even more, his spatial understanding of the heavenly tabernacle authenticates Christ's function as high priest as convincing and authentic for those Jewish Christians who would not accept a non-Levitic high priest in the temple in Jerusalem.[78] The author declares that that is the place where Christ found or obtained redemption once and for all (9:12). As the author says in 1:3, after he made purification, he sat down at the right hand of the Father (1:3, 8; 8:1; 10:12). The hermeneutic importance of Ps. 110:1 (109 LXX) is indicated in 1:3 and 10:12: the author states that when Christ had offered for all time a single sacrifice for sins, "he sat down at the right hand of God," and since then has been waiting "until his enemies would be made a footstool for his feet." The author combines the early church confession of the sacrifice of Christ with this description of him as offering his sacrifice then "sitting" and "waiting" enthroned in heaven. The information does not correspond well with confining the location of the offering for the atonement on the cross. The description of Christ "sitting and waiting" after he died on the cross leaves no room for the three days in the tomb after his death on the cross, his resurrection, the over 500 post-resurrection appearances and his ascension. No place exists without a time, so . . . where in time is the location of the author's description of place?

The author does not discuss how his teaching fits into the sequence of events in the gospel narratives, but it unlikely that he was unaware of the central confessions about Jesus's death, resurrection, and ascension transmitted in the oral tradition that are included in the Gospels and the Pauline corpus. In fact, one may infer with

---

[76] For identification of 9:11-14 as a minor discourse peak, see Westfall, *Hebrews*, p. 205.

[77] While this material has some relative prominence, and certainly plays a role in our understanding of the author's use of space, there is no signaling in the text that would mark v. 11 as the "heart of the discourse," as claimed by Albert Vanhoye, *Structure and Message of the Epistle to the Hebrews* (Rome: Editrice Pontificio Instituto Biblico, 1989), p. 36. See a critique of Vanhoye's symmetrical arrangement which is the rationale for Vanhoye's claim that 9:11 is the keystone of the discourse in Westfall, *Hebrews*, p. 10.

[78] The extensive description and defense of Jesus's priesthood according to the Melchizedek would be unnecessary for a Gentile audience. The purpose of the vivid spatial description is to provide the recipients with a concrete context (tabernacle), together with an effective procedure (priesthood, sacrifice, and covenant) which enables the recipients to draw near to God, which reflects the heart of the message. See Westfall, *Hebrews*, p. 241.

confidence that the oral tradition about the life and teaching of Jesus refers to the content of the confession that he wants the recipients to hang onto (2:1; 4:14; 10:23), and he clearly wants to assume basics as a given such as the resurrection of the dead in 6:2 (ἀναστάσεώς τε νεκρῶν) in order to move on to more advanced teaching (6:1). Regardless, the most natural understanding of the relationship between the heavenly sanctuary and the atonement is that the author wanted the recipients to believe that it was a real and concrete place that a real and concrete resurrected (embodied) Jesus entered, and that was the time when the process of the atonement was completed. If we follow the author's hermeneutic, the time span needed for Jesus's atonement would differ by necessity from the time span of the Day of Atonement in Leviticus 16—the passage of time (e.g., "Day") had no semantic value because the author's exegesis was based on spatial references.[79] He associates the entrance of the high priest into the Holy of Holies with the time of Jesus's enthronement and he is not concerned with the passing of hours or days. In fact, some scholars correlate Jesus's second coming in 9:28 with the reappearance of the High Priest to the people.[80] Regardless of discrepancies in timing that shift with the application of a Christological lens, the correspondence of place and process stay the same, and the final act of the atonement does not occur in the place where the sacrifice occurs.

How do we interpret the space and time of the atonement?

I have described the author's language about the heavenly sanctuary and the earthly tabernacle in terms of Firstspace and Secondspace, arguing that the heavenly sanctuary is described as a finite physical and concrete place that is literally occupied by a physical and concrete Jesus. However, when composing a theology of atonement, we interpret the author's language and find theological meaning that is consistent with our own understanding of reality or theology.[81] Twenty-first century interpreters cannot adopt the worldview of a Second Temple Jew, but perhaps spatial theory and the "recovery" of the meaning of place can bring the two worldviews into dialogue.

There seems to be an assumption among many scholars that if the heavenly tabernacle is unseen, then it must be either abstract, metaphorical, or "a future reality that shapes our present according to our contemporary definitions." The assumptions

---

[79] But with the position that the atonement was completed on the cross, the timing, place, and process of atonement differ far more radically.

[80] For example, see Brooke Foss Westcott, *The Epistle to the Hebrews* (3rd ed.; London: Macmillan, 1909), p. 278. However, as Attridge says, "the phrase indicates that Christ's second coming will not have the atoning function of the first," in *Hebrews*, p. 266.

[81] For example, Schenck, *Eschatology in Hebrews*, p. 8, argues that the author must be using the tabernacle in "several different metaphorical ways that do not cohere with one another," rejecting any literal referent in heaven primarily because of the need for cleansing of the heavenly tabernacle in 9:23, saying, "How could something in heaven need cleansed (*sic*)?" Such a necessity is obviously inconsistent with Schenck's theology of heaven, so much that he assumes that the author had to be dealing with metaphors. However, the author's correlation of the cleansing of the Mosaic tabernacle with the cleansing of the heavenly sanctuary is actually an excellent illustration of the literal hermeneutic that the author was using. We cannot access the author's intention or assume a discrepancy between his language and his theology without further evidence.

of allegory or metaphor or eschatology are therefore sometimes taken as a starting point, which conveniently relativizes the problem of timing. However, perhaps in view of the contemporary recovery of the importance of place, we should be reluctant to dismiss the significance of the author's spatial references, adjectives that describe space and the hermeneutics of the author. In fact, the message of the author explicitly specifies that the heavenly tabernacle is not abstract. The author is committed to making the heavenly tabernacle as more physical and concrete than the earthly tabernacle in the OT narrative, which, significantly, was also unseen—it had not been used for centuries. That is why the author devotes unusual attention to the description of the earthly tabernacle, and then states that he wanted to add more detail but was unable to do it—he did not have the time or space to do an exhaustive analysis (9:5; cf. 11:32). As Koester says, the author's description and the details "serve[s] as a reflection of the glory of the sanctuary in which Jesus ministers."[82] For example, the description of the golden figures of the winged cherubim who overshadowed the mercy seat evokes the seraphim flying over the throne of God in the scene of the heavenly sanctuary in Isaiah 6. Each detail of the earthly tabernacle is meant to evoke the more concrete and real heavenly tabernacle. However, the author is not concerned about making the chronology explicit, so our theological task would seem to be to account for the claims of Scripture with the least interpretive problems, and I am still looking for the Scripture that states the atonement was a single act in time completed on the cross. In 1 Cor. 5:17, Paul baldly states, εἰ δὲ Χριστὸς οὐκ ἐγήγερται, ματαία ἡ πίστις ὑμῶν, ἔτι ἐστὲ ἐν ταῖς ἁμαρτίαις ὑμῶν (if Christ was not raised, your faith is useless; you are still in your sins). This would seem to be consistent with the process of atonement as described in Hebrews, and say that Paul believed that the atonement was a process that was completed after the resurrection.

The supposed advantage of choosing to interpret the author's description as a metaphor is that we can retain our focus on the importance of Christ's sacrificial death on the cross. However, the Hebrews author recognized the essential importance of Jesus's death.[83] He said that a will/covenant cannot go into effect without a death (9:16-18), and without the shedding of blood there is no forgiveness (9:22). One can say that Jesus's death is the "synecdoche *par excellence*" and it is the sine qua non for the process of the atonement. But the Hebrews author specifically demonstrates how everything written about Jesus in the law of Moses, the prophets, and the psalms about the atonement was fulfilled when the process was completed with the offering in the heavenly tabernacle (Lk. 24:44).

Conclusion

I suggest that in the current debate about the place and timing of the atonement, the interpreter of Hebrews stands at a crossroads: we can either take the author's spatial description of the atonement literally or we can spiritualize it. However, the

---

[82] Koester, *Hebrews*, p. 402.
[83] Contra Moffitt, see n. 76.

author's description of the place of atonement would not be understood as an abstract metaphor in the context of Second Temple Judaism—his message was dependent on the argument that the place of atonement was concrete. Furthermore, a metaphoric interpretation runs against the nature and the importance of place in the Second Temple worldview. If our objective is discovering authorial intent, we should lean toward a literal reading. If we are comfortable with reinterpreting the author's argument by overlaying it and reinterpreting it with our traditional theology of the cross and our devotion to it, as well as our own assumptions of the nature of reality, we might be able to support a metaphorical understanding of the argument in Hebrews in which the dominant view on the timing of the atonement stays in place. But I would count the cost. If you transform the heavenly tabernacle into a metaphor, what other aspects about the atonement of Jesus that the author claims as realities do you relativize by implication?

Faith in Hebrews and Its Relationship to Soteriology: An Interpretation in the Context of the Concept of Fides in Roman Culture[1]

Gabriella Gelardini

Fides quaerens intellectum?

In his work *Zwei Glaubensweisen* (*Two Types of Faith*) published in Zurich in 1950, Martin Buber famously described "the faith of Judaism and the faith of Christendom [as] . . . by nature different."[2] In his view, there were in principle two types or basic forms of conduct toward the infinite or God. For him, the Hebrew kind of faith, *emunah*, is the human's pure and unconditioned trust in God, unmediated by any mediator, but which is embedded in previously experienced guidance, namely in the memory of the testing of the faithfulness of many generations of the Jewish people in history. For Buber, the Christian kind of faith, the Greek πίστις, "was born outside the historical experiences of nations, so to say in retirement from history, in the souls of individuals, to whom the challenge came to believe that a man crucified in Jerusalem was their saviour."[3] Πίστις, the Christian type of faith, thus consists essentially in saying "I believe that it is so."[4] It is an acceptance of the truth of certain tenets of faith. As is well known, Buber sees Paul as the typical representative of Greek πίστις but regards Jesus as belonging to the Hebrew *emunah* type.[5]

In the fourth chapter of his work, Buber also refers to the epistle to the Hebrews. He interprets Heb. 11:1 as a definition by the "author of the epistle," in which the "two aspects stand unconnected beside each other" but are, equally, "a Jewish and a Greek concept of faith": both the "*assurance* of what is hoped for" and the "conviction of

---

[1] I am grateful to Dr. David E. Orton for proofreading this chapter.
[2] Martin Buber, *Two Types of Faith* (trans. Norman P. Goldhawk, The Martin Buber Library; Syracuse: Syracuse University Press, 2003), p. 173.
[3] Ibid., p. 172.
[4] Ibid.
[5] Karl-Josef Kuschel has made important remarks on the Christian and Jewish reception history of Buber's *Zwei Glaubensweisen* and his interpretation of Christianity in the introduction to volume 9 of the *Werkausgabe* (see pp. 50–71 of Martin Buber, *Schriften zum Christentum* (vol. 9 of *Werkausgabe*, ed., intro. and annotated by Karl-Josef Kuschel; Gütersloh: Gütersloher Verlagshaus, 2011)).

things unseen," as Buber puts it in his translation.⁶ Buber, by the way, reverts to Luther's translation of ὑπόστασις with "assurance" (*Zuversicht*), which is why he sees a reference in the first part of Heb. 11:1 to the Israelite understanding of faith. The second part, he says, adds "*elenchos*," familiar from Greek philosophy, the "proof" or "demonstration," or, in recognition of the element of personal belief, "conviction."⁷ Buber adds, "The first part has as its object that which is to come, that which does not yet exist, which as such cannot yet be perceived, the second that which cannot in any way be perceived, the unseen and unseeable, that is, the eternal in distinction from the temporal." For Buber, then, according to the epistle to the Hebrews "he who has faith . . . has received proof of the existence of that, the existence of which admits of no observation."⁸

Buber has seen something here which recent research on the understanding of faith in Hebrews has expressed as follows (by Erich Grässer in particular): namely, that the author, though rooted in the OT concept of *emunah*, also introduces a certain rationalization, has a "rationalistic . . . basic attitude," in which his Greek-influenced background is articulated.⁹ Attention is often drawn to this intellectual character in relation to Hebrews as a whole,¹⁰ although it is evaluated in quite different ways.

For Ernst Käsemann, at any rate, talk of rationalism or intellectualism is not so felicitous, because it obscures the paradoxical moment of faith in Hebrews, according to which the divine cannot be explored by intellectual experiments. In line with kerygmatic theology, he thus emphasizes that in the letter to the Hebrews faith is "the echo of the objective divine word" (*das Echo des objektiven göttlichen Wortes*) and "therefore . . . is an objectively justified assurance and a certainty transcending all earthly possibilities in sureness" (*folglich . . . eine objektiv begründete und an Sicherheit alle irdischen Möglichkeiten überragende Gewissheit ist*),¹¹ but precisely a certainty and thus also a knowledge. Faith conveys insight and knowledge. According to Grässer, the rationalistic concept of faith in Hebrews directly counters a *theologia naturalis* which makes the divine visible on the basis of the capacities of reason. Reason is needed, but without faith it is not capable of insight into the divine.¹² So Benjamin Schliesser, in his important, recently published essay "Glauben und Denken im Hebräerbrief und bei Paulus," reminds us of the *fides quaerens intellectum* of Anselm of Canterbury,¹³ speaking of the "interconnectedness of rationality and the paradoxicality of faith" (*Ineinander von Rationalität und Paradoxalität des Glaubens*).¹⁴

---

[6] Buber, *Two Types of Faith*, pp. 36–37.
[7] Ibid., p. 37.
[8] Ibid.
[9] Erich Grässer, *Der Glaube im Hebräerbrief* (Marburger Theologische Studien, 2; Marburg: Elwert, 1965), p. 56; cf. also Benjamin Schliesser, "Glauben und Denken im Hebräerbrief und bei Paulus: Zwei frühchristliche Perspektiven auf die Rationalität des Glaubens" in *Glaube* (ed. Jörg Frey, Benjamin Schliesser, and Nadine Ueberschaer; WUNT, 373; Tübingen: Mohr Siebeck, 2017), pp. 503–60 (520).
[10] Schliesser refers in particular to numerous writings by Cesla Spicq; see Schliesser, "Glauben und Denken im Hebräerbrief und bei Paulus" pp. 512-13.
[11] Ernst Käsemann, *Das wandernde Gottesvolk: Eine Untersuchung zum Hebräerbrief* (FRLANT 55; 2nd ed.; Göttingen: Vandenhoeck & Ruprecht, 1957), p. 22.
[12] Erich Grässer, *An die Hebräer* (EKKNT 17; vol. 3; Zurich: Benziger; Neukirchen-Vluyn: Neukirchener, 1997), p. 106; cf. also Schliesser, "Glauben und Denken im Hebräerbrief und bei Paulus," p. 524.
[13] Schliesser, "Glauben und Denken im Hebräerbrief und bei Paulus," p. 525.
[14] Ibid., p. 521.

When Buber, however, says that in Hebrews the Israelite type of faith is combined with the "Greek method of thought,"[15] a fundamental criticism is implied. In support of this he refers to Heb. 11:6, where he reads: "Whoever cometh to God must believe that He is...."[16] For Buber, in Israelite belief the existence of God is a "truism,"[17] not an article of faith, so to speak, but a self-evident matter of fact.[18] However, if the concern here is with a "holding true" of the existence of God, then it is precisely with the fundamental self-evidence "of the existence of God as the fundamental [fact] among all invisible facts" (*der Existenz Gottes als die grundlegende unter allen unsichtbaren Tatsachen*),[19] regardless of whether the subtext is a criticism of ancient atheism.[20] But at least this shows that, despite his clear dependence on philosophical rhetoric, the author has addressees in mind whose thinking is already at home with religious beliefs from the OT/Jewish understanding of trust in God's faithfulness. Backhaus, in his interpretation of Hebrews 11, calls this the "habitus of basic trust" (*Habitus des Urvertrauen*).[21] In this respect, the "the Greek way of thinking" certainly has a persuasive function. But the work of persuasion is carried out on those in whom the confessional tradition is already alive, or at least still awake, in whom faith lives and breathes.

Bicultural interaction, not syncretism

Recent cultural anthropological studies of the NT have taught us that the ancient Mediterranean only became an entity, as it were, through first Greek rule and then Roman rule. Andrew Wallace-Hadrill, in particular, has highlighted the bilingualism of the Mediterranean Roman world, that is, the ability to use the vernacular in addition to mastery of literary language or everyday use of Koine Greek or Latin.[22] But even where—as was the case for many Diaspora Jews—Hebrew or Aramaic was the exclusive province of the elite, while elsewhere it existed mainly in only rudimentary form, it should be noted that people's own ethnic and cultural identity was always situated within a tradition of bicultural exchange. In this context Wallace-Hadrill applies the concept of "code-switching,"[23] a key capability in bilingualism research. The concept of biculturalism has replaced older terms and interpretative concepts like "Hellenization," "syncretism," and, more recently, "hybridity." The point is that competent Jewish Koine speakers, such as Paul but also the author of Hebrews, stood in dialogue or interaction with their Greco-Roman cultural environment in the Diaspora, "borrowing" certain concepts while eschewing others, aiming to stay in touch with their Jewish heritage

---

[15] Buber, *Two Types of Faith*, p. 36.
[16] Following Buber's translation (*Two Types of Faith*, p. 38).
[17] Buber, *Two Types of Faith*, p. 38.
[18] Ibid.
[19] Knut Backhaus, *Der Hebräerbrief* (RNT; Regensburg: Pustet, 2009), p. 387.
[20] Ibid.
[21] Backhaus, *Der Hebräerbrief*, p. 382.
[22] Andrew Wallace-Hadrill, *Rome's Cultural Revolution* (Cambridge: Cambridge University Press, 2008).
[23] For a detailed discussion of the approach to bilingualism research, see Wallace-Hadrill, *Rome's Cultural Revolution*, pp. 9–28.

and identity, inwardly as well as outwardly. They already, of course, stand within a broad tradition of bilingualism or biculturalism in Greek-speaking Judaism.

The key factor, however, is that this linguistic competence was accompanied by cultural "code-switching." Bilingualism also meant biculturalism, the capacity for a cultural interaction. This includes the possibility of asserting one's own cultural identity—despite the "code-switching." Picking up on recent ethnicity research, Wallace-Hadrill points out that ethnic and thus religious and cultic identities are formed in interactions, in "borrowing" and "exchange," both internally and externally.[24] Philo could write Greek competently and express his own Jewish identity in interaction with Greek culture and philosophy. The same applies to Paul and particularly to the author of Hebrews. Conversely, however, as Wallace-Hadrill has shown,[25] Jewish literary concepts also influenced the discourse of the Roman elite in the Augustan era.

Fides and πίστις

If, therefore, we read the epistle to the Hebrews against the background of a long-established tradition of bicultural interactions in the Hellenistic-Roman Mediterranean, we need to take due account of this—constant—process of negotiating identity. There is never a pure type; it is something that changes according to context. And this applies not least when—as in Hebrews—the addressees are those who refer in their "confession" to Jesus, the "pioneer (or founder: ἀρχηγός) and perfecter of πίστις" (Heb. 12:2). Therefore, if together with derivatives of the stem, πίστις is, as it were, a key term in the book's vocabulary,[26] we may also discern the traces of the culturally dominant Roman context, which was determined by the Latin noun *fides*, but also influenced the Greek word πίστις semantically. In Pauline research, this contextualization has already yielded fruitful results, in the work of Thomas Schumacher, for example, in relation to early Christian language as a whole, especially Pauline language,[27] and in Teresa Morgan's work in relation to early Jewish or early Christian writings as a whole.[28]

In relation to Hebrews I would like to make an initial attempt here. It is significant that classical and philological studies have pointed to the great importance of the πίστις or *fides* culture in the Roman Empire. In his article *"Fides, Pistis und Imperium"* Hubert Cancik discusses the function of *fides* for relations in society, within the state and between states.[29] He has shown that, despite the various sociohistorical differences

---

[24] Cf. Wallace-Hadrill, *Rome's Cultural Revolution*, pp. 39–40.
[25] See Andrew Wallace-Hadrill, "The Golden Age and Sin in Augustan Ideology," *Past & Present* 95.1 (1982), pp. 19–36.
[26] In fact, the noun πίστις is most often found in Hebrews, a total of thirty-two times (4:2; 6:1,12; 10:22,38,39; 11:1,3,4,5,6,7,7,8,9,11,13,17,20,21,22,23,24,27,28,29,30,31,33,39; 12:2; 13:7); next most frequently the adjective πιστός, namely five times (2:17; 3:2,5; 10:23; 11:11); then twice each the verb πιστεύω (4:3; 11:6) and the opposite of belief ἀπιστία (3:12,19).
[27] Thomas Schumacher, *Zur Entstehung christlicher Sprache: Eine Untersuchung der paulinischen Idiomatik und der Verwendung des Begriffs "pistis"* (BBB, 168; Göttingen: V & R Unipress, 2012).
[28] Teresa Morgan, *Roman Faith and Christian Faith: Pistis and Fides in the Early Roman Empire and Early Churches* (Oxford: Oxford University Press, 2015).
[29] See Hubert Cancik, "Fides, Pistis und Imperium," in *Römische Religion im Kontext: Kulturelle Bedingungen religiöser Diskurse* (ed. Hildegard Cancik-Lindemaier; Gesammelte Aufsätze I; Tübingen: Mohr Siebeck, 2008), pp. 178–97.

between the Greek πίστις concept and the Latin *fides* concept, it was Roman ideas that prevailed, to the point that a Greek author, Epictetus, could, as it were, borrow the concept of πίστις from the Roman way of thinking—which would be "the only instance of Greek philosophy enriching itself from Rome" (*der einzige Fall, in dem sich griechische Philosophie aus Rom bereichert hat*).[30]

Cancik's article refers to the fact that the term πίστις is far from common in Greek literature.[31] Others have pointed out that although the Greek πίστις concept is quite similar to the Roman/Latin one, there are also differences. For one thing, reciprocity is crucial for the Roman concept of *fides*. It marks a reciprocal, albeit hierarchically structured, relationship between the patron and his client in public, private, and also official contracts, as in alliances. *Fides* and *foedus*, faithfulness and covenant, belong together, but so do justice/righteousness and salvation, *iustitia* and *salus*.[32] And in the religious context this is manifest in the very fact that *Fides* is a deity. She is described with her right hand outstretched, which is considered a gesture of contract by handshake, but also of assurance by an oath, seen as a vow of allegiance and a guarantee. Valerius Maximus, the first-century Roman writer, put it as follows in his *Memorabilia*:[33]

> *Cuius imagine ante oculos posita venerabile fidei numen dexteram suam, certissimum salutis humanae pignus, ostentat. Quam semper in nostra civitate viguisse et omnes gentes senserunt.*

> When her image is set before our eyes the venerable divinity of Faith displays her right hand, the most certain pledge of human welfare. That she has always flourished in our community all nations have perceived. (*Facta et dicta memorabilia* 2.6.6)[34]

Valerius Maximus is talking about respect for international law, which demands *fides*. In Hebrews, the noun *pistis* takes up most space in terms of word statistics, but is never used in reference to God, possibly to avoid any echo of the Greco-Roman goddess Πίστις or *Fides*. But in Heb. 10:23 God is said to be πιστός, that is faithful to his promises. The reliability of God is manifest in his mighty word as Creator and not least in the fact that he has now, finally, spoken through his Son (Heb. 1:2). And often there is mention of the oath or vow that God has made—as his own witness, the supreme witness, as it were. He himself is the one who, bound by his oath, offers a guarantee, as when giving his promise to Abraham (Heb. 6:13) or appointing Christ as priest forever (7:17, 21). Christ is also called πιστός—faithful. He remains faithful to God, as high priest and expiator for the sin of the people (Heb. 2:17); and as "apostle or ambassador and high priest of our confession" Jesus is "faithful to God," who "appointed" him (3:2). But the noun πίστις is the very word Hebrews uses in relation to the attitude of the

---

[30] Cancik, "Fides, Pistis und Imperium," p. 196; he cites Richard Heinze here, "Fides" (1929), in *Vom Geist des Römertums: Ausgewählte Aufsätze* (ed. Erich Burck, 3rd ed.; Stuttgart: Teubner, 1960), pp. 59–81 (80).
[31] See Cancik, "Fides, Pistis und Imperium," p. 192.
[32] Incidentally, where the Vulgate translates σωτηρία, it always uses *salus*.
[33] In Book 6, under the title "De fide publica."
[34] Valerius Maximus, *Memorable Doings and Sayings, Volume II: Books 6–9* (ed. and trans. D. R. Shackleton Bailey, LCL 493; Cambridge, MA: Harvard University Press, 2000), pp. 66–67.

wandering people of God, since ancient times and now in the end-times as well.³⁵ And it is also associated with the keyword διαθήκη, Latin *foedus*. The concern is with the "covenant," the New Covenant, that of God with humanity, whose "mediator" is Christ (Heb. 9:15), and so with "salvation." Accordingly, πίστις can be explicitly mentioned as a means of σωτηρία, salvation, for instance in Heb. 11:7. There we read:

> Πίστει χρηματισθεὶς Νῶε περὶ τῶν μηδέπω βλεπομένων, εὐλαβηθεὶς κατεσκεύασεν κιβωτὸν εἰς σωτηρίαν τοῦ οἴκου αὐτοῦ δι᾽ ἧς κατέκρινεν τὸν κόσμον, καὶ τῆς κατὰ πίστιν δικαιοσύνης ἐγένετο κληρονόμος.³⁶
>
> By faith Noah, after he was warned (by God) about things not yet seen, in pious fear constructed an ark for the salvation of his house, with which/ (sc. faith) he condemned the cosmos and became an heir of the righteousness that corresponds with faith.³⁷

But also in Heb. 10:37-39, the lines introducing the great encomium on πίστις in chapter 11, the theme of faithfulness, justice, and salvation from perdition is set, familiar from the history of interpretation of Habakkuk 2, as in the letter to the Romans. Salvation through faithfulness is here characterized as περιποίησις ψυχῆς, that is, as the "acquisition" or "production" of (eternal) life—the word does indeed have the basic meaning of the manufacture of commodities. This is reminiscent of Noah's very practical construction of the ark as a means of rescue from the flood, on divine command. And present here in Heb. 10:39 too, of course, is the paraenetic motif that constantly accompanies πίστις: the call to perseverance and patience, and the avoidance of shrinking back or turning away. Grässer has then labeled Heb. 10:39 somewhat dramatically, if quite plausibly, as the "*skopos* of Hebrews in general" (*Skopos des Hebr überhaupt*).³⁸

It should also be mentioned that alongside *fides* and *foedus*, πίστις and διαθήκη, *salus* and σωτηρία, the theme of empire, important to the Roman conception, also belongs in this context. It was precisely the Roman Empire, Roman rule over the *orbis terrarum*, the world, that ultimately celebrated covenants and friendships with its subject peoples in the Temple of *Fides* on the Capitol. Valerius Maximus, as I have mentioned, emphasized precisely this rule of the *Fides* of Rome and its clientele: *omnes gentes senserunt*—all peoples have noted and understood it. The *fides publica*, the relationship of loyalty between Rome's citizens and rulers as well as between its allies everywhere, is the very foundation of social, state, and interstate life. It should also be noted that in the understanding of πίστις in Hebrews empire-critical undertones may well also resonate. An author who speaks in Heb. 12:22 "of the city (πόλις) of the living God," the heavenly Jerusalem, who says in Heb. 13:14 that "we have no lasting city (πόλις) here," but are looking for "the city that is to come," who speaks in Heb. 2:5

---

[35] Remarkably, the author never uses the present participle as a noun to designate believers, such as Paul.
[36] According to the *Novum Testamentum Graece* (founded by Eberhard and Erwin Nestle, ed. Barbara and Kurt Aland et al., 28th rev. ed., ed. Institut für Neutestamentliche Textforschung, Münster/Westphalia under the direction of Holger Strutwolff; Stuttgart: Deutsche Bibelgesellschaft, 2014), p. 676.
[37] My translation.
[38] Grässer, *An die Hebräer*, p. 82.

of "the coming world (οἰκουμένη)," and in Heb. 11:14,16 of the "heavenly homeland (πατρίς)" is not locating his empire in Rome but in heaven. And unlike many Augustan court poets, such as Virgil,[39] he hardly considers Rome to be the *imperium sine fine*, the empire without borders in space and time, nor Rome the *urbs mansura*, the lasting and eternal πόλις. Rather, this is the "unshakable kingdom" in heaven (the author of Hebrews is referring to Daniel at this point), where Christ has already arrived as πρόδρομος—forerunner—and is enthroned at the right hand of God. It is precisely toward this heavenly, everlasting reign that hope, patience, perseverance, and of course πίστις are directed. Precisely as the one who by faith set out for an unknown land, Abraham is explicitly referred to as the witness of faith who was always waiting for "the πόλις that is firmly established, whose builder and founder is God" (Heb. 11:10). All the great witnesses of faith in history enumerated in Hebrews reached out for this promised πόλις, which God has "prepared" for them (as the author says in Heb. 11:16). Christ, however, is the one who, with his obedience through suffering in the end-times, is the leader (ἀρχηγός) or initiator, but also the "perfecter (τελειωτής) of the πίστις." For as he has already reached heaven and reigns at the right hand of God (Heb. 12:2), he is the "leader of the salvation" (2:10) of many "sons [and daughters]," whom he wants to "lead to glory," but who have not arrived there yet. It is this empire-critical subtext that in my opinion also underlines the capacity for bilingual or bicultural identity politics that I mentioned. Borrowing and rejection belong together in code-switching.

The cloud of witnesses

It is noteworthy that, in its great historical outline in chapter 11, Hebrews lists the series of heroes of faith in the biblical order, starting with Abel. It begins with the much-discussed definition (some, with Attridge, consider this designation to be correct while others have their doubts).[40] The definition reads: Πίστις is a ὑπόστασις of things hoped for, an ἔλεγχος of invisible things. As mentioned above, with Luther, Buber translates ὑπόστασις as "assurance" (*Zuversicht*). Other, more recent translations prefer "reality" or "actuality."[41] Helmut Koester's article in TDNT informs us that the basic meaning of ὑπόστασις, influenced by the natural sciences and philosophy, is akin to the "precipitation" (*Niederschlag*) of something, hence something that forms a sediment.[42] This suggestion has much in its favor, providing πίστις is indeed a reality, but precisely the substrate of something else. And these are the things hoped for. And the meaning of ἔλεγχος? The interpretation "conviction" favored by Buber and others is rejected in the relevant article in the TDNT by Büchsel.[43] It is not a matter of subjective conviction, but of objective proof. Which means: faithfulness is proof or evidence of invisible things.[44] If one interprets the transition to paraenesis in Heb. 12:1, following

---

[39] See Virgil, *Aeneid*. 1.278–9; 3.85–6.
[40] For the discussion see Harold W. Attridge, *Hebrews* (Hermeneia; Philadelphia: Fortress, 1989), pp. 307–8.
[41] So for instance Backhaus, *Der Hebräerbrief*, p. 376; Attridge, *Hebrews*, p. 305.
[42] Helmut Köster, "ὑπόστασις," *TWNT* pp. 8:571–88 (572–73).
[43] See Friedrich Büchsel, "ἐλέγχω, ἔλεγξις, ἔλεγχος, ἐλεγμός," *TWNT*, pp. 2:470–47 (473).
[44] Cf. the usage of language, especially in the papyrus documents by Friedrich Preisigkenach Friedrich Preisigke, *Wörterbuch der griechischen Papyrusurkunden: Mit Einschluss der griechischen*

chapter 11, as something like a summary instruction for reading, then it is striking that the examples of faith are called a "cloud of witnesses" (νέφος μαρτύρων). "Cloud" is a fixed metaphor for a large amount or mass. Of course, as Karrer has remarked, this points upward to heaven as the goal of the path of faith.[45] And in Heb. 12:23 there may also be an implication that in heavenly Zion or Jerusalem there is already a congregation, an ἐκκλησία, consisting not only of angels and Christ, but also of "the spirits of the perfected righteous"—perhaps these are simply the ranks of the faithful ones or heroes of faith[46] since Abel. The word "witnesses," however, seems more important at this point. Because a forensic meaning seems implied here. This is quite remarkable in the context of Hebrews 11, as verses 2, 4, and 39 emphasize that God himself commended these heroes of πίστις. This forensic context fits well with Heb. 11:1, where I translated ἔλεγχος as proof or evidence. In legal language, πίστις can certainly mean credible witness, which is why Karrer[47] has emphasized in his commentary that the forensic rhetoric of Hebrews 11 should not be overlooked.[48] If, therefore, according to Heb. 11:3, πίστις emphasizes the ability to perceive, here specifically to know that the cosmos was created by the Word of God, then the function of witness or proof seems at least to have significance from a noetic point of view. To that extent, there is something to be said for the often emphasized—most recently by Benjamin Schliesser—"intellectual" element of the understanding of faith in Hebrews.[49] But I think the clearly skilled use of Koine rhetoric, especially with the emphasized contextual link with the comprehensive Greco-Roman concept of *pistis/fides*, is of additional importance. In the end it could be ironic that a *fides* concept, which Christian Strecker calls "a kind of identity marker of Roman culture and domination" (*eine Art von identity marker römischer Kultur und Herrschaft*),[50] was used in Hebrews—in accordance with biblical tradition, of course— to culturally strengthen allegiance to the celestial empire. For arguably, for the author of Hebrews the fall of the Roman Empire is a done-and-dusted thing.

Inschriften, Aufschriften, Ostraka, Mumienschilder usw. aus Ägypten (ed. Emil Kissling; vol. 1; Berlin: Selbstverlag der Erben, 1925), col. 467.

[45] See Martin Karrer, *Der Brief an die Hebräer* (ÖTK 20; Gütersloh: Gütersloher Verlagshaus, 2002–08), p. 2:300.

[46] The perception that the faith or faithfulness of people who lived under challenging circumstances was rewarded by transfer to heaven, to the heaven of heroes, was familiar to Romans too. Josephus, at least, tells us that during the siege of Jerusalem the commander Titus promised precisely this to soldiers willing to storm the third and last city wall (Josephus, *War.* 6.34–53).

[47] See Karrer, *Der Brief an die Hebräer*, p. 2:270.

[48] At this point I would also like to refer to rabbinical passages where—with reference to Exod. 32:13–14 and Deut. 9:27–29—the faith of the patriarchs Abraham, Isaac, and Jacob may even be claimed as atonement for one's own sins. See especially *Exod. Rab.* 44 on Exod. 32:14; but also Philo, *Praem. Poen.* 166; *Exod. Rab.* 41 on Exod. 32:6; *Lev. Rab.* 36–37 on Lev. 26:42; *Lam. Rab.* Introduction; *Pesiq. Rab.* 27/28,1; and *Pirqe R. El.* 45. For precise details on the references in the German translation of the sources, see Gabriella Gelardini, "*Verhärtet eure Herzen nicht" der Hebräer, eine Synagogenhomilie zu* (Tischa be-Aw, BINS 83; Leiden: Brill, 2007), pp. 343–45, 347–48.

[49] Schliesser, "Glauben und Denken im Hebräerbrief und bei Paulus," 505 et passim.

[50] Christian Strecker, "Fides – Pistis – Glaube: Kontexte und Konturen einer Theologie der 'Annahme' bei Paulus," in *Lutherische und Neue Paulusperspektive: Beiträge zu einem Schlüsselproblem der exegetischen Diskussion* (WUNT 182, ed. Michael Bachmann; Tübingen: Mohr Siebeck, 2005), pp. 223–50, 231.

16

The Church and Atonement in Hebrews[1]

Harold W. Attridge

The epistle to the Hebrews offers the most comprehensive and complex treatment of the effects of Christ's death in the NT. It does so within the context of a symbolic presentation of the life of the Church, developed through two intersecting metaphors, the wandering people of God and the family or household of God. The homilist frames the treatment of Christ's death as an atoning sacrifice that works precisely as a covenant inaugurating event that creates the Church by proclaiming God's forgiveness of sin and offering the model by which a faithful life is to be led.

Presuppositions about Hebrews

Before exploring how Hebrews handles ecclesiology and atonement, it is useful to review some general assumptions about Hebrews.[2] Although part of the Pauline corpus since at least the early third century, Hebrews is probably not a composition of the Apostle, but perhaps of someone in his general orbit or school, someone, that is, who shares a hope in a future defined by Christ applicable to all, Jews and Gentiles alike.[3] His "word of encouragement" as he calls it (13:22), written sometime in the last third of the first century, is more homily than epistle, although it concludes with epistolary formulas that suggest that the piece was forwarded to a distant congregation. The rhetorical situation that the homily addresses, whether real or fictive, is of a congregation whose ardor for the faith needs bolstering. The addressees have experienced persecution and alienation from their environment (10:32–39). They may have begun to doubt some

---

[1] This chapter is an expansion and revision of a paper given at the Evangelical Theology Society on November 21, 2014. I am grateful to Jon Laansma for his many helpful criticisms and suggestions on the version of the paper presented at that time.
[2] The basic understanding of the fundamental issues about Hebrews remains what was presented in Harold W. Attridge, *Hebrews: A Commentary on the Epistle to the Hebrews* (Hermeneia; Philadelphia: Fortress, 1989).
[3] While it shares important features with Pauline letters, some of which will be examined here, it does not formally pretend to be a composition by the apostle, nor am I persuaded that it might be a more subtle form of pseudepigraphy. For that position, see Claire Rothschild, *Hebrews as Pseudepigraphon: The History and Significance of the Pauline Attribution of Hebrews* (WUNT, 235; Tübingen: Mohr Siebeck, 2009).

of the eschatological hopes that they once eagerly embraced. Some may even have stopped attending common assemblies (10:25). Many interpreters, perhaps including the second-century Christians who gave the text a title, also suspect that the addressees had a Jewish background and were attracted to the cult of the Jerusalem Temple or the communities that supported it, rather than the fellowship of believers in Christ of which they were a part.[4]

Whatever the precise details of the rhetorical situation, the author responds with his "word of encouragement," in which he tries to bolster faith by painting a new image of Christ as High Priest and a new understanding of what his priestly sacrifice means for the lives of the addressees.

The Church as wandering people and household of God

Hebrews begins with a focus on the Son, now enthroned at the right hand of the divine majesty (1:1-13). Much of the homily explores how he came to be there and what the significance of his heavenly session might be, but before developing that exposition, the homilist says something about the community that will receive it. After drawing a verbal image of the enthroned Son and delivering his first "warning" (2:1-4), the homilist turns toward those effected by the Son's life and death, not "angels" but "the world to come" (2:5). And it soon becomes clear that the "world to come" involves the "sons of men."

Hebrews 2:6-9 famously rereads Ps. 8:5-7 not as a reference to the exalted status of human beings, but as a summary of the story of the Son, made "lower than the angels" for a "little while," then "crowned with glory and honor." The opening lines of the citation "what is a human being that you should remember him or the child of a human being (literally 'son of man') that you should watch over him" (Heb. 2:6) are intriguingly polyvalent. The language of "man" and "son of man" may indeed refer to Jesus, as vv. 8 and 9 will interpret the terms, but it may also refer, as it does in the original psalm, to all of humankind, as the next pericope (2:10-18) confirms.

The homilist begins his attention to the community in 2:10 affirming that it was "fitting" for God to "perfect" the Son through suffering, since he was the "forerunner" (ἀρχηγός) involved in leading many children to heavenly glory. The next verse (2:11) suggests that the "perfecting" involves a process of "sanctification," since both "the sanctifier" and "sanctified" are from one source. The two verses weave together several themes related to an understanding of the Church, which is, first and foremost, a collection of people on the move. This phrasing hints at the association of the addressees with the desert generation of ancient Israel, which will be explicitly developed in the next chapter, and repeated again in the catalogue of the faithful in ch. 11. The motif served as the basis for the famous monograph on Hebrews by Ernst Käsemann, who,

---

[4] For a recent attempt to explore anew the identity of the community addressed, see Ole Jakob Filtvedt, *The Identity of God's People and Paradox of Hebrews* (WUNT, 2.400; Tübingen: Mohr Siebeck, 2015).

however, read it within a Gnostic framework.[5] While that framework, based on a problematic religio-historical theory, is not persuasive, Käsemann's recognition of the importance of the motif was certainly correct. The "wandering people of God" is the first of the two major images through which Hebrews defines the Church.

The two verses (2:10-11) make other contributions to the understanding of the Church. The people on the move have a leader, their "forerunner" (ἀρχηγός). The title will appear again, also playfully associated with the notion of "perfection" at 12:3. The journey of the people of God toward heavenly glory is, in effect, a formative pilgrimage, but exactly how the "perfecting" takes place remains to be seen. A key to that process, however, is the fact that the leader and the led, sanctifier and sanctified, are in solidarity. They are "from one" (ἐξ ἑνός, 2:11).

The following verses, reinforcing the notion that the forerunner and his followers are intimately connected, introduce the second major image for the Church. Three scriptural verses, cited in Heb. 2:12-13, help to make the case. The first is from Ps. 22:23 (21:23 LXX), and the next two from Isa. 8:17 and 18. The homilist (v. 11) highlights the specific point made by the first citation, that the Son calls those who follow him "brothers (and sisters)." But the psalm does more. For the first time in the homily, the audience now hears the voice of Jesus. Speaking through the psalmist, he says, "I shall announce your name to my brothers (and sisters), in the midst of the assembly (ἐκκλησίας) I shall sing your praise (ὑμνήσω σε)."

The verse indeed speaks of the solidarity between the leader and the people on their way, but it also defines the people itself as the ἐκκλησία, a people "called out," as the etymology of the word suggests. The verse intimates that the calling took place through the proclamation of the divine name made by the Son. It also suggests something of what takes place in the "assembly." The voice of the Son there sings God's praise. The voices of the "brothers and sisters" will eventually join that song.

Before they do so, the "brothers and sisters" must learn to imitate the Son. In the first verse from Isaiah the Son defines his relationship to the Father as one of trusting faith (ἔσομαι πεποιθώς, 2:13). It is precisely as an exemplar of that virtue that the Son will lead the other members of the assembly (12:1-3). Finally, the last verse from Isaiah, separated from the immediately preceding verse to highlight its distinctive point, returns to the motif sounded in v. 11. The Son refers to himself and "the children" (τὰ παιδία, v. 13) God has given him. In these carefully selected verses the homilist proposes the second major motif used to define the Church: the "family" or "household" of God.

The same two images, wandering people and household of God, recur repeatedly in other passages reflecting on the community. Both appear separately in the following section of Hebrews, an example of the homiletic form in miniature. The introductory segment (3:1-6) offers a comparison or *synkrisis* comparing Moses unfavorably to Jesus. The homilist frames the comparison with the image of a "house" or "household" (οἶκος, 3:3, 5), of which Moses is, as Num. 12:7 LXX indicates, simply a "faithful servant" (πιστὸς . . . θεράπων, v. 5). In contrast, Jesus is the "son who is over the

---

[5] Ernst Käsemann, *The Wandering People of God: An Investigation of the Epistle to the Hebrews* (trans. Roy A. Harrisville and Irving L. Sandberg; Minneapolis: Augsburg, 1985); translation of *Das wandernde Gottesvolk: eine Untersuchung zum Hebräerbrief* (Göttingen: Vandenhoeck & Ruprecht, 1939).

house" (υἱὸς ἐπὶ τὸν οἶκον, v. 6), who, moreover, has "fashioned" (ὁ κατασκευάσας, v. 3) it. What is said of Jesus here echoes phrases from the first two chapters. He was named "Son" in Ps. 2:7, cited at 1:5. While he was the agent of the world's creation (1:2), his "fashioning" of the house is a more specific event, the proclamation (2:12) to his "brothers and sisters" (ἀδελφούς, 2:11), the "children" (υἱοὺς, 2:10, παιδία, 2:13) whom he leads.

The rest of the little homily of chs. 3 and 4 takes as its text Psalm 95, the call to the people of Israel to hear the voice of God "today" and not be hard hearted like their ancestors.[6] The homilist thus invokes the typology explicit in the psalm between the wandering people of God of old and his current addressees. The household or family of God is a new version of wandering Israel, on the way to a true heavenly rest (3:11; 4:3-7).[7] To achieve its goal, that pilgrim people must pay attention to the word of its preacher, who articulates that penetrating "word" of God (4:12-13).

The central part of Hebrews, 4:14 to 10:18, reflects on the significance of Christ's sacrificial death, to which we shall return. The ecclesial framework for that reflection, with its tensive structure of family and wandering people, continues in the hortatory chapters that follow.

The two themes of wandering people and household of God are interwoven in the roster of the faithful in chapter 11.[8] The interweaving is particularly prominent in the portion of the catalogue devoted to the patriarchs of ancient Israel (vv. 8-22), which lies at the heart of the chapter. Abraham was summoned to a place that he would inherit, not knowing where he was going (v. 8). He, Sarah (v. 11), and their wondrously conceived offspring (v. 12) all looked to their inheritance from afar, confessing that they were "strangers and sojourners on the earth" (v. 13). Thus the biblical type of the family called into being by God recognizes its status on the way to its heavenly home (v. 16). One curious detail in the report about Jacob reemphasizes the point. In v. 21 the homilist sketches the scene described in Genesis 47, where Jacob on his deathbed summons Joseph and asks not to be buried in Egypt. When Joseph swears to do as his father requested, Jacob, according to the Hebrew, "bowed himself on the head of his bed" (וישתחו ישראל על ראש המטה). The LXX of Gen. 47:31, cited at Heb. 11:21, translates that verse as "and he worshiped on the head of his staff" (προσεκύνησεν ἐπὶ τὸ ἄκρον τῆς ῥάβδου αὐτοῦ). The homilist does not explain the significance of that verse, but the context suggests what he probably read in it. Jacob leaning on his staff is, like Abraham, ready to move on. The household formed by God is ever on the way.

---

[6] In citing the negative example of the desert generation of ancient Israel the homilist here uses a common homiletic trope, also in evidence in 1 Cor. 10:1-13.

[7] For a discussion of the typology of the passage see Harold W. Attridge, "'Let us strive to enter that Rest': The Logic of Hebrews 4:1-11," *HTR* 73 (1980) pp. 279-88, repr. in idem, *Essays on John and Hebrews* (WUNT 264; Tübingen: Mohr Siebeck, 2010), pp. 260-67.

[8] On this chapter, see especially Michael R. Cosby, *The Rhetorical Composition and Function of Hebrews 11: In Light of Example Lists in Antiquity* (Macon, GA: Mercer University Press, 1988); Pamela M. Eisenbaum, *The Jewish Heroes of Christian History: Hebrews 11 in Literary Context* (SBLDS, 156; Atlanta: Scholars, 1997); and R. W. L. Moberly, "Exemplars of Faith in Hebrews 11: Abel," in *The Epistle to the Hebrews and Christian Theology* (ed. Richard Bauckham, Daniel Driver, Trevor Hart, and Nathan MacDonald; Grand Rapids, MI: Eerdmans, 2009), pp. 353-63.

The final portion of Hebrews' hortatory section formally balances the two ecclesiological themes. After summarizing the catalogue of the faithful "cloud of witnesses" (12:1), the homilist points again to the prime example of fidelity, Jesus, the "inaugurator and perfector of faith" (12:2), whose willingness to accept the shame of the cross is proposed as the model that his followers should consider for themselves (12:3).

The homilist then turns to the faithful followers and urges them first to endure whatever suffering comes their way, understanding it to be a form of divine "education" (12:4-11). Proverbs 3:11-12 grounds the appeal and makes the point that children need parental discipline. To be a member of the household of God is thus not always pleasant.[9]

After a warning passage invoking the case of Esau, who gave up his birthright and thereby his status in the household of Israel (12:12-17), the homilist returns to the image of the wandering people and compares his addressees to the children of Israel encamped at Mount Sinai (12:18-24). Their encampment is not, however, in the presence of a fearsome theophany, but a heavenly Jerusalem (12:23), an "assembly" (ἐκκλησία) composed of "firstborns" (πρωτοτόκων) enrolled in the divine presence, "spirits of perfected righteous ones" (πνεύμασι δικαίων τετελειωμένων). The language used here echoes all the notes that appeared in the first sketch of "familial" ecclesiology in ch. 2, but it does so in a context evocative of the motif of the wandering people.

To all of this the homilist adds a note that ties the imagery of the Church to the exposition of Christ's sacrificial death. The people gathered before the heavenly Jerusalem also confront "the mediator of the New Covenant, Jesus," and "the sprinkled blood that speaks a better word than the blood of Abel" (12:24: αἵματι ῥαντισμοῦ κρεῖττον λαλοῦντι παρὰ τὸν Ἄβελ). What forms the household and wandering people of God, the voice that calls them out and assembles them on their pilgrim path, is the voice of the "mediator" (μεσίτῃ), whose sacrificial death, his crying "blood," created a New Covenant. How did that happen?

Contemporary understanding of sacrifice

Hebrews, following the lead of many other early Christians, presents the death of Christ as a sacrificial act that has as its effect the atonement of sin, an event foundational for the life of the Church. Before exploring how the homilist frames that atoning action, it is necessary to step back for a moment from the exegetical task and review briefly how recent scholars have come to understand ancient notions of "sacrifice."

Interest in the practice of sacrifice in antiquity in general,[10] in the biblical tradition in particular,[11] and in early Christian discourse has expanded dramatically in recent

---

[9] On this passage, see N. Clayton Croy, *Endurance in Suffering: Hebrews 12:1-13 in Its Rhetorical, Religious, and Philosophical Context* (SNTSMS, 98; Cambridge: Cambridge University Press, 1998).

[10] Christopher A. Faraone and F. S. Naiden, *Greek and Roman Animal Sacrifice: Ancient Victims, Modern Observers* (Cambridge: Cambridge University Press, 2012).

[11] Jonathan Klawans, *Purity, Sacrifice, and the Temple: Symbolism and Supersessionism in the Study of Ancient Judaism* (New York: Oxford, 2005); James W. Watts, *Ritual and Rhetoric in Leviticus: From Sacrifice to Scripture* (New York: Cambridge University Press, 2007); Christian A. Eberhart,

scholarship. Most of the literature has been carefully reviewed in recent treatments by Robert Daly, who has long been a leading contributor to the study of the phenomenon and to the Christian theology of sacrifice, and by Sarah Coakley.[12] Within this scholarship there has been attention to the category of sacrifice in Hebrews.[13] Space does not permit a summary of this scholarly literature, but several points that undergird the analysis of this essay are worth noting.

The first preliminary point, stressed especially by John Dunnill,[14] questions the widespread modern presupposition that "sacrifice" is equivalent to "giving something up." If one wanted to risk offering some general definition of "sacrifice," it would have more to do with gift giving and sharing than with deprivation. A corollary of this general observation is that interpretations of sacrifice that focus on the act of killing, particularly of animals, regularly misinterpret sacrificial rituals by ignoring large parts of what actually takes place in them. The same may be true of theological appropriations of the category of sacrifice.

The second important preliminary point is the complexity of sacrificial practices, which calls into question any simple "definition" of sacrifice. Within the two major cultural traditions interwoven in the pages of the NT, the Israelite and the Greco-Roman, lie a number of ancient ritual and non-ritual actions labeled as "sacrifice." The ancient sources sometimes attribute to these acts certain ends or results, although the way in which they accomplish those results is usually *not* explained. There are also some ancient observers of sacrificial practices who make note of that opacity.

Alongside the complexity of sacrificial practices, there arose in antiquity, and particularly in the biblical tradition, a set of language games that used sacrificial categories for various purposes. This discourse has often been dubbed "spiritualization," a category severely criticized as vague and imprecise by scholars such as Jonathan Klawans,[15] and defended and refined by scholars such as Stephen Finlan, who is

---

ed., *Ritual and Metaphor: Sacrifice in the Bible* (SBLRBS, 68; Atlanta: SBL, 2011), particularly the essays by Jeffrey S. Siker, "Yom Kippuring Passover: Recombinant Sacrifice in Early Christianity," pp. 65–82, and Stephen Finlan, "Spiritualization of Sacrifice in Paul and Hebrews," pp. 83–98.

[12] Robert J. Daly, *Sacrifice Unveiled: The True Meaning of Christian Sacrifice* (London: T&T Clark, 2009). See also George Heyman, *The Power of Sacrifice: Roman and Christian Discourses in Conflict* (Washington, DC: Catholic University of America, 2007) and Sarah Coakley, *Sacrifice Regained, Reconsidering the Rationality of Religious Belief* (Cambridge: Cambridge University Press, 2013).

[13] Stephen Holmes, "Death in the Afternoon: Hebrews, Sacrifice and Soteriology," in *The Epistle to the Hebrews and Christian Theology* (ed. Richard Bauckham, Daniel Driver, Trevor Hart, and Nathan MacDonald; Grand Rapids, MI: Eerdmans, 2009), pp. 229–52; Ekkehard W. and Wolfgang Stegemann, "Does the Cultic Language in Hebrews Represent Sacrificial Metaphors? Reflections on Some Basic Problems," in *Hebrews: Contemporary Methods – New Insights* (ed. Gabriella Gelardini; BIS, 75; Atlanta: SBL, 2005), pp. 13–23; and A. N. Chester, "Hebrews: The Final Sacrifice," in *Sacrifice and Redemption* (ed. S. W. Sykes; Cambridge: Cambridge University Press, 1991), pp. 57–72. Note also Guy G. Stroumsa, *The End of Sacrifice: Religious Transformations in Late Antiquity* (trans. Susan Emanuel; Chicago: University of Chicago Press, 2009), esp. p. 72 on Christianity as a religion "centered on sacrifice, even if it was a reinterpreted sacrifice."

[14] John Dunnill, *Sacrifice and the Body: Biblical Anthropology and Christian Self-Understanding* (Ashgate New Critical Thinking in Religion, Theology and Biblical Studies; Surrey; Burlington, VT: Ashgate, 2013).

[15] Jonathan Klawans, *Purity, Sacrifice, and the Temple: Symbolism and Supersessionism in the Study of Ancient Judaism* (New York: Oxford, 2005).

particularly attentive to sacrificial metaphors in Christian sources.[16] The ancient writers who engage in one or another form of this discourse do various things with the language of "sacrifice." Some criticize the rituals performed on altars or at temples and suggest that something else, a moral life, for instance, is the offering that God truly wants. Some ancients try to provide an interpretation of scarcely understood ritual actions that they may still want to preserve but to which they want to apply a meaning derived from a moral or intellectual sphere. "Sacrifice" then becomes a metaphor or symbol of something else. Some lay the foundation for what scholars such as Dunnill take to be misleading modern notions of sacrifice by applying the category to the actions of people, like Greek heroes or the Maccabean martyrs, who lay down their lives in defense of home or country. What modern readers explore when interpreting passages dealing with sacrificial language in the NT are examples of one or more of the forms of "sacrificial" discourse available in the first-century world of Hellenized Judaism. As one interprets such texts, it is necessary to take account not only of modern cultural reconstructions about how sacrificial rituals functioned in ancient societies, what anthropologists call the "etic" or behavioral dimensions of action, but also what ancient people were doing conceptually, or the "emic" dimensions of their engagement with ritual practices and their metaphorical applications.

One final word about presuppositions: this chapter offers an interpretation of a sacred text. Those who wrestle with the category of "sacrifice" in such texts should be aware of two temptations, the Scylla and Charybdis of the interpretive enterprise. On the one side, lie modern theological concerns. Christians have been reflecting on the "sacrificial" language of the NT for two millennia, wondering about how exactly the "sacrifice" of Christ does its atoning, salvific work and how it is connected with its ritual remembrance. A theologically sensitive interpreter wants the sacred texts to make some sense that accords with a theological system deemed rational and coherent. Interpreters might then be tempted to overinterpret or read into the text something that is not there. They might defend the project as a theological reflection inspired by the sacred text, but that is a reading of a special sort. On the other hand—and this is a common temptation in dealing with Hebrews—interpreters have a tendency to oversimplify what an ancient author can do with multivalent terms such as "sacrifice." Complex symbolism can too easily be dismissed as conceptual confusion or a mixing of disparate sources and, the subtlety of a sophisticated ancient exposition can be missed. One should keep those two interpretive headlands in mind and judge whether our interpretation has in fact crashed on one or another of them.

Sacrifice and atonement in the tradition behind Hebrews

In painting his verbal picture, the homilist offers an interpretation of the death and resurrection/exaltation of Jesus. He takes for granted many basic teachings of the Christian movement and alludes to that fact at one point, chiding his addressees

---

[16] See his *Background and Content of Paul's Atonement Metaphors* (Leiden: Brill, 2004) and idem, *Options on Atonement in Christian Thought* (Collegeville, MN: Liturgical, 2007).

that they need to move to a deeper level of understanding (5:11–6:3). Among the presupposed "facts" is probably the understanding that the death of Jesus is a "sacrifice" of some sort. The metaphorical use of the category for a martyr's death may well have been part of the background, but it is surely more than that, since many of our early Christian authors explicitly applied to Christ's death both the language of noble death and cultic images taken from the biblical tradition.

The Fourth Gospel, for instance, refers to the death of Jesus in sacrificial terms, but those references create as many problems as they solve. They begin with John the Baptist's identification of Jesus as the Lamb of God who takes away the sins of the world in Jn 1:29. The kind of Lamb that the evangelist has in mind is made clear by his account of the crucifixion. That scene ends with soldiers coming to break the legs of the crucified ones to hasten their demise. They do not need to do so for Jesus since he was already dead (Jn 19:33); instead they pierced his side. This all happened, says the evangelist, so that the scripture might be fulfilled that "no bone of his shall be broken," a reference to Exod. 12:10 and 46 and the required treatment of the Passover Lamb. Fair enough, Jesus is the Passover Lamb, who takes away the sins of the world. The only problem with that identification is that Passover Lamb was not ordinarily understood to be a sacrifice that did that kind of work.

This is not the place to solve that little conundrum in the Fourth Gospel. Many scholars ground their hermeneutical ships on the rock that equates the evangelist's move here with an unreflective assimilation of Passover to Yom Kippur, a "Yom Kippurization of Passover," to quote Jeffrey Siker.[17] Like many other tensive moves that the Fourth Evangelist makes, this one too is, I think, designed to stimulate reflection. It is a riddle, "How does a sacrifice not designed to take away sin take away sin?" The solution to that riddle lies elsewhere in the Fourth Gospel's construal of how the revelation of the Divine Word works.[18]

At this point this chapter is simply exploring the kinds of things that the author of the epistle to the Hebrews might have assumed. Many sacrificial images appear in Paul's letters, applied in an almost casual and indiscriminate way at various points in his correspondence. So Paul can call Christ's death a Passover sacrifice (1 Cor. 5:7). At a climactic point in Romans, explaining how God has graciously dealt with the problem of universal and pervasive sin (Rom. 3:25), Paul can allude to the ritual of Yom Kippur, calling Christ's death a ἱλαστήριον, the "mercy seat" over the ark of the covenant, on which the high priest sprinkled cleansing blood on the Day of Atonement. Translations often fail to catch the allusion. The NRSV translates this word as "a sacrifice of atonement"; the NAB translates as "expiation." Neither captures quite what Paul says. Jesus is, in his image, the sacred place where atoning blood is sprinkled.[19] Paul may

---

[17] Jeffrey S. Siker, "Yom Kippuring Passover: Recombinant Sacrifice in Early Christianity," pp. 65–82; see n. 1.

[18] That the Fourth Gospel works with an understanding of sin as willful ignorance will be discussed in my forthcoming commentary. For a related example of how the Gospel develops its sometimes perplexing theological positions, see Harold W. Attridge, "Divine Sovereignty and Human Responsibility in the Fourth Gospel," in *Revealed Wisdom: Studies in Apocalyptic in Honour of Christopher Rowland* (ed. John Ashton; Leiden, New York: Brill, 2014), pp. 183–99.

[19] On the difficulties of this verse, see Joseph Fitzmyer, *Romans* (AB, 33; Garden City, NY: Doubleday, 1993), pp. 349–50 and Robert Jewett, *Romans: A Commentary* (Hermeneia; Minneapolis: Fortress, 2007), pp. 283–87.

allude to another cultic image at 2 Cor. 5:21 when he says that God made Jesus, who knew no sin, to be "sin" so that we might become God's righteousness in him. Some interpreters discern here a cultic metaphor, in which Paul says that Jesus became a "sin offering," reflecting the way in which the Greek translation could refer to the חטאת or sin offering of Leviticus as a "for sin" (περὶ ἁμαρτίας). Some interpreters read 2 Cor. 5:21 instead as a reference to the scapegoat ritual of Yom Kippur, in which the High Priest laid the sins of the people on the head of a goat sent out to the wilderness (Lev. 16:20-22). If so, 2 Cor. 5:21 is the only allusion in the NT to this particular ritual.[20] Paul gestures toward another sacrificial act in Rom. 8:32. His reference to God not sparing his own son may allude to the *Aqedah*, or "Binding" of Isaac by Abraham in Genesis 22.[21] Paul, in brief, calls upon a number of images of sacrifice in association with the death of Jesus.

The author of Hebrews drew on other early Christian traditions. Many early Christians also understood Jesus, as a result of his resurrection, to have been seated in an honored place in heaven and endowed with a special name. The best-known example of that belief is perhaps the Christ Hymn of Phil. 2:6-11, but this way of thinking about the resurrection and ascension of Jesus is quite common. One way in which the sacred authors expressed their belief was the application to Christ of Ps. 110:1, a royal psalm in which God addresses an Israelite king being installed at God's right hand. The verse is cited frequently in the NT, for example, in Acts 2:34; Eph. 1:20, Col. 3:1.

Sacrifice and atonement in Hebrews, constructing the argument

References to Christ's exaltation and to his death as some sort of sacrificial act are the foundational elements on which our homilist builds his new portrait of Christ. It is not possible to determine the way in which he developed his argument, how the *inventio*, as ancient orators called the process of constructing a speech, would have worked. He may have simply begun, reflecting on data in the Pauline corpus, from the premise that Christ's death was a "sacrifice," then speculated on what kind of sacrifice it might be. He might also have begun with the notion that if Christ's death was a sacrifice, it needed a competent officiant. He would then have wondered how Christ could qualify. The homilist may have developed his argument in other ways, but however he did so, he came to grips with the claim that Christ's death was a sacrifice of some sort.

The homilist also needed to show how the death and exaltation of Christ was relevant to the lives of his congregation. How did that sacrificial death and glorious exaltation really work for them? This rhetorical necessity may well have driven the homilist to his reflection on sacrifice and priesthood, or he may have been driven by questions about the meaning and true function of what people called sacrifices. Whatever the path his

---

[20] For discussion of the interpretive options, see Victor P. Furnish, *II Corinthians* (AB, 32A; Garden City, NY: Doubleday, 1984), p. 330. Furnish finds not a cultic metaphor but a general allusion to the sinful state of humanity.

[21] For the history of this interpretation, see Fitzmyer, *Romans*, pp. 531-32, and Jewett, *Romans*, pp. 536-38, who is skeptical about such an allusion.

solution to that particular problem is, in many ways, the most creative aspect of his reflection on Christ's death as a sacrifice.

Our homilist's basic and obvious conceit is that the pattern of Christ's death and exaltation is analogous to the actions of the High Priest on the Day of Atonement, as prescribed in Leviticus. Christ's death maps onto the ritual in which blood is used as a means of purifying the mercy seat (the ἱλαστήριον) and Christ's one-time session at the right hand of God in heaven corresponds to the annual entry of the High Priest into the Most Holy part of the Tabernacle.

Before exploring in more detail how the reflection proceeds, it is worth noting that the homilist probably considered other options for dealing with Christ's death as a sacrifice. In addition to the Yom Kippur analogy, developed in chs. 8–10, he obviously knows of the daily sacrifices of the Levitical cult. He casually mentions these in the initial job description of a high priest (5:1), which involves tending "to things pertaining to God, so as to offer gifts and sacrifices for sin." This is fairly neutral language. The homilist is a bit more disdainful when he mentions the daily sacrifices in his summary paragraph of ch. 7, which makes the connection between Christ and Melchizedek. He is *much* more disparaging in the context of the exposition of the Yom Kippur analogy, where he refers (8:9) to the "gifts and sacrifices"—the same terms used at 5:1—of the cult of the tabernacle. These, he claims, do not cleanse conscience but only deal with issues of ritual purity. That judgment on daily and annual sin offerings reappears in the next paragraph, which unfavorably contrasts the blood of Christ with the blood of bulls and goats (9:13), which only effects cleansing of the flesh. The homilist adds here a gesture toward yet another ritual, that of the red heifer of Num. 19:9-17, whose blood has special cleansing power for certain kinds of ritual impurities. One might debate whether that ritual should be considered a "sacrifice" like many of the others in the roster, but for our homilist it is of a piece with the general category of "gifts and sacrifices," the rituals that "those who serve at the tabernacle" (13:10) perform.

Other sacrifices are also mentioned in passing, including, at 11:17-19, the *Aqedah*. The reference here is not, as in Paul's letter (Rom. 8:32), an indirect allusion but a clear account of the story of Genesis 22. Yet the relevance of the story to the homilist's program is not focused on Isaac's brush with death, but on the conviction that motivated Abraham's action, a belief imputed to him that God would raise Isaac from the dead to make good on the promise of offspring through Isaac. This is an ingenious twist to the story, but it says nothing about sacrifice. One wonders if our homilist may be saying to other Christians who found the story attractive, "If you are going to use Genesis 22, this is how you should do it."

The catalogue of sacrifices mentioned in Hebrews includes Passover, mentioned at 11:28, as something that the faithful one, Moses, courageously celebrated in Egypt. There may be an oblique gesture in this reference to Christ's sacrifice, since it appears in the context of the author's selective account of Moses as one who "preferred the reproach of Christ to the treasures of Egypt," but our homilist makes no direct connection of Passover and Jesus's death.[22] In fact, he does not even label the Passover ritual a sacrifice, perhaps because he is so concerned with sacrifices that deal with sin.

---

[22] As noted above, through its citation of Exod. 12:10, 46 at Jn 19:36, the Fourth Gospel explicitly draws the typology between the sacrifice of the Passover Lamb and the death of Christ. Later interpreters

One last type of sacrifice appears in the middle of the reflection on Yom Kippur, at 9:18-22, the ritual described in Exodus 24 whereby Moses sanctified the people of the desert generation, in effect inaugurating the "Old Covenant." The oxen sacrificed that day are said to be "offerings of well-being" (זבחים שלמים; in the LXX θυσίαν σωτηρίου, literally, a "sacrifice of salvation") to the Lord. When Moses sprinkles their blood on people, he says, and the homilist quotes him, "This is the blood of the covenant which the Lord made with you" (Exod. 24:8). This citation is important and we shall return to it. For now it is important to note simply that our homilist knows various possibilities for exploring the meaning of sacrifice and chooses his own, almost unique, path. He focuses on Yom Kippur, but somehow connects it with the passage in Exodus 24.

Not only does our homilist know about different kinds of biblical sacrifice, he also knows about ways in which people criticized sacrifice and used it as a metaphor for something else. The critique is as old as the prophets who proclaimed that Yahweh did not want the blood of animals, but a true heart and deeds of mercy (Hos. 6:6; 8:13; cf. Amos 4:4-6).[23] Such critiques were part of the intellectual landscape of the first century, mounted not only by Jewish prophets and teachers,[24] but also by Hellenistic philosophers thinking about the traditional sacrificial cults of the Greco-Roman world. "Why," those philosophers asked, "are we attempting to give the gods something with our sacrificial offerings? The Divine does not need anything."[25] Such critiques, clearly biblical and possibly philosophical, may lie behind the disparaging comments on other sacrifices in ch. 9 of Hebrews. Such critiques are explicitly part of the point of the citation of Ps. 40:7-9 in Heb. 10:5-7. As his comment at 10:8-9 makes clear, our homilist takes that quotation to be not simply a passing criticism, but a rejection of the sacrifices mentioned and their replacement with something else. The character of that something else requires more attention.

Hebrews, the argument and its surprising twists

We have considered the homilist's rhetorical situation, and the array of resources at his disposal, including early Christian confessional claims and attitudes toward sacrifice. A hint about his conclusions has emerged, but not the path through which he reaches it. To understand his path it is important to recognize Hebrews as a sophisticated

of Hebrews and John, from the Fathers through Thomas Aquinas, will read the symbolism of the two texts together. The phenomenon of such intra-canonical references is a common part of the tradition of theological interpretation of the New Testament. For some other examples in the Church Fathers, see Harold W. Attridge, "Jesus the Incarnate High Priest: Intracanonical Readings of Hebrews and John," in *Hebrews in Context* (ed. Gabriella Gelardini and Harold W. Attridge; Leiden: Brill, Forthcoming, 2016).

[23] The prophetic critique of cult can be read either as a comparative preference ("God did not want *merely* animal sacrifice"), not an absolute preference, implying rejection ("God wants mercy, and not sacrifice"). Whatever the original meaning of the prophetic texts, Hebrews understands them in the latter, rejecting, fashion.

[24] Cf. Mark 12:33, where Jesus seems to speak in favor of the comparative preferential understanding of the prophetic motif.

[25] See Harold W. Attridge, *First-century Cynicism in the Epistles of Heraclitus* (Harvard Theological Studies, 29; Missoula: Scholars, 1976), and idem, "The Philosophical Critique of Religion under the Early Empire," in *ANRW* 2.16.1 (Berlin: De Gruyter, 1978), pp. 45–78.

rhetorical work. It does conceptual analysis but does not do it in a simple and direct way. It interprets scripture and tradition subtly and with wit, with a view toward its rhetorical impact. Ignoring the rhetorical web obscures the theological point.

The treatment of Christ's sacrificial death comprises the central portion of Hebrews, from 7:1 to 10:18. The homilist begins by making the point that, all appearances to the contrary notwithstanding, Christ is a priest. This argument, comprising most of ch. 7, involves the interpretation of the two biblical texts that mention Melchizedek, Ps. 110:4 and Gen. 14:17-20. It may be inspired by speculation about Melchizedek in Jewish circles, but our homilist does not commit to any version of such speculation.[26] No, what counts for him is that scripture testifies that the fatherless, motherless, genealogy-less Melchizedek "lives." Therefore, if the psalm is addressed to the Son and calls him a priest "according to the order of Melchizedek," one can infer that Christ is a priest of an eternal order. Apart from the playful exegesis, ch. 7 thus offers a perspective on Jesus and his work that plays a major role in the chapters that follow. Jesus, the eternal and exalted Son, is a high priest of a very special sort, one who belongs to a heavenly, eternal, perhaps even ideal reality.

What follows builds on the evocation of the eternal order in the chapter on Melchizedek. The argument from 8:1 to 10:18 is itself a well-defined little homily, structured in a way very similar to the homily on Psalm 95 found at 3:1-4:13. An introductory paragraph, here, 8:1-6, sets out some themes; scripture is cited (8:7-13), and then elements of the biblical text and the initial themes are explored in an orderly and symmetrical way (9:1-10:10), until the rhetorical flourish (10:11-18), which reminds the audience of the key points of the scriptural citation.

This whole segment of Hebrews is structured around several antitheses, contrasting heaven and earth, new and old, exterior and interior.[27] The way in which our homilist manipulates those antitheses is important for the points he finally wants to make. The opening paragraph establishes the axis of heaven and earth, based upon the account in Exod. 25:39-40 about God showing to Moses the heavenly plan for or model (Heb. תבנית) of the earthly tabernacle. The contrast between earth and heaven governs the exposition of Yom Kippur rituals in ch. 9, which first describes the earthly "shadows" of the heavenly reality in 9:1-10, and then as the "heavenly" reality, depicts Christ's ascension to God's right hand in 9:11-14. The homilist evokes the "heavenly" realm again in 9:23-24, pushing the imagery that he has been using to an extreme.

The contrast of heavenly ideal with earthly realities can be construed in various ways. Many readers have found here in Hebrews an evocation of the Platonic idealism adopted by the first-century Jewish philosopher Philo of Alexandria.[28] There are indeed touches pointing in this direction, including the contrast of reality and shadow (8:5),

---

[26] On possible Jewish backgrounds and an argument that Hebrews takes them seriously, see Eric F. Mason, *"You Are a Priest Forever": Second Temple Jewish Messianism and the Priestly Christology of the Epistle to the Hebrews* (STDJ, 74; Leiden: Brill, 2008).

[27] See Harold W. Attridge, "The Uses of Antithesis in Hebrews 8–10," *HTR* 76 (1986), pp. 1–9 [G. W. E. Nickelsburg and George W. MacRae, S. J., eds., *Christians Among Jews and Gentiles* (Philadelphia: Fortress, 1986), pp. 1–6], repr. in *Essays on John and Hebrews* (WUNT 264; Tübingen: Mohr Siebeck, 2010), pp. 273–80.

[28] Most recently, see James W. Thompson, *The Beginnings of Christian Philosophy: The Epistle to the Hebrews* (CBQMS, 13; Washington, DC: Catholic Biblical Association of America, 1982) and idem, *Hebrews* (Paideia; Grand Rapids, MI: Baker Academic, 2008).

reminiscent of Plato's Myth of the Cave, or the insistence that in heaven there are the "holy things *themselves*" (9:23), which is the kind of technical terminology that Plato uses for ideas or forms. Whether or not there is an allusion to a Platonic scheme, the imagery is quite provocative. It is a very strange kind of heavenly realm, into which literal "blood" can be brought, as it must be if the analogy between the Christ event and the action of the High Priest on Yom Kippur is to have any validity. By the time that the first-century audience of this homily reaches the end of ch. 9, they might be a little anxious to see how our preacher would hold this rather tensive structure together.

He does so by connecting or rather transforming the vertical dichotomy of heaven and earth into the antithesis of old and new. He had introduced that contrast as part of the Scripture cited in 8:8-13, a quotation from Jer. 31:31-34, the longest citation of a text from the OT anywhere in the New. In that passage, the prophet, speaking for Yahweh, promises to establish a New Covenant with his people, better than the old one that they did not keep. The first little surprise that our audience experienced in hearing this homily was in fact the citation of just this passage. "What," an attentive hearer might have asked, "does this text have to do with the matter of Christ as a High Priest, or his death as a sacrifice?" "Stay tuned, impatient one," the homilist might have said, had "tuning" been part of his vocabulary.

Part of the answer to our concerned listener about the relevance of Jeremiah to the topic of the homily has to do with the way in which our homilist deploys the "old-new" antithesis. It is part of the contrast in ch. 9 between the Yom Kippur of scripture and the Yom Kippur of Christ's act, but it comes back in spades at the beginning of ch. 10, right at the point where the antithesis of heaven and earth has been most sharply—and most bafflingly—drawn.

The attentive listener had been left asking at the end of ch. 9 how blood gets into heaven and how it is that "heavenly things themselves" needed purification. The answer has been lurking in the details of the homilist's remarks all along, in his references to the "cleansing" of "consciences" (9:9, 14). The realities to be cleansed are not in some transcendent heavenly space or realm of ideas. They are here, in this realm of flesh and blood; they are within us. That the space that the Great High Priest enters to effect his ideal Yom Kippur sacrificial act is, in fact, the hearts and minds of his followers, becomes clear in the final section of his exposition, 10:1-10. Here the homilist reverts to the antithesis of "old and new." He turns, that is, from the vertical axis that had dominated the previous section of his exposition to a horizontal axis and offers a new interpretation of key elements of the vertical axis. He now operates with another familiar trope, the distinction of a shadow and the body that casts it, used in Col. 2:17. In ch. 8, the trope underlay the distinction between the heavenly ideal tabernacle and its shadowy counterpart on earth, the tabernacle of Exodus. Here the shadow is the Law of old (10:1), and the body that casts that shadow is none other than the body of Christ (10:10), offered once for all, as the concluding verse of the section proclaims.

What makes that body cast its shadow? It is what the homilist portrays Christ as saying, "when he comes into the world," as he puts it at 10:5. What Christ says, in this, his second speech in Hebrews—his first was at 2:12-13—is another citation from the OT: Ps. 40:7-9. The citation works particularly well for the homilist's purpose, because the Greek of the LXX translates the Hebrew (אזנים כרית לי) "Ears you have cut out for me," as "you have prepared a body for me." Christ, in the body, makes a commitment to be faithful to God, saying, "See, God, I have come to do your will" (10:7). As our homilist puts it in v. 10, "It is by this will that *we* are sanctified." That "will" is not to be found in an abstract, heavenly realm, but in "the offering of the body of Jesus Christ once for all" (v. 10). This is the "body" prepared for him mentioned in Psalm 40 and it is the "body" that casts the shadow (10:1). The "will" or "intent" embodied in the action of Jesus who conforms himself in fidelity to God's will is the source of sanctification for his followers.

The psalmist cited here had contrasted the commitment to do God's will with "holocausts and sacrifices for sin," invoking the prophetic critics of sacrificial ritual. It is somewhat ironic, then, that the "sacrifice" of Christ on the ultimate "Yom Kippur" should serve as the elimination of any external sacrificial ritual, but that irony seems to be intentional. For Hebrews the principle of "doing your will, O God," takes away (ἀναιρεῖ) the principle of sacrifice (v. 9).

The citation of the psalm put on the lips of Jesus discloses what our homilist takes to be the essential component of at least the "ultimate" sacrifice, not a ritual action or external gift to God, but a personal commitment of one's self to do God's will. In offering this interpretation of this particular sacrifice, the homilist stands not only within the prophetic tradition, but also closely resembles the position of at least one theologically informed Jewish thinker of the period, namely Philo. In *Spec.* 1.271–72 (Colson; LCL 320, pp. 256–257), he writes,

> (271) . . .God is not pleased even though a man bring hecatombs to his altar; for he possesses all things as his own, and stands in need of nothing. But he delights in the minds of the friends of God . . . (272) And even if they bring nothing else, still when they bring themselves, the most perfect completeness of virtue and excellence, they are offering the most excellent of all sacrifices, honoring God, their Benefactor and Savior, with hymns and thanksgivings . . . the worshippers making their exclamations and invocations with their soul alone, and only appreciable by the intellect, and there is but one ear, namely, that of the Deity which hears them.

Many interpreters have explored the possible relationship between our homilist and the Jewish philosopher and exegete, which cannot be pursued in this chapter.[29] It is not necessary to commit to a position that Hebrews is heavily indebted to Philo to see the close resemblance at this point. For both, the true "sacrifice" is the offering of oneself to God. Whether or not he knows Philo, our homilist thinks with him on this point.[30]

But that is not the end of our homilist's account of sacrifice. He is part of a tradition, or rather, he is committed to a tradition, that understands the sacrificial death of Christ to have an effect on his followers. The grand goal of this homily was to remind the audience of that effect, perhaps to offer something of an explanation of it to those who might be in doubt about it, but certainly to instill a renewed appreciation of it. The

---

[29] For more on Philo and worship, see Jutta Leonhardt, *Jewish Worship in Philo of Alexandria* (Texts and Studies in Ancient Judaism, 84; Tübingen: Mohr Siebeck, 2001).

[30] Another interesting text potentially relevant to Hebrews is Philo, *Migr.* 104, where the soul enters Holy of Holies with song; and *Sacr.* 107, where we are the dough of sacrificial bread.

explanation that Christ's death was an act of submission to God's will and therefore counts as a "sacrifice" does not quite do the trick.

The device that the homilist relies on to show the ongoing relevance of the sacrificial death of Christ, understood as an act of willing submission to God, lurks back in the source of the "old-new" antithesis, in the citation from Jeremiah. The move that the homilist wants to make was probably the ultimate reason for the citation of Jeremiah in the first place. Even if our homilist was inspired by other uses of Jeremiah, his own application of the text is unique. The solution to the question of the relevance of Christ's death to our lives is the notion of a "New Covenant," anticipated by such passages as 7:12 that connect a change of priesthood with a change of law. In making his point our homilist could probably rely on the assumption of his addressees that they were indeed in a "new covenantal" relationship with God and that God has somehow "written on their hearts." Paul, in any case, seems to allude to precisely this understanding in his image-laden letter 2 Corinthians, when he speaks at 3:1-11 about the way in which his "letters of recommendation" are written on the hearts of the Corinthians.

Yes, the notion of a "New Covenant" provides a vehicle with the potential for talking about the ongoing relationship of the community with God, but like so many other clever solutions in Hebrews, this one too comes with a problem. How does one make the connection between Christ's death and the promise of the "New Covenant"? One might simply say, "Look, my brothers and sisters, Christ gave us an example of how we should relate to God in his 'sacrificial' act of wholehearted commitment; go, follow his example, and do likewise!" But some wag at the back of the assembly might raise a hand and ask, "I really don't get the connection between the prophecy and the exhortation. Help me, please!"

What our homilist does in the very center of his exposition of the relationship between Christ's death and Yom Kippur rituals is to anticipate and answer this question. He does so by two interconnected moves, one a play on words and one an evocation of another scriptural text. Both of these moves might seem to us superficial, facetious, even extraordinarily playful, and so they are, but they frame what our homilist takes to be profound truth.

The pun is difficult to reproduce in English and requires some sort of footnote to get the point across. It appears in Heb. 9:15-17, which is worth citing. The NAB reads:

> 15 For this reason he is mediator of a new covenant: since a death has taken place for deliverance from transgressions under the first covenant, those who are called may receive the promised eternal inheritance. 16 Now where there is a will, the death of the testator must be established. 17 For a will takes effect only at death; it has no force while the testator is alive.

The NRSV is very similar here.[31] The pun, or to use the technical rhetorical term, the *antanaclasis*, is a play on the Greek word διαθήκη, which might be best translated generically as a "legal disposition." It is a word that includes contractual arrangements

---

[31] NRSV: (15) For this reason he is the mediator of a New Covenant, so that those who are called may receive the promised eternal inheritance, because a death has occurred that redeems them from the transgressions under the first covenant. (16) Where a will is involved, the death of the one who

and wills or testaments. The play on the different applications of the word is found elsewhere in the NT, in Gal. 3:15-17. Hence, our homilist has not invented the pun but has put it to good use. He says, in effect, that the διαθήκη that Jeremiah was talking about was in fact a testamentary διαθήκη, through which Jesus provided an "inheritance." But what is the content of that inheritance?

Many things might qualify to be part of the estate sketched in Jesus's last will and testament. At the middle of 9:15, the sentence framed by references to the "will" and the "inheritance," stands the "promise" that those who are called will receive. The promise to which the Church looks forward included the "heavenly rest" promised in Psalm 95 (Heb. 4:8-10). It includes the heavenly Jerusalem around which members of the wandering household of God finally gather (12:18-24), the "promise" that Abraham and his immediate family did not receive (11:13). The contents of the inheritance, then, are complex. It involves union with God in the fellowship of those who have been sanctified, but it also involves the way to attain that union, the "new and living way" that the homilist mentions in 10:19 at the start of his final, lengthy exhortation to a life of faith, hope, and love.

The inheritance was not simply a hope for the future but an example for the present. The content of that example in the "will" left by Jesus will soon be expressed in the words of the psalm, written as the psalm itself seems to say, "about him," the words, "I have come to do your will, O God." The exemplary act of dedication and commitment, the commitment that defined his death as a sacrifice, stands at the heart of the inheritance left by Jesus.

But "Wait, wait!" the voice of the perplexed member of the congregation in the back pew might be saying, "I understand about moral examples, and how his response to God might be part of what Jesus left as an inheritance, but what about the blood?" Anticipating that potential objection and supplementing the pun with a scriptural text, the homilist, immediately after finishing his play on διαθήκη, introduces the other half of the keystone to his exposition of Christ's death, linking it to the inauguration of the first covenant. This little reflection is bounded by two comments, 9:18: "Hence not even the first covenant was inaugurated without blood," and 9:22: "Indeed, under the law almost everything is purified with blood, and without the shedding of blood there is no forgiveness of sin." For those familiar with Levitical thinking about ritual, these comments evoke the fundamental principle established at Lev. 17:11 "for, as life, it is the blood that makes atonement." Blood does indeed function as a cleansing substance in many sacrifices designed to deal with sin.[32] Yet that principle is hardly a universal one. Not all sacrifices that atone for sin involve blood.[33] The principle, like other bold generalizations made in Hebrews,[34] serves the purpose of the argument. The evocation

made it must be established. (17) For a will takes effect only at death, since it is not in force as long as the one who made it is alive.

[32] These include the blood of bulls for the sins of a priest (Lev. 4:4-7), the blood of a bull for the unintentional sins of whole congregation (Lev. 4:16-20), the blood of a goat for the sins of a ruler (Lev. 4:25), the blood of a female goat for the unintentional sins of the people (Lev. 4:34), the blood of turtledoves and pigeons for those who cannot afford a more costly sacrifice (Lev. 5:9).

[33] Those who cannot afford even two turtledoves can offer one-tenth of an ephah of choice flour (Lev. 5:11).

[34] Cf. 6:16, on the function of oaths; 7:7, on the blessing by the greater; 7:12 on the relationship between priesthood and Law.

of the principle here is no more than that, an evocation that remains to be clarified by the moves that the homilist makes in ch. 10. The "blood" of Jesus is indeed simply his life, offered to God upon his death,[35] but also, as the introduction to the quotation from the psalm at 10:5 indicates, from the moment of his entry into the world. The "blood" that inaugurates a covenant and provides "forgiveness of sin" is that life which he lived and in which his followers now participate.

"But wait, wait, how does the blood do the atoning thing?" our querulous critic might ask. "Is it magic? Is there a ransom being paid to Satan or to Sin? Is the life taken by God as recompense for sin, as if God needed recompense? What, please tell me, is going on with the blood?" Is it the case that blood is an offering for the "redemption" (ἀπολύτρωσις) of sin, mentioned at 9:15, and that offering simply conforms to the paradigm of the various sin offerings in Leviticus? Pushed to this point, we might, as some interpreters do, throw up our hands and say that our homilist, though offering some clever, Philonic-like moves relating to Jesus's death as sacrifice, has not really developed a coherent theology of atonement. Instead he struggles with primitive notions trying to invest them with some new meaning. He certainly has not solved our conceptual problem of how Christ's death provides atonement.

Ah, but if so we would be giving up on the very threshold of success. The evocation of the scriptural quote in 9:20 from Exod. 24:8 is central to the interpretation that the homilist offers. The scriptural verse is what Moses says as he sprinkles on the congregation the blood that inaugurates this covenant, "This is the blood of the covenant which God has made with you." Our homilist, following up with a bit of playful misdirection, says in v. 21 that Moses sprinkled blood on the tabernacle and the liturgical implements, but as the biblical text says, and as noted in v. 19, Moses scattered it on the *people*. The blood, the life, *marked the people* as a people in covenant with God. The blood, the life that marks the people of the New Covenant, identifies them as God's own, as people of the covenant. It does no more and no less than that. What is sprinkled with the blood of the sacrificial victim is not a heavenly altar or mercy seat, but a people whose lives are now marked by the life for which that blood stands. The purification and the sanctification provided by the act of sprinkling is not a magic act; it is the state of being in that covenant relationship, the commitment to the life that the blood symbolizes.

When the people of the wandering household stand before God in that covenant relationship, listening to Jeremiah's voice, they hear the promise of what the covenant entails. To make sure the point does not escape us, our homilist repeats that voice in the peroration of his exposition at 10:16-17, in what could well be understood as the content of the testament put into effect upon the Son's death:

"This is the covenant that I will make with them
After those days," says the Lord:

---

[35] The interpretation of the atonement theology of Hebrews by David M. Moffitt focuses, too narrowly I believe, on this point. See his *Atonement and the Logic of Resurrection in the Epistle to the Hebrews* (NovTSup, 141; Leiden: Brill, 2011). See also his "Blood, Life, and Atonement: Reassessing Hebrews' Christological Appropriation of Yom Kippur," in *The Day of Atonement: Its Interpretations in Early Jewish and Christian Traditions* (ed. Thomas Hieke and Tobias Nicklas; Themes in Biblical Narrative 15; Leiden: Brill, 2012), pp. 211-24.

"I will put my laws in their hearts, and I will write them on their minds."
He also adds (says our homilist),
"I will remember their sins and their lawless deeds no more."

The "promise" that the covenant offers and that "those called" receive through the death of Jesus (9:15) is not simply the fulfillment of eschatological hope. It is a more immediate benefaction that guarantees the realization of the hope. The covenant relationship, in other words, involves two gracious gifts of God. One is the writing of God's "law" on the heart. This is probably not what Jeremiah envisioned, a heartfelt adherence to Torah. Rather, it is the acceptance of the example of Christ's dedication and the covenantal life lived in faith, hope, and love.[36] The second element of the covenant relationship is a divine promise that sins would be remembered no more. The promise is not made in view of a gift that is given, a debt paid, or a ransom delivered. It is gracious divine amnesia pure and simple. It is that amnesia that provides "redemption" (9:12, 15).

The sacrifice of the Great High Priest and the life of the Church

The sacrifice of Christ works by creating a people of a New Covenant. That covenant is based on a divine promise, expressed in the words of the prophet Jeremiah, that those who follow the example of his Son receive his gracious forgiveness of sin. How is that gracious gift lived out in the lives of the wandering household of God?

Hebrews does not spend a great deal of attention to the ongoing life of the Church. It does not provide the advice to disciples that the Gospel of Matthew does in several of the sermons of Jesus, nor does it describe what the liturgical practices or pious observances of the new ἐκκλησία might be. It does, however, offer hints of how the ways in which the inaugurating event impacts the life of Jesus's followers.

The members of the wandering household have, first and foremost, been "perfected" (10:14), not in the sense that they have attained the apex of virtue. No, they are still very much a people "on the way," looking to their ἀρχηγός for inspiration and listening to their homilist's "word of exhortation" (13:22). Their "perfection" resembles that of the Great High Priest, who became "qualified" for his eternal priesthood by his life of obedience to God's will (2:18; 5:9).[37] They too have been "qualified" for their entry into a sacred space. Another way of describing that qualification is that they have been "sanctified" (10:10) and thus made eligible to serve at the place where the true altar

---

[36] For exploration of the resumption of the covenant theme in the final chapter of Hebrews, see Jason A. Whitlark, *Getting "Saved": The Whole Story of Salvation in the New Testament* (Grand Rapids, MI: Eerdmans, 2011), 72–91.

[37] On the theme of perfection, see David G. Peterson, *Hebrews and Perfection: An Examination of the Concept of Perfection in the Epistle to the Hebrews* (SNTSMS, 47; Cambridge: Cambridge University Press, 1982), and more recently, Jason A. Whitlark, "Cosmology and the Perfection of Humanity in Hebrews," in *Interpretations and the Claims of the Text: Resourcing New Testament Theology* (ed. Jason A. Whitlark, Bruce W. Longenecker, Lidija Novakovic, and Mikeal C. Parsons; Waco: Baylor University Press, 2014), pp. 117–30.

resides. The connection between "perfection" and "sanctification" echoes the initial description of the Son's salvific activity (2:10-11).

The archetypical "sanctification" or "cleansing" of the covenant people took place, as we have seen, when Moses sprinkled blood on them (9:20-22). The cleansing sanctification of the New Covenant people takes place when they too were "sprinkled" (ῥεραντισμένοι) in their hearts and "washed in body with pure water" (λελουσμένοι τὸ σῶμα ὕδατι καθαρῷ, 10:22). Not surprisingly, then, entry into the household or incorporation into the wandering people, took place in the baptismal ritual practiced by most Christians. If, as is likely, Pauline teaching lies in the background of Hebrews, the baptismal act envisioned here was also a participation in the death of Christ and an opening to a new life with him (Rom. 6:4; Col. 2:12).

The unique sacrifice of Christ in which they symbolically participate has qualified the people of the New Covenant for their role in worship, but the process of their sanctification continues (10:14) as they move in the footsteps of Jesus. Their lives are grounded in the grand triad of theological virtues, faith (10:22), hope (10:23), and a love that works to stimulate their mutual service (10:24). They endure, with self-confident boldness (10:35) in the face of opposition, inspired by a long line of faithful wanderers with whom they share an eschatological goal (11:40).

As they make their way to the heavenly Jerusalem (12:22) where their true "rest" is to be found (4:1-11) the wandering family also engages in acts of worship. Hebrews points to this reality in two ways in the concluding chapter. The homilist begins by actually involving the addressees in the kind of worship he has in mind. In response to God's promise never to forsake or abandon them (13:5), the church ("we") prays Ps 118:6 (117:6 LXX), cited at 13:6: "The Lord is my helper and I will not be afraid, what can anyone do to me?" In doing so "we" imitate the faithful worship in which Jesus himself has been engaged earlier in Hebrews. The "I" of the psalmist, who had been Jesus, now becomes the "we" of the Church at prayer.[38]

The prayer of the Church is directed to the Lord mentioned in the psalm, who may be the God to whom Jesus prayed. Or, more likely, their "Lord" is Jesus himself, the one who sits on the "throne of grace," and from whom they can expect grace, mercy, and support (4:16).[39] As an eternal High Priest, he is there for his followers, his brothers and sisters, ready to intercede for them (7:25). Note that the wandering people approach that throne not for forgiveness of sin, but for "timely aid" (εὔκαιρον βοήθειαν), the kind of support that a persecuted people need.

The wandering people also worship in some other way, at an "altar" (θυσιαστήριον) to which priests of old have no access (13:10). More than any other allusive reference to the continuing life of the wandering family, this passage has provoked scholarly debate. Is it a reference to the Eucharistic table, understood as a site of ongoing "sacrifice," as later Catholic theology will hold? Or is this simply an allusion to the "sacrifice of

---

[38] On Hebrews' use of the Psalms to engage the addressees in the Son's dialogue with the Father, see Harold W. Attridge, "Giving Voice to Jesus," in *Psalms in Community* (ed. Harold W. Attridge and Margot Fassler; Atlanta: SBL; Leiden: Brill, 2004), pp. 101–12; repr. in *Essays on John and Hebrews* (WUNT, 264; Tübingen: Mohr Siebeck, 2010), pp. 320–30.

[39] On the ambiguous allusions to the Christ-centered worship life of the community, see most recently Filtvedt, *Identity*, pp. 173–87.

praise" (θυσίαν αἰνέσεως) that they offer with "lips confessing his name" (13:15).[40] The latter is somewhat more likely, but in either case, the sacrifice that the community now offers is simply a participation in the once-for-all sacrifice of Jesus.[41] That event made available to the new wandering household the gracious gift of God's merciful forgiveness of sin. It called them as it marked them to be people who would live as Jesus lived.

Conclusion

Hebrews understands the Church to be a body of people that stands in continuity with ancient Israel but which is distinguished from it in an important way. Like ancient Israel it is a family called into being by God and summoned to move from the safe and familiar territory toward an eschatological goal. What called this people into being and toward its mission was the life and death of its "forerunner" in faith, the Great High Priest, Jesus. His death, like the rituals of the Day of Atonement, provided release from sin, in a profound way modeling and inspiring the life of the wandering people. The release from the burden of sin was achieved precisely by identifying the people as the "heirs" of the promise of God's covenant/testament, an event that "wrote" fidelity "on the hearts" of its heirs and gave assurance of God's gracious forgiveness.

---

[40] In a different set of circumstances, in critical opposition to the Temple at Jerusalem and its priesthood, the sectarians at Qumran (1QS 9.3-5) also proposed a displacement of blood sacrifice by an "offering of the lips."

[41] Several early Christian sources operate with a similar set of categories to frame their worship. Particularly striking is *1 Clement*, a text that probably knows Hebrews. *1 Clem.* 52 cites Ps. 50:14-15, mentioning "sacrifice of praise" and Ps. 51:17, which claims "sacrifice ... is a broken spirit," to support the proposition that "the Master, brothers, has no need of anything at all. He requires nothing of anyone except to make a confession to him" (Michael W. Holmes [ed. and trans.], *The Apostolic Fathers* [3rd ed.; Grand Rapids, MI: Baker Academic, 2007], pp. 114–15).

Bibliography

Abba, Raymond, "The Origin and Significance of Hebrew Sacrifice", *BTB* 7.3 (1977), pp. 134–35.

Adams, Edward, *The Stars Will Fall from Heaven: "Cosmic Catastrophe" in the New Testament and its World* (LNTS 347; London: T&T Clark, 2007).

Aitken, Ellen Bradshaw, "The Body of Jesus Outside the Eternal City: Mapping Ritual Space in the Epistle to the Hebrews", in *Hebrews in Contexts* (Edited by Gabriella Gelardini and Harold W. Attridge; Ancient Judaism and Early Christianity, 91; Leiden: Brill, 2016), pp. 194–209.

Allen, David M., *Deuteronomy and Exhortation in Hebrews: A Study in Narrative Re-Presentation* (WUNT 2:238; Tübingen: Mohr Siebeck, 2008).

Anatolios, Khaled, *Retrieving Nicaea: The Meaning and Development of Trinitarian Doctrine* (Grand Rapids, MI: Baker Academic, 2011).

Anatolios, Khaled, "The Soteriological Grammar of Patristic Christology", *The Thomist* 78.2 (2014), pp. 165–88.

Anatolios, Khaled, "Creation and Salvation in St. Athanasius of Alexandria", in *On the Tree of the Cross: George Florovsky and the Patristic Doctrine of Atonement* (Edited by Matthew Baker, Seraphim Danckaert, and Nicholas Marinides; Jordanville, NY: Holy Trinity Seminary Press, 2016), pp. 59–72.

Anderson, Gary, *Sacrifices and Offerings in Ancient Israel: Studies in the Social and Political Importance* (HSM 41; Atlanta, GA: Scholars Press, 1987).

Anderson, Gary, *Sin: A History* (New Haven, CT: Yale University Press, 2009).

Anderson, Gary, *Charity: The Place of the Poor in the Biblical Tradition* (New Haven, CT: Yale University Press, 2013).

Ando, Clifford, *The Matter of the Gods: Religion and the Roman Empire* (Transformation of the Classical Heritage, 44; Berkeley, CA: University of California Press, 2008).

Andrews, Mary M., "*Peirasmos*: A Study in Form-Criticism", *AThR* 24 (1942), pp. 229–44.

Andriessen, P. C. B., "La Teneur Judéo-Chrétienne de He I 6 et II 14b-III 2", *NovT* 18.4 (1976), pp. 293–313.

Anizor, Uche, *Kings and Priests: Scripture's Theological Account of Its Readers* (Eugene, OR: Pickwick, 2014).

Aquinas, Thomas, *Commentary on the Epistle to the Hebrews* (Translated Chrysostom Baer; South Bend, IN: St. Augustine's, 2006).

Aquinas, Thomas, *Commentary on the Letter of Saint Paul to the Hebrews* (Edited by J. Mortensen and E. Alarcón; Translated by F. R. Larcher, O.P.; Lander, WY: The Aquinas Institute for the Study of Sacred Doctrine, 2012).

St. Athanasius the Great of Alexandria, *On the Incarnation: Greek Original and English Translation* (Preface by C.S. Lewis; Translation and Introduction by John Behr; Yonkers, NY: St. Vladimir's Seminary Press, 2011).

Attridge, Harold W., *First-century Cynicism in the Epistles of Heraclitus* (Harvard Theological Studies 29; Missoula, MT: Scholars Press, 1976).

Attridge, Harold W., "The Philosophical Critique of Religion under the Early Empire", *ANRW* 2.16.1 (Berlin: De Gruyter, 1978), pp. 45–78.

Attridge, Harold W., *Hebrews: A Commentary on the Epistle to the Hebrews* (Hermeneia; Philadelphia, PA: Fortress Press, 1989).

Attridge, Harold W., "God in Hebrews", in *The Epistle to the Hebrews and Christian Theology* (Edited by Richard Bauckham, Daniel Driver, Trevor Hart, and Nathan MacDonald; Grand Rapids, MI: Eerdmans, 2009), pp. 95–110.

Attridge, Harold W., "Giving Voice to Jesus", in *Psalms in Community* (Edited by Harold W. Attridge and Margot Fassler; Atlanta, GA: SBL; Leiden: Brill, 2004), pp. 101–12; repr. in *Essays on John and Hebrews* (WUNT 264; Tübingen: Mohr Siebeck, 2010a), pp. 320–30.

Attridge, Harold W., "The Uses of Antithesis in Hebrews 8–10", *HTR* 76 (1986), pp. 1–9 [G. W. E. Nickelsburg and George W. MacRae, S. J., eds., *Christians Among Jews and Gentiles* (Philadelphia, PA: Fortress Press, 1986), pp. 1–6]; repr. in *Essays on John and Hebrews* (WUNT 264; Tübingen: Mohr Siebeck, 2010b), pp. 273–80.

Augustine, *The City of God* (Translated by Marcus Dods; *The Nicene and Post-Nicene Fathers*, Series 1, vol. 2; 14 vols; Grand Rapids, MI: Eerdmans, 1956).

Augustine, *On Genesis* (Translated by E. Hill; New York, NY: New City Press, 2002).

Augustine, *Saint Augustine Confessions: A New Translation by Henry Chadwick* (Translated by Henry Chadwick; Oxford World's Classics; Oxford: Oxford University Press, 2008).

Augustine, *The City of God. De civitate dei* (Translated by William Babcock; *The Works of Saint Augustine: A Translation for the 21st Century*; Hyde Park, NY: New City Press, 2013).

Backhaus, Knut, *Der Hebräerbrief* (RNT; Regensburg: Pustet, 2009).

Barrett, C. K., "The Eschatology of the Epistle to the Hebrews", in *The Background of the New Testament and its Eschatology: Studies in Honour of C. H. Dodd* (Edited by W. D. Davies and D. Daule; Cambridge: Cambridge University Press, 1954), pp. 363–93.

Barth, Karl, *Church Dogmatics*, Volume Four: *The Doctrine of Reconciliation*, Part One (Edited by G. W. Bromiley and T. F. Torrance; London: T&T Clark, 1956).

Barth, Karl, *Church Dogmatics III.1* (Translated by. J. W. Edwards, O. Bussey, and H. Knight; Edinburgh: T&T Clark, 1958).

Barth, Karl, *Church Dogmatics III.2* (Translated by H. Knight, G. W. Bromiley, J. K. S. Reid, and R. H. Fuller; Edinburgh: T&T Clark, 1960).

Basker, Bianca, *Original Copies: Architectural Mimicry in Contemporary China (Spatial Habitus)* (Honolulu, HI: University of Hawaii Press, 2013).

Bauckham, Richard J., *Jesus and the Eyewitnesses: The Gospels as Eyewitness Testimony* (Grand Rapids, MI: Eerdmans, 2006).

Bauckham, Richard J., "The Divinity of Jesus Christ in the Epistle to the Hebrews", in *The Epistle to the Hebrews and Christian Theology* (Edited by Richard Bauckham, Daniel Driver, Trevor Hart, and Nathan MacDonald; Grand Rapids, MI: Eerdmans, 2009), pp. 15–37.

Bavinck, Herman, *Sin and Salvation in Christ* (Edited by John Bolt; Translated by John Vriend; Reformed Dogmatics, 3; Grand Rapids, MI: Baker Academic, 2006).

Bayes, J. F., *The Weakness of the Law: God's Law and the Christian in New Testament Perspective* (Paternoster Biblical Monographs; Eugene, OR: Wipf & Stock, Publishers, 2006).

Beard, Mary, John North, and Simon Price, *Religions of Rome. Vol. 1: A History. Vol. 2: A Sourcebook* (Cambridge: Cambridge University Press, 1998).

Beasley-Murray, G. R., *Jesus and the Kingdom of God* (Grand Rapids, MI: Eerdmans, 1986).

Beavis, Mary Ann, and Hye-Ran Kim Cragg, *Hebrews* (Edited by Barbara E. Reid and Linda Maloney; Wisdom Commentary Series, 54; Collegeville, MN: Liturgical Press, 2015).

Becker, E.-M. "'Gottes Wort' und 'Unser Wort': Bemerkungen zu Heb 4,12-13," *BZ* 44 (2000), pp. 254-62.

Becking, Bob, "Nehemiah 9 and the Problematic Concept of Context (*Sitz im Leben*)", in *The Changing Face of Form Criticism for the Twenty-First Century* (Edited by Marvin A. Sweeney and Ehud Ben Zvi, Grand Rapids, MI: Eerdmans, 2003), pp. 253-65.

Beeke, Joel R., and Sinclair B. Ferguson, eds., *Reformed Confessions Harmonized* (Grand Rapids, MI: Baker, 1999).

Berceville, Gilles, O. P., "Le sacerdoce du Christ dans le *Commentaire de l'épître aux Hébreux* de saint Thomas d'Aquin", *RevThom* 99 (1999), pp. 143-58.

Berman, Joshua, *The Temple: Its Symbolism and Meaning Then and Now* (Northvale, NJ: J. Aronson, 1995).

Berquist, Jon L., "Critical Spatiality and the Book of Hebrews," in *Hebrews in Contexts* (Leiden: Brill Academic, 2016), pp. 181-93.

Bick, Ezra, "Tamid" (etzion.org.il/en; Yeshivat Har Etzion - Virtual Beit Midrash, 1997), pp. 1-8.

Blenkin, Hugh, *Immortal Sacrifice* (London: Darton, Longman and Todd, 1964).

Blocher, Henri, "Yesterday, Today, Forever: Time, Times, Eternity in Biblical Perspective", *Tyndale Bulletin* 52 (2001), pp. 183-202.

Botner, Max, "What Has Mark's Christ to Do with David's Son? A History of Interpretation", *CBR* 16 (2017), pp. 50-70.

Boring, M. E., *Mark: A Commentary* (NTL; Louisville, KY: Westminster John Knox, 2006).

Boyancé, Pierre, "Les Romains, peuple de la *fides* [1964]", in *Études sur la religion romaine* (Edited by l'École française de Rome; Collection de l'École française de Rome, 11; Rome/Paris: École française de Rome, 1972), pp. 135-52.

Boyarin, Daniel, *Dying for God: Martyrdom and the Making of Christianity and Judaism* (Stanford, CA: Stanford University Press, 1999).

Boyarin, Daniel, *The Jewish Gospels: The Story of the Jewish Christ* (New York, NY: The New Press, 2012).

Boyle, John F., "'On the Relation of St. Thomas' Commentary on Romans to the *Summa theologiae*", in *Reading Romans with St. Thomas Aquinas* (Edited by Matthew Levering and Michael Dauphinais; Washington, DC: Catholic University of America Press, 2012), pp. 75-82.

Braun, Herbert, *An die Hebräer* (HNT, 14; Tübingen: Mohr Siebeck, 1984).

Braund, Susanna Morton, "The Anger of Tyrants and the Forgiveness of Kings", in *Ancient Forgiveness: Classical, Judaic, and Christian* (Edited by C. L. Griswold and D. Konstan; Cambridge: Cambridge University Press, 2012), pp. 79-96.

Bremmer, Jan N. (ed.), *The Strange World of Human Sacrifice* (Studies in the History and Anthropology of Religion; Leuven: Peeters, 2006).

Bremmer, Jan N., "Greek Normative Animal Sacrifice", in *A Companion to Greek Religion* (Edited by D. Ogden; Malden, MA/Oxford: Wiley-Blackwell, 2007), pp. 132-44.

Briggs, Richard S., "Speech-Act Theory", in *Dictionary for Theological Interpretation of the Bible* (Edited by Kevin J. Vanhoozer, Craig G. Bartholomew, Daniel J. Treier, and N. T. Wright; Grand Rapids, MI: Baker Academic, 2005), pp. 763-66.

Bruce, F. F., *The Epistle to the Hebrews* (NICNT; Grand Rapids, MI: Eerdmans, 1964).

Bruce, F. F., *The Canon of Scripture* (Downers Grove, IL: IVP, 1988).
Bruce, F. F., *The Epistle to the Hebrews* (rev. ed.; NICNT; Grand Rapids, MI: Eerdmans, 1990).
Brueggemann, Walter, *The Land: Place as Gift, Promise, and Challenge in Biblical Faith* (2nd ed.; Minneapolis, MN: Fortress Press, 2002).
Buber, Martin, *Two Types of Faith* (Translated by Norman P. Goldhawk, The Martin Buber Library; Syracuse, NY: Syracuse University Press, 2003).
Buber, Martin, *Schriften zum Christentum* (Vol. 9 of *Werkausgabe*, Edited, introduced and annotated by Karl-Josef Kuschel; Gütersloh: Gütersloher Verlagshaus, 2011).
Büchsel, Friedrich, "ἐλέγχω, ἔλεγξις, ἔλεγχος, ἐλεγμός", *TWNT*, pp. 2: 470–47.
Bultmann, Rudolf, *Theology of the New Testament* (Translated by Kendrick Grobel; 2 vols; London: SCM, 1952).
Burkert, Walter, *Greek Religion* (Translated by J. Raffan; 1977 repr., Cambridge, MA: Harvard University Press, 1985).
Burrell, David B., C. S. C., *Towards a Jewish-Christian-Muslim Theology* (Oxford: Wiley-Blackwell, 2011).
Bynum, Caroline Walker, *Wonderful Blood: Theology and Practice in Late Medieval Northern Germany and Beyond* (Philadelphia, PA: University of Pennsylvania Press, 2007).
Bynum, Caroline Walker, "Why Paradox? The Contradictions of My Life as a Scholar", in *Journeys in Church History: Essays from the* Catholic Historical Review (Edited by Nelson H. Minnich; Washington, DC: Catholic University of America Press, 2015), pp.29–51.
Calhoun, Robert M., *Paul's Definitions of the Gospel in Romans 1* (vol. 2; WUNT 2.316; Tübingen: Mohr Siebeck, 2011).
Cancik, Hubert, "Fides, Pistis und Imperium", in *Römische Religion im Kontext: Kulturelle Bedingungen religiöser Diskurse* (Edited by Hildegard Cancik-Lindemaier; Gesammelte Aufsätze I; Tübingen: Mohr Siebeck, 2008), pp. 178–97.
Cancik, Hubert, Helmuth Schneider, and Manfred Landfester (eds.), *Brill's New Pauly: Encyclopedia of the Ancient World* (22 vols; Leiden: Brill, 2002–2012).
Carbon, Jan-Mathieu, and Vinciane Pirenne-Delforge, "Priests and Cult Personnel in Three Hellenistic Families", in *Cities and Priests: Cult Personnel in Asia Minor and the Aegean Islands from the Hellenistic to the Imperial Period* (Edited by M. Horster and A. Klöckner; Religionsgeschichtliche Versuche und Vorarbeiten, 64; Berlin: De Gruyter, 2013), pp. 65–120.
Casey, Edward S., *Getting Back into Place: Toward a Renewed Understanding of the Place-World* (Bloomington, IN: Indiana University Press, 1993).
Casey, Edward S., *The Fate of Place: A Philosophical History* (Berkeley: University of California Press, 1997).
Casey, Edward S., *Getting Back into Place: Toward a Renewed Understanding of the Place-World* (2nd ed.; Bloomington, IN: Indiana University Press, 2009).
Cessario, Romanus, O. P., *The Godly Image: Christ and Salvation in Catholic Thought from Anselm to Aquinas* (Petersham, MA: St. Bede's, 1990).
Chaniotis, Angelos, "Illness and Cures in the Greek Propitiatory Inscriptions and Dedications of Lydia and Phrygia", in *Ancient Medicine in its Socio-Cultural Context II* (Edited by P. J. van der Eijk, H. F. J. Horstmanshoff, and P. H. Schrijvers; Papers read at the Congress held at Leiden University, April 13–15, 1992; Amsterdam: Rodopi, 1995), pp. 323–43.
Chapman, David W., and Eckhard J. Schnabel, *The Trial and Crucifixion of Jesus: Texts and Commentary* (WUNT, 344; Tübingen: Mohr Siebeck, 2015).

Charlesworth, J. H. (ed.), *Old Testament Pseudepigrapha* (2 vols; Peabody, MA: Hendrickson, 1983).
Chester, A. N., "Hebrews: The Final Sacrifice", in *Sacrifice and Redemption* (Edited by S. W. Sykes; Cambridge: Cambridge University Press, 1991), pp. 57–72.
Childs, Brevard S., *The Struggle to Understand Isaiah as Christian Scripture* (Grand Rapids, MI: Eerdmans, 2004).
Clarkson, M. E., "The Antecedents of the High-Priest Them in Hebrews", *ATR* 29 (1947), pp. 89–95.
Cockerill, Gareth Lee, *The Epistle to the Hebrews* (NICNT; Grand Rapids, MI: Wm. B. Eerdmans, 2012).
Cody, A., *Heavenly Sanctuary and Liturgy in the Epistle to the Hebrews: The Achievement of Salvation in the Epistle's Perspectives* (St. Meinrad, IN: Grail, 1960).
Collins, A. Y., "The Charge of Blasphemy in Mark 14:64", *JSNT* 26 (2004), pp. 379–401.
Collins, Adela Yarbro, *Mark: A Commentary* (Hermeneia; Minneapolis, MN: Fortress Press, 2007).
Compton, Jared, "Review of *Atonement and the Logic of Resurrection in the Epistle to the Hebrews*," *TJ* 36 (2015), pp. 133–35.
Coppens, Joseph, "Les affinités qumraniennes de l'Épître aux Hébreux", *NRTh* 84 (1962), pp. 128–41.
Coppens, George W., *To the Hebrews: Translation, Comment and Conclusion* (AB 36; Garden City, NY: Doubleday, 1972).
Cortez, Felix H., "From the Holy to the Most Holy Place: The Period of Hebrews 9:6-10 and the Day of Atonement as a Metaphor of Transition", *JBL* 125 (2006), pp. 527–47.
Cosby, Michael R., *The Rhetorical Composition and Function of Hebrews 11: In Light of Example Lists in Antiquity* (Macon, GA: Mercer University Press, 1988).
Cross, Anthony R., "The Meaning of 'Baptisms' in Hebrews 6.2", in *Dimensions of Baptism: Biblical and Theological Studies* (Edited by Stanley E. Porter and Anthony R. Cross; London/New York, NY: Sheffield Academic, 2002), pp. 163–86.
Croy, N. Clayton, *Endurance in Suffering: Hebrews 12:1-13 in its Rhetorical, Religious, and Philosophical Context* (SNTSMS 98; Cambridge: Cambridge University Press, 1998).
Cyril, *Fragments on Hebrews* in *Sancti patris nostri Cyrilli archiepiscopi Alexandrini in D. Joannis evangelium* (vol. 3; Edited by P. E. Pusey; Oxford: Clarendon Press, 1872) pp. 362–423.
Daley, Brian, *God Visible. Patristic Christology Reconsidered* (Oxford: Oxford University Press, 2018).
Daly, Robert J., *Sacrifice Unveiled: The True Meaning of Christian Sacrifice* (London: T&T Clark, 2009).
de Lubac, Henri, S. J., *The Four Senses of Scripture*, vol. 2 in *Medieval Exegesis* (Translated by E. M. Macierowski; Grand Rapids, MI: Eerdmans, 2000).
de Silva, David A. *Perseverance in Gratitude: A Socio-Rhetorical Commentary on the Epistle "to the Hebrews"* (Grand Rapids, MI: Eerdmans, 2000).
Dautzenberg, Gerhard, "Psalm 110 im Neuen Testament", in *Liturgie und Dichtung. Ein Interdisziplinäres Kompendium 1* (Edited by Hansjakob Becker and Riener Kaczynski; Pietas Liturgica 1–2; Sankt Ottilien: EOS, 1983).
Déaut, Roger Le, *La nuit pascale: Essai sur la signification de la Pâque juive à partir du Targum d'Exode XII 42* (Rome: Institut biblique pontifical: 1963).
Dekker, Wisse "De 'Geliefde Zoon' in de Synoptische Evangelien", *NedTTs* 16 (1961), pp. 94–106.

Detienne, Marcel, and Jean Pierre Vernant, *The Cuisine of Sacrifice among the Greeks* (Translated by P. Wissing; repr. 1979, Chicago, IL: University of Chicago Press, 1989).

Docherty, Susan E., *The Use of the Old Testament in Hebrews* (WUNT 260; Tübingen: Mohr Siebeck, 2009).

Dodd, C. H., *According to the Scriptures: The Sub-Structure of New Testament Theology* (London: Nisbet, 1952).

Dodds, Eric R., *The Greeks and the Irrational* (Sather Classical Lectures; Berkeley, CA: University of California Press, 1951).

Dohrmann, Henning, *Anerkennung und Bekämpfung von Menschenopfern im römischen Strafrecht der Kaiserzeit* (Europäische Hochschulschriften, 2.185; Frankfurt: Lang, 1995).

Dunn, J. D. G., "'Are You the Messiah?': Is the Crux of Mark 14:61-62 Resolvable?", in *Christology, Controversy, and Community: New Testament Essays in Honour of David R. Catchpole* (Edited by David Catchpole, David Horrell, and Christopher M. Tuckett; Leiden: Brill: 2000), pp. 1–22.

Dunn, James D. G., *Jesus Remembered: Vol. 1: Christianity in the Making* (Grand Rapids, MI: Eerdmans, 2003).

Dunnill, John, *Sacrifice and the Body: Biblical Anthropology and Christian Self-Understanding* (Ashgate New Critical Thinking in Religion, Theology and Biblical Studies; Surrey: Ashgate, 2013).

Dyer, Bryan R., *Suffering in the Face of Death: The Epistle to the Hebrews and Its Context of Situation* (LNTS 568; London: T&T Clark, 2017).

Eberhart, Christian, *Studien zur Bedeutung der Opfer im Alten Testament: Die Signifikanz von Blut- und Verbrennungsriten im kultischen Rahmen* (WMANT 94; Neukirchen: Neukirchener, 2002).

Eberhart, Christian, "A Neglected Feature of Sacrifice in the Hebrew Bible: Remarks on the Burning Rite on the Altar", *HTR* 97.4 (2004), pp. 485–93.

Eberhart, Christian, "Characteristics of Sacrificial Metaphors in Hebrews", in *Hebrews: Contemporary Methods—New Insights* (Edited by G. Gelardini; Leiden: Brill, 2005), pp. 37–64.

Eberhart, Christian, *Ritual and Metaphor: Sacrifice in the Bible* (SBLRBS 68; Atlanta, GA: SBL, 2011a).

Eberhart, Christian, *The Sacrifice of Jesus: Understanding Atonement Biblically* (Minneapolis, MN: Fortress Press, 2011b).

Eberhart, Christian, *Kultmetaphorik und Christologie: Opfer- und Sühneterminologie im Neuen Testament* (WUNT, 306; Tübingen: Mohr Siebeck, 2013).

Eger, Otto, "Eid und Fluch in den maionischen und phrygischen Sühne-Inschriften", in *Festschrift Paul Koschaker. Vol. III* (Weimar: Böhlau, 1939), pp. 281–93.

Eisenbaum, Pamela, *The Jewish Heroes of Christian History: Hebrews 11 in Literary Context* (SBLDS 156; Atlanta, GA: Scholars Press, 1997).

Eisenbaum, Pamela, "Ritual and Religion, Sacrifice and Supersessionism: A Utopian Reading of Hebrews", in *Hebrews in Contexts* (Edited by Gabriella Gelardini and Harold W. Attridge; Ancient Judaism and Early Christianity, 91; Leiden: Brill, 2016), pp. 343–56.

Eliade, Mircea, *The Myth of the Eternal Return: Cosmos and History* (Translated by William R. Trask; Princeton, NJ: Princeton University Press, 1954).

Ellingworth, Paul, *The Epistle to the Hebrews: A Commentary on the Greek Text* (NIGTC; Grand Rapids, MI/Carlisle, PA: Eerdmans/Paternoster, 1993).

Embry, Brad, "The *Psalms of Solomon* and the New Testament: Intertextuality and the Need for a Re-Evaluation", *JSP* 13 (2002), pp. 99–136.

Emery, Gilles, O. P., "Biblical Exegesis and the Speculative Doctrine of the Trinity in St. Thomas Aquinas's *Commentary on John*", in *Reading John with St. Thomas Aquinas: Theological Exegesis and Speculative Theology* (Edited by Michael Dauphinais and Matthew Levering; Washington, DC: Catholic University of America Press, 2005), pp. 23–61.

Ernest, James D., *The Bible in Athanasius of Alexandria* (Boston, MA and Leiden: Brill, 2004).

Eschner, Christina, *Gestorben und hingegeben "für" die Sünder. Die griechische Konzeption des Unheil abwendenden Sterbens und deren paulinische Aufnahme für die Deutung des Todes Jesu Christi* (WMANT, 122; 2 vols; Neukirchen-Vluyn: Neukirchener Verlag, 2010).

Eubank, Nathan, "Ineffably Effable: The Pinnacle of Mystical Ascent in Gregory of Nyssa's *De vita Moysis*", *International Journal of Systematic Theology* 16.1 (2014), pp. 25–41.

Euripides (Translated by David Kovacs; Loeb Classical Library; 5 vols; Cambridge, MA: Harvard University Press, 1994–2002).

Faraone, Christopher A., and F. S. Naiden, *Greek and Roman Animal Sacrifice: Ancient Victims, Modern Observers* (Cambridge: Cambridge University Press, 2012).

Feder, Yitzhaq, "On *Kuppuru, Kippēr* and Etymological Sins That Cannot Be Wiped Away", *VT* 60.4 (2010), pp. 535–45.

Finlan, Stephen, *Background and Content of Paul's Atonement Metaphors* (Leiden: Brill, 2004).

Finlan, Stephen, *Options on Atonement in Christian Thought* (Collegeville, MN: Liturgical Press, 2007).

Finlan, Stephen, "Spiritualization of Sacrifice in Paul and Hebrews", in *Ritual and Metaphor: Sacrifice in the Bible* (Edited by Christian A. Eberhart; SBLRBS 68; Atlanta, GA: SBL, 2011), pp. 83–98.

Fletcher-Louis, Crispin, "The Revelation of the Sacral Son of Man: The Genre, History of Religions Context and the Meaning of the Transfiguration", in *Auferstehung—Resurrection. The Fourth Durham-Tübingen Research Symposium. Resurrection, Transfiguration and Exaltation in Old Testament, Ancient Judaism and Early Christianity (Tübingen, September 1999)* (Edited by F. Avemarie and H. Lichtenberger, WUNT 135; Tübingen: Mohr Siebeck: 2001), pp. 247–98.

Foley, Helen P., *The Homeric Hymn to Demeter: Translation, Commentary, and Interpretive Essays* (Princeton, NJ: Princeton University Press, 1994).

Fortenbaugh, William W., Pamela Huby, Robert Sharples, and Dimitri Gutas (eds.), *Theophrastus of Eresus. Sources for his Life, Writings, Thought and Influence* (2 vols; Leiden: Brill, 1992).

France, R. T., *The Gospel of Mark* (NIGTC; Grand Rapids, MI: Eerdmans; Carlisle, PA: Paternoster Press, 2002).

Friedrich Schleiermacher, *The Christian Faith* (Edited by H. R. Mackintosh and J. S. Stewart; Translated by D. M. Baillie, W.R. Matthews, Edith Sandbach-Marshall, A.B. Macualay, Alexander Grieve, J.Y. Campbell, R.W. Stewart, H.R. Mackintosh; Edinburgh: T&T Clark, 1989).

Frisch, Peter, "Über die lydisch-phrygischen Sühneinschriften und die 'Confessiones' des Augustinus", *EA* 2 (1983), pp. 41–45.

Froehlich, Karlfried (with Mark S. Burrows), *Sensing the Scriptures: Aminadab's Chariot and the Predicament of Biblical Interpretation* (Grand Rapids, MI: Eerdmans, 2014).

Gäbel, Georg, "'[…] inmitten der Gemeinde werde ich dir lobsingnen' Hebr 2,12: Engel und Menschen, himmlischer und irdischer Gottesdienst nach dem Hebräerbrief", in *Gottesdienst und Engel im antiken Judentum und frühen Christentum* (Edited by Jörg Frey and Michael R. Jost; WUNT 2/446; Tübingen: Mohr Siebeck, 2017), pp. 185–239.

Gane, Roy E., *Cult and Character: Purification Offerings, Day of Atonement, and Theodicy* (Winona Lake, IN: Eisenbrauns, 2005).

Gayford, S. C., *Sacrifice and Priesthood: Jewish and Christian* (2nd ed.; London: Methuen, 1953).

Gelardini, Gabriella, "Hebrews, An Ancient Synagogue Homily for *Tisha Be-Av*: Its Function, Its Basis, Its Theological Interpretation", in *Hebrews: Contemporary Methods—New Insights* (Edited by Gabriella Gelardini; Leiden: Brill, 2005), pp. 107–27.

Gelardini, Gabriella, *"Verhärtet eure Herzen nicht": der Hebräer, eine Synagogenhomilie zu* (Tischa be-Aw, BINS 83; Leiden: Brill, 2007).

Gelardini, Gabriella, "The Inauguration of Yom Kippur according to the LXX and Its Cessation or Perpetuation according to the Book of Hebrews: A Systematic Comparison", in *The Day of Atonement: Its Interpretations in Early Jewish and Christian Traditions* (Edited by Thomas Hieke and Tobias Nicklas; Themes in Biblical Narrative, 15; Leiden: Brill, 2011), pp. 225–54.

Gelardini, Gabriella, "Charting 'Outside the Camp" with Edward W. Soja: Critical Spatiality and Hebrews 13", in *Hebrews in Contexts* (Edited by Gabriella Gelardini and Harold W. Attridge; Ancient Judaism and Early Christianity, 91; Leiden: Brill, 2016a), 210–37.

Gelardini, Gabriella, "Existence Beyond Borders: The Book of Hebrews and Critical Spatiality", in *The Epistle to the Hebrews: Writing at the Borders* (Edited by R. Burnet, D. Luciani, and G. Van Oyen; Leuven: Peeters, 2016b), pp.187–204.

Geller, Stephen A., "Blood Cult: Toward a Literary Theology of the Priestly Work of the Pentateuch", *Prooftexts* 12.2 (1992), pp. 97–124.

Gese, H., "The Atonement", in *Essays on Biblical Theology* (Translated by K. Crim; Minneapolis, MN: Augsburg, 1981), pp. 93–116.

Gordon, Richard, "Raising a Sceptre: Confession-Narratives from Lydia and Phrygia", *JRA* 17 (2004), pp. 177–96.

Gorman, Frank H., "Priestly Rituals of Founding: Time, Space, and Status", in *History and Interpretation: Essays in Honour of John H. Hayes* (Edited by M. Patrick Graham, William P. Brown, and Jeffrey K. Kuan; Sheffield: JSOT, 1993), pp. 47–64.

Gorman, Michael J., *The Death of the Messiah and the Birth of the New Covenant: A (Not So) New Model of the Atonement* (Eugene, OR: Cascade, 2014).

Graf, Fritz, "One Generation after Burkert and Girard: Where are the Great Theories?", in *Greek and Roman Animal Sacrifice: Ancient Victims, Modern Observers* (Edited by C. A. Faraone and F. S. Naiden; Cambridge: Cambridge University Press, 2012), pp. 32–51.

Gräßer, Erich, *An die Hebräer* (EKKNT 17; 3 vols; Zürich: Benziger; Neukirchen-Vluyn: Neukirchener Verlag, 1990–97).

Grässer, Erich, *Der Glaube im Hebräerbrief* (Marburger Theologische Studien, 2; Marburg: Elwert, 1965).

Grässer, Erich, "Das wandernde Gottesvolk Zum Basismotiv des Hebräerbriefes," in *Aufbruch und Verheißung: Gesammelte Aufsätze zum Hebräerbrief* (Edited by Martin Evang and Otto Merk; Berlin: De Gruyter, 1992), 231–50.

Grässer, Erich, *An die Hebräer* (EKKNT 17; vol. 3; Zurich: Benziger; Neukirchen-Vluyn: Neukirchener, 1997).

Grassi, Joseph A., "Abba, Father (Mark 14:36): Another Approach", *JAAR* 50 (1982), pp. 449–58.

Greenstein, Edward L., "Presenting Genesis 1, Constructively and Deconstructively", *Prooftexts* 21.1 (2001), p. 4.

Greer, Rowan A., *The Captain of our Salvation. A Study in the Patristic Exegesis of Hebrews*. (Beiträge zur Geschichte der Biblischen Exegese; Tübingen: J.C.B. Mohr, 1975).

Griswold, Charles L., "Plato and Forgiveness", *Ancient Philosophy* 27 (2007), pp. 269–87.

Gruenwald, Ithamar, "God the 'Stone/Rock': Myth, Idolatry, and Cultic Fetishism in Ancient Israel", *JR* 76 (1996), pp. 428–48.

Guggenheim, Antoine, *Jésus Christ, grand prêtre de l'ancienne et de la nouvelle Alliance. Étude du Commentaire de saint Thomas d'Aquin sur l'Épître aux Hébreux* (Paris: Parole et Silence, 2004).

Guthrie, George H., *The Structure of Hebrews: A Text-Linguistic Analysis* (Supplements to Novum Testamentum 73; Leiden/New York, NY: E.J. Brill, 1994).

Guthrie, George H., *Hebrews* (NIVAC; Grand Rapids, MI: Zondervan, 1998a).

Guthrie, George H., *The Structure of Hebrews: A Text-Linguistic Analysis* (Grand Rapids, MI: Baker, 1998b).

Guthrie, George H., "Hebrews' Use of the Old Testament: Recent Trends in Research", *Currents in Biblical Research* 1 (2003), pp. 271–94.

Guthrie, George H., "Hebrews", in *Commentary on the New Testament Use of the Old Testament* (Edited by G. K. Beale and D. A. Carson; Grand Rapids, MI: Baker Academic, 2007), pp. 919–95.

Hanson, A. T., *The Living Utterances of God: The New Testament Exegesis of the Old* (London: Darton, Longman, & Todd, 1983).

Hanson, R. P. C., *The Search for the Christian Doctrine of God: The Arian Controversy 318-381 AD* (New York, NY: T&T Clark, 1988).

Harris, R. Laird, "Exegetical Notes: Meaning of Kipper", *JETS* 4.1 (1961), p. 3.

Hayes, Christine, *What's Divine about Divine Law? Early Perspectives* (Princeton, NJ: Princeton University Press, 2015).

Hays, Richard, *Echoes of Scripture in the Letters of Paul* (New Haven, CT: Yale University Press, 1989).

Hays, Richard, "Christ Prays the Psalms: Paul's Use of an Early Christian Exegetical Convention", in *The Future of Christology: Essays in Honor of Leander E. Keck* (Edited by Abraham J. Malherbe and Wayne A. Meeks; Minneapolis, MN: Augsberg, 1993), pp. 122–36.

Healy, Mary, *Hebrews* (Catholic Commentary on Sacred Scripture; Grand Rapids, MI: Baker Academic, 2016).

Heck, Sarah, "Space, Politics and Occupy Wall Street" (MA Thesis, Georgia State University, 2014).

Heen, Erik M. and Philip D. W. Krey, *Hebrews* (Ancient Christian Commentary on Scripture, New Testament 10; Downers Grove, IL: Intervarsity Press, 2005).

"The Heidelberg Catechism (1563)", in *Reformed Confessions of the Sixteenth Century* (Edited by Arthur Cochrane; Louisville, KY: Westminster John Knox, 2003), pp. 305–31.

Heinze, Richard (1929), "Fides", in *Vom Geist des Römertums: Ausgewählte Aufsätze* (Edited by Erich Burck, 3d ed., Stuttgart: Teubner, 1960), pp. 59–81.

Helm, Paul, "Eternity" in *The Stanford Encyclopedia of Philosophy* (Spring 2014 Edition), Edward N. Zalta (ed.), URL = https://plato.stanford.edu/archives/spr2014/entries/eternity/.

Hengel, Martin, *Studies in Early Christology* (Edinburgh: T&T Clark, 1995).

Herodotus (Translated by A. D. Godley; LCL; 4 vols; Cambridge, MA: Harvard University Press, 1920–1925).
Herrmann, Peter, *Der römische Kaisereid. Untersuchungen zu seiner Herkunft und Entwicklung* (Hypomnemata, 20; Göttingen: Vandenhoeck & Ruprecht, 1968).
Hesiod (Translated by Hugh G. Evelyn-White; Loeb Classical Library, 57; Cambridge, MA: Harvard University Press, 1936).
Heyman, George, *The Power of Sacrifice: Roman and Christian Discourses in Conflict* (Washington, DC: Catholic University of America, 2007).
Hicks, Frederick C. N., *The Fullness of Sacrifice: An Essay in Reconciliation* (3rd ed.; London: SPCK, 1953).
Himmelfarb, Martha, *Ascent to Heaven in Jewish and Christian Apocalypses* (New York, NY: Oxford University Press, 1993).
Hoch, Carl B., Jr., *All Things New: The Significance of Newness in Biblical Theology* (Grand Rapids, MI: Baker, 1996).
Hofius, Otfried, *Katapausis: Die Vorstellung vom endzeitlichen Ruheort im Hebräerbrief* (WUNT 1/11; Tübingen: Mohr Siebeck, 1970).
Hofius, Otfried, "Inkarnation und Opfertod Jesu nach Hebr 10,19f. [1970]", in *Neutestamentliche Studien* (WUNT, 132; Tübingen: Mohr Siebeck, 2000), pp. 210–19.
Holmes, Michael W. (ed. and trans.), *The Apostolic Fathers* (3rd ed.; Grand Rapids, MI: Baker Academic, 2007).
Holmes, Stephen, "Death in the Afternoon: Hebrews, Sacrifice and Soteriology", in *The Epistle to the Hebrews and Christian Theology* (Edited by Richard Bauckham, Daniel Driver, Trevor Hart, and Nathan MacDonald; Grand Rapids, MI: Eerdmans, 2009), pp. 229–52.
Homer (Works of Homer, translated by A. T. Murray; rev. William F. Wyatt; Loeb Classical Library; 4 vols; Cambridge, MA: Harvard University Press, 1919–1925).
Homer *Hymns* (Rev. and trans. Martin L. West; Loeb Classical Library, 496; Cambridge, MA: Harvard University Press, 2003).
Hughes, Dennis D., *Human Sacrifice in Ancient Greece* (London: Routledge, 1991).
Hughes, Graham, *Hebrews and Hermeneutics: The Epistle to the Hebrews as a New Testament Example of Biblical Interpretation* (SNTSMS 36; Cambridge: Cambridge University Press, 1979).
Hunsinger, George, "Jesus as the Lord of Time According to Karl Barth", *Zeitschrift für Dialektische Theologie* 4 (2010), pp. 113–27.
Hurst, L. D., *The Epistle to the Hebrews: Its Background of Thought* (SNTSMS 65; Cambridge: Cambridge University Press, 1990).
Hurtado, Larry W., *Lord Jesus Christ: Devotion to Jesus in Earliest Christianity* (Grand Rapids, MI: Eerdmans, 2003).
Huizenga, Leroy A., *The New Isaac: Tradition and Intertextuality in the Gospel of Matthew* (NovTSup 131; Leiden/Boston, MA: Brill, 2009).
Isaacs, Marie, *Sacred Space: An Approach to the Theology of the Epistle to the Hebrews* (JSNTSup, 73; Sheffield: Sheffield Academic Press, 1992).
Jackson-McCabe, Matt, "What's in a Name? The Problem of Jewish Christianity", in *Jewish Christianity Reconsidered: Rethinking Ancient Groups and Texts* (Edited by Matt Jackson-McCabe; Minneapolis, MN: Fortress Press, 2007a), pp. 10–38.
Jackson-McCabe, Matt (ed.), *Jewish Christianity Reconsidered: Rethinking Ancient Groups and Texts* (Minneapolis, MN: Fortress Press, 2007b).
Jamieson, R. B., "Hebrews 9.23: Cult Inauguration, Yom Kippur and the Cleansing of the Heavenly Tabernacle", *New Testament Studies* 62 (2016), pp. 569–87.

Jamieson, R. B., "When and Where Did Jesus Offer Himself? A Taxonomy of Recent Scholarship on Hebrews", *Currents in Biblical Research* 15 (2017), pp. 338–68.

Jamieson, R. B., *Jesus' Death and Heavenly Offerings in Hebrews* (SNTSMS 172; Cambridge: Cambridge University Press, 2018).

Janowski, Bernd, "Schöpferische Erinnerung : zum 'Gedenken Gottes' in der biblischen Fluterzählung", in *Sprachliche Tiefe - Theologische Weite* (Edited by Oliver Dyma and Andreas Michel; Biblisch-Theologische Studien, 4; Neukirchen-Vluyn: Neukirchener, 2008), pp. 220–21.

Jobes, Karen H., "Rhetorical Achievement in the Hebrews 10 'Misquote' of Psalm 40", *Bib* 72 (1991), pp. 387–96.

Jobes, Karen H., "The Function of Paronomasia in Hebrews 10:5-7", *TJ* 13 (1992), pp. 181–91.

Johnson, Adam, "A Fuller Account: The Role of 'Fittingness' in Thomas Aquinas' Doctrine of the Atonement", *International Journal of Systematic Theology* 12 (2010), pp. 302–18.

Johnson, Luke T., "The Scriptural World of Hebrews", *Interpretation* 57 (2003), pp. 237–50.

Johnson, Luke T., *Hebrews: A Commentary* (NTL; Louisville, KY: Westminster John Knox, 2006).

Johnson, William G., "The Cultus of Hebrews in the Twentieth Century", *ExpTim* 89 (1978), pp. 104–08.

Jones, Christopher P., *Between Pagan and Christian* (Cambridge, MA: Harvard University Press, 2014).

Joslin, Barry, *Hebrews, Christ, and the Law: The Theology of the Mosaic Law in Hebrews 7:1–10:18* (Paternoster Biblical Monographs; Exeter: Paternoster, 2008).

Jugie, M., *Nestorius et la controverse nestorienne* (Paris: Beauchesne, 1912).

Kajava, Mika, "Religion in Rome and Italy", in *The Oxford Handbook of Roman Epigraphy* (Edited by C. Bruun and J. Edmonson; Oxford: Oxford University Press, 2015), pp. 397–419.

Karrer, Martin, *Der Brief an die Hebräer* (ÖTK 20; Gütersloh: Gütersloher Verlagshaus, 2002-2008).

Käsemann, Ernst, *The Wandering People of God: An Investigation of the Epistle to the Hebrews* (Translated by Roy A. Harrisville, and Irving L. Sandberg; Minneapolis, MN: Augsburg, 1985); translation of *Das wandernde Gottesvolk: eine Untersuchung zum Hebräerbrief* (Göttingen: Vandenhoeck & Ruprecht, 1939).

Käsemann, Ernst, *Das wandernde Gottesvolk: Eine Untersuchung zum Hebräerbrief* (FRLANT 55; 2nd ed.; Göttingen: Vandenhoeck & Ruprecht, 1957).

Käsemann, Ernst, *Das wandernde Gottesvolk: Eine Untersuchung zum Hebräerbrief* (4th ed.; Göttingen: Vandenhoeck & Ruprecht, 1961).

Keating, Daniel A., and Matthew Levering, "Introduction" to St. Thomas Aquinas, *Commentary on the Gospel of John: Chapters 1-5* (Edited by Daniel A. Keating and Matthew Levering; Translated by Fabian Larcher, O. P., and James A. Weisheipl, O. P.; Washington, DC: Catholic University of America Press, 2010), pp. ix–xxx.

Keener, Craig S., *The Historical Jesus of the Gospels* (Grand Rapids, MI: Eerdmans, 2009).

Kibbe, Michael H., "Is It Finished? When Did It Start? Hebrews, Priesthood, and Atonement in Biblical, Systematic, and Historical Perspective", *Journal of Theological Studies* 65.1 (2014), pp. 25–61.

Kibbe, Michael H., *Godly Fear or Ungodly Failure? Hebrews 12 and the Sinai Theophanies* (BZNW 216; Berlin: De Gruyter, 2016).

Kidner, Derek, "Sacrifice: Metaphors and Meaning", *TynBul* 33 (1982), pp. 119–36.

Kim, Lloyd, *Polemic in the Book of Hebrews: Anti-Judaism, Anti-Semitism, Supersessionism?* (PTMS 64; Eugene, OR: Wipf & Stock, 2006).

Kistemaker, Simon, *Psalm Citations in the Epistle to the Hebrews* (Eugene, OR: Wipf & Stock, 1961).
Kiuchi, Nobuyoshi, *The Purification Offering in the Priestly Literature: Its Meaning and Function* (JSOTSup, 56; Sheffield: Sheffield Academic, 1987).
Kiuchi, Nobuyoshi, *Leviticus* (Apollos Old Testament Commentary 3; Downers Grove, IL: IVP Academic, 2007).
Klauck, Hans-Josef, "Die kleinasiatischen Beichtinschriften und das Neue Testament", in *Geschichte – Tradition – Reflexion* (Festschrift M. Hengel; Edited by H. Lichtenberger; Tübingen: Mohr-Siebeck, 1996), pp. 64–87.
Klawans, Jonathan, *Purity, Sacrifice, and the Temple: Symbolism and Supersessionism in the Study of Ancient Judaism* (New York, NY: Oxford University Press, 2005).
Kleinig, John W., *Leviticus* (Concordia Commentary; Saint Louis, MO: Concordia, 2003).
Knöppler, Thomas, *Sühne im Neuen Testament: Studien zum urchristlichen Verständnis der Heilsbedeutung des Todes Jesu* (WMANT 88; Neukirchen: Neukirchener, 2001), on Rom 3:25–26, 113–120; on Hebrews, 188–291; on John, 220–51.
Koester, Craig R., *Hebrews: A New Translation with Introduction and Commentary* (AB, 36; New York, NY: Doubleday, 2001).
Konstan, David, *Before Forgiveness: The Origins of a Moral Idea* (Cambridge: Cambridge University Press, 2010).
Konstan, David, "Assuaging Rage: Remorse, Repentance, and Forgiveness in the Ancient World", in *Ancient Forgiveness: Classical, Judaic, and Christian* (Edited by C. L. Griswold and D. Konstan; Cambridge: Cambridge University Press, 2012), pp. 17–30.
Köster, Helmut, "ὑπόστασις", *TWNT* 8: pp. 571–88.
Kuma, Hermann V. A., *The Centrality of Αἷμα [Blood] in the Theology of the Epistle to the Hebrews: An Exegetical and Philological Study* (Lewiston, NY: Mellen, 2010).
Kurtz, Johann, *Offerings, Sacrifices and Worship in the Old Testament* (Translated by James Martin; Peabody, MA: Hendrickson, 1863).
Laansma, Jon, *I Will Give You Rest: The "Rest" Motif in the New Testament with Special Reference to Mt. 11 and Heb. 3-4* (Tübingen: Mohr, 1997).
Laansma, Jon, "Hebrews and the Mission of the Earliest Church" in *New Testament Theology in Light of the Church's Mission: Essays in Honor of I. Howard Marshall* (Edited by Jon Laansma, Grant R. Osborne, and Ray F. Van Neste; Eugene, OR: Cascade, 2001), pp. 327–46.
Laansma, Jon, and Daniel J. Treier (eds.), *Christology, Hermeneutics, and Hebrews. Profiles from the History of Interpretation* (LNTS 423; London: T&T Clark, 2012).
Laansma, Jon, *The Letter to the Hebrews: A Commentary for Preaching, Teaching, and Bible Study* (Eugene, OR: Cascade, 2017).
Laansma, Jon, "The Living and Active Word. A Theological Reading of Hebrews", in *Listen, Understand, Obey: Essays on Hebrews in Honor of Gareth Lee Cockerill* (Edited by Caleb T. Friedeman; Eugene, OR: Wipf and Stock, 2017).
Lane, William L., *Hebrews 1-8* (WBC; Nashville, TN: Nelson, 2009).
Langenhoven, Hanno, Eliska Nortjé, Annette Potgieter, Yolande Steenkamp, "The Day of Atonement as a Hermeneutical Key to the Understanding of Christology in Hebrews", *Journal of Early Christian History* 1 (2011), pp. 85–97.
Latte, Kurt, *Römische Religionsgeschichte* (Handbuch der Altumswissenschaft, 4; repr. 1960, München: Beck, 1992).
Leach, Edmund, "The Logic of Sacrifice", in *Anthropological Approaches to the Old Testament* (Edited by Bernhard Lang; Issues in Religion and Theology 8; Philadelphia, PA: Fortress Press, 1985), pp. 136–50.

Lee, Gregory W., *Today When You Hear His Voice: Scripture, Covenants, and the People of God* (Grand Rapids, MI: Eerdmans, 2017).
Lefebvre, Henri, *Le Droit à la ville* (Paris: Anthropos, 1968).
Lefebvre, Henri, *The Production of Space* (Oxford: Blackwell, 1991).
Lehne, Susanne, *New Covenant in Hebrews* (JSNTSup; Sheffield: JSOT, 1990).
Leonhardt, Jutta, *Jewish Worship in Philo of Alexandria* (Texts and Studies in Ancient Judaism, 84; Tübingen: Mohr Siebeck, 2001).
Leschert, Dale, *Hermeneutical Foundations of Hebrews: A Study in the Validity of the Epistle's Interpretation of Some Core Citations from the Psalms* (Lewiston, NY: Edwin Mellon, 1994).
Levenson, Jon D., *The Death and Resurrection of the Beloved Son: The Transformation of Child Sacrifice in Judaism and Christianity* (New Haven, CT: Yale University Press, 1993).
Levering, Matthew, *Christ's Fulfillment of Torah and Temple: Salvation according to Thomas Aquinas* (Notre Dame, IN: University of Notre Dame Press, 2002).
Levering, Matthew, *Sacrifice and Community: Jewish Offering and Christian Eucharist* (Oxford: Blackwell, 2005).
Levering, Matthew, *Jewish-Christian Dialogue and the Life of Wisdom: Engagements with the Theology of David Novak* (London: Continuum, 2010).
Levering, Matthew, *Engaging the Doctrine of Creation: The Wise and Good Creator and His Theophanic, Fallen, and Redeemed Creatures* (Grand Rapids, MI: Baker Academic, 2017).
Levine, Baruch A., "The Descriptive Tabernacle Texts of the Pentateuch", *JAOS* 85.3 (1965), pp. 307–18.
Levine, Baruch A., *Va-Yikra/Leviticus* (JPS Torah Commentary; Philadelphia, PA: Jewish Publication Society, 1989).
Lewicki, T. *"Weist nicht ab den Sprechenden!": Wort Gottes und Paraklese im Hebräerbrief* (Padorborner Theologische Studien 41; Paderborn: Schöningh, 2004).
Lhôte, Éric, *Les lamelles oraculaires de Dodone* (École Pratique des Hautes Etudes, Sciences historiques et philologiques III; Geneva: Droz, 2006).
Libanius (Translated by A. F. Norman; Loeb Classical Library; 4 vols; Cambridge, MA: Harvard University Press, 1969–1992).
Lindars, Barnabas, SSF, *The Theology of the Letter to the Hebrews* (New Testament Theology; Cambridge: Cambridge University Press, 1991).
Lipka, Michael, *Roman Gods: A Conceptual Approach.* (Religions in the Graeco-Roman World, 167; Leiden: Brill, 2009).
Lloyd-Jones, Hugh, *The Justice of Zeus* (Sather Classical Lectures; Berkeley, CA: University of California Press, 1971).
Loader, William R. G., "Christ at the Right Hand: Ps. 110:1 in the New Testament", *NTS* 24 (1978), pp. 199–217.
Loader, W., *Sohn und Hoherpriester: Eine traditionsgeschichtliche Untersuchung zur Christologie des Hebraerbriefes* (WMANT 53; Neukirchen-Vluyn: Neukirchener Verlag, 1981).
Locher, Gottfried W., *Die Theologie Huldrych Zwingli sim Lichte seiner Christologie, Erster Teil: Die Gotteslehre* (Zürich: Zwingli Verlag, 1952).
Löhr, Hermut, "Wahrnehmung und Bedeutung des Todes Jesu nach dem Hebräerbrief. Ein Versuch", in *Deutungen des Todes Jesu im Neuen Testament* (Edited by J. Frey, and J. Schröter; WUNT, 181; Tübingen: Mohr Siebeck, 2005), pp. 455–76.
Longenecker, Richard N., *Biblical Exegesis in The Apostolic Period* (Grand Rapids, MI: Eerdmans, 1975).

Loofs, F., *Nestoriana* (Halle A. S.: Niemeyer, 1990).
Low, Bernard, "The Logic of Atonement in Israel's Cult", *Scripture and Interpretation* 3.1 (2009), pp. 5–32.
Luther, Martin, *Lectures on Genesis: Chapters 1-5* (*Luther's Works*; American Edition 1; Saint Louis, MO: Concordia Publishing House).
Lyonnet, Stanislas, and Leopold Sabourin, *Sin, Redemption, and Sacrifice: A Biblical and Patristic Study* (Rome: Biblical Institute, 1970).
Mackie, Scott D., *Eschatology and Exhortation in the Epistle to the Hebrews* (WUNT, 223; Tübingen: Mohr Siebeck, 2007).
MacMullen, Ramsay, *Paganism in the Roman Empire* (repr. 1981, New Haven, CT: Yale University Press, 1983).
MacRae, G. W., "Heavenly Temple and Eschatology in the Letter to the Hebrews", *Semeia* 12 (1978) pp. 179–99.
Malay, Hasan, "New Confession-Inscriptions in the Manisa and Bergama Museums", *EA* 12 (1988), pp. 147–52.
Malpas, J. E., *Place and Experience: A Philosophical Topography* (Cambridge: Cambridge University Press, 1999).
Marshall, I. Howard, "Soteriology in Hebrews", in *The Epistle to the Hebrews and Christian Theology* (Edited by R. J. Bauckham, Daniel Driver, Trevor Hart, and Nathan MacDonald; Grand Rapids, MI: Eerdmans, 2009), pp. 253–77.
Martin, Francis, "The Spiritual Sense (*Sensus Spiritualis*) of Sacred Scripture: Its Essential Insight", in *Sacred Scripture: The Disclosure of the Word* (Edited by Francis Martin; Naples, FL: Sapientia Press, 2006), pp. 249–75.
Martínez, Florentino García, and Eibert J. C. Tigchelaar (eds.), *The Dead Sea Scrolls: Study Edition* (2 vols; Leiden: Brill, 1997–1998).
Mason, Eric F., *"You Are a Priest Forever": Second Temple Jewish Messianism and the Priestly Christology of the Epistle to the Hebrews* (STDJ, 74. Leiden: Brill, 2008).
Maximus the Confessor, *St. Maximos the Confessor. On Difficulties in Sacred Scripture. The Response to Thalassios* (Translated by Maximos Constas; Fathers of the Church, A New Translation Washington, DC: Catholic University of America Press, 2018).
McCaffrey, James, *The House with Many Rooms: The Temple Theme of Jn. 14, 2-3* (Rome: Pontifical Biblical Institute, 1987).
McCarthy, Dennis J., "The Symbolism of Blood and Sacrifice", *JBL* 88.2 (1969), pp. 166–76.
McCollough, J. C., "Anti-Semitism in Hebrews?", *IBS* 20 (1978), pp. 30–45.
McCormack, Bruce L., "The Identity of the Son: Karl Barth's Exegesis of Hebrews 1.1–4 (and Similar Passages)", in *Christology, Hermeneutics, and Hebrews: Profiles from the History of Interpretation* (Edited by Jon C. Laansma and Daniel J. Treier; Library of New Testament Studies; London: T&T Clark, 2012), pp. 155–72.
McGuckin, John Anthony, *St. Cyril of Alexandria. On the Unity of Christ* (Crestwood, NY: St. Vladimir's Seminary Press, 1995).
McKelvey, R. J., *Pioneer and Priest: Jesus Christ in the Epistle to the Hebrews* (Eugene, OR; Pickwick, 2013).
Meier, J. P., "Symmetry and Theology in the Old Testament Citations of Heb. 1:5-14", *Biblica* 66 (1985), pp. 504–33.
Meier, J. P., *A Marginal Jew: Rethinking the Historical Jesus: Vol. 2: Mentor, Message, and Miracles* (ABRL; New York, NY: Doubleday, 1994).
Metzler, Karin, *Der griechische Begriff des Verzeihens. Untersucht am Wortstamm συγγνώμη von den ersten Belegen bis zum vierten Jahrhundert n.Chr.* (WUNT, 2.44; Tübingen: Mohr Siebeck, 1991).

Metzler, Karin, and K. Savvidis, *Athanasius: Werke, Band I. Die dogmatischen Schriften, Erster Teil, 2.Lieferung* (Berlin: De Gruyter, 1998).
Michel, Otto, *Der Brief an die Hebräer: Übersetzt und Erklärt* (KEK, 13; Göttingen: Vandenhoeck & Ruprecht, 1966).
Milgrom, Jacob, "On the Origins of Philo's Doctrine of Conscience", *Studia Philonica* 3 (1974-1975), pp. 41-44.
Milgrom, Jacob, *Cult and Conscience: The Asham and the Priestly Doctrine of Repentance* (SJLA, 18; Leiden: Brill, 1976).
Milgrom, Jacob, *Studies in Cultic Theology and Terminology* (SJLA, 36; Leiden: Brill, 1983).
Milgrom, Jacob, *Leviticus 1-16: A New Translation with Introduction and Commentary* (AB, 3; New York, NY: Doubleday, 1991).
Miller, James, "Paul and Hebrews: A Comparison of Narrative Worlds", in *Hebrews: Contemporary Methods —New Insights* (Edited by Gabriella Gelardini; Leiden: Brill, 2005), pp. 245-64.
Milligan, William, *The Ascension and Heavenly Priesthood of Our Lord: The Baird Lecture 1891* (London: Macmillan, 1892).
Moberly, R. W. L., "Exemplars of Faith in Hebrews 11: Abel", in *The Epistle to the Hebrews and Christian Theology* (Edited by Richard Bauckham, Daniel Driver, Trevor Hart, and Nathan MacDonald; Grand Rapids, MI: Eerdmans, 2009), pp. 353-63.
Moffatt, James, *A Critical and Exegetical Commentary on The Epistle to the Hebrews* (ICC; Edinburgh: T&T Clark, 1924).
Moffit, David M., "'If Another Priest Arises': Jesus' Resurrection and the High Priestly Christology of Hebrews", in *A Cloud of Witnesses: The Theology of Hebrews in Its Ancient Contexts* (Edited by Richard Bauckham, Daniel Driver, Trevor Hart, and Nathan MacDonald; London: T&T Clark, 2008).
Moffitt, David M., *Atonement and the Logic of Resurrection in the Epistle to the Hebrews* (NovTSup, 141; Leiden: Brill, 2011a).
Moffitt, David M., "Jesus the High Priest and the Mosaic Law: Reassessing the Appeal to the Heavenly Realm in the Letter 'To the Hebrews'", in *Problems in Translating Texts About Jesus: Proceedings from the International Society of Biblical Literature Annual Meeting, 2008* (Edited by Mishael Caspi and John T. Greene; Lewiston, NY: Mellen, 2011b), pp. 187-224.
Moffitt, David M., "Blood, Life, and Atonement: Reassessing Hebrews' Christological Appropriation of Yom Kippur", in *The Day of Atonement: Its Interpretations in Early Jewish and Christian Traditions* (Edited by Thomas Hieke and Tobias Nicklas; Themes in Biblical Narrative, 15; Leiden: Brill, 2012), pp. 211-24.
Moffitt, David M., "Serving in the Tabernacle in Heaven: Sacred Space, Jesus's High-Priestly Sacrifice, and Hebrews' Analogical Theology", in *Hebrews in Contexts* (Edited by Gabriella Gelardini and Harold W. Attridge; Ancient Judaism and Early Christianity, 91; Leiden: Brill, 2016), pp. 259-80.
Moffitt, David M., "Jesus' Heavenly Sacrifice in Early Christian Reception of Hebrews: A Survey", *JTS* 68 (2017a), pp. 46-71.
Moffitt, David M., "Hebrews", in *T&T Clark Companion to Atonement* (Edited by Adam J. Johnson; London: Bloomsbury T&T Clark, 2017b), pp. 533-36.
Moffitt, David M. "Modelled on Moses: Jesus' Death, Passover, and the Defeat of the Devil in the Epistle to the Hebrews", in *Mosebilder: Gedanken zur Rezeption einer literarischen Figur im Frühjudentum, frühen Chrsitentum und der römisch-hellenistischen Literatur* (Edited by M. Sommer, E. Eynikel, V. Niederhofer, and E. Hernitscheck; WUNT 1/390; Tübingen: Mohr Siebeck, 2017c), pp. 279-97.

Moffitt, David M., "Wilderness Identity and Pentateuchal Narrative: Distinguishing between Jesus' Inauguration and Maintenance of the New Covenant in Hebrews", in *Muted Voices of the New Testament: Readings in the Catholic Epistles and Hebrews* (Edited by Katherine M. Hockey, Madison N. Pierce, and Francis Watson; LNTS 565; London: Bloomsbury T&T Clark, 2017d), pp. 153–71.

Moore-Gilbert, Bart, Gareth Stanton and Willy Maley, *Post-colonial Criticism* (London: Longman, 1997).

Morales, L. Michael, *The Tabernacle Pre-Figured: Cosmic Mountain Ideology in Genesis and Exodus* (Leuven: Peeters, 2012).

Morales, L. Michael, *Who Shall Ascend the Mountain of the Lord? A Theology of the Book of Leviticus* (Downers Grove, IL: IVP Academic, 2015).

Morgan, Teresa, *Roman Faith and Christian Faith: Pistis and Fides in the Early Roman Empire and Early Churches* (Oxford: Oxford University Press, 2015).

Morna, D. Hooker, "Christ, the 'End' of the Cult", in *The Epistle to the Hebrews and Christian Theology* (Edited by Richard Bauckham, Daniel Driver, Trevor Hart, and Nathan MacDonald; Grand Rapids, MI: Eerdmans, 2009), pp. 188–212.

Morris, Leon, *The Gospel According to John* (rev. ed.; NICNT; Grand Rapids, MI: Eerdmans, 1995).

Müller, H. P., "Das Motiv Für Die Sintflut. Die Hermeneutische Funktion Des Mythos Und Seine Analyse", *ZAW* 97.3 (1985), pp. 295–316.

Musser, Sarah S., "Sacrifice, Sabbath, and the Restoration of Creation" (unpublished doctoral dissertation, Duke University, 2015).

Naiden, Fred S., "Blessèd are the Parasites", in *Greek and Roman Animal Sacrifice: Ancient Victims, Modern Observers* (Edited by C. A. Faraone, and F. S. Naiden; Cambridge: Cambridge University Press, 2012), pp. 55–83.

Naiden, Fred S., *Smoke Signals for the Gods: Ancient Greek Sacrifice from the Archaic through Roman Periods* (New York, NY: Oxford University Press, 2013).

Nelson, Richard D., *Raising Up a Faithful Priest: Community and Priesthood in Biblical Theology* (Louisville, KY: Westminster John Knox, 1993).

Nestorius, *First Sermon against the Theotokos* (Translated by Richard A. Norris, *The Christological Controversy*; Sources of Early Christian Thought; Philadelphia, PA: Fortress Press, 1980).

Nestorius, *The Bazaar of Heraclides* (Translated by G. R. Driver and Leonard Hodgson; Oxford: Oxford University Press, 1925; Reprinted in Eugene, OR: Wipf & Stock, 2002).

Nichols, Aidan, O. P., "St. Thomas Aquinas on the Passion of Christ: A Reading of *Summa Theologiae* IIIa, q. 46", *SJT* 43 (1990), pp. 447–59.

Nickelsburg, George W. E., *Glory at the Right Hand: Ps. 110 in Early Christianity* (SBLMS 18; Nashville, TN: Abingdon, 1973).

Novum Testamentum Graece (Founded by Eberhard and Erwin Nestle, Edited by Barbara and Kurt Aland et al., 28th rev. ed., ed. Institut für Neutestamentliche Textforschung, Münster/Westphalia under the direction of Holger Strutwolff; Stuttgart: Deutsche Bibelgesellschaft, 2014).

Nyssa, Gregory, *Life of Moses* (Translated by Abraham Malherbe and Everett Ferguson; Classics of Western Spirituality; New York, NY: Paulist, 1978).

O'Donovan, Oliver, *Resurrection and Moral Order: An Outline for Evangelical Ethics* (Grand Rapids, MI: Eerdmans, 1994).

Osborne, Robin, "Unity vs. Diversity", in *The Oxford Handbook of Ancient Greek Religion* (Edited by E. Eidinow and J. Kindt; Oxford: Oxford University Press, 2015), pp. 11–20.

Owen, John, *Exposition of Hebrews 11:1-13:25* (Edinburgh: Banner of Truth Trust, 1991).

Pannenburg, Wolfhart, *Jesus – God and Man* (2nd ed.; Philadelphia, PA: Westminster, 1977).
Pannenberg, Wolfhart, "Eternity, Time, and the Trinitarian God", in *Trinity, Time, and Church* (Edited by C. E. Gunton; Grand Rapids, MI: William B. Eerdmans, 2000), pp. 62–70.
Parke, Herbert W., *The Oracles of Zeus: Dodona, Olympia, Amman* (Oxford: Blackwell, 1967).
Parke, Herbert W., and Donald E. W. Wormell, *The Delphic Oracle* (Oxford: Oxford University Press, 1956).
Peeler, Amy, "Desiring God: The Blood of the Covenant in Exod. 24", *BBR* 23 (2013), 187–205.
Perrin, Nicholas, "Sacraments and Sacramentality in the New Testament", in *The Oxford Handbook of Sacramental Theology* (Edited by Hans Boersma and Matthew Levering; Oxford: Oxford University Press, 2015), pp. 52–67.
Perrin, Nicholas, *Jesus the Priest* (London: SPCK; Grand Rapids, MI: Baker Academic, 2018).
Peterson, David G., *Hebrews and Perfection: An Examination of the Concept of Perfection in the Epistle to the Hebrews* (SNTSMS, 47; Cambridge: Cambridge University Press, 1982).
Pettazzoni, Raffaele, *La confessione dei peccati* (Bologna: Zanichelli, 1937).
Pettazzoni, Raffaele, *Essays on the History of Religions* (Studies in the History of Religions, 1; Leiden: Brill, 1954).
Petzl, Georg, *Die Beichtinschriften Westkleinasiens* (Epigraphica Anatolica, 22; Bonn: Habelt, 1994).
Petzl, Georg, *Die Beichtinschriften im römischen Kleinasien und der Fromme und Gerechte Gott* (Nordrhein-Westfälische Akademie der Wissenschaften: Geisteswissenschaften; Vorträge, G 355; Opladen/Wiesbaden: Westdeutscher Verlag, 1998).
Philo (Translated by F. H. Colson, J.W. Earp, Ralph Marcus, and G.H. Whitaker; Loeb Classical Library; 12 vols; Cambridge, MA: Harvard University Press, 1929–1962).
Pliny (Translated by H. Rackham, W.H.S. Jones, and D.E. Eichholz; Loeb Classical Library; 12 vols; Cambridge, MA: Harvard University Press, 1938–1969).
Polen, Nehemia, "Leviticus and Hebrews… and Leviticus", in *The Epistle to the Hebrews and Christian Theology* (Edited by Richard Bauckham, Daniel Driver, Trevor Hart, and Nathan MacDonald; Grand Rapids, MI: Eerdmans, 2009), pp. 213–25.
Polyandro, D. Johanne, "Disputation 42: On the Calling of those who Minister to the Church, and on Their Duties", in *Synopsis Purioris Theologiae*, volume 2: *Disputations 24–42* (Edited by Henk arvan den Belt; Translated by Riemer Faber; Studies in Medieval and Reformation Traditions 204; Leiden: Brill, 2016).
Porter, Stanley E., *Verbal Aspect and the Greek New Testament with Reference to Tense and Mood* (SBG; New York, NY: Peter Lang, 1989).
Poulet, Georges, *Proustian Space* (Baltimore, MD: Johns Hopkins University Press, 1977).
Preisigke, Friedrich, *Wörterbuch der griechischen Papyrusurkunden: Mit Einschluss der griechischen Inschriften, Aufschriften, Ostraka, Mumienschilder usw. aus Ägypten* (Edited by Emil Kissling; vol. 1; Berlin: Selbstverlag der Erben, 1925).
Preus, James Samuel, *From Shadow to Promise: Old Testament Interpretation from Augustine to the Young Luther* (Cambridge, MA: Harvard University Press, 1969).
Price, Simon R. F., *Rituals and Power: The Roman Imperial Cult in Asia Minor* (repr. 1984, Oxford: Oxford University Press, 1998).
Prügl, Thomas, "Thomas Aquinas as Interpreter of Scripture", in *The Theology of Thomas Aquinas* (Edited by Rik Van Nieuwenhove and Joseph Wawrykow; Translated by Albert K. Wimmer; Notre Dame, IN: University of Notre Dame Press, 2005), pp. 386–415.

Psalmi cum Odis, Septuaginta Vetus Testamentum Graecum 10 (Edited by Alfred Rahlfs; Göttingen: Vandenhoeck & Ruprecht, 1979).

Quinot, Bernard, "L'influence de l'Épître aux Hébreux dans la notion augustinienne du vrai sacrifice," *Revue d' Etudes Augustiniennes et Patristiques* 8.1 (1962), pp. 129–68.

Ragavan, Deena (ed.), *Heaven on Earth: Temples, Ritual, and Cosmic Symbolism in the Ancient World* (Oriental Institute Seminars, 9; Chicago, IL: Oriental Institute of the University of Chicago, 2013).

Rainey, A. F., "The Order of Sacrifices in Old Testament Ritual Texts", *Bib* 51.4 (1970), pp. 485–98.

Ramirez, Andres, *Other Spaces, Plural Narratives of Space in Berlin's SO 36* (Berlin : Universitätsverlag der TU Berlin, 2015).

Rascher, Angela, *Schriftauslegung und Christologie im Hebrärbrief* (BZNW, 153; Berlin: De Gruyter, 2007).

Relph, E. *Place and Placedness* (London: Pion, 1976).

Ribbens, Benjamin J., "Levitical Sacrifice and Heavenly Cult in Hebrews" (unpublished doctoral dissertation, Wheaton College, 2013).

Ribbens, Benjamin J., *Levitical Sacrifice and Heavenly Cult in Hebrews* (BZNW 222; Berlin: De Gruyter, 2016).

Ribbens, Benjamin J., "The Ascension and Atonement: The Significance of Post-Reformation, Reformed Responses to Socinians for Contemporary Atonement Debates in Hebrews", *Westminster Theological Journal* 80 (2018), pp. 1–23.

Ricl, Marijana, "The Appeal to Divine Justice in the Lydian Confession-Inscriptions", in *Forschungen in Lydien* (Edited by E. Schwertheim; Asia Minor Studien, 17; Bonn: Habelt, 1995), pp. 67–73.

Ricl, Marijana, "CIG 4142 – A Forgotten Confession-Inscription from North-West Phrygia", *EA* 29 (1997), pp. 35–43.

Ricl, Marijana, "Society and Economy of Rural Sanctuaries in Roman Lydia and Phrygia", *EA* 35 (2003), pp. 77–101.

Ricl, Marijana, "Observations on a New Corpus of Inscriptions from Lydia", *EA* 44 (2011), pp. 143–52.

Ridgway, Brunilde S., *Roman Copies of Greek Sculpture: The Problem of the Originals* (Ann Arbor, MI: University of Michigan Press, 1984).

Rindge, Matthew S., "Reconfiguring the Akedah and Recasting God: Lament and Divine Abandonment in Mark", *JBL* 131 (2011), pp. 755–74.

Roberts, J. J. M., *The Bible and the Ancient Near East: Collected Essays* (Winona Lake, IN: Eisenbrauns, 2002).

Rooke, Deborah W., "Jesus as Royal Priest: Reflections on the Interpretation of the Melchizedek Tradition in Heb 7", *Biblica* 81 (2000), pp. 81–94.

Rostad, Aslak, "Human Transgression – Divine Retribution: A Study of Religious Transgressions and Punishments in Greek Cultic Regulations and Lydian-Phrygian Reconciliation Inscriptions" (unpublished doctoral dissertation; Bergen, Norway: University of Bergen, 2006).

Rüpke, Jörg, Jörg Rüpke, *The Religion of the Romans* (Edited and Translated by R. Gordon; 2001 repr., Cambridge/Malden, MA: Polity, 2007).

Rüpke, Jörg, "Gifts, Votives, and Sacred Things: Strategies, not Entities," *Religion in the Roman Empire* 4 (2018), pp. 207–36

Sanders, J. T., *The New Testament Christological Hymns* (SNTSMS 15; Cambridge: Cambridge University Press, 1971).

Schaff, Philip, and Henry Wace (eds.), *A Select Library of Nicene and Post-Nicene Fathers of the Christian Church.* (28 vols in 2 series. 1886–1889repr.)

Scheid, John, *Religion et piété à Rome* (Paris: Découverte, 1985).
Scheid, John, *Romulus et ses frères. Le collège des frères arvales, modèle du culte public dans la Rome des empereurs* (Bibliothèque des Écoles françaises d'Athènes et de Rome, 275; Rome: École française, 1990).
Scheid, John, "Roman Animal Sacrifice and the System of Being", in *Greek and Roman Animal Sacrifice: Ancient Victims, Modern Observers* (Edited by C. A. Faraone, and F. S. Naiden; Cambridge: Cambridge University Press, 2003a), pp. 84–98.
Scheid, John, *An Introduction to Roman Religion* (Translated by J. Lloyd; 1998 repr., Edinburgh: Edinburgh University Press, 2003b).
Scheid, John, *Quand faire c'est croire: les rites sacrifiels des Romains* (Paris: Aubier, 2005).
Schenck, Kenneth L., "Keeping His Appointment: Creation and Enthronement in Hebrews", *JSNT* 66 (1997), pp. 91–117.
Schenck, Kenneth L., *Understanding the Book of Hebrews: The Story Behind the Sermon* (Louisville, KY: Westminster John Knox Press, 2003).
Schenck, Kenneth L., *Cosmology and Eschatology in Hebrews: The Settings of the Sacrifice* (SNTSMS, 143; Cambridge: Cambridge University Press, 2007).
Schenck, Ken, "God Has Spoken: Hebrews' Theology of the Scriptures", in *The Epistle to the Hebrews and Christian Theology* (Edited by Richard Bauckham et al.; Grand Rapids, MI: Eerdmans, 2009), pp. 321–36.
Schenck, Kenneth L., "An Archaeology of Hebrews' Tabernacle Imagery", in *Hebrews in Contexts* (Edited by Gabriella Gelardini and Harold W. Attridge; Ancient Judaism and Early Christianity, 91; Leiden: Brill, 2016), pp. 238–58.
Schierse, Franz Joseph, *Verheißung und Heilsvollendung. Zur theologischen Grundfrage des Hebräerbriefes* (Müchener Theologische Studien; München: Zink, 1955).
Schlesinger, Eugene R., "Trinity, Incarnation and Time: A Restatement of *The Doctrine of God* in Conversation with Robert Jenson", *Scottish Journal of Theology* 69 (2016), pp. 189–203.
Schliesser, Benjamin, "Glauben und Denken im Hebräerbrief und bei Paulus: Zwei frühchristliche Perspektiven auf die Rationalität des Glaubens" in *Glaube* (Edited by Jörg Frey, idem, and Nadine Ueberschaer; WUNT, 373; Tübingen: Mohr Siebeck, 2017), pp. 503–60.
Schmitt, Mary, "Restructuring Views on the Law in Hebrews 7:12", *JBL* 128 (2009), pp. 189–201.
Schnabel, Eckhard J., "Divine Tyranny and Public Humiliation: A Suggestion for the Interpretation of the Lydian and Phrygian Confession Inscriptions", *NovT* 45 (2003), pp. 160–88.
Schnelle, Udo, *Theology of the New Testament* (Translated by M. E. Boring; ET Grand Rapids, MI: Baker Academic, 2009).
Scholer, John M., *Proleptic Priests: Priesthood in the Epistle to the Hebrews* (JSNTSup 49; Sheffield: Sheffield Academic Press, 1991).
Schoot, Henk, and Pim Valkenberg, "Thomas Aquinas and Judaism", in *Aquinas in Dialogue: Thomas for the Twenty-First Century* (Edited by Jim Fodor and Frederick Christian Bauerschmidt; Oxford: Blackwell, 2004), pp. 47–66.
Schumacher, Thomas, *Zur Entstehung christlicher Sprache: Eine Untersuchung der paulinischen Idiomatik und der Verwendung des Begriffs "pistis"* (BBB, 168; Göttingen: V & R Unipress, 2012).
Scullion, James P., "A Traditio-Historical Study of the Day of Atonement" (unpublished doctoral dissertation, Catholic University of America, 1990).
Seeley, David, *The Noble Death: Graeco-Roman Martyrology and Paul's Concept of Salvation* (JSNTSup, 28; Sheffield: JSOT Press, 1990).

Seneca (Translated by John W. Basore; Loeb Classical Library; 10 vols; Cambridge, MA: Harvard University Press, 1917–2002).

Shelfer, Lochlan, "The Temple as Courtroom: The Confession Stelai of Imperial Lydia" (unpublished doctoral dissertation; Baltimore, MD: Johns Hopkins University, 2010).

Sheppard, Anne R. R., "Pagan Cults of Angels in Roman Asia Minor", *Talanta* 12–13 (1980–81), pp. 77–101.

Siker, Jeffrey S., "Yom Kippuring Passover: Recombinant Sacrifice in Early Christianity", in *Ritual and Metaphor: Sacrifice in the Bible* (Edited by Christian A. Eberhart; SBLRBS 68; Atlanta, GA: SBL, 2011), 65–82.

Signer, Michael A., "King/messiah: Rashi's Exegesis of Psalm 2", *Proof* 3 (1983), pp. 273–78.

Skarsaune, Oskar, *In the Shadow of the Temple: Jewish Influences on Early Christianity* (Downers Grove, IL: IVP Academic, 2008).

Skarsaune, Oskar, and Reidar Hvalvik, (eds.), *Jewish Believers in Jesus: The Early Centuries* (Peabody, MA: Hendrickson, 2007).

Sklar, Jay, *Sin, Impurity, Sacrifice, Atonement: The Priestly Conceptions* (Hebrew Bible Monographs 2; Sheffield: Sheffield University Press, 2005).

Small, Brian C., *The Characterization of Jesus in the Book of Hebrews* (Biblical Interpretation, 128; Leiden: Brill, 2014).

Smith, Jonathan Z., "The Domestication of Sacrifice", in *Violent Origins: Ritual Killing and Cultural Formation* (Edited by R. G. Hamerton-Kelly; Stanford, CA: Stanford University Press, 1987), pp. 191–205.

Snaith, Norman H., "Sacrifices in the Old Testament", *VT* 7.3 (1957), pp. 308–17.

Soja, Edward W., *Thirdspace: Journeys to Los Angeles and Other Real-and-Imagined Places* (Cambridge, MA: Blackwell, 1996).

Sommer, Benjamin, *The Bodies of God and the World of Ancient Israel* (Cambridge: Cambridge University Press, 2011).

Son, Kiwoong, *Zion Symbolism in Hebrews: Hebrews 12:18-24 as a Hermeneutical Key to the Epistle* (Milton Keynes: Paternoster, 2007).

Soskice, Janet Martin, *Metaphor and Religious Language* (Oxford: Clarendon, 1985).

Soulen, R. Kendall, *The God of Israel and Christian Theology* (Minneapolis, MN: Fortress Press, 1996).

Spicq, Ceslas, *L'Épître aux Hébreux* (2 vols; Paris: Gabalda, 1952–1953).

Stegeman, Ekkehard, and Wolfgang Stegeman, "Does the Cultic Language of Hebrews Represent Sacrificial Metaphors? Reflections on Some Basic Problems", in *Hebrews: Contemporary Insights—New Methods* (Edited by Gabriella Gellardini; Leiden: Brill, 2005), pp. 13–23.

Steinleitner, Franz S., *Die Beicht im Zusammenhange mit der sakralen Rechtspflege in der Antike. Ein Beitrag zur näheren Kenntnis kleinasiatisch-orientalischer Kulte der Kaiserzeit* (Leipzig: Dieterich'sche Verlagsbuchhandlung, 1913).

Stephens, W. P., *The Theology of Huldrych Zwingli* (Oxford: Clarendon, 1986).

Steyn, Gert J., "Psalm 2 in Hebrews", *Neotestamentica* 37 (2003), pp. 262–82.

Steyn, Gert J., *A Quest for the Assumed LXX Vorlage of the Explicit Quotations in Hebrews* (FRLANT 235; Göttingen: Vandenhoeck & Ruprecht, 2011).

Stibbs, Alan M., *The Finished Work of Christ* (London: The Tyndale Press, 1954).

Strabo, *The Geography* (Translated by Horace Leonard Jones; Loeb Classical Library; 8 vols; Cambridge, MA: Harvard University Press, 1917–1932).

Strecker, Christian, "Fides – Pistis – Glaube: Kontexte und Konturen einer Theologie der 'Annahme' bei Paulus", in *Lutherische und Neue Paulusperspektive: Beiträge zu einem Schlüsselproblem der exegetischen Diskussion* (WUNT 182, Edited by Michael Bachmann; Tübingen: Mohr Siebeck, 2005).

Stroumsa, Guy G., *The End of Sacrifice: Religious Transformations in Late Antiquity* (Translated by Susan Emanuel; Chicago, IL: University of Chicago Press, 2009).
Svendsen, Stefan Nordaard, *Allegory Transformed: The Appropriation of Philonic Hermeneutics in the Letter to the Hebrews* (WUNT 2, 269; Tübingen: Mohr Siebeck, 2009).
Tapie, Matthew A., *Aquinas on Israel and the Church: The Question of Supersessionism in the Theology of Thomas Aquinas* (Eugene, OR: Pickwick, 2014).
Tasker, R. V. G., Gospel in the Epistle to the Hebrews (2nd ed.; London: Tyndale Press, 1956).
Tasker, R. V. G., *The Gospel According to St. John* (TNTC; Grand Rapids, MI: Eerdmans, 1960).
Telscher, Guido, *Opfer aus Barmherzigkeit. Hebr 9,11-28 im Kontext biblischer Sühnetheologie* (FzB, 112; Würzburg: Echter, 2007).
Theodoret, "Letter of Alexander to Alexander of Byzantium", in *Ecclesiastical History* (*NPNF*; Peabody, MA: Hendrickson, 1995).
Theodoret of Cyrus, *Commentary on the Letters of St. Paul.* (Volume 2; Translated by Robert Charles Hill; Brookline, MA: Holy Cross Orthodox Press, 2001).
"Theognis", in *Greek Elegiac Poetry* (Translated by Douglas E. Gerber; Loeb Classical Library, 258; Cambridge, MA: Harvard University Press, 1999), pp. 166–385.
Thompson, James W., *The Beginnings of Christian Philosophy: The Epistle to the Hebrews* (CBQMS, 13; Washington, DC: Catholic Biblical Association of America, 1982).
Thompson, James W., *Hebrews* (Paideia; Grand Rapids, MI: Baker Academic, 2008).
Thiessen, Matthew, "Hebrews 12.5-13, the Wilderness Period, and Israel's Discipline", *New Testament Studies* 55.3 (2009), pp. 366–79.
Torrance, Thomas F., "Doctrinal Consensus on Holy Communion", *SJT* 15 (1962), pp. 4–21.
Torrance, Thomas F., *The Christian Doctrine of God: One Being, Three Persons* (London: T&T Clark, 2001).
Treier, Daniel J., "Speech Acts, Hearing Hearts, and Other Senses: The Doctrine of Scripture Practiced in Hebrews", in *The Epistle to the Hebrews and Christian Theology* (Edited by Richard Bauckham, Daniel Driver, Trevor Hart, and Nathan MacDonald; Grand Rapids, MI: Eerdmans, 2009), pp. 337–50.
Trevaskis, Leigh M., *Holiness, Ethics and Ritual in Leviticus* (Sheffield: Sheffield Phoenix, 2011).
Turcan, Robert, *The Gods of Ancient Rome: Religion in Everyday Life from Archaic to Imperial Times* (Edinburgh: Edinburgh University Press, 2000).
Turner, C. H., "Ο ΥΙΟΣ ΜΟΥ ΑΓΑΠΗΤΟΣ", *JTS* 27 (1926), pp. 113–29.
Valerius, Maximus, *Memorable Doings and Sayings, Volume II: Books 6–9* (Edited and Translated by D. R. Shackleton Bailey, LCL 493; Cambridge, MA: Harvard University Press, 2000).
Van Vliet, Hendrik, *No Single Testimony: A Study on the Adoption of the Law of Deut. 19:15 par. into the New Testament* (Utrecht: Kemink & Zoon, 1958).
VanderKam, James C., *Enoch: A Man for All Generations* (Studies on Personalities of the Old Testament; Columbia, SC: University of South Carolina Press, 1995).
Vanhoye, Albert, "Longue marche ou accès tout proche?: Le contexte biblique de Hébreux 3,7-4,11", *Biblica* 49 (1968), pp. 9–26.
Vanhoye, Albert, *Situation du Christ: Hébreux 1-2* (LD 58; Paris: Cerf, 1969).
Vanhoye, Albert, *Structure and Message of the Epistle to the Hebrews* (Rome: Editrice Pontificio Instituto Biblico, 1989).

Várhelyi, Zsuzsanna, "'To Forgive is Divine': Gods as Models of Forgiveness in Late Republican and Early Imperial Rome", in *Ancient Forgiveness: Classical, Judaic, and Christian* (Edited by C. L. Griswold and D. Konstan; Cambridge: Cambridge University Press, 2012), pp. 115-33.

Varinlioğlu, Ender, "Eine Gruppe von Sühneinschriften aus dem Museum von Uşak", *EA* 13 (1989), pp. 37-50.

Versnel, Hendrik S., "Self-Sacrifice, Compensation and the Anonymous Gods", in *Le sacrifice dans l'antiquité* (Edited by J. Rudhardt and O. Reverdin; Entretiens sur l'antiquité classique, 27; Vandoeuvres/Geneva: Fondation Hardt, 1981), pp. 135-85.

Versnel, Hendrik S., "Quid Athenis et Hierosolymis? Bemerkungen über die Herkunft von Aspekten des 'effective death'", in *Die Entstehung der jüdischen Martyrologie* (Edited by J. W. Van Henten; SPB, 38; Leiden: Brill, 1989), pp. 162-96.

Versnel, Hendrik S., "Making Sense of Jesus' Death: The Pagan Contribution", in *Deutungen des Todes Jesu im Neuen Testament* (Edited by J. Frey and J. Schröter; WUNT, 181; Tübingen: Mohr Siebeck, 2005), pp. 213-94.

Versnel, Hendrik S., *Coping with the Gods: Wayward Readings in Greek Theology* (Religions in the Graeco-Roman World, 173; Leiden: Brill, 2011).

Vis, Joshua M., "The Purification Offering of Leviticus and the Sacrificial Offering of Jesus" (unpublished doctoral dissertation, Duke University, 2012).

Vögtle, Anton, *Das Neue Testament und Die Zukunft des Kosmos* (KBNT; Düsseldorff: Patmos, 1970).

Von Rad, Gerhard, "Es ist noch eine Ruhe vorhanden dem Volke Gottes", *Zwischen den Zeiten* 11 (1933) pp. 104-11.

Von Rad, Gerhard, *Old Testament Theology* (2 vols; New York, NY, Harper and Row: 1962), p. 147 n. 23.

Vos, Geerhardus, *Biblical Theology: Old and New Testaments* (Edinburgh: Banner of Truth, 1948).

Wainwright, Geoffrey, *For Our Salvation: Two Approaches to the Work of Christ* (Grand Rapids, MI: Eerdmans, 1997).

Walker, P. W. L., *Jesus and the Holy City: New Testament Perspectives on Jerusalem* (Grand Rapids, MI: Eerdmans, 1996).

Wallace-Hadrill, Andrew, "The Golden Age and Sin in Augustan Ideology", *Past & Present* 95.1 (1982), pp. 19-36.

Wallace-Hadrill, Andrew, *Rome's Cultural Revolution* (Cambridge: Cambridge University Press, 2008).

Wallace, David, "The Use of Psalms in the Shaping of a Text: Psalm 2:7 and Psalm 110:1 in Hebrews 1", *ResQ* 45 (2003), pp. 41-50.

Watts, James W., "'ōlāh: The Rhetoric of Burnt Offerings", *VT* 56.1 (2006), pp. 125-37.

Watts, James W., *Ritual and Rhetoric in Leviticus: From Sacrifice to Scripture* (New York, NY: Cambridge University Press, 2007).

Watts, E., "The Lord's House and David's Lord: The Psalms and Mark's Perspective on Jesus and the Temple", *BibInt* 15 (2007), pp. 307-22.

Webster, John, "One Who is Son: Theological Reflections on the Exordium to the Epistle to the Hebrews", in *The Epistle to the Hebrews and Christian Theology* (Edited by Richard Bauckham, Daniel Driver, Trevor Hart, and Nathan MacDonald; Grand Rapids, MI: Eerdmans, 2009), pp. 69-95.

Weinandy, Thomas G., O. F. M. Cap., "The Supremacy of Christ: Aquinas' *Commentary on Hebrews*", in *Aquinas on Scripture: An Introduction to His Biblical Commentaries* (Edited by Thomas G. Weinandy, O. F. M. Cap., Daniel A. Keating, and John P. Yocum; London: T&T Clark International, 2005), pp. 223-44.

Weinfeld, Moshe, "Jeremiah and the Spiritual Metamorphosis of Israel", *ZAW* 88 (1976), pp. 17–56.
Weiss, Hans-Friedrich, *Der Brief an die Hebräer: Übersetzt und Erklärt* (KEK, 13; Göttingen: Vandenhoeck & Ruprecht, 1991).
Wenham, Gordon J., "The Theology of Old Testament Sacrifice", in *Sacrifice in the Bible* (Edited by Roger T. Beckwith and Martin J. Selman; Carlisle, PA: Paternoster, 1995), pp. 77–80.
Westcott, Brook Foss, *The Epistle to the Hebrews: The Greek Text with Notes and Essays* (3rd ed.; London: MacMillan and Co., 1903).
Westcott, Brook Foss, *The Epistle to the Hebrews* (3rd ed.; London: Macmillan, 1909).
Westfall, Cynthia Long, *A Discourse Analysis of the Letter to the Hebrews: The Relationship between Form and Meaning* (LNTS 297; London: T&T Clark, 2005).
Westfall, Cynthia Long, "Running the Gamut: The Varied Responses to Empire in Jewish Christianity", in *Empire in the New Testament* (Edited by Stanley E. Porter and Cynthia Long Westfall; Bingham Colloquium Series; Eugene, OR: Pickwick, 2010), pp. 230–58.
Whitlark, Jason A., *Getting "Saved": The Whole Story of Salvation in the New Testament* (Grand Rapids, MI: Eerdmans, 2011).
Whitlark, Jason A., "Cosmology and the Perfection of Humanity in Hebrews", in *Interpretations and the Claims of the Text: Resourcing New Testament Theology* (Edited by Jason A. Whitlark, Bruce W. Longenecker, Lidija Novakovic, and Mikeal C. Parsons; Waco, TX: Baylor University Press, 2014), pp. 117–30.
Whitsett, Christopher G., "Son of God, Seed of David: Paul's Messianic Exegesis in Romans 1:3-4", *JBL* 119 (2000), pp. 661–81.
Williamson, R., *Philo and the Epistle to the Hebrews* (ALGHJ 4; Leiden: Brill, 1970).
Windisch, Hans, *Die Hebräerbrief* (2nd ed.; NTG 14; Tübingen: Mohr [Siebeck], 1931).
Winter, Bruce W., *Divine Honours for the Caesars: The First Christians' Responses* (Grand Rapids, MI: Eerdmans, 2015).
Wissowa, Georg, *Religion und Kultus der Römer* (Zweite Auflage; 1902 repr., München: Beck, 1912).
Wright, David P., "The Gesture of Hand Placement in the Hebrew Bible and in Hittite Literature", *JAOS* 106.3 (1986), pp. 433–46.
Wright, N. T., *New Testament and the People of God* (London: SPCK, 1992).
Wright, N. T., *The New Testament and the People of God* (Minneapolis, MN: Fortress Press, 1996a).
Wright, N. T., *Christian Origins and the Question of God: Vol. 2: Jesus and the Victory of God* (London: SPCK; Minneapolis, MN: Fortress Press, 1996b).
Wyatt, Nicolas, *Space and Time in the Religious Life of the Near East* (Sheffield: Sheffield Academic, 2001).
Young, Frances, "Christological Ideas in the Greek Commentaries on the Epistle to the Hebrews", in *Christology, Hermeneutics, and Hebrews. Profiles from the History of Interpretations* (The Library of New Testament Studies; Edited by Jon Laansma and Daniel Trier; London: T&T Clark, 2014), pp. 33–47.
Zimmermann, Daniël, *Heinrich Bullinger on Prophecy and the Prophetic Office (1523-1538)* (Reformed Historical Theology 33; Göttingen: Vandenchoeck & Ruprecht, 2015).
Zwingli, Huldrych, "The Clarity and Certainty of the Word of God," in *Zwingli and Bullinger* (Edited by G. W. Bromiley; Library of Christian Classics; Louisville, KY: Westminster John Knox, 2006), pp. 59–95.

Index of References to Premodern Sources

HEBREW BIBLE/OLD TESTAMENT

Genesis
1	181
1:1–2:3	31
2	14
2:2	13, 177, 178
2:2-3	179
4:4	169
6:5-7	29
6:9	33
6:24 LXX	189
8	28
8:21	29
12	203
12:1	203
12:2	203
12:1-3	203
12:4	203
14	198
14:13	203
14:17-20	203, 268
14:18	63
14:19	204
14:19-20	204
15:1	142
15:7	39
15:11	203
17:1	33
17:11	203
21:2	203
22	6, 28, 34, 57, 58, 204, 265, 266
22:1	59
22:1-19	203
22:2	29, 57
22:8	59
22:11	57
22:12	57
22:12-14	204
22:15	57
22:16	57
22:16-17	204
22:17	204
47	260
47:31 LXX	260
50:25	205

Exodus
1:8-10	205
6:7	196, 201
10:25	29
12	140
12:5	132, 137
12:10	264, 266
12:42-51	205
12:46	264, 266
14:21-31	205
15:17-18	55
15:25	172
16:4	172
19	205
19:12-13	205
20:2	39
20:20	172
22:27	60
23:18	222
24	10, 29, 133, 134, 237, 267
24:1-11	82
24:3	201
24:3-8	205
24:5-8	29
24:7	201
24:8	22, 23, 133, 221, 267, 273
25	134
25:9	30
25:40	163, 190
25–30	19, 235, 237, 239, 242
25–31	205
25:8-9	188
25:16-21	212
25:39-40	268
25:40	188, 242
25:40 LXX	237
28:30 LXX	39
28:43 LXX	39
29:10	221
29:21	221
29:35-37	29
29:38-46	29
29:42	45 30
30:28	30
31:9	30
32:6	256
32:13-14	256
32:14	256
33:14	182
34:6-7	151
34:25	222
35:16	30
35–40	19
35–40 LXX	235
35–40	237, 239, 242
38:1	30
40:6	30
40:9	221
40:10	30
40:29	30

Leviticus
1:1-17	30
1:1-6:7	30, 32
1:2	33
1:2-3	214, 215

1:3	33, 215	6:8–7:38	30	9:18-19	221
1:4	212	6:13	215	9:23	216
1:5	214	6:14	222	10:3	216
1:9	137, 222	6:23	212	10:10	185
1:13	222	7:3	214	10:11	217
1:14	215	7:7	212	10:17	212
1:17	222	7:8-9	214	11:45	39
2:1	214, 215	7:11-13	214	12:7-8	212, 221
2:1-15 LXX	163	7:13	215		
2:2	222	7:15	222	13:6–7	221
2:4	214, 215	7:16	215	13:13	221
2:4-5	215	7:18	214	13:17	221
2:7	215	7:27	216	13:23	221
2:8	214	7:29	215	13:28	221
2:11-14	214	7:29-30	214	13:34–35	221
2:12-13	215	7:33	214	13:37	221
2:13	215	7:38	214, 215	13:59	221
2:14	222	8	213, 215	14:2	221
3:1	215	8–9	213	14:4	221
3:1-6	215	8:2	216, 221	14:4-6	221
3:3	222			14:7–8	221
3:6	214, 215	8:6	58, 214	14:11	221
3:9	214, 222	8:10	134	14:14	221
4	147	8:11-12	221	14:17–20	221
4:4-7	272	8:15	221	14:18-21	212
4:5	216	8:14	221	14:20-22	222
4:7	30	8:15	147, 212, 213	14:23	221
4:10	30			14:25	221
4:16-20	272	8:17	221	14:28–29	221
4:18	30	8:22	216	14:29	212
4:20	212	8:26	216	14:31	212, 221
4:23	214, 215	8:28-29	216	14:48	221
4:24-25	30	8:31	216	14:53	212
4:25	30, 272	8:33	216	14:57	221
4:26	212, 222	8:34	212, 213	15:13	221
4:30	30	9	32, 213, 216	15:15	212
4:31	212			15:28	221
4:32	215	9:1	216	15:30	212
4:34	30, 272	9:1 LXX	216	16	19, 36, 82, 131, 133, 213, 214, 215, 216, 219, 222, 237, 239, 243, 244, 246
4:35	212, 222	9:4	217, 221		
5	135	9:5	216		
5:6	212	9:6	216		
5:9	135, 272	9:7	212, 213, 216		
5:10	135, 212				
5:11	272	9:7-8	216		
5:13	212	9:9	147		
5:16	212	9:13	216	16 LXX	235
5:18	212	9:15	215	16:3	221
5:26	212	9:17-18	216	16:5	221

16:6	212, 221, 222	23–25	30	*Judges*	
		24:10-23	60	13	36
16:9	215, 222	25:29	219	13:20	36
16:10-11	212	25:48	219		
16:11	213, 221, 222	26:31	31, 165	*1 Samuel*	
		26:42	256	2:6	10, 127
16:12-13	38			15:22	35
16:15	221	*Numbers*		26:19	178
16:15-16	245	3:10	216		
16:16	221	4:19	216	*2 Samuel*	
16:16-17 LXX	213	7:89	212	7:10	55
16:16-18	212	12:7 LXX	259	7:11-16	197
16:18	213	12:8	106, 111	7:14	196
16:19-20	219, 221	14:1-10	202, 206	22:3 LXX	48
16:20	212	14:22	172	23:5	196
16:20-22	265	15:7	35	24:24	34
16:22	222	15:30	138		
16:23-24a	213	15:30-31	60	*2 Kings*	
16:24	36, 212, 213	16:46-50 MT	164	18:11-12	206
		18:5	164	25:4-7	206
16:25	222	18:16	219		
16:27	141, 212	19	58, 131, 133	*1 Chronicles*	
16:29-30	128			6:34	30
16:30	212, 219, 221	19:1-10	216, 221	15:1	238
		19:9	132	16:40	30
16:32	216	19:9-17	266	17:11-14	197
16:32-34	212	19:18-20	221	21:26	30
17:4	215	24:6 LXX	235	21:29	30, 238
17:11	147, 212, 272	28	29		
		28–29	30, 31	*2 Chronicles*	
18:6	216			1:3	238
18:19	216	*Deuteronomy*		5:4-5	238
19:18	35	5:28	155	6:16	197
19:22	212	6:5	35	29:18	30
19:33	216	6:7	196, 201		
20:16	216	6:10 LXX	38	*Ezra*	
21:6	215	9:27-29	256	6:10	34
21:8	215	11:29 LXX	38		
21:10	216	12:6	31	*Nehemiah*	
21:17	215	12:11-14	31	9:7	39
21:17-18	216	17:6	15, 185		
21:21	215, 216	18:1-5	160	*Job*	
21:23	216	19:5	15, 185	9:33-35	119
22:3	216	25:19	178		
22:4	221	29	122	*Psalms*	
23:2	30	30:6	35	2	5, 6, 15, 51, 52, 53, 54, 55, 56, 57, 59, 60,
23:25-28	36	32:14	221		
23:24	36	32:35-36	49		
23:27	36	32:39	10, 128		
23:28	212	33:10	31, 34		

	61, 62, 63, 64	49:13 50:14-15	221 276		216, 223, 268	
2:1-2	55	50:23	139, 141	110:4b	53, 54	
2:6	52	51:16	136	118:6	275	
2:7	6, 52, 53, 54, 57, 62, 196, 260	51:15-16 51:16-17 51:17 69:4	130 35 130, 276 10, 128	132:13f 146:6 *Proverbs*	178 10, 127	
2:7b	53, 54	89:3-4	197	2:14	138	
2:7-9	197	94 LXX	171	3:11	154	
2:12 LXX	48	94:7-11	49	3:11-12	261	
8	16, 42, 196, 197, 207	95	13, 16, 171, 177, 178, 179, 180, 202, 260, 268, 272	3:12 8:22 14:22 16:4 21:3	154 88 129 10, 12 35	
8:4-6	50					
8:5-7	258					
15:2	33					
16:5	133	95:7	150	*Isaiah*		
16:10	10, 127, 140	95:11 95:11 LXX	177, 178 202	1:11 1:13	138, 221 10, 130	
17 LXX	48	99:6	58	1:15	138	
18:49	41	101 LXX	196	1:16	58	
21 LXX	40, 42	101:6	132	4:4	58, 132	
21:23 LXX	5, 47, 48	102:25	106	6	238, 247	
21:24 LXX	47	102:26	171	7	130	
22	150	107:20	127	7:14	48	
22:22	47, 113, 150	109:1 LXX 109:1	207 196	8 8 LXX	130 40, 42	
22:23	259	110	5, 6, 16, 51, 52, 53, 54, 56, 57, 59, 60, 61, 63, 64, 111, 161, 172, 190, 195, 196, 198, 212, 214, 229, 239, 242	8:14 LXX	48	
23:5	35			8:17 LXX	48, 49	
34:1	141			8:17	259	
36:8-9	36			8:17-18 LXX	5, 47, 48, 49	
38:9	139			8:18	48, 49, 259	
39 LXX	40, 42, 43, 44, 45			9:6-7	49	
39:7 LXX	44			11:1	48	
39:7-9 LXX	5, 42, 43, 46, 49			11:10 12	48 130	
40	37, 38, 45, 116, 198, 215, 218, 270	110:1	19, 53, 54, 196, 223, 235, 238, 239, 246, 265	12:1 LXX 12:2 LXX 12:4 LXX 19:21 24:5	48 48 48 142 127	
40:6	136					
40:6-7	35					
40:6-8	106, 137	110:4	112, 162, 190, 197, 198, 199, 200, 212, 213,	24:9	10, 126	
40:7-9	267, 269			29:13	131	
41:10	140			35:8	130	
44:7 LXX	196			40:28	178	
45:6	106			49:4	138	

50:23	141	*Lamentations*		15:8	131
52–53	10, 126	1:12	10, 126	18:16	185
53	125, 222			25:34	225
53:3	126	*Ezekiel*		26:28	134
53:7	136	22:26	186	26:36-46	37
53:12	141, 222, 223	36:25-26	184	26:39	10, 126
		36:25-33	58	27:26	96
53:12 LXX	222	44:23	186	27:46	46
57:18	141				
59	130, 132	*Daniel*		*Mark*	
59:19	132	7	36, 60	1:1-3	57
		7–8	131	1:9-11	52, 53, 57
Jeremiah				1:10	59, 61
6:29	138	*Hosea*		1:11	57, 58, 61
7:22	138	6:6	22, 35, 267	8:11	59
8:6	138			8:27-38	58
11:15	137	8:13	22, 267	9:1-18	58
14:10-12	165	8:13-14	165	9:2	58
31	9, 22, 37, 112, 114, 173, 199	14:2	139, 141	9:5	58
				9:7	58
		Amos		10:2	59
31:1	114	4:4-6	22, 267	11:17–12:40	60
31:2	114	5:20-27	165	11:27-33	62
31:4	114			12:15	59
31:6	114	*Micah*		12:33	267
31:9	114	6:6-8	35	12:35-37	6, 52, 59, 60, 62
31:11	114	6:7	10, 130		
31:12	114	7:19	58	13	60
31:14	114			14:22-25	63
31:17	114	*Habakkuk*		14:32-42	58
31:18	114	2	254	14:36	59
31:20	114	3:4	131	14:38	58
31:22	114			14:53-65	6, 60
31:23	114	*Zechariah*		14:55-59	185
31:25	114	1	131	14:61	59, 60
31:26	114	6:13 LXX	235	14:62	60
31:28	114	9:11	142	15	59
31:30	114	13:1	58	15:34	47
31:31-34	22, 86, 114, 115, 117, 120, 122, 201, 217, 269			15:38	58, 61
		Malachi		15:38-39	59
		1:11	139		
				Luke	
		NEW TESTAMENT		1:5-25	58
31:32	201	*Matthew*		3:21-22	53
31:33	183, 200	1:21	132	11:21	10, 128
31:34	84, 200, 202	3:13-17	53	18:13	73
		6:3-4	142	24:44	247
31:35-37	114	6:20	142		
31:38-40	114	10:28	128	*John*	
38:33 LXX	183, 184	13:35	225	1:29	264

Index of References to Premodern Sources

Reference	Page
5:17	14, 179
5:30	89
6:55	127
8:17	185
10:18	126
14:30	10, 128
19:30	157, 158
19:33	264
19:36	266
19:37	48

Acts

Reference	Page
2:34	265
17:11	4

Romans

Reference	Page
1:4	52
2:17-29	186
3:25	264
5:14	97
5:15	97
6:4	275
6:23	136
8:3	136
8:11	164
8:32	265, 266
8:34	13, 174
8:35-36	174
10:9	174
11:33	155
11:36	10, 127
12:1	130
12:1-2	100
14	186
15	41
15:3	41
15:8-9	41
15:9	41
15:10	48

1 Corinthians

Reference	Page
1:23	81
2:2-5	81
5:7	264
5:17	247
10:1-3	260
10:11	138
15:22	97
15:24-26	206

2 Corinthians

Reference	Page
3:1-11	22, 271
5:14-15	92
5:21	136, 265
13:1	185

Galatians

Reference	Page
3:15-17	272
3:19-20	9, 113
3:21–4:7	113
4:9	113
4:10	186
5:2-3	186

Ephesians

Reference	Page
1:4	225
1:20	265
2:8	139
5:2	35

Philippians

Reference	Page
1:23	128
2	95
2:6-11	265

Colossians

Reference	Page
2:12	275
2:14	95
2:15	98
2:17	269
3:1	265
3:2	243
3:2-4	243

1 Thessalonians

Reference	Page
2:14	241
5:23	154

1 Timothy

Reference	Page
1:15-16	113
2:3-4	113
2:5	9, 113
5:19	185

Hebrews

Reference	Page
1	42, 56, 111, 197
1–2	162
1:1	40, 45, 79, 110, 144, 149, 203, 204, 240
1:1-2	151, 159, 230
1:1-4	11, 14, 56, 86, 106, 109, 182
1:1-13	258
1:1-2:4	110
1:1–4:13	111
1:2	40, 46, 52, 78, 80, 144, 149, 196, 226, 260
1:2-3	116, 117
1:3	78, 83, 84, 85, 94, 145, 149, 158, 173, 197, 198, 229, 235, 239, 244, 245
1:3b	53
1:3c	197
1:3-4	148
1:4	88
1:5	41, 48, 79, 196, 260
1:5-13	53, 152
1:5-14	144
1:5–2:9	106, 109
1:5a	53
1:6	38, 41, 48
1:7	162
1:8	41, 79, 106, 117, 196, 245
1:9	41
1:10	106
1:10-12	41, 226
1:11	196
1:12	171, 196
1:13	41, 48, 53, 78, 196, 197, 206, 207

1:14	107, 162, 166, 167, 170, 205	2:11-15	80	3:5	205, 252, 259
		2:12	11, 41, 42, 47, 48,	3:5-6	122
2	39, 42, 53, 127, 131, 136, 197, 198, 201, 206		113, 150, 260	3:6	79, 150, 152, 197, 201, 260
		2:12-13	5, 49, 259, 269	3:7	11, 150
		2:13	42, 47, 48, 49, 259, 260	3:7b	150
2:1	174, 246, 253			3:7-19	177
				3:7-4:10	206
2:1-4	242, 258	2:13a	48, 49	3:7-4:13	84, 106, 111
2:2	174	2:13b	48		
2:2-3	79	2:14	44, 82, 136, 197, 198, 202, 205, 206	3:11	202, 260
2:3	107			3:12	202, 252
2:4	110, 149			3:14	11, 13, 108, 177
2:5	254, 258				
2:5-8	48	2:14-15	10, 92, 108, 127, 190	3:14-15	150
2:5-9	110, 111			3:15-4:7	171
2:5-10	42			3:17-4:13	177
2:5-3:1	243	2:15	50, 107, 128	3:18	79
2:6	95, 258			3:18ff	108
2:6-9	258	2:16	201	3:19	202, 252
2:7	149	2:17	20, 50, 73, 83, 84, 85, 86, 105, 107, 150, 162, 197, 198, 252, 253	4	177, 180, 225, 260
2:8	50, 53, 192, 207			4:1	13, 177
2:8-9	196			4:1-11	275
2:8-18	78			4:2	82, 202, 252
2:9	9, 47, 80, 85, 92, 106, 125, 126, 149			4:3	17, 202, 225, 252
		2:17-18	81, 216		
		2:18	80, 274	4:3-7	260
2:9-10	108, 216	3	260	4:3-10	207
2:10	5, 10, 47, 49, 50, 80, 85, 92, 115, 127, 149, 202, 205, 255, 258, 260	3-4	13, 14, 49, 180, 202	4:4	202
		3:1	53, 83, 85, 88, 108, 150, 152, 159, 243	4:5	48
				4:6	79
				4:7	48, 204
				4:8-10	272
				4:9	202
		3:1-2	86	4:10	202
2:10-11	86, 259, 275	3:1-6	11, 106, 111, 259	4:11	79
				4:11-13	243
2:10-18	106, 258	3:1-4:13	22, 53, 268	4:12	11, 153, 154, 155
2:11	50, 85, 95, 108, 150, 172, 173, 174, 212, 258, 259, 260	3:2	20, 88, 150, 205, 252, 253	4:12-13	152, 260
				4:13	154
		3:3	205, 259, 260	4:14	53, 79, 81, 83, 159, 175, 200, 246, 260
2:11-13	40	3:4	205		

Index of References to Premodern Sources

4:14-15	98	5:11-6:3	264	7:8	146, 162
4:14-16	106, 111, 158, 159	5:11-6:6	242	7:9	97, 196, 199
		5:11–6:20	112		
4:14–5:10	111	5:12	202	7:11	108, 173, 198, 199
4:14–10:18	53, 111	5:14	108		
4:15	78, 81, 83, 88, 98, 115, 136, 164, 198	6	198, 203, 204	7:11-12	195
				7:11-28	36
		6:1	82, 246, 252	7:12	15, 122, 189, 190, 199, 271, 272
4:15-16	108	6:3	253		
4:16	201, 216, 242, 243, 275	6:2	62, 145, 246		
				7:13-16	199
		6:4	108	7:14	160, 161, 187, 197
5	198, 202	6:4-6	138		
5:1	78, 95, 121, 124, 139, 161, 214, 215, 216	6:5	149	7:15	146
		6:6	80	7:15-16	161, 162
		6:8	154	7:16	83, 108, 112, 116, 146, 147, 148, 149, 197
		6:9	107		
		6:11	108		
5:1-4	215	6:12	82, 205, 252		
5:1-10	213				
5:1-7:28	159	6:12ff	107	7:17	51, 253
5:1–10:18	111	6:13–8	54	7:18	122, 185, 199
5–10	145, 150	6:13-14	204		
5:1	266	6:16	198, 272	7:19	107, 108, 112, 115, 155, 173, 191, 199, 200, 216
5:1ff	107	6:17	112, 113, 198		
5:3	78, 215, 216				
		6:19-20	147		
5:4	216	6:20	83, 85, 162, 198	7:20	199
5:4-5	149				
5:4-6	53	7	112, 146, 158, 160, 161, 198, 200, 203, 266, 268	7:21	198, 201, 253
5:5	6, 62, 79, 83, 216			7:22	50, 107, 108, 112, 115, 195, 199, 201
5:5-6	86, 161				
5:5a	53				
5:5-10	56	7–8	16		
5:7	44, 124, 139, 146, 215, 244	7–10	15, 186		
		7:1	112, 150, 203	7:23	124, 140, 190, 198
5:7-8	62	7:1-28	22, 213	7:23-28	115
5:7-9	37, 81, 96	7:1–10:18	22, 50, 268	7:24	150, 190, 198, 201
5:8	78, 115				
5:8-9	80	7:1–10:25	86	7:24-27	37
5:8-10	158, 160, 216	7:2-3	161	7:25	11, 12, 85, 86, 107, 108, 112, 158, 167, 168, 172, 173, 174,
		7:3	83, 146, 162		
5:9	107, 149, 162, 216, 274	7:4	203		
		7:6	203, 204		
5:10	83, 86	7:7	272		

	198, 201, 275	8:8–13 8:9	22, 269 201, 266		131, 201, 219, 221,
7:26	147	8:10	15, 183,		244, 245,
7:26-28	81, 83, 112, 215, 216	8:11 8:12	200, 202 202 84, 200	9:12-14 9:13	274 190, 198 80, 82, 84,
7:27	38, 78, 81, 216, 217, 244	8:13 8:13–9:19	122, 238 123 10, 22, 131, 267,		131, 132, 191, 219, 221, 223, 266
7:27-28	235		268, 269	9:13-14	131, 191,
7:28	79, 216		124, 128		200
8	112	9–10	37, 112,	9:14	44, 80, 82,
8–10	236, 266	9:1-10	245, 268		85, 107,
8:1	81, 83, 112, 158, 197, 235, 239, 245	9:1-14 9:1–10:10 9:4	37, 243 268 195 84, 132,		117, 125, 132, 151, 164, 191, 198, 200,
8:1-4	158, 161, 168	9:5	163, 212, 247		215, 219, 221, 269
8:1-5	109, 243				
8:1-6	37, 268	9:6	10	9:15	50, 78,
8:1-10:18	22, 37, 112, 268	9:7	80, 82, 128, 129, 215		107, 112, 113, 116, 133, 150,
8:1-10:20	159				195, 201,
8:1–10:22	243	9:7-8	236		206, 218,
8:2	147, 235	9:7-9	107		244, 254,
8:3	78, 188, 198, 214, 215, 216, 242	9:8 9:8-11 9:9	130, 131, 244 130 10, 78,	9:15-16	272, 273, 274 196
8:3-4	215		115, 130,	9:15-17	22, 133,
8:3-5	236		132, 173,		271
8:3–10:18	213		200, 215,	9:15-21	217
8:3ff	107		269	9:15-22	221
8:4	147, 160, 161, 162, 185, 187, 244	9:10 9:11	82 83, 109, 116, 147, 191, 236,	9:16 9:16-17 9:16-18 9:17	133, 244 195 247 133, 203
8:5	125, 163, 188, 205, 230, 237, 242, 268	9:11-12 9:11-14	237, 245 81, 221 37, 112, 116, 245,	9:18 9:18-20	82, 133, 217, 218, 272 80, 200
8:6	50, 112, 113, 115, 150, 195, 198, 201	9:11-15 9:11-28	268 37 17, 84, 218, 219, 220, 223	9:18-22 9:19 9:19-20	267 80, 134, 273 205
8:7-13	114, 217, 268	9:12	44, 80, 81, 82, 85,	9:19-22 9:19ff.	10, 133 191
8:8	201, 206		107, 125,	9:20	82, 195,
8:8-10	195				273

Index of References to Premodern Sources

9:20-22	275		200, 236,		197, 198,	
9:21	82, 134,		237, 269,		215, 239,	
	273		270		245	
9:21-22	80	10:1-2	137	10:12-13	111	
9:22	82, 84,	10:1-3	236	10:12-14	158	
	107, 135,	10:1-4	37	10:13	80, 197,	
	147, 196,	10:1-10	22, 37,		206, 207	
	217, 244,		113, 269	10:14	78, 107,	
	247, 272	10:1-14	46		108, 138,	
9:22b	224	10:1-18	38, 79		173, 174,	
9:22-23	81	10:2	84, 107		200, 201,	
9:23	10, 78,	10:4	10, 82,		205, 225,	
	135, 136,		107, 130,		227, 274,	
	173, 222,		137		275	
	246, 269	10:5	41, 44, 45,	10:15	46	
9:23-24	268		46, 80,	10:15-18	217	
9:23-25	147		116, 137,	10:16	15, 46,	
9:23-28	79		198, 269,		183, 195	
9:24	4, 39, 79,		273	10:16-17	23, 37,	
	81, 82, 85,	10:5-6	137		273	
	108, 145,	10:5-7	5, 40, 42,	10:17	201	
	191, 198		43, 44, 45,	10:17-18	107	
9:24-26	158		106, 137,	10:18	79, 145,	
9:24-28	109		267		201, 202,	
9:25	80, 215,	10:5-8	217		217, 260	
	236	10:5-9	137	10:19	82, 107,	
9:25-26	17, 78,	10:5-10	37		138, 202,	
	224, 225	10:5-14	80, 81,		272	
9:26	81, 116,		109	10:19-20	200	
	125, 136,	10:6	45	10:19-22	36, 37,	
	145, 221,	10:7	46, 137,		107, 108,	
	222, 227		270		201, 238,	
9:26-28	7, 8, 107	10:8	215, 236		242, 243,	
9:27	136	10:8-9	267		244	
9:28	13, 80, 81,	10:9	22, 270	10:19-23	159	
	113, 116,	10:9b-10	37	10:19–13:25	111	
	136, 166,	10:10	44, 80, 81,	10:20	81	
	167, 170,		86, 108,	10:21	148	
	171, 172,		174, 198,	10:22	44, 82, 84,	
	198, 201,		200, 201,		138, 151,	
	207, 215,		244, 269,		198, 200,	
	246		270, 274		201, 216,	
9:28–10:2	215	10:10-18	173		252,	
10	22, 44, 46,	10:10ff	173		275	
	49, 198,	10:11	38, 78,	10:23	20, 85,	
	215, 269,		138, 145		107, 159,	
	273	10:11-12	173		175, 246,	
10:1	18, 19, 46,	10:11-18	86, 268		252, 253,	
	82, 108,	10:12	81, 83, 85,		275	
	122, 173,		147, 148,	10:24	275	

10:25	170, 175, 258	11:7	21, 252, 254	12:1	144, 202, 205, 239, 255, 261
10:26	79, 138, 175, 185	11:8	203, 252, 260	12:1-2	85, 144
10:26-31	84	11:8-22	260	12:1-3	243, 259
10:26ff	107	11:9	203, 252	12:2	79, 80, 83, 107, 145, 197, 239, 252, 255, 261
10:27	84	11:10	21, 170, 255		
10:28	15, 185				
10:28-29	139	11:11	149, 252, 260		
10:29	82, 108, 139, 173, 185, 195	11:11-12	203, 204	12:3	259, 261
		11:12	203, 260	12:4	82, 124, 140
10:30	48, 49	11:13	203, 204, 252, 260, 272	12:4-11	86, 261
10:32	108			12:5-11	79, 201
10:32-34	83			12:5-13	154
10:32-39	257	11:14	21, 255	12:7	215
10:34-36	107	11:14-15	204	12:12-17	261
10:35	142, 275	11:16	21, 170, 255, 260	12:14	107, 108, 202
10:36-39	80				
10:37	170	11:17	203, 204, 215, 252	12:18	150
10:37-39	21, 254				
10:38	82, 252	11:17-19	266	12:18-21	151, 200
10:39	82, 107, 252, 254	11:19	145, 204	12:18-24	261, 272
		11:20	252	12:18-29	113, 155
11	107, 108, 116, 142, 152, 203, 204, 239, 251, 254, 255, 256, 258, 260	11:21	252, 260	12:19	151
		11:22	205, 252	12:20	206
		11:23	140, 252	12:21	150, 205
		11:23-28	140	12:22	21, 84, 140, 170, 202, 254, 275
		11:24	252		
		11:25-26	205		
		11:26	106, 116, 205		
				12:22-23	151
11–12	107	11:27	205, 252	12:22-24	204
11:1	20, 21, 236, 249, 250, 252, 256	11:28	82, 124, 140, 252, 266	12:22-28	243
				12:22-29	107
				12:23	108, 206, 256, 261
11:1-3	18, 236	11:29	252		
11:1-40	144	11:30	252	12:23-24	80
11:2	19, 205, 239, 240, 256	11:31	252	12:24	21, 50, 80, 82, 113, 116, 124, 140, 150, 151, 168, 169, 174, 195, 197, 207, 261
		11:32	247		
		11:33	252		
11:3	21, 149, 252, 256	11:35	145		
		11:35-38	239		
11:4	79, 140, 169, 215, 252, 256	11:38	239		
		11:39	252, 256		
11:4-5	124	11:39-40	168, 173	12:25	11, 86, 149, 150, 151, 152, 155
11:5	252	11:40	206, 275		
11:6	20, 142, 251, 252	12	111, 116, 150		

Index of References to Premodern Sources 311

12:26b	151	13:22	257, 274	*Sirach*	
12:27	171, 193			10:2	132
12:27-28	205	*1 Peter*		24:19	140
12:28	85, 86, 202	1:20	225	34:4	132
		2:24	222	34:19	164
12:29	84	3:18	136	41:4	128
13	113, 202				
13:5	275	*2 Peter*		*2 Baruch*	
13:5-8	108	2:18	10, 128	4:2-6	15, 189
13:6	23, 275				
13:7	154, 252	*1 John*		*Psalms of Solomon*	
13:8	11, 12, 107, 109, 116, 152, 153, 155, 156, 226	1:7-9	174	17.21-25	5, 56
		1:7–2:2	174	17.26	56
				17.30	56
		Revelation		PSEUDEPIGRAPHA	
		1:8	10, 127	*1 Enoch*	
13:9	239	5:5	10, 128	9:1	15
13:10	168, 238, 266, 275	5:6	131	*2 Enoch*	
13:10-11	235	12:18-29	12	22.8-10	58
13:11	79, 82, 141	13	131		
		13:8	225	*3 Enoch*	
13:11-12	141, 214	17	131	12	58
13:11-16	124	17:8	225		
13:12	79, 80, 82, 83, 107, 108	21:1	171	*Epistle of Barnabas*	
		21:2	170	6:2	4
		21:10	170		
13:12-13	85			*Jubilees*	
13:13	79, 242	DEAD SEA SCROLLS		17.15–18.19	59
13:13-14	240			17.16	59
13:14	21, 107, 171, 254	*1QS*		18.19	59
		9.3-5	276		
13:15	23, 79, 85, 118, 141, 142, 276	*4Q174*	5, 55	*Letter of Aristeas*	
		4Q400 frag.		97	58
		1 1.1-4	15, 188	*Odes of Solomon*	
13:15-16	239			2:14	221
13:16	142	*Testament of Levi*			
13:17	79	3.4-6	15, 189	RABBINIC WORKS	
13:20	5, 39, 47, 50, 80, 82, 86, 107, 124, 142, 146, 148, 156, 195, 198, 201	APOCRYPHA		*b. Hag.*	
		1 Esdras		12b	15, 189
		8:63	221	*Gen. Rab.*	
				69.7	15, 189
		Wisdom of Solomon			
		1:13	136	*Exod. Rab.*	
13:20-21	86, 149, 172, 174	2:10-11	10, 125	41	256
		2:20	10, 125	44	256
13:21	79, 107, 108, 148, 156, 207	6:7	10, 127	*Lev. Rab.*	
		9:1	188	36–37	256
		9:8	15, 188		

Num. Rab.			292–93	73	Josephus	
12.12	15, 189				Antiquities of the Jews	
			Cato			
Song. Rab.			On Agriculture		3.216-17	58
48.8	15, 189		139	71	3.189–191	168
Lam. Rab.			Cicero		Apion	
Introduction	256		De domo suo		2.8	237
			121	68	103-109	237
Pesiq. Rab.						
27/28,1	256		Tusculanae		Wars of the Jews	
40.6	15, 189		Disputationes		5:5	237
			1.116–17	75	6.34–53	256
Pirqe R. El.			1.89	75		
45	256		2.52	75	Libanius of Antioch	
					Aristides	
GRECO-ROMAN			Dionysius Halicarnassus		30.33	68
LITERATURE			The Art of Rhetoric			
Aelius Aristides			2.5	75	Musonius Rufus	
Orations					14 7	5
48.44	75		Epictetus			
51.24–25	75		Discourses		Nestorius	
			2.7.3	75	Author	96
Aeschylus						
Prometheus			Euripides		First Sermon against the	
1026–29	75		Alcestis		Theotokos	
			155	75	125	94
Antoninus Liberalis			284	75		
Metamorphosis					On Heb 3.1	
25.2	76		Herodotus		232-42	95
			Histories			
Apollodorus			1.50	73	The Bazaar of Heraclides	
Bibliotheca			7.220	75	251-52	95
2.5.11,10	75					
1.106	75		Hesiod		Philo	
			Theogony		General	229,
Aristotle			526–532	75		268–9
Nicomachean			535–61	66		
Ethics					De confusione linguarum	
1.6	72		Works and Days		169	48
1110a24–26	72		238–47	71		
1109b18–					De migratione Abrahami	
1111a2	72		Homer		104	270
1109b30–32	72		Iliad			
1149b4–6	72		1.386	73	De opificio mundi	
			1.472	73	41	48
Callimachus			15.496–97	75	70	48
Hymnus in Cererem						
368–69	73		Odyssey		De plantatione	
268–74	73		3.435	67	171	48

Index of References to Premodern Sources 313

De praemiis et poenis
166 256

De sacrificiis Abelis et Caini
107 270

De sobrietate
8 48

De somniis
1.166 48
2.19 48

De specialibus legibus
1.67 15, 188
1.271-272 22, 270

Legatio ad Gaium
306 168

Legum allegoriae
3.102 242
3.4 48

Quaestiones et solutiones in Exodum
2.52 242

Quis rerum divinarum heres sit
2.122 48

Quod omnis probus liber sit
106 75

Philostratos
Life of Apollonius
7.12 75

Pliny
Epistulae
10.35 83

Panegyricus
94.1-2 83

Plutarch
Amatorius
761E 75

Apophthegmata Laconica
217d 66
229d 66
236d 66

Poseidonios from Halicarnassus
Author 74

Quintilian
Institutio Oratoria
9.3.66 43

Seneca
De Clementia
2.7.1-2 72

Epistulae morales ad Lucilium
24.6 75

Strabo
Geographica
4.4.6.4 74

Suetonius
Nero
34.4 72

Theodoret
Letter of Alexander to Alexander of Byzantium
1.4.1-61 89

Theognis
Poetry
373-82 70
743-46 70

Theophrastus
Frag. 584A 67

Valerius Maximus
Memorabilia
2.6.6 253

Virgil
Aeneid.
1.278-9 255

3.85-6 255
SEG XL 1109 74
IG IV 607 75
IG IV 7577 75

EARLY CHRISTIAN WRITINGS
1 Clement
10:4 48
10:6 48
14:5 48
15:3 48
15:4 48
52 276

Aquinas, Thomas
Author 9, 18, 124, 267

Commentary on the Letter of Saint Paul to the Hebrews
Whole work 123
§39 127
§122 125
§126 126
§127 127
§128 127
§142 128
§144 128
§255 139
§256 139
§257 140
§367 140
§384 137
§426 128, 129
§427 129, 130
§429 131
§§429-30 129
§430 130
§431 131
§439 131
§440 131
§441 131
§442 131
§443 132
§446 132
§448 133
§451 133
§456 134

§457	134	*On the Incarnation*		Eusebius	
§458	134	Whole work	88, 91,	*Ecclesial History*	
§459	135		101	6.14.4	186
§460	133, 135	9	92		
§462	135	10	92, 93	Gregory of Nazianzus	
§463	135			*Oratio in laudem Basilii*	
§464	136	*Orations against the Arians*		4.102	82
§468	136				
§470	136	Whole work	88, 92, 93	*Oration*	
§475	136	2.7	90-91	30.14	157
§477	136	2.9	89		
§482	137	3.29	89	Gregory Nyssa	
§482	137			*Life of Moses*	
§487	137	Augustine		91-93	151
§488	138	Author	8, 14, 17,		
§490	137		88, 122,	Heidelberg	
§492	138		126	Catechism	11, 148
§515	138	*City of God*			
§516	139	10	99	Irenaeus of Lyons	
§529	139	10.6	100	Author	9
§568	140	19.23	74	Jerome	
§621	140			Author	126
§712	140, 141	*Confessions*			
		11	225	Maximus the Confessor	
§743	141	11.14.17	209	Author	8, 88, 101
§746	141				
§751	141	*On Genesis*		*To Thalassius*	
§752	141	IV.34	181	21	98, 99
§754	142	IV.35	181	36	99
§768	142				
		Boethius		Origen	
Summa theologiae		*The Consolation of Philosophy*		*Commentary on the Gospel of John*	
Whole work	123				
I–II, Q. 99			225	1.11	187
a. 6, ad 3	131				
I–II, Q. 102		Chrysostom		Q. Aurelius Symmachus	
a. 3	133	General	126	*Relatio*	
I–II, Q. 102				3.8	82
a. 3, ad 1	134	Cyril of Alexandria			
I–II, Q. 102		Author	8, 96, 97,	Theodoret of Cyrus	
a. 3, ad 2	134		101	*Commentary on the Letters of St. Paul*	
I–II, Q. 102					
a. 5, ad 4	131	*Fragments on Hebrews*		136	88
III, Q. 49		367–70	94		
a. 5, ad 1	131			*Letter of Alexander to Alexander of Byzantium*	
		On the Unity of Christ			
Athanasius					
General	99	Whole Work	88	1.4.1–61	89

Index of Authors

Abba, Raymond 33
Adams, Edward 151
Aitken, Ellen Bradshaw 233
Allen, David M. 152
Allen, Michael 11, 144, 228
Anatolios, Khaled 7, 87, 88, 92, 93, 94, 97
Ando, Clifford 68, 82, 86
Andriessen, P. C. B. 39
Anizor, Uche 110, 153
Attridge, Harold W. 5, 21, 37, 41, 42, 48, 50, 51, 82, 99, 120, 162, 163, 170, 171, 183, 187, 192, 210, 215, 217, 224, 229, 236, 239, 240, 246, 255, 257, 260, 264, 267, 268, 275

Backhaus, Knut 251, 255
Barrett, C. K. 230, 243
Barth, Karl 14, 18, 144, 178, 179, 182
Basker, Bianca 237
Bauckham, Richard 41, 65, 83, 109, 146, 152, 155, 161, 186, 193, 260, 262
Bavinck, Herman 119
Bayes, J. F. 199
Beard, Mary 68
Beasley-Murray, G. R. 62
Beavis, Mary Ann 195
Becker, E.-M. 154
Becking, Bob 54
Beeke, Joel R. 111
Berceville, Gilles 126, 132, 133, 137, 142
Berman, Joshua 33, 34
Berquist, Jon L. 232, 233, 238
Bick, Ezra 29, 30
Blenkin, Hugh 35
Blocher, Henri 209
Boring, M. E. 57
Botner, Max 60
Boyancé, Pierre 82
Boyarin, Daniel 239, 240
Boyle, John F. 127
Braun, Herbert 83

Braund, Susanna Morton 72, 80
Bremmer, Jan N. 66, 76
Briggs, Richard S. 42
Brixhe, H. 78
Bruce, F. F. 27, 44, 45, 146
Brueggemann, Walter 229, 234
Buber, Martin 20, 249, 250, 251
Buchanan, George W. 51
Büchsel, Friedrich 255
Bultmann, Rudolf 183
Burkert, Walter 66, 69
Burrell, David B. 130
Burrows, Mark S. 129
Bynum, Caroline Walker 143

Calhoun, Robert M. 52
Calvin, John 122
Cancik, Hubert 252, 253
Carbon, Jan-Mathieu 74
Casey, Edward S. 229, 234
Cessario, O. P. Romanus 123
Chaniotis, Angelos 76
Chapman, David W. 81
Chester, A. N. 262
Childs, Brevard S. 130
Clarkson, M. E. 51
Coakley, Sarah 262
Cockerill, Gareth Lee 217
Cody, A. 236, 244
Collins, Adela Yarbro 57, 60
Compton, Jared 166
Constas, Maximos 98
Coppens, Joseph 51
Cortez, Felix H. 211
Cosby, Michael R. 260
Cragg, Hye-Ran Kim 195
Cross, Anthony R. 62
Croy, N. Clayton 261

Daley, Brian 97
Daly, Robert J. 262
Dautzenberg, Gerhard 54

D'Costa, Gavin   125
Dekker, Wisse   57
De Lubac, Henri   129
DeSilva, David A.   241
Detienne, Marcel   67, 69
Docherty, Susan E.   43, 44, 49
Dodd, C. H.   62
Dodds, Eric R.   71
Dunn, James D. G.   62, 63
Dunnill, John   262
Dyer, Bryan R.   242

Eberhart, Christian A.   34, 81, 82, 163, 164, 261–2
Eger, Otto   76
Eisenbaum, Pamela   192, 260
Eliade, Mircea   189
Ellingworth, Paul   27, 39, 206
Embry, Brad   55
Emery, Gilles   127
Ernest, James D.   91
Eschner, Christina   75, 76
Eubank, Nathan   151

Faraone, C. A.   66, 67, 70, 261
Feder, Yitzhaq   27
Ferguson, Sinclair B.   111
Filtvedt, Ole Jakob   258, 275
Finlan, Stephen   262–3
Fitzmyer, Joseph   264, 265
Fletcher-Louis, Crispin   58
Foley, Helen P.   73
Fortenbaugh, William W.   67
France, R. T.   57
Frisch, Peter   76
Froehlich, Karlfried   129
Furnish, Victor P.   265

Gäbel, Georg   161, 162
Gane, Roy E.   33, 163, 164
Gayford, S. C.   35
Gelardini, Gabriella   20, 81, 114, 163, 187, 188, 192, 210, 229, 233, 256, 262, 267
Geller, Stephen A.   28, 31, 36
Gese, Harmut   27
Gignilliat, Mark S.   13, 176
Gordon, Richard   76
Gorman, Frank H.   31
Gorman, Michael J.   112

Gräßer, Erich   82, 83, 84
Graf, Fritz   66
Grässer, Erich   20, 170, 183, 250, 254
Grassi, Joseph A.   59
Greenstein, Edward L.   31
Greer, Rowan A.   87
Gruenwald, Ithamar   187
Guggenheim, Antoine   123, 132, 140
Gunkel, Hermann   178
Gutas, Dimitri   67
Guthrie, George H.   16, 27, 37, 48, 152, 159, 209, 212, 213, 214, 215, 217

Hahn, Scott W.   122
Hanson, A. T.   153
Hanson, R. P. C.   90
Harris, R. Laird   27
Hayes, Christine   184
Hays, Richard B.   5, 41, 48, 50
Heck, Sarah   242
Heen, Erik M.   87
Helm, Paul   225
Hengel, Martin   54, 76
Herrmann, Peter   83
Heyman, George   262
Hicks, Frederick C. N.   35
Himmelfarb, Martha   190
Hoch, Carl B., Jr.,   105
Hofius, Otfried   81, 170, 171
Holmes, Stephen   262
Hooker, Morna D.   186, 194
Huby, Pamela   67
Hughes, Dennis D.   76
Hughes, Graham   51, 152
Huizenga, Leroy A.   57
Hunsinger, George   226
Hurst, L. D.   231
Hurtado, Larry W.   107
Hvalvik, Reidar   240

Isaacs, Marie E.   187, 190, 191, 236

Jackson-McCabe, Matt   240
Jamieson, R. B.   210, 211, 217, 221, 224
Janowski, Bernd   33
Jewett, Robert   264
Jobes, Karen H.   5, 40, 43, 44, 152
Johnson, Adam   127
Johnson, Luke T.   27, 87, 149, 151, 152, 154, 199, 206

Index of Authors

Johnson, William G.   230
Jones, Christopher P.   81, 86
Joslin, Barry   184, 186, 187
Jugie, M.   94

Kajava, Mika   81
Karrer, Martin   256
Käsemann, Ernst   20, 159, 250, 259
Keating, Daniel A.   128
Keener, Craig S.   62
Kibbe, Michael Harrison   12, 147, 155, 158, 202, 228
Kidner, Derek   31, 34, 36
Kim, Lloyd   241
Kindt, J.   65
Kistemaker, Simon   37
Kiuchi, Nobuyoshi   33, 147
Klauck, Hans-Josef   76, 77
Klawans, Jonathan   188, 189, 261, 262
Kleinig, John W.   29, 30, 34
Koester, Craig R.   84, 85, 114, 187, 217, 241, 242, 247, 255
Konstan, David   72
Krey, Philip D. W.   87
Kuma, Hermann V. A.   191
Kurtz, Johann   32, 35
Kuschel, Karl-Josef   249

Laansma, Jon C.   2, 3, 51, 52, 91, 98, 109, 124, 125, 140, 147, 177, 257
Lane, William L.   39, 146, 217, 230, 231, 235
Langenhoven, Hanno   211
Latte, Kurt   68
Leach, Edmund   33, 36
Le Deaut, Roger   59
Lee, Gregory W.   122, 123, 153
Lefebvre, Henri   231, 232, 233
Lehne, Susanne   195, 199
Leonhardt, Jutta   168, 270
Leschert, Dale   153
Levenson, Jon D.   27, 57
Levering, Matthew   9, 62, 120, 122, 123, 125, 127, 128
Levine, Baruch A.   30, 31
Lewicki, T.   152
Lhôte, Éric   74
Lichtenberger, H.   58

Lindars, Barnabas   118, 193
Lipka, Michael   69
Lloyd-Jones, Hugh   71
Loader, W.   28
Loader, William R. G.   54
Locher, Gottfried W.   153
Löhr, Hermut   85, 86
Longenecker, Richard N.   221, 274
Loofs, F.   95
Low, Bernard   33, 35
Luther, Martin   14, 180, 181
Lyonnet, Stanislas   28, 35

McCaffrey, James   39
McCarthy, Dennis J.   28
McCollough, J. C.   241
McCormack, Bruce L.   109
McGuckin, John Anthony   96, 97
McKelvey, R. J.   37
Mackie, Scott D.   206
MacMullen, Ramsay   70
MacRae, G. W.   229
Malay, Hasan   76
Maley, Willy   233
Malherbe, Abraham J.   41
Malpas, J. E.   244
Marshall, I. Howard   65, 84, 228
Martin, Francis   129
Mary Andrews, M.   59
Mason, Eric F.   268
Meeks, Wayne A.   41
Meier, J. P.   53, 61
Metzler, Karin   72, 91
Michel, Otto   191
Milgrom, Jacob   33, 35, 191, 192
Miller, James   203
Milligan, William   158, 168
Minkowski, Hermann   228
Moberly, R. W. L.   260
Moffatt, James   51, 160
Moffitt, David   11, 12, 16, 17, 37, 39, 41, 44, 46, 47, 145, 146, 147, 148, 157, 158, 160, 161, 162, 163, 165, 166, 171, 176, 186, 187, 190, 193, 207, 209, 210, 211, 212, 214, 215, 218, 219, 220, 224, 228, 229, 230, 235, 243, 244, 247, 273
Moo, Douglas   228

Moore-Gilbert, Bart 233
Morales, L. Michael 4, 27, 28, 29, 31, 33, 39, 214
Morgan, Teresa 252
Morris, Leon 158
Muller, H.P. 29

Naiden, F. S. 66, 67, 70, 79, 81, 261
Nelson, Richard D. 33, 35
Nichols, Aidan 127
Nickelsburg, George W. E. 239
North, John 68
Nortje, Eliska 211

O'Donovan, Oliver 14, 179, 180
Osborne, Grant R. 3
Osborne, Robin 65, 66
Owen, John 152

Panayotou, K. A. 78
Pannenberg, Wolfhart 18, 52, 226
Parke, Herbert W. 73, 74
Peeler, Amy A.B. 15, 195, 206
Perrin, Nicholas 5, 51, 62, 64
Peterson, David G. 162, 187, 191, 274
Pettazzoni, Raffaele 77
Petzl, Georg 76, 78
Philip, Mayjee 129, 134, 135
Pirenne-Delforge, Vinciane 74
Polen, Nehemia 193
Polyandro, D. Johanne 152
Porter, Stanley E. 62, 235, 240
Potgieter, Annette 211
Poulet, Georges 234
Preisigke, Friedrich 255
Preus, James Samuel 130
Price, Simon R. F. 68, 69, 76
Prügl, Thomas 129
Pusey, P. E. 94, 95

Quinot, Bernard 100

Ragavan, Deena 189
Rahlfs, Alfred 43
Rainey, A. F. 31
Ramirez, Andres 232, 233, 239
Rascher, Angela 82
Relph, E. 233, 234
Ribbens, Benjamin 17, 38, 120, 147, 155, 212, 225

Ricl, Marijana 76, 77
Ridgway, Brunilde S. 237
Rindge, Matthew S. 57
Roberts, J. J. M. 54
Rooke, Deborah W. 160
Rosenberger, Veit 71
Rostad, Aslak 76, 77
Rothschild, Claire 257
Rüpke, Jörg 69, 79

Sabourin, Leopold 28, 35
Sanders, J. T. 51
Savvidis, K. 91
Scheid, John 69, 70, 82
Schenck, Kenneth L. 109, 152, 187, 203, 231, 246
Schierse, Franz Joseph 80
Schleiermacher, Friedrich 124
Schlesinger, Eugene R. 225, 226
Schliesser, Benjamin 20, 250
Schmitt, Mary 190
Schnabel, Eckhard J. 6, 7, 65, 76, 77, 81
Schnelle, Udo 51
Scholer, John M. 216
Schoot, Henk 130
Schumacher, Thomas 252
Schwertheim, E. 76
Scullion, James P. 28, 37
Seeley, David 75
Sharples, Robert 67
Shelfer, Lochlan 76, 77
Sheppard, Anne R.R. 76
Signer, Michael A. 56
Siker, Jeffrey S. 262, 264
Skarsaune, Oskar 240
Sklar, Jay 28, 147
Small, Brian C. 107
Smith, Jonathan Z. 66
Snaith, Norman H. 34
Soja, Edward W. 229, 231, 232, 233
Sommer, Benjamin 192
Son, Kiwoong 39
Soskice, Janet Martin 187
Soulen, R. Kendall 121
Spicq, Ceslas 35, 189, 230, 250
Stanton, Gareth 233
Steenkamp, Yolande 211
Stegeman, Ekkehard 262
Stegemann, Wolfgang 262
Steinleitner, Franz S. 76

Stephens, W. P. 153
Steyn, Gert J. 37, 43, 45, 47, 48, 54
Steyn, Pace 60
Stibbs, Alan M. 157, 166, 169
Strecker, Christian 256
Stroumsa, Guy G. 262
Svendsen, Stefan Nordaard 184, 186, 187, 193

Tapie, Matthew A. 123
Tasker, R. V. G. 158, 191
Telscher, Guido 82
Thiessen, Matthew 14, 154, 183
Thompson, James W. 151, 171, 268
Torrance, T.F. 1, 144, 179
Treier, Daniel J. 2, 8, 42, 98, 105, 109, 150, 152
Trevaskis, Leigh M. 29, 33, 35
Turcan, Robert 68
Turner, C. H. 57

Valkenberg, Pim 130
VanderKam, James C. 190
Vanhoye, Albert 51, 171, 245
Van Neste, Ray F. 3
Van Vliet, Hendrik 185
Várhelyi,, Zsuzsanna 72, 80, 84
Varinlioğlu, Ender 76
Vernant, Jean-Pierre 67, 69
Versnel, Hendrik S. 71, 74, 75, 77, 83, 85
Vis, Joshua M. 192
Vögtle, Anton 151

Von Rad, Gerhard 178
Vos, Geerhardus 176

Wainwright, Geoffrey 108
Walker, P. W. L. 27
Wallace, David 52, 53
Wallace-Hadrill, Andrew 251, 252
Watts, James W. 27, 28, 30, 31, 32, 34
Watts, Rikki E. 56
Webster, John 109, 155
Weinandy, Thomas G. 123, 124, 127, 137, 140
Weinfeld, Moshe 184
Weiss, Hans-Friedrich 183
Wenham, Gordon J. 33
Westcott, B. F. 160, 246
Westfall, Cynthia Long 18, 38, 228, 239, 240, 243, 245
Whitlark, Jason A. 192, 274
Whitsett, Christopher G. 52
Williamson, R. 131
Windisch, Hans 51
Winter, Bruce W. 83
Wissowa, Georg 68
Wormell, Donald E.W. 73, 74
Wright, David P. 33
Wright, N.T. 42, 62, 203, 234
Wyatt, Nicolas 38

Young, Frances 97

Zimmermann, Daniël 154
Zwingli, Huldrych 11, 153

www.ingramcontent.com/pod-product-compliance
Lightning Source LLC
Chambersburg PA
CBHW070014010526
44117CB00011B/1563